WORKS ISSUED BY
THE HAKLUYT SOCIETY

Series Editors
Gloria Clifton
Joyce Lorimer

JAPANESE TRAVELLERS IN SIXTEENTH-CENTURY EUROPE

THIRD SERIES
NO. 25

THE HAKLUYT SOCIETY
Council and Officers 2012–2013

PRESIDENT
Captain M. K. Barritt RN

VICE-PRESIDENTS

Peter Barber OBE
Professor Roy Bridges
Anthony Payne

Dr Nigel Rigby
Professor W. F. Ryan FBA
Dr Sarah Tyacke CB

Professor Glyndwr Williams

COUNCIL
(with date of election)

Professor Jim Bennett (2011)
Dr Jack Benson (co-opted)
Dr Surekha Davies (2011)
Dr Margaret Deacon (2008)
Professor Felipe Fernández-Armesto (2009)
Professor Peter Hulme (2009)
Bruce Hunter (2011)
Major Anthony Keeley (2010)
Jonathan King (2010)
Lionel Knight (2012)

Dr Roger Morriss (2008)
Lt Cdr Lawrence Phillips (2008)
Dr Maurice Raraty (2012)
Royal Geographical Society
 (Dr John H. Hemming CMG)
Catherine Scheybeler (2009)
Professor Suzanne Schwarz (2009)
Dr Silke Strickrodt (2012)
Dr John Smedley (co-opted)
Professor Charles W. J. Withers FBA (2010)

CUSTODIAN TRUSTEES

Professor Roy Bridges
Professor W. E. Butler

Dr John H. Hemming CMG
Dr Sarah Tyacke CB

HONORARY TREASURER
David Darbyshire FCA

HONORARY JOINT SERIES EDITORS
Dr Gloria Clifton   Professor Joyce Lorimer

HONORARY EDITOR (ONLINE PUBLICATIONS)
Raymond Howgego

HONORARY ARCHIVIST
Dr Margaret Makepeace

ADMINISTRATION
(to which queries and application for membership may be made)
Telephone: 0044 (0)1428 641 850   Email: office@hakluyt.com   Fax: 0044 (0)1428 641 933

Postal Address only
The Hakluyt Society, c/o Map Library, The British Library,
96 Euston Road, London NW1 2DB, UK

website: www.hakluyt.com

Registered Charity No. 313168   VAT No. GB 233 4481 77

INTERNATIONAL REPRESENTATIVES OF THE HAKLUYT SOCIETY

Australia Dr Martin Woods, Curator of Maps, National Library of Australia, Canberra, ACT 2601

Canada Dr William Glover, 163 Churchill Crescent, Kingston, Ontario K7L 4N3

Central America Dr Stewart D. Redwood, PO Box 0832-1784, World Trade Center, Panama City, Republic of Panama

France Contre-amiral François Bellec, 1 place Henri Barbusse, F92300 Levallois

Germany Thomas Tack, Ziegelbergstr. 21, D-63739 Aschaffenburg

Iceland Professor Anna Agnarsdóttir, Department of History and Philosophy, University of Iceland, Reykjavík 101

Japan Dr Derek Massarella, Faculty of Economics, Chuo University, Higashinakano 742-1, Hachioji-shi, Tokyo 192-03

Netherlands Dr Leo M. Akveld, Hammerfeststraat 48, 3067 DC Rotterdam

New Zealand John C. Robson, Map Librarian, University of Waikato Library, Private Bag 3105, Hamilton

Portugal Dr Manuel João Ramos, Av. Elias Garcia 187, 3Dt, 1050 Lisbon

Russia Professor Alexei V. Postnikov, Institute of the History of Science and Technology, Russian Academy of Sciences, 1/5 Staropanskii per., Moscow 103012

Spain Ambassador Dámaso de Lario, Glorieta López de Hoyos, 4, 28002 Madrid

USA Dr Edward L. Widmer, The John Carter Brown Library, Box 1894, Providence, Rhode Island 02912

DE MISSIONE
LEGATORVM IAPONEN
sium ad Romanam curiam, rebusq; in
Europa, ac toto itinere animaduersis
DIALOGVS
EX EPHEMERIDE IPSORVM LEGATORVM COL-
LECTVS, & IN SERMONEM LATINVM VERSVS
ab Eduardo de Sande Sacerdote Societatis
IESV.

In Macaensi portu Sinici regni in domo
Societatis IESV cum facultate
Ordinarij, & Superiorum.
Anno 1590.

Title page of *De Missione*.
By permission of Toyo Bunko, Tokyo.

JAPANESE TRAVELLERS IN SIXTEENTH-CENTURY EUROPE

A Dialogue Concerning the Mission of the Japanese Ambassadors to the Roman Curia (1590)

Edited and annotated with an introduction by
DEREK MASSARELLA

Translated by
J. F. MORAN

Published by
Ashgate
for
THE HAKLUYT SOCIETY
LONDON
2012

© The Hakluyt Society 2012

All rights reserved. No part of the publication may be reproduced, stored in a retrieval system, or transmitted in any form or by any means, electronic, mechanical, photocopying, recording or otherwise without the prior permission of the publisher.

Published for The Hakluyt Society by

Ashgate Publishing Limited
Wey Court East
Union Road
Farnham
Surrey GU9 7PT
England

Ashgate Publishing Company
110 Cherry Street
Suite 3–1
Burlington, VT 05401–3818
USA

Ashgate website: http://www.ashgate.com
Hakuyt Society website: http://www.hakluyt.com

British Library Cataloguing in Publication Data
Japanese travellers in sixteenth-century Europe : a dialogue concerning the mission of the Japanese ambassadors to the Roman curia (1590). – (Hakluyt Society. Third series ; v. 25)
1. Japanese – Europe – History – 16th century – Sources. 2. Europe – Description and travel – Early works to 1800. 3. Travellers' writings, Japanese – Translations into English. 4. Valignano, Alessandro, 1538–1606. 5. Jesuits – Missions – Japan – History – 16th century. 6. Jesuits – History – 16th century – Sources. 7. Europe – Foreign Relations – Japan. 8. Japan – Foreign relations – Europe. 9. Japan – Foreign relations – 1185–1600.
I. Series II. Massarella, Derek, 1950– III. Hakluyt Society.
914'.04232'089956-dc23

Library of Congress Cataloguing-in-Publication Data
LCCN: 2012026020

ISBN 9781908145031 (hbk)
ISBN 9781409452645 (ebk – PDF)
ISBN 9781409472230 (ebk – ePUB)
ISSN 0072 9396

Typeset by Waveney Typesetters, Wymondham, Norfolk

Printed and bound in Great Britain by the MPG Books Group, UK

To the memory of:

Gerald Aylmer,
Imai Hiroshi,
Marius B. Jansen,
Joseph F. Moran
and
Tamura Hideo

CONTENTS

Figures and Maps — xii
Preface — xv
Acknowledgements — xvi
Abbreviations — xvii
A Note on Currency — xviii
Romanization of Japanese and Chinese Names — xix

INTRODUCTION
  Background to *De Missione* — 1
  Objectives of the Embassy and the Individuals Chosen — 6
  Publication of *De Missione* — 15
  Authorship of *De Missione* — 20
  Sources of *De Missione* — 21
  Contextualizing *De Missione* — 23
  Evaluating *De Missione* and the Tenshō Embassy — 26
  The Boys after their Return to Japan — 28
  Conclusion — 31

A DIALOGUE CONCERNING THE MISSION OF THE JAPANESE AMBASSADORS TO THE ROMAN CURIA

Imprimatur — 35
Nihil obstat — 36
Alessandro Valignano of the Society of Jesus to the pupils of the Japanese seminaries — 37
Duarte de Sande to Claudio Aquaviva, Superior General of the Society of Jesus — 38
Contents of these Colloquia — 40
Colloquium I: The reasons for the Japanese embassy — 43
Colloquium II: The journey from Japan to Macao, the gateway to China, and from there to the Straits of Singapore — 51
Colloquium III: The approach to the city of Malacca, in the Golden Chersonese, and from there to the city of Cochin, in Nearer India — 62
Colloquium IV: The coming of the Portuguese to India, and the spread of the Portuguese empire — 71
Colloquium V: About the Indian race, and the houses of the Society in India — 80
Colloquium VI: The Voyage from India to Portugal — 92
Colloquium VII: About the things of Europe in general, and firstly of the sacred or ecclesiastical monarchy, and other lower ranks — 107

Colloquium VIII: About the secular monarchy, and various dignities belonging to it 122

Colloquium IX: Of the splendour and opulence of the kings and rulers of Europe in what concerns the treatment of the body, food, and accommodation, and of their great costs and expenses 132

Colloquium X: Of the multitude of servants and the pomp which the princes of Europe use at home and abroad 142

Colloquium XI: About the agreeable and honourable exercises which the nobles of Europe engage in, and of the noble education of their children 149

Colloquium XII: The arrangements and customs of Europeans with regard to the administration of kingdoms and republics 159

Colloquium XIII: Of the wars which are usually waged in Europe, the way of setting up an army, and land battles 171

Colloquium XIV: Of the naval battles in which they usually engage in Europe 181

Colloquium XV: Of the size of the cities, the splendour of the churches, and the magnificence of other buildings 191

Colloquium XVI: Reverting to the account of the journey, with a description of Lisbon, capital of the kingdom of Portugal 200

Colloquium XVII: Which gives an account of the things which took place in Lisbon, and then in Évora and Vila Viçosa, and then proceeds into the kingdom of Castile, to Toledo and to Mantua Carpetana or Madrid 222

Colloquium XVIII: Of the power of King Philip of Spain, and the oath by which the nobles of the kingdom swore allegiance to his son as his successor, and of the visit which the ambassadors made to both 234

Colloquium XIX: Of various works built by King Philip, especially the work of the Escorial, and of the approach to the city of Alón or Alicante 244

Colloquium XX: The voyage from Spain to Italy, the visit to the grand duke of Tuscany, and things noted in Pisa and Florence 255

Colloquium XXI: Of the delights and pleasures of the Pratolino villa of the duke of Tuscany, and of things observed at Siena, Viterbo, and on the remainder of the journey to Rome 263

Colloquium XXII: Of the entrance into the celebrated city of Rome, and the audience with the Supreme Pontiff Gregory XIII, and of the sacred palace and the most august church of St Peter 273

Colloquium XXIII: Continues with things noted at the pope's solemn masses and elsewhere 283

Colloquium XXIV: Of what took place in Rome up until the death of Pope Gregory XIII 300

Colloquium XXV: How the funeral of a pope is carried out, and the way in which another pope is chosen, and to what great and universal applause Sixtus V was proclaimed pope 309

Colloquium XXVI: The cavalcade with which the pope made his way to the church of St John Lateran, and the ambassadors, invested with the insignia of knighthood, departed the city; and of the most noble city of Naples, and the church of the Blessed Virgin of Loreto 317

Colloquium XXVII: The journey through other cities, especially Ancona, Bologna, Ferrara, and Venice, and the things seen there   329

Colloquium XXVIII: Gives an account of notable things observed in Venice, and of the honour with which the Japanese ambassadors were treated by its august Senate   341

Colloquium XXIX: More about things in Venice, but also dealing with the access of the ambassadors to other cities, principally Padua, Verona, Mantua, Cremona, and Milan, and the rejoicing with which they were received in them   357

Colloquium XXX: More about things noted in Milan and in Pavia, and about their entry into the city of Genoa and the voyage to Spain   373

Colloquium XXXI: Of the city of Coimbra and the famous college of the Society there, the generous treatment extended to the ambassadors in Lisbon, by order of King Philip, with regard to the voyage to India, and the reasons for the wealth of Europe   389

Colloquium XXXII: The Voyage from Portugal to India, and from India to the Kingdom of China   401

Colloquium XXXIII: The kingdom of China, its customs and administration   416

Colloquium XXXIV: A summary description of the whole world, and a statement as to which is its principal and noblest part   438

BIBLIOGRAPHY   451

INDEX   471

FIGURES AND MAPS

Figures

Frontispiece. Title page of *De Missione*. By permission of Toyo Bunko, Tokyo.

Figure 1. 'Anon-Moreira' world map. By permission of the owner. — 19

Figure 2. The departure from Nagasaki, engraving by Abraham van Diepenbeeck, in Cornelius Hazart, *Kerckelycke historie van de gheheele wereldt*, Antwerp, 1667, vol. I, facing p. 63. By permission of Professor Tominaga Michio. — 52

Figure 3. Drawing of Michael Chijiwa by Urbano Monte, July 1585, in B. Gutierrez, *La prima ambascieria giapponese in Italia*, Milan, 1938, following p. 56 (unpaginated). By permission of Gakushuin Women's College, Tokyo. — 94

Figure 4. Drawing of Mancio Itō by Urbano Monte, July 1585, in B. Gutierrez, *La prima ambascieria giapponese in Italia*, Milan, 1938, following p. 40 (unpaginated). By permission of Gakushuin Women's College, Tokyo. — 95

Figure 5. Drawing of Martin Hara by Urbano Monte, July 1585, in B. Gutierrez, *La prima ambascieria giapponese in Italia*, Milan, 1938, following p. 56 (unpaginated). By permission of Gakushuin Women's College, Tokyo. — 96

Figure 6. Drawing of Julian Nakaura by Urbano Monte, July 1585, in B. Gutierrez, *La prima ambascieria giapponese in Italia*, Milan, 1938, following p. 72 (unpaginated). By permission of Gakushuin Women's College, Tokyo. — 97

Figure 7. Drawing of Diogo de Mesquita, S.J., by Urbano Monte, July 1585, in B. Gutierrez, *La prima ambascieria giapponese in Italia*, Milan, 1938, following p. 72 (unpaginated). By permission of Gakushuin Women's College, Tokyo. — 98

Figure 8. Audience with King Philip II, engraving by Abraham van Diepenbeeck, in Cornelius Hazart, *Kerckelycke historie van de gheheele wereldt*, vol. I, Antwerp, 1667, facing p. 64. By permission of Professor Tominaga Michio. — 241

Figure 9. Audience with Gregory XIII, engraving by Abraham van Diepenbeeck, in Cornelius Hazart, *Kerckelycke historie van de gheheele wereldt*, vol. I, Antwerp, 1667, facing p. 68. By permission of Professor Tominaga Michio. — 275

Figure 10. Commemorative medal struck by Gregory XIII to mark the embassy. By permission of Biblioteca Apostolica Vaticana, with all rights reserved. — 303

Figure 11. Mural in the Vatican Library of Sixtus V's procession to St John Lateran, 5 May 1585. By permission of Nagasaki Bunkensha. — 318

Figure 12. Autographs of Mancio Itō, Michael Chijiwa, Martin Hara, Julian Nakaura and Diogo de Mesquita, in Yūki Ryōgo, *Roma wo mita*: *Tenshō shōnen shisetsu*, Nagasaki, 1982, frontispiece. By permission of the Nihon Nijūroku Seijin Kinenkan, Nagasaki Insatsu KK and the Archivum Romanum Societatis Iesu, Rome. 412

Figure 13. *Newe Zeyttung/ auß der Insel Japonien*, Augsburg, 1586. By permission of Kyoto University Library. 445

Maps

Map 1. The voyage to Europe and back to Japan, February 1582–August 1584, April 1586–July 1590. Drawn by Daisy Fearns. xx

Map 2. The mission's travels through Portugal and Spain, August 1584–February 1585, and August 1585–April 1586. Drawn by Daisy Fearns. xxi

Map 3. The mission's travels through Italy, March 1585–August 1585. Drawn by Daisy Fearns. xxii

PREFACE

Joseph Moran began his translation of *De Missione* in 1998. Illness, and his untimely death in 2006, prevented him from preparing a scholarly apparatus to accompany the translation. I am extremely grateful to his widow, Chihoko Moran, for making the translation available to me and for entrusting me with the task of preparing such an apparatus. I hope that my efforts have done justice to his fine translation.

In completing this edition of *De Missione*, I would like to thank a number of people for their advice, support and encouragement. These include Michael Ainge, Roger Batty, Beatrice Bodart-Bailey, Alexander Bruce, Michael Cooper, Fukushima Masahiro, Sheelagh M. Fullerton, Joseph S. O'Leary, Kenneth Nebenzahl, Geoffrey Parker and Tominaga Michio. I also thank Daisy Fearns, for drawing the maps, and Luís Filipe Barreto, director of the Centro Científico e Cultural de Macau. For permission to reproduce material in their possession, I am most grateful to the following individuals and institutions: Kyoto University Library; Toyo Bunko, Tokyo; Nagasaki Bunkensha; the director of the Archivum Romanum Societatis Iesu, Rome; the present owner of the 'Anon-Moreira' map; and the Vatican Library. The staff of the reference section of Chuo University Library have been especially helpful, not only with their customary professionalism, but also with their suggestions and help in securing permission for the reproduction of some of the illustrations that accompany the text. In addition, I am grateful to the staff of Kirishitan Bunko in Sophia University, Tokyo, for allowing me access to material in their possession and for their patience in dealing with my requests. I am extremely grateful to Joyce Lorimer, the series editor, for her care in editing this book. Finally, I wish to thank my students who, sometimes without being aware of it, have contributed greatly to shaping my ideas about the nature of European–Japanese relations.

Derek Massarella
Shimoda, April 2012

In addition, Chihoko Moran would like to thank the bishop emeritus of Aberdeen, Peter A. Moran, and Adriana Boscaro.

ACKNOWLEDGEMENTS

The Hakluyt Society thinks it appropriate that the generosity of donors should be recorded in the book which their donations have helped to make possible. The editor and the Society wish to express their enormous gratitude to the Japan Foundation, London, and the Great Britain Sasakawa Foundation, which made generous grants as a contribution to the costs of publishing this volume.

ABBREVIATIONS

ARSI   Archivum Romanum Societatis Iesu, Rome
RAHM   Real Academia de la Historia, Madrid

A NOTE ON CURRENCY

Monetary values in *De Missione* are given in *sestertium* (sesterces) and *aurei* (gold coins). The value ascribed to the *sestertium* is difficult but not impossible to unravel. On p. 86 of the original edition (p. 134 below) no European king is said to have an annual income of less than '*quadringentes sestertium, hoc est decies centena millia aureorum*' ('forty million *sestertium* which is one million gold coins'). According to the humanist Guillaume Budé (Budaeus), however, when the Romans wrote '*centies sestertium*' (10 million *sestertium*) they were in fact abbreviating '*centies centena milia sestertium*' or 100 × 100,000 sesterces. Hence '*quadringentes sestertium*' is equivalent to '*quadringentes centena milia sestertium*' or 40 million sesterces. *De Missione* gives this as equivalent to 1 million gold coins, making one *sestertium* equal to 0.025 gold coins. But, according to Budé, and Polydore Vergil, one *sestertium* was equal to 25 *écus* or gold coins, which would make 40 million *sestertium* the equivalent of 1,000,000,000 gold coins. This is patently absurd. No European monarch had such a fabulous income. In his book, however, Budé distinguishes between small sesterces and large sesterces. One large sesterce was worth 1,000 small sesterces. In *De Missione* it appears that when *sestertium* is employed it refers to small sesterces, in which case one small sesterce equals 0.025 gold coins and therefore 40 million sesterces is indeed equivalent to 1 million gold coins.[1] As for *aurei*, we know from other sources that Sixtus V endowed the Jesuit mission in Japan with 6,000 ducats and on p. 68 of *De Missione* he is credited with assigning '*sex aureorum millia*' or 6,000 thousand gold coins to the Society in Japan (p. 116 below). It is, therefore, safe to assume that an *aureus* is the equivalent of a Spanish *ducado* or ducat (a Spanish unit of account worth 375 *maravedís*) and has been translated as such. Valignano, for example, gives the figures for the running costs of the Japan mission in ducats.[2]

---

[1] Guillaume Budé, *Extraict ou abbrege du liure De asse de feu Mo[n]sieur Bude: auquel les monnoyes, poix, & mesures anciennes sont reduictes à celles de maintenant*, Paris, 1549, ff. 6–8v. The original Latin version was published in 1514 (Budaeus, *De asse et partibus eius*, Paris, 1514). Vergil, *On Discovery*, p. 219 (the first edition was published in 1499 and more than a hundred editions in eight languages followed, ibid., p. viii).

[2] Valignano, *Sumario*, pp. 311, 338.

ROMANIZATION OF JAPANESE AND CHINESE NAMES

Japanese words, names and titles are Romanized according to the revised Hepburn system. As is the convention, macrons have been omitted from well-known names and terms such as Kyoto and shogun. Macrons have also been omitted from the term daimyo in the Introduction and footnotes but in the Colloquia themselves *daimyō* has been italicized and the macron retained. Japanese and Chinese personal names appear with the family name first except in citations from European-language sources where the family name follows the given name. Chinese names and places are given in Pinyin except for Ming era titles, which are given according to the Wade-Giles system used in the most accessible reference work (Hucker, *Dictionary*), and for familiar historical names such as Canton (rather than Guangzhou).

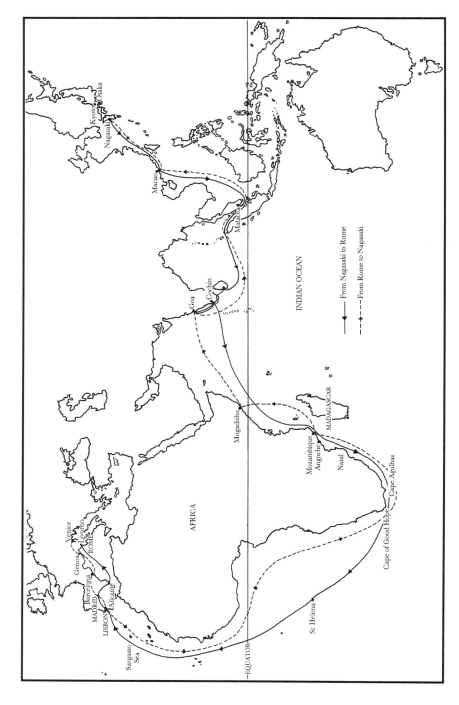

Map 1. The voyage to Europe and back to Japan, February 1582–August 1584, April 1586–July 1590. Drawn by Daisy Fearns.

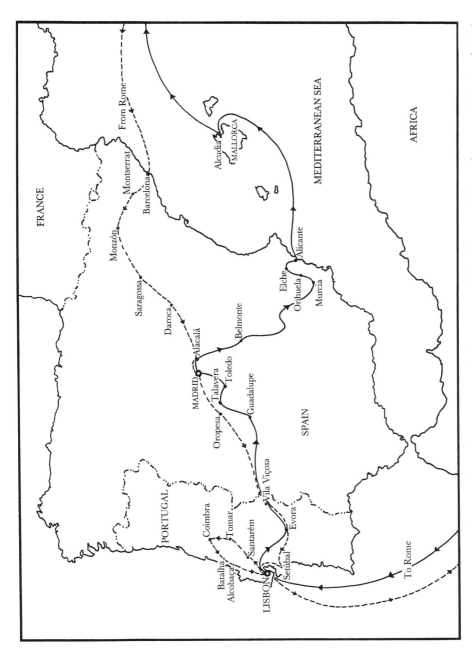

Map 2. The mission's travels through Portugal and Spain, August 1584–February 1585, and August 1585–April 1586. Drawn by Daisy Fearns.

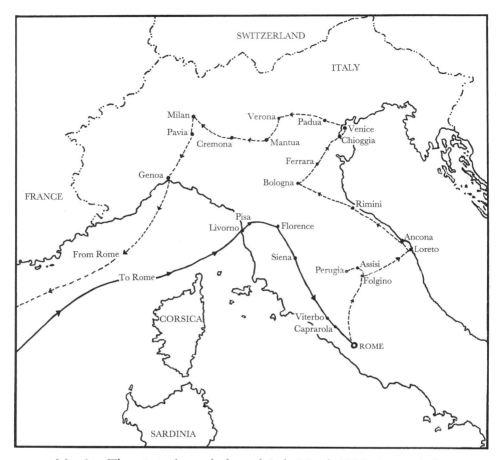

Map 3. The mission's travels through Italy, March 1585–August 1585.
Drawn by Daisy Fearns.

INTRODUCTION

Background to *De Missione*

The decision to send a number of young Japanese to Europe was made spontaneously in the autumn of 1581 by Alessandro Valignano, *visitator* (visitor or inspector) of the Jesuit missions in the East Indies, covering the area from Goa to Japan. Preparations for such an ambitious and dangerous undertaking were made hurriedly not long before the boys themselves left their homeland. Valignano did not envisage the visit as a formal embassy, even if that is how it came to be seen in Europe and that is how Valignano himself referred to it retrospectively. It did, however, have an official character in that two of the boys chosen went as representatives of three of the most important Christian daimyo in western Japan to perform obeisance to the pope, acknowledging him as their pastor.

The boys left Japan on 20 February 1582. In addition to the places they visited on the outward and return voyages, they travelled from Lisbon, where they disembarked on 11 August 1584, through Portugal, Spain and Italy as far as Rome, the highpoint of their journey, before returning to the Portuguese capital, from where they finally set sail on the long voyage home on 13 April 1586. They reached Nagasaki on 21 July 1590, amidst great rejoicing, more than eight years after their departure. During their travels in Europe they had audiences and less formal meetings with the most powerful European monarch, Philip II, two popes, Gregory XIII and Sixtus V, and were received by many of the most important political, ecclesiastical and social figures in the places they visited. Determined to capitalize on the successful outcome of this remarkable journey, Valignano conceived of the idea of a book based on the boys' travels, one that could also be used for teaching purposes in Jesuit colleges in Japan. The outcome was *De Missione*, published in Macao early in 1590, although printing had begun in the middle of the previous year.[1]

The visit is known retrospectively in Japanese as the *Tenshō shōnen shisetsu* (the Tenshō era boys' embassy) or *Tenshō ken-Ō shisetsu* (Tenshō era embassy to Europe). Sixteenth-century Europeans, unlike their modern counterparts for whom the words 'embassy' and 'ambassador' have become technical terms with more limited usage, had no difficulty in considering the visit an embassy and the boys as ambassadors or, in the humanists' favoured terminology, *legati*. By the 1580s a hierarchy had emerged among the various European powers and authorities recognized as having the right to send and receive diplomatic representatives, as had the modern practice of permanent diplomacy and resident ambassadors. The hierarchy was not rigid; nor did it contain a standard or widely accepted terminology to classify such representatives and their functions. In the thirteenth

---

[1] ARSI, Jap.Sin 11: I, f. 157v; Schütte, 'Der Lateinische Dialog', p. 268; Valignano, *Apología*, p. 55.

century the canon lawyer Gulielmus Durandus wrote that '[a] *legatus* ... is anybody sent by another'. Commenting on the first diplomatic textbook, written by Bernard du Rosier in 1436, Garrett Mattingly noted that the 'the occasions for sending ambassadors [were] as numerous as the kinds of advantages to be obtained'. Mattingly, following Rosier, divides embassies into 'embassies of ceremony' and 'embassies of negotiation'. Such distinctions were well understood in sixteenth-century Europe and for contemporaries the Japanese visit was an embassy of ceremony.

The embassy was not the first of its kind to reach Europe from the distant lands that the Portuguese encountered during the golden age of their overseas voyages. Nor was it the first to receive widespread publicity and comment, or indeed to inspire a major publication such as *De Missione*.[1] Among a number of such embassies to reach Europe in the fifteenth and sixteenth centuries, that from the Ethiopian emperor, or *negus*, Lebna Dengel (David II), deserves particular mention because it attracted much attention at the time, and because the Japanese embassy was later compared highly favourably with it. The Ethiopian emperor's ambassador was a Portuguese religious, Francisco Álvares, who had been a member of the Portuguese embassy to Ethiopia in 1520 and who wrote a valuable and much praised description of the country.[2] Álvares performed obeisance before Clement VII on behalf of the Ethiopian ruler in the presence of another emperor, Charles V, at Bologna on 29 January 1533, although some, including the pope himself, doubted the embassy's authenticity. This may account for the rumours about the legitimacy of the Japanese mission and questions about the status of the boys that began to circulate in Europe during their visit. A published account of the Ethiopian embassy, *Legatio Dauid Aethiopiae Regis, ad Sanctissimum D. N. Clementem Papam VII. vnà cum obedientia, eidem sanctiss. D. N. praestita ...*, appeared in February 1533 in Bologna. French, German and Italian versions quickly followed.[3] The title of the present work, *De Missione Legatorvm Iaponensium ad Romanum curiam ...*, which, amongst other things, is an account of the Japanese mission, is a conscious reference to this earlier publication.

Álvares's embassy is mentioned in the dedication of Guido Gualtieri's account of the Tenshō embassy. He compared the Japanese visit to the adoration of the Magi and judged it more impressive than its Ethiopian predecessor because the boys

---

[1] Such distinctions did not confuse people in the 16th century although their modern counterparts, for whom the words 'embassy' and 'ambassador' have become technical terms, have difficulties with them. See Mattingly, *Renaissance Diplomacy*, pp. 15–60, esp. pp. 23, 26–7, 30; Carter, 'Ambassadors of Early Modern Europe', *passim*. Viewed from Japan, which had had official relations with China (severed after 1557) and with Korea, but not with any European power, the boys' mission was not an embassy officially sanctioned by the Japanese state. Nor, given the fact that the country was still rent by civil wars, could it have been, for as the wars approached their conclusion, the 16th-century Japanese state was undergoing a process of state re-formation and no single Japanese ruler had yet emerged with sufficient control over its apparatus to authorize such a mission even in the highly unlikely event that he would have wished to do so.

[2] See Beckingham and Huntingford, *Prester John*, *passim*.

[3] On the embassy and on the various editions of the *Legatio Dauid*, see Matos, *L'Expansion portugaise*, pp. 186–204, 564–5. On the doubts concerning the embassy's authenticity, see the reports by the English ambassador in Gairdner, *Letters and Papers Henry VIII*, VI, nos 63, 109, 156, 175. On previous actual and alleged embassies from African rulers, see Matos, *L'Expansion portugaise*, p. 186; Lowe, '"Representing" Africa', *passim*.

themselves were Japanese; they had travelled much further at greater risk to their well-being, and were from a pagan land not an ostensibly Christian one somewhat closer to home.[1]

The architect of the Tenshō embassy, Valignano, a towering and controversial presence in the history of the Jesuit mission in Asia, was a native of Chieti in the kingdom of Naples, then a possession of the Spanish monarchy. He had been appointed visitor in August 1573 and left Europe in March 1574, never to return. He reached India in September, and arrived in Japan, the first of three visits, in July 1579. During his stay in Japan, Valignano undertook an extensive consultation process which resulted in a number of recommendations to place the highly promising Japan mission on a new and, it was hoped, secure footing.[2] As Valignano was fully aware, policies which appeared to deviate from the Society's established way of proceeding, *noster modus procedendi*,[3] required the approval of the Jesuit superior general. Those which might deviate from established canon law and practice, especially in the aftermath of the Council of Trent, required the approval of the Holy See.

Valignano left Japan in 1582 along with the four boys. His purpose was to return to Europe to seek approval for his recommendations concerning Japan and the governance of the province of Goa, and also to seek rulings on matters relating to the Japan mission which were unclear in canon law, such as the sanctioning of marriage between Japanese Christian converts and non-Christian Japanese. The boys accompanied him as part of his overall strategy to further the Jesuit mission in Japan. After reaching Cochin in October 1583, however, Valignano was shocked and greatly disappointed to receive orders from Claudio Aquaviva, the Jesuits' fifth superior general and a personal friend, to remain in India as provincial. Valignano was too important an individual to risk losing on a voyage to Europe and back. As a result, the boys proceeded to Europe accompanied by a Portuguese Jesuit, Diogo de Mesquita.[4] Mesquita was not Valignano's first choice for this task. He would have preferred that Alfonso Pacheco accompany them. Pacheco, a Spanish Jesuit from a noble Castilian family, was well known to, and trusted by, Valignano. They had journeyed together to India in 1574. Six years later Pacheco had been dispatched to Europe as procurator and in the course of his duties had met with Philip II and Gregory XIII. He returned to Goa in 1581. He died on 15 July 1583 along with four other Jesuits, including Rodolfo Aquaviva, a nephew of the Jesuit general, and fifteen Indian Christians, in an attack at Salsete, to the south of Goa. This was an area where Portuguese missionary activity had met with fierce resistance from both Hindus and Muslims. The Hindus in particular resented the triumphalist and provocative policy (strongly supported by Valignano) of erecting churches on the sites of Hindu temples destroyed by the

---

[1] Gualtieri, *Relationi*, dedication, Aiiir–v.

[2] A preliminary consultation was held in the Shimo (for the Jesuits this meant Kyushu excluding the province of Bungo) in the summer of 1580 and three larger ones in Usuki, Azuchi and Nagasaki between October 1580 and December 1581. See Schütte, *Valignano's Mission Principles*, I: 1, pp. 368–73 and I: 2, pp. 7–50, 131–6, 214–49; Valignano, *Sumario*, pp. 73 n. 17, 1101.

[3] On 'our way of proceeding', sometimes called the Jesuit 'Institute', see O'Malley, *First Jesuits*, pp. 4–9, esp. p. 8.

[4] *Documenta Indica*, XII, pp. 828, 833. On Mesquita see below p. 50 n. 1. Valignano was reappointed visitor in September 1595.

missionaries.¹ Valignano felt that while Mesquita was fully qualified to look after the boys he was unknown in Europe, unlike Pacheco, and lacked the necessary experience and diplomatic polish to handle meetings and attend to business with the powerful people he would encounter. Later, after Mesquita and the boys returned from Europe, Valignano acknowledged that despite these shortcomings he had done a sterling job as chaperon.²

Valignano had wanted to accompany the boys on the long, hazardous, unfamiliar journey because they had been entrusted to his care, and they in turn trusted him. Moreover, he had wanted to argue his case about the future policy and governance of the vice province of Japan in person before the relevant authorities: the Jesuit superior general and the Holy See in Rome, and Philip II in Spain.³ En route, in Europe, he would also have taken the opportunity to promote and canvass the support of influential individuals for the Japan mission which he described as 'without doubt the most important and beneficial of all in these parts of the Orient, even of all the discoveries'.⁴ The written word alone, he felt, was inadequate to convey his intentions and, inevitably, words were open to misinterpretation, especially as some of his recommendations would appear novel and controversial to many in Europe. Documents alone were unable to communicate just how different Japan was from other places where the Jesuits were active, a leitmotiv in his numerous writings.⁵ However, as an obedient son of Ignatius of Loyola, the Jesuits' founder, he accepted the general's order to remain in India, but requested that on the boys' return from Europe he should accompany them back to Japan, mentioning 'the great love that I have' for that country where, with God's assistance, he had adapted himself so well, that he felt Japan had become 'my proper vocation'.⁶

Among Valignano's novel proposals for the future governance of the Japan mission, was the stipulation that European Jesuits must accommodate themselves to Japanese manners and customs.⁷ The concept of accommodation was not new. The issue had been raised in 1558 by Juan Alfonso de Polanco, the Society's first secretary and a trusted

---

¹ *Documenta Indica*, XII, pp. 4*, 5*, 117–18, 193–4, 249–50, 274–5, 916–32, 987; Álvarez-Taladriz, 'En el IV centenario de la embajada', p. 130 esp. n. 20; Xavier, *A invenção de Goa*, pp. 333–79.

² *Documenta Indica*, XII, p. 833; ARSI, Jap.Sin 10: II, ff. 288r–v, printed in Álvarez-Taladriz, 'En el IV centenario de la embajada', pp. 153–4.

³ After the union of the crowns in 1581, also Filipe I of Portugal.

⁴ Valignano, *Sumario*, p. 131, see following note.

⁵ *Documenta Indica*, XII, pp. 827–44. Valignano's recommendations for the future of the Japan mission are set out in the records of the consultations held during his visit and the resolutions passed (see Schütte, *Valignano's Mission Principles*, I: 2, pp. 214–57); in the *Advertimentos e avisos acerca dos costumes e catangues de Jappão*, referred to hereafter by the title of the modern published edition as Valignano, *Il cerimoniale*; and in Valignano's personal assessment of Japan and the Jesuit mission, 'Sumario de las cosas que pertenecen a la Prouincia de Jappón y al gouierno della, compuesto por el Padre Alexandro Valegniano [*sic*], Visitador de las Indias de Oriente dirigido a N. P. General Claudio Aquaviva', largely completed before he left Japan, and generally known as the *Sumario de las cosas de Japón* or *Sumario* after its definitive modern edition. A French translation is also available (Bésineau, *Jésuites au Japon*). Valignano had already expressed his keen desire to return to Europe in October 1580 when he had written to the superior general mentioning that he would like to be able to fly to Rome to give the pope and the general a personal briefing on his proposals. See Schütte, *Valignano's Mission Principles*, I: 2, p. 57.

⁶ *Documenta Indica*, XII, p. 848.

⁷ See Schütte, *Valignano's Mission Principles*, I: 2, pp. 240–49; Valignano, *Sumario*, ch. 23; *Il cerimoniale*, *passim*.

companion of Loyola. In the following decade the Jesuits in Japan recognized the need to adapt Christianity to, what they viewed as, the special circumstances of Japanese society if they were to make any progress and sought guidance from higher authorities about a number of questions concerning relations between Christians and non-Christians.[1] The novelty of Valignano's proposals, however, lay in the extent he wanted to stretch the concept and practice of accommodation. Accommodation was to be achieved by organizing Jesuit institutions in Japan along the lines of Buddhist monasteries, particularly those of the *gozan* or Five Mountain monasteries of the Rinzai school of Zen Buddhism, a major departure from 'our way of proceeding'.[2]

Among the controversial aspects of Valignano's propositions were two requests: firstly that, contrary to the rulings of the Council of Trent which had emphasized episcopal jurisdiction and authority, no bishop should be sent to Japan for the present; secondly that Japan should be reserved exclusively for the Jesuits. The mendicant orders, the senior service of Catholic missionary activity whose presence in Asia, although not continuous, dated back to the thirteenth century and who had first arrived in India at the beginning of the sixteenth century, were to be excluded from Japan.[3] Although these requests are sometimes portrayed as originating with Valignano, they had been aired before his appointment as visitor. The question of sending a bishop to Japan had been suggested as early as 1555 and in 1566 Melchior Carneiro, one of the Society's most distinguished early members, was appointed bishop of Japan, although he did not outrank the Jesuit superior there. He reached Macao in 1568 where, too infirm to travel further, he remained, his authority ignored by Valignano. During the consultations in Japan, Valignano's attitude towards the appointment of a bishop was inconsistent. Eventually he agreed with those who argued that the first bishop of Japan to be appointed should be Japanese, presiding over a Japanese clergy. This would take time to achieve, and in the interim a Jesuit should be sanctioned to perform such necessary functions as consecrating chrism and holy oils for sacramental and other purposes.[4]

The question of keeping the Japan mission exclusively for the Jesuits had likewise been raised before Valignano's appointment as visitor. Again, opinion among the Jesuits was divided. The third Jesuit general, Francisco de Borja, doubtless recalling Francis Xavier's insistence that Japan should be open to all religious orders, was in favour of other missionaries joining the undermanned mission, although he was well aware of the

---

[1] Leturia, 'Un significativo documento de 1558', pp. 102–17, esp. p. 110; *Documenta Indica*, IV, pp. 72–80, esp. p. 74; Pinto and Pires, '"Resposta que alguns padres de Japão mandaram perguntar"', *passim*.

[2] Valignano, *Il cerimoniale*, pp. 82–92; Moran, *Japanese and the Jesuits*, pp. 56–7. Although the Jesuits were much impressed by the organization of the *gozan* monasteries, these were past the peak of their influence. The Zen monasteries of Daitokuji, which had been excluded from the *gozan* network in 1386, and Myōshinji, which had not been part of the network, were being patronized by the new elites emerging from the turmoil of the civil wars. See Collcutt, *Five Mountains*, pp. 91, 112, 123–9.

[3] The mendicants had not yet reached the country. They first arrived in 1584 when a junk bound for Manila from Macao was blown off course. They were made welcome by the Japanese. Ten years later the Franciscans were given permission to establish a mission in Japan by Toyotomi Hideyoshi, the second of the three unifiers and hegemons who emerged in the later 16th century.

[4] On the bishop question see Valignano, *Sumario*, pp. 138–42; Schütte, *Valignano's Mission Principles*, II: 2, pp. 15–18, 53–7, 220–24, 279–80; López-Gay, *El catecumenado*, pp. 175–81; Cooper, *Rodrigues the Interpreter*, pp. 108–9; Moran, *Japanese and the Jesuits*, pp. 161–5; Bourdon, *Compagnie de Jésus et le Japon*, pp. 553–7; and below p. 35 n. 1.

opposition to such a policy among some of the Jesuits in Japan.[1] Valignano, who had first voiced his objections to allowing other missionaries to enter Japan while still in Goa in 1576 before even reaching Japan, was unyielding in his opposition to opening up the mission and sought to obtain a categorical ruling from Rome that Japan would remain exclusively a Jesuit mission. He cited the division of Japanese Buddhism into a number of irreconcilable sects to justify the unusual request. The Japanese, he firmly believed, should not come to see Christianity as similarly divided, a situation that would be likely to arise were the mendicants, with their own missionary ethos, permitted to come to Japan. Valignano saw the mendicants' dependence on alms as impractical for raising funds to sustain and develop missionary activity, and one that would demean all missionaries in the eyes of the Japanese.[2]

The question of alms touched upon an additional mundane, but nevertheless vital, reason why Valignano wanted to proceed to Europe: money, the *sine qua non* for any missionary activity in Japan. Unless the Japan mission was put on a secure financial footing, it had no future. The running costs for 1582 were 12,020 ducats, covered by rents from lands in India. In the *Sumario*, Valignano wrote that the mission needed at least an annual income of 10,000 ducats to cover running costs and a further endowment of 30,000 or 40,000 ducats to fund new houses and colleges and to tide the mission over in years when no shipping arrived from Macao. He noted, tartly, that his request was paltry in comparison with the amount of money lavished on the Roman College or the German College and confidently predicted that, if the money was forthcoming, 'before thirty years have passed, all or the most part of [Japan] would be converted'.[3]

The dispatch of the four boys to Europe, then, was not the primary reason for Valignano's (aborted) trip to Europe. But, as he put it in the detailed instructions he gave to Nuno Rodrigues, the rector of the Jesuit college in Goa, who was going to Rome to attend a conference of Jesuit procurators and to whom he entrusted the boys and the documents concerning the future of the Japan mission, their presence would significantly boost the case for his policies. They would be a 'carta viva', a living letter or embodiment of what Valignano was writing about Japan.[4]

Objectives of the Embassy and the Individuals Chosen

As Valignano originally conceived it, the boys' journey had two objectives.[5] First, the presence of noble and refined ambassadors should raise awareness of Japan amongst the

---

[1] *Documenta Indica*, VII, pp. 489–90, 593–4, 628–9. There were 77 Jesuits in Japan in 1581, including 20 Japanese. See Costa, 'Os Jesuítas no Japão', pp. 304, 329, 330, which revises earlier figures by Schütte, *Introductio ad Historiam Societatis Jesu*, p. 321. On Xavier's recommendation that Japan be open to all religious orders, see Ruiz-de-Medina, *Documentos del Japón*, I, pp. 167, 315.

[2] *Documenta Indica*, X, pp. 688–90; Valignano, *Sumario*, pp. 143–9.

[3] Schütte, *Monumenta Historica Japoniae I*, pp. 142–5; Valignano, *Sumario*, pp. 338–9. Elsewhere, in a letter to Aquaviva of 12 December 1583, he puts the figure for an endowment at 50,000 cruzados (Álvarez-Taladriz, 'En el IV centenario de la embajada', p. 143).

[4] ARSI, Jap.Sin 22, f. 53 printed in Álvarez-Taladriz, 'En el IV centenario de la embajada', p. 142. On Rodrigues, see below, p. 93 n. 1.

[5] Valignano stated his objectives for the embassy in several letters: to Aquaviva, Macao, 17 December 1582 (ARSI, Jap.Sin 9: I, f. 117v) and Cochin, 28 October 1583 (ARSI, Jap.Sin 9: II, f. 174); to Father Manuel

clerical and secular elites in Europe and demonstrate that what the Jesuits had been writing about Japan, some of which had been published and circulating for almost thirty years, was not, as was put about by some of Society's detractors, a fabrication. Valignano was very concerned about the quality of writing on Japan that appeared in Europe. Shortly after he first arrived in Japan, he wrote a highly perceptive memo on the superficial, inaccurate and misleading nature of the reports sent to Europe by Jesuits, some of which later appeared in print. The memo remains a salutary warning about the pitfalls of first impressions and superficial generalizations about Japan. Valignano complained that the reports differed greatly from the reality of Japan as he understood it. He attributed these shortcomings to the fact that when European Jesuits arrived in Japan they had neither linguistic competence nor any meaningful knowledge of Japanese society and culture. These deficiencies led them to make snap judgements. The visit by the boys would make the pope and other European rulers appreciate the importance of Japan as a missionary territory, support it, and underwrite its costs. Second, the visit would impress upon the four youths the glory and grandeur of the Christian religion, the majesty of the European rulers who had embraced it, the richness and splendour of Europe's kingdoms and cities, and the honour and authority that the Christian religion enjoyed throughout Europe.[1]

Valignano emphasized the latter point because he considered that the Japanese knew nothing concrete about Europe and tended to view the missionaries as people of low standing in their native lands who had come to Japan ostensibly to preach the gospel but in reality to make their fortune. He claimed that the Japanese held in contempt the Portuguese merchants and seamen who frequented Nagasaki, which from 1570 had become the terminus for the Portuguese trade between Macao and Japan, and that this

---

Rodríguez, Goa, 15 December 1583 (ARSI, Jap.Sin 9: II, f. 223r–v); to Teotónio de Bragança, archbishop of Évora (*Cartas*, II, ff. 88v–89); and in the 'Regimento e instrução' which he drew up for Father Nuno Rodrigues who accompanied the boys to Europe (ARSI, Jap.Sin 22, ff. 51–8v, esp. ff. 52r–v). The relevant passages of the letters are printed in Valignano, *Apología*, pp. 59–61 n. 25. The letter to Aquaviva of 28 October 1583 is printed fully in *Documenta Indica*, XII, pp. 827–44, esp. pp. 833–4, and in Álvarez-Taladriz, 'En el IV centenario de la embajada', pp. 126–36, esp. p. 129–30. The 'Regimento e instrução' is printed fully in ibid., pp. 136–51, esp. pp. 139–40, and partially in Abranches Pinto and Bernard, 'Les instructions', pp. 392–403, esp. pp. 395–6. Valignano repeated the objectives in his *Apología*, pp. 57–61.

[1] Below pp. 38–9; Abranches Pinto and Bernard, 'Les instructions', pp. 395–6; Álvarez-Taladriz, 'En el IV centenario de la embajada', pp. 139–40. According to Valignano, the more prejudiced Jesuits considered that their interpretations of Japanese people's outward behaviour could be applied willy-nilly to the whole society and culture, and rashly proceeded to categorize all Japanese as simple and devout or cunning and secretive and so on. Others, he noted caustically, while having a better grasp of Japanese society and culture, produced edifying commentaries that caused people in Europe to think that the Japanese were imbued with 'truth and an inner spirit' (i.e. they had already accepted the Christian revelation and had experienced regeneration without the precondition of baptism, absurdities from the missionary viewpoint). Others again wrote about the spiritual fervour with which people had embraced Christianity on the orders of their lords who wanted to have the Portuguese ships call at their ports. This gave the impression that the whole country was motivated by such spiritual fervour. Finally, some writers who found little good in some or other aspect of Japan then proceeded to paint the whole society with a negative brush. To counter such deficiencies, he intended to write a practical and more edifying history. He repeated these criticisms of the reporting of Japan over the years and frequently referred to his planned history. It was never completed. See ARSI, Jap.Sin 8: II, ff. 243r–v, printed in Valignano, *Historia*, pp. 483–4; Abranches Pinto and Bernard, 'Les instructions', p. 396 n. 46; Álvarez-Taladriz, 'De la primera visita', pp. 90–91. See also *Documenta Indica*, XV, p. 63; Moran, *Japanese and the Jesuits*, p. 39.

assessment had coloured Japanese perceptions of the Jesuits.[1] To counter such negative images, and to heal the 'great disunion and aversion' that existed between the European Jesuits and the Japanese *irmãos* or brothers,[2] it was essential that a few intelligent, young Japanese of high social status should see for themselves the reality of Europe – or rather, what Valignano intended them to see – and report back to their compatriots what they had witnessed. The boys were to be treated well, befitting their high status, and the trip was to be instructive. They were to be constantly chaperoned and screened from discovering anything unedifying or controversial about the state of Christianity in Europe which, if reported back to Japan, might hinder the progress of the church there. The list of censored information extended far beyond the most obvious – the division of Christendom into rival Protestant and Catholic states – to include the discord, jealousies and rivalries that existed at the Spanish court and among the clergy in Spain, the quarrels between Philip II and the papacy, the differences between Philip II and the Jesuits (who, the monarch believed, had acted against him during the Portuguese succession crisis and who, he suspected, were trying to make themselves financially independent of the crown to further their own interests), and finally discord within the Jesuit order itself and the schismatic tendencies among the Spanish Jesuits. The boys were not to be permitted to remain in Rome to pursue their studies as Valignano had promised their parents they would return as soon as possible. Two of the boys, Michael and Julian, were only surviving sons of widowed mothers.[3]

The boys chosen for this bold experiment in Jesuit diplomacy were known to the fathers in Japan. Although Michael, who represented the daimyo of Ōmura and Arima, is the main speaker in *De Missione*, the senior member of the party was Mancio Itō Sukemasu, representing Ōtomo Yoshishige (or Sōrin), daimyo of Bungo. Mancio was a grandson of Itō Yoshisuke, lord of Hyūga, who had been hostile to Christianity, but who had fled to Bungo (to whose ruler he was connected by marriage) with his dependants when he lost his domains in 1578. Yoshishige had been baptized in 1578, taking the Christian name Francisco. Yoshishige's first choice as his representative was his grandnephew (and Mancio's cousin), Jerónimo Itō Yoshikatsu, but the latter was studying at the Jesuit seminary in Azuchi, near Kyoto, where the first of the country's three hegemons, Oda Nobunaga, had established his headquarters, and would have been unable to reach Nagasaki before the scheduled departure. As a result, Mancio was substituted. Michael (or Miguel) Chijiwa Seizaemon was a nephew of Ōmura Sumitada, daimyo of

---

[1] Valignano, *Il cerimoniale*, p. 172; also taken up in Colloquium VII below.

[2] ARSI, Jap.Sin 8: II, f. 298, Valignano to the Jesuit general, 27 October 1580, printed in Schütte, *Valignanos Missionsgrundsätze für Japan*, I: 2, p. 489.

[3] *Documenta Indica*, XII, p. 833; Abranches Pinto and Bernard, 'Les instructions', pp. 400–401; Álvarez-Taladriz, 'En el IV centenario de la embajada', p. 149. On the broader issues of relations among Philip II, the Jesuits and the papacy, see *Documenta Indica*, XII, pp. 259–61, 407, 604, and XIV, pp. 1*, 67, 71, 327 n. 13; Wicki, 'Philip II und die Jesuiten', *passim*; Lynch, 'Philip II and the Papacy', pp. 23–42; *idem*, *Spain under the Habsburgs*, pp. 257–70; Parker, *Grand Strategy*, pp. 7, 80–81, 96–7, 190–91; Marques, 'Confesseurs des princes', pp. 213–28; Alden, *Making of an Enterprise*, pp. 79–91, 96–109; 670–73; Padberg et al., *For Matters of Greater Moment*, pp. 10–13; García Cárcel, 'Las relaciones de la monarquía de Felipe II', pp. 232–41; Navarro, *La Compañía de Jesus*, pp. 98–117; Dandelet, *Spanish Rome*, ch. 3; Levin, *Agents of Empire*, *passim*; Palomo, 'Para el sosiego y quietud del reino', *passim*; Bireley, *Jesuits and the Thirty Years War*, pp. 273–5; Disney, *History of Portugal*, I, pp. 173–6, 192–7.

Ōmura and the first daimyo to be baptized in 1563, taking the Christian name Bartolomeu. Michael was also a cousin of Arima Harunobu, daimyo of Arima who was baptized in 1579, taking the Christian name Protasio. The two other boys, Julian (or Julião) Nakaura and Martin Hara (sometimes called Martinho Campo in Portuguese, a direct translation of his family name), went along as companions of Michael and Mancio, although they were also treated as if they were envoys. Julian's father had been the castellan of a fort between Hirado and Ōmura but had lost control of it during the civil wars. Little is known about Martin's family except that his sister had married a brother of Ōmura Sumitada and his younger brother was (presumably the titular) castellan of one of the most important forts in the Ōmura domains.[1] A Japanese Jesuit, the *irmão* Jorge Loyola (one of the Fathers' star pupils), accompanied the boys as their Japanese language and literature tutor, although of a weak constitution. Two young Japanese, Constantino Dourado and Agostinho, are mentioned as being among the servants and attendants.[2] When they left Japan the four boys were about fourteen years old.[3]

The other speakers in *De Missione*, Leo (or León) and Lino, are described respectively as 'brother of the king of Arima' and 'brother of the prince of Ōmura, both of whom are cousins of Michael on their fathers' side' who had 'never been out of Japan'.[4] They were indeed historical persons and Michael's cousins. Leo was Arima Sumizane (or Matazaemon), younger brother of Arima Harunobu,[5] and Lino was Ōmura Suminobu, a son of Ōmura Sumitada and younger brother of Ōmura Yoshiaki, Sumitada's heir. Lino's taste for Portuguese clothes, which he ordered from Macao, was well known.[6]

The final decision to send the boys to Europe was made in December 1581, not long before Valignano and his charges left Japan. He made the decision in consultation with the daimyo concerned. In some ways such an embassy had been anticipated. Ōmura Sumitada and Ōtomo Yoshishige had already received letters from Gregory XIII, who took a special interest in Japan. One such letter to Sumitada, dated 3 October 1573, congratulated him on becoming a Christian, the other to Yoshishige, dated 20 December 1578, thanked him for his favours to Christians.[7] The idea of sending a delegation to Rome might even have been suggested by one of the daimyo themselves and was certainly not inimical to them. In September 1578, before Valignano's arrival in Japan, Ōtomo

---

[1] Valignano, *Sumario*, pp. 87, 89 n. 79, 102, 103; *Apología*, pp. 56–7; Fróis, *Première ambassade*, pp. 9–16; Matsuda, *Kinsei shoki Nihon kankei*, pp. 807–52, esp. pp. 833, 840; Oishi, *Tenshō ken-Ō shisetsu*, pp. 107, 117.

[2] On Loyola, see below p. 50 n. 2. On Constantino, see Álvarez-Taladriz, 'El Escorial', pp. 7–9; Cooper, *Japanese Mission*, pp. 183–4, and below p. 53 n. 5. Nothing is known about Agostinho beyond the references to him in Fróis, *Première ambassade*.

[3] In the annual Japan letter for 1581, dated 15 February 1582, just before their departure, Gaspar Coelho says that the boys 'had not [yet] passed fourteen'. Valignano, writing to the superior general from Cochin en route to Goa with the boys in October 1583, says they were aged fifteen (*Cartas*, II, f. 17v; *Documenta Indica*, XII, p. 828). These are the most reliable estimates of their ages. The Jesuit historian and rector of the Jesuit college in Belmonte in Spain, Luís de Guzman, whom they met, commented profusely that although 'they appeared to be boys in age, in judgement and discretion they were men' (Guzman, *Historia*, II, p. 294).

[4] Below p. 39.

[5] Valignano, *Sumario*, p. 83; Fróis, *História de Japam*, V, pp. 188, 336; Yūki, 'Arima-ke no kirishitan daimyō', pp. 14–15; *Hanshi daijiten*, VII, p. 236.

[6] *Cartas*, I, f. 400v; Valignano, *Sumario*, p. 76 n. 35; *Hanshi daijiten*, VII, p. 199.

[7] Magino, *Pontifica Nipponica*, I, pp. 14–15, 22–3.

Yoshimune, who was not yet a Christian but who had nominally taken over the government of Bungo from his father, had asked the Jesuit, Luís Fróis, whether, on becoming a Christian, a Japanese 'king' was obliged to send an 'ambassador' to the pope to perform obeisance.[1] Meanwhile, Gregory XIII had expressed a wish that some Japanese should come to Rome. When he arrived in Goa with the boys on 28 November 1583, Valignano was elated to hear this news and took it as an indication of Providence's care for the Society.[2]

Doubts about the boys' status and rumours that they were not Japanese began to circulate in Europe during the visit and controversy about their social status and the authenticity of the mission has resonated ever since.[3] Among the first to allege fraud was a Spanish Jesuit, Pedro Ramón. On 15 October 1587, Ramón sent a letter from Ikitsuki to the Jesuit general in which he made a number of allegations. First, he claimed that the boys were low born and that had they not attached themselves to the Jesuits they would have been nobodies. Mancio, he said, he knew well. He had taken pity on the boy when he was destitute and had given him clothing and shelter in the church at Funai. Second, Ramón took issue with the title 'king' used in Europe to describe the daimyo whom the boys represented and in the letters that the pope and others had addressed to these rulers. The Japanese term *yakata*, he contended, was not equivalent to king; in European parlance they were dukes or nobles, not monarchs. Third, and more seriously, he alleged that Ōtomo Yoshishige had no prior knowledge of the boys' journey, that Mancio Itō had been chosen to represent him without his permission, and that the letter (the original of which is no longer extant) presented by Mancio to the pope and signed by Yoshishige had not been written by him.[4] Ramón's charges anticipate those made more publicly nine years later by the mendicants.[5]

However, as the editor of the published version of the full text of Ramón's letter notes, when one considers the letter in its entirety, and an earlier one of 10 November 1585, Ramón's allegations appear in a different light, not primarily as an attack on the embassy itself but a critique of Valignano's stewardship of the mission. Ramón's command of Japanese was excellent and his knowledge of the country extensive, greater than Valignano's in his own opinion. He criticized the visitor for managing the affairs of the Japan mission in such a way that opinions contrary to his own were not reflected in the final report prepared after the consultations. Valignano's high-handed and personal management style, he suggested, had concentrated too much power at the top. In Ramón's

---

[1] Fróis, *Historia de Japam*, III, p. 31; Álvarez-Taladriz, 'A cada cosa', p. 18.

[2] ARSI, Jap.Sin 8: II, f. 223, printed in Álvarez-Taladriz, 'En el IV centenario de la embajada', pp. 184–5, and Valignano, *Apología*, p. 60.

[3] Richard Cocks, head of the English East India Company's factory in Japan 1613–23, whose sources were Franciscan, repeated the charges of fraud while others, such as the Jesuit historian Joseph de Jouvency, rejected them. See Farrington, *English Factory*, I, p. 257; de Jouvency, *Historiae Societatis Jesu Pars Quinta*, pp. 582–3; Boscaro, 'Manoscritto inedito', p. 38 n. 54.

[4] ARSI, Jap.Sin 10: II, ff. 282–5v, printed in Álvarez-Taladriz, 'A cada cosa', pp. 7–16, esp. pp. 9–13. On the question of the correct translation of *yakata*, see below p. 129 n. 2.

[5] The mendicant critique was made most forcefully by the Franciscan, Fray Martín de la Ascensión, who visited Japan in the summer of 1596, in two memoranda, one to the commissary general of the Franciscan order in the Indies, the other to Philip II. The texts are printed in Álvarez-Taladriz, *Documentos Franciscanos*, pp. 41–145. Valignano responded to the charges in his *Apología* (pp. 52–76).

assessment, the boys' visit and the deceitful manner in which it was arranged were, from the perspective of 1587 – when Japan's new hegemon, Toyotomi Hideyoshi, had issued a decree ordering the missionaries to leave Japan – further illustrations of the mission's organizational flaws. These flaws, Ramón believed, had contributed to the promulgation of the decree and put the whole mission in jeopardy. In fact, the decree was not strictly enforced and only a few Jesuits left Japan while others, including Ramón, took refuge in Hirado and other places until things settled down.[1]

In recent times, the accusation that Valignano consciously perpetrated a fraud has been repeated by Jurgis Elisonas who bases much of his argument on Ramón's letter. Elisonas dismisses the embassy contemptuously as a 'masquerade' and a 'farce', aided and abetted 'by the lords along the boys' route' who had been 'well coached beforehand' (by whom is not stated) on how to receive the visitors.[2] To buttress his case, Elisonas draws attention to discrepancies (originally noted by the Japanese historian, Matsuda Kiichi) in a copy of a letter from Ōtomo Yoshishige to the Jesuit general. In the letter, the characters used for Mancio's family name, Itō, are given as 伊藤 rather than 伊東 and Yoshishige's monogram was one he no longer used. On the basis of these errors Elisonas pronounces the letter 'a palpable forgery'.[3] But, the evidence of forgery is not conclusive. In his comments on the letter, Matsuda makes much of Yoshishige's reference to Itō Jerónimo, his first choice as his representative, as '*itoko Itō Jeronimo*', which Matsuda gives as 'our cousin Itō Jerónimo'. Matsuda points out that Jerónimo was not Yoshishige's cousin but his niece's son, or grandnephew, which indeed he was.[4] It is possible, however, to read '*itoko*' not only as 'our cousin' but also as 'our beloved child' or 'our dearest child', in other words as a term of affection.[5] In the same letter Mancio is referred to as '*itoko Manshiyo*' which Matsuda reads as 'cousin' whereas 'beloved' or 'dear child' is a more likely reading for a Japanese document

---

[1] Álvarez-Taladriz, 'A cada cosa', pp. 1–20, esp. pp. 5, 9, 17. One of Ramón's suggested solutions to the structural problems facing the mission was the erection of a fortress in a place like Nagasaki where, under the protection of the Portuguese monarch, the fathers and their charges would be secure. Such a proposal was anathema to Valignano. It was dismissed in Rome when Ramón's 1587 letter was read with Aquaviva's comment that only Providence knew when and how the Japanese 'kings' would become Christians and that, as had been the case with the early church, fortitude and patience would overcome 'these difficulties'. The general also dismissed the suggestion, in the letter, that the boys were accepted in Rome as 'princes'. They were, he noted, known to be nobles carrying letters from 'these *yakata* which are equivalent to kings'.

[2] Elisonas, 'Acts, Legends, and Southern Barbarous Japanese', pp. 16–17; 'Fables and Imitations', p. 13 n. 5; 'Journey to the West', pp. 33–47, esp. p. 39. The charges of fraud have been dismissed by Schütte (*Valignano's Mission Principles*, I: 2, pp. 258–63), Pacheco ('Los cuatro legados', pp. 21–5 and *Os quatro legados*, pp. 10–13), Yūki (*Tenshō shōnen shisetsu*, 1992, *passim*) and Cooper (*Japanese Mission*, p. 16).

[3] *Dai Nihon Shiryō*, XI: 1, pp. 318–19; Matsuda, *Tenshō ken-Ō shisetsu*, pp. 70–71; Elisonas, 'Journey to the West', p. 33 n. 6. The original is in ARSI, Jap.Sin 186a, unfoliated.

[4] Matsuda, *Kinsei shoki Nihon*, p. 840; *Tenshō ken-Ō shisetsu*, pp. 70–71. Nephew is how Jerónimo is described in the Spanish version of this letter and Mancio is described, correctly, as Jerónimo's cousin (*Dai Nihon Shiryō*, XI: 1, p. 275). The same is true for the Spanish translations of Yoshishige's letters to the 'King of Portugal', Cardinal Henrique and the pope (RAHM, MS 09-02663, ff. 326–7v), although, in the Portuguese version of Yoshishige's letter to Aquaviva, Jerónimo is described as '*meo primo*' or 'my cousin', clearly a copyist's error (Fróis, *Première ambassade*, p. 175).

[5] See *Kōjien*. This is also the reading shared by the editors of Fróis, *Première ambassade*, in their discussion of Mancio's genealogy (p. 14). To complicate matters, in a letter to Cardinal Carafa, written in 1587, Arima Harunobu uses a different word for Michael, referring to him as '*warera jūshi*' or 'our cousin' (*Dai Nihon Shiryō*, XI: 2, p. 302).

of this period.[1] There are a number of inconsistencies concerning the relationships between Mancio, his grandfather (the former daimyo of Hyūga) and Yoshishige in the extant sources, but the majority, including a note describing the boys and their party that accompanies Spanish and Italian translations of the daimyo's various letters among the Jesuit archives, do not say there was a blood relationship with Yoshishige.[2] After the Franciscan charges of fraud were made, Valignano felt compelled to put to rest the misunderstandings about Mancio. Writing to Aquaviva from Macao in October 1588, he stated correctly that Mancio was the grandson of Itō Yoshisuke and a cousin of the restored daimyo of Hyūga, Itō Suketaka, and was not a blood relation of Yoshishige.[3]

On the question of monograms, raised by Professor Matsuda, the charge of forgery is inconclusive. The translation of a subsequent letter from Yoshishige to Aquaviva, dated 20 November 1584, in which Yoshishige asks for a fragment of the Cross and advocates the beatification of Francis Xavier, bears a monogram different from that affixed to the earlier letter to Aquaviva.[4] Two additional problems (not addressed by Professor Elisonas) undermine the reliability of Ramón's letter. One is Ramón's assertion that Jorge Loyola was a substitute for another Jesuit brother, a native of Kyoto, who was in Bungo at the time and could not make it to Nagasaki before the boys' departure. Here Ramón, who admits that his memory is somewhat hazy, confuses the substitution of Mancio for Jerónimo. The other problem is that Ramón wrongly asserts that the boys' fathers were all dead. Martin's was very much alive and welcomed his son home in Nagasaki.[5]

Allegations of fraud are further undermined by the contents of the annual letter to the Jesuit general for 1581 sent with all the other documents from Japan in the vessel which carried Valignano and his charges. In the letter, dated 15 February 1582, the vice provincial, Gaspar Coelho, wrote, as had Valignano, that the boys' journey to Europe would demonstrate the great importance of the '*empresa*' or undertaking that the Society had taken on in Japan and that he expected that the boys would return edified and impressed with what they had seen, to the future benefit of Christianity in Japan. He

---

[1] Matsuda, *Tenshō ken-Ō shisetsu*, p. 70. I am extremely grateful to Professor Tominaga Michio for his suggestions about reading this letter.

[2] ARSI, Jap.Sin 33, f. 16; Fróis, *Première ambassade*, pp. 10–12.

[3] Valignano, *Apología*, p. 56. Oddly, in his account of the visit, Fróis says that Mancio was Yoshishige's nephew rather than great-nephew (*Première ambassade*, p. 6).

[4] ARSI, Jap.Sin 33, ff. 43–4, part of a correspondence of which little survives. It should be noted that the dates given in the European-language translations are wrong. They are direct translations from the Japanese, unadjusted to the European calendar. For example, Yoshishige's letter to Aquaviva is dated 11 January 1582 while the Japanese version is dated '*shōgatsu juichi nichi*' or the eleventh day of the first month of the lunar calendar, i.e. 3 February. Also in Ōmura Sumitada's letter to the Jesuit general, now in the University of Kyoto Library, Michael is referred to twice as 'Don Migeru', not in *hiragana* script but in *kanji*, and the character used is 鈍 which can be pronounced either as *don* or *nibui*, meaning 'dull' or 'dim-witted' (*Dai Nihon Shiryō*, XI: 1, p. 319). We cannot know whether this is an insult, irony, a humble expression, or the truth. I am most grateful to Professor Tominaga for noting the latter point. The editors of Fróis, *Première ambassade* (p. 90 n. 346) assert that after Valignano heard of Philip II's accession to the Portuguese throne he ordered new letters from the daimyo addressed to Philip to be drawn up. This is conjectural. There is no reason to suppose that the letters had not been written in Japan as Valignano had originally planned that the boys would meet the king. See Álvarez-Taladriz, 'En el IV centenario de la embajada', p 140. Letters addressed to the Cardinal King of Portugal, Henrique, were, however, discarded. Two are now in ARSI, Jap.Sin 186a, unfoliated.

[5] Álvarez-Taladriz, 'A cada cosa', pp. 11–12; Fróis, *História de Japam*, V, p. 188.

described correctly Mancio's and Michael's relationships with the daimyo they each represented, and the substitution of Mancio for Jerónimo, and noted that Valignano had met with Ōmura Sumitada several times both in Nagasaki and in Ōmura after the visitor's return from Kyoto in the autumn of 1581. During the meetings, the question of sending the boys certainly came up. The Portuguese Jesuit Afonso de Lucena, who worked in the Ōmura domain from 1578 until 1614, says that Valignano discussed the idea with Sumitada who felt it was 'made in heaven' and offered his assistance to help bring it about. For his part, Coelho believed that the embassy must have been ordained by Providence because of the ease with which these 'great lords' had given permission for the boys to accompany the visitor on such a long and dangerous voyage, and because their mothers, despite having no other sons, had agreed to let them go, something unprecedented in Japan.[1] There is no indication of fraud here and while it may be objected that Lucena's account is suspect because it was written retrospectively (sometime between 1614 and 1623 at a time when the controversy surrounding the embassy was already public), it would be a grand slander to suggest that Coelho was, in cahoots with Valignano, lying to his superior. The embassy may have been hurriedly put together but it was no fraud.

Further evidence to support this view dates from after the boys returned to Japan. Once home, they were visited by various daimyo in western Japan and feted by Arima Harunobu and Ōmura Sumitada's son and successor, Yoshiaki. Furthermore, they were warmly received in Kyoto by none other than the *kampaku* or regent himself, Toyotomi Hideyoshi, who knew exactly who they were. Hideyoshi showed much affection to Mancio telling him that he had confirmed his cousin, Itō Suketaka, in the Itō household's traditional landholdings in Hyūga, and that he was willing to confer favours on Mancio as well.[2] In addition, in October 1590, Michael wrote to Cardinal Carafa in Rome mentioning that his family was joyous at his safe return and that Arima Harunobu and Ōmura Yoshiaki were very pleased with the letters they had received from Europe and with the boys' reception there.[3] In the same month Valignano wrote to Aquaviva declaring the visit a success and mentioned that it was a complex time-consuming task to translate various letters from Arima and Ōmura to the pope and Philip II, amongst others, because of the various languages involved (a reminder of how easy it was for copyists to make mistakes).[4] Had both the embassy and Ōtomo's letter been fraudulent and had there been a connection between the embassy and Hideyoshi's expulsion decree in 1587, rather than being feted, meeting the *kampaku*, and supervising translations of letters from the Christian daimyo who had sponsored the embassy, Valignano would have been expelled from Japan, if not executed. *Lèse-majesté* was no less severe a crime in Japan than in

---

[1] ARSI, Jap.Sin 46, ff. 59v–60; *Cartas*, II, f. 17v; Lucena, *Erinnerungen*, pp. 128–9; Schütte, *Valignano's Mission Principles*, I: 2, pp. 261–2.

[2] ARSI, Jap.Sin 11: II, f. 290; ARSI, Jap.Sin 51, ff. 327–8v; Fróis, *História de Japam*, V, pp. 187–8, 280–81, 285, 307, 334–8; Pacheco, 'Los cuatro legados', pp. 23–5, 27–8 and *Os quatro legados*, pp. 10–13, 15–16. In Kyoto, Hideyoshi asked Michael if he was related to Arima Harunobu. After some prodding, Michael replied that there was a connection but did not intimate precisely what it was (Fróis, *História de Japam*, V, p. 308).

[3] ARSI, Jap.Sin 11: II, f. 210. The letters from Europe to Ōmura were addressed to Sumitada who died in 1587.

[4] ARSI, Jap.Sin 11: II, f. 226. For copies and drafts of the letters from Arima and Ōmura, see ARSI, Jap.Sin 33, ff. 52–64.

Europe. In short, Valignano did not conspire to pass off the boys as hereditary princes travelling as accredited ambassadors of major Japanese potentates.

During the travels recounted in *De Missione* neither the Jesuits nor anyone else arranged for the boys to be welcomed with theatrical display. In his letters and instructions on how the boys should be treated, Valignano emphasized the need for modesty in their appearance and behaviour and a lack of ostentation in the manner of their reception. The boys were to be given the best accommodation in Jesuit colleges, but apart from the other residents because, as he noted, the colleges were not accustomed to receiving such young guests. They were to be treated well and shown respect and affection. Attention was to be paid to cleanliness concerning their food and dress. Their presence was in no way to disturb the colleges' routine. In their spare time the boys were to devote themselves to their studies of Japanese, Latin and music. Their visit was to have a religious character and tone, especially as the boys intended to become Jesuits. It was not to cause bother or expense either for the king or the pope, as it would if they were treated as issue and ambassadors of the lords who sent them.[1]

Valignano's insistence that the visit be conducted in an unostentatious way was ignored in Europe for reasons beyond the visitor's control, as Aquaviva later informed him. The decision to receive the boys in Rome in a public consistory with 'pomp and public honour' was made by Gregory XIII and some of his cardinal advisors. It was intended, amongst other things, to show Protestants how far the 'glory of the Holy Roman Church which they persecute' extended.[2] While it is true, as is made clear in *De Missione* and elsewhere, that both Gregory XIII and Sixtus V ordered the various authorities within the Papal States to give the boys a festive welcome on their travels, this did not involve, as Professor Elisonas suggests, 'coaching'.[3] The public ceremonial with which they were greeted in Italy and elsewhere was the norm not the exception for receiving important visitors. The Portuguese as well as Philip II, the Venetian Republic, the d'Este in Ferrrara, and the Gonzaga in Mantua all had their own reasons (notably smoothing relations with the papacy) for ensuring that the boys were received within their jurisdictions, but they did not need coaching from outsiders about the etiquette and protocols for receiving distinguished visitors. As Peter Burke has pointed out, '[m]agnificence was the outward sign of magnanimity, the greatness of spirit which is a central virtue in Aristotle's *Ethics*'.

---

[1] ARSI, Jap.Sin 9: I, f. 117v, and II, ff. 175v–6 (published in *Documenta Indica*, XII, pp. 842–3), 223r–v. His comments touching these matters are gathered conveniently in Valignano, *Apología*, p. 59 n. 25. See also Abranches Pinto and Bernard, 'Les instructions', pp. 394–5; Álvarez-Taladriz, 'En el IV centenario de la embajada', pp. 138–40. Valignano's modest expectations for the embassy were shared by others, including the Latin translator of *De Missione*, Duarte de Sande (*Documenta Indica*, XII, pp. 899, 972–3). On the cramped, overcrowded living conditions in the Jesuit college in Lisbon at this time, see *Documenta Indica*, XIV, p. 52. For a contemporary eyewitness account of the routine in the Jesuits' English College in Rome with its austerity and strict discipline, with punishments for misdemeanours, which included self-flagellation before fellow students at dinner, practices which Valignano was fully aware would have scandalized the boys, see Munday, *English Roman Life*, pp. 35–44. On flagellation and other forms of mortification in India, see *Documenta Indica*, XVI, pp. 885, 1047; and, more generally, Maher, 'Jesuits and Ritual', pp. 206–7.

[2] Valignano, *Apología*, p. 62; Fróis, *Première ambassade*, p. 143 n. 526; Cooper, *Japanese Mission*, pp. 84–5. The original of Aquaviva's letter to Valignano is no longer extant. See *Documenta Indica*, XIV, pp. 161, 426.

[3] Below, pp. 271, 325; RAHM, MS 09-02663, f. 441v.

It was the indispensable manner with which to receive, honour and impress visitors.[1] On learning of the embassy's reception in Europe Valignano did not complain that his instructions had been ignored. He was elated. The visit had gone better than he could ever have imagined.[2]

Publication of *De Missione*

Determined to capitalize on this success, Valignano conceived of the idea of a book based on the boys' travels, one that could also be used for teaching purposes in Jesuit colleges in Japan. The outcome was *De Missione*. The volume was published in Macao early in 1590, although printing, as has been mentioned, had begun in the middle of the previous year.[3] It was the third work to be published on the printing press that Valignano had requested for use in Japan.[4] The press accompanied the boys on their return from Europe and was taken to Japan. Valignano had long wanted to produce Latin books because, as he put it in a letter to Aquaviva in January 1586, of 'the impossibility and infinite cost' of having books sent regularly from Portugal. Luís Fróis had similarly requested that a press be sent, noting that the European Jesuits in Japan were wasting precious time copying texts instead of furthering their Japanese studies while the Japanese students, for obvious reasons, could not be expected to copy out their own textbooks.[5]

The reasons for publishing such a lengthy work in Latin are set out in Valignano's preface to the book, in his letter to Aquaviva of 25 September 1589 from Macao, and in the prefatory letter to Aquaviva at the beginning of the book by Duarte de Sande, the individual responsible for putting it into Latin. Both men emphasized that *De Missione* was not intended for a European readership but as a text for Latin studies in Jesuit seminaries and as a guide for the Japanese to things European.[6] In his letter, written while printing was underway, Valignano gave three reasons for deciding not to send the complete text to Rome for an *imprimatur*, a departure from the established practice. First, the boys had to have 'a perfect account' of their travels to take back to Japan to inform their compatriots of what they had seen and done during their travels. Second, the book was only of marginal interest in Europe and was intended for use in Japan. Valignano noted that the book had been carefully compiled and dealt with things that 'I have found from experience' will guide and please Japanese students and not give offence so that if any vernacular translation were to be made it should follow the original exactly. Third, he hoped the book would confound the charges of fraud already circulating. An additional,

---

[1] Burke, *Historical Anthropology*, pp. 132–49 esp. 134; Stinger, *Renaissance in Rome*, pp. 29, 140; Bertini, 'Marriage of Alessandro Farnese', esp. pp. 52, 54, 56–7.

[2] ARSI, Jap.Sin 10: II, f. 288, printed in Álvarez-Taladriz, 'En el IV centenario de la embajada', pp. 152–3.

[3] ARSI, Jap.Sin 11: I, f. 157v; Schütte, 'Der Lateinische Dialog', p. 268; Valignano, *Apología*, p. 55.

[4] The first was *Oratio habita À Fara D. Martino Iaponio*, Goa, 1588; the second João Bonifacio, *Christiani Pveri Institvtio, Adolescentiaeqve perfugium: autore Ioanne Bonifacio Societatis Iesv*, Macao, 1588. See Laures, *Kirishitan Bunko*, pp. 29–32. On the former, see below p. 414.

[5] Laures, *Kirishitan Bunko*, pp. 8–9; Schütte, 'Christliche Japanische Literatur', pp. 269 n. 127, 271–2.

[6] Below p. 39; ARSI, Jap.Sin 11: I, f. 157; Schütte, 'Der Lateinische Dialog', p. 261; Moran, *Japanese and the Jesuits*, p. 148.

unstated, reason for publishing in Macao was to pre-empt any unwelcome and improper editing in Rome of the sort Valignano had experienced with his own *Catechism*, written in Japan in collaboration with Japanese knowledgeable about Buddhist teaching and intended for use by Japanese *irmãos*. The *Catechism* had been sent to Portugal in manuscript form and then translated and published in Latin in 1586, much to the author's surprise and initial embarrassment.[1]

While the literary quality of *De Missione* has been rightly praised as 'written in a Humanistic rhetorical style of the first water',[2] opinion is divided as to how effective it would have been as a Latin textbook in Japan. The Jesuit historian Josef Franz Schütte claims that it would have been highly effective.[3] Others are less convinced.[4] No matter, Latin was an essential part of the Jesuit curriculum. In Japan command of Latin was essential for those aspiring to become Jesuits or secular priests. Without competence in Latin hopefuls would not be able to pursue their theological studies. Accordingly, Latin, along with the study of Japanese, was emphasized in the daily routine for young seminarians, set out in the *Regimento que se ha de guarder nos semynarios* (1580).[5] Valignano's opinion about the ability of Japanese students to master Latin varied from optimism (at the time of *De Missione*'s composition), to moderate pessimism (after

---

[1] ARSI, Jap.Sin 11: I, f. 157; Valignano, *Apología*, p. 55; Burnett, 'Humanism and the Jesuit Mission to China', p. 439 n. 60; Moran, *Japanese and the Jesuits*, pp. 147–8 and 'Real Author', pp. 10, 12. To fend off censure for his unorthodox behaviour, Valignano sent parts of the text to the superior general and to Portugal as they came off the press. See ARSI, Jap.Sin 11: I, f. 157v, and II, f. 188v; Schütte, 'Christliche Japanische Literatur', pp. 273–4; Laures, *Kirishitan Bunko*, p. 33; Moran, *Japanese and the Jesuits*, p. 147; Valignano, *Apología*, p. 55. On Valignano's *Catechism*, see below p. 37.

[2] Burnett, 'Humanism and the Jesuit Mission to China', p. 426.

[3] Schütte, 'Der Lateinische Dialog', pp. 289–90.

[4] Moran, *Japanese and the Jesuits*, p. 153; Cooper, *Japanese Mission*, p. 198.

[5] ARSI, Jap.Sin 8: I, f. 265, printed in Álvarez-Taladriz, 'Apendice documental', p. 55–6; Schütte, *Valignano's Mission Principles*, I: 1, pp. 351–3. In 1581, while still in Japan, Valignano had given instructions for a Latin dictionary and grammar to be prepared. In September 1589 he wrote to Aquaviva that he hoped these would be well-advanced on his return to Japan. See ARSI, Jap.Sin 11: I, f. 157v; Laures, *Kirishitan Bunko*, p. 50; Moran, *Japanese and the Jesuits*, p. 149. Valignano had clear-cut ideas about suitable textbooks from which the Japanese could learn Latin. In a letter to Diogo de Mesquita, dated Cochin, 25 December 1584, he urged Mesquita to acquire *Emmanvelis Alvari e Societate Iesv, De Institutione Grammatica Libri Tres* by the Portuguese Jesuit, Manuel Álvares (first edn, Lisbon, 1572, with many subsequent ones), which was used widely in Jesuit colleges, and dictionaries by Jerónimo Cardoso. The latter included *Hieronymi Cardosi Lamacensis Dictionarium ex Lusitanico in latinum sermonem* (Lisbon 1562); *Dictionarium iuventuti studiosae admodum frugiferum* (2nd edn, Coimbra, 1562) and *Dictionarium latinolusitanicvm et vice versa Lusitanicolatinvm* (Coimbra, 1570). On no account was Mesquita to acquire works by Virgil or Ovid, or other works which mentioned 'profane matters' because it was not possible to profit from them nor to use them as yet in Japan. See *Documenta Indica*, XIII, pp. 761–2. Álvares was acquired, and an abridged version was printed in Japan in 1594 with conjugations in both Latin and Japanese and containing numerous examples from the Japanese classics. The Latin dictionary, based on Ambrosio Calepino's *Dictionarium Latino-Lusitanicum ac Iaponicvm*, was published in Amakusa in 1595 (Laures, *Kirishitan Bunko*, pp. 49, 50–51; Moran, *Japanese and the Jesuits*, p. 155). On 22 December 1586 Valignano wrote to Aquaviva requesting the general to send 600 or 800 copies of Lucius Coelius Firmianus Lactantius, a Christian apologist of the 3rd century whom he believed would be an appropriate author for Japan. The work he had in mind is unknown but the *Divine Institutions*, which was included in many editions of his works in the 16th century, seems the most likely. See *Documenta Indica*, XIV, p. 775; Schütte, 'Christliche Japanische Literatur', pp. 270–71; Moran, 'Real Author', p. 16.

returning to Japan in 1590) and deeper pessimism (during his third visit from 1598 until 1603).[1]

Valignano intended that a Japanese version of *De Missione* should appear shortly after the original (as de Sande mentions in his prefatory letter) but the individual to whom this daunting task was to be entrusted, Jorge Loyola, died in Macao on 16 August 1589.[2] Eventually, Valignano hoped translations into various European languages would appear.[3] None did. In 1610, in his history of the Jesuits' mission in Asia, Daniello Bartoli wrote that a thousand copies of *De Missione* had been printed in Macao in 1598 and 'distributed throughout Japan'. He does not say whether this was the original Latin version or a Japanese translation and there is no other mention of such a printing. Such a large print-run is highly unlikely.[4] In his edition of Valignano's *Adiciones*, José Luis Álvarez-Taladriz speculates that, after returning to Japan in 1590, and reviewing the precarious situation of the mission and the unpredictability of Hideyoshi's behaviour towards the missionaries and Japanese Christians, the visitor had second thoughts about the wisdom of a Japanese translation. He might well have feared that Japanese readers, Christian and non-Christian alike, might be angered by the negative presentation of their country and that Hideyoshi's hostility towards Christianity would be inflamed by the excessive praise lavished on Philip II and accounts of his military might, about which much is made in *De Missione*. As Álvarez-Taladriz emphasizes, this is speculation.[5] Nevertheless, it is a highly plausible supposition. The arrival in Japan of Pedro de Ribadeneira's *Vida del bienaventurado Padre San Ignacio de Loyola, fundador de la Compañía de Jesús* (Madrid, 1583), in which there was an account of Philip II's war with Paul IV, caused alarm among the European Jesuits. Mesquita, who was by then the minister in the Jesuit college in Amakusa, wrote to Aquaviva in November 1593 urging that the relevant chapter should be deleted from any future editions. The content ran counter to what the Jesuits were teaching, and – although he did not mention this explicitly – to what was written in *De Missione*, regarding the impossibility of wars between the secular European rulers and the papacy. It also contradicted the assertion in Colloquium XXIV that the Jesuits had no intention of aligning with the Christian daimyo to seize power in Japan because such a coup would be contrary to Christian teaching.[6] Moreover, when the existence of what

---

[1] Moran, *Japanese and the Jesuits*, pp. 151–3, 162–3, 165–8. See also Hubert Cieslik who suggests that a number of Japanese seminarians were proficient in Latin ('Training of a Japanese Clergy in the Seventeenth Century', p. 312). Ironically, in a letter to Aquaviva in September 1577, Valignano admitted that his own ability to write Latin was rusty (see *Documenta Indica*, X, p. 905). In the same letter he adds that, although he would prefer to write his correspondence with Rome in Italian, as he had done until then, henceforth he would do so in Spanish, although he self-mockingly called himself a 'base Castilian'. Writing in Portuguese, he conceded, would be useless as it was not widely understood in Italy (ibid., pp. 905–6).

[2] ARSI, Jap.Sin 11: I, f. 157v; Schütte, 'Der Lateinische Dialog', p. 263; Laures, *Kirishitan Bunko*, p. 33; Moran, *Japanese and the Jesuits*, p. 150; Schütte, *Monumenta Historica Japoniae I*, p. 284. On Loyola's command of Latin, see his letter to Aquaviva from Goa in 1587 (*Documenta Indica*, XIV, pp. 741–6).

[3] ARSI, Jap.Sin 11: I, f. 157v; Valignano, *Apología*, p. 55.

[4] Bartoli, *Historia*, p. 174; Laures, *Kirishitan Bunko*, p. 34; Moran 'Real Author', pp. 15–16. The editors of Fróis, *Première ambassade*, suggest, without evidence, that a Japanese translation was made some time after 1592 (p. xxix).

[5] Valignano, *Adiciones*, p. 558.

[6] See Álvarez-Taladriz, 'El Padre Diogo de Mesquita', p. 103, and below, pp. 305–6. Mesquita and the Portuguese Jesuits in Japan learned about the war for the first time from Ribadeneira's book.

has become known as the 'Anon-Moreira world map' (Fig. 1), produced sometime between 1590 and 1614 and possibly made by Ignacio Moreira who came to Japan along with Valignano and the boys in 1590,[1] is taken into consideration the case for Valignano having cold feet about a Japanese translation of *De Missione* becomes even stronger. The map, which re-emerged in 1986, depicts the then-known world but with Europe, an eastwardly expanding Muscovy, the Ottoman Empire, the Middle East, a huge Ethiopian empire in Africa, Ceylon, parts of the Americas, and even Greenland emblazoned with crosses, indicating that they were Christian territories and suggesting that Christianity was more widespread and entrenched than it actually was. Confessional differences within Christendom, the Ottoman threat to Latin Christendom, and, interestingly, the Spanish presence on Luzon, with which Hideyoshi became familiar in the early 1590s, are ignored in this work of Christian propaganda. It is possible that the map was produced in conjunction with, and intended to illustrate the content of *De Missione*.[2] If so, the visual information contained in the map, which would have been much more easily understood and absorbed by a Japanese audience than the obscure Latin text of *De Missione*, would have fuelled the suspicions of Hideyoshi and others about Christian expansionist ambitions in the world, and especially in Japan. It is quite reasonable, then, to suppose that Valignano had second thoughts about producing a Japanese version.[3]

In the event, only a portion of *De Missione* appeared in a European vernacular, part of Colloquium XXXIII, on China. This was published in English by Richard Hakluyt in the second edition of *The Principal Navigations* in 1599 under the title 'An excellent treatise of the kingdome of China, and of the estate and government therof: Printed in Latine at Macao a citie of the Portugals in China, An. Dom. 1590 and written Dialogue-wise. The speakers are Linus, Leo, and Michael.' Hakluyt obtained the volume from the booty of the Portuguese vessel the *Madre de Dios*, seized on her homeward voyage by English privateers off the Azores in 1592. In the Epistle Dedicatory to Sir Robert Cecil in the second volume, Hakluyt described *De Missione* as being 'inclosed in a case of sweete Cedar wood, lapped vp almost an hundred fold in fine calicut-cloth, as though it had beene some incomparable iewell'.[4] It was also one of the books which Hakluyt cited in a paper he prepared for the directors of the newly chartered East India Company to use when lobbying the queen, to reassure her that their intended voyages would be to places beyond the Spanish monarchy's 'power, Jurisdiction or comaunde'.[5]

After Hakluyt, references to *De Missione* appeared in works by the Jesuit historian, Luis de Guzman, and the compiler of the first Jesuit bibliography, Pedro de Ribadeneira. In 1727, in the introduction to his translation of Engelbert Kaempfer's *History of Japan*,

---

[1] On Moreira, see Schütte, 'Ignacio Moreira', *passim*.

[2] On the map, see Marques, 'A cartografia portuguesa e o Japão', pp. 327–34; Nebenzahl and Marques, 'Moreira's Manuscript', pp. 21–3; Headly, 'Geography and Empire', pp. 1149–50, which erroneously states that Valignano visited the Japanese emperor in 1585.

[3] Hideyoshi's suspicions had violent repercussions in 1592. Following an audience with the Dominican Juan Cobo, emissary of the governor of the Philippines, where he learnt for the first time that Philip II was king of both Spain and Portugal, Hideyoshi ordered that the churches and Jesuit properties in Nagasaki be razed (Massarella, 'Exceptionalism versus Universalism', pp. 149–52).

[4] *Principal Navigations*, VI, pp. 348–77; ibid., I, p. lxxii; Bovill, '*Madre de Dios*', pp. 129–52; Boxer, 'Taking of the *Madre de Dios*, 1592', pp. 82–4; Quinn, *Hakluyt Handbook*, I, pp. 305–6.

[5] Brayman and Mancall, 'Richard Hakluyt the Younger's Notes', pp. 433–4.

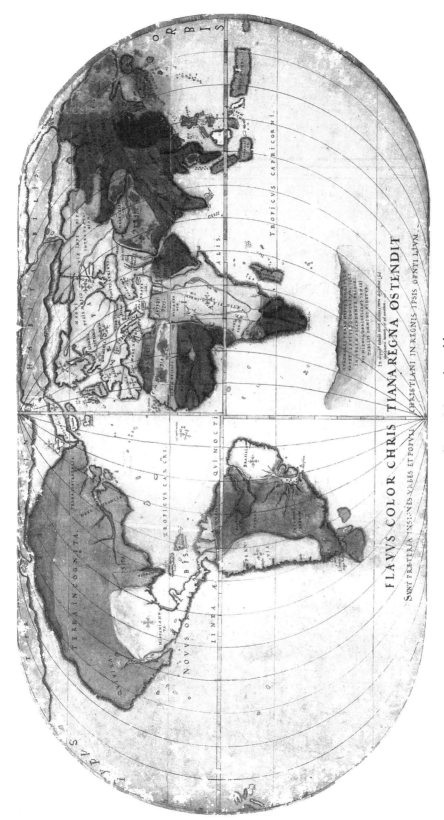

Figure 1. 'Anon-Moreira' world map.
By permission of the owner.

J. G. Scheuchzer referred to *De Missione* as a 'rare and curious Treatise' which, 'were the whole work now reprinted, I do not doubt, but that it would yet meet with a favourable reception'.[1] Subsequently, and inaccurately, Léon Pagès, among others, asserted that European translations or editions had appeared in Spanish (1591) and Latin (1593).[2] In fact, until now only a partial translation into Portuguese,[3] and complete translations into Japanese,[4] and Portuguese have appeared,[5] although the book has been referred to and quoted from in various scholarly works.

Authorship of *De Missione*

The question of authorship of *De Missione* – whether it was Valignano or de Sande, himself a distinguished Portuguese humanist scholar and one of the most intellectually-gifted among the Jesuits in Asia – which was previously believed to have been settled conclusively, remains, at least for some, a matter of controversy.[6] The title page says that it was 'put into Latin by Duarte de Sande' ('*in sermonem Latinvm versvs ab Eduardo de Sande*') and this is correct. De Sande himself would have preferred that the Spanish version, from which he worked, had been sent to Rome where, he modestly noted, others more capable than himself, could have put it into Latin, but Valignano was adamant that the translation had to be done in Macao.[7] De Sande accepted his assignment, albeit reluctantly, doubtless unhappy about the prospect of having Valignano constantly breathing down his neck.[8] It is unknown whether the Spanish text de Sande worked from was drafted by Valignano himself, or drawn up under his supervision, but we do know that the visitor had been working on a text before departing from Goa for Macao which, as with many of his literary projects, he had failed to complete before reaching Macao.[9] Once there, as Valignano describes it in his prefatory letter, he asked de Sande 'to put the collected and ordered writings of the ambassadors themselves into Latin, and, in order to make them clearer and more useful to you, to make them into a dialogue'. In his own prefatory letter to the Jesuit general, de Sande said that Valignano asked him to 'put into

---

[1] Guzman, *Historia*, II, pp. 660–61; Pedro de Ribadeneira, *Bibliotheca scriptorvm Societatis Iesv*, Antwerp, 1608; Kaempfer, *History of Japan*, I, pp. lxviii–ix.

[2] Pagès, *Bibliographie japonaise*, p. 7; Medina, *Nota bibliográfica*; Garnett, 'On the "*De Missione legatorum Japonensium*"', pp. 176–7, which, while useful on this point, is inaccurate in many other respects.

[3] *Archivo Pittoresco*, vols V (1862) and VI (1863).

[4] Hamada et al., *Tenshō nenkan*; Izui et al., *De-Sande*.

[5] Sande, *Diálogo*. This was first published in 1997 and has been republished together with the Latin text in 2009 as Sande, *Embaixadores Japoneses*. A facsimile edition of the original Latin was published by the Toyo Bunko in 1935.

[6] The case for Valignano, rather than de Sande, as the author of *De Missione* is made by Moran in 'Real Author', *passim*. The case for de Sande is made by Américo da Costa Ramalho in 'Portugueses e Japoneses', pp. 346–68, and Sande, *Embaixadores Japoneses*, I, pp. 11–12. Laures (*Kirishitan Bunko*, p. 33) splits the difference and says that Valignano compiled the rough draft and de Sande gave it its final form. On de Sande see Schütte, 'Der Lateinische Dialog', pp. 263–8; Burnett, 'Humanism and the Jesuit Mission to China', pp. 427–43.

[7] ARSI, Jap.Sin 11: I, f. 169.

[8] ARSI, Jap.Sin 11: I, f. 169; Schütte, 'Christliche Japanische Literatur', p. 274; Burnett, 'Humanism and the Jesuit Mission to China', p. 439 n. 60.

[9] *Documenta Indica*, XIV, pp. 123–4; Bernard, 'Valignani ou Valignano', p 87; Schütte, 'Der Lateinische Dialog', p. 260; Moran, 'Real Author', p. 11.

Latin the excellent notes made by those noble youths, and afterwards arranged in order', in the form of a dialogue not as a 'continuous history, which could perhaps be somewhat boring'.[1] The Spanish original, the existence of which both Valignano and de Sande attest, is no longer extant.

Most scholars ascribe the authorship of the Spanish document on which *De Missione* is based to Valignano.[2] However, other individuals contributed to the book. Certainly de Sande did rather more than merely making changes (such as abbreviating, changing the order and arrangement), but always in consultation with Valignano.[3] Other likely contributors were Diogo de Mesquita, who kept his own account of the trip; Nuno Rodrigues, who accompanied the boys on the return journey from Rome; the rector of the Jesuit college in Macao, Lourenço Mexia, a Portuguese; and Fathers Nicolão de Ávila and Diogo Antunes, respectively Spanish and Portuguese, who checked and approved de Sande's Latin.[4] Valignano, was immensely satisfied with the result. Nobody in these parts could have done it better then de Sande, he said, and he felt sure that the quality of the translation would be much appreciated in Europe.[5]

In brief, *De Missione* was the outcome of a collaborative effort put together under the driving force and firm supervision of an editor-in-chief, Valignano. No single authorial 'I' speaks out from its pages.

Sources of *De Missione*

To impress the intended Japanese readership, both Valignano and de Sande emphasized that the book was based on journals kept by the boys during their trip, and that the boys, whose time was strictly governed, had been diligent in keeping them. Unfortunately, these journals are no longer extant and we have no knowledge about which language they used for writing them, although fragments (descriptive not analytical) found their way into Fróis's account of the visit. These are in Portuguese but there is no way of knowing whether or not they are translations from Japanese or polished versions of notes made in Portuguese.[6] Another two short narratives of the embassy survive among the Jesuit archives in Rome. One, partly written by Mesquita, is dated 10 August 1585, and records

---

[1] See below, pp. 37, 39. A continuous history was, of course, the form adopted by Luís Fróis in his 'Tratado dos embaixadores Japões que forão à Roma no anno de 1582', written after *De Missione*. Two manuscript versions of Fróis's *Tratado* survive. It was finally edited and printed in 1942 and is an essential companion piece to *De Missione*. See Fróis, *Première ambassade*, *passim* but esp. pp. xxiii–iv.

[2] ARSI, Jap.Sin 11: I, f. 157; Bernard, 'Valignani ou Valignano', pp. 87–9; Schütte, 'Der Lateinische Dialog', pp. 261–2; Valignano, *Apología*, p. 54 n. 13; Moran, 'Real Author', *passim*. Ramalho, who champions de Sande, is the exception. See Sande, *Embaixadores Japoneses*, I, p. 12; *idem*, *Diálogo*, pp. 14–15.

[3] ARSI, Jap.Sin 11: I, f. 169; Burnett, 'Humanism and the Jesuit Mission to China', p. 440.

[4] ARSI, Jap.Sin 11: I, f. 157; Bernard, 'Valignani ou Valignano', p. 88; Schütte, 'Der Lateinische Dialog', p. 263; Valignano, *Apología*, p. 54 n. 13.

[5] ARSI, Jap.Sin 11: I, f. 157; Bernard, 'Valignani ou Valignano', p. 88; Valignano, *Apología*, p. 54 n. 13.

[6] See Fróis, *Première ambassade*, 98–106 (the Escorial and Madrid). Frois's description of the Vila Viçosa (pp. 50–53) and Toledo (pp. 64–8) also incorporates notes made by Constantino. Guzman notes that the boys were meticulous in writing down everything they saw and heard. See Guzman, *Historia*, II, p. 294; Cooper, *Japanese Mission*, pp. 194–5.

the journey from Japan to Madrid (20 February 1582–October 1584).[1] The other is a narrative of the trip from Lisbon to Alicante with a brief description of what the boys did after returning to Portugal, including the visit to Coimbra.[2] A few of the letters of Nuno Rodrigues have survived from the return trip to Lisbon. Material from these sources was incorporated into *De Missione* as were reports from the Jesuits ordered to accompany the boys on their travels in Europe. One of these individuals, Alessandro Leni, accompanied the boys from Rome to Lisbon and then sailed in the same fleet as them to start a career in India. Once in India, he gave Valignano first-hand information about the visit.[3] Official records, such as the *Acta Consistorii* (the official account of the obeisance before Gregory XIII), as well as the *avvisi* or newsletters, some of which were printed during the boys' travels, also provided material for *De Missione* and it is possible that Guido Gualtieri's *Relationi*, published in 1586, was another source.[4]

Other sources were used to flesh out the descriptions of Lisbon, Rome and Venice. The detailed and invaluable description of Lisbon before the catastrophic earthquake struck in 1755 owes nothing to Valignano, who spent only three months in Portugal, mostly preparing for his new assignment in the Indies.[5] Both de Sande and Mesquita were Portuguese, as were Mexia and Antunes. All would have been familiar with the description of Lisbon by their fellow-countryman, Damião de Góis, *Urbis Olisiponis Descriptio*, published in 1554. The influence of de Góis's famous publication is easily detectable in *De Missione*. Ironically, de Góis had been condemned as a heretic by the Portuguese Inquisition in 1572 and imprisoned in the monastery of Batalha, which the boys visited, where he died in mysterious circumstances in 1574. His chief accuser had been Simão Rodrigues, one of Loyola's original companions, the first Jesuit provincial of Portugal, and a controversial and divisive figure in early Jesuit history.[6] The description of the Roman churches draws upon Andrea Palladio's *Descritione de le chiese, stationi, indulgenze & reliquie de Corpi Sancti, che sono in la città de Roma* (1554). The description of Venice, a city which gets much attention in *De Missione*, relies heavily on Francesco Sansovino's

---

[1] ARSI, Jap.Sin 22, ff. 59–73v. The text in folios 59 to mid 63v is written in Italian, the remainder is in Spanish, in Mesquita's hand and autographed by him at the end. It has the appearance of having been put together in a hurry, possibly from other notes.

[2] ARSI, Jap.Sin 22, ff. 76–83. This is in Spanish. The author notes (f. 82v) that what the Japanese did after departing from Alicante for Italy until their return to Lisbon he would leave to Lazaro Catano, an Italian brother who accompanied them, to write about. Unfortunately, this was not done, but the fact that it was intended suggests that the Jesuits in Europe planned to produce their own account of the visit. They may have abandoned this plan in view of the numerous publications that appeared concerning the embassy.

[3] The Jesuit reports are contained in ARSI, Ital. 159. They have been translated into Japanese. See Yūki, 'Shinshiryō'. On Leni, who had originally intended to serve in Spain but, on the recommendation of Nuno Rodrigues, had been allowed to proceed to India, see ARSI, Jap.Sin 10: II, f. 214v; *Documenta Indica*, XIV, pp. 15*, 45–6, and XV, p. 195.

[4] On the many printed works resulting from the visit see Boscaro, *Sixteenth Century European Printed Works*. Some of the private letters and diplomatic correspondence from the *relazioni* or formal reports which ambassadors of the Italian states sent to their masters are published in *Dai Nihon Shiryō*, XI: 1 and XI: 2, although none of this would have been available for the writing of *De Missione*.

[5] Schütte, *Valignano's Mission Principles*, I: 1, pp. 64–91.

[6] On de Góis, see *Documenta Indica*, I, pp. 88–9; Hirsch, *Damião de Góis, passim*; Matos, *L'Expansion portugaise*, pp. 436–74. On Rodrigues, see O'Malley, *First Jesuits*, pp. 31–2, 308–9, 329–34; Alden, *Making of an Enterprise*, pp. 25–8, 671; below, p. 394 n. 1.

Venetia citta nobilissima et singolare, Descritta in XIIII. Libri (1581), although Valignano himself had no fondness for Venice having been detained in prison there for more than a year, from late 1562 until March 1564, and then banned from Venetian territory for four years over an incident involving a sword cut administered to the face of one Franciscina Throna.[1]

Contextualizing *De Missione*

To a modern reader and critic *De Missione* appears to boast endlessly, even arrogantly and smugly, about the superiority of Europe vis-à-vis Japan. Having said that, *De Missione* is not an easy work to categorize. Unlike José de Acosta's more famous and influential work, the *Historia natural y moral de las Indias*, it cannot be neatly pigeonholed as an early contribution to ethnology.[2] But this does not mean that it can be dismissed, as its detractors suggest, as crude propaganda, the product of a deeply entrenched Eurocentrism embedded in the heart of the Christian missionary project which, in the case of Japan, contributed greatly to a disastrous – and for some, inevitable – failure.

De Missione is a far richer and more complex work than its detractors allow and can be identified within certain established sixteenth-century literary traditions, the most obvious being the dialogue, a genre which especially flourished in Italy during the sixteenth century before suffering a decline in the seventeenth. It is notoriously difficult to define exactly what the dialogue, which Virginia Cox has called 'this most slippery of terms',[3] constitutes, but first and foremost the dialogue was a means of presenting and communicating information to an audience in an effort to win it over to the author's point of view. In other words, it was didactic and its models were the dialogues of Cicero and Plato. Cox has argued that the dialogue enjoyed widespread popularity in Italy during the sixteenth century because it created 'an elusive union between the spoken and written word'. At a time when the print revolution was still relatively young, the dialogue provided an antidote to the alienating effects of the printed medium by linking the impersonal quality of text with earlier but still familiar oral methods and practices of argumentation. As Cox puts it, 'the dialogue offers the closest approximation possible within a written text to the responsiveness of the spoken word'.[4] In the context of the Jesuit mission in Japan, and Valignano's aspirations for Jesuit pedagogy there, one can easily see the attractions of writing *De Missione* in the form of dialogue as a way to bridge the divide between European and Japanese ways of thought and debate. In a telling, if somewhat inelegant, characterization of the Italian context within which the sixteenth-century dialogue thrived, Cox describes the genre as 'the means by which a subject-matter of socially dubious status can assert a sort of squatters' right to residence in

---

[1] See Schütte, *Valignano's Mission Principles*, I: 1, p. 32 esp. n. 106.
[2] The *Historia* was first published in Seville in 1590 and was soon translated into other European languages. The first English translation appeared in 1604. For a modern English edition, see Acosta, *Natural and Moral History*.
[3] Cox, *Renaissance Dialogue*, p. 2; Snyder, *Writing the Scene of Speaking*, p. 1.
[4] Cox, *Renaissance Dialogue*, pp. 44, 103, 105, 112–13.

courtly discourse'.¹ In other words, the means by which something – and, by extension, someone – outside official, established circles could become inside; in Japanese, for something or someone *soto*, outside the house or household (and by extension, Japan), to become *uchi*, a part of the house or household.² The Jesuits were fully aware of this important Japanese concept and the quest to find ways to cross the formidable barrier separating *soto* and *uchi* lay at the very heart of the policy of accommodation. *De Missione* was a vital part of the Jesuit ambition to secure squatters' rights for Europe within Japan's epistemological and cognitive worlds and, ultimately, permanent residency within Japanese society and culture.³

By the later sixteenth century, in the post-Tridentine world, the dialogue had lost much of its Ciceronian character as a form of discussion and exploration among equals, and acquired a distinctly more Platonic and absolutist character, one which sought to impose rather than impart truth to its readers. The Jesuits' *Ratio studiorum* (1599), for example, has such an absolutist quality.⁴ But *De Missione* retains a number of the Ciceronian characteristics of the dialogue, such as a concern for verisimilitude, necessity not will as the point of departure (which puts Michael, ostensibly involuntarily, into the driving seat), spontaneity, and the flattery of inclusion (by assigning lesser roles to real people, Leo and Lino). These attributes are all on display in *De Missione* especially in the first colloquium.⁵

Another context within which to understand *De Missione* and its jarring praise of Europe and things European is the *laudes civitatum* or civic *descriptiones* which date back to the Middle Ages. These *descriptiones* followed certain simple conventions for describing or 'praising' a city. This genre was transformed somewhat after the thirteenth century by authors who organized their work more systematically and purposefully, adding statistical material to the descriptions and praising the positive qualities of the citizenry, their distinctiveness, their superiority over rival cities and their claims to a greater ancient lineage than their rivals. The most influential of these medieval *descriptiones* was *Mirabilia Urbis Romae* (c. 1143) which became a popular guidebook for pilgrims. The *Mirabilia*, which circulated widely in Europe, draws attention to the eternal city not only as a destination for pilgrims but as a distinct polity in which, as J. K. Hyde has put it, 'the local and the universal coincided'. The Renaissance *descriptiones*, while manifesting a measure of continuity with their medieval predecessors transformed the genre by employing rhetoric to describe a city's physical characteristics and using it as a vehicle to convince readers that the sum of a city's parts equalled its

---

¹ Ibid., p. 39.

² On *soto* and *uchi*, 'outside' the house or household (the fundamental unit of Japanese society), and 'inside', see *Vocabvlario*, ff. 227, 270.

³ After his return to Japan in 1590, Valignano realized the immensity of this challenge even within the Jesuit institutions in Japan, never mind the broader society. Such a challenge was far greater than he had imagined a decade previously, when, in the *Sumario*, he had written about the need to maintain a 'spiritual union' ('*unión de los ánimos*') between the Japanese *irmaōs* and *dōjuku* (assistants) and the European Jesuits, without which the whole enterprise in Japan would collapse. See Valignano, *Sumario*, p. 198; *Adiciones*, pp. 567–83, esp. pp. 574–6; Moran, *Japanese and the Jesuits*, pp. 169–77.

⁴ Cox, *Renaissance Dialogue*, pp. 68–9.

⁵ On these characteristics, see Cox, *Renaissance Dialogue*, pp. 12–13, 30, 38, 41–2. On other aspects of the 16th-century dialogue, see Snyder, *Writing the Scene of Speaking*, pp. 1–38.

excellence and its superiority over rivals.¹ Such rhetorical attributes are all displayed in *De Missione*.

One of the most striking examples of such Renaissance *descriptiones* was Leonardo Bruni's panegyric, *Laudatio Florentinae Urbis* (c. 1403–4), modelled on the Greek rhetorician Aelius Aristedes's second-century panegyric *Panathenacius*. The opening words of Bruni's work, which was a *laudatio* of Florentine republican virtue contrasted with Milanese despotism, provide a useful comparison with the aspirations and rhetorical tone of *De Missione*:

> Would that God immortal give me eloquence worthy of the city of Florence, about which I am to speak, or at least equal to my zeal and desire on her behalf; for either one degree or the other would, I think, abundantly demonstrate the city's magnificence and splendour. Florence is of such a nature that a more distinguished or more splendid city cannot be found on the entire earth, and I can easily tell about myself, I was never more desirous of doing anything in my life. So I have no doubt at all that if either of these wishes were granted, I should be able to describe with elegance and dignity this very beautiful and excellent city. But because everything we want and the ability granted us to attain what we wish are two different things, we will carry out our intention as well as we can, so that we appear to be lacking in talent rather than in will.²

De Missione is firmly situated within this other humanist, rhetorical tradition of how Europeans and European polities projected themselves to each other. Its uniqueness lies in the fact that the authors intended it to be used as a vehicle to project Europe, or at least the idealized Europe of the Counter Reformation, to a non-European audience. But this was an audience that was totally unfamiliar with the literary conventions and rhetorical style it incorporated. As a result, the possibilities for misunderstanding were huge.

In the following century the Jesuits produced another, shorter work which attempted to explain Europe to non-Europeans, this time to a Chinese readership, Giulio Aleni's *Xifang dawen* (1637). Like *De Missione*, *Xifang* aimed to counter a lack of knowledge about Europe among its intended readership – Chinese officials and intellectuals rather than Jesuit seminarians. It covered some of the same ground as *De Missione*, always trying to show Europe in a favourable light, and, while critical of some Chinese practices, notably concubinage and geomancy, the tone is generally respectful of China. Structured in a simple question and answer format, shorn of the humanist rhetoric that permeates *De Missione*, *Xifang* reflects a different, but no less ambitious, missionary agenda and strategy than those deployed previously in Japan.³

---

¹ On medieval and renaissance descriptions, see Hyde, 'Medieval Descriptions of Cities', esp. p. 322; Fasoli, 'La coscienza civica nelle "Laudes civitatum"', pp. 40–41; Frugoni, *Distant City*, p. 54; Góis, *Lisbon in the Renaissance*, pp. xxviii–xxx; Lowe, 'Understanding Cultural Exchange', p. 15.

² Kohl and Witt, *Earthly Republic*, p. 135.

³ Ironically, *De Missione* was written at a time when Japan was emerging from protracted civil wars which greatly influenced Jesuit perceptions of the country, as is evident in the book, whereas when *Xifang* was composed, China was entering a period of extended warfare during which the Ming dynasty would be supplanted by the Qing. *Xifang dawen* is reprinted and translated in Mish, 'Creating an Image of Europe for China', pp. 1–87. On Aleni, an Italian who entered China in 1613, eventually becoming vice-provincial of southern China, see Luk, 'A Serious Matter of Life and Death', pp. 177–97.

Evaluating *De Missione* and the Tenshō Embassy

As has been emphasized, the boys' visit was not the principal reason why Valignano intended to return to Europe in 1582, and yet the boys served as the perfect showcase with which to advertise the visitor's plans for the Japan mission. As the numerous contemporary publications (including Protestant ones) testify, the embassy was hailed as a success. Valignano himself was both relieved and overjoyed when he heard about the favourable reaction to the visit.[1] In the long term, alas, the visit's success proved to be of little benefit for Valignano's ambitions in Japan.

On 24 December 1584, Aquaviva wrote to Valignano informing him that, after careful study, he approved of the visitor's recommendations for the Japan mission, but with some reservations. These concerned the proposals to imitate what the general saw as the ostentation of the Buddhist clergy. He was afraid that imitation of Buddhist protocols might corrode the Christian message and the Jesuit way of proceeding, which above all else should emphasize poverty and humility, especially within the Society's seminaries and colleges. The general was confident, however, that the boys' experience in Europe would contribute greatly to overcoming such problems. He noted that that while the boys had been able to witness for themselves 'the greatness of the Holy See, the dignity of the cardinals, the power of his Catholic Majesty and the splendour of the other Christian princes they have easily been able to discern that it is our Faith that makes people poor by choice and that it is need and wretchedness that make man base'.[2] Given the controversy that was brewing within the Society over what some members saw as the conflict between its spiritual and secular roles with some, notably among the Spanish Jesuits, critical of the Society's increasing worldliness, Aquaviva's letter was generous and indulgent concerning the visitor's plans.[3]

Rather than accepting the general's letter as an endorsement of his policy of accommodation, Valignano replied lengthily and testily, almost declaring that in matters concerning Japan he, with his greater knowledge of the country and its social and political institutions, should be the arbiter of policy.[4] The letter displays Valignano's much-observed character defects which included arrogance and self-righteousness. These faults did not always work in the best interests of the mission and provided ammunition for his enemies, of whom there were a number both within and without the Society, notably his fiercest critic, the former Jesuit superior of Japan and later provincial of Goa, Francisco Cabral.[5] Nevertheless, Valignano deserves the credit for gaining official recognition of

---

[1] *Documenta Indica*, XIV, pp. 138, 698; ARSI, Jap.Sin 11: II, f. 226; Purchas, *Hakluytus Posthumus*, XII, pp. 254–7; Lach, *Asia in the Making*, I: 2, p. 702. The visit's success may even have encouraged him to contemplate another embassy to Europe, from the Chinese emperor to the Holy See, so that Chinese mandarins could also see first-hand the great authority that the pope had over the kings of Europe and come to realize that the missionaries intended no harm in China. He mentioned this idea in a letter of 10 November 1588 to Aquaviva. See ARSI, Jap.Sin 11: I, ff 5r–v, printed in Álvarez-Taladriz, 'El proyecto de embajada', p. 79.

[2] Valignano, *Il cerimoniale*, pp. 37–41, 315–24, esp. 323; Boscaro, *Ventura e sventura*, pp 209–14, esp. p. 214.

[3] On the controversy within the Society, see Certeau, 'La réforme de l'intérieur', *passim*; O'Malley, 'Society of Jesus', pp. 234–5.

[4] Valignano's reply is printed in *Sumario*, pp. 250–70. See also *Il cerimoniale*, pp. 42–50.

[5] For Cabral's criticism of Valignano, see *Documenta Indica*, XVI, pp. 541–51; and on Valignano's short temper and high-handedness, see ibid., IX, pp. 484, 614; XIV, pp. 289–90, 551–2, 584–6; XVI, pp. 101–2.

accommodation, a policy that was soon to play out on a much bigger stage, in China, with momentous consequences.

Concerning finances, the visit appeared to augur well. Sixtus V increased the papal subvention for Japan, granted by his predecessor in 1583 for twenty years, from 4,000 to 6,000 ducats. Unfortunately, such generosity did nothing to alleviate the financial difficulties of the cash-starved mission. The increase was paid only in the first and last years of Sixtus's short reign. Clement VIII cut the subvention back to 4,000 ducats in 1603 and payments remained intermittent. As a result, the Jesuits continued to finance their mission from their controversial participation in the silk trade.[1]

Two of the other recommendations which Valignano wanted Rome to approve – that no bishop should be sent to Japan for the present, and that the Japan mission should remain closed to other orders – were not accepted. On the bishop question, Valignano had become flexible and he was not dissatisfied with the appointment of a bishop for Japan, especially as the individual selected was a Jesuit. On the question of keeping the friars out of Japan, a policy about which the visitor was unyielding and which he sought to extend to China, he scored a Pyrrhic victory. In January 1585, before the boys' arrival in Rome but in accordance with Valignano's lobbying, Gregory XIII issued a brief (*Ex pastorali officio*) making Japan an exclusive Jesuit missionary field and forbidding the mendicants from entering the country.[2] Philip II had already issued a letter in 1584, unrelated to Gregory's brief, ordering the Franciscans to stay out of Japan. This was intended to soothe Portuguese feelings in the aftermath of the union and was part of a vain attempt to halt the illicit trade that was developing between Acapulco, Manila and east Asia to the detriment of the economic interests of the Spanish metropolis.[3] But, when he learned of Gregory's brief, Philip was greatly displeased and ordered his ambassador in Rome to see that it was revoked. The Spanish monarch was annoyed that the papacy, with Jesuit encouragement, was intervening unilaterally in matters pertaining to the royal prerogatives, the governance of the church in Spain and of the Spanish *patronato*. As a result, for Philip II and his successor, Gregory XIII's brief was a dead letter.[4]

Sixtus V (himself a Franciscan) did not share his predecessor's support for this Jesuit aspiration concerning Japan and in November 1586 he issued a brief (*Dum ad uberes*) which, while not specifically revoking *Ex pastorali officio*, allowed the Franciscans to found missions throughout the East Indies. The Jesuits insisted on interpreting the new brief as excluding Japan; the mendicants ignored such Jesuit special pleading and, with the support and encouragement of the authorities in Manila, proceeded to Japan and set up their mission there.[5] From the 1590s, the mendicant orders established a strong presence. Finally in 1608, after years during which the mendicants had been operating in a grey

---

[1] Valignano, *Apología*, pp. 203–6; Schütte, 'Die Wirksamkeit der Päpste', pp. 205–6, 221; Cooper, *Japanese Mission*, pp. 171–3.

[2] *Documenta Indica*, XIII, pp. 829, 832; XIV, pp. 91–2. On Valignano's desire to keep the mendicants out of China, the case for which he built using the same arguments as for Japan, see ARSI, Jap.Sin 11: I, ff. 7r–v printed in Álvarez-Taladriz, 'El proyecto de embajada', pp. 87–8.

[3] *Documenta Indica*, XIII, p. 579; XVI, pp. 196–7; Álvarez-Taladriz, 'En el IV centenario del breve "Ex Pastorali Officio"', p. 105 n. 22; Boyajian, *Portuguese Trade in Asia*, p. 65.

[4] *Documenta Indica*, XIV, pp. 7–9, 17–18, 327 and n. 13, 719–20; Álvarez-Taladriz, *Documentos Franciscanos*, p. 174, n. 31, and 'En el IV centenario del breve "Ex Pastorali Officio"', pp. 105–6.

[5] Ibid., pp. 112–13; Massarella, 'Exceptionalism versus Universalism', pp. 145ff.

area of canon law, Paul V, recognized the de facto situation in Japan and ruled that all religious orders should have access to Japan. In the interim, the mendicant presence had set in motion one of the most bitter inter-missionary divisions and feuds which, even after 1614 when Christianity was outlawed by the Tokugawa shogunate, continued to poison Jesuit–friar relations. Both sides publicly, indecorously, spitefully, and, at times, pettily, blamed the other for losing Japan.[1] Valignano and his stubborn, well-publicized insistence on exclusivity shares part of the blame for this outcome.[2]

While this is not the place to discuss and analyse this bitter division, it should be mentioned that Valignano's determination to keep Japan for the Jesuits was not solely a matter of interreligious rivalry and jurisdiction. It touched on the delicate question of the respective jurisdictions of the Portuguese *padroado* and the Spanish *patronato*, the royal prerogative, and commerce as the Portuguese in Macao sought to maintain their privileged position in east Asian trade and the Spanish in Manila sought to undermine it. Moreover, Valignano's zeal and was not shared by all members of the Society. A number of his colleagues in Japan, as aware as he of the difficulties facing the mission, especially, the shortage of manpower, favoured admitting the friars. Once they were established in Japan (the Franciscans had been given permission to stay in Japan by Hideyoshi in 1594), Mesquita, who had been a supporter of Valignano's position, believed the fait accompli should be accepted and that, for the greater good of the mission, concord rather than discord should prevail.[3] Valignano would have done well to have heeded such counsel. More importantly, once the Japanese themselves had encountered the friars, the first of whom arrived in 1584, they warmed to them and requested that more should come. Ōmura Sumitada himself, who met one of the first Franciscans to reach Japan in 1584, was so impressed by the friar's demeanour and simple attire, that he was moved to say that were he not already a Christian such was the power of what he had seen and heard from the friar that he would become one immediately. He believed that the friar's mien and conduct could exist only to serve one purpose: the salvation of souls.[4] On the question of the plurality of orders in Japan, the ground was cut from under Valignano by forces beyond his (and that of his superiors in Rome) control.

The Boys after their Return to Japan

Once back in Japan the four young men, as they had become, underwent a role reversal. In Europe, dressed in Japanese clothes, they had been representations of Japan. In Japan, dressed in the European clothes given them by Gregory XIII, and ever-willing to display

---

[1] Only the three Jesuits among the twenty-six martyrs crucified in Nagasaki in 1597 were included in a painting of the event hanging in the Jesuit church, San Andrea al Quirinale, in Rome. The others, including the six Franciscans, were left out. The Franciscans reciprocated by omitting the Jesuit martyrs from a Franciscan engraving of the martyrdom commissioned in France. See Gregory, *Salvation at Stake*, p. 468 n. 7.

[2] He cited *De Missione* in the *Apología* to refute the Franciscan charge that the boys had been sent to Rome specifically to obtain Gregory XIII's bull excluding the mendicants from Japan (pp. 29–31). While this is literally true (it was not indeed the purpose of the embassy), Valignano was determined to secure such a papal brief.

[3] Álvarez-Taladriz, 'Opinión de un teólogo de la Compañía de Jesús', *passim*, and 'El Padre Diogo de Mesquita', *passim*; Massarella, 'Exceptionalism versus Universalism', pp. 140–42.

[4] Lucena, *Erinnerungen*, pp. 144–7; Álvarez-Taladriz, *Documentos Franciscanos*, p. 59 n. 73.

their knowledge about Europe and their accomplishments on European musical instruments, they portrayed Europe. In Valignano's words, they had become 'so Portuguese-like and accustomed to our world' that they seem like Europeans, much to the astonishment of the Japanese brothers.[1] They accompanied Valignano, in his capacity as ambassador of the Portuguese viceroy in Goa, on his visit to Hideyoshi in Kyoto in 1591. On the way, Valignano used every opportunity to show off the young men before Japanese notables. They relished their role as teachers on such occasions. Speaking in Japanese, and utilizing the books and instruments, including an astrolabe and globe, they had brought back from Europe, they described their travels. According to Frόis, they did this more effectively and skilfully than most Europeans in similar circumstances would have been able to do.[2] These impromptu tutorials were a *tableau vivant* of the colloquia in *De Missione* and a rehearsal for how the book was planned to be used. In Kyoto, at Hideyoshi's magnificent new residence, the Jurakutei, where the *kampaku* had received the emperor Go-Yōzei in 1588, and in a ceremony symmetrical to the one before Gregory XIII in Rome, Valignano appeared before Hideyoshi and the 'principal lords of Japan' with great 'pomp and solemnity', as he described it. He removed his biretta and paid reverence to Hideyoshi, genuflecting three times.[3]

After the visit to Kyoto, the young men who had undertaken the remarkable eight-year journey from Japan to Europe and back, were eager to fulfil their ambition and become Jesuits. They were able to do so despite some initial obstacles. Mancio, who managed to persuade his younger brother, Justo, to enter the Society as well, had to overcome the strong opposition of his mother who threatened to appeal to Hideyoshi to stop him. Michael had to face the joint opposition of his mother and Arima Harunobu who wanted the young man to enter his service where he would have been of great use. According to Frόis, and doubtless with Valignano's encouragement, the young men were determined to press ahead. After a few days pursuing the *Spiritual Exercises* to determine their state of mind, and after finally securing the approval of their mothers and the daimyo, the boys got their way. On 25 July 1591, the feast of St James or Santiago, the patron saint of Spain, they were admitted to the Society. In a major departure from the usual manner of receiving novices, the young men were accepted after a solemn high mass in which organs and other musical instruments were played. In addition, there were festive celebrations and a banquet attended by their families and the daimyo. Valignano permitted this departure from the usual austere manner of admission to the Society because, as he put it, it was the custom in Japan to mark such occasions with ceremony and that as they were men of status it would please (or rather, under the circumstances, appease) their families.[4]

---

[1] ARSI, Jap.Sin 23, f. 203v, printed in Álvarez-Taladriz, 'En el IV centenario de la embajada', p. 154.
[2] Frόis, *Historia de Japam*, V, pp. 189, 225–6, 280–81.
[3] Kleiser, 'P. Alexander Valignanis Gesandtschaftsreise', p. 97 n. 44; Álvarez-Taladriz, 'Relación del P. Alejandro Valignano', pp. 44–5.
[4] Frόis, *Historia de Japam*, V, pp. 353–4; Álvarez-Taladriz, 'Relación del P. Alejandro Valignano', p. 55. The fast-tracking of the young men's admission to the Society can be compared with the lengthier process which the future saint, Aloysius Gonzaga, eldest son of the marquis of Castiglione, endured before finally having his wish to join the Jesuits fulfilled. As was the case with Mancio and Michael, there was strong family opposition to such a move (see below, pp. 111–12).

In September 1608, Mancio, Julian and Martin, who had all remained in the Society, were ordained in the presence of Diogo de Mesquita, their chaperon in Europe and then rector of the Jesuit college in Nagasaki, and by the bishop of Japan, Luis Cerqueira, whose office they had personally lobbied Philip II to establish. Mancio died in Nagasaki in 1612. Julian remained in Japan after the decree ordering all religious to leave Japan was issued in 1614 and was arrested in 1632, tortured, and martyred the following year. Martin left Japan in 1614, died in Macao in 1639 and was buried in the Jesuit church of São Paulo where Valignano's remains had been interred in 1606. Michael, the principal speaker in *De Missione*, left the Jesuit order around 1603 when his name disappears from Jesuit personnel records, and subsequently (exactly when is unknown) apostatized. His later career is unclear and there are conflicting accounts of his activities, economic situation and fate, although it seems likely that he entered the service of the Ōmura. What is clear is that he married, had four sons, and, on the basis of the names on a tombstone discovered in 2003 in Isahaya City near Nagasaki, it has been suggested that he died in 1633, an adherent of the Nichiren sect of Buddhism.[1] Whether or not he was the author of the anti-Christian tract *Kirishitan kanagaki* remains unproven. Jurgis Elisonas asserts that he was. But the postscript to the tract, cited by Professor Elisonas as proof, can be read as suggesting that he was merely a source of information about the Jesuits rather than its author.[2] Of the four boys, Martin Hara was considered the most able translator into Japanese. Mesquita described him as 'the best interpreter we have in Japan, he does excellent work translating spiritual books into the language and script of Japan'. Michael is described (as indeed were Mancio Itō and Julian Nakaura) in the 1593 catalogue of Jesuits in Japan as 'not knowing much of the letters of Japan'.[3] If one believes that Michael was the author of *Kirishitan kanagaki*, which appeared around 1606, about three years after he left the Jesuits, the author's fluency in Japanese would be a remarkable (but highly unlikely) tribute to his ten years of Jesuit education.

As for Leo (Arima Sumizane) and Lino (Ōmura Suminobu), the former angered his brother, Harunobu, during the Okamoto Daihachi affair. This was a complex intrigue which brought about Harunobu's downfall and contributed directly to the passing of the first anti-Christian edicts in 1614. Amongst other charges, Harunobu was accused of paying for and receiving letters bearing the forged seals of Tokugawa Ieyasu and plotting the murder of a high Tokugawa official. Harunobu was dispossessed, forced into exile and ordered to commit suicide in 1612. Leo was banished to Yushima (now Dangōjima, in Nagasaki Prefecture) where he died.[4] Lino accompanied his brother, Yoshisake, to Korea during Hideyoshi's first invasion in 1592 but appears to have remained there after his brother returned in 1596, or at least that is when he disappears from history.[5]

---

[1] Valignano, *Sumario*, p. 87; Farrington, *English Factory*, I, p. 257; Pacheco, 'Los cuatro legados', *passim*, and 'Os quatro legados', *passim*; Cooper, *Japanese Mission*, pp. 184–92; Oishi, *Tenshō ken-Ō shisetsu*, pp. 84–122; Elisonas, 'Journey to the West', pp. 48–9.

[2] Ibid., pp. 48–9; *Kirishitan kanagaki*, esp. p. 259.

[3] Pacheco, 'Diogo de Mesquita', p. 441; Schütte, *Monumenta Historica Japoniae I*, pp. 317–18.

[4] Boxer, *Christian Century*, pp. 314–15; *Cambridge History of Japan*, Volume 4, pp. 366–7; http://www2.u-netsurf.ne.jp/~koga/ushima%.

[5] Lucena, *Erinnerungen*, p. 264 n. 123; http://www.page.sannet.ne.jp/kuranosuke/ohmura.html.

Conclusion

Valignano's major writings on Japan as well as the Tenshō Embassy and *De Missione* all reflect his ambitions to encourage Europeans and Japanese to shed their mutual prejudices and misconceptions and attempt to engage with each other in a manner that would produce a 'union of minds'. Such a union was essential to advance the mission and capitalize on what had been achieved thus far with relatively few resources of men and money since Xavier's arrival in 1549. This accomplishment would not have been possible had not many of those who became Christian felt a genuine attraction and commitment to the faith. To this extent, the missionaries had succeeded in crossing the threshold from outside (*soto*) to inside (*uchi*). The policy of accommodation was intended to produce even greater success. But accommodation had to proceed in both directions so, obversely, and this is something which figures unmistakably in *De Missione*, the Japanese were expected to step outside the confines of their world. As an inducement, they were offered membership in the nascent global, Roman Catholic, community portrayed so vividly in the book. But, in the late-sixteenth and early-seventeenth centuries, Japan's new rulers rejected this particular global vision. As the civil wars drew to an end, the Japanese house or state was being reconstructed, first by Hideyoshi and then, building upon his achievement, by the Tokugawa shogunate. In performing this task, Japan's new leaders decided to use existing, familiar materials drawn from indigenous and deeply rooted sources of tradition and legitimacy. Exotic foreign materials of dubious provenance, alien to Japan's traditional cultural world, were excluded lest they undermine the foundations. Japan's leaders, especially the Tokugawa, judged that Christianity, already too entrenched on the still insecure western periphery of the country, posed a threat to the new order. As a result, it had to be extirpated.

Unlike *Kirishitan kanagaki* and other anti-Christian tracts which appeared in the seventeenth century, *De Missione*, despite its authors' intentions, made no lasting impact on Japanese perceptions of Europe. It was inconsequential. This was not the case with the information about Europe provided by another Jesuit source, the Italian Giovanni Battista Sidotti, who entered Japan illegally from the Philippines in 1708 and was put to death in Edo in 1714. Drawing mainly upon his conversations with Sidotti, the Confucian scholar Arai Hakuseki produced an account of Europe, *Seiyō kibun*, which greatly influenced Japanese *kokugaku* (national learning) scholars in the eighteenth century and helped shape Japan's subsequent response to European and American overtures and threats in the nineteenth.[1] By then, of course, the Japanese had become very much impressed by the magnificence of Europe and they sought ways to emulate such majesty for their own ends. Christianity was not one of the means chosen to achieve that goal.

---

[1] See Elison, *Deus Destroyed*, pp. 237–41; Wakabayashi, *Anti-Foreignism and Western Learning*, pp. 93–7. For an English translation of *Seiyō kibun*, see 'Sei Yo Ki-Bun'.

A Dialogue concerning the Mission of the Japanese Ambassadors to the Roman Curia, and Things which they observed in the Course of their Journey, in Europe and elsewhere,
Based on their own Diary, and put into Latin
By Duarte de Sande, Priest of the Society of Jesus.

In the house of the Society of Jesus, in the Port of Macao, in the Kingdom of China, with the Permission of the Bishop and Superiors
In the year 1590.

I, Leonardo de Sá,[1] Bishop of China and Japan and Apostolic Inquisitor in the same diocese, entrust to the Reverend Father Alessandro Valignano, Visitor of the Society of Jesus, and to others to be appointed by him, the examining of the book composed by Father Duarte de Sande of the same Society about the mission of the Japanese ambassadors to the Roman Curia, and things which they observed in the whole course of their journey, in Europe and elsewhere; and I give him permission to have it printed after those same fathers have given their signed approval.

Given in the city of Macao, 5 September 1589

Bishop Leonardo

---

[1] Leonardo de Sá (the original edition, A1v, gives Saà), bishop of Macao, 1576–97 (his death), a member of the Order of Christ (Ordem de Cristo). He arrived in Macao for the first time in 1581. The Jesuits suspected him of being hostile to them. See *Documenta Indica,* XIV, pp. 67, 726; XV, p. 94; López-Gay, 'Don Pedro Martins, SJ', p. 80. On the basis of some 17th-century information, various authorities – notably Manuel Teixeira (*Macau e a sua diocese,* vol. 2, pp. 85–8), Hubert Cieslik ('Zur Geschichte der kirchlichen Hierarchie', pp. 204–5) and Josef Schütte ('Die Wirksamkeit der Päpste', pp. 191–2) – say that in 1590 de Sá was held captive in Acheh, having been seized on a return voyage from Goa to Macao in either 1586, 1587 or 1588, and was released only in 1594. This is contradicted by his imprimatur to *De Missione* and by references to his activity in other contemporary sources (*Documenta Indica,* XV, pp. 94, 650). A separate diocese for Japan had finally been established by a consistorial charter on 19 February 1588 with the establishment of an episcopal see in Funai, which the charter (inaccurately) suggests was a thriving city. Until then Japan had been part of the diocese of Macao, established in 1576 as a suffragan diocese of Goa with the right of nomination, as a part of the Portuguese *padroado real,* awarded to the Portuguese monarch. The first bishop appointed to the new diocese of Japan, Sebastião de Morais (or Moraes), the Jesuit provincial of Portugal who helped ensure that the boys' stay in Portugal went smoothly, died near Mozambique en route to Japan on 19 August 1588. His successor, Pedro Martins SJ, 1592–8, reached Japan in 1596 but stayed for just over a half-year before being expelled by Toyotomi Hideyoshi. See Fróis, *Première ambassade,* pp. 32, 37, 39, 256, 263; Schütte, *Monumenta Historica Japoniae I*, p. 1230; Cieslik, 'Zur Geschichte der kirchlichen Hierarchie', pp. 207–14; Elison, *Deus Destroyed*, p. 410 n. 43; López-Gay, 'Don Pedro Martins, SJ', pp. 79–94; Cooper, *Japanese Mission,* pp. 174–5, who misdates Morais's appointment, giving February 1587 instead of February 1588.

I, Alessandro Valignano, Visitor of the Society of Jesus in the Oriental Province, and Fathers Diogo Antunes[1] and Nicolão de Ávila[2] of the same Society, having been entrusted by the Most Reverend Leonardo de Sá, Bishop of China etc., with the reading and examining of the book about the mission of the Japanese ambassadors to the Roman Curia, and things which they observed in the whole course of their journey, in Europe and elsewhere, composed by Father Duarte de Sande of our same Society, find nothing in it opposed to the Christian religion or to good morals; indeed we judge it to be truly useful and necessary for the Church of Japan, and in testimony to this we have signed below.
4 October 1589

Alessandro Valignano   Diogo Antunes   Nicolão de Ávila

---

[1] Born in Crato, Portugal, c. 1552, he entered the Society in 1570 or 1571, and worked in Macao from December 1587 until his death around July 1610. See Schütte, *Monumenta Historica Japoniae I*, pp. 216, 309, 485, 496, 511, 513. On the bishop question, see Introduction p. 5.

[2] Born in Villacastín, Spain, c. 1551, he entered the Society 1572 and served in Japan from 1598 to 1614 when the missionaries were expelled. He died in Macao in 1618. See Schütte, *Monumenta Historica Japoniae I*, pp. 309, 411, 585, 601, 654, 663, 784.

Alessandro Valignano of the Society of Jesus to the pupils of the Japanese seminaries. S.D.[1]

Here now, excellent boys, you see published, as a third testimony to my love for you, this dialogue about the mission of the Japanese ambassadors and the things they observed on their journey. My first concern was to ensure, as far as was in my power, by composing a catechism and later having it printed in Latin in Europe,[2] that your souls would be strengthened in the Christian faith through a knowledge of the main points of our religion. Nor have I been disappointed with the outstanding example you have already given in embracing the faith with your whole heart. After this foundation had been laid I strove further to have printed some book to instruct you in the virtues pertaining to conduct, and I believe I accomplished this with the printing of the book *De honesta puerorum institutione*, by João Bonifacio, priest of the Society of Jesus.[3]

There remained the need for some book to provide you with instruction about European things, which are so closely linked with, and indeed in large part drawn from Christian devotion. It is fortunate, therefore, that this book has now made its appearance. All the things in it were diligently noted by the ambassadors from your own country sent to the Roman curia, and passed on with my full approval to Father Duarte de Sande of our Society, who now lives in the Kingdom of China. He was formerly dedicated to the study of the humanities, and was always interested in anything to do with you, and I asked him to put the collected and ordered writings of the ambassadors themselves into Latin, and, in order to make them clearer and more useful to you, to make them into a dialogue taking place between the ambassadors and their companions and their relatives. You have to persuade yourselves, therefore, that it is no foreigner that you are listening to, but that it is your own people who are speaking, and that, since they were not able to talk to everyone and tell them about Europe, they are now gladly communicating to the whole nation of Japan, in this dialogue, everything that they learned in the whole of their journey.

For my part, I would ask you not to reject these offerings as trifling or lightweight, but to accept them with a grateful heart as truly useful and profitable, acknowledging my paternal solicitude for you, and to give back to God the cultivator of all things, with much increase, the hoped-for fruit from these seeds.

---

[1] '*Salutem dicit*', sends greetings.

[2] Alessandro Valignano, *Catechismus Christianae Fidei*, Lisbon, 1586. Only two copies of this work survive. See Schütte, *Valignano's Mission Principles*, I: 2, pp. 67–89; Laures, *Kirishitan Bunko*, pp. 27–9; Elison, *Deus Destroyed*, pp. 37–42.

[3] João Bonifacio, *Christiani Pueri Institutio, Adolescentiaeqve perfugium: autore Ioanne Bonifacio Societatis Iesv*, Macao, 1588, first published in Salamanca in 1575 with numerous editions thereafter. Valignano prepared his edition from a manuscript version of the Burgos edition, possibly sent to him by Bonifacio himself. It was intended to strengthen Japanese seminarians' virtue and as an aid for Latin studies. He made a number of modifications, including the addition of an anecdote about the piety and heroism of two Japanese youths. Only two copies of the Macao edition are extant, one in the Biblioteca da Ajuda in Lisbon, the other in Det Kongelige Bibliotek, Copenhagen. See Laures, *Kirishitan Bunko*, pp. 30–32; Shinzo Kawamura, 'Humanism, Pedagogy and Language'; Oliveira, 'A construção de conhecimento', p. 946 n. 8.

To the Most Reverend Father in Christ Claudio Aquaviva,[1] Superior General of the Society of Jesus, Duarte de Sande. S.D.

Most reverend Father in Christ, the news that an embassy was being sent from Japan, that embassy which, we are told, was welcomed with such joy and to such acclamation by the Supreme Pontiffs Gregory XIII[2] and Sixtus V[3] (whom God preserve) and by other Christian princes, gave us great hopes of ever more abundant fruit from the Japanese field. This is not the place to list all the benefits which it was hoped would accrue from the embassy, but one particularly important one was that these youths with their education, their intelligence, and their eagerness to learn about our things, would bear the first fruits of the Japanese harvest to Europe and to the Roman Curia, and would then return to their own country of Japan, where knowledge of Europe and of Christianity is as yet inadequate, to communicate to their compatriots their own knowledge, developed and verified in the course of their long journey.

    Anyone with any knowledge of Japan is well aware how difficult it has been up till now, and how much perseverance has been necessary, for the fathers of our Society to be able to convince the Japanese of the majesty of the Supreme Pontiff, of the authority wielded by cardinals and other prelates, and of the power and the greatness of Christian kingdoms. The Japanese are not aware of the distinction between religious and secular jurisdiction, the former of a higher order than the latter, nor of the ends proposed or the means employed by each of the two, nor of the idea that state or country is to be administered in accordance with justice and natural law. They do not grasp how widespread the Christian religion is in various countries of the world, nor do they appreciate the great difference that there is in worship and in discipline between religious persons and persons who devote themselves to transitory things. They have no notion of the numbers of men and women in Christendom who, intent on the good which is everlasting, spurn the pleasures of this life, and take the road of the evangelical counsels, the direct way to heaven; nor any understanding of what it is that moves these religious men to put themselves in the most extreme danger, traversing land and sea, many lands and many seas, in order zealously and eagerly to proclaim the name of Christ to peoples and nations to whom it is unknown. Together with Christian teaching the fathers have provided the Japanese with information on all these and other similar matters, but they have had very limited success in convincing them of these things, and in rooting out the erroneous opinions which they have conceived about both their own and our things, the former opinions bequeathed to them by their ancestors, the latter an assemblage of fatuous hearsay. For this reason our fathers never forgot that one of the principal objectives of this embassy was that these high-born youths should bring back to their own country and impart to their compatriots full information about our things, and they reminded them insistently that they must not fail to observe, to note down, and to preserve in writing everything that they experienced throughout all the

---

[1] Or Acquaviva, born in Atri in 1543, youngest son of Giovanni Antonio Donato d'Aragona, the Duke of Atri. He entered the Society in 1567, the year after Valignano. He was elected fifth Superior General of the Jesuits at the Society's fifth congregation in Rome in 1581 and remained in office until his death in 1615. He was a personal friend of Valignano. They had studied together in Rome.

[2] r. 1572–85.

[3] r. 1585–90.

length of their pilgrimage. They, admirable as they are in their character and in their obedience to the fathers, promptly recorded in their journal whatever things seemed to them notable and worth remembering, and although, in conformity with Japanese manners, they gave no outward sign of surprise, they regarded all those things as truly wonderful, and kept them lodged securely in their senses and in their minds.

Father Alessandro Valignano, Visitor of the whole oriental region, was concerned that all their work should not simply be lost, and that the memory of their journey and of the many things they had noted should not fade with the passage of just a few years. He wanted a record of it to be kept and used, and wanted the whole Japanese people to be aware of these things, and children to be steeped in and formed by an awareness of them from an early age. Accordingly the Father Visitor decided that all that these noble youths had informally committed to paper should be written up in a more mature style in Latin, so that the Japanese who were learning Latin would have a book about this embassy to study from; and afterwards it would be translated into Japanese for the benefit of those ignorant of Latin, and the printed versions of both the Latin and the Japanese would be, as it were, a perpetual storehouse and most agreeable reminder of these so necessary and useful things.[1]

When the time came, therefore, to embark on this work, the same father decided that it should take the form not of a continuous history, which could perhaps be somewhat boring, but of a dialogue, featuring the following speakers: the legates Mancio and Michael, their companions Martin and Julian, and also Leo, brother of the king of Arima, and Lino, brother of the prince of Ōmura, both of whom are cousins of Michael on their fathers' side, Leo, Lino, and Michael being the sons of three brothers. Leo and Lino, who have never been out of Japan and have as yet no knowledge of our things, ask many questions of the others, who are knowledgeable about many things, and answer fully. It may be that the reader will be somewhat irritated to have things explained in such exhaustive detail, but he must remember that this book has been composed, according to the instruction of the reverend Father Visitor, not for Europeans, who are already very well informed, but for the Japanese, who are beginners, with no knowledge of these things.

So it fell to me, with advice from the same reverend father, to put into Latin the excellent notes made by those noble youths, and afterwards arranged in order. I was very conscious of the many years which had intervened since I abandoned the study of the classics in order to cultivate more demanding muses, and gave all my time, as holy obedience required, to mastering Chinese. But such is the power of obedience that it easily found me a place in my old school and restored me to favour with the humanities. But if the restoration seems ill-patched, as the renowned author said,[2] and our dialogue seems to savour more of Chinese than of Latin, I am quite content to be known more for my obedience than for my eloquence. I am therefore happy to offer and commit this work in the first place to God, to whom my efforts are directed, and then to your Paternity and to the Father Visitor, whom I acknowledge in place of God, trusting that it will be useful to the Japanese and acceptable to the Europeans. I hope that I shall have no regrets about this book and that on the contrary through its teaching, as by a timely irrigation, the Japanese field may produce ever more excellent fruit, to the gladdening of all Christendom.

---

[1] A Japanese version was finally printed in 1942 (Hamada et al., *Tenshō nenkan*).
[2] The author in question is Horace and the reference is to the *Epistles* (I.3.31) where Horace compares a broken friendship to a wound that stitches have failed to close.

CONTENTS OF THESE COLLOQUIA

Colloquium I: The reasons for the Japanese embassy

Colloquium II: The journey from Japan to Macao, the gateway to China, and from there to the Straits of Singapore

Colloquium III: The approach to the city of Malacca, in the Golden Chersonese, and from there to the city of Cochin, in Nearer India

Colloquium IV: The coming of the Portuguese to India, and the spread of the Portuguese empire

Colloquium V: About the Indian race, and the houses of the Society in India

Colloquium VI: The Voyage from India to Portugal

Colloquium VII: About the things of Europe in general, and firstly of the sacred or ecclesiastical monarchy, and other lower ranks

Colloquium VIII: About the secular monarchy, and various dignities belonging to it

Colloquium IX: Of the splendour and opulence of the kings and rulers of Europe in what concerns the treatment of the body, food, and accommodation, and of their great costs and expenses

Colloquium X: Of the multitude of servants and the pomp which the princes of Europe use at home and abroad

Colloquium XI: About the agreeable and honourable exercises which the nobles of Europe engage in, and of the noble education of their children

Colloquium XII: The arrangements and customs of Europeans with regard to the administration of kingdoms and republics

Colloquium XIII: Of the wars which are usually waged in Europe, the way of setting up an army, and land battles

Colloquium XIV: Of the naval battles in which they usually engage in Europe

Colloquium XV: Of the size of the cities, the splendour of the churches, and the magnificence of other buildings

Colloquium XVI: Reverting to the account of the journey, with a description of Lisbon, capital of the kingdom of Portugal

Colloquium XVII: Which gives an account of the things which took place in Lisbon, and then in Évora and Vila Viçosa, and then proceeds into the kingdom of Castile, to Toledo and to Mantua Carpetana or Madrid

Colloquium XVIII: Of the power of King Philip of Spain, and the oath by which the nobles of the kingdom swore allegiance to his son as his successor, and of the visit which the ambassadors made to both

Colloquium XIX: Of various works built by King Philip, especially the work of the Escorial, and the approach to the city of Alón or Alicante

Colloquium XX: The voyage from Spain to Italy, the visit to the grand duke of Tuscany, and things noted in Pisa and Florence

Colloquium XXI: Of the delights and pleasures of the Pratolino villa of the duke of Tuscany, and of things observed at Siena, Viterbo, and on the remainder of the journey to Rome

Colloquium XXII: Of the entrance into the celebrated city of Rome, and the audience with the Supreme Pontiff Gregory XIII, and of the sacred palace and the most august church of St Peter

Colloquium XXIII: Continues with things noted at the pope's solemn masses and elsewhere

Colloquium XXIV: Of what took place in Rome up until the death of Pope Gregory XIII

Colloquium XXV: How the funeral of a pope is carried out, and the way in which another pope is chosen, and to what great and universal applause Sixtus V was proclaimed pope

Colloquium XXVI: The cavalcade with which the pope made his way to the church of St John Lateran, and the ambassadors, invested with the insignia of knighthood, departed the city; and of the most noble city of Naples, and the church of the Blessed Virgin of Loreto

Colloquium XXVII: The journey through other cities, especially Ancona, Bologna, Ferrara, and Venice, and the things seen there

Colloquium XXVIII: Gives an account of notable things observed in Venice, and of the honour with which the Japanese ambassadors were treated by its august Senate

Colloquium XXIX: More about things in Venice, but also dealing with the access of the ambassadors to other cities, principally Padua, Verona, Mantua, Cremona, and Milan, and the rejoicing with which they were received in them

Colloquium XXX: More about things noted in Milan and in Pavia, and about their entry into the city of Genoa and the voyage to Spain

Colloquium XXXI: Of the city of Coimbra and the famous college of the Society there, the generous treatment extended to the ambassadors in Lisbon, by order of King Philip, with regard to the voyage to India, and the reasons for the wealth of Europe

Colloquium XXXII: The Voyage from Portugal to India, and from India to the Kingdom of China

Colloquium XXXIII: The kingdom of China, its customs and administration

Colloquium XXXIV: A summary description of the whole world, and a statement as to which is its principal and noblest part

COLLOQUIUM I

The reasons for the Japanese embassy

Leo: Dear brother Michael, it is not easy to put into words the joy we felt when we saw you, Mancio, Martin, and Julian entering this fortress of Arima,[1] amid such general excitement and such applause.

Michael: My dear Leo, I know without you telling me how glad you and Lino, our most loving brother, were to have us back here in our own country. We expected no less, given the closeness of our blood relationship and the love we used to have for one another, especially as we for our part are so delighted to see you grown up, and in such good health, and so grateful to you for the happiness we all feel.

Lino: A further reason for our joy, besides the one mentioned by Leo, was that we were intensely keen to hear from you about all the things that happened to you on your immensely long journey.

Mancio: I am very pleased to hear you say so, for any experienced judge would agree that the best way to come to a knowledge of so many things would have been to be with us over the eight and a half years spent on this voyage.

Lino: Dear God! Is it eight and a half years since you set out?

Mancio: It is, or just a few days short of it. We left Nagasaki on 20 February in the year of Our Saviour 1582,[2] and it was not until July of the present year of 1590 that the ship docked at this port.[3]

Lino: That is such a very long time that you have probably forgotten at least the things that happened at the beginning of the voyage. I'm sure Martin and Julian will agree.

---

[1] The boys arrived in Arima, on the Shimabara peninsula in present-day Nagasaki prefecture, in May 1591 after their visit to Kyoto as part of Valignano's embassy to Hideyoshi. For an account of their reception in Arima, see Fróis, *História de Japam*, V, pp. 334–8.

[2] The original edition (pp. 1–2) gives '*vigesimo*' corrected to '*decimo namque calendas Martij*', i.e. ten days before the Kalends of March (1 March) or 20 February. Fróis, erroneously, gives 28 February (*Première ambassade*, p. 8).

[3] 21 July 1590.

Martin: That is indeed what you would expect, given the length of time and the way time usually consigns the past to oblivion: but in this case the things were of such importance that they are impressed and fixed in our minds as if they had happened only recently.

Julian: Martin is right. Minor and trivial things are soon forgotten, but our experience, of major and important things, carved out, as it were, in the depths of our minds, will not be lost however long the time.

Leo: That is exactly what we have been hoping you would say. Both Lino and I are longing to hear from you about everything that happened to you on your journey, and about all the things in all those places on which your eyes could feed and your minds feast. This is the reason, the only reason, why we were so eager to meet you today. If it's not asking too much, do please tell us all about it.

Michael: We are very keen indeed and more than willing to do what you want, but time is a problem. In the short time we have it is almost impossible for us to give you an account of everything that happened in the course of those eight years.

Mancio: I agree. We saw, or experienced, or in some way came to know about so many things, and such important things, which we had never heard of before, that it just would not be possible to get across to you in a short time what it was all really like.

Lino: We are well aware of that, and we never had any intention of restricting you to one day. We do have time, and we have arranged to come together every day for several days so that you can tell us all about it. We are looking forward to it very much indeed.

Leo: Absolutely. Those who have to make a living by their labour or their skill always have to be looking for an occupation, and this leaves them no leisure, but in this and other points the nobility are different, and no occupation could be more agreeable than our present one.

Michael: Your arrangements as far as time is concerned are fine. Now we are going to get Mancio to act as narrator, and if he happens to leave anything out we can easily add it in.

Mancio: No, no. I'm not going to be the narrator. That's your job, Michael, here in the fortress of Arima, in front of your beloved brothers, who are so eager to hear from you about it, and will accept it so much more gladly if they have it from you. My turn will come when we get to Bungo.[1] There will be no lack of people there expecting me to tell the story.

Martin: I agree with Mancio. When he reaches Bungo there will be plenty of people ready to listen to him and begging him to tell his story.

---

[1] In fact the boys proceeded to Ōmura rather than Bungo following their visit to Arima (Fróis, *História de Japam*, V, p. 338).

Julian: I think Mancio is right, too. Words are sweeter to the ear and more acceptable to the mind when you are bound to the speaker by ties of blood and of love.

Leo: As far as we are concerned it makes no difference whether Michael or Mancio takes the part of narrator, but since all of you are at one in assigning this task to Michael we are perfectly content with your decision, especially as it is inevitable that, with so much material to deal with, sometimes the one and sometimes the other will have to act as narrator.

Lino: You are quite right. Now we mustn't spend all our time discussing who does what. Michael, could you start it off for us, and begin with an account of the reasons why you made this huge journey; when you left we were too young to be able to comprehend them, and a recapitulation would lay an excellent foundation for your story.

Michael: Since it's the wish of all of you I'll be glad, with Mancio's' permission, to do as you ask. For my part I ask you, Mancio, and my other companions for the help of your prayers as I embark upon our story, and if I stray from the right path I would be grateful if you would speak out and lead me back. The main reason that I have the confidence to begin is that I have you, witnesses of all the things I am going to speak about, here listening to my words. Anyone speaking of matters which are at once important and unfamiliar to his hearers runs the risk, if there is no witness present, either of going beyond the truth by exaggerating certain points, or of stopping short of the truth by failing to mention others. But if there are witnesses present who will criticize any inaccuracy he will naturally be more cautious and careful in what he says, and will keep his eyes fixed on truth as the lodestar of his voyage, as I undertake to do today.

Leo: Michael, what's all this talk of witnesses? The esteem in which we hold you, and the nature of the matters of which you will be treating, mean that falsification is out of the question. Men of noble blood are not in the habit of allowing their name to be sullied by being branded as liars, and in any case when you are dealing with such foreign matters there is no possibility of attachment to self, or self-love, inclining you to deviate from the truth. So don't keep us in suspense any longer, but start, as Lino recommended, with the reasons why your long journey was arranged.

Michael: You ask, dear brothers, about the reasons for our expedition. There were many different important reasons, and we understood them much better after we got to Europe. I'll deal briefly with just some of them. The first reason was that Father Alessandro Valignano, Visitor of the Society of Jesus, judged it expedient. After he had arrived in Japan, having sailed from Europe, he learned by experience that the customs of Japan are in many ways very different from those of Europe; he also realized that, because of the vast distance between the two, the scale and magnificence of provinces and kingdoms in Europe, the majesty and power of their leading men, and many other admirable things, had reached the islands of Japan only as a sort of distant rumour; he understood besides that the fathers of the Society, who spoke of these things to the Japanese, were not entirely believed, and this had many unfortunate results, to the detriment of souls and with at best a reduction in the crop of that most desirable fruit. The said father, after full discussion of the matter, determined that it was essential that some princes and nobles from our country should go to Europe to see with their own eyes and, so to speak, touch with their own hands the condition of that region and all those things of which till then word had reached us only from foreigners. These nobles were to return to their own country here, bringing incontrovertible witness of those things to their own people, so that our countrymen would no longer suspect that they were being told lies, and their minds would be freed of the many false opinions which they conceive about European things.

Leo: An excellent explanation indeed; but to help us understand it, could you explain what region is meant by the name Europe.

Michael: That's a very good question, and very relevant to what I'm going to be talking about. Since the Japanese live in these islands, at an enormous distance from that, so to speak, other world, and have had little commerce or other contact with its peoples, we have until now had definite and reliable information only about our own Japan, and about kingdoms near to it, China[1] and Siam,[2] apart from some, as I said, rather vague reports about the kingdom of the *nambanjin*,[3] that is, of the people from the south, which we call *namban* and the Chinese call *nanfan*, i.e. the south, from where, we used to be told, the merchants and the priests of the Society come. But now that we have been there our eyes are opened, as it were, as if a darkness surrounding them had been dispersed, and we know that there are many other kingdoms and many provinces all over the world. They are known for their size and almost infinite in their number, so that the three regions of Japan, China, and Siam seem by comparison like portions of some miniature world.[4] Let me put before you briefly the principal parts of the world: the earth is divided, according to the most learned of scientists, into five principal parts, namely Europe, Africa, Asia, America, and, lastly, that land which writers call *terra incognita*, the unknown land. Sailors voyaging from west to east have sometimes taken too southerly a route and have seen that land, and before eventually being carried beyond it they have observed that it is very extensive indeed. Nevertheless it is not yet certain what peoples inhabit it, what their customs are,

---

[1] The first embassy from Japan to reach China is recorded as 57 CE. Thereafter there was a long history of Sino-Japanese diplomatic relations. After 1557 the Chinese broke off official relations between the two empires (which had lapsed anyway) in response to the ravages of the *wakō* 倭寇 or Japanese pirates along China's maritime provinces. In reality many of the *wakō* and their leaders were Chinese taking advantage of the upheavals of Japan's civil wars by using the numerous islands and inlets off and around Kyushu as bases. See *Cambridge History of Japan, Volume 4*, pp. 239–62.

[2] I.e. India and, more generally, South-east Asia.

[3] 南蛮人 *nambanjin* or southern barbarians, the name for the Portuguese in Japan.

[4] According to Fróis, writing in 1565, the Japanese divided the world into three parts: Japan, China and Siam. Initially the Jesuits believed that Siam was the birthplace of the historical Buddha and that Buddhism was transmitted from Siam and China to Japan, hence the identification of Siam with India. João Rodrigues put the record straight, correctly identifying India as the birthplace of the Buddha. The Jesuits, and the Portuguese more generally, were not interested in Siam in the 16th century and other missionaries made little headway there. See *Cartas*, I, f. 172; Fróis, *História de Japam*, I, pp. 30, 165; Lach, *Asia in the Making*, I: 1, pp. 285–6; *Cambridge History of Southeast Asia*, vol. 1, p. 414; Cooper, *João Rodrigues's Account*, pp. 17, 19 n. 2, 66. See also *Vocabvlario*, f. 218: '*Sangocu. Mitçuno cuni.i [Sankoku. Mitsu no kuni] ... China, Siāo, Iapāo*' (the three kingdoms, China, Siam, Japan). Japan's longstanding and extensive dealings with Korea and its trading relationship with the Ryūkyū kingdom (present-day Okinawa) were largely unfamiliar to the early Jesuit writers.

what sort of climate or soil they have, so the land is generally called *incognita* or unknown.[1] The regions of Japan, China, and Siam, already known to us, belong to the part called Asia, which also contains many other provinces and kingdoms, so many that it would be tedious to list them.[2] In the course of our voyage we did indeed spend time in certain Asian kingdoms which are far from here, and we passed along the shores of Africa; but since Europe, that most noble region, was the longed-for objective of our journey, I feel justified in according it special mention in this first account of our experience.

Lino: You are saying extraordinary things, Michael, and in listing these parts of the world for us you are providing us with plenty of material to question you about.

Michael: There will indeed be no lack of matter for questioning, but it will be better to wait for the appropriate time, so as to deal with things in their proper order. If we try to explain things all at once there is bound to be a loss of clarity in the telling, since an immediate and full answer to every question would mean so many digressions that it would be very difficult to keep to our story and provide a coherent account. We have to make it a rule, therefore, that everything will be treated in its proper place, and the audience will be patient and allow the narrator as far as possible to keep to the proper order. For the moment, then, it is enough to have spoken of those five parts of the world, though I shall have something to say later on about the form, so to speak, of the world as a whole.

Leo: Michael is quite right. If we want to ask a question every time he makes any statement, and to make enquiries at that point about the form of the whole universe, how can he give a proper answer to our first question about the reasons for this expedition?

Michael: The second reason was this: when the fathers of the Society came to Japan in order to communicate to us the light of divine truth which had previously been given to them by God, and to promulgate the law which comes from the supreme legislator, this law and teaching was so completely unknown to our people, whose minds were imbued with the false religion of the *kami* and *hotoke*,[3] that it was always extremely difficult for the

---

[1] Ortelis's world map of 1570 names the vast unknown continent '*Terra Avstralis nondum cognita*' and it appears on the 'Anon-Moreira' Map (Fig. 1). Whether or not the Portuguese reached the north-western coast of Australia in the first half of the sixteenth century (the source material is inconclusive), they showed no interest in the area. The Spanish, sailing from Peru, took an interest in Pacific exploration but it was the Dutch, notably Abel Tasman, who put New Holland, what was later to become Australia, on the map. See *Dicionário*, I, pp. 103–4; Williams, *Great South Sea*, pp. 1–12, 56–68; Nebenzahl and Marques, 'Moreira's Manuscript', pp. 18–19.

[2] For such a list and description, see Cooper, *João Rodrigues's Account*, ch. 1 *passim*.

[3] *Kami* 神 or Shinto deities, and, by extension, Shinto, the traditional religion of Japan. *Hotoke* 佛 (modern character 仏) Buddha, one who has attained nirvana. There are many Buddhas in Mahayana Buddhism (practised in Japan, China and Korea) but only one, the historical Buddha, in Theravada Buddhism (practised in south-east Asia). The principal Buddhist sects in Japan venerate different Buddhas. The Jesuits were perfectly aware of the difference between Shinto and Buddhism and struggled to understand the complexities of Buddhism in Japan, not least because they knew that many Japanese considered Christianity a Buddhist sect. They regarded Buddhist images as idols. See *Vocabvlario*, ff. 34v (*Cami*), 304 (*Xintô*), 351v (*Fotoqe*). The earliest surviving account of Japan by Jorge Álvarez, composed around the end of 1546 and written at the request of

fathers to wean the Japanese away from their vain opinions, and to persuade them that the doctrine they taught was entirely in accord with the truth. For although they were admirably prompt in expressing an intellectual assent to the doctrine which they heard from the fathers, their wills were held back by long habit from exchanging the antiquated law of their empty deities for the most true teaching of God, especially as they were not yet convinced as to how very widespread this teaching was, how many peoples throughout all the world had accepted it, and the distinction and splendour of its adherents. So since the fathers who had come to Japan up till that time lived among the Japanese in their normal way, that is with a very modest and unostentatious lifestyle, and with no power or authority in public affairs, their appearance and their way of life gave no indication to our people of the majesty and grandeur of Christianity; rather they would have thought, and indeed did think, judging from what they could observe externally, that the law which they were promulgating was associated with some inferior manner of life, and they suspected various other things too. As a result their minds were distracted by all sorts of ideas, and this was no small obstacle to the progress of Christianity. This was why it was necessary that some men of noble birth from this land of ours should travel to that part of the world where Christianity is flourishing, so as to grasp, no longer vaguely, distantly, through uncertain hearsay or scraps of rumour, but by seeing, by hearing, by daily contact and personal experience, the lustre and distinction which the light of divine truth brings to the human mind, how much Christianity contributes to good and holy living, and further, what a difference there is between those illumined with this light and those who still walk in the dark; they would then come back to their own country with this certain knowledge and first-hand experience and would share their knowledge with all their compatriots.

Mancio: I really have to interrupt at this point to add my witness in confirmation of what Michael has said; it would have been impossible for us ever to have imagined anything so magnificent as the condition of Christendom if we had not seen it with our own eyes; and we are uncomfortably aware that no matter what we say we can do no more

---

Francis Xavier, with whom Álvarez was friends, makes the distinction but does not use the word *kami*. See Ruiz-de-Medina, *Documentos del Japón*, I, pp. 1–24, esp. pp. 16–24, partially translated into German and English in Schurhammer, *Shin-tō*, pp. 161–4. It was clear even before Xavier reached Japan that Buddhism with its numerous sects, institutions, sacred texts and rituals would be the missionaries' nemesis. See Nicolao Lancillotto's 'informatione de una insula che se è discoperta novamente ... chiamata Giapan' (Ruiz-de-Medina, *Documentos del Japón*, I, pp. 44–69). Both Álvarez and Lancillotto relied heavily on information provided by a Japanese from Kagoshima, Anjirō, who became acquainted with Xavier in the Mollucas and converted to Christianity, taking the name Paul. He went with Xavier to Japan but seems later to have apostatized, ending his days as a *wakō* or pirate on the China coast (Ruiz-de-Medina, *Documentos del Japón*, I, pp. 31*–32*, 297). These accounts, together with Xavier's earliest letters from Japan, soon circulated in Europe and influenced the writings of Guillame Postel. See Bernard-Maitre, 'L'Orientaliste Guillaume Postel', pp. 83–108; Elisonas, 'An Itinerary', pp. 25–68. Valignano devoted a short chapter to Japanese religion in the *Sumario*, mentioning that there were '*sectas*', among which the *kami* was native to Japan and the *hotoke* was introduced from China (*Sumario*, ch. 3). Towards the end of his life, in the *Principio*, he commented, wearily and patronizingly, that much had been written about 'these sects' in various letters, many of which had been published in Europe, but that he himself would not deal with them 'because it is a large confusing subject of no benefit' (printed in Valignano, *Sumario*, p. 58, n. 2; Üçerler, 'Sacred Historiography', II, p. 36).

than convey merely a shadow of the excellence of what we saw, without in any way doing it justice.

Lino: What most persuades me to believe without any problem what you tell us is the emphasis with which you tell it; and I am very much struck by that second reason which you put before us.

Michael: I can cap it with a third, and I think you will find this one persuasive as well. You have already heard, and it should not be forgotten, that there is as it were a supreme governor, or pontiff, of the whole Christian people, who holds on earth the place of Christ, true God and founder of the Christian faith, and who, for centuries past, has had his seat in Rome, a most noble and famous city of Europe, which has almost always held sway over the greater part of the world; and from there, as if from a most certain oracle for the whole world, the Supreme Pontiff prescribes laws, provides answers to weighty questions, and moderates the entire Christian state as supreme pastor. To him come the most prominent of men, the most senior of priests; nay, sometimes kings themselves, if they can, come to him, all of them subjecting themselves as suppliants to him as father of all; and in the intervals between their visits, when it is not possible for them to go themselves, they acknowledge through their ambassadors his supreme majesty and sanctity on earth; and thus the proper union between body and head, between flock and shepherd, is maintained.

Now, by divine favour, a considerable portion of our people had heard and accepted the law of Christ, and had gone over to the side of the same Lord and His Supreme Vicar, and been numbered among so blessed a people; however, because of the enormous distance between there and here, only vague stories had reached us about Rome and the Supreme Roman Pontiff, and likewise he had heard only the faintest of rumours about Japan and the Japanese leaders, so that he could have no idea what sort of people the Japanese were, in these so remote regions, whether they were dull or sharp of mind, whether they cared for honour and reputation, whether they were in any way concerned about the glory and fame of a famous name, whether they practised the noble arts or were backward and ignorant. There were many other things of which he could have no knowledge, except for things selected from the letters of the Fathers, so given that the Japanese lords themselves, those who had already committed themselves to Christ, were not able to make the journey to the pope and eagerly prostrate themselves to kiss his feet, as other princes, their co-religionists, are accustomed to do, it seemed absolutely necessary that they at least send some young men, blood relatives of theirs; these should take upon themselves the role of legates, and should perform this role in the name of the Japanese lords. Thus the name of Japan, until now barely heard or known, would be celebrated in Rome itself, the most famous location in the whole world; and the supreme father would embrace these his recently born sons, absent though they were, in paternal love and benevolence, and with the signs of this love and benevolence would draw those not yet enlightened with the Christian faith to adopt that faith with all speed.

These were the principal reasons why Father Alessandro Valignano, Visitor of the Society of Jesus, after speaking about it to Francisco and Protasio, kings of Bungo and of Arima, and Bartolomeu the prince of Ōmura, planned this embassy. He explained the reasons to them, and arranged that they should send Mancio and me, together with our dear companions Martin and Julian, as their ambassadors to the Supreme Pontiff. To ensure that things would go smoothly he decided, to the great joy of all, that he, Father Diogo de Mesquita,[1] and Brother Jorge Loyola,[2] our compatriot, would be our constant companions; he himself as our leader on the journey, Father de Mesquita as teacher and instructor, and Brother Jorge to make sure we did not forget Japanese. And with these most happy auguries our voyage began.

Leo: We are satisfied with your account of the reasons for the journey; I'd like you to move on now to the journey itself.

Michael: Dear Leo, you have noticed, surely, that my talk has already taken us well into the night. If you don't mind, let's go to bed now, and continue tomorrow the story begun today.

Lino: Michael is right. We should take a break from the story at this point and have a short sleep. We'll be all the more eager to resume tomorrow. I wish you a peaceful night's rest.

Michael: And we too wish you a very good rest tonight, with a happy day to look forward to tomorrow.

---

[1] Born in Meiaofrio, Portugal, 1553, he died in Nagasaki, 1614. He entered the Society 1574 in Goa and was sent to Japan 1577. He became fluent in Japanese and was highly regarded by Valignano. Mesquita favoured the ordination of Japanese Jesuits and maintained his friendship with the boys after their return to Japan. He introduced various fruits and vegetables into Japan, including figs and olives. See Valignano, *Il cerimoniale*, p. 118 n. 2 (which inaccurately gives the year of his birth as 1533 instead of 1553); Schütte, *Monumenta Historica Japoniae I*, esp. pp. 310, 442; *Documenta Indica,* XIII, pp. 658, 674; XIV, p. 656; Pacheco, 'Diogo de Mesquita'; Álvarez-Taladriz, 'De arboricultura', *passim*; Correia, 'Father Diogo de Mesquita'; Cooper, *Japanese Mission*, pp. 181–3.

[2] Loyola was born in Isahaya, near Nagasaki in 1562. He entered the Society in 1580 as an *irmão* or brother and died in Macao on 16 August 1589. See Schütte, *Monumenta Historica Japoniae I*, pp. 174–5, 218, 284; *Documenta Indica,* XIV, pp. 16*–17*, 741–6; Cooper, *Japanese Mission*, pp. 20–21, 184. See also Introduction, p. 9.

COLLOQUIUM II

The journey from Japan to Macao, the gateway to China, and from there to the Straits of Singapore

Leo: We enjoyed yesterday's meeting so much, and we have been looking forward so much to the time scheduled for today's meeting, that the space between the two, both last night and today, has seemed unusually long.

Michael: That's what usually happens; when you really want something even a short delay seems long. But since you are so keen you will have no difficulty in remembering where we left off yesterday.

Lino: You finished dealing with the reasons for your expedition, so you should start now from the beginning of your journey.

Michael: I'll be starting today from the time when we set off, but first I want to say something about obstacles which were put in our way. The enemy of the human race was aware that our voyage would provide abundant fruit for many souls, and this he was unwilling to accept; so he made sure (such are his wiles, such his persistent cunning) that just as we were about to sail various obstacles would be put in our path. Notable among these were the ones which came as it were hidden behind the veil of our parents' love for us, and our pious duty to them. The snares most difficult to recognize are after all those which appear in the guise of duty. So our mothers, who at first had readily given permission for us to make the journey because they did not think the plan would really be carried out, tried with prayers and tears and in other ways to dissuade us from going when they saw us all equipped to go and everything ready for sailing.[1] And besides these entreaties from our mothers we also had to face deep fear, for there were many who put to us the dangers of the enormously long voyage, the difficulties and inconveniences, the small hope of ever coming back safely to our own country, and even the certainty of death. Our spirits were assailed, indeed, by such attacks, but, fortified by the help of God, which is the beginning and the completion of all good, they were by no means

---

[1] In his instructions to Father Nuno Rodrigues, Valignano alludes to the boys' parents' anxieties and orders Rodrigues to ensure that they return to Japan as soon as possible after completing their mission. He added another reason for Rodrigues to ensure their early return: the boys were not to be permitted to acquire a taste for Roman life (Abranches Pinto and Bernard, 'Les instructions', p. 401; Álvarez-Taladriz, 'En el IV centenario de la embajada', p. 149). Valignano need not have worried. In Rome the boys became homesick and longed to return to Japan (*Dai Nihon Sihryō*, II: 1, p. 269).

Figure 2. The departure from Nagasaki, engraving by Abraham van Diepenbeeck, in Cornelius Hazart, *Kerckelycke historie van de gheheele wereldt*, Antwerp, 1667, vol. I, facing p. 63.
By permission of Professor Tominaga Michio.

overcome, for God usually gives, to those who are led by his great love to approach Him, the strength of soul to be able to overcome all difficulties, be they never so great. And in the same way the Providence of God, which governs all things, saw to it that the impediments interposed by our common enemy were removed easily enough. For afterwards even our mothers were able to base their judgment on reason rather than on private feeling, and to put the importance of the voyage before our suffering and their own wishes; and their trust firstly in God and His help, and secondly in the love of the Father Visitor for us, easily dispelled and dispersed all that thick dark cloud of terrors. Just to see the Father Visitor, with his more than paternal love for us, was enough to persuade us that whatever dangers he was willing to face, we too should most gladly confront together with him. A further weighty reason for remaining faithful to our commitment to undertake the journey was the shame that any revocation would inevitably bring on our names, the more so if the occasion for retraction was mere talk of danger and terrors.

So it was that at Nagasaki, on 20 February of the year 1582,[1] with God as our leader and the Father Visitor as, so to speak, the standard bearer for our coming battle with the ocean and the waves, we joyfully boarded the ship of the Portuguese nobleman Ignacio de Lima.[2] He and the Father Visitor were bound to each other by strong ties of long acquaintance and of love, and in his solicitude for the Father Visitor and for us he had prepared excellent cabins and quarters for our long journey. With the four of us went, besides the Father Visitor, his personal associates Father Lourenco Mexia[3] and Brother Oliverio Toscanello,[4] and also Father Diogo de Mesquita and Brother Jorge Loyola, plus the servants and attendants assigned to us.[5]

After we had set sail and were out at sea heading for Macao, gateway to the kingdom of China (which, as you know, is to the west from Japan), we began soon enough to feel the effects of the rough seas. There was nothing wrong with the size, the design, or the structure of the ship, but as the wind got up the ship, rather than being carried along by the waves and the air, seemed sometimes to be being carried away, and sometimes even to be jumping along. None of this made us despond or lose heart, however, especially as the Father Visitor was assiduous in keeping our spirits up with his calm and comforting words. However, we did suffer severely from seasickness. It afflicts most people who are on their

---

[1] See above, p. 43 n. 2. The Errata list corrects '*vigesimo*' to '*decimo*' here.

[2] The *capitão-mor* or captain-major of the Japan voyage in 1581, and a benefactor of the Jesuits in Asia. See Boxer, *Great Ship*, p. 41; Fróis, *Première ambassade*, p. 263 n. 924.

[3] Born in Olivença, Portugal, in 1539, he died in Macao in 1599. He entered the Society in 1560 but did not accompany the boys to Europe, instead he remained in Macao. See Schütte, *Monumenta Historica Japoniae I*, pp. 109, 216, 306; Fróis, *Première ambassade*, p. 8 n. 50.

[4] Born in Macerata, Italy, 1542 or 1543, he died in Macao in 1601. He entered the Society in 1567 or 1568. See Schütte, *Monumenta Historica Japoniae I*, pp. 218, 311.

[5] Among those assigned were Constantino Dourado (c. 1567–1620) and Agostinho. Dourado, like Jorge Loyola, was a native of Isahaya. He was a *dōjuku* or catechist and entered the Society in 1595. Possibly his father was Portuguese. Dourado spoke and wrote Portuguese well but was poor in written Japanese. Exiled from Japan in 1614, he was ordained in Malacca around 1616 and became superior of the seminary in Macao in 1618. He died sometime thereafter. Some of the notes he made during the embassy were incorporated into Fróis's text (Fróis, *Première ambassade*, pp. 50–53, 64–8; Schütte, *Monumenta Historica Japoniae I*, pp. 447, 588, 677, 781; Alvarez-Taladriz, 'El Escorial', pp. 7–9; Cooper, *Japanese Mission*, pp. 183–4). All that is known about Agostinho is contained in Fróis (*Première ambassade*, pp. 87, 97, 220).

first voyage, as we were. Both head and stomach are so affected that you find you are revolted by the idea of food. What happens is that the humours which are dispersed through the stomach and innermost parts are upset, and then you feel as if not only the humours but your intestines themselves were being vomited up. All of us suffered, but Mancio less than the rest, so that he was sometimes able to laugh at all our moaning, though he had some dizzy spells himself.

Mancio: It is true that in my minor trouble the sight of your affliction acted as a consolation. But on the other hand you were better off in that your seasickness made you less acutely aware of the dangers of the voyage: my stomach indeed was less disturbed than yours, but I was gripped and shaken by the fear of death.

Martin: But don't you think seasickness is itself something close to death, so that when we suffered that seasickness we were experiencing something close to extinction.

Julian: Martin is right. My seasickness was slightly less severe, and yet at times it seemed to me that I was breathing my last.

Leo: No doubt you must have sometimes wished, when the condition of your stomach allowed any wishing, that you were in your own country, in a safe haven like this fortress of ours, and had never challenged the unfamiliar dangers of the sea.

Michael: Those who are far from home and finding their work very hard will naturally think from time to time of their native land, but all the same I believe we were all thinking not of that but of reaching Macao as soon as possible.

Martin: I was not in any way troubled by the memory of my homeland when I experienced severe bouts of seasickness and other types of suffering; for one pain drives out another, as one key keeps another out. It is well-known, after all, that a second disaster can cure the first

Mancio: So that seasickness was certainly not without its usefulness, since it freed you from pining for your homeland and from the fear of danger. The rest of us, who were not so ill, were harrowed by the fear of dying so that we found it hard to look at the sea so convulsed by the wind or the ship so threatened by the waves. The Sea of Japan and China is shallow, with many islands around, and it rages more violently, and is rough more often, than that part of the sea which extends over a vast reach, with no islands to break it up, like an immense flat plain, as we ourselves saw on our journey from India to Europe; so it is in our own sea that ships are subject to more violent tossing.[1]

Lino: I am very surprised to hear you say that such large ships are tossed so violently by the waves.

---

[1] Much of the East China Sea has a depth of less than 200 m.

Michael: You shouldn't be surprised about the size of the ships; the one which transported us could even be regarded as being on the small side compared to others that we saw in the course of our travels.[1]

Lino: What do you mean? Are there even larger ships than those which come to our ports almost every year?

Michael: There certainly are, much larger; so much larger that the difference in size between them and those others which we saw is as great as the difference between our little Japanese ships and the foreign ones which come to Japan.[2]

Leo: How is it, then, that these great ships can be driven by the winds and the sea?

Mancio: Is it surprising, dear Leo, that ships should be driven by wind and sea? Many very large ships are not merely driven, but violently shaken, or even sometimes suddenly capsized, and they can even be swallowed up by the abyss of the ocean, with not one of the unfortunate passengers ever being seen again. It may perhaps help to give you a better understanding of the violence and ferment of the waves if I mention an experience that we had now and again. The movement of the sea and the waves was sometimes so strong that the small boat which usually goes with the ship, roped to the stern, often disappeared from sight because of the heavy swell and the high waves, and then, as the waves plunged, would reappear from the depths, and we found this way the boat had of disappearing and reappearing extremely disturbing.

Lino: When the winds and waves were so strong would it not have been possible to take down the sails so as to have the ship proceed more calmly?

Mancio: They were all down, one only excepted, that one being necessary to help control the steering; and only a part of that one sail was left hoisted, only the topsail,[3] to catch some part of the wind. Portuguese sails have two parts, and the lower part can be separated from the upper.

---

[1] In 1570 King Sebastião had ordered that *nau* or great ships of the *Carreira da Índia* should be between 300 and 450 tons. Experience had shown that these were more seaworthy and easier to handle. Previously *nau* had reached up to 800–900 tons. After the union of the crowns, the law was allowed to lapse and larger ships were commissioned, some up to 2,000 tons. The *nau* sailing to Japan averaged about 1,200–1,600 tons until 1618 when they were replaced by smaller galliots which could be manoeuvred more easily to avoid Dutch attacks (Boxer, *Fidalgos*, pp. 13–15; *Great Ship*, p. 13; Godinho, *Os descobrimentos*, III, pp. 50–53; Massarella, *A World Elsewhere*, p. 40).

[2] At this time Japanese ships were small compared with European ones, although Father Organtino was impressed by some warships Nobunaga had built for use in Osaka Bay, describing them as about the same size as Portuguese carracks, each equipped with three pieces of heavy ordnance. See Lamers, *Japonius Tyrannus*, pp. 155–6; Farris, 'Shipbuilding and Nautical Technology', esp. p. 277.

[3] Original edition (p. 12) '*suppara*' from '*supparus, supparum*' topsail.

Leo: All this sounds extraordinarily trying; there is certainly something in the saying that one should view the sea from a safe place, but cling to the land as to a parent.[1] But what happened after that?

Michael: When a few days had passed the strength of the winds began to ease up and the ferocity of the waves to diminish; if there was no let up of the stormy weather, after all, the sea would not be navigable. The Supreme Author has set this variety in all things, in a wonderful weaving together of prosperity and adversity, so that while human life is not wholly hateful to us, neither is it totally favourable and delightful. When calm was restored, then, we sailed on, and in due time came as planned to the kingdom of China; on the seventeenth day after our departure the islands of China, which in that area are almost innumerable, came into view, and at last on 9 March we came into the port of Macao, and were welcomed by the bishop of that city,[2] the royal governor,[3] and the fathers of the Society, amid great and general enthusiasm.

Leo: I would be glad if you would tell me what people live in that port and city of Macao.

Michael: The people are mostly Portuguese, the same as those who come here on the ship every year. In years gone by they came to that port of China, and to start with they carried on trade but were more or less confined to their ships, because the Chinese were extremely suspicious, and lived in great fear of losing their kingdom. Gradually, however, the Chinese got used to the Portuguese, their fear diminished, and they assigned them a particular place and allowed them to set up dwellings there.[4] In time it developed into a middle-sized town, and there live not only the Portuguese, but also many Chinese who have been converted to the Christian religion. To Macao come also many pagan merchants from every province of that country, with their goods, so that now that city is a famous Portuguese market, frequented by many merchants from the whole of the East.

Lino: You had now arrived in the kingdom of China, so I would very much like to hear from you about the customs and the character of the Chinese, some of whom we sometimes see here in Japan.

---

[1] This maxim might have been contained in a tract similar to that composed by Shimazu Tadayoshi, the daimyo of Satsuma, in 1545 for the guidance of his sons. Tadayoshi's tract is written as a poem listing various maxims for correct moral conduct. In any case the maxim was one that the boys shared. For Tadayoshi's tract, see López-Gay, 'El código de un samurai', pp. 245–59. I am most grateful to Professor Tominaga Michio for this reference.

[2] De Sá.

[3] João de Almeida, who died in office in 1582, and was succeeded in December 1582 by Aires Gonçalves de Miranda (Boxer, *Fidalgos*, p. 41).

[4] The Portuguese had tried to establish a presence in China using both diplomacy and force in the 1510s and early 1520s. Thereafter they traded illegally until around 1555 when they were given permission by the authorities in Canton to establish a settlement at a place known in Chinese as *Ao-Men* (Gate of the Bay) which the Portuguese preferred to call *A-ma-ngao* (Bay of the goddess Ama), soon shortened to Macao. Macao was a subordinate market to Canton from where the Portuguese acquired the silk on which their highly profitable trade with Japan depended. The classic account of this trade is Boxer, *Great Ship*.

Michael: I have many things to say about the vast kingdom of the Chinese, but I'll leave that till I come to our return from Europe.[1] For the moment it is enough to know that we lived there for ten months, until it came to the time for us to leave.

Leo: What do you mean by 'the time for us to leave'? Can't you leave port at any time?

Michael: By no means. The nature of the sky in all the East is such that it is not opportune to sail anywhere at just any time, but only at particular times of the year, when particular winds are blowing. At a certain time, when the wind blows strongly from the south, you can sail to us here; at another time, with another wind, namely a north wind, the way to India is open, since for part of the way there you are heading south, although later you turn back north.[2]

Lino: So how did you pass your ten months of leisure?

Michael: Absence of leisure would be more accurate. In the company of religious men you are never less idle than when you are at leisure, nor less free than when you have no commitments. We had a very suitable place to live, and what with the various very proper things to do, reading, writing, playing musical instruments, and so on, our time was not wasted; and while we were there we were very happy to be able to enjoy the regular and most agreeable company of the priests.

Lino: What are the fathers of the Society doing in that city?

Michael: The same as they do in other cities, namely to attract to the Christian faith those who are strangers to it, and to call Christians to return to the old disciplined way of life. There is besides in the city a hospice equipped to receive those who have undertaken the enormous and often very dangerous journey from Europe, so as to come here to us, and for our benefit.[3]

Leo: Great indeed and grave are the dangers which the fathers face for our sakes; but clearly we are dealing here with men who look to God for the reward of their labours.

Michael: To help you understand the dangers, which we shall often have to mention, I'll content myself with just one example which is appropriate to the place we are now at. In that year, when we were in the port of Macao, the Portuguese ship which had left the port of Goa turned back to the same port, and there was no other ship to sail with the merchandise to Japan. The Portuguese merchants in Macao accordingly designated two Chinese ships, which they call junks, for the task. These ships, as you know, are very different from the Portuguese ships in form, in structure, and in armaments, and are less

---

[1] See Colloquium XXXIII below.
[2] The Portuguese sailed from Macao to Japan catching the south-west monsoon from the end of June to early August and set out on the return voyage with the prevailing northerly winds between November and March.
[3] Run by the Santa Casa da Misericórdia. The Macao branch was established in 1569 (Souza, *Survival of Empire*, pp. 27–9). See also below, p. 208 n. 1.

capable of standing up to an attack from a raging sea. When therefore those two ships, loaded with merchandise set out for these islands, it happened that one of them, the larger and stronger of the two (this is how it is with voyages, and conditions vary so much from voyage to voyage), through the carelessness of the captain, struck the rocks of the island popularly known as 'the beautiful island'[1] and was wrecked. There the fathers who were on board, as well as the other Portuguese, shipwrecked and cast up on the shore, suffered the damage and extreme discomfort of shipwreck, and they lost all the things that were being carried on that boat for the support of the fathers here in Japan and the ornamentation of the churches and the liturgy. However, with divine assistance, which is usually available to those who work for God, it came about that a new raft was constructed, not without great difficulty, from pieces and remnants of the lost ship linked and connected together, and on this the poor passengers were brought back to the port of Macao, from which that island is not very far away, and were received with profound sympathy, for they were suffering severely from hunger and thirst, they were almost naked, and they were exhausted from their labours.[2] The next year a number of fathers arrived from India, and nine set out from the port of China and arrived here successfully.

Leo: I had almost forgotten, but now you have revived my memory of it. For I remember also that in those places in that year, when one ship arrived, the great concern of the fathers was for the other ship, all of them dreading what might have happened to it; and I remember that afterwards, on the next voyage, nine of the fathers came to us, among whom was Father Pedro Gómez, who was afterwards the superior of those who lived in Bungo.[3]

Michael: You remember correctly, but, to come back to our story, after that time had passed we again embarked on the ship of the same Ignacio de Lima for the voyage to India.

Mancio: But when we boarded that ship, how great was the care and providence for us of God, the best and the greatest.[4]

Michael: It is indeed wonderful. What I am going to tell you is an excellent illustration of it, and we all owe thanks to Mancio for reminding us of it.

---

[1] Ilha Formosa, Taiwan.

[2] The junks in question left Macao on 10 July. The one that was shipwrecked carried, among others, the Jesuit Alonso Sánchez, a critic of Valignano and an advocate of a Spanish invasion of China, a project that met with disapproval in Spain and Rome. Sánchez had reached Macao from Manila at the end of May 1582 carrying orders for the Portuguese in Macao to take the oath of allegiance to Philip II of Spain as Filipe I of Portugal following the union of the Spanish and Portuguese crowns in 1581. The other junk reached Japan on 12 August. See Boxer, *Great Ship*, pp. 43–5; idem, *Fidalgos*, p. 41; Borao Mateo, *Spaniards in Taiwan*, pp. 2–15; Cooper, *Japanese Mission*, pp. 29–30, 216 n. 11.

[3] He was born in Antequera in the diocese of Seville in 1534 and died in Japan in 1600. Gómez entered the Society in 1553. He arrived in India in 1579, and in Macao in 1581. Finally, he reached Japan after returning to Macao from the shipwreck on Taiwan, in July 1583. He was superior of Bungo and finally vice-provincial of Japan, 1590–1600. See Schütte, *Monumenta Historica Japoniae I*, pp. 113–19, 154–5, 221–2, 234–5, 356.

[4] The original edition (p. 15) gives '*Dei Optimi Maximi*'. *Deo Optimo Maximo* or DOM (To God, the Best and the Greatest) was adapted by the early Christians from the Roman dedication to Jove (*Iovi Optimo Maximo*) and was used as an inscription in many churches. The expression occurs several times in *De missione*.

Lino: Was there something that happened as you set out again, the memory of which now affects you so strongly?

Michael: There were three ships ready for the voyage to India, one Chinese and two Portuguese. The other Portuguese one, which belonged to a merchant, was very large and very strongly built, and everybody said it was a better ship than de Lima's. The captain and owner of that ship, who, as I said, was a wealthy merchant, tried very hard to get the Father Visitor to board his ship, and to bring all his party and his equipment, saying that the ship was spacious, very well sealed with absolutely no leaks, and that there were superbly equipped cabins for all. The Father Visitor was moved by the urgings of this man, his friend, and he began to deliberate with himself about which ship to choose, but after considerable deliberation he decided that it would be unworthy of his authority to desert Ignacio de Lima, who was besides a nobleman, and who had deserved well of him, and to choose the other ship, even though it was a larger and more robust vessel. So he thanked the merchant, and to forestall any complaint that he was being forsaken by the priests of the Society he assigned two to his ship, one a priest, the other not yet ordained; we and the Father Visitor himself went back to the ship of de Lima. This was a decision made out of regard for courtesy, and an excellent decision it was. Our ship therefore successfully reached the Golden Chersonese,[1] but the other ship ran aground on rocks, with losses of four hundred thousand ducats for the master and passengers. And the two from the Society who were on board were gravely afflicted by the shipwreck, for one was very seriously ill, and the other died in the Malacca college, almost as soon as he set foot on the ground, from the violent shaking to which he had been subjected and the persistent fever which had been affecting him from some time before.

Martin: That is what happened, and it certainly gave us good reason for giving thanks to God for our own safety. But that's enough now about the perils of the sea. Don't forget to say something about how much we enjoyed watching the fishermen of the Straits of Singapore.[2]

Michael: I shall, and at the same time I shall say something about the straits themselves. Before you reach the city of Malacca there are various islands, a large number of them; some of these lie right beside the mainland and form the Straits of Singapore, famous throughout Asia. The straits are so extremely narrow that to have gone through them with such large ships seems to betoken rashness if not lunacy;

---

[1] Ptolemy's name for the Malay peninsula. On its identification with the Malay Peninsula, see Wheatley, *Golden Khersonese*, pp. 144–7.

[2] The Old Straits, on the southern side of the island, were used by the Portuguese and then the English and Dutch. They could be difficult to navigate. Jacques de Coutre, who lived in Malacca in the 1590s and sailed through these waters, has left a description of the people, the Selates, or Orang Selat, living in or near the Old Straits which complements the following description. On his outward voyage in 1637, John Weddell passed through the Old Straits. Peter Mundy mentions them and the Selates living on their boats covered with *cadjan* (*kajang*) coverings. See Yule and Cordier, *Cathay and the Way*, II, pp. 156–7; de Coutre, *Andanzas asiáticas*, pp. 95–6, 420–22; Mundy, *Travels*, III: 1, pp. 139 n. 4, 146–8, esp. n 3; III: 2, p. 322 n. 1; IV, p. xiii; Gibson-Hill, 'Singapore', *passim*.

neither the famous Hellespont, between Europe and Asia,[1] nor the Thracian[2] or Cimmerian Bosphorus,[3] can be compared with them, so narrow they are, so churned up the water, and so tortuous the way which has to be followed for at least three miles.

But leaving aside the danger which threatened us (for in avoiding the whirlpool we almost came to grief in the shallows), it was a real delight to see for the first time the fishermen native to those straits; I call them 'native to those straits' because they have no hut or other lodging except a very small boat, over which, as protection against the weather and the elements, they hang a sort of covering made out of palm leaves. When there is a severe storm they attach the boat to the shore, and with that they regard themselves as completely safe. They are black in colour and nearly naked, and fishing is almost their sole support. Their method of fishing is as follows: two of them turn the boat round, and usually it is a man and wife, for the women are very skilled at this work. One of them is in the prow, grasping an iron-tipped spear and looking for a fish; the other, in the stern, following the instructions of the one on the lookout, turns the boat incredibly rapidly, harrying the fish until, when the right opportunity comes, the one in the prow lets fly, and hardly ever misses, so that the fish is speared and caught. In this way, without nets, buckets, or anything, a great quantity of a fish something like a mullet is caught, and they are sold to passengers on ships going through there, who enjoy and benefit from the results of the fishing.

Leo: You said those fishermen are black in colour. I would like to know if some of the Portuguese too are like that. We have seen many of those black people brought to us on the ships, but they are slaves of the merchants, and we have heard that among these Portuguese the nobles are white in colour, but the base-born are black, as if born to slavery.

Michael: If you had sailed to Portugal you would easily have been disabused of that false opinion and of others similar to it. For neither the Portuguese nor any other men in all Europe are black or deformed of face, or crooked of feature. On the contrary, it is certain, as will become more evident as our story progresses, that they have excellent faces, with the members of the body admirably structured and of an agreeable colour, together with other notable gifts of nature and of art. But those Ethiopians, or people of any other dark colour, who come to us with the merchants, are slaves bought in various regions of the East; it is not noble or humble birth which decides a man's colour, but the nature of his country and its climate. Accordingly, as there are on the earth various regions and climates, so there is a great variety of colour such that the earth does not produce any people in Europe which is not white and of excellent colour, while almost all those that it produces in Africa, and many in Asia, are dark in colour.[4]

---

[1] Connecting the Aegean Sea and the Sea of Marmora.
[2] Thracian Bosphorous, connecting the Sea of Marmora with the Black Sea.
[3] Cimmerian Bosphorus, now known as the Strait of Kerch, connecting the Black Sea and the Sea of Azov.
[4] This matter is discussed more fully below in Colloquium V.

Lino: Truly those who have never set foot outside their native land can hardly be called men, so many and so false are the opinions that they conceive, judging everything solely from the point of view of their own country and its customs.[1]

Michael: That is a very valid point, and you would be much more convinced of its truth if you had travelled all those seas and lands with us. But we have yet to speak about our approach to the Golden Chersonese. Since there is a good deal to say I suggest we leave it to tomorrow to speak about it.

Leo: Agreed. In the meantime you take a rest from your labours, and all of us will refresh our bodies in the quiet of the night.

---

[1] The point is made again more fully in Colloquium XXXIV.

COLLOQUIUM III

The approach to the city of Malacca, in the Golden Chersonese, and from there to the city of Cochin, in Nearer India

Lino: I want to tell you where you were yesterday, so that my remembering it will show clearly how attentive we are, and how keen. You had just reached the Straits of Singapore, and were on the point of telling us about the Golden Chersonese.

Michael: That's right; we passed through the straits and reached the Golden Chersonese. The Europeans give the name 'peninsula' in Latin, and 'chersonese' in Greek, to any notable piece of land which stretches far out into the sea, almost making an island. The strip of land we are talking about now is like that; nowhere else in Asia does the land project out like a promontory, so far out that it almost stretches to the point which the astrologers call the equinoctial line, or the Equator, while the other parts of Asia are further to the north. Thus it is that for those sailing from the kingdom of China their route as far as Malacca is from the north, but then, if they are sailing for Nearer India, they have to head north again after they have made the circumnavigation which is necessary because of that very long promontory. And it is called the Golden Chersonese because of the abundance it has of merchandise and of other precious things. It is situated in that part of India which is further away for those coming from Europe, that is to say it is beyond the river Ganges; the part on the near side of the Ganges is called Nearer India.[1] At the far end of this famous promontory, which is opposite the island once known as Taprobane but now as Sumatra, is situated a very famous city called Malacca, which in years past was taken under the sovereignty of the Portuguese.[2] But since I have to deal later with the spread of Portuguese sovereignty in India, here and now I'll say just a few things about our arrival in Malacca. We were welcomed very kindly by the governor of the city and the commander of the citadel, and enjoyed the generous hospitality of the fathers of the Society for eight days.[3]

Leo: Don't forget to tell us what the distance is from here in Japan to Macao the port of the kingdom of China, and from that port to Malacca; and also what people besides

---

[1] Original edition (p. 18) gives '*ulterior*' and '*certerior*' Ganges. Ptolemy labelled them '*India intra Gangem*' and '*India extra Gangem*'.

[2] The Portuguese seized Malacca in 1511. Camões (*Lusíadas*, X, 107:3, 124:3) identified Ceylon with Ptolemy's Taprobane, while Garcia de Orta in his *Coloquios dos simples, e drogas he cousas medicinias da India* (Goa, 1563) preferred Sumatra, first visited by the Portuguese in 1509. Other contemporaries were similarly confused. See Linschoten, *Voyage*, I, p. 107; Lach, *Asia in the Making*, I: 1, pp. 166, 193, 339, 342; I: 2, p. 503.

[3] The *capitão* was Roque de Melo Pereira who became the *capitão-mor* of the Japan voyage in 1591.

the Portuguese live in Malacca, for, as is clear from what you have already said, the Portuguese travel throughout the Orient as outsiders and foreigners.

Michael: From the port of Nagasaki, the Japanese city, to the port of Macao the Portuguese reckon it 300 leagues, and one of their leagues is more than one of ours by a third, so it should be counted as 450 of our leagues, which is 900 miles.[1] From the port of Macao to Malacca is a distance of 600 leagues, which, as has been said, can easily be converted to our leagues or to miles.[2] The inhabitants of the city of Malacca are the native Malays, and all that region and its language are called Malayan after them. But many of the inhabitants have now accepted the Christian faith and live together amicably with the Portuguese.

Lino: On the way to Malacca from the port of China did you not put in at any other port?

Michael: On that voyage the Portuguese do not usually put in anywhere else, but there are various others at which other ships starting from that same port usually do call. Now since the Chinese region and the region of Malacca are both part of the same continental land, namely (to use the general name) Asia, there are many kingdoms in between, such as Cochinchina, Champa, Cambodia, Siam, of which we need not treat. In fact, if I can put this in at this point, this same land which I have called Asia, runs all the way to the Arabian Gulf, which separates it from Africa; and Africa extends for a very long way, from there to Europe, in which Portugal is, and is divided from Europe by the Mediterranean Sea. And the furthest parts of all these lands are washed by the ocean, as is evident in the shape of the whole world, which I promised I would show to you.

In the city of Malacca, as I told you, we stayed eight days, and then, having recovered our strength, we boarded the same ship again for the voyage to Nearer India. The force of illness in the early stages of that voyage was remarkable. Since Malacca, as I explained above, is situated close to the equinoctial region, although the climate is relieved by frequent rains, when rain and wind do fail it is the worst possible thing for the voyage. And that is what happened at the start of our voyage. For after we had gone a short distance from the port there was no breath of wind, and what with the total calm of the sea, and the burning heat of the air the ship could make no progress, and we could not avoid serious illnesses. Of us all the most dangerously ill, apart from Father Diogo de Mesquita, was our Mancio, who was so ill that we almost gave up hope of his recovering. But the care

---

[1] If one Portuguese league is one third more than a Japanese one then 300 leagues would equal approximately 400 Japanese leagues not 450 which would be one and a half times the value of a Portuguese league. Below (p. 131) a Japanese league is given as approximately one and a half times that of a Portuguese league and that is the value that Ignácio Moreira gave it after his own fieldwork and after consulting various Japanese. The precise value of a Japanese league (里 or *ri*) at this time is difficult to estimate for its value varied within Japan itself. The Roman league was equivalent to three miles and this is the value used by Valignano for a Portuguese league. See Rodrigues, *Arte da lingoa de Iapam*, f. 219v; Valignano, *Principio*, ch. 2 printed in *Adiciones*, pp. 350–51, 384–5, 387; Cooper, *João Rodrigues's Account*, p. 119; Schütte, 'Ignacio Moreira', pp. 116–28, esp. p. 123; Nakamura, 'Japanese Portolanos', pp. 39–40.

[2] Voyaging in the other direction in 1581, Pedro Gómez gives the distance as about 600 leagues and the duration as 37 days (Schütte, *Monumenta Historica Japoniae I*, p. 115).

and solicitude of the Father Visitor in caring for him in his sickness was such that, except for God and His help, Mancio owes his recovery entirely to him. The Father Visitor was so very concerned about us that we feared that his dedicated work in caring for the sick would lead to his coming down with some grave illness, and this would leave all the rest of us bereft of our essential and only consolation. He however remained healthy and unaffected throughout, when others were in very real danger.

Leo: Were you so gravely ill, Mancio?

Mancio: Yes, I was; and, as Michael said, I owe my recovery first to the divine help, but after that to the efforts and work of the Father Visitor, who was with me night and day, giving me all his attention, supporting me as far as was possible in my weakness with his words. With his prayers he vanquished the dreadful sickness which gripped me. What would I not do, and what food, even though my stomach was rejecting it as loathsome, would I not ravenously devour at his request?

Michael: The heat was really extremely severe, and this affected all of us with the fear of falling very seriously ill. And since the length of the voyage was unusually protracted it reached the point where we began to suffer from a shortage of food and especially of water, so much so that it was necessary for the captain, that noble man of whom I spoke, to take charge of the conservation and distribution of the water, because if some improvident man were to have used it up quickly we would all have been in very great danger. The delay became so long and so troublesome that many would have chosen to go back to the port of Malacca, but as there was not the slightest breath of wind anywhere we were not at liberty either to go on or to return to Malacca. We therefore had recourse to divine help, with constant prayers to God, to the Blessed Virgin, and to all the angels and saints, daily invoking all of their names, in the manner customary with the fathers of the Society on their voyages. And with that, little by little, a wind began to blow, and it caught the sails more strongly each day, so that we passed those islands which lie near Taprobane, and then crossed that long stretch of sea which is beyond them, and at last were brought to that port in the island of Ceylon which the Portuguese hold.[1] Here I could tell you a great deal about how agreeable this island is, but I really must hasten on to the Indian mainland. In passing, however, I can say that the island is rich in many things, especially in its splendid cinnamon, which is exported from there to various parts of Europe by the Portuguese. It is incomparably better than the cinnamon brought to Japan from China.[2]

We left the port of Colombo, in the island of Ceylon, and were brought by sail and by prayer, as I said, to the shore of India, for we came very close to losing the ship and our lives. What happened was this: as between the Golden Chersonese and Taprobane there

---

[1] Colombo where the Portuguese had built a fort in 1518. By the end of the 16th century the Portuguese – who had involved themselves in, and skilfully manipulated, the conflicts among the various rulers on the island – had extended their control to most of the coastal areas. See Strathern, *Kingship and Conversion*, passim.

[2] Cinnamon had attracted the Portuguese to Sri Lanka in the first place. Linschoten judged the cinnamon of Sri Lanka the best. It was much admired for its medicinal qualities (Linschoten, *Voyage*, II, pp. 76–8).

is a rather narrow stretch of sea, so also between Ceylon and the promontory of India called Comorin[1] there is a certain shallow and dangerous strait, very famous for its sandbanks and its shallows, called in Chinese the Chilaica, that is to say laborious, shallows.[2] There is, you should know, a persistent rumour that the Chinese once came to India and brought many kingdoms under their rule, and there are still many traces of them, and many words from the Chinese language have been preserved.[3] Now when we were heading for Cochin, which is on the far side of the Comorin promontory, the shore had not yet come in sight, but the pilot persuaded himself that he had already rounded the promontory, and under full sail made, so he thought, for the port of Cochin. But in reality the situation was very different; for we were still on the near side of the promontory, and our course was taking us rapidly into sandbanks and shallows. And now the Father Visitor, who with our safety in mind was not disposed to leave even questions of navigation entirely to others, was doubtful about whether we had indeed passed the promontory, and being concerned he spoke with the pilot and the captain of the ship, and implored them to take soundings with a lead instrument to check the depth of the sea.[4] The captain and the pilot laughed at this and declared that there was no danger. Then the Father Visitor said, 'Ignacio, just to humour me, tell them to let down the plumb bob; I have some kind of presentiment about this.' The captain, since he held the Father in very high regard, ordered it done, and a sailor diligently carried out the task, and found that the sea was just fifteen fathoms deep. All were taken aback, and soon, when the sailor was again told to test the depth of the seabed, he found that the sea was a mere six fathoms deep. Then all were petrified with fear, for they understood only too well from this that we had not yet rounded the promontory, and that we were heading for the shallows with all speed. With all haste, therefore, at the sign given, the direction of prow and stern were reversed, in an effort to get away from those rocky places; and if that had not been done then within an hour the ship would not have been able to escape being dashed against the rocks.[5]

---

[1] Kanyakumari.

[2] Ma Huan, the interpreter of the Chinese admiral Zheng He, who commanded the early Ming voyages to south-east Asia, India and east Africa, calls Sri Lanka 'Hsi-lan sha'n (Mills, *Ma Huan*, p. 292). Couto speculates, fancifully, that the name Ceylon was derived from a dangerous reef near the island, Cinlao, on which Chinese vessels were wrecked and that the name Cinlao was used by Persian and Arab seafarers for the whole island. See Couto, *Da Ásia*, Decada 5, pt 1, pp. 77–8. François Valentijn plagiarized Couto's account. See Arasaratnam, *François Valentijn's Description*, p. 99. For the etymology of the name Ceylon (from *Sinhala* or *Sihala*, lions' abode), see Yule and Burnell, *Hobson-Jobson*, pp. 181–2.

[3] The first embassy from Sri Lanka to China was in 405 and in the 6th century Sri Lanka (from the Chinese perspective) became a part of China's world order or tributary system, although official relations lapsed after 1459. Several of Zheng He's expeditions visited the island and parts of India, including Calicut. See Yule and Cordier, *Cathay and the Way Thither*, I, pp. 67–8, 75–8; Mills, *Ma Huan*, pp. 8–14; Gibb and Beckingham, *Travels of Ibn Baṭṭūṭa*, IV, pp. 812–14, which includes a fine description of a Chinese junk; Needham, *Science and Civilization*, IV:3, pp. 522–3; Malekandathil, *Portuguese Cochin*, pp. 32–3. On the folk memory of the Chinese in India, see Needham, *Science and Civilization*, IV: 3, p. 508. On the early contacts between China and India, see Liu, *Ancient India and Ancient China*. For a revisionist view of the Zheng He voyage, which sees them as 'proto-colonialism', see Wade, 'Zheng He Voyages', *passim*.

[4] Valignano had an impressive layman's knowledge of the sea routes and weather patterns in Asian waters. See *Documenta Indica*, XIII, pp. 62–70, 316–18.

[5] Ibn Baṭṭūṭa had had a similar experience in these waters. See Gibb and Beckingham, *Travels of Ibn Baṭṭūṭa*, IV, p. 857.

Leo: Great indeed and very clear was God's goodness to you.

Mancio: Great, and never to be forgotten, and the greater because those who had charge of the ship's navigation believed that we were immune from danger.

Michael: For God kept the Father Visitor alert, so that in that situation he refused to be satisfied without frequent checks on the depth of the water. So on that day, in the afternoon, we saw land, and we realized that despite the day's efforts we had not managed to pass the Comorin promontory. Imagine what our case would have been if we had not changed course! The reason why that day's labour achieved so little was, as later experience proved, that there was a very strong current in the shallow water at that place. When the sails had been taken down and the anchors lowered into the sea we recognized that this was the stretch of land commonly known as the Fishery Coast, so named because of the very famous pearl fishing. And since there had been fathers of the Society living on that coast for many years past, the Father Visitor sent a letter to tell them of our arrival. They hastened to us with tubs full of whatever they could bring, rice, meat, fruit of various kinds, and gave a very enthusiastic welcome to the Father Visitor and all of us. And since all of us were exhausted by the long voyage the father decided that we should go ashore and rest for a short time, to recover our strength, in one of the villages which there are along that coast. So we took leave of the captain and other companions, went down into the boats, and very soon were able at last to set foot on the shore of Nearer India, and there we spent some days with the fathers and with some natives of that coast who were pious Christians.[1]

Martin: The joy in our hearts at standing for the first time on that land is almost impossible to describe (as is usually the case after a long voyage), and we were able to add to that our relief at having escaped the danger of the following night.

Michael: Your memory is quite right. That night, the ship which we had left was in great danger of running on the rocks. As I said a few moments ago, the rocks were not far away, and it happened that the anchors which had been let down were dragged by the wind and by the force of the currents, so that the ship went back unintentionally a whole league, and almost struck the rocks. Furthermore two of the ropes to which the anchors were attached were broken and destroyed by the violence of the sea, and the passengers were only just saved by the other unaffected ropes; the sailors worked hard to tie two of the ropes together so as to retard the ship and keep it from slipping away. The following day, when we looked for the ship, we were startled to see it a league away, in the direction of the rocks, but extremely glad that we had escaped that danger and all the labour of that night.

Leo: You really were very fortunate. But please tell us about that tract of land called the Fishery Coast.

---

[1] The Parava, an ancient Tamil low-caste people, living on the Fishery Coast. Tirunelveli, in present-day Tamilnadu, had been home to pearl divers and fishermen for centuries. Xavier and his successors scored their biggest missionary success in India here. Initially, at the instigation of their leaders, the Parava converted to Christianity in return for Portuguese protection. The area became a focus of tension and discord among the Jesuits, the authorities of the *Estado da Índia* and local Indian powers. See Lach, *Asia in the Making*, I: 1, pp. 269–71; Subrahmanyam, *Portuguese Empire in Asia*, pp. 263–7.

Michael: The Comorin promontory protrudes about 200 leagues into the sea. The nearer side is called the Fishery Coast, and the further side Travancore, and on both sides there are numerous different native villages. The natives of both sides, and of the whole region, are called the Malabars. As I told you, the Fishery Coast got its name from the famous pearl fishing there; fishermen live there who, at particular times of the year, fish out the precious shells in which pearls are found.

Leo: But what are the fathers of the Society doing there?

Michael: They are, so to speak, fishing for souls, which they, quite rightly, judge to be more precious than pearls. They seek, as far as possible, to establish themselves among the natives, even at the risk of their lives, so as by dealing with them, by talking to them, and especially by the example of their lives, to attract them to the Christian faith; and as a result there are 80,000 Christians on shores on the two sides of Comorin, which is no small number in those places, where native kings hold sway, but where the fathers have made a remarkable conquest of their souls.[1]

Lino: It is strange, however, that those kings themselves have not yet joined with their people in consenting to submit to the yoke of Christ.

Michael: The reason is that they are under a different yoke, that of their own pleasures and vices, and, blinded and in darkness, they do not see the brilliance and splendour of the Christian law. For it often happens that vices cloud our minds with a sort of darkness as of night, and this does not permit our eyes to seek the celestial light. The same thing happens here in Japan, never mind in those places, where the natives, being blackish in colour, are of low intelligence, and by nature inclined to vice. But the fathers, by their work, have overcome these difficulties, for we saw there not only Christians, but some excellent examples of the Christian life.

Leo: Did you stay long in that Fishery Coast area?

Michael: We soon left that place; at first we were in a village called Trichanduri, then we went on to another called Manapar, while Father Mesquita and others who were ill stayed in a larger settlement called Tutocorin.[2]

Mancio: Since you have mentioned various villages in which we were, it will be appropriate, at this stage of the story, to explain how we travelled. We went neither on foot nor on horseback, but in a different way, one that is commonly used in that region. They

---

[1] In his *Sumario de la India*, Valignano estimated the number of Christians on the Travancore side at between 12,000 and 15,000 and on the Fishery Coast at between 40,000 and 50,000, and mentions the fact that missionary activity inland was all but impossible because the gentiles there belonged to higher castes and were not at all receptive to the mission (*Documenta Indica*, XIII, pp. 41, 179, 183). Other estimates of Christian converts vary from 90,000 to 130,000 (Lach, *Asia in the Making*, I: 2, p. 271).

[2] Where the Jesuits had a college and seminary to train a native clergy; it is now a diocese. See *Documenta Indica*, XIII, p. 184.

use a type of litter, normally carried by four men. It is spread with mattresses and cushions, and whoever travels in it is so comfortable on his journey that the shaking of it inclines him to sleep or to rest. And since the heat is sometimes extreme they travel by night, and sometimes cover eight or ten leagues at a stretch.

Michael: In the way described by Mancio we passed through villages on the nearside of that promontory and arrived at the other side, and there we found a small Portuguese vessel[1] and travelled in it to the Portuguese fortress at Quilon;[2] there we found a ship about to depart for the city of Cochin, and we reached the port of Cochin after one full day.

Mancio: Michael, don't forget the danger from which we were saved, by the divine goodness, on that short voyage.

Michael: You tell it yourself, Mancio. Your remembering it shows clearly how afraid you were.

Mancio: We were all afraid, very afraid, and especially the Father Visitor, who was extremely concerned, for us rather than for himself. About the middle of the night, when we were going to board the Quilon ship, we were called by the captain to the skiff which was to take us out to the ship. But the trip on the skiff was delayed, and when day began to dawn the ship was still a considerable distance away, and two Malabar pirate vessels[3] appeared and bore down on us with full sail. What were we to do? The ship was a third of a league away, the shore much further, and all the efforts of our oarsmen could not match the speed of the galleys. God was our only refuge. We prayed to God, and at the same time sent a signal to the sailors in the ship to bring our danger to their notice. They were affected either by the signal, or by the sight of the galleys, or rather perhaps by divine prompting, and they took up the anchor and headed for us under sail, and thus the ship came between us and the pirates and by the divine goodness we were snatched just in time from the hands and the swords of the pirates.[4]

Lino: The favours you received from God were indeed many.

Mancio: Many indeed, and such that we ought never to forget them. But now let Michael proceed with his story.

---

[1] The original edition (p. 24) gives '*myoparone*' (*myoparo-onis*, a kind of small, light, easily manoeuvrable vessel favoured by pirates).

[2] Or Coulão, now known as Kollam.

[3] The original edition (p. 24) gives '*myoparones*'.

[4] Attacks by Malabar corsairs or pirates were a constant problem on the Malabar coast They are mentioned by Pliny the Elder (*Natural History*, Book VI, ch. 26). Valignano was already familiar with the danger they posed (*Documenta Indica*, XIII, p. 317). For a discussion of the Malabar pirates and their place in the political and economic struggles among the coastal states (including the Portuguese possessions), see Bouchon, 'L'évolution de la piraterie'; Malekandathil, *Portuguese Cochin*, pp. 131–3, 224–6.

Michael: We arrived in the noble Portuguese city of Cochin in April of 1582,[1] and we were there until the month of October, hibernating, as it were. Then in October it was possible to sail to Goa, and of course we pursued our usual occupations during that time.

Leo: Tell us a little more about that city of Cochin, its situation and its native inhabitants.

Michael: The city is situated, as I said, in Nearer India, on the Malabar coast in the kingdom of Cochin, from which the city takes its name. Next to Goa it is the most famous city both for the quantity of its merchandise and for the size of its buildings. It was founded in that place by the Portuguese, with the permission of the king of Cochin, who himself lives in another town some distance from the coast of the same name.[2]

Lino: What reason did that king have for allowing the Portuguese to build that city in his kingdom?

Michael: It happened that the king of Cochin was actively prosecuting a war with another very powerful king of the same Malabar coast, called the zamorin. The Portuguese had come there from Europe to trade, and the king of Cochin appealed to them to join him and help him. They were so successful, with their bravery and their military skill that the zamorin, after many defeats, could barely maintain himself within his own lands, and the kingdom of the king of Cochin expanded in all directions. The king, being greatly indebted to the Portuguese for what they had done for him, gave them permission to build that city in his kingdom.

Leo: That king behaved very honourably.

Michael: So did the Portuguese. They gave their help to the king, but did not keep for themselves anything of what their sweat and blood had produced in that long war.

Lino: How were they able to persuade themselves to behave in that way?

Michael: Those men were bound by an alliance, and linked by ties of friendship to the king of Cochin, and their only care was for his advantage; and although they put their lives in very great danger, and shed much blood for the preserving of their friend the king and his kingdom, all they sought for themselves was glory. The towns and places which they had captured they magnanimously handed over to the king of Cochin.

---

[1] *Sic* 1583, on 7 April.
[2] The raja of Cochin's palace was in Clavethy. Religious, caste and business interests determined the composition of the port of Cochin which the Portuguese called *Cochin de cima* (upper Cochin), now Mattancherry. The area beside the sea was given to the Portuguese by the raja. They named it Santa Cruz and it is now called Fort Cochin. See Malekandathil, *Portuguese Cochin*, pp. 36–7.

Lino: That integrity of the Portuguese is incredible.[1]

Michael: It is remarkable, and among our own people it is something unusual, as can be seen in another example. The Portuguese have conquered a large part of India, a place far removed from Europe, but there has never yet been a case of anyone rebelling against the king and claiming absolute power for himself.

Lino: That Portuguese nation deserves to be praised by their king, and to be awarded many honours.

Michael: The Portuguese are highly regarded, and justly so, not only by their own kings, but also by those of other countries; and all the peoples of India consider themselves fortunate if in their lands they have a town, or at least a settlement, of Portuguese merchants, for they find it greatly to their advantage, and we too can vouch for this from the coming of the Portuguese to Japan.

Leo: Now then Michael, when you are talking about the Portuguese and their power in India, start again from the beginning and tell us in more detail how it was that they first came to India, and what authority they have there.

Michael: An excellent subject and field for us to develop, but we'll enjoy it even better if we leave it till tomorrow.

Lino: Let's leave it for just now then, and ask you to begin from that point tomorrow.

---

[1] Cochin and Calicut had been visited by Pedro Álvares Cabral in 1500. Cabral was not made welcome in Calicut and his men were attacked, some forty being massacred. In reprisal he bombarded and burnt down the town. In 1502 the Portuguese were given permission by the raja of Cochin to establish a factory in his domain and they quickly became embroiled in the historical rivalry between the zamorin, the ruler of Calicut, and the raja of Cochin. Portuguese military assistance was vital in securing the raja's rule after an invasion from Calicut. Thanks to Portuguese patronage, Cochin prospered at the expense of Calicut, which, until the arrival of the Lusitanians, had been a powerful, rich state and one of India's major emporia. Relations between the Portuguese and the raja were never as cordial as *De Missione* suggests, although Cochin was never a mere client-state of the Portuguese. See Chaudhuri, *Trade and Civilisation in the Indian Ocean*, pp. 162–3; Pearson, *Portuguese in India*, pp. 45–8; Bouchon, 'Sixteenth Century Malabar', pp. 162–84, esp. pp. 170–71; Malekandathil, *Portuguese Cochin*, pp. 37–40 and *passim*; Prakash, *Portuguese in India*, I, ch. 1, esp. pp. 8–11. For Valignano's description of the religious institutions in Cochin, see *Documenta Indica,* XIII, pp. 32–6, 173–8.

COLLOQUIUM IV

The coming of the Portuguese to India, and the spread of the Portuguese empire.

Leo: Last night, Michael, you left us eagerly anticipating your account of how the Portuguese came to India, and why it was that they developed an empire there.[1]

Michael: The whole question of the coming of the Portuguese to India and their exploits there is matter for a lengthy history, and you can find it truly and elegantly written by Jerónimo Osório, bishop of Silves;[2] here I shall merely be outlining the main points, and I shall begin with the kingdom of Portugal. You should know firstly that Portugal is a part of the western edge of Europe, much of it washed by the ocean, and its people are famous especially for their nobility, their power, their wealth, and their military prowess. And since Africa, which is held by the Saracens, most aggressive enemies of the Christian religion, is not far distant, the Portuguese princes have always considered it to be their duty to send excursions into Africa to punish wrongs done to Christ, and to expel the enemies of the Christian name far from their neighbouring countries. And things worked out to their advantage, for in many encounters they put their enemies to flight, and they built a number of fortresses in Africa, to the very great ignominy of the Saracen name, and have now been holding them, with great honour and glory, for three hundred years.

Now among these princes the most illustrious Prince Henry,[3] son of King João I,[4] and brother of King Duarte,[5] a man distinguished not only for his royal blood, but for wisdom and valour, conceived the idea of something greater than an African expedition. Burning with ardour to propagate the Christian religion, he decided to send ships to explore the whole maritime coast of Africa right down to the promontory of Good Hope, which is far distant from Portugal, and to open the route to India, known to art and science, but not known by experience and untried in practice. He was convinced that this would advance and bring glory to the Christian religion and the name of Portugal. He initiated the enterprise, and when his death intervened the signs were favourable and the prince

---

[1] Valignano provides a somewhat different, more geopolitical, narrative of the rise of the *Estado da Índia* in his *Historia* (ch. 6).

[2] Jerónimo Osório (1506–80), author of *De Rebvs Emmanvelis regis Lvsitaniae invictissimi virtvte et avspicio gestis libri dvodecim*, Lisbon, 1571. It was intended for a European readership and has little original to say about Asia. See Lach, *Asia in the Making*, I: 1, p. 196.

[3] 1394–1460.

[4] r. 1385–1433.

[5] r. 1433–8.

bequeathed it as his most noble inheritance to the kings of Portugal.[1] King João II[2] carried it on as long as he lived, and King Manuel,[3] whose memory is especially famous among the Portuguese, brought it to a happy conclusion.

When he first took up the royal insignia he sent Vasco da Gama, a man noble, wise, and vigorous, with four ships to explore the Indies in order to export to Portugal the goods which in that region are many and precious, and thus to enrich his kingdom; and also so that the light of the Christian religion, which had shone on the Europeans for a long time, should be communicated with piety and love, by upright and religious men, to the Indian peoples. So this Vasco da Gama, having survived many dangers, suffered the hardships of the long voyage, and travelled along the coast of the whole of Africa and much of Asia, at last reached the Indies, his objective, and came to the kingdom and to the port of the zamorin, who at that time was the most famous among the kings.[4] He presented to him the message from King Manuel, and discussed the question of a treaty, and initially he was courteously received. Later, however, the king was deceived by the Saracens, who are numerous in that kingdom, and persuaded to change his mind, and Vasco da Gama, a man otherwise much disposed to promote peace and agreement, was subjected to injuries which, for the sake of the dignity of the Christian and Portuguese name, could not be ignored.[5]

In the expedition of the following year another most noble man, Pedro Álvares Cabral,[6] followed in the steps of Vasco da Gama, and on the orders of King Manuel spared no effort to try to bring the zamorin, who was caught in a web of trickery, to some genuine goodwill, and to discussion and negotiation about the things agreed, as is normal between honourable kings. But the wiles of the Saracens prevailed, together with the evil of avarice, as is usually the case with minds clouded by superstitions about false gods, so much so that although the king had previously given Cabral permission to build a house, at his own expense, for purposes of trade, and there were already seventy Portuguese buyers living there peacefully, a Saracen army of six thousand men made a sudden attack on the house, destroyed it with fire, sword, and every sort of contrivance, impiously and wickedly robbed the Portuguese, to whom they were bound by ties of hospitality, universally regarded as sacred, and killed them; and all this not just with the connivance, but actually on the orders of the king, who by now was alienated from the Portuguese.

In this most grave crisis Christ, whom the Portuguese religiously worship, did not abandon his own, for from that massacre, astonishingly, twenty men were saved; they inflicted great slaughter on their enemies and escaped to the ships. Then the king of

---

[1] For an assessment of Henry the Navigator, see Russell, *Prince Henry 'the Navigator'*.

[2] r. 1481–95.

[3] Manuel I, r. 1495–1521.

[4] Da Gama arrived near Calicut on 20 May 1498, but he himself did not set foot on Indian soil until 28 May. The zamorin or samudri at the time was Mānavikraman Raja.

[5] He seized a number of hostages. On his stay in Calicut, see Disney, *History of Portugal*, II, pp. 122–5.

[6] Cabral's voyage (with 13 ships, 1,500 soldiers and sailors, and some Franciscan missionaries) was a much larger enterprise than da Gama's. He had orders to establish factories at Sofala and Calicut. The voyage lasted from March 1500 until July 1501, during which he famously 'discovered' Brazil and, as has been mentioned, burnt Calicut. As a result of the voyage the Portuguese decided that in future they would pursue their objectives in the Indies by force rather than by peaceful means. See Greenlee, *Voyage of Pedro Álvares Cabral*; Diffie and Winius, *Foundations*, pp. 220–23; Godinho, *Os descobrimentos*, II, 169–70; Malekandathil, *Portuguese Cochin*, pp. 37–40.

Cochin, who had long been at enmity with the zamorin, of his own accord offered all Portuguese who were in foreign countries and without any help his protection and favour, inviting them to trade, and providing them with hospitality and with all necessary guarantees. Cabral, being in a critical situation, did not reject such favour and benevolence, and he signed with him, in the name of King Manuel, treaties pledging friendship and perpetual partnership, and declared war without quarter on the zamorin, most malevolent enemy of both of them. This therefore was how the Portuguese first came to India, and how with just cause the Portuguese empire began to develop.

Leo: The zamorin indeed gave the Portuguese good reason for hate and aversion when, for no other cause than the deceit of the Saracens and his own greed, he perpetrated such a perfidious crime; there is no doubt that the Portuguese were justified in declaring war on him.

Michael: That is correct, and in the same way the king of Cochin gave the Portuguese good reason to embrace him with all love and kindness for the generous hospitality which he had extended to them as foreigners.

Leo: Were there no Portuguese towns, with Portuguese living in them, in India at that time?

Michael: None at all. They just came with their merchandise to the Indian ports, stayed for a short time to trade, and then headed back for Portugal as soon as they were able to sail.

Lino: So was it merely for the sake of trade that the Portuguese opened up the route to India and faced such danger to life and limb?

Michael: That was the attitude of the merchants, who were concerned with their own advantage. But God usually implants in kings, especially those imbued with Christian piety, a much higher and more sublime spirit, and the intention of the kings, as I said before, was to extend far and wide the empire of Christ, to which they had all pledged themselves. Their intention was to elevate the people of the whole of Asia, an almost infinite multitude of people savage and barbarous, who were like cattle, living without any certain law or religion; to ennoble these people with Christian piety, and to teach them a better way of life.

Lino: Now with regard to the merchants, I would like to know what merchandise they brought from Europe to India, and again what things were taken back from India to Portugal.

Michael: From Portugal they bring firstly silver with which to buy the goods from the Indies; then wine pressed from grapes, and oil made from olives; and Europe produces abundant quantities of these liquids, which are highly regarded in India. They bring besides many kinds of clothing, linen, silk, woollen, gold-embroidered, and other similar things, which Europe, an extremely fertile region, produces and develops in many ways.

And from India pepper, ginger, cinnamon, cloves, and other spices, plus a great quantity of cotton clothing, are taken back to Europe. And thus, with merchandise going back and forward in a sort of exchange both regions, Europe and the Indies, profit greatly.

Lino: It seems that India profits more, since it receives both silver and excellent merchandise.

Michael: Nevertheless, it is for commercial reasons that the Portuguese risk all those voyages, and they derive very considerable profit from them; for the spices of India, which you hold in no very high regard, are prized, and delightful to taste, and they have other virtues, so that when they go from Portugal to various parts of Europe they are sold for a great weight of silver and make a remarkable profit for the Portuguese, so that the money invested in them comes back to the merchants sometimes doubled, sometimes even trebled.

Leo: Now then, explain to us how the Portuguese first came to have towns and colonies in India.

Michael: The first colony of the Portuguese in India was the city called Cochin,[1] situated in the kingdom of the king of Cochin. For when the zamorin, that perfidious king, tried in his hatred to persuade the king of Cochin into perfidy and deception, but found that his approaches did not succeed, he took to arms, and launched an all-out war on the neighbouring king, who suffered losses and was struggling to keep his territory. He therefore begged the Portuguese for help and support, and gave them full permission to build a citadel and a town in his lands. And this town, starting from small beginnings, grew so much in the course of time that now it is deservedly numbered among the principal cities of India, a city busy with the arrival of Portuguese merchants, the crowding in of Indian people, and the wide variety of goods available, so that the king himself derives no small advantage from all the duties and taxes.

Leo: And what was the cause and origin of the other colonies?

Michael: That example of goodwill and friendship given by the king of Cochin to all the others, and also the impressive evidence of the advantage which had accrued to him. For when the other kings realized what benefits his goodwill had brought to the king of Cochin, they were not slow to extend their favour to the Portuguese, and to invite them, with promises and entreaties, to establish towns on their lands. In this way fortresses were built in the lands of a number of kings, namely the kings of Cananore, Quilon, Cranganore, and Chaul,[2] and the Portuguese, previously unknown or suspect in India, began to be favoured and welcomed by those peoples, so much so that even the zamorin himself, despite his consciousness of the crime he had previously committed, became very

---

[1] The Portuguese were given permission to establish a factory at Cochin in 1500 and afterwards a fort was built and paid for by the raja (Malekandathil, *Portuguese Cochin*, pp. 72–3).

[2] The Portuguese established forts in these places in, respectively, 1505, 1503, 1507 and 1521. See, *Dicionário*, I, p. 325; Malekandathil, *Portuguese Cochin*, pp. 148–9.

eager to enter into an alliance with them;[1] and the Saracens, who hated the very name of Christian, were expelled from the territories of many kings, lost a number of their own towns, and were forced to submit to the Portuguese yoke.[2] And Goa, the most famous city in India and formerly the most secure home of Saracen impiety, became so to speak the splendid headquarters of the Portuguese and of Christianity, from where the banners of fortitude and of religion are carried to all other peoples.[3]

Lino: Which king formerly ruled over Goa, that most famous city, which you call the headquarters of the Portuguese empire in India?

Michael: One of the kings of the Saracens, who formed an alliance with the zamorin and with other Saracens, enemies of the Christian name, in order to annihilate the Portuguese; and they inflicted great losses on the Portuguese, and provoked them to war. Now, under the leadership of the invincible Afonso de Albuquerque, the Portuguese not only expelled the Saracens from Goa but also added Ormuz, most noble city of the lands of Persia, and Malacca, shining light of the Golden Chersonese, to the lands under their empire, and performed many other celebrated exploits, to which I have neither the time nor the eloquence to do justice.[4] I shall say merely that among all the peoples of India the Portuguese name is held in the highest respect and, so to speak, veneration, for celebrated exploits and singular virtue, and all revere it as something holy and august.

Leo: It is very remarkable that the Portuguese, a people external and foreign, should have accomplished such deeds in India.

Michael: You would find it much more remarkable, dear Leo, if you were to some degree familiar with the histories of the Portuguese. I would like you to take note of the three causes of all the things which they have accomplished, namely loyalty to their king, invincible fortitude of spirit, and lastly an ardent zeal for the Christian religion. Since they were adorned with these three virtues nothing was too arduous or difficult for them to undertake, and there was no goal which they could not achieve.

Leo: One question which it occurs to me to ask in this context is who is to be given the administration of the Portuguese people in India, given that the king is separated from them by such a huge distance?

---

[1] The zamorin finally made peace with the Portuguese in 1583–4 (see, *Dicionário*, I, p. 167).

[2] The original edition (p. 30) gives '*Lusitanorum iugum subire sint coacti*' referring to the Saracens rather than the friendly rulers.

[3] This account is an oversimplification heavily biased in favour of the Portuguese. For modern accounts of Portuguese strategy and activity on the Malabar coast and the war in the Indian Ocean against the Egyptian Mamluks who were allied to Portugal's other rival, Venice, see Bouchon, 'Sixteenth Century Malabar', *passim*; Subrahmanyam, *Portuguese Empire in Asia*, pp. 60–69.

[4] The Mamluk challenge to the Portuguese in India was broken when Francisco de Almeida destroyed the Mamluk fleet at Diu in 1509. Thereafter, under Afonso de Albuquerque, the individual most responsible for laying the foundations of Portugal's maritime empire in Asia, the Portuguese acquired Goa (1510), Malacca (1511) and Hormuz (1514). For the seizure of Goa from the Bijapur sultanate, see Diffie and Winius, *Foundations*, pp. 248–54.

Michael: The moderator of the Portuguese virtues, as of all other things, is prudence. Adorned with that virtue they are extraordinarily proficient in the science of government. In brief, their king, distant though he is from India, at a prescribed time sends some member of the nobility, noted for experience in military matters and for fortitude, to be his viceroy and representative, and all the Portuguese respect him as they would the king himself, with total loyalty and devotion, so that the absence of the king in no way impedes the observance of the law whether secular or sacred. And subject to this viceroy there are many other leaders and prefects appointed to the various cities and strongholds in India, so that there is no hint of any departure from due order in government.[1]

Leo: This viceroy must be a person of great dignity and grandeur.

Michael: He is, being always a person of distinguished and illustrious birth, and throughout India upholds the authority of the office which the king has assigned to him.

Lino: Is there no danger that this viceroy, with all the power and majesty that he has, might raise a rebellion, desert his king, and take power, or tyranny, over all India?

Michael: None, if the virtue of the Portuguese, tried and tested over so long a time, is taken into account. The very idea of usurpation never enters their heads, and even if perchance the possibility of such a terrible crime were to occur to them, there would be no one so sunk in perfidy as to conspire with the viceroy in plotting treason. Nor among Christian princes is it in any way common for lower officials to foment sedition against a king, nor would any dare to encourage or support such a plot.

Leo: Oh that here in Japan the Christian religion flourished as it does in Europe, so that the thoughts of Japanese men, so quick to move to treachery and rebellion, might be restrained, there could be an end to all the many wars, and we could at last live in tranquillity.

Michael: May God the immortal bring us to such a happy outcome, for that would be the best way imaginable to extinguish the fires of war in Japan.

Lino: The state of things in Japan is such that it may reasonably be doubted whether even the remedy you recommend would suffice. For since Japan is split up into so many and such various domains, under kings, princes, and dukes, there is no way of avoiding frequent outbreaks of civil war, when hate and envy cause them to move against one another.

Michael: Still, I don't think my opinion is mistaken, for the power of the Christian religion is such that it binds the souls of Christians together with a sort of marvellous chain, and keeps them obedient to their own kings and in a relationship of trust with neighbouring princes. Besides, the Christian law for the most part holds in check the

---

[1] On the government of the Portuguese empire in Asia where the viceroy's power was far less than is suggested here, see Disney, *History of Portugal*, II, pp. 159–65.

cupidity which so often incites to the coveting of the possessions of others, teaches, with many precepts, that each should live content with his lot, and is insistent in putting before us, as the model to be imitated, Christ the author of all peace and concord; with the result that then all Christian peoples, governed though they are with so many Christian kings and princes, live entirely at peace and secure in their possessions.

Leo: May God again grant that that golden peace, foretold by celestial herald at the most holy birth of Christ, may come upon us, together with a growth in Christianity, and that the many upheavals of the wars by which we are continuously upset may be stilled at last But explain to us now how long you stayed at Cochin, and why you did not immediately head for Goa, the splendid seat of the viceroy of Portugal.

Michael: The reason was that changing winds and rainstorms meant that we never had suitable weather, and were therefore forced to winter in Cochin, for we reached there on 7 April, and rested there till the end of September. But during that time the viceroy himself,[1] in a letter brought along the coast by a very fast small boat, welcomed and congratulated the Father Visitor with every sign of love, and he charged the royal officials all along the coast to see to it that we should have an abundant supply of everything.

Leo: You say you reached the port in April, so what do you mean by saying that you wintered there?

Michael: Because in India, as well as the time when the days are shorter and it gets cooler, the time when, nature duly providing, the extreme heat is tempered by frequent rain, and strong winds from the sea make sailing impossible, is also called winter. This period normally begins in May, and lasts a good three or four months. So it was in the beginning of October,[2] when that season had run its course, that we took ship, and in a matter of a few days were brought, by favourable winds and by prayer, to that city to which we had looked forward so much, that most famous settlement of the Portuguese. There we were welcomed with joy by a great assembly of fathers of the Society, by the whole city, and by the viceroy.[3] After a short rest we called on the viceroy, who spoke most kindly with us. We presented to him the letters from Kings Francisco and Protasio and Prince Bartolomeu, and the viceroy made clear how delighted and happy he was to receive them.[4]

Lino: At this point I would like to know how you dressed in India, and in the other places where you stayed, particularly when you visited the viceroy and other princes.

---

[1] Francisco Mascarenhas. See below, p. 80 n. 1.

[2] In fact they arrived in Goa in what had become late November, not in October. The Portuguese authorities in the Indies adopted the new Gregorian Calendar (promulgated the previous year in Rome), on 14 November 1583, which then became 24 November. Besides, at the end of October Valignano wrote to Aquaviva from Cochin. See *Documenta Indica,* XII, pp. 827, 844; Fróis, *Première ambassade,* p. 20.

[3] Details of the Jesuit presence in India are given below (pp. 89–91). Fróis provides some additional detail of the stay in Goa, mentioning, in particular, their studies which included Japanese and Latin. In Cochin they had also studied Latin and music. See Gualtieri, *Relationi,* p. 41; *Dai Nihon Shiryō,* XI: 1, p. 56; Fróis, *Première ambassade,* pp. 21–5.

[4] The letters are no longer extant.

Michael: It was decided, on the prudent advice of the Father Visitor, that we should follow the usage of the regions where we were staying, and should as far as possible use their clothing and language. When we went to visit the foremost men of Europe, however, and to explain to them the condition and the character of the Japanese, we were to wear Japanese dress, since they would be more taken with that.[1] So dressed like this we visited the viceroy of India, Cardinal Albert of Portugal, nephew of the king of Spain on his sister's side,[2] King Philip himself, his sister the wife of the late emperor, and lastly the pope himself, to whom our embassy was principally sent. However, we wore in addition, so as to be better dressed, some Portuguese items of clothing, namely these shirts, stocks, and beautifully made velour caps.

Lino: In what way did this adding of European clothing make you better dressed?

Michael: Oh, it made a big difference. In Europe it is considered unbecoming to go out with head, neck, or arms uncovered, so adding some European clothes did make a considerable difference to the way we were turned out.

Lino: To my eye that kind of clothing is acceptable enough, but it looks uncomfortable, tight somehow, and constricting.

Michael: You think it is inconvenient because you are not familiar with it, not accustomed to it. Think about it and you will see that it really is convenient in various ways; it does not get in the way of any movement, and it's a great help against the cold; there's no need to be putting your arms and hands inside the fold of your tunic or kimono. And also if the shirt is changed every day, and it usually is, the collar of the tunic does not get dirty; so whether you are thinking of style or of cleanliness you have to admit that it is a very convenient item of clothing.

Lino: You have certainly provided excellent reasons to recommend it; I am only surprised that it is not in use in Japan.

Michael: Japan, being contained in these far distant islands, has customs very different from those of other peoples; we have hardly any intercourse with any other nations, so we use only our own things, which, perhaps by being used, come to seem to us attractive and beautiful, but in Europe, where various peoples are linked together by common custom and experience, each people adopts many things which they find useful from the inventions and skill of others.

Lino: So you think European clothing superior to ours?

---

[1] Valignano spelled this out in his instructions. See Álvarez-Taladriz, 'En el IV centenario de la embajada', p. 139; Abranches Pinto and Bernard, 'Les instructions', p. 395. Lowe ('"Representing" Africa', p. 119) claims that '[r]itual "Europeanisation" was required even before their entrance [to Rome], and cultural assumptions about dress were very rigid.'

[2] 1559–1621, archduke of Austria, son of the emperor Maximilian II and empress María, viceroy of Portugal 1583–93 and later governor-general of the Spanish Netherlands.

Michael: I had never intended to compare the one to the other, but rather to leave it to your judgement, now that you have seen these elegant, sober, well-finished European clothes. The doublet and the shirt, though, I do approve of, and I think they should be both be added to our range of clothes, since that would leave us better dressed and better defended against the cold.[1]

Leo: I think Michael is quite right. If it was left to me I would straight away have both of them added to our clothes.

Mancio: If Leo and Lino both agree, and both persuade their brothers, then it can be done, with Leo persuading Protasio of Arima, Lino Sancho of Ōmura,[2] and they having this custom introduced in both Arima and Ōmura.[3]

Leo: But you will be better able to persuade our princes and brothers, since you have recently come from Europe.

Michael: As time moves on we'll be able to judge what should be done in these and other similar matters. But now there are some people here almost falling asleep, and that suggests we should be retiring for the night.

Leo: I have so enjoyed listening to what you say that I feel I don't need sleep, but very well, we'll end today's colloquium here.

---

[1] There was a short-lived boom for *namban* clothes, and other southern barbarian artefacts, among the Japanese elite during the second half of the 16th century.

[2] Ōmura Yoshiaki (1568–1615), baptized as Sancho, who succeeded Ōmura Sumitada in 1587. He apostatized in 1606 and became a persecutor of Christianity although he himself had been forced to give control of his domains to his son, Sumiyori, after siding against Tokugawa Ieyasu in 1600.

[3] This is clearly an in-joke as Lino had a penchant for Portuguese clothing.

COLLOQUIUM V

About the Indian race, and the houses of the Society in India.

Lino: Our colloquium last night ended with a discussion of differences between Japanese and European dress, and this took us away a little from the thread of your story. It would be right now, Michael, to take it back to the point where the digression began.

Michael: That digression has done us no harm; indeed to insert digressions of that kind will mean adding variety to the narrative, with questions and answers, and that will make it more agreeable, and will be a good defence against the boredom which non-stop narration so often produces.

Leo: I accept that an audience likes variety, but I don't accept that there is any possibility of being bored when listening to you. So do go on now and tell us what happened next.

Michael: We were just beginning our visit to the viceroy of India, a position held at that time by Francisco Mascarenhas, Count of Vila da Horta,[1] of the illustrious Mascarenhas family, ennobled for many exploits at home and abroad. He, being a gentleman of refinement and courtesy, received us cheerfully and kindly, embraced us warmly, and, urging us to remember him by it, generously fastened round the neck of each of us a gold chain with a skilfully made repository for a sacred relic. He also ordered the royal officials to see to it that we should be provided with everything we might need with regard to food and accommodation on the voyage to Portugal. And indeed the money involved was no small sum, with as much as 3,000 ducats spent for various purposes.[2]

---

[1] He was governor 1581–4. The Mascarenhas family was indeed illustrious and was one of the most important families in Portugal's overseas expansion. Amongst other positions, the family furnished two viceroys of India in the 16th century and a governor of Macao in the following century. The Mascarenhas Archipelago or Mascarene Islands, east of Madagascar, were named in honour of Pedro de Mascarenhas (?–1535) and his namesake (1484?–1555) served as João III's ambassador in Rome at the time of the founding of the Jesuits. In Rome, Loyola was his confessor and he was instrumental in facilitating the passage of the first Jesuits to Goa, where he himself served as viceroy 1554–5. His kinswoman Leonor de Mascarenas, whom the boys would meet in Madrid, royal governess to two of the daughters of Charles V, was an early and important sponsor of the Jesuits. See Rodrigues, *História da Companhia de Jesus*, I: 1, pp. 200–204, 212–16; *Dicionário*, II, pp. 704–9; Hufton, 'Altruism and Reciprocity', pp. 337–8.

[2] In a letter of 5 December 1583 to Aquaviva, de Sande mentions the viceroy's generosity (*Documenta Indica*, XII, p. 899).

Leo: With that degree of generosity to foreign persons that viceroy certainly left you much indebted to him.

Michael: Very much so; but he was not the only one to put us in his debt. The liberality of many other European princes, through whose territory our journey took us, left us similarly obliged.

Lino: It is truly remarkable that those European princes should be so open-handed towards foreigners, given that they did not know them and had no expectation of the favour being reciprocated.

Michael: The cause of this liberality is the abundance which they have of money and property, but also a largeness and loftiness of spirit which sets no store by gold and silver. But we shall be speaking elsewhere at greater length about the princes of Europe, to tell you more about their splendour and dignity, so we needn't say any more for the moment.

Lino: That is a very rich subject, it seems to me, with a great deal to be said about it, so you are right to leave it for another time. Now, when you have been speaking about the cities of Cochin and Goa, is the time to say something about the peoples of India.

Michael: The inhabitants of those cities are for the most part Portuguese, either merchants or soldiers, and they are certainly not to be regarded as natives, with the possible exception of those who are of the Portuguese race but born in India, for there are many Portuguese married couples living in various cities of India.[1]

Leo: So who are the natives, properly so called?

Michael: That word should properly be used of the people of India, those who were living in the various regions of India before the Portuguese arrived in India. There is a race of men more or less black in colour, not unattractive in facial features, mean spirited but at the same time quite ready to resort to arms, as well as the Saracens, with whom the Portuguese are at war, who are not originally from India, but from Persia and Arabia, and who have a more advanced knowledge of military matters.

Leo: If I understand you rightly it follows that there is a great multitude of people black in colour; for, if I am not mistaken, you said that both the Malays and the inhabitants of the Fishery Coast are of that colour, so I imagine the number of people of that colour must be very large.

Michael: From Malacca to Goa, as I said earlier, is a distance of 600 leagues, and this whole area is inhabited by peoples black of face. But as well as these there are far more

---

[1] *Casados* or officially recognized Portuguese settlers in Asia. Most were married to Asian women. Their children were labelled either as *castiço* (of Portuguese descent) or *mestiço* (mixed blood) and met with various degrees of prejudice. In filling the highest positions in state and church in Portuguese India, European-born Portuguese were preferred. See Boxer, *Portuguese Seaborne Empire*, pp. 296–307; Disney, *History of Portugal*, II, pp. 147–8.

other peoples. For all of that stretch of Africa, not to mention other places, between India and Portugal, which contains 3,000 leagues, is inhabited by certain people known to the Latins as Ethiopians,[1] but commonly called Kaffirs,[2] and they are very black of face, curly-haired, and different from the Indians in other physical characteristics; and I have said nothing about enormous stretches of territory in Asia and Africa inhabited by peoples of the same colour. So we have to conclude that they are not fewer than those born with white faces.

Lino: There is a major problem which occurs to me about the colour of these peoples: for if all men stem from their first parents, Adam and Eve, and if they, as seems certain, were born white and beautiful, how can it have come about that so many peoples gradually took on a black colour?[3]

---

[1] Original edition (p. 37), '*Æthiopes*'. 'Etiópia' was one of the Portuguese names for sub-Saharan Africa. See, for example, Camões, *Os Lusíadas*, I-43: 6, IV-62: 7 and -101:8, V-6: 8, VII-61:7.

[2] Port. *Cafre* which generally referred to inhabitants of southern Africa (ibid., V-47: 3, X-38: 1); from the Arab *Kafir*, an infidel. See also *Vocabvlario*, f. 67: '*Curobô. Cafre. Ou homem negro*', black man. At the time this was not a pejorative term in Japanese. Later, in the 18th century, as *kuro(n)bon* 黒(ん)坊 it became very much so as did other disparaging epithets for Europeans. See Leupp, 'Images of Black People', pp. 3, 4–6; Fujita, 'Edo jidai ni okeru Nihonjin', esp. pp. 241–65.

[3] In what follows one detects the voice of Valignano. The visitor comments on skin colour on several occasions in his writings. In the *Sumario de la India* he stated that not only did the people of the Indies differ from Europeans in appearance, dress, language, customs, governance, and so on, but all, with the exception of the Chinese and Japanese, were black-skinned, although of various shades (*Documenta Indica*, XIII, pp. 5, 144). The Chinese and the Japanese, on the other hand, were, as Valignano, and other European observers noted, 'gente blanca' white people, like Europeans, people of the temperate zone. See Greenlee, *Voyage of Pedro Álvares Cabral*, p. 109; *Documenta Indica*, XIII, pp. 5, 202; Valignano, *Sumario*, pp. 5 n. 10, 131; Valignano, *Historia*, pp. 126–7; Cooper, *João Rodrigues's Account*, p. 120. This distinction between white and dark-skinned people was not based on racial ideology as that came to be understood in the 19th century, although some contemporaries studied the variety of humankind and divided the species into types, unintentionally laying the groundwork for a division of humankind into races (Hannaford, *Race*, chs 5 and 6). In the *Sumario de la India*, Valignano associated dark skin with poverty, nakedness, oppression, disregard for learning (although, as he noted, the use of letters was common in India), deceitfulness and the loss of the faculty of reason occasioned by idolatry. Such people did not embrace the Christian message as a matter of inner, spiritual conviction like the Japanese but, but rather as a way to escape temporal hardship or as a means to gain reward or favour (*Documenta Indica*, XIII, pp. 9, 146). In the *Historia*, he moderated (somewhat) this harsh assessment (pp. 23–4, 28, 30). The white-skinned, civilized Japanese became Christian, in Valignano's opinion, because, possessed of right reason, they exercised free will (*Documenta Indica*, XIII, pp. 9–10; Valignano *Sumario*, pp. 131–2, 181 n. 2). Valignano's division of the people of the Indies has some features in common with José de Acosta's ranking of non-European people (excluding Jews and Moslems) according to their level of civilization. For Acosta, who was influenced by his fellow-Jesuits' writings from Japan, the Japanese and the Chinese were at the top: they lived in organized polities, with institutions and laws, had fortified cities, enjoyed commerce and thanks to their books and academies had achieved high levels of learning (Acosta, *De Procuranda Indorum salute*, I, p. 63). Both Valignano and Acosta believed that the Japanese and the Chinese could be converted to Christianity by arguments based on natural law precepts and right reason, not by force. As the following comments make clear, Valignano, although clearly puzzled by colour difference, was stumped to account for it. One suspects too that there was also an element of aesthetic prejudice involved. Valignano did not find dark-skinned people attractive. (See also Rubiés, *Travel and Ethnography*, pp. 7–8, 171–6.) But aesthetic prejudice (or preference) should not be equated with racism, even if one cares to label it ethnocentric for, as David M. Goldenberg has suggested, '[e]thnocentrism is not tantamount to racism. The former recognizes physical reality, the latter orders that reality into a hierarchy of domination' (*Curse of Ham*, p. 198). See also the perceptive comments on 'whiteness' and 'Portugueseness' in Sá, 'Charity and Discrimination', esp. p. 58.

Michael: You are right to call it a major problem, and you could add that it is a very complicated problem; but I'll leave it to Mancio, or one of the others, to sort it out for you. I'll be quiet for a little while, and pick up the story again afterwards.

Mancio: I have indeed heard many things about this important question, but they are all known to Michael. I know he is the narrator, but he should take on the role of philosopher as well, and discourse to us about the various causes.

Michael: Since Mancio won't accept the task we'll give it to Martin, who has committed to memory, and to writing, all the different opinions about this topic, and how to deal with the complexities of the whole question.

Martin: Come on, Michael, don't keep the audience in suspense. Of course all this is part of the role you have taken on.

Michael: All right, then, I'll begin, since that's what you want, and I'll put various opinions which I have heard about this question. First of all there are those who assert that the cause of this black colour is excessive heat; for many geographers and philosophers declare that that middle part of the world known as the torrid zone, which lies in the equinoctial region between the two tropics, is so scorched by the fierce heat of the sun that all the peoples who inhabit that region take on that black colour.

Lino: Michael, you show plainly that you have been to Europe, foster-mother of the arts, when you speak of the equinoctial regions and the tropics; but we need a little more explanation of all these things.

Michael: So as to have a foundation for a fuller explanation let me start from the shape of the sky. It has to be accepted as proved that it is round, and not, as the Japanese believe, quadrangular, and this is evident from what we can see with our own eyes and from the turning of the celestial spheres, not to mention other reasons.[1] For, as astrologers have

---

[1] These, and subsequent, comments on Japanese cosmology are crude and ill-informed. In Chinese cosmology, which influenced that of Japan, there were two major schools. The first, Gaitian (*Kai t'ien*) or hemispherical dome theory, in its mature form, held that the heavens provided a hemispherical covering for the earth, which itself resembled an upturned bowl. Pictured together, they were like two concentric domes. According to this theory, the earth was square, surrounded on all sides by four seas. The movement of the celestial vault, to which the sun and moon were attached, accounted for the variations between the seasons. According to the second school, Huntian (*Hun t'ien*), or celestial sphere, the heavens were spherical, like a hen's egg with the earth in the position of the yolk. This theory became orthodox after the 6th century, was favoured by Neo-Confucianists from the 12th century, and was the prevailing one when the Jesuits reached China. It influenced Japanese cosmology. Another, less influential school, influenced by Buddhism, was Xuanye (*Hsüan yeh*) or infinite empty space, according to which the sun, moon and stars float freely in empty space, in motion or motionless. This theory also allowed for the possibility of galaxies besides our own. See Needham, *Science and Civilisation*, III, pp. 209–24; Nakayama, *History of Japanese Astronomy*, pp. 24–43, 87. João Rodrigues, who benefited greatly from Ricci's knowledge of China, provides a far more informed discussion of Japanese cosmology and emphasizes the Buddhist contribution, the influence of both the Gaitian and Xuanye schools, and the importance of Islamic intellectuals in the transmission of knowledge eastwards (Cooper, *João Rodrigues's Account*, bk II, chs 8–16, esp. p. 360).

admirably pointed out, the sky, like some most perfect globe, moves in an orbit, and rests on two axes or poles, of which one is called the Arctic and the other the Antarctic, the former located in the north, the latter in the south. These most learned astrologers divide the sky into five main parts and circles; the first, named after the Arctic axis, is called the Arctic circle; the second, the Tropic of Cancer; the third, the equinoctial line, which cuts across the middle of the sky; the fourth, the Tropic of Capricorn; and the fifth is called the Antarctic circle. Now the place which is between the two tropics, and is divided in its centre by the equinoctial line, is the proper path of the sun, and every year it follows this path, tending sometimes towards Cancer, sometimes towards Capricorn, but never overstepping these limits assigned to it by nature. And the power of this path of the sun is such that all change of seasons, and the difference of day and night, depends entirely on it. For whenever the sun veers towards the Tropic of Cancer, which is to the north, then the days are shorter and the cold usually more severe in the south; and in the north the same thing happens as soon as the sun takes a course to the south; and the four-part alteration of the year, from spring to summer to autumn to winter, corresponds to the greater or lesser degree of the movement of the sun towards those two lines. And when the sun holds to that centre circle which I called the equinoctial line, then the days and nights are found to be of equal length. And these same astrologers also divide the earth, which is spherical and solid, into five parts, corresponding to those five in the heavens. The ancient astrologers went astray, however, in thinking that that central portion of the earth which lies beneath the equinoctial zone, is subject to such violent heat from the sun that it could never be inhabited by man; and that the two portions under the zones from the Arctic and Antarctic to the two poles suffer from such cold that there was no place for human habitation in either. I say, however, that the ancient astrologers were mistaken, for those three regions, which they considered untouched by any human attention, are in fact inhabited by various peoples. The one in the middle, which is beneath the torrid zone, is occupied by Ethiopians, that is, people black in colour. For although those three parts are disagreeable, one because of the heat, the others because of the cold, nature, with an eye to man's advantage, has provided various remedies by which the inconveniences are very considerably alleviated.[1] But this subject is a little difficult, so I want you to look at a model of the sky which the astrologers use.[2] In this sphere that you are looking at you can see those two axes on which the sky in a sense rests and on which it turns; then these five circles which I mentioned. The Zodiac, cutting through the middle circle and touching the circles of Cancer and of Capricorn, indicates clearly to us the path the sun follows. As I said before, the sun does not go beyond its set limits at Cancer and Capricorn. When it coincides with the middle equinoctial circle it makes night and day equal, and in moving towards or away from those limits it produces the changing of the seasons.[3]

[1] In his *Natural and Moral History of the Indies*, Acosta devotes much space to refuting the belief of the Ancients that the torrid zone was uninhabitable (bk II, *passim*).

[2] Probably an armillary sphere which had either been included among the presents given to the boys in Europe or was brought to Japan by Moreira.

[3] While a student at the Roman College, Valignano had studied mathematics in 1567–8 under Clavius. Another of Clavius's students, and a protégé of Valignano, was Matteo Ricci. Clavius insisted that a solid grounding in mathematics was essential for a study of philosophy even if this involved contradicting the Ancients, and that the study of natural phenomena helped one understand better the spiritual world. See Schütte,

Leo: It's extremely interesting for us to examine this model of the sky, made by the hand of some uncommonly skilled craftsman, which you put before us. It is easy to see from this how poor the learning and science is of our Japanese priests, whom we call *bonze*s,[1] when they philosophize. They will have it that the sky is square, and that the sun revolves round a stone like a clepsydra, and they say that the alternation of day and night, and the vicissitudes of heat and cold, are caused by its rising and sinking.

Michael: I have to say that I don't know whether to laugh or to marvel at their opinion, for our own eyes testify that the sky is round or spherical, and this stone round which they say the sun revolves is simply an invention, a fiction, and no reasoning can show us where it is located or positioned. But it is not surprising to find that, where good arts and disciplines do not flourish, the door is open to errors. These errors are contrary to both reason and sense, but with the passage of time they establish themselves in the minds of ignorant men, become very difficult to root out, and are accepted as certain truth by the people.

Lino: That is certainly true. But from what you have said I suppose that the cause of the black colour is almost certainly the heat.

Michael: I would not say it was almost certain, since there are a number of weighty arguments against that opinion.

Lino: I would be glad if you could rehearse those arguments for us.

Michael: I'll state just what seem to me the two or three principal ones. The first is, that if that black colour was brought about simply by an excess of heat from the sun, it would necessarily follow that only the natives of the tropical zone would be born with that colour, and within that zone the closer a part was to the equinoctial line, the blacker the people living under that zone would be, because the periods when they are deprived of the sun are shorter. But experiment has shown that this is not the case, for the Malaccans and others like them, who are almost directly under the equinoctial line, are much less black than some others who live under the tropics; and this is very clear, since examination has shown that those Ethiopians who live at the Cape of Good Hope, a full 35 degrees south, and located right outside the tropical zone, are very black, and have very

---

Valignano's Mission Principles, I: 1, p. 34; Spence, *Memory Palace*, pp. 142–4, 146. Clavius's books included manuals for the construction and use of scientific equipment (see ibid., p. 148). It should, of course, be remembered that Catholic dogma at this time completely rejected the idea of a heliocentric universe even as, thanks to the invention of the telescope, the evidence for heliocentrism was becoming irrefutable. Catholic dogma also prohibited the Jesuits from introducing heliocentrism into China until 1760. See, Needham, *Science and Civilisation*, III, pp. 442–7; Waley-Cohen, *Sextants*, pp. 107–12.

[1] *Bōzu* 坊主, a Buddhist monk or priest, or, as was favoured by the missionaries, *bonze*, i.e. *bonsō* or *bonzō* 凡僧, '*Religioso commun, sin dignidade*', a lowly monk without dignity (*Vocabvlario*, f. 25). The Jesuits used the term indiscriminately and pejoratively when referring to the Buddhist and Shinto clergy. It was first used by the Portuguese merchant Jorge Alvarez in a letter of 1546 or 1547 to Xavier. The name was used frequently by Xavier and his successors thereafter. See *Sumario*, p. 9 n. 33; Ruiz-de-Medina, *Documentos del Japón*, I, pp. 18, 145; Xavier, *Letters and Instructions of Francis Xavier*, p. 299.

curly hair. And this can't be put down simply to extreme heat, since Portuguese sailors experience severe cold and shorter days when they are in that area, rounding the promontory. So the black colour cannot be attributed just to the heat.[1]

Lino: That's a good argument, but one which can be refuted by another. If I wanted to dispute with you I would say that there are Ethiopian people, living under the torrid zone, who have changed their place of residence and moved south, and there they have produced children like themselves.

Michael: But this argument supports mine; if the cause of that colour was simply an excess of heat, the effect would necessarily disappear if you removed the cause, and this would mean that the longer those Ethiopian people lived in southern regions the more they would be free of that black colour. But that simply does not happen; even with the passing of ages, of centuries, black people still produce black people. So it seems that that colour should be attributed not just to heat, but to the seed and nature of the parents, according to the axiom of the philosophers, who assert that like begets like. And experience supports this view; if two Ethiopians go to Portugal or to another region where the inhabitants are white, and there, in due time, give birth to children, these children are no less black, and no different in their other features. But on the other hand if one of the couple is white, and he marries an Ethiopian woman, their children show much less of their mother's colour, and with the passage of time it gradually comes about that the grandchildren, the great-grandchildren, and those who come after are gradually cleansed of the stain with which they were branded by that first mother, and they come back to being completely white. Finally, if a white couple emigrate to Ethiopian lands and there produce offspring, all of the offspring are born the same white colour; but if white are joined in matrimony with blacks, that mark of the black colour is passed on like a stain, but again, by marriage with white spouses, is gradually removed. Thus it seems, surely, that the colour must be ascribed not to the heat but to some generative cause.

Lino: Now I am inclined to your opinion; but I do wonder what that generative cause could be, given that all men are born of Adam and Eve, our first parents, as from an original stem, and they were totally without any such stain. How can it have come about, then, that without any other later intervention from the heavens, Ethiopians are there in certain regions?

---

[1] Marvel at skin colour was not limited to Europeans. It puzzled the Japanese as well. In March 1581 Nobunaga and other Japanese were much intrigued by a black slave in Valignano's entourage. When the individual visited Nobunaga in Kyoto, the hegemon refused to believe that the man was naturally black and had him washed and scrubbed several times in the false belief that he had been painted black. The man was in his mid-twenties, powerfully-built, master of a number of skills and could speak Japanese. Nobunaga insisted on taking him into his service and he showed him off around the capital so much so that rumours began to circulate that they were lovers and that Nobunaga intended to make him a *tono*. See RAHM, MS 09-02663, f. 249v; *Cartas*, II, ff. 2, 3v, 17; Fróis, *Segunda parte*, p. 242, n. 1; Valignano, *Sumario*, pp. 149*–50*; Ōta, *Nobunaga kōki*, II, p. 213. There were, of course, a number of Africans and Malays in Portuguese service, vividly represented in *namban* folding screens, and they would not have been unfamiliar in the streets of Nagasaki. In the 17th century the Dutch and English had people whom Richard Cocks called '*caffro*' in their service as did various daimyo including those of Hirado and Satsuma. See Cocks, *Diary*, I, pp. 26, 92, 109, 124, 168, 207, 216, 238; II, pp. 205, 238–9.

Michael: That's the real problem, to explain this colour, newly introduced in a certain race of men. There are some who try to explain it by reference to divine justice and punishment for sin, and they say that when Noah, after the universal flood, was treated with less than due reverence by one of his sons, Ham by name, moved by just indignation he immediately cursed his son, and because of that curse that stain, never wholly to be erased, came upon him and his descendants.[1]

Leo: If indeed that was how it was it would surely have come down to us in the sacred scriptures, but they make no mention of that punishment.

Michael: If it had been handed down to us in the sacred scriptures no occasion would remain for doubt. It is not in the sacred books, so it is not entirely certain; but neither should it be totally rejected just because it is not set down in those holy books. We know that many things which did take place, and were recorded by most weighty authors, were not included by the writers of the sacred scriptures. But the idea that it was a punishment of some kind arises not only because the Ethiopians are black in colour, but also because they are for the most part sad and misshapen of face, rough and primitive in their nature, and prone to all inhumanity and savagery. Thus it seems credible that that race of men is cursed because of the fault of some ancestor. It can also reasonably be said that the cause of that colour and of those features is some celestial influence unknown to us which combines the heat of the sun with some unknown causes, by which not only the Ethiopians by the blackness of their bodies, but also other peoples are marked off one from another by the diversity of their features. We Japanese, and the Chinese, with our smaller and deeper eyes, and our flatter snub noses, differ from the Europeans. So it is not surprising if through some hidden celestial cause, combined with the heat of the sun, some people gradually began to go black, and their hair to become twisted, and that this vice of nature, as it were, should have been passed down to their descendants. In fact this seems the best explanation, for it does not entirely reject heat as a cause, nor does it take refuge in divine miracles as the solution to all puzzles, but instead refers this colouring partly to heat, partly to a cause unknown, and partly to the seed of the parents.

Lino: And in this way the differing views of the various authors can be reconciled. But tell us now why it is that the ancient philosophers and astrologers judged that there could be no human habitation either in the torrid zones or in the Arctic or Antarctic circles.

Michael: It is not surprising that the Ancients, whose thought was concerned only with the nature of things and had no grounding in experience, should have come to that conclusion. Since the closer the sun comes to a place the stronger the heat to which that place is exposed and the longer the days, and in the opposite case it gets cold and the days are shorter, it was not entirely unreasonable to judge that the torrid zone, which the sun

---

[1] According to the Bible, Ham saw the nakedness of his father Noah, and reported this to his brothers, but it was Canaan and his issue, not Ham and his, who were cursed with eternal slavery (Genesis 9:18–27). Subsequently it was believed that the curse had been transferred to the descendents of Ham who were identified with black Africans. See Goldenberg, *Curse of Ham*, esp. pp. 141–77, which amongst other things disproves the conventional view, repeated here, that Ham and his descendants were black.

never leaves, and the places under the two axes, which, whether its course tends to the north or to the south, the sun never reaches, could not provide any appropriate habitation for men. But in fact the author of nature, who in his great wisdom is wont to consider and provide for all human needs, has provided remedies to temper the rigour of both heat and cold, so as not to debar men from making a home in those regions.

Lino: List the remedies with which the author of nature has tempered the heat of the central regions.

Michael: In the first place I list the winds which almost continuously cool all of that torrid zone, and which are so frequent, so mild, and so wholesome that the summer heat in Europe and Japan comes near to surpassing the heat of the torrid zone. In fact at a particular time of the year in certain parts of the torrid zone the winds, especially winds blowing from inland areas, are cold enough to make extra warmer clothing necessary; and the water cools sufficiently to provide a most agreeable drink for the natives of that region, especially in the afternoon, when the wind dies down, the day heats up, but the water keeps the cool of early morning. In the second place the inhabitants of those regions have heavy rain, especially at the time when the sun, climbing to a point directly overhead, would burn the land especially fiercely but for the rain clouds coming between and shutting it out. Thirdly they have a far larger number of rivers than other places have, and these, flowing most pleasantly, so irrigate the land as not to allow it to be scorched by the heat of the sun. And finally, other considerations aside, they have very dark forests of trees whose leaves bar the heat of the sun very effectively, especially as almost all the trees are of such kinds that at no time of the year is there a total lack of foliage, since though some leaves fall others do not; and they are so agreeable, and their fruits so sweet, that they are a wonderful benefit for the natives.

Leo: With those excellent remedies provided by God that zone can be called not torrid but temperate. But what are the appropriate remedies which nature has set against the strength and asperity of the cold within the Arctic and Antarctic circles?

Michael: We have never been to those places, but from what we have heard and what we have read in books we gather that there too the people have certain advantages. With regard to the continuous night, which in certain places, under both poles, lasts one, two, three, and even six months: first, this infliction is less severe at those times called twilight, which last longer in those places; second, when the sun is absent for a long time, the light from the moon and the stars is much stronger; furthermore, with the many trees that there are they have such fires and bonfires that they seem brighter than daylight. There are also ways of moderating the cold: apart from that continuous burning of wood, and the heat from fires in the home, there are not lacking many animals of various sorts, from whose skins,[1] fastened together and woven, they make excellent clothing for keeping out the cold; not to mention the hypocausts, crypts, and other similar places where fires are always kept burning, so that they manage to live with an acceptable degree of comfort. There is, in fine, no place so plagued by heat or cold that it does not have some relief

---

[1] In the Errata '*pellibus*' (original edition p. 43) is changed to '*velleribus*'.

either provided by nature or supplied by art, and it is because they did not appreciate this that the ancient philosophers and mathematicians bequeathed to us the notion that those middle and extreme lands, that is to say those lands situated under the torrid zone and under the farthest circles, were totally empty of men.

Leo: In learning about all these different places on the earth and their various particular characteristics we have developed a great desire to be able to pass this knowledge on to others who have not yet heard about it. But tell us, please, by what laws and what religion these people are held bound, these people who, as you say, are so many in number and born black in colour.

Michael: We can call those people totally lawless and irreligious, for they are constrained to duty by no fixed laws or religion, but live for the most part like cattle, which nature has left prone and obedient to their stomachs, addicted to their desires and vices, and lacking all refinement and all sense of human culture. Therefore it is rightly said by a certain European philosopher that those people are born simply to serve.[1] And with regard to religion, the figments and absurdities of these people concerning their gods are such that they will serve as excellent evidence of the degree to which all pagans are fallen into error, inventing such preposterous fables and dreams; and this can also be seen in those of the Japanese who are still pagans.

Leo: You are quite right, Michael, for we can see with our own eyes differences so many and so great among the absurd sects, that it does appear that our people are mired in chaos.

Michael: This is a very strong argument for the falsity of paganism and the truth of Christianity. The pagans, in all the various regions in which they are dispersed, make up their own religion according to their own sense and judgement, and their gods are almost as many as their different senses and judgements; whereas Christians consider things to do with religion not only by the light of their own intelligence, but also and mainly by the splendour of the divine light, and although they are separated in various remote provinces and regions, speaking different languages and following different customs, they preach the one God and bear witness to Him by the example of their lives, for truth is one and simple, not to be pulled apart or torn asunder.

Lino: If only the Japanese would follow that one simple truth with one mind and one heart. But I would like to know what houses the fathers of the Society have in India, and how they live there.

Michael: In India the fathers of the Society have many colleges, and houses, and private dwellings. In Cochin there is a very well constructed college, in which twenty-five of the Society live, as well as a number of other people;[2] and besides that within the same

---

[1] Aristotle, *Politics*, bk I, ch. 5. See also *Documenta Indica,* XIII, pp. 5–6, 144; Valignano, *Historia*, p. 24. On the theory of natural slavery, see Hanke, *Aristotle and the American Indians*; Pagden, *Fall of Natural Man*, ch. 3 *passim*.

[2] Valignano provides more detail in the *Sumario de la India* (*Documenta Indica,* XIII, pp. 32–6, 173–8).

kingdom of Cochin they have other smaller residences, especially among those who are popularly called the Thomas Christians, for at the very beginning of Christendom St Thomas, one of the most holy apostles of Christ, brought them from false superstition to Christian piety. With the passing of time, however, they had come to adopt a less strict discipline, and the fathers of the Society call them back to the old norm of Christian teaching; and they have a seminary for boys, where boys receive an excellent education and later, when they have been instructed in holy things, are able to teach Christian precepts to their own people.[1] In those regions the fathers also have regard to the health and well-being of those whom, by their labour and industry, they have persuaded to commit themselves to Christ; and there are many of them spread all along that maritime coast as far as the fortress of Quilon, and there too there is a house of the Society; and from there all the next stretch, called Travancore, on the near side of the Comorin promontory, and the other stretch beyond the promontory, known as the Fishery Coast, has many private houses of the fathers of the Society, with at least two living in each of them, and they are in control of all those people, once primitive, but now splendidly accomplished in their Christian observance. For these they have two seminaries, one in Quilon, the other on the Fishery Coast, and it is hoped that in each of them boys will be nobly and religiously educated, and in the course of time will become excellent priests and ministers of divine things.[2]

In Goa, the centre of Portuguese rule, the fathers have three very fine houses, in which one hundred and sixty of the Society live. The first is the house of the professed, new, with the building not yet quite completed, but in form and structure it can easily stand comparison with the most spacious and magnificent of European buildings, and already it holds forty of the Society, who live there very suitably provided for on the alms most generously donated by the citizens.[3] The second is the College of St Paul, an old and magnificent building, with a church so noble that its renown is high throughout India, and it is larger than any other church in India. In this college live those who are still zealously applying themselves to the liberal arts, and they are eighty in number. The third is the house of the tyros, or novices, where those who having turned their backs on the goods and pleasures of this world exercise themselves seriously in the Christian militia, and apply their minds and their abilities to overturning the power of the devil, so that

---

[1] On the Thomas Christians, see Neill, *History of Christian Missions*, pp. 122–6; Moffett, *History of Christianity in Asia, Volume 1*, pp. 22–39; 266–70; 498–503; Gillman and Klimkeit, *Christians in Asia*, pp. 159–66, 188–201. The Synod of Diamper (Udayamperur), 1599, ostensibly brought to an end the independent existence of a Christian tradition as old as that of Rome. Latin uniformity was imposed and the Thomas Christians absorbed into the Latin church. This did not go unopposed and a schism occurred in 1653 (Gillman and Klimkeit, *Christians in Asia*, pp. 200–201). The expression 'call them back to the old norm' is misleading. The Thomas Christians, as Valignano noted in the *Sumario de la India*, and whose numbers he estimated at 100,000, had never adhered to the Roman rite. They were being taken over. Unlike his accommodation policies in Japan and China, Valignano was uncompromising in his dealings with the Thomas Christians and refused to countenance any departure from the rulings of the Council of Trent. See *Documenta Indica*, XIII, pp. 34, 176–8; XIV, pp. 103–9; Wicki, 'Die unmittelbaren Auswirkungen', pp. 228–33, 242–6. On the seminary, a project much favoured by Valignano, see *Documenta Indica*, XIII, pp. 35, 177; XIV, pp. 106, 109.

[2] Valignano gives a detailed account of the Jesuit presence in India in the *Sumario de la India* (*Documenta Indica*, XIII, pp. 13–48, 151–88).

[3] The professed house was established on 21 October 1584 (ibid., pp. 12*–14*, 678–96, 769–70).

afterwards they may study in the colleges, may end up as perfect soldiers, and may cast the yoke of sin off from the necks of wretched men.[1]

Lino: Why so many houses in one and the same city? Would it not be better to have those fathers dispersed in various cities and towns, so that more abundant fruit could be gathered from many different kinds of work?

Michael: In this matter the fathers make wise and effective provision. For those who are dispersed throughout the various regions have first laid aside, in the novitiate, bad habits learned from associating with irreligious men, and have grown accustomed to bearing the arms of Christ; thereafter they transfer to the colleges, from which, after advanced studies in arts and doctrine, they emerge as excellent teachers and masters of Christian law, easily able to instruct other ignorant men in the divine precepts. And these fathers do not remain permanently in Goa, but after first arming themselves in those two houses, of virtue and of learning, either they transfer to the professed house, to the benefit of the citizens of Goa, or they travel to the various provinces of India, some of them very remote, or to the islands of the Moluccas, or even to China and here to Japan, and they cover the whole oriental region. There are also a number of other houses of the fathers in the northern part of India, but we did not go there, so I pass them over in silence.[2] Now we should move on to the voyage to Portugal, but first we need to call a halt to the story so as to have some rest.

Lino: Very well. We would have been delighted if you had continued talking, but we'll reserve the pleasure for tomorrow.

---

[1] The College of St Paul was founded in 1541 and officially taken over by the Jesuits in 1551. It was their principal college in India functioning as a seminary to train future secular clergy, with students from many nations attending, and as a school for Portuguese, Indians and *mestiço* children. See *Documenta Indica,* XIII, pp. 13–19, 151–8; Wicki, 'Der einheimische Klerus in Indien', pp. 17–31; Alden, *Making of an Enterprise,* p. 44; Worcester, *Cambridge Companion to the Jesuits,* p. 155.

[2] They are described in the *Sumario de la India* (*Documenta Indica,* XIII, pp. 166–73).

COLLOQUIUM VI

The Voyage from India to Portugal

Michael: Time now demands that our story move from India to Portugal, since we have dwelt at some length on things Indian, and many other things remain if we are to give an account of the whole of our journey. So in tonight's meeting we should, I think, deal with the voyage to Portugal, and leave out certain other matters more agreeable than necessary.

Leo: Many of the things you have been speaking about in these colloquia make us eager to know more; but let us leave our questions aside, for we very much want to hear about the voyage to Portugal, and to have your account come at last to the wide expanse of the things of Europe.

Michael: After that short stay, only a few days, in Goa, we took ship for Portugal when a suitable opportunity occurred. We took leave of the Father Visitor and the other fathers of the Society, not without many tears shed on both sides, and they made clear to us the great hopes they had as they saw us off.

Leo: What do you mean when you say that you took leave of the Father Visitor? Did he not go with you on that voyage, as your leader, as he said here that he would?

Michael: That was always the intention of the Father Visitor, and he did not alter it lightly, but just when we were ready to depart a letter brought from Rome tore him away from us. In that letter the Father General of the Society imposed on him the task of being Provincial Superior of East India, a task which he could neither refuse, nor turn over to someone else, and if he was to perform the task he could not leave India, so our hopes of his leadership and his company were cut short.[1]

Lino: That must have dampened your happiness considerably, for you would be making your way less happily to Europe, another world, without such a leader and standard-bearer, especially as the Father had protected you and had taken you under his wing.

Michael: There is no denying that the loss of the presence and company of the said Father was a great blow to our happiness; the love by which we were joined to him was not less than the love of children for their parents. But that same principle, of total obedience

---

[1] The letter is no longer extant but Valignano's replies are. See *Documenta Indica*, XII, pp. 827–56. See Introduction, p. 4.

to the Father General, was a great consolation to us in that situation, especially when by experience we came to realize that the fathers of the Society were so linked to one another by the bond of charity that they were all of one mind, one spirit, one sense, so that as we proceeded on our journey, even without the Father Visitor, the kindness and love shown to us by the European fathers would leave nothing to be desired. Nor were we mistaken about this; for although, throughout our enormously long journey, we came in contact with many fathers of different languages and different nations, dispersed in separate places, we found manifested in all of them the same spirit, as if they were of the one language and from the same place. Besides, although the Father Visitor was no longer with us, and that was a great loss, (as well as having with us Father Diogo de Mesquita, our beloved instructor and teacher) we were provided with another leader of the whole party, namely Nuno Rodrigues, a man of great virtue and authority, who was at that time rector of the Goa college,[1] and his presence did much to make up for the absence of the Father Visitor. With Father Rodrigues as leader we took ship and were soon at the port of Cochin, where the merchandise of India is brought and loaded on to the Portuguese ships. We left Cochin happily on the 20 February 1584, and on the 10 August of that same year we reached the most celebrated port of Lisbon, in Portugal.[2]

Leo: You have covered the whole voyage in just a few words, but in reality it was very long, for if you work it out it took you just ten days short of six months.

Michael: Indeed, dear Leo, that's right. The voyage from India to Portugal takes longer than any other yet discovered, and is also fraught with more danger, discomfort, and difficulty.[3] But God, who treated us on that journey with great indulgence, like his little

---

[1] Portuguese, Rodrigues was born in 1538, entered the Society in 1559, and was professed of the four vows in 1577 (*Documenta Indica*, XIII, p. 602). Although Rodrigues was given overall responsibility for the boys, his main purpose in going to Europe was in his capacity as procurator (i.e. representative) to attend a congregation of Jesuit procurators, scheduled to begin in Rome on 15 November 1584. Valignano stressed that this assignment was to take precedence over accompanying the boys. Rodrigues was to leave his charges in Lisbon and proceed in haste to Rome and Valignano requested the provincial of Portugal, Sebastião de Morais, to appoint someone suitable to replace Rodrigues. See *Documenta Indica*, XIII, pp. 418–27 (Valignano's instructions to Rodrigues as procurator), 452–3 (Valignano to Morais); Álvarez-Taladriz, 'En el IV centenario de la embajada', pp. 137, 141; Abranches Pinto and Bernard, 'Les instructions', pp. 392, 400. The second general congregation of the Society, held in 1565, stated that procurators should be sent to Rome from all provinces every three years to vote on whether or not a general congregation should be called. On this specific office (there were procurators with other functions in the Society), including its relevance to Japan, see Schütte, *Valignano's Mission Principles*, I: 1, pp. 364–5; I: 2, pp. 34, 53, 237, 302–4; Padberg et al., *For Matters of Greater Moment*, pp. 117, 127.

[2] The boys sailed on the *Santiago*, one of five ships returning to Lisbon. The other four ships departed before the *Santiago*. The boys were assigned to the captain's quarters (Gualtieri, *Relationi*, pp. 42–3; *Dai Nihon Shiryō*, XI: 1, pp. 58, 61–2; Fróis, *Première ambassade*, p. 23). For the arrival date in Lisbon the original edition (p. 48) gives '*sexto Idus Augusti*' or 8 August, but the errata list changes this to '*quarto*' or 10 August. Fróis says they arrived at Cascaes on the 10th and entered Lisbon the following day (*Première ambassade*, pp. 27–8).

[3] For Valignano's account of the voyage from Lisbon to Goa, see *Historia*, pp. 9–16. On the dangers, conditions and hardships of the voyages of *Carreira da Índia* and on Spanish Indies fleets, see Boxer, '*Carreira da Índia*', *passim*; Cooper, *Rodrigues the Interpreter*, pp. 27–32; Pérez-Mallaína, *Spain's Men of the Sea*, pp. 129–89 *passim*. On mortality rates on Portuguese voyages, which could be as high as 50 per cent, see Boxer, '*Carreira da Índia*', p. 58. The mortality rate among crew on Spanish New World fleets has been estimated at 12.3 per cent, three times higher than the average for people on land (Pérez-Mallaína, *Spain's Men of the Sea*, p. 186). For mortality rates on Dutch East India Company ships, which were also quite high, see Bruijn et al., *Dutch-Asiatic Shipping*, pp. 162–4.

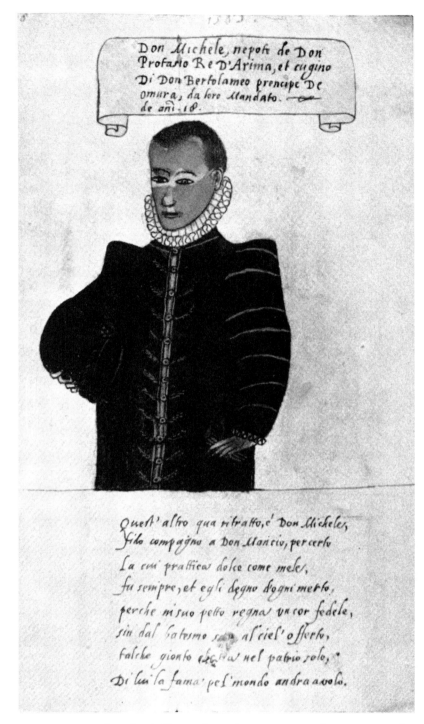

Figure 3. Drawing of Michael Chijiwa by Urbano Monte, July 1585, in B. Gutierrez, *La prima ambascieria giapponese in Italia*, Milan, 1938, following p. 56 (unpaginated). By permission of Gakushuin Women's College, Tokyo.

Figure 4.   Drawing of Mancio Itō by Urbano Monte, July 1585, in B. Gutierrez, *La prima ambascieria giapponese in Italia*, Milan, 1938, following p. 40 (unpaginated). By permission of Gakushuin Women's College, Tokyo.

Figure 5. Drawing of Martin Hara by Urbano Monte, July 1585, in B. Gutierrez, *La prima ambascieria giapponese in Italia*, Milan, 1938, following p. 56 (unpaginated). By permission of Gakushuin Women's College, Tokyo.

Figure 6. Drawing of Julian Nakaura by Urbano Monte, July 1585, in B. Gutierrez, *La prima ambascieria giapponese in Italia*, Milan, 1938, following p. 72 (unpaginated). By permission of Gakushuin Women's College, Tokyo.

Figure 7. Drawing of Diogo de Mesquita, S.J., by Urbano Monte, July 1585, in B. Gutierrez, *La prima ambascieria giapponese in Italia*, Milan, 1938, following p. 72 (unpaginated).
By permission of Gakushuin Women's College, Tokyo.

children, made that dangerous way safe, clear of all danger, so that without any difficulty, and with constantly favourable winds, so that there were only a couple of occasions when we had to take in the sails, we completed the voyage. On the way back to India, however, we found ourselves treated as more experienced campaigners, caught up in difficulties and dangers of many different kinds.

Lino: It is extraordinary, like a dream, that a man should be carried along for full six months in a ship, where the cabins can't be very roomy or spacious, and there are many other difficulties to be borne, but especially being enclosed like that in the ship as if in a prison; no one would be able to stay for six months shut in and enclosed in a house, not even if it was put to them that the house would be furnished as for royalty, never mind a ship uncomfortable in so many ways.

Michael: I agree, Lino, for the discomforts of a ship outdo even the difficulties of a prison. But as in other human affairs the accomplishing of some wished-for end diminishes the harshness of the means through hope and expectation of a most sweet conclusion (as for example with leaders and soldiers in war, who in the hope of obtaining victory submit themselves to all kinds of dangers to their lives, and to the uncertain fortunes of war), so also it was with us; the great desire we had of reaching Portugal and Europe assuaged the troubles and the boredom of the voyage, and the longer we spent on the journey, the more we were sustained by the hope of reaching port.

Leo: How, or with what occupation, did you while away the time and the days, which must have seemed extremely long?

Michael: During storms and tempests the time of the voyage is occupied with difficulty and extremely hard work, but when it is calm, and the wind favourable, there are plenty of distractions to help the voyager pass his time not disagreeably. For most of the time that is how it was with us; we were sometimes busy with the Latin language, sometimes playing musical instruments, quite often fishing for various fish or relaxing in the delightful company of other passengers, and our regular prayers to God and the saints were not forgotten.

Lino: You were at sea, then, for those six months, without ever touching land, or even passing by any land and seeing it?

Michael: On that voyage to Lisbon the only port or land that you reach or touch is a certain island, which takes its name from St Helena. This island is on the way from the Cape of Good Hope to the equinoctial line, a long way from the Cape, and God most provident has set it there as a welcome refuge for those who undergo the voyage. Travellers replenish their supplies of water, recover their strength, and provide themselves with food from the plentiful supplies of meat and of fruit which there are there.[1]

---

[1] The first Portuguese to reach St Helena was João da Nova in 1502, on St Helen's Day. The island became an important resting place and rendezvous for returning ships of the *Carreira da Índia* during the 16th and 17th centuries until the island was taken over by the English East India Company in 1673. Linschoten mentions that

Leo: So you seldom see land at all? How can it be then, that the pilots of the ships know what region of the world they are at, and whither they are to direct their course, especially when some wild tempest in the skies blocks the view of the stars, and the sea offers no marker or boundary line to guide them on their way?

Michael: In this most important matter there is an art on which they can rely, for over the course of time various instruments have been developed, and they have a tried and tested art of navigating with the use of these instruments, such that they know for certain on any given day where they are, where they should be heading, and what places to steer clear of. They use mainly the astrolabe or planisphere, a navigational chart, and a compass, and with these instruments they can easily master the method of navigating. For with the astrolabe they ascertain the distance from the position of the sun, and then from the pole and from the Equator; on the chart, which maps the coastlines of all the seas, they circle with a pair of compasses the place they have reached; then with the compass they check where north and south are, and thus they know what course they should be setting; when they have taken account of all this, and also read through the observations of other sailors or pilots, which they carry with them in written form, and made use of their own judgement and experience, they can usually solve all problems, and rarely stray from their intended route.

Leo: That is remarkable, and it is news to us. Could you explain what each instrument can do, and what it is for, so as to give us a better idea of them.

Michael: Gladly; and I'll let you see each of them. Boy, bring the instruments which are hanging on nails in my room, which I often use to soothe my soul. We knew, of course, that our own people here would be extremely eager to know all about our experiences on the journey, so we made a point of getting hold of anything which we thought would help us to explain them more easily.

Here we are then; in the first place I'll show you the astrolabe, which, as I said, indicates to the navigator, when he observes the rise and decline of the sun, the height of the pole and how near or far he is from the Equator.[1] To make it easier for you to understand how it is used, note that mathematicians who profess the science of celestial things, divide the whole circle of the sky into four parts: each of them runs from one of the poles to the equinoctial line, and has ninety portions, which they call degrees. Thus the whole circle, which runs from the Arctic pole past the equinoctial line and on to the Antarctic pole, and then from that Antarctic pole, again passing the equinoctial line, comes back to the Arctic pole, contains 360 degrees; and each of the four equal main parts has ninety degrees, from

---

when the men caught sight of the island during his return voyage 'there was so great ioy in the ship, as if we had bene in heaven', and Pyrard felt that the island had been placed in such a favourable place in the middle of a vast ocean by Providence. Sick members of Portuguese ships were left on the island to recover and joined the following year's ships. According to Linschoten, most survived thanks to the island's favourable climate, although Mundy found it bitterly cold in October. See Linschoten, *Voyage*, II, pp. 250–60, esp. p. 250; Pyrard, *Voyage*, II, p. 795; Mundy, *Travels*, III: 2, pp. 411–16.

[1] An astrolabe was among the instruments Moreira brought to Japan and which he used for his fieldwork (Schütte, 'Ignacio Moreira', p. 123).

the pole to the equinoctial line. Each of these degrees is then divided into sixty even more minute parts, known as minutes. These mathematicians, using the same principle, divide the whole sphere of the earth, which lies under the sky, into the same number of sections, and they know from careful observation that each degree of the earth, if you travel directly north to south, is made up of seventeen and a half leagues, and this can easily be converted, as we said above, either to our leagues or to Italian miles. This means that the whole of the earth, which is round, spherical, and has thirty-six sections, has a circumference of six thousand three hundred leagues.[1] So the divisions of the sky and the earth are known, and this astrolabe is constructed so cleverly that it sets before our eyes all those sections of the sky, and this needle, with these two holes in the central part of it, points to all the various degrees. In order to calculate the correct degree for each day, the sailors hold the astrolabe in their hands at midday and point the needle at the sun, so that the beam of the sun penetrates directly through the two holes, and the figure that the upper part of the needle or rotating arm then points to is the correct distance in degrees from the position of the sun. Thus they can easily work out how far they are from the sun, and taking into account the veering of the sun towards or away from the south or the north they calculate how far away they are from the equinoctial line.[2] This known, they take this chart in their hands and mark on it the point or the area of the place where they are, and the distance from the equinoctial line. For in this same chart, as you can see, they have the celestial circles and degrees, but they also have the outline of all the sea coasts, and they can calculate how far away they are from them. They do this every day, and this allows them to estimate how much of their journey they have covered, and how far away they are from this or that place.

But for plotting the course of the ship this needle, which you see here,[3] is extremely useful. It is made of iron and is balanced on the point of a rod, and when the two ends of it are rubbed with a certain stone, which is called a magnet, the power of that stone is communicated by the rubbing to the needle or indicator itself, with the result that, without anything else being done to it, one end of the needle always points north and the other end south; and with the guidance of this instrument the sailors, however far out at sea they are, and however cloudy and dark the sky, steer the ship to the north or to the south, as required. In addition to these two principal indicators there are also other lines, as you can see, leading off from the circle, and these show them not only the four main winds, namely the north, south, east, and west, but also the others in between. The ship is steered this way and that according to the changing of the winds and the destination predetermined by the sailors, and the sails are adjusted and adapted now this way, now

---

[1] According to the authority on 16th-century nautical matters, Martín Cortés de Albacar's *Breve compendio de la sphera y de la arte de navegar*, known simply as the *Arte de navegar* (1551), translated into English by Richard Eden as *The Arte of Nauigation* (1561), on which the following discussion is based, the value of a degree was either 16⅔ or 17½ leagues, with Cortés favouring the latter (Waters, *Art of Navigation*, p. 64).

[2] The original edition (p. 50) gives '*foramen*' (s.) 'hole' instead of '*foramina*' (pl.) 'holes', a mistake because the astrolabe has two holes. See Sande, *Embaixadores Japoneses*, I, p. 391 n. 38. However, the contention there that what is translated here as 'the veering of the sun' ('*accessus solis*', original edition p. 51) should be translated as 'the place' or '*loci*' (Port. 'lugar'), is open to debate. D. W. Waters makes it clear that longitude was determined after taking into account the transit above the horizon of the sun (or star) being observed through the astrolabe (Waters, *Art of Navigation*, pp. 56–7; idem, 'Science and the Techniques of Navigation', pp. 208–12).

[3] The compass was the most important instrument on a 16th-century ship. For a full discussion and depiction of the compass, see Waters, *Art of Navigation*, pp. 21–30.

that, to catch the strength of the wind. There is also the skilful judgement and long experience of the sailors, and the observations, written down and frequently referred to, of other expert pilots, and with assistance from all these sources at once they are not likely to go astray.

Leo: I am delighted to have been able to examine these instruments, and although this is the first time I have had them explained I can see well enough how they are used. However, I have some questions about them, and would be glad if you could answer them.

Michael: I'll answer them as well as I can, and if I omit something my companions will supply it from the thorough grasp they have of all these things. I believe they have investigated them much more searchingly than I have, and I am sure that they are much less likely than I am to forget what they have been told.

Leo: Firstly I want to know what the sailors do when the sky is covered with clouds and shrouded in thick darkness, and the sea is agitated with various winds and storms. I don't see how, when the sun is hidden, they can work out their distance from it or calculate the degrees accurately.

Michael: If the weather on the voyage is as rough and difficult as you described just now they leave aside the astrolabe and put almost all their trust in the needle, which always indicates those two parts of the sky, as I said. There is also the expertise and the past experience of the sailors, who remember the readings taken in the prior calm, judge the distance covered since the storm got up, and taking into account the objective towards which the ship was headed, whether the wind, from the poop or tending to one side or the other, strengthens or slackens off, and various other circumstances too, as experience teaches them, they know pretty well where they are in the sea, and where they should be aiming; until the clouds disperse, the sun reappears, and the exact course to steer can be calculated with the instrument.

Leo: That's fine, but supposing the course is not directly north or south? In that case I don't see how you can work out the number of leagues to each degree, unless somehow it's exactly the same whatever direction the ship is sailing.

Michael: No, the number of leagues is not the same. It varies, depending where the ship is heading, and the more the course deviates from north or south the bigger it gets. But since the sailors know very well the number of leagues in each degree, whatever their course, depending on where it is that the voyage is headed, they can easily work out how much progress they have made each day. If their course takes them directly from east to west, or vice-versa, however, the distance from the pole and the equinoctial line stays the same, so they all have to rely on familiarity and long experience to help them judge how much way they have made each day, however strong or otherwise the wind. Of course the sailors most notable for their expertise, judgement, and experience are the ones least likely to err.

Lino: It occurs to me to ask also how it can be that, if one degree contains seventeen and a half leagues, it can be contained on this chart within such narrow bounds?

Michael: That is easily grasped if you realize that the space of land and sea is represented on this map not in its actual size but in an imagined, artificial size. The distance between two points is very short on the map, but in the mind it is thought of as containing ten, twenty, or thirty leagues, so that the measuring of the distance, short or long, between the points is always accurate, and in this way we can measure any distance, however great, on the earth. When you draw a man who is ten palms tall in a picture only one hand high, you will represent his real size in those smaller imagined dimensions, and you will not claim that the picture is the same size as the man. It is no different with this chart, this picture on parchment; stretches of sea and land are represented there, but by the use of a different scale the space they occupy is shrunk. Note also, however, that the proportions of the degrees vary according to the size of the chart, so that if you try to use on another chart the scale which is right for calculating degrees on this chart you are likely to get things wrong. So whether the chart is large or small, if the degrees are to scale the measuring, and the calculating of distances in leagues, is always completely accurate.

Leo: You have explained the chart to us very well. But now explain more about the power of the navigating needle, and how it is that it always points to the north and south.

Michael: I said before that it comes from the power of a certain stone called a magnet. If you rub one point of the needle against one end of the stone that point indicates south, and if you rub the other point against the other end it indicates north. And whenever the power taken from the stone becomes weaker it can be restored by applying it to and rubbing it against the stone again. This secret of applying the needle to the magnet was revealed to us by a natural human process of observation and examination, and we needn't marvel at this innate power of the magnet, since God provides abundantly for all the necessities of human life, not the least of which is navigation.

Leo: This is the Cape of Good Hope, isn't it, shown protruding into the sea like that on this map?

Michael: That is the famous Cape of Good Hope, known for being very dangerous, and for the storms which frequently arise there. We, however, by the divine favour, rounded it on 10 May in beautiful weather and with a favourable wind, and we celebrated the crossing to the far side, as it were, with cheering and rejoicing.

Lino: What was the reason for the cheering and rejoicing after you passed the Cape?

Michael: The reason is that until they round that promontory the sailors do not guarantee to reach Europe, because of the contrary winds which often blow before you make that crossing, especially if you have been rather late leaving India. The winds blowing from the bow often force the ships to stay long in the same place, and it's all they can do to withstand the force of the winds and the waves. And if that continues for a long time either the ships are severely shaken, or they are carried backwards, or it can even happen that enormous cracks appear, with great danger to life and property. Because of this it sometimes happens that the sailors do not dare to stand up any longer to the force of the wind and the waves, and are obliged to go back, at great expense, to a certain fortress of the Portuguese called Mozambique, which is 600 leagues away from the Cape of Good Hope, and to wait there for a full six months for an opportune time to sail; and this means the voyage takes a year and a half. And that is not the end of their trouble and labour, because the climate in Mozambique is very unhealthy, plagued by heat and other problems, which means that the health of the passengers is in great danger, and there are many who are carried off by illness, and end their lives before they end the voyage. And this is why everybody thinks there is good cause for rejoicing when they have passed the Cape of Good Hope; but in our case especially there was very good reason for rejoicing and giving many thanks to God, for we passed the promontory without any extra danger, and without rough seas or contrary winds.[1]

Lino: Indeed, for those who have never been in danger at all should be no less grateful than those who have been subjected to its terrors before escaping.

Mancio: How great God's goodness was to us in that place you will easily understand from what happened next, for the other ships which were in our group were beset by severe storms. One of them was struck so violently by the rough seas that the force of the waves surging on to the ship tore off the whole of the gallery which you usually have on the prow, and, disastrously, snatched up with it the captain, and his brother's son, who happened to be there.[2] They were calling desperately for help and begging for ropes, but the sailors could do nothing for them against the force of the sea, and both of them were buried in the depths of the sea, as in a sepulchre, to the profound grief of those who watched.

Michael: Mancio is right to remember that heartrending event. It plunged all who were there into the depths of sorrow, for they could see those poor men struggling with the waves, they could hear their shouting and wailing, and, knowing that there was nothing they could do for them as they died, they were overwhelmed with grief.

Leo: Dear God! That must indeed have been a most piteous spectacle, and it makes me realize how great the dangers are on these voyages.

Michael: You will learn the same thing from the dangers of our return journey to India; but we should go back now to pick up the thread of our story. Seventeen days after we passed the Cape of Good Hope, that is on the 27 May, we reached the port of the island of St Helena. This island is 500 leagues away from the Cape, and is situated out at sea at sixteen degrees, on the way to the equinoctial line, and this was the first and the only port where we landed during the voyage before we got to Europe.[3]

---

[1] Despite its reputation for disease and high mortality, Mozambique was the principal port of call for outward voyages of the *Carreira da Índia*. The companies of returning ships were indeed joyous if they could make it round the cape and on to St Helena. See Boxer, 'Principal Ports of Call', pp. 35–47, and 'Moçambique Island', *passim*.

[2] The captain was Estêvão Alvares and the ship was the *Salvador*. The boys saw the damage on their arrival in Lisbon (Fróis, *Première ambassade*, p. 28 n. 107).

[3] St Helena lies at latitude 15° 55′ 59″, 3,132 km from Cape Town.

Lino: It must be a great joy and thrill for both sailors and passengers when they reach that island, situated in the middle of the sea, an ideal resort and refuge, it seems, on such a long and troublesome journey, especially if there are people there to cultivate it, and it has in plenty other things needed for the voyage.

Michael: The island is entirely lacking in human habitation, except that one of those people who used to be called hermits sometimes stays on the island, leading a solitary life, and cultivates it (it's a common enough case) sufficiently to provide for the needs of the Portuguese who arrive there. So apart from the one or at most two who sometimes stay there, others are prohibited by order of the king from living on that island, since a few suffice to cultivate it and keep it fertile, and if there was a larger number of inhabitants they would easily consume all that it produces, on account of the poverty of the soil and the surroundings. But as far as those who arrive there are concerned it has, in the first place, abundant and permanent water sources, an ideal supply of water, and abundant herds, mainly of smaller animals, such as goats; also birds, both domestic such as hens, and wild, like partridges and others of that kind; initially they were left there by the Portuguese, but with the course of time they have produced offspring in abundance. There is besides a plentiful supply of delicious fruit from a variety of trees. As long as they are here the Portuguese make full use of all these items of nourishment, and they load great quantities of them on to the ships for food and bodily comfort.[1]

As well as the above advantages this island also offers excellent opportunities for hunting and fishing, and this provides not only physical recreation, but also adds not a little, by way of salt meat, to the food supplies for the voyage. So for eleven days we took advantage of all the delights that this most pleasant island had to offer; we procured a fine supply of food for the remainder of the voyage, and then we boarded the ship again, the winds were with us all the way, and on 10 August we reached the port of Lisbon, to which we had looked forward so much. The flood of joy we experienced as we entered that port is almost beyond the power of words to express; because it was the end, at last, of the troubles and difficulties with which we were from time to time afflicted in the course of that six month long voyage, and also because we could now feast our eyes on an amazing range of new things.[2]

We were enormously impressed in the first place, as we came into the famous port of that city, by the almost infinite multitude of ships which were there at anchor in that port; we counted more than 300 larger ships. With regard to the different types of ship, some were beaked, some not, some were longer, some shorter, some were cargo vessels,

---

[1] At this time a hermit was indeed living on the island. He informed the captain of the *Santiago* that the other ships in the voyage had left for Lisbon shortly before. This was a cause for concern because return voyages made their rendezvous at the island in order to proceed together to Lisbon for better protection from corsairs. The hermit was eventually repatriated on the orders of the king (Gualtieri, *Relationi*, pp. 46–7; *Dai Nihon Shiryō*, XI: 1, p. 65; Linschoten, *Voyage*, II, p. 257; Guzman, *Historia*, II, p. 232). As was the custom, the boys left messages, in Japanese, about themselves and their journey on the walls of the chapel on the island. Fróis mentions that they enjoyed fishing from the ship's deck during their stay on the island. See Fróis, *Première ambassade*, pp. 26–7; Pyrard, *Voyage*, I, p. 47; ibid., II, p. 791; Mundy, *Travels*, III: 2, pp. 415–16.

[2] During the final stages of the voyage, while crossing the Sargosso Sea, 32 of the people on board perished (Fróis, *Première ambassade*, p. 27). The original edition (p. 56) gives '*sexto idus Augusti*' for the day of their arrival but see above, p. 93 n. 1.

some swift-sailing, to say nothing for the moment of the triremes, galleys, yachts, and the multitude of skiffs and wherries; we were enormously impressed by both the quantity and the variety. As to the appearance of that vast city, who could do justice to it? Magnificent houses, lofty buildings, the high structure of walls and towers, all present themselves to the beholder, who has difficulty in deciding which to admire more, the scale of the city, the magnificence of the buildings, the great size of the churches, or the infinite multitude of people. In European cities the structure, the massive bulk and lofty elevation of the buildings, is such that anyone accustomed to seeing our walls and buildings cannot but be overwhelmed with admiration when they see it. But here I'll say no more about the grand scale of everything in Lisbon and Europe, since I'll be dealing with it a little later.

We were very happy when, as soon as the anchors were down in the sea, a great number of fathers of the Society, who knew of our coming from other ships in our group, came to meet us in very fast skiffs, delightedly celebrating our longed-for arrival, and welcoming us with every sign of love and benevolence. We were told that when we disembarked we would be greeted with some great and solemn display and procession, but we were tired from the long voyage, and were glad to turn to the fathers of the Society, who were ready to greet us with loving hospitality, rather than to wait for a public welcome from the people. And we were not disappointed, for we could see that the fathers in the professed house had the same love for us which we had experienced with the fathers in India and at home in Japan, and knew that all were truly of one heart and mind.

Lino: As soon as you reached Lisbon did you pay a visit to some leading man, or governor, as you did in Goa?

Michael: Yes, we paid a visit to Cardinal Albert, viceroy of the whole of Portugal, nephew of King Philip of Spain, and son of the king's sister, who was the wife of the emperor, and now, since her husband's death, lives in Spain.[1]

Leo: I remember that earlier in your story you mentioned the emperor, kings, princes, dukes, counts, and also prelates and bishops. We would be very glad if you would explain those names to us, and their different offices, and whether they have in Europe the names *dairi*, *kubō*, *kuge*, *yakata*, *kunishu*,[2] as we have, and indeed if you could deal with the whole matter of public office.

Michael: Gladly; I'll deal with the whole question of nobility and rank in Europe, provided we can leave it till tomorrow, since it will take quite some time, and it's already late.

Lino: Indeed; we should all call a halt to the story, and say goodnight.

---

[1] The emperor Maximilian II died in 1576 and María, who continued to interfere in imperial affairs to the annoyance of her sons, often on behalf of her brother's interests, returned to Spain heavily indebted in 1582 and took up residence in the Monasterio de las Descalzas Reales, Madrid (Fichtner, *Emperor Maximilian II*, pp. 209–13, 218).

[2] On these names see below, pp. 129–31.

COLLOQUIUM VII

About the things of Europe in general, and firstly of the sacred or ecclesiastical monarchy, and other lower ranks

Lino: The question Leo put last night was such a crucial one, and I have been so looking forward to hearing your answer to it that the hours of the day till the time of this meeting have seemed to last longer than usual. So now please begin your story with the ranks and offices of Europe.

Michael: There really are so many things, and such things, in Europe, that although I and my companions have often considered how best to go about explaining them, I have never been convinced that I have found any really satisfactory way to do it. Since things in Europe and in Japan differ (as they say) in genus and form,[1] it is not easy to explain to our people the way things are in Europe.[2] I am not well qualified to judge of these matters, but I'll do the best I can, and I'll spend the whole of tonight's colloquium treating of the twofold structure of government in Europe; for this twofold jurisdiction, on the one hand the sacred, or, to use the more common term, ecclesiastical, on the other the profane, generally known as the secular, forms the basis of all government and power in Europe. To the sphere of sacred jurisdiction belongs the disposal of everything conducing to the pious and religious performance of the worship of God, the best and the greatest; the refuting and banishing of errors about religion, however low or high the men who produce them; and the directing of the immortal souls of men, which are made for a life of eternal happiness, to that same end, which is above all of nature; directing them by the right path, according to both the laws hallowed by Christ, and those others which have come into being over the course of time. It belongs to the other jurisdiction, which I call profane and temporary, since it is common even to peoples wanting in true religion, although much better ordered among Christians, to keep to their duty in solid justice and the other virtues men who are subject to civil and political society, so as to keep the human

---

[1] Original edition (p. 58) '*genere ac forma (ut aiunt)*'. Aristotle analyses genus and species in the *Topics* as does Cicero in his *Topica* where he equates form with species (*Topica*, VII).

[2] Japan and Europe as opposites was a common trope among the Jesuits in Japan, although it was not deployed, as it was in the 19th century, to present Japan as a quaint, exotic topsy-turvy land. Rather it was deployed to emphasize and promote the need for a different, and in many respects unique, approach to missionary activity in Japan. Luís Fróis wrote a short tract on the matter, unpublished until the last century, *Tratado em que se contêm muito susinta e abreviadamente algumas contradições e diferenças de costumes entre a gente de Europa e esta província do Japão* (1585). See the editions by Schütte (*Kulturgegensätze*) and Garcia (Fróis, *Europa/Japão*), and the detailed analysis in Jorisssen, *Das Japanbild*. See also Fróis, *História de Japam*, III, pp. 177–8.

community in complete peace and tranquillity, without insurrection, brigandage, murder, adultery, and other public and antisocial crimes. The first of these two powers, therefore, is power over souls, and the second is said to provide for bodies. Both of these ways of administering human affairs have their origin in God, the best and the greatest, that most abundant source of all good and all order; but the one which rules the maintenance of bodies and of the human community can be discovered by the light of nature which is in the minds of men, whereas the other, much nobler and higher, is established by a supernatural light specially communicated to man by God.

From this it follows that among men of every nation, except for nations wholly rude and barbarous, there is always someone who defends civil society, and leads the people in the observance of duty, and this person normally has the title of king, or prince, or some similar name. This power is common to both Christian people and other peoples, but it is much better preserved among Christian people, and in a way much more attuned to the common good. But the sacred power, instituted for souls, is proper to Christendom, and specially instituted by Christ, the true Son of God, who came down from heaven to earth and showed to man the perfect example of right living, perfect in every respect. He designated one of his apostles, named Peter, His Vicar, and willed that the same power should be conserved in perpetuity by the continuous line of his successors. He is the Vicar of Christ who is called pope, that is father of fathers, and supreme pontiff, and supreme bishop, and all other power of government over the members of the Christian people is derived from him as from the supreme head. All other men in power, even profane power, recognize him as set in the place of Christ, and they frankly accept that they are his inferiors.

Besides this supreme pontiff and ecclesiastical monarch there are other ministers of divine things who are high in rank and authority; in the first place among these stand those who are as it were the hinges of this whole divine edifice, and are commonly called cardinals, and the Supreme Pontiff discusses with them, as with brothers and counsellors, all matters of great weight and moment; and it is they alone who, when the Supreme Pontiff dies, vote for another to replace him from their own number and assembly. These high-ranking priests, whom I called cardinals, hold the second place after the Supreme Pontiff, the maximum of honour is paid to them by other men, and sons of kings and princes regard themselves as very privileged if they are co-opted by the Supreme Pontiff to this most solemn and sacred order. The Supreme Pontiff, however, has more regard in his nomination and co-opting of cardinals to great virtue, notable wisdom, and outstanding merit, than to blood and nobility.[1]

---

[1] The relationship between the sacred and the profane is, of course, far more complex than is portrayed here. The secular authorities were as jealous of their prerogatives as the sacred and attempted to influence the conclaves to elect a new pope. At the time of *De Missione*'s composition, Spain was still attempting to exercise veto power. Moreover, the institutional powers of the College of Cardinals vis-à-vis the pope had already been weakened, the culmination of a long process. Popes tried to exercise control over the College and to reduce the influence of the secular rulers by creating cardinals from Italy, a good number of whom came from the Papal States. By the time of *De Missione* the College of Cardinals was becoming akin to a service nobility. Among the Cardinal Nephews, whom many popes employed in their administrations, were many highly competent individuals dedicated to serving the broader interests of the church rather than the narrower ones of their family. See Wright, *Early Modern Papacy*, pp. 47–52, 68–81, 113–14; Ippolito, 'Secretariat of State', pp. 132–57; Mara DeSilva, 'Senators or Courtiers', pp. 154–73.

Leo: High indeed is the rank of those fathers, on whose votes that supreme power depends, and from whose number is chosen he who is raised to the supreme summit. But I would like to know if there is a fixed number of fathers of that order, and where they have their seat.

Michael: The number is not entirely fixed, but generally the cardinals number sixty, and since they are counsellors to the Supreme Pontiff, they almost always have their domicile in Rome, with him.[1] Sometimes, however, they are sent to other provinces and countries in the name of the supreme bishop to deal with matters of great moment, and there they are received with all honour by the Christian kings and princes, and when the business is concluded they return to the Supreme Pontiff, whom they do not leave for other than weighty reasons. After these come, in descending order, the patriarchs,[2] archbishops, and bishops or pontiffs. The bishops take on the governing of dioceses and jurisdictions distributed by the pope, and each of them can refer particularly important questions to the archbishops,[3] who in turn are subordinate to the patriarchs, whose power extends to many provinces and kingdoms. All of these, as I said, are attentive to the supreme head of the Christian republic, namely the pope, and to his will and command, and it is by his authority, with advice from the cardinals, that the cardinals themselves, the patriarchs, the archbishops, and the bishops have their episcopal or other rank. Now since their dignity is very high, and adorned with both honours and revenues, how exalted must be the majesty of the supreme power, on which all depend for management, administration, and support. Besides all these there are also many other important priests who are subject to the bishops, with different responsibilities and duties, such as abbots, canons, and, among the canons, deans, archpriests, schoolmasters, and many others, each with his rank, his duties, and his dignity; and all of them have in abundance, and in accordance with their various positions, the income necessary to uphold the dignity of their positions.

But besides all these priests, who are said to be of the order of St Peter,[4] there are also many other religious men who are committed to sacred and divine things, but whose role is not so much to exhibit that ecclesiastical majesty and authority, but rather to renounce all external good things, binding themselves by solemn vows of poverty, chastity, and obedience, and to live a common and religious life in monasteries or colleges, according to the various different rules which the distinct groups profess. All of them, however, have their own governors of their houses, monasteries, and provinces, and all the orders acknowledge their own general superiors, all of whom, however, are subject to the pope as supreme head of all, for there is no member of this body, namely

---

[1] During the 16th century the size of the College had been increasing. In 1586 Sixtus V (1585–90) set the maximum membership of the College of Cardinals at 70, a figure that was maintained until John XXIII. Also in the course of the 16th century, cardinals increasingly came to reside in their dioceses. See Broderick, 'Sacred College of Cardinals', pp. 14–15, 20, 37, 45–6; Wright, *Early Modern Papacy*, pp. 51, 68–9.

[2] Originally the patriarchs were the bishops of early Christianity's most important sees: Rome, Alexandria, Antioch, Constantinople and Jerusalem. In the early modern period the heads of the various orthodox churches called themselves patriarchs and those who joined the Roman rite retained the title. The archbishops of Aquilea, Venice and Lisbon were styled patriarchs but this was honorific. See Wright, *Early Modern Papacy*, p. 317.

[3] The original edition (p. 60) gives '*ad archipraesules, siue archiepiscopos*'. *Archipraesules* is redundant.

[4] I.e. the secular clergy.

the Christian people, no member however distinguished or elevated, whose governance does not depend on that supreme head. And the fathers of the Society, who come to us here from Europe, belong to these families and orders of religious men, for the Society of Jesus is one of the families of religious men who devote themselves to living out the Christian life perfectly.

Leo: My dear Michael, it gives me great joy and delight to hear you discourse so aptly and appositely on these most grave matters; but to help us understand this question more clearly, explain about these religious men, who pronounce those three solemn vows, not being subject like others to the bishops of the various dioceses.

Michael: Since the religious men of whom we are speaking have committed themselves totally to divine worship, and live outside the press of other men, it was right that they should have their own moderators and superiors, as I said, who are subject to their general superiors, and whose duty it is to keep them to their proper rule of life; at the same time, however, they treat the ordinary and ecclesiastical bishops whose helpers they are with all reverence and honour; they are inducted by them into holy orders, so as to offer the august sacrifice of the most holy Eucharist, and they receive from them the faculties of preaching to and teaching the people, and of hearing confessions of sins; and by them, finally, they are assigned the role of assistants and helpers of their own pastors in all things necessary for the instruction of the people. In domestic and institutional matters, however, and in matters concerning their own religious family, they obey their own moderators, prefects, and superiors, and they in turn obey the Supreme Pontiff himself.

Lino: Do the men of these families, or orders, who profess the three vows, all have the same rule of life with regard to food and clothing, or are there differences in certain things between one order and another?

Michael: Just as the members of the human body have the same predetermined end of preserving life, but all have different functions, so all religious orders of men pursue the same end, the perfect Christian life, but make use of different means. Just as in the case of the two most holy sisters, Martha and Mary,[1] both of whom received Christ very well when long ago He was living on earth, but each of whom received Him in a different way, so also some of these religious men give themselves entirely to action in pursuit of those things which pertain to the common good, while others have their eyes fixed totally on the contemplation of divine things; others again take, as far as possible, both parts, being sometimes active, sometimes contemplative, and using various means for the feeding and building up of the body. This variety in the means gives rise to the variety of orders; far from upsetting this body, it gives it a most beautiful form.

Leo: From that account of their way of living it appears to me that our priests in Japan, ministers of false religion, are remarkably similar to the religious men of Europe, if you consider their way of living in monasteries, and their bearing and refinement.

---

[1] Luke 10:38–42. Martha was the more active sister; Mary the more contemplative.

Michael: Looking at externals I would say that between the two there is indeed some similarity of appearance and form, but that when you penetrate to the things within the Christians and Europeans are as far from Japanese religious men as the highest point in the heavens from the centre of the earth, as you will easily appreciate from what follows. If I set myself to point to differences between the two, I would say first that our men enter religion because they are suffering from poverty and penury, and in order to enjoy a finer and more abundant style of life, and for that reason they choose, in so far as in them lies, to live in certain very wealthy monasteries and opulent temples. Rather than cutting themselves off from the empty and transitory things of this life, they pursue those things more keenly and avidly after committing themselves to the (as they falsely think) religious life; if, therefore, they could find another way of acquiring a large income, honour and rank, riches and property, they would never enclose themselves within the walls of a monastery.[1] In the religious families of European men, on the other hand, things are very different. There, wealthy and noble men, who could have led a profane life with the highest honours and an abundance of human things, disengage themselves from all vain goods, knowing that they are hindrances to the perfect life, and flee from the polluted stream of men as from a raging sea to the harbour of the religious life; there they profess the three vows of poverty, chastity, and obedience, and live modestly, chastely, and submissively, allowing no stain of vice to defile their souls; and this is not at all how it is with our *bonze*s.

And although there are in Europe, as I said, various orders of religious, full of noble and illustrious men, since only the fathers of the Society have come to Japan, and we were brought up among them, and sent together with them on this embassy, in order to support the point I was making just now let me take a few examples only from among men of this Society. When we ourselves were staying in Rome, we saw, as eyewitnesses, that certain noble men, who previously had prospered, with riches, resources, and nobility, and who had every prospect of carrying off major honours, were co-opted into the Society. Among them was one of the clerics of the Camera,[2] whose dignity is such that from that office they are very frequently enrolled in the College of Cardinals, that most elevated senate. He, however, spurning great revenues and casting away the certain expectation of higher rank, gave himself totally to God and the Society.[3] The second was the son of the duke of Terra Nova and governor of Milan, who in the same way turned his back on all the pleasures and riches of life, entered the same Society, and gave himself up totally to the religious life.[4] The third case which we saw was a certain most illustrious marquess of noble birth, of

---

[1] The wealth and ostentation of Buddhist monasteries had been criticized by Japanese as well. In the early Muromachi period (1336–1573) the temples had become rich but during the civil wars their wealth, landholdings and political power declined, although the *gozan* monasteries emerged in better shape from the conflicts than others. See Collcutt, *Five Mountains*, pp. 249–81; McMullin, *Buddhism and the State*, pp. 29–58, 240–42.

[2] The Apostolic Camera, the body charged with administering the finances of the papacy, at the time one of the most important branches of the Roman curia.

[3] Giovanni Baptista Lambertini of Bologna. See Sacchini, *Historiae Societatis Iesv Pars Qvinta*, p. 236.

[4] Simeone Tagliavia d'Aragona (1550–1604), son of Carlo Tagliavia d'Aragona, duke of Terranova, prince of Castelvetrano, viceroy of Sicily and Catalonia, governor of Milan 1583–92. Simeone became a cardinal deacon in 1583 and received the red hat in 1585. He is buried in the Jesuit Gesù church in Rome. The boys met him in Rome and his father in Milan.

the famed Gonzaga family, who scorned honours, a great name, and other things in order to consecrate himself wholly to reaching the summit of the perfect Christian life.[1]

I can also refer you here to the Superior General of the whole Society, the reverend Father Claudio Aquaviva, still living now, and to whose charity, benignity, and other outstanding virtues we ourselves, who were there with him in Rome, can bear witness; he was the son of the duke of Atri, he enjoyed a very high degree of authority and of favour under Pope Pius V, and there is no doubt that he would very soon have been raised to the cardinalate, since in fact his nephew, the son of his brother, was afterwards made a cardinal in his place.[2] All these things, however, he repudiated, choosing a safer life in the Society, and he made such progress in virtue and Christian piety that he was raised to the office of Superior General, with the full approval of the fathers. Not less worthy of memory and record is the example of another Superior General, namely Father Francisco de Borja, who had the governance of the whole Society not many years ago. He was the most illustrious duke of the city of Gandia, in Spain, with an abundance of wealth and resources of all kinds, and governed and steered all of Catalonia, but under divine inspiration he renounced all those things for which men so ardently long, and made for the safe anchorage of the Society, where being outstanding in every kind of virtue he was eventually elected general with the votes of all the fathers, and while in that office, and busy with other important matters, he passed away gloriously from this life.[3]

Lino: Is it possible that men so rich and noble should prefer poverty to wealth and obedience to nobility?

Michael: I don't have far to look for witnesses, since my companions are here, and they saw several of those to whom I have been referring.

Mancio: What need is there of our testimony? All over Italy and Spain we spoke to men of the highest nobility, sons of dukes, marquesses, and counts, who were living a holy life in the Society, and we were in admiration at their greatness of soul in spurning all the fleeting and empty things of this life.

---

[1] The future St Aloysius Gonzaga (1568–91), son of Ferdinand I, marquess of Castiglione. He entered the Society 25 November 1585, the same day as Lambertini, by which time the boys had already left Rome (Sacchini, *Historiae Societatis Iesv Pars Qvinta*, p. 236). However, he was in Mantua when they visited the city and his decision to enter the Society, against his parents' wishes, was finalized while they were there. See ARSI, Ital. 159, f. 85v; Yūki, 'Shinshiryō', p. 190; Grendler, *University of Mantua*, pp. 41–4. Not all families were happy to see their firstborn enter the Society. The parents of Antonio de Padilla, son of the governor of Castile and the countess of Buendía and inheritor of these titles, unsuccessfully tried to prevent their offspring from becoming a Jesuit at age fifteen. He went on to become an outstanding professor of theology and preacher. See Sánchez, 'La Compañía de Jesús', pp. 196–7.

[2] His nephew was Giulio Aquaviva d'Aragona (1546–74) who became a cardinal in 1570. His brother, Ottavio, became a cardinal in 1591. The family furnished a number of cardinals.

[3] Francisco de Borja (1510–72), son of Juan de Borja, duke of Gandía, succeeded to the title 1543. He married Eleanor de Castro Melo e Menezes with whom he had eight children. After her death he entered the Society of Jesus in 1548 and was elected general in 1565. He was canonized in 1671. He took a great interest in the Japan mission. When he decided to enter the Society Loyola recommended him to keep his decision secret, which he did for a few years, 'for the world does not have ears to hear such a clack (*estampida*)'. See O'Neill and Dominguez, *Diccionario histórico*, II, pp. 1605–11, esp. p. 1606.

Martin: These are all matters of common knowledge, and need no further testimony; but if we look for examples even from antiquity, we can read, recorded in ancient documents, how many princes, kings, emperors left their principalities, kingdoms, and empires, to devote all their efforts and attention to acquiring the riches of heaven.

Julian: In support of the same argument there is also the point that we find in the Christian republic not only men, who are by nature stronger in spirit, but also many women, who are of the weaker and more fragile sex, including very noble women, who declare war on the things of this world, subject to the changes of time, and who devote and consecrate themselves totally to the worship of God, most joyously offering the flower of their virginity to Christ their heavenly spouse, living religiously in convents set up for this purpose, far from familiar association with men; so much so that they scarcely allow themselves to be seen even by their relatives, giving all their time to divine prayer and singing, and to the contemplation of heavenly things, and none to idleness or vain and useless chatter; and, with the example of Christ the Lord before their eyes, Christ who willed to be obedient even unto death, they allow themselves to be totally ruled and directed by the judgment and will of superiors commonly known as abbesses. It is difficult to tell you how great the number is of these women and these convents throughout Europe, or how well everything concerning these holy virgins is administered, either by the prelates charged with their care, or by men of the religious order or family of the same name. And it would be a mistake to think that these virgins are women who are unable to marry well because of family poverty, for we ourselves witnessed how the daughter of the emperor,[1] who holds the highest and first of all worldly ranks, despising all the titles and riches of this life, entered a convent together with other very distinguished women, providing, with her virtue, a remarkable example not only for the living, but for all posterity; and, partly because she wished to imitate her, her mother too, wife of the emperor and sister of King Philip, after the death of her husband entered the same convent, and although she did not take solemn vows she resolved to live there piously and religiously for the remainder of her life.

Leo: What you relate about religious men and women in Europe is indeed remarkable; for we, judging the things of Europe by our own measure, assumed that only the needy, and those suffering from poverty, would take refuge in religious life as a solution; but now you have shown us that that is far from being the case.

Michael: We too carried that idea with us when we knew nothing of European things, but when we had travelled through Europe, and seen and, so to speak, handled those things, we abandoned that opinion and came to a very different one, for we recognized that these extraordinary examples of a deliberate change of life must indeed be attributed to the power of Christian faith. This power is so great that it can easily free souls caught in all sorts of business and riches, and impel them to care only for divine things, like Matthew, apostle of the most blessed Christ, who left his tables and his money bags, and

---

[1] Margaret of Austria (1567–1633), daughter of the emperor Maximilian II and María of Austria. She became a nun in the Monasterio de las Descalzas Reales, Madrid.

found himself led by Christ the Lord away from money and profit to the perfect and apostolic way of life.¹

But let us proceed to the second difference between religious men in Europe, and our religious men, which is as follows: ours differ in their behaviour, their treatment of the body, and their way of life, and similarly they differ from one another in their religion; large numbers of families of religious men have taken root throughout Japan, and the number of different opinions, or rather errors, about religion and divine worship is just as large. But in Europe religious men, even if they differ in their treatment of the body and their manner of life, and wear the special insignia of various saints, nevertheless worship the one God and the one Christ, Son of God, they hold the same faith and the same law, they take the same vows of poverty and obedience, and all strive wholeheartedly towards the same end; and this is a very strong argument for the truth and certainty of the Christian religion, which so many orders and degrees of persons follow in exactly the same way. Just as there is one spirit and one heart in one body, so also in the Christian republic there is one spirit and one will. The result is that when the most holy fathers have convened from different nations to remove errors which have from time to time arisen, there has always been a unanimous consensus, they have come to the same conclusion, and they have kept constant the faith handed down by Christ and the Apostles, complete, and without change to any part.

Lino: I am very satisfied with this point, and it seems to me a very sound argument for the Christian religion. But with regard to corroboration of the Christian religion, all of that is dealt with very well in the catechism composed by the fathers,² so we should leave it and return to our theme.

Michael: The third difference between men here and European men committed to religion and divine worship is this: the Japanese do not profess either poverty, or chastity, or obedience. Where their way of life and personal property are concerned all of them are very keen to have riches and possessions. With regard to bodily integrity, it is not for me to try to give you an account of the sordid degradation and filth in which they engage. And as for obedience, each of them insists on having his own way, and thus the *bonzes* rely not on true and solid virtue, but on shadows and images, that is to say on their external rites and ceremonies.³ In the Christian republic, on the other hand, men committed to divine

---

¹ Matthew 9:9.

² See above, pp. 16, 37.

³ For Valignano's discussion of Buddhism, see *Historia*, ch.19 *passim*; *Sumario*, ch. 3 *passim*. Álvarez-Taladriz (Valignano, *Adiciones*, p. 393 n. 4) suggests that Valignano and other Jesuits kept their remarks about Buddhism and its origins deliberately short, reflecting St Paul's dictum not to 'give heed to fables and endless genealogies' (Timothy 1:4). There is, nevertheless, a wealth of information about Buddhism throughout the Jesuit writings on Japan. Moreover, if imitation is a high form of flattery, then Valignano's insistence that Jesuit houses in Japan be organized in the manner of the *gozan* monasteries rates highly on a mimetic scale. Unlike other Buddhist institutions, Zen monasteries had largely kept out of the civil wars. See Valignano, *Il cerimoniale*, ch.1 *passim*, and above, p. 5. The 'sordid degradation and filth' Valignano refers to is presumably *shudō* 衆道, the expression for *nanshoku* 男色 or male love as practised in Buddhist temples in Japan. *Shudō* was indeed common in Buddhist monasteries and openly acknowledged, unlike in European religious institutions, although it was not without its Japanese critics. Male love was also tolerated in secular society, as the Jesuits knew well. The Jesuits, from Xavier on, commented upon the prevalence of sodomy in Buddhist monasteries in Japan and condemned

worship aim for a true and solid basis of virtue, and when they establish this in their inmost soul, they cannot but show it with many signs and evidences in their external bearing and manner; but all of that proceeds and springs from that root in the soul. And the same thing that I have said of men also applies to the women, who, withdrawn in their convents in Europe, similarly outdo the *bikuni*; where the *bikuni* grasp only the shadow, the nuns have true and solid virtue.¹

Lino: You are quite right, and I think the difference between the two is the same as the difference between the two religions, the Christian true and certain, the pagan an empty shadow.

Leo: That is indeed true, but I should like to know how those religious men, with their profession of poverty, manage to support themselves.

Michael: They rely on the divine promise, transmitted to us by Christ in the Sacred Scripture, that nothing will be lacking to him who casts away vain and fleeting things for the sake of Christ, but that on the contrary he will have all things in abundance. Therefore religious men live in poverty and in affluence, in moderation and in abundance, having nothing, as St Paul says, and possessing all things.² This may seem contradictory, so let me explain further. The religious men give up, as far as they can, everything which is theirs by right; but the princes and kings instructed in the Christian religion do not allow them to die of hunger or thirst, but most generously provide the monasteries where they live with ample income, so that although no individual there has anything of his own, the community has an abundant supply of all things. The result is that the individual is not troubled about providing for himself, nor does he suffer from the want of anything in his community. And the same is true of their houses and monasteries, which although they may have no annual income, nevertheless live fittingly and appropriately on the alms with which they are abundantly provided.

Leo: It is not difficult for us to accept that it is as you say in Europe, but how is it that the fathers of the Society here in Japan, so far from Europe and possessing nothing,

---

the practice. Valignano specifically equated the introduction of Buddhism into Japan and the beginning of sodomy in a society which until then, he claimed, had not known the practice (*Historia*, pp. 138–9). Sodomy was common in China as well and, ironically, the celibate Jesuits were suspected of being sodomites. See Spence, *Memory Palace*, pp. 220–31; Schalow, 'Kūkai and the Tradition of Male Love', pp. 215–30; Faure, *Red Thread*, esp. chs 5 and 6. In Renaissance and Reformation Europe sodomy was officially condemned. In practice, trials, punishment, and toleration, varied according to time, place and confession. In Italy, despite the draconian punishment (burning alive for those found guilty) a thriving homosexual underworld existed, including within religious institutions. In Aragon, a number of sodomy trials before the Inquisition involved members of monastic institutions and resulted in death sentences for the defendants. See Ruggiero, *Boundaries of Eros*, esp. ch. 6; Trexler, *Public Life in Renaissance Florence*, pp. 379–82, 388, 470, 475, 541; Wiesner-Hanks, *Christianity and Sexuality*, pp. 87–9, 126–8; Najemy, *History of Florence*, pp. 244–9.

¹ 比丘尼 (Sanskrit, *bhikkuṇi*) Buddhist nuns, many from imperial or aristocratic families. Nuns and nuns' temples were important in Japanese Buddhist traditions.

² II Corinthians 6:10.

nevertheless incur such costs, building so many colleges, and churches, and seminaries, and feeding so many of their own members and of the boys in the seminaries?

Michael: Those costs and expenses, which you see incurred by the fathers, are covered by money supplied from the divine treasures, which the Lord Himself promised would never be exhausted; for although the fathers of the Society have no lands in Japan they construct so many residences, they feed such a number of their own members and of boys, as well as spending money on other things, that it is right to credit the availability of funds to Divine Providence. However, neither is the care and solicitude of the Supreme Pontiffs lacking, especially of Pope Gregory XIII of happy memory, and of the present Pope Sixtus V (whom God preserve unharmed) who, observing from their high watchtower the needs of Japan, magnanimously decreed that six thousand ducats be assigned annually to the fathers for their expenses. But since the annual outgoings are at least twice that amount, it is clear that God provides very well for the fathers. Nor are the Portuguese kings lacking in generosity, for they provide kingly help for the fathers resident in Japan with liberal alms from their treasury.[1]

Lino: Why is it that popes and kings provide in this way for the fathers who live so far away?

Michael: The first reason is that mutual Christian charity so strongly urged by Christ, and which will earn a great reward in heaven. Then there is their zeal for the common good; the Christian princes appreciate the abundance of the fruit resulting from the arrival and the residence of the fathers in Japan, and it is only reasonable for them to give to religious men a good part of the good things which God in his great goodness has given to them. And the pope, being the supreme head of the whole Christian republic, that being as it were the body, the supreme head which provides for the needs of all the other members, is concerned not only for the Christians whom he has close by, but also for those far distant from him, such as the Japanese, and he relieves their need as if they were present before him in his sight; and he looks out with great providence on the fathers who are intent on striving to benefit the Japanese people. We Japanese ought to be greatly ashamed about this, since the very law of nature as well as the divine precept prescribes that those who work in a place should get from that place fruit sufficient to sustain life;

---

[1] In his brief *Mirabilia* (13 June 1583) Gregory XIII created an annual subsidy of 4,000 ducats for the Japan mission payable for 20 years. His successor, Sixtus V, increased the sum by 2,000 ducats on 23 May 1585, one of the results of the embassy. In fact the additional sum appears to have been paid only in the first and last years of Sixtus's pontificate. Gregory XIV and Clement VIII revised the subsidy back to its original 4,000 ducats but payment was irregular and often considerably less than the given subsidy. In December 1586 Valignano estimated the money raised in Portugal, India and China for Japan at 3,303,900 *réis* while the actual expenditure in Japan was 4,452,000 *réis*. The Jesuits made up for the shortfall from benefactions from the Christian daimyo and by trading in silk of which they had an official annual allotment of 50 *peculs*, secured by Valignano in negotiations in 1578 and 1584. But shipwrecks and other unforeseen events meant that the mission's cash flow was often in a parlous state. As Valignano put it, the fate of the mission hung by a 'thread'. Jesuit involvement in the silk trade with Japan was controversial among the Jesuits and was fiercely attacked by the mendicants. See *Documenta Indica*, XIII, 406–7, 451; XIV, pp. 37, 56–7, 82, 498, 500, 627 esp. n. 22; Valignano, *Apologia*, pp. 203–8; Schütte, 'Die Wirksamkeit der Päpste', pp. 205–6; Cooper, 'Mechanics', pp. 423–33; *idem*, *Rodrigues the Interpreter*, pp. 244–7.

the fathers of the Society, however, come to us from far distant provinces and kingdoms, and not only lay out all their effort and industry for our salvation and advantage, but also bring with them from outside food and resources to cover essential expenses, and share a large part of these with our men and youth. The reason for this is on the one hand the penury of our people, on the other the upheavals of the wars which constantly threaten us.

Leo: I fully appreciate how little the crop so far harvested from the Japanese field corresponds to the labour and diligence of the fathers, and I think this is to be ascribed to the causes you have identified. There will come a time, if God hears our prayers, when many powerful princes accept Christianity; the tumult of wars will be stilled, and with the advent of peace everywhere it will be possible for them to remunerate the fathers who have deserved so well of us with assistance, even with an annual income, and thus to treat them as liberally and generously as they used to treat the priests of false religion. But I would like to know if there are any from those families of religious men that you have told us about who are appointed as cardinals, or bishops, or archbishops.

Michael: To those religious whom I spoke of the way is open not only to those ranks which you mentioned, but also to the supreme seat of the papacy, which is now held by the most holy pontiff Sixtus V,[1] of the Franciscan order, who rose through all the ranks of honour, amid the highest praise, to that most exalted position; and in the same way many others from the families of religious men have been raised to the cardinalate and the papacy. It is easy for them to rise to those most eminent seats, since those chosen for positions of high ecclesiastical rank are men distinguished for virtue and learning, in which these families of religious abound.

Lino: Is there no order of religious men barred from access to those highest of positions?

Michael: None, as far as I know, except for the Society of Jesus, which itself wanted to close off its own access to those distinguished degrees of dignity. Because of this, when the three solemn vows which we spoke about before are pronounced in the Society, one more is added to them, a vow in no way to aspire to those honours and titles of rank, and firmly and persistently to reject them if they are offered; with the possible exception of cases where the fathers of the Society are compelled to accept them by the Supreme Pontiff's command, which no one is permitted to break or violate.[2] And although the Society has had, up till now, such an abundance of men of outstanding virtue, and honours of that sort have very frequently been offered to them, none of them so far has ever accepted any, apart from those who were chosen for the expedition to Ethiopia,[3] and took on their

---

[1] Felice Peretti (24 April 1585–23 August 1590), a Franciscan born into a poor family.

[2] The fourth vow is one of 'special obedience to the sovereign pontiff regarding missions' (O'Malley, *First Jesuits*, pp. 298–301, esp. p. 298).

[3] In 1554, at the instigation João III of Portugal, Ignatius supported the consecration of three Jesuits who were to be sent to Ethiopia along with twelve other Jesuits in the expectation that Portuguese assistance to the Ethiopians in their war against Muslims would bring about a union between the Ethiopian and Roman churches. The mission was a failure. See ibid., pp. 327–8.

shoulders the heavy burden of a province abounding not in wealth and resources but in labour and difficulties. One of these was the most reverend Sebastião de Morais, chosen to be Bishop of Japan, but who died on the way here, so we have heard, to the sorrow of all and to the detriment of our country of Japan.[1] At the moment the Japanese field is fertile not in wealth and power but in labour, trouble, and danger, so it is clear that whoever has the responsibility for farming it and is appointed bishop, must be regarded as having been given a very heavy burden rather than any gratifying honour.

Leo: I would very much like to know why it is that, although the way is open to those honours for men of outstanding virtue and virtue and wisdom from the other families of religious, the Society closes that road off to its own people and completely blocks the entrance.

Michael: When we stayed in Rome and other places we made repeated enquiries about that, and I shall give you in brief the result of our investigations. The first reason is that, although religious men from all the orders are raised to honours and dignities of this kind, and in these positions they bear good fruit for the Christian republic, the Society has excluded itself from these offices so as to be able to devote itself in peace and freedom to the occupations of its Institute,[2] and to be able the better to attain to the perfection which it professes, without any temptation to exchange its proper state for another; especially since on the one hand there is no lack of men eminently suitable for those dignities, and very ready to accept them, and on the other there are not quite so many ready to give themselves to the occupations and exercises of the Society. The second reason is that although these honours and offices are very fruitful for Christendom, and buttress the splendour and majesty of Christendom, by their very nature, as exalted ranks, they are desirable, and they easily move the wills of men to pursue them; and since attachments of this kind are incompatible with the submission of soul and other virtues which the Society professes, the Society is right to bar the way to those urges which belong to ambition, fearing that if the way was open to these honours, the way would also be wide open to ambition, and this would impede the perfecting of submission and other virtues. Thirdly, although the men raised to the rank of pontiff from the religious orders serve the Christian republic exceedingly well, those religious orders suffer no small loss, being deprived of men outstanding in knowledge and in virtue, and lament the snatching away of those on whose shoulders they depended as prop and support. The Society, therefore, seeing what a disadvantage this could be, and learning from the harm which others had suffered, refuses to allow itself to be deprived of those whose defence, like veteran soldiers, can repel any enemy attack, and whose strength, as of well brought up and full-grown sons, can support parental old age. And these are the main reasons which led Ignatius,

---

[1] Provincial of Portugal and first bishop of Japan, Morais died en route in Mozambique in August 1588. These and a number of other appointments were exceptions to Loyola's intention to exempt Jesuits from church office.

[2] 'The "Institute" of the Society of Jesus, in Jesuit parlance, is the sum total of papal documents, statutes (*Constitutiones*) of the founder, enactments (*decreta*) of general congregations, and ordinances and instructions of generals which contain ascetical, juridical, and methodological norms for the life and work of its members' (Schütte, *Valignano's Mission Principles*, 1: 1, p. 45, n. 12). O'Malley states it 'was a manifestation of the character and of the deepest values and sensibilities of the organization' (*First Jesuits*, pp. 370–75, esp. p. 370).

first and most holy founder of the Society, to refuse to open the way for his sons to ranks and honours of that kind.[1]

Leo: This kind of rule of life seems to me right, but at the same time I am afraid that the Society may remain somewhat inferior to other orders, to whom the way to the highest honours is not barred; and that there may be few who wish to be co-opted into an order so opposed to honours and dignities.

Michael: On the contrary. To despise honours is to put oneself in direct opposition to the desires and appetites of human nature, which send us hurtling along towards glory and high position; therefore all men appreciate how great and how solid is the virtue of the Society, which totally rejects honours. And when they have this idea of the Society, aristocrats and leading men are so far from despising it that for this very reason they are in admiration at the virtue of the Society in despising human things. And we can confidently bear witness from our own experience to this opinion which people have of the Society, since we not only heard many nobles and prelates recount wonderful things of the Society, but were also dumbfounded by the public declarations of the Supreme Pontiffs Gregory XIII and Sixtus V about the Society, and the glad acclamation, so to speak, which they accorded it.

Lino: What you have said makes me appreciate something else, namely the great mistake our people are making when they convince themselves that the fathers of the Society have migrated here because forced to do so by poverty and want; or at least that they are using their zeal for the propagation of the Christian faith as a sort of veil to mask their intention and determination to obtain some supreme power in Japan, and cunningly, like the *bonze* of Osaka,[2] to incite the people to defect from our own rulers. The Society's

---

[1] Loyola had insisted that Jesuits should not accept honours nor become involved in worldly affairs and the fifth general congregation expressly forbade Jesuits from involving themselves in 'what is secular and belongs to political affairs and the governance of states'. However, for the founder, and his successors, there was a difference between what was said, and decreed, and what was done. In practice Jesuits became involved in secular matters whether by accepting office (Valignano himself became, albeit once, an ambassador of the viceroy of India on his return to Japan in 1590) or becoming confessors to princes, an issue which caused great controversy among the early Jesuits when it first arose in Portugal in the 1550s. Loyola himself provided the ultimate justification for Jesuit involvement in secular affairs: whatever promoted the greater glory of God. See Padberg et al., *For Matters of Greater Moment*, p. 12; Marques, 'Confesseurs des princes', pp. 213–28; Höpfl, *Jesuit Political Thought*, pp. 53–63; Navarro, *La Compañía de Jesus*, pp. 47–81.

[2] Kennyo Kōsa (1543–92), eleventh abbot of Ishiyama Hongan-ji, a *Jōdo Shin*, or True Pure Land, temple in Osaka. Kennyo had fortified the temple and resisted Oda Nobunaga's attempts to disarm and pacify it until 1580. Kennyo was a bogeyman for the Jesuits who were sensitive to any suggestion that they had similar ambitions to advance their religious agenda with the use of force. During Hideyoshi's Kyushu campaign in 1586–7, the then vice-provincial, Gaspar Coelho, whom a fellow Jesuit described as more a 'captain of arms than a pastor of souls', foolishly involved himself in the conflict, contrary to Valignano's orders, by promising to furnish Hideyoshi with Portuguese armaments and saying that he would ensure that the Christian daimyo of Kyushu would support him against his enemies. These daimyo were appalled and warned Coelho that he was damaging the Christian cause in Japan. They were right. One of the reasons Hideyoshi gave for banishing the missionaries in 1587 was that they were behaving too much like the *bonze* of Osaka. Later, in 1598, Valignano used the example of the *bonze* of Osaka as an argument against the presence of the mendicants in Japan. See *Cartas*, II, f. 174v; Álvarez-Taladriz, 'El padre vice provincial Gaspar Coelho', p. 47; 'La persecución de 1587', pp. 96–7, 104, 105; *Documenta Indica*, XVI, pp. 547–8; Valignano, *Apologia*, pp. 49–50; Elison, *Deus Destroyed*, pp. 119–23; Tsang, *War and Faith*, pp. 29–30, 223–4, 227–33.

most praiseworthy principle of repudiating honours, even sacred honours, totally uproots and removes this suspicion from our minds.

Michael: This error which you have referred to is rooted entirely in ignorance firstly of Christian things, and secondly of the constancy of the fathers of the Society in despising office and the privilege which attends it. For those who know nothing of charity, the root of all good deeds, nor of the labour which Christ, the supreme teacher, undertook for our salvation, nor of the zeal of religious men in imitating Him and proclaiming His deeds, cannot convince themselves that there are men who hasten to us from far distant kingdoms, making such journeys by sea and by land, with no hope or wish for riches, honour, or dominion. But we, who not only saw or heard of all the things which are in Europe, but engraved and imprinted them on our inmost senses, know with total certainty, first, that the fathers of the Society live much more comfortably in Europe, in a way much more conducive to an agreeable life, and troubled by no lack of necessities (in some cases they spurn great wealth in order to enter the Society, but in the same Society they have abundant provision from income and alms), so that when they come to Japan it is solely in order to procure our salvation; secondly, we know that when they live here, for the sake of Christ they go without many things which make for a comfortable life, and to which they have been accustomed from childhood, in order to garner a more desirable fruit, namely the salvation of our souls. And if our people could throw off the darkness of this error and direct the light of their minds to these things, they would see that the fathers of the Society, who bring money and provisions to Japan from elsewhere, and indeed alleviate our poverty, seek no material advantage in Japan, and lack none in their own countries. Is it credible, besides, that foreigners, strangers, should abandon their homeland and condemn themselves to the misery of exile in order to pursue honours and power, when they can more easily and more happily obtain these honours and power, if they wish to, in their own countries, where, as we can testify, they are held in high honour, the more so because, as we already said, they very often do have these things offered to them and reject them. We should therefore accept, since it is clearer than daylight, that in coming to us the fathers are in quest of nothing human, temporary, and vain, but of what is immortal, perpetual, and eternal.[1]

Their zeal to bring these benefits to all takes them not only here to Japan, but also to an infinite number of other parts of the world, and there they live holily, religiously, and for the common good, no longer as Europeans, but doing without the comforts and delights of their own land, where it is normal and natural for all to find happiness, they adopt the customs of the Japanese, the Chinese, the Indians, or whatever people they are living among. All this can be understood from what I have already said. I have said, for example, that throughout India many fathers have built houses and are living according to the different customs of the various peoples there, sharing the way of life of the indigenous peoples so as to be able to give them the Christian religion. It is almost impossible to describe how unpalatable their experiences in this can be, and the ordeals to which they submit in adapting themselves to peoples rude and barbarous, and in toiling mightily to learn the languages of so many nations. Those who undertake all this, often

---

[1] On Japanese suspicions and accusations that the missionaries had only come to Japan to improve their material lot, see Valignano, *Sumario*, pp. 146–7; *Adiciones*, pp. 668–9, 718–19; *Apologia*, p. 49.

in the face of many insults, while turning away the honours offered to them in their own country, must be adjudged to be motivated not by rank, power, wealth or resources, but by zeal for some higher good.

But there is no need to bring forward as testimony the things to which they subject themselves in foreign countries and provinces; here in Japan we can see for ourselves how the fathers, in order to win over the hearts and minds of our people, adapt themselves to Japanese usage and custom in food, clothing, language, and other matters, and change their own nature, brought up to other things, for something very different, meanwhile being subjected by the pagans to attacks and harassment of various kinds.[1] Their tolerance of all these things, as I said, grows like a branch from the root which is charity. We know from experience that the European fathers, rooted in this same charity, wish above all else to suffer much hardship and frustration for Christ. For the more letters they receive from Japan, letters in which they are told of labours borne, dangers faced, trials suffered, the more astonishingly eager they are to undergo the same labours, trials, and dangers for Christ. They compare themselves with the fathers who are here with us, rejoicing for them because they are on the direct road to heaven, the road passing, as it should, through the Cross of Christ; and greatly grieving for themselves because they have a life of comfort, which acts as a distraction, deflecting them from their ultimate heavenly target. But this most agreeable subject has kept us talking well into the night, and we must call a halt and retire for the night.[2]

Leo: We were enjoying your talk so much that sleep was forgotten. But enough. We meet again tomorrow for further colloquium.

---

[1] In October 1581 Lourenço Mexia wrote from Funai that the European Jesuits in Kyoto no longer ate bread and only drank sake rather than wine, and usually slept on the tatami mats not in beds (RAHM, MS 09-02663, f. 282).

[2] In the course of the 16th century many editions of edifying letters came off the presses. The first collection relating to Japan was published in Coimbra in 1565. As has been mentioned, Valignano was critical of the quality of these publications. See Valignano, *Historia*, pp. 19*–31*; Lach, *Asia in the Making*, I: 1, pp. 314–31; and above, Introduction, p. 7. The letters inspired young Jesuits to apply for missionary work. Numerous letters of application or *litterae Indipetae* written by aspiring missionaries eager to serve in the Indies to the general in Rome (preserved in the Jesuit archives in Rome) testify to the influence of these edifying reports from the frontlines of missionary activity. They provoked a backlash from some Jesuits who argued that new recruits should be willing to serve in the '*Indie di qua*' (the Indies here) in Europe where superstition and ignorance continued to flourish. See Prosperi, 'The Missionary', esp. pp. 178–9; Roscioni, *Il desiderio delle Indie*, pp. 72–9, 97–107, 180–98; Selwyn, *Paradise Inhabited*, pp. 98–105; Cushner, *Why Have You Come Here?*, pp. 22–7.

COLLOQUIUM VIII

About the secular monarchy, and various dignities belonging to it

Leo: We were so taken with yesterday's talk about the sacred or ecclesiastical monarchy, and so much enjoyed hearing about its various offices, that we have been looking forward very much indeed to today's meeting and colloquium, in which you are to treat of the secular monarchy, and from which we hope to derive no less intellectual pleasure.

Michael: I am convinced that it really will be so. Since a knowledge of European things is of no small advantage to our people we consider it one of the major benefits gained from our immensely long voyage that we bring back from Europe to our country information about things so new and unheard of. Part of the reason we were sent to Europe, after all, was that, besides taking our embassy to the pope, we should become thoroughly familiar with European things through use and experience, and should then communicate our knowledge of them to our own people. Now, to link today's subject with yesterday's it should be borne in mind that in the Christian state, besides the ecclesiastical monarchy, which is divine and above all nature, there is also another monarchy, which is secular, or temporal, and which other nations, nations deprived of the Christian religion, also have; the secular monarchy in the Christian state, however, being divinely inspired by the sacred monarchy, is very much superior to the monarchies and powers of other peoples, as will be clear from what I am about to say.[1]

Now in order to come back to the very foundation and root of this whole subject we should note that the first beginning, the first introduction into the world, of government and power was the superiority to others of outstanding men, and the reverence of men of a lower kind for those distinguished for their valour. And when the human race spread far and wide and became divided into many peoples and nations, each nation or people by common consent took for their ruler or governor the man whom they knew to be eminent for valour and fortitude. This governor of the whole people and state came in the course of time to be called lord, or sometimes prince, or finally king, or by some such title. In the appointment of a king or prince the pagans had various customs. Sometimes they gave the principality or kingdom to someone on the principle that it would be handed on to his sons, or grandsons, or other posterity, by right of heredity, and that only those born of that family and blood could succeed to that principality. Other pagans recognized no

---

[1] At the end of the 5th century Pope Gelasius I distinguished between the sacred authority of bishops, the church, and the royal or secular power. The extent of their powers and boundaries of their respective jurisdictions dominated political debate during the Middle Ages and was still a burning issue at the time of *De Missione*. See *Cambridge History of Medieval Political*, pp. 288–9 and ch. 14 *passim*.

hereditary right, but simply the custom of choosing and appointing each king after mature deliberation. There were also cases where, as sometimes happens, principles were overthrown by violence, and those were raised to that supreme position who had the power and the resources to seize it.

In this matter there were in the kingdoms of Europe, before the Christian faith, all the variety and vicissitudes to which human things, in their sphere-like revolutions, are subject, because of the fragility of nature itself, and as punishment for the sin common to all, vicissitudes such as we ourselves, here in Japan, experience daily. Thus after a variety of occurrences and events a certain people in a famous province of Europe, by name Italy, built the most celebrated and splendid city of Rome, known throughout the whole world. This city began so to flourish in wealth and power, with the strength, prudence, and industry of its citizens, that first it subjected and brought under its authority various peoples throughout Italy; then, having taken that province, which was like a brilliant light to all others, it gradually and for various reasons entered into agreements with other peoples. It waged war against these people when they did not keep faith, brought under its yoke the main provinces of Europe, Asia, and Africa which were then open to it, made many kings its tributaries, and finally became, as it were, mistress of the world. In the course of these events the deeds of the Romans, in both peace and war, were so many that many books of the Ancients, which still exist today, are full of them, and the memory of these exploits is very well preserved.

In the government of this city, however, there were great and remarkable changes. In its first two hundred and forty-three years it was governed by kings, then for almost four hundred and fifty years maintained the form of a republic, to the highest praise and to the glory of its name; eventually, labouring under its own greatness, and assailed by various civil wars, it was taken over by one of its own citizens, namely Julius Caesar, a man of the utmost valour, but at the same time extremely ambitious; and thereafter it, together with the great part of the world subject to it, was governed by a succession of emperors. These emperors flourished for many centuries, ruling with all power and success, and governing many provinces and kingdoms. But there is nothing firm and stable in human affairs, and about the nine-hundredth year from the time when Rome began to be dominant in the world, the power of the emperors was gradually reduced, and many kings withdrew various kingdoms from its jurisdiction, and themselves exercised supreme power in various provinces.[1]

This is now the condition of that monarchy which was so flourishing. There is still an emperor with some provinces subject to him, but he does not now have the splendour and power which were originally his; and the kings, although they recognize the emperor as first in rank, live each in his own kingdom, with his own jurisdiction and his own laws, in no way dependent in their administration on the will of the emperor.[2] This, therefore,

---

[1] The traditional dates for the founding of the Roman republic are 509 BCE or 507 BCE. In 49 BCE Caesar crossed the Rubicon and was assassinated in 44 BCE. Octavian became the first Roman emperor, as Augustus, in 27 BCE. Romulus Augustus was overthrown by Odoacer in 476, the end of the empire in the West.

[2] The Holy Roman Emperor. On Christmas Day 800, Charlemagne was crowned emperor by Pope Leo III. For most of its existence, until 1806 when the last emperor, Francis II, resigned, the geographical and jurisdictional core of the empire was in central and eastern Europe. By the time of *De Missione*'s composition, the power and aspirations of the emperors to universal sovereignty had been checked by the papacy and the sovereign rulers who had long since secured inalienable possessions and rights. The description here of the contemporary

is first and supreme among the profane ranks, and there is no doubt that it has precedence over the others. Close behind it is royal rank, that is the rank of the kings who administer and have jurisdiction over certain great kingdoms or provinces, and rule without deferring to any other secular prince, although they respect the emperor as being above them in rank. Below the emperor and kings there are four types of power, namely princes, dukes, marquesses, and counts; and I should add a fifth rank, lower than the others, who are known as viscounts and barons. All of these together we can refer to as rulers. None of them is subject to any of the others, but all recognize as their superior either the emperor or the king within whose jurisdiction they have their revenues. Some of the princes and dukes, however, have such power and authority, and are so little dependent on the emperor, that they are kings in all but name, and in other things, namely wealth, land, and income, no different from kings. Some of these are in Italy, some in France, and some are in other provinces, especially in Germany, where at the present day the emperor has his proper seat, and, as I have explained, he is honoured as the first of all of them by the princes, dukes, and other rulers.

With regard to royal seats, there are a very large number of kingdoms in Europe which in former times were held each by its own king, and which still retain the name and insignia of kingdoms; many of these, however, have by the course events have taken been resolved into one, and now obey one and the same king. As a result there is a long list of different kingdoms, but the list of kings who administer them is much shorter.

Leo: Could you tell us by what means these dignities are obtained nowadays from men? Is it a matter of heredity, or are they elected by the people, or is it by the use of some kind of force?

Michael: With regard to force, that has no place among Christian princes, since they are men imbued with the Christian religion, which controls and constrains unbridled cupidity, so among them the way is open to right and justice, not to the desire to rule; whereas here in Japan, by contrast, we see all human and divine rights shaken by force, by arms, and by the desire to rule.[1]

So with regard to the position of emperor, after a long period during which the pattern of succession was not fixed, he came in the end to be consecrated by the supreme pontiffs, and in our own time the procedure is as follows: on the death of an emperor his successor is chosen by the votes, not of the whole people, or of the army, as used to happen, but of seven very distinguished rulers known as the imperial electors. And to allow this to be done without any pressure it is customary for whoever is to take over his post to be chosen while the emperor is still living, and that person is known as the King of the Romans, and he is referred to by this name until such time as he assumes the imperial dignity and power.

European states' system reflects the pretensions of the Counter-Reformation papacy and its adherents, and draws heavily upon the Roman humanist rhetoric of the late 15th and early 16th centuries. Ernst Kantorowicz's characterization of these pretensions with reference to England at the beginning of the 17th century as 'like some quaint remnant from a distant past' is also an apposite characterization of the assertions in *De Missione*. See Kantorowicz, *King's Two Bodies*, p. 317; Stinger, *Renaissance in Rome*, pp. 238–46.

[1] The recent case of Spain's annexation of Portugal by force is ignored, although it would have repercussions in Japan when Hideyoshi learned about it.

And although the electors are at liberty to choose for this highest of offices whomever they judge most worthy, generally they designate a son of the current emperor, if he has one, or a close blood relative. As a result of this for many years past now the imperial dignity has always been within the leading family of the Austrians, and many from that family have received the highest praise for their governance of the empire. And after the proclamation is made as to who is to take over this highest of positions, petition is made to the pope, vicar of Christ our Saviour, King of Kings and Lord of all Lords, to ratify the appointment and to bestow on him the diadem and other insignia of the emperors; and after the pope has been assured that the virtues of the appointee are adequate for the role which he is to undertake he is considered solidly established as emperor, he receives the imperial insignia which are handed over to him either by the pope or by an accredited replacement, and he is then held in the highest honour and veneration by all as the defender of the whole of Christendom.

With regard to the kings, they generally have their kingship by hereditary right, passed on from parents to children and grandchildren; and if there are no children or grandchildren, those who are the deceased king's closest blood relatives take it over. If there is no blood relative at all the people and citizens assembled together are at liberty to appoint a king for themselves from some very noble family.

Lino: Who are those that you called the imperial electors?

Michael: They are seven in number, three of them with secular offices, three with sacred, and the seventh a king. Those of secular dignity are the duke of Saxony, the marquess of Brandenburg, and the count Palatine, so that each of the main titles is represented in this election. Those eminent for their sacred dignity are the archbishops or archprelates of the three major dioceses, namely Mainz, Cologne, and Trier. To these six, who sometimes do not agree in their voting, is added a seventh, the most illustrious king of Bohemia, who acts as arbiter in these disagreements and as judge of the whole controversy. In this way the most august emperor is elected by majority vote, and is accorded the highest honour by all Christian princes.[1]

Lino: I would like to know from you whether those who rise to the rank of king are also confirmed in it by the approval of the pope.

Michael: Since kings, as I said, attain to their royal office either by hereditary right or by the votes of the people, they need no special confirmation in order to assume that office. In some cases, however, it is customary for them to receive the royal insignia which are given to them by the pope with great pomp and ceremony. But even if there is no place for this solemn tradition, that does not prevent them from exercising their office, and in any case, whatever the form in which they have commenced the administration of their office, they send legates to the pope, and through them they acknowledge him as supreme

---

[1] The electoral college of the Holy Roman Empire was established in 1356 by the emperor and king of Bohemia, Charles IV, in the Golden Bull. By the 16th century the imperial crown was in the possession of the Habsburgs, not by right but by election. The Emperor Maximilian's coronation in 1562 was the last at which all the electors were present. See Wilson, *Europe's Tragedy*, pp. 16–25.

head of Christendom; and they do the same whenever one pope leaves the land of the living for the realms above and another takes his place. The pope can also raise a great prince or ruler to the rank of king, and he can even deprive kings themselves, and the emperor, of their royal or imperial rank, if on account of some defection on their part, or for some most just and grave reason, he should judge this to be for the good of Christendom. And we know from most certain European records that this has sometimes actually happened.[1]

Lino: Great indeed and incredible is the majesty of the Supreme Pontiff, who can abrogate the right of kingship for one and create it for another, on whose authority the emperor is wholly dependent for the stability of his most high office, and whom Christian kings hold in such reverence and veneration.

Michael: You will understand how great the majesty of the Supreme Pontiff is from what I shall be saying in the course of these colloquia about our happy arrival in the city of Rome. However, if I am not to omit matters which our present subject and purpose require, it is very important that you should know how the Supreme Pontiff, the emperor, and the kings conduct themselves whenever they come together for some most grave cause. For firstly, when the emperor and kings approach the Supreme Pontiff (to say nothing, for the moment, of the universal rejoicing and satisfaction with which they are received) before approaching the seat of the Supreme Pontiff they genuflect three times, and the third time they reverently prostrate themselves on the ground, and submitting themselves totally, body and soul, they kiss the sacred feet of the Supreme Pontiff, and piously and religiously venerate and adore him as the vicar of Christ.[2] But then immediately the Supreme Pontiff receives them in his embrace, and most courteously and paternally invites them to take the seats assigned to them. And if the Supreme Pontiff wishes to take his place with all solemnity at table, the custom is that they pour water on his hands, as servants do for their lord, and offer him a towel to wipe them with, and then lay the first dishes before him. This rite of veneration performed he most kindly invites them to the banquet; they reverently take their places and, like sons, most joyously share the feast with him who is father to all of them. Even more remarkably, if it happens that

---

[1] Most famously in 1076 when Gregory VII deposed the emperor Henry IV, setting the stage for the Investiture Controversy and the subsequent trials of strength and debates over respective power, authority and jurisdictions of the spiritual and the secular realms. *De Missione* reflects the consensus among Jesuit theologians who considered it self-evident that the papacy had the power to depose a secular ruler if the latter became a heretic in order to protect the souls of the faithful. By the beginning of the 17th century, Jesuit theologians had become embroiled in a wider controversy about whether the deposing power extended to acts that secular rulers considered to be political not spiritual, such as James VI and I's Oath of Allegiance and the Venetian Republic's assertion of juridical authority over the clergy and the disposition of ecclesiastical property (Höpfl, *Jesuit Political Thought*, ch. 14 *passim*, esp. pp. 344–7, 362–3). These same theologians further asserted, however, that the deposing power did not extend to non-Christian rulers for, as Cardinal Bellarmine put it, 'the foundation of dominion is not in grace but in nature'. See Skinner, *Foundations of Modern Political Thought*, II, pp. 166–71, esp. p. 167; Höpfl, *Jesuit Political Thought*, p. 363.

[2] The *osculum pedis*, kissing the pontiff's foot, a symbolic act derived from the *proskynesis* of the eastern Roman empire. On this ritual, which was routinely performed (Montaigne, for example, performed it), see Montaigne, *Journal*, pp. 192–3; Ullmann, *Growth of Papal Government*, pp. 144, 257, 315; Burke, *Historical Anthropology*, pp. 169, 171, 173, 175; Lowe, 'Understanding Cultural Exchange', p. 10.

the Supreme Pontiff wishes to make a journey on horseback, with full ceremony, and in the company of all the nobility, the emperor and the kings, if they are present, hold the sacred feet of the Supreme Pontiff as he mounts, and they hold the bridle reverently and accompany him for some distance as he sets out, till he most courteously invites them to mount the horses prepared for them. The fact that the emperor and the kings submit themselves to him in this manner and show him such reverence shows clearly the veneration of other princes for the Supreme Pontiff.[1]

Leo: What you tell us of the authority of the Supreme Pontiff is remarkable indeed, and hearing these things stirs us most profoundly and moves us to venerate him.

Michael: When I tell you of our arrival in the city of Rome it will be easier for you to understand how great is the grandeur and majesty of the Supreme Pontiff, how striking and resplendent his state, adorned as it is with such humanity, charity, and other pre-eminent virtues, and how wonderfully he represents to us in both the dignity of his state and the sweetness of his ways Christ the greatest and best, whose vicar he is.

Lino: You said before that the city of Rome was the first seat of the empire, but that since then the emperor has usually resided in Germany. I would like to know whether the secular power over the city of Rome belongs to the emperor or to the Supreme Pontiff.

Michael: You do well to ask, and it is a point which I have been wanting to explain. When the emperors of old first came to know the truth of Christianity and adopted it, there was one named Constantine who above all others was celebrated, famed, and renowned. He was so ardently zealous in spreading the Christian religion that he not only had splendid churches built, saw to it that Christianity was propagated throughout all the kingdoms subject to him, and spared no expense in promoting everything Christian, but he also decided to make manifest by his deeds the regard in which he held the authority and the majesty of the Supreme Pontiff. Accordingly he gladly assigned to him the whole city of Rome, together with many other provinces, and he moved away from Rome and established a new Rome for himself in Thrace.[2] Later on the capital there was troubled by tumult and war, and in the end the seat of the emperor was established in

---

[1] On papal ritual more generally at this time, see Burke, *Historical Anthropology*, ch.12 *passim*.

[2] In 330 Constantine moved the capital to Byzantium which was renamed Constantinople and which finally fell to the Ottoman Turks in 1453. The so-called Donation of Constantine (*Constitutum domini Constantini imperatoris*), fabricated in the mid-8th century by author or authors unknown for reasons unknown, reached Rome in the 11th century as part of a collection of Frankish canon law. The document was quickly seized upon by advocates of papal supremacy. It claims that the emperor Constantine I donated jurisdiction over the territories of the western empire and primacy over the eastern patriarchs to Sylvester I (314–35) as a reward for converting him to Christianity and curing him of leprosy. The document also says that Constantine furnished the pope with a bejewelled crown (the *phrygium*) and in recognition of the superiority of the sacred power over the profane held the bridle of the pope's horse and acted as his groom. In 1440 Lorenzo Valla provided perhaps the most notable debunking of the document. At the time of the writing of *De Missione* canon lawyers still judged the document authentic. See Valla, *Discourse*; *Cambridge History of Medieval Political*, pp. 212–13, 230–31. On the notion of a *translatio imperii* (i.e., that the Roman Empire had passed from Romans to Greeks and finally to the Franks), which was implicit in the coronation of Charles the Great by pope Leo III in 800 as 'emperor of the Romans', see ibid., pp. 165–6, 249–50.

Germany. And not only the Emperor Constantine, but also many others, acted with the same magnificence, and greatly increased the temporal jurisdiction of the Supreme Pontiff, with the result that, although in the course of time there was a great decline in the Roman Empire, the city of Rome, from the time when it first came to dominate, has always held both secular and sacred dominion over the whole world; so that a certain Latin poet, foremost of all the poets, is not wrong to have God say 'I have given you an empire without end';[1] and elsewhere, of the Capitol, which is the immovable rock of the citadel of Rome, no power can destroy it.[2] And the truth of the matter is that Rome now is much more dominant throughout the world, since it is from Rome that all Christian peoples have the certain guarantee of religion.[3]

Leo: Indeed; for although the Japanese are almost as far away from it as it is possible to be, we too, when we embrace the Christian religion, venerate Rome, the seat of the Supreme Pontiff, and the Pontiff himself, as the father whom all nations have in common; and from this I can readily appreciate that the jurisdiction of the Roman empire has never before extended so far and wide. But come now, tell us more clearly and more in detail about the other official ranks.

Michael: As well as kingdoms and royalty, there are also in Europe some republics, which possess power no less than royal power, but are answerable only to themselves, with their own special laws, free and exempt from all royal jurisdiction, and these hold great authority in Christendom. Pride of place among these goes to the most celebrated republic of Venice, founded many centuries ago, pre-eminent in its wealth and in its power both at sea and on land, and whose jurisdiction is acknowledged by very distinguished lords who are governors of provinces and islands. These and other similar republics are to be regarded as of royal rank. But with regard to Venice, we shall have more to say about it in another colloquium.

Leo: Could you tell me now whether people acquire the rank of prince, duke, marquess, count, by right of heredity or by election.

Michael: With regard to those ranks below the rank of king, the eldest sons of kings are called princes, and the others are popularly known as 'infantes', meaning sons of kings, and they outrank all others, whatever their titles or distinctions. Next come other princes, who although not sons of kings nevertheless are specially granted this title because of their greatness. After them come dukes, and there are two kinds of dukes, for some of them are subject to no king, as I said before, and are themselves kings in all but name, being almost the equal of kings in power, wealth, and resources, and having subject to them marquesses, counts, and other powerful figures; but there are also dukes of another kind, who live under the jurisdiction of kings or of the pope. For since, as I have said, the sovereignty of the Supreme Pontiff is very large, it embraces dukes, marquesses,

---

[1] Virgil, *Aeneid*, I: 279, '*imperium sine fine dedi*'.
[2] Ibid., IX: 448 '*Capitoli immobile saxum*'.
[3] In reality the Catholic church was marginal as a global presence. Until 1700 approximately nine-tenths of the world's Catholics lived in Europe (Broderick, 'Sacred College', p. 46).

and counts. So among those who are subject either to the Supreme Pontiff or to kings there are firstly princes, secondly dukes, thirdly marquesses, and fourthly counts, and although some are more powerful than others, they all recognize the order of rank which I have indicated. All of these degrees of nobility, then, normally descend by right of heredity from parents to children; sometimes, however, they are conferred, by pope, emperor, or kings, on men who have deserved especially well of them, together with the appropriate revenues. And after all of those of whom I have spoken come viscounts, barons, and other nobles, descended from the same families or from other noble families.

Leo: These European lords seem to me very similar to our Japanese lords, for the one we call the *dairi*[1] is like the emperor, those we call *yakata*[2] are like the kings, the ones we

---

[1] 内裏 literally the inner grounds of the imperial palace designated for the emperor's use but also a name for the emperor himself (*Vocabvlario*, f. 70). The name was one of a number used for the emperor. The best contemporary European discussion of the nomenclature is Rodrigues, *Arte breve*, ff. 83–4. In his *Sumario*, and more fully in ch. 5 of the *Principio*, Valignano describes the historical and contemporary political nomenclature of Japan. Despite errors and shortcomings, it remains a valuable synthesis. In his writings, Valignano sees the broad sweep of Japanese history as one in which the *dairi*, originally 'the universal lord of Japan', and the court aristocracy lost power to an unstable military class, so much so that by the mid-16th century an impoverished emperor and court did the bidding of the prevailing military strongman (Valignano, *Sumario,* pp. 8–14; *Principio*, printed in *Adiciones*, pp. 393–409; *Historia*, pp. 132–3). However, regardless of straitened circumstances and political impotence, but not political irrelevance, the imperial institution remained an essential source of legitimacy and the three unifiers, Nobunaga, Hideyoshi and Tokugawa Ieyasu, legitimized their power by seeking and accepting offices and titles that the imperial court could bestow. They further strengthened their connections with the court by such means as rehabilitating the imperial finances. On the relations between the three unifiers and the court at this time, see, inter alia, Berry, *Hideyoshi,* pp. 168–205; Butler, *Emperor and Aristocracy*, pp. 124–68. The earliest surviving Jesuit account of Japan, written the year before Xavier reached Japan by Nicalao Lanchillotto, based on information furnished by a Japanese samurai from Kagoshima, introduced the supposed distinction between the emperor as the spiritual leader (like the pope) of Japan, and the shogun as the temporal leader (like the Holy Roman Emperor) (Ruiz de Medina, *Documentos del Japón*, I, pp. 61–2). The distinction long remained current in European writing about Japan (see, for example, Bodart-Bailey, *Kaempfer's Japan*, pp. 23, 48–9, 89).

[2] 屋形 or 館. Originally the designation for a Shinto shrine the name was gradually applied to the residences of the nobility and then to the nobles themselves, although only with the permission of the shogun and then only to a limited number. Here, and one detects Valignano's intervention, the definition of *yakata* is far more nuanced than in Valignano's earlier one in the *Sumario* where he says that *yakata* 'in a certain manner correspond to kings'. The reason for this greater precision reflects the Visitor's concern over the questions raised in Europe about the status of the rulers the boys represented and Pedro Ramón's critique. Later, Valignano devoted a chapter of the *Principio* to a detailed discussion of the use of the word 'king' in descriptions of Japan and the confusion such usage had caused in Europe, and cited this passage in his analysis. See Valignano, *Sumario*, p. 12; *Principio*, printed in *Adiciones*, pp. 393–409. In Rodrigues's *Arte breve* (f. 79v) and the *Vocabvlario* (f. 316), *yakata* is rightly regarded as synonymous with the most powerful of the daimyo. Writing in 1586, Fróis says *yakata* is synonymous with 'king' but his later history, written in the early 1590s, is, like *De Missione*, more nuanced. See *Cartas*, II, f. 188v; Fróis, *História de Japam*, I, pp. 8–9. Ironically, in view of the use that has been made of Ramón's letter to attack the embassy, Martin Hara, writing around 1624, praised João Rodrigues for intending to translate *yakata* as 'duke' rather than 'king' in his *História*, a project on which Hara collaborated. He emphasized this point and was pleased because it would counter the friars' calumnies about the embassy and force them to stop their needling. Nevertheless, Rodrigues's manuscript refers to the 'kingdoms and states' of Japan. See RAHM, Jesuítas 7236, ff. 317v, 318, 323v; Schütte, 'A "História inédita dos bispos da Igreja do Japão"', pp. 314–15; idem, *Monumenta Historica Japoniae I*, p. 350; Álvarez-Taladriz, 'A cada cosa', pp. 4, 10; Cooper, *João Rodrigues's Account*, p. 67 n. 2.

refer to as *kuge*[1] and *kunishū*[2] correspond to dukes, marquesses, and counts, and those we call *tono*[3] or *samurai*[4] represent the barons, viscounts, and others that you have referred to as nobles.

Michael: That is more or less correct, although there is some difference between European kings and our Japanese *yakata*. *Yakata* can indeed be called kings in that as they possess entire kingdoms, have under their power various *kunishū*, who are like marquesses and counts, raise great armies, live by their own laws, and can make war on their enemies. But in that their jurisdiction is much more strictly limited and their revenues far smaller, and in that they acknowledge as their superior the *dairi*, and also the *kubō*,[5] who takes the place of the *dairi*, they by no means correspond to European kings. I would say rather that they are equivalent to great dukes, who although they are first among other nobles, are in some sense under the emperor, and defer to kings; equivalent, I mean, not in revenues, but in the scope of their jurisdiction and the authority of their regime. But we can affirm most certainly that the *dairi* is of royal rank, and that the *kuge* and *kunishū* are like marquesses and counts, so that we call them, to use the general term, *daimyōshu*, that is men of great name,[6] in the way that in Europe we speak of 'the nobility' or 'the aristocracy'.

In addition to these ranks of the nobility, of which I have been speaking until now, there are very many ranks of office in the service of both the sacred and secular

---

[1] 公家 court nobility (Rodrigues, *Arte breve*, f. 85; *Vocabvlario*, f. 63v).

[2] 国衆 provincials (also known as 国人 *kokujin*) men of substance whose political and military power derived from their local or provincial landholdings. By the second half of the 16th century some of these individuals had established themselves as independent rulers. Their authority proved invaluable to the *sengoku daimyō* 戦国大名 who rose to power during the civil wars at the expense of the *shugo daimyō* 守護大名 or military governors who had been appointed by the Muromachi shogunate in the middle of the fourteenth century but who lacked any local power base. Fróis's description of them as akin to *fidalgos* (*Cartas*, II, ff 136, 153) is closer to the reality than the grander titles ascribed to them here and in Valignano's *Historia* (p. 452). On Valignano's confusion about these titles, see Álvarez-Taladriz's learned comment in the *Sumario* (p. 12 n. 55). It is important to remember that Valignano and others were inconsistent in their definitions of the titles associated with Japan's political and social institutions. The most informed and impressive Jesuit discussion of those titles is Rodrigues, *Arte breve*, ff. 75v–96.

[3] 殿 equivalent to daimyo (not samurai), which is how Valignano describes it in the *Sumario* (pp. 8–9 and n. 31 where he equates it with counts, marquesses and dukes). The *Vocabvlario* defines it as territorial lord (f. 261). It was also used by aristocratic wives as an honorific to address their husbands and similarly by vassals to address their lords. The English in Hirado referred to the daimyo with this honorific as *tono-samma*. See, for example, Satow, *Voyage of Captain John Saris*, p. 79.

[4] 侍 one who serves, the warrior elite divided into lord and vassal hierarchies. By the 1580s the samurai were increasingly divorced from the peasantry and the land, living in castle towns and cities in the service of their lords. The *Vocabvlario* gives '*saburai. Fidalgo ... homem honrado*' (f. 214). The supplement to the *Vocabvlario* gives '*samurai daixô. saburaino taixô. capitão de gente nobre*', captain of a nobleman, or, more literally, 'warrior two swords', samurai having the privilege of carrying two swords (f. 376v).

[5] 公方 the term for shogun used by Jesuit writers. It was originally applied to the emperor and imperial court. During the Kamakura period (1185–1333) it signified both the shoguns and their deputies in the Kanto area. See Valignano, *Sumario*, p. 10 n. 40; *Adiciones*, pp. 399–400; Rodrigues, *Arte breve*, f. 85v; *Vocabvlario*, f. 62. The last Muromachi shogun, Ashikaga Yoshiaki, was deposed by Nobunaga in 1573.

[6] 大名衆 more commonly daimyo or 'great name', *dai* meaning 'great' and *myō* derived from *myōden* 名田 or 'name land' the designation for waste land that had been converted into rice fields. Those who cleared the land became the proprietor and received a name.

monarchies, just as in Japan we have *kampaku*,[1] *daijō daijin*,[2] *kubō*, and very many others, all of them most honourable, but distinguished by their different functions, being variously concerned with the governing of the people, the administering of the royal palaces, or military organization and preparation for war.

Lino: I wish to know whether those European kingdoms and states have abundant wealth and prosperity, and whether they are superior in power and resources to ours in Japan.

Michael: Your question, dear Lino, moves me and my companions to laughter. It is not surprising, however, given that you have never crossed the seas nor visited foreign countries. But as we proceed with more of these colloquies you will come to appreciate how wealthy and powerful the kingdoms of Europe are. I leave other considerations for another occasion, but it is certain that the smallest European kingdoms contain at least eighty or a hundred leagues, which equals a hundred and fifty of ours; so the whole of Japan, divided as it is into sixty-six kingdoms, would, if measured by European standards, amount to only about three middle-sized kingdoms, while in Europe there are many other larger ones. And with regard to the population and wealth of European cities and towns, they were so great as to leave us astonished; it will be possible to grasp something of this from the splendour and magnificence which attend their kings, and the lavishness of their expenditure. But since there is a lot here to deal with let us postpone it until tomorrow and allow ourselves the due time for rest.

Lino: I agree to that, although we have been so enthralled with the colloquium that we were not in the least concerned about resting.

---

[1] 関白 imperial regent, a title first bestowed by the emperor Kōkō (r. 884–7). Various romanizations of this title were used by the Europeans. Just before his death Nobunaga was offered the title. Hideyoshi accepted and received the title in 1585 and kept it until 1591 when he became *taikō* 太閤 or retired regent. Hideyoshi ensured that the title was passed on to his nephew and heir, Hidetsugu. It did him no good. Relations with his uncle became strained after the birth of Hideyoshi's son, Hideyori, in 1593. A possible power struggle was avoided when Hideyoshi exiled his nephew in 1595 and ordered him and his retainers to commit suicide. Hidetsugu's children and his female retainers were publicly executed in Kyoto. See *Vocabvlario*, f. 204, '*Quanbacu*'; Berry, *Hideyoshi*, pp. 58, 178–81, 218–23; Lamers, *Japonius Tyrannus*, pp. 213–14.

[2] 太政大臣 grand minister of state, another title bestowed on Hideyoshi by the imperial court in 1587.

COLLOQUIUM IX

Of the splendour and opulence of the kings and rulers of Europe in what concerns the treatment of the body, food, and accommodation, and of their great costs and expenses

Lino: We are delighted to be together again as usual this evening, dear Michael, to listen to you telling us about the scale of spending to which the princes of Europe are usually committed, and of the magnificence of their adornment and refinement.

Michael: I am happy to tell you about it, and I shall begin with some very famous words which a certain queen of Sheba addressed to Solomon the king of Jerusalem, who, as it says in the sacred writings, prefigured and adumbrated in many things Christ Our Lord and Saviour. Rumour and report had reached this queen of the wisdom and the power of the said king, so that she was moved by a great desire to see him, and set off in haste on the long journey from her own kingdom to his. And when she saw and experienced for herself, with evidence ample and varied, the incredible magnificence and splendour of that king, his wealth, the resources at his command, the almost infinite multitude of servants ministering to him, all in perfect order; when she experienced, besides, the peerless wisdom of the king, conjoined with the utmost felicity, in all matters of administration, she was overwhelmed with an extreme admiration, and said to the king, in the words of Sacred Scripture:

> And she said to the king: The report is true, which I heard in my own country, concerning thy words, and concerning thy wisdom. And I did not believe them that told me, till I came myself, and saw with my own eyes, and have found that the half hath not been told me: thy wisdom and thy works, exceed the fame which I heard. Blessed are thy men, and blessed are thy servants, who stand before thee always, and hear thy wisdom. Blessed be the Lord thy God, whom thou hast pleased, and who hath set thee upon the throne of Israel, because the Lord hath loved Israel for ever, and hath appointed thee king, to do judgment and justice.[1]

And just as that queen pronounced all those words, as is recorded in Sacred Scripture, so we too could well have done the same when first we saw the rulers of Europe, their majesty and magnificence, the scale and structure of their buildings, the dignity and pomp with which they are served; when we saw, besides, how very well-ordered their government is, and realized that all these things are in reality just as the fathers had told us they were, whereas previously we had not entirely believed what they had told us. And I am confident that you too will come to the same conclusion about these things if you resolve to accept

---
[1] I Kings 10:6–9 (Douay-Rheims translation).

what I am going to be telling you. I'll be speaking about these things at your request, and I would like you to appreciate that in dealing with them I am not going to go one inch beyond the truth, and am more likely to understate their qualities, as my companions who are here present can testify.

And to begin my exposition I would have you know first of all that Europe differs greatly from Japan in the way in which annual income is reckoned. For here in Japan the way that income is normally reckoned is that the lord of a particular district is regarded as possessing the entire income from the land within his jurisdiction, the total of the whole of the crop harvested from the area subject to him, even though he himself does not keep possession of all the fruits of the land, but distributes the greater part of them to subordinate lords, such as the *tono* and others like them. So when we say that some *yakata* harvests so many thousands of measures of rice every year, that is not to be understood as meaning that he keeps all of it stored in his barn; on the contrary, he divides it among all those who recognize and submit themselves to his jurisdiction, so that it reaches right down to the farmers who till the fields, with the result that the *yakata* really keeps for himself barely one eighth of the whole. Thus the man who is reckoned to have fifty thousand of the measures which we call *koku*[1] devotes only six or seven thousand to his own use, so that the real and genuine extent of the income of *yakata* or ruler cannot properly be based on this huge tally of measures of rice, since the greater part of it goes to other subordinate lords, and only the portion which he and his family have for their own use should be regarded as belonging to him.

In Europe, however, things are very different, and in reckoning income it is not a matter of counting the measures of rice or other crops, but of calculating the total amount of money; and the princes and rulers to whose jurisdiction the people are subject do not arbitrarily apportion lands, nor take them from some and give them to others, but just as the great lords have a degree of jurisdiction of their own, so also the subordinate lords have lands which belong to them, and the crop which the land yields is theirs, and they buy, sell, or exchange them, and indeed make use of them as their own independent property in any way they wish. There are some lands, however, the so-called royal lands, which are a special case. These are given by the kings to an annual list of men who have deserved well of them, and are inalienable by any contract unless with the express permission of the kings.

So when it is said that the total of the royal income is such and such, it is not a question of the value of the whole of the land in that kingdom, and indeed that is a reckoning

---

[1] 石, about 180 litres or 5 US bushels of unpolished rice. It was the base measure of the *kokudaka* or tax assessment introduced by Hideyoshi. While the boys were away Hideyoshi, drawing upon precedents set by Oda Nobunaga and other lords, had further consolidated his power through a series of cadastral surveys or *kenchi* starting in 1582. The surveys laid the basis for an improved system of land registration and taxation. Henceforward, land whether that of the daimyo, court nobility or religious institutions was possessed by Hideyoshi and distributed according to his, and later the Tokugawa shogunate's, prerogative. The system survived until the Land Tax Reform in the early Meiji period (Berry, *Hideyoshi*, pp. 111–31). Valignano elaborates on the income of the daimyo in the *Principio*, and quotes this paragraph, attributing it to de Sande. He also suggests that one *koku* is equivalent to one ducat (*Principio*, ch. 6, printed in *Sumario*, pp. 324–5). Hideyoshi's landholdings are estimated to have been around 2 million *koku* while Philip II's revenue is calculated to have risen from 8.7 million to 12.9 million ducats between 1577 and 1598. See Berry, *Hideyoshi*, p. 130; Thompson, *War and Government*, pp. 68–9.

which is hardly ever made, but just of the income which belongs personally to the king himself, as his own. Yet no king receives less than forty million sesterces, or one million ducats, every year, and in the same kingdom where the king enjoys such ample revenues there are also many dukes, marquesses, and other rulers, who have four, five, or six hundred thousand, or even a million ducats, in income and tribute, every year.

Therefore in calculating the total income of a king or prince it is not the wealth of the entire kingdom or jurisdiction which is counted, but the amount of income accruing to that individual person. And from this you can easily see that our *yakata*, although they may have jurisdiction over more extensive lands than many of those dukes, marquesses, and counts who are subject to the king, and although they may also have larger numbers of vassals, cannot compete with them in wealth and income; and although those whom we call *kunishū* and *daimyō* are indeed similar to the dukes and other rulers of Europe, they cannot match them in their resources and personal property. And I am convinced that the kings of Europe so outdo our *yakata* in wealth and power that with the exception of the monarch of the whole of Japan, whom we call the Lord of the Tenka, meaning Lord of everything,[1] no other can stand comparison with the kings of Europe.

Lino: What you tell us of the power and wealth of the European kings, and also of the ample resources of those rulers who are subject to them, is indeed remarkable. But when I think about it I find myself very puzzled as to how it can be that those kings allow such powerful rulers to live and to exercise power within their kingdoms, without any fear of rebellion or conspiracy.

Michael: You don't know the nature and disposition of Europeans, and the customs normally followed in that region. You must remember that rulers there possess their income and their lands in such a way that there is no possibility of their being deprived of them by the kings, unless they commit the crime of treason, a crime to which the European mind has a very strong aversion. And even if those nobles were to plot treason, they are so controlled and constrained by the power of the kings that they would never be able to carry it through. And since the kings know this with certainty, they regard the number and the wealth of those nobles as a support rather than as any kind of threat.

Leo: I can easily imagine, from their greatness and power, their store of wealth, and their treasure chests overflowing with gold and silver.

Michael: The leaders of Europe are more concerned to spend magnificently than to hoard money in their treasuries, so that every year their expenses exceed their incomes. The kings, however, the grand dukes, and the free republics, do for the most part make a point of setting aside large sums of money in their treasuries to cover the expenses of wars,

---

[1] 天下 literally 'below heaven', i.e. the world or the polity (*Vocabvlario*, f. 254, '*Tenca. Amega shita. Monarchia ou imperio*'). Both Nobunaga and Hideyoshi considered themselves lords of the Tenka but their understanding of the concept differed. The former saw himself as the legitimate ruler of the Tenka because he, and he alone, had provided, and could continue to guarantee, peace and stability in the polity. Hideyoshi, like Nobunaga, obtained mastery of the Tenka by force but claimed legitimacy by virtue of the office of *kampaku* (Katsumata, 'Development of Sengoku Law', pp. 119–24).

should these happen to break out, or for other similar eventualities with which they can sometimes be faced.¹

Leo: You speak of war as if it affected only those whom you have mentioned, but do lesser dukes, marquesses, and counts not also sometimes make war on one another?

Michael: No, they don't. Only the supreme rulers, who owe obedience to no one, and the free republics, can make war. If other rulers, who are subject to the kings, find themselves for some reason in contention, they put their entire disagreement in the hands of the royal senate or public magistracy, and the quarrel, however grave, is ended by their decision and judgment, in accordance with the ancient rights and laws established with due counsel and in all maturity by their forebears. Thus they live in perfect peace and tranquillity, with no place for wars or strife.² I shall have more to say about these things as I proceed with my explanation, but to come back to the wealth and resources of the princes of Europe, these are on such a scale that it is scarcely possible for any who have not seen it with their own eyes to believe it. Perhaps the best evidence of it is the fact that even if a man of noble birth has an annual income of two or three thousand ducats, this does not mean that he is considered to be rich; indeed this income may be barely enough to match his annual expenditure, and it is not difficult to understand this, given the splendour of their dwellings, apparel, lifestyle, and other things.³

Leo: We would love to hear more from you about the cost of all the different things; it would help our imaginations to get a grasp of the magnificence of such riches.

Michael: I'll deal first with their houses, which are most splendidly and skilfully constructed. The houses of the nobility, not to mention the royal houses and the palaces of the kings and rulers, are of wonderful workmanship, built of lime and polished stone, on three or four stories. They have spacious galleries, halls, colonnades, entrance chambers, balconies, various bedrooms, ladies' rooms, and guest-rooms; all of these buildings, both because there are so many of them and because they are so elegantly fashioned, cannot be completed without very great expense. We ourselves saw many residences in many cities built, in some cases, at a cost of forty, fifty, or even sixty thousand ducats, so you can imagine what it cost to build the palaces of the kings. And it is not only in the cities that there are houses of this sort, but also on estates in the country, where the nobles go for relaxation, and there too they are at pains to construct the most magnificent buildings.

---

¹ European governments went into debt handsomely – and, in the case of Spain, recklessly – to finance their ambitions. Spain, the first global power with expenses to match but not meet its ambitions, had to borrow heavily to finance its policies. Under Philip II there were frequent defaults. Despite the general European unease with Spain's apparent attempt to establish a 'universal monarchy', by the end of the 16th century European, and not a few Spanish, observers, judged that Spain was already in decline. See Thompson, *War and Government*, pp. 72–3; 'Impact of War', p. 266; Kamen, *Spain's Road to Empire*, pp. 292–8; Elliott, *Empires of the Atlantic World*, pp. 25–6.

² Between 1578 and 1595 banditry and lawlessness were endemic in the Papal States. Those involved included disaffected nobility fighting against the centralizing pretensions of the papacy. See Pastor, *History of the Popes*, XX, pp. 513–41; XXI, pp. 75–94; Delumeau, *Vie économique et sociale de Rome*, pp. 541–66.

³ In 1590 the Roman aristocratic family, the Orsini, had an income of about 70,000 *scudi* but debts of about 500,000 *scudi* thanks to their lifestyle and building projects (Burke, 'Southern Italy in the 1590s', p. 179).

The European cities therefore present a very pleasing aspect, with so many houses exhibiting a most striking and splendid appearance, and the fields and the countryside itself, adorned as they are with very fine villas, present to the eye a much more agreeable sight. The interiors of the houses are also highly decorated, for the floors are made of boards very neatly joined together, but also of tiling, mosaic, and intricate inlaid work; the roofs are secured by panelling adorned with gold and paintings, or are supported by an arch constructed of lime, plaster, or other similar material, and ornamented with various figures and images; and finally the walls are decorated with gold and various other colours, so that it seems that everything in the house makes a display of splendour, magnificence, and distinction.

Leo: How can it be that the nobility of Europe build such very costly houses, when constructing them could empty their treasuries?

Michael: Well, I said before, didn't I, that not every man who is of the nobility, even though most of them have two or three thousand a year in gold, is reckoned to be wealthy or moneyed, for even all that may be little enough to cover his regular expenses. The richer they are the more magnificent the houses they build, but all the same, all of them have houses which can be called magnificent and impressive.

Leo: Tell us now whether these houses have furnishings to match their magnificence.

Michael: They do indeed. Since all this splendour derives from their plentiful revenues, their finely constructed houses have in them very beautiful and ornate furnishings. In the first place the walls of their houses are usually adorned with very fine tapestries and hangings, appropriate to each season; for the spring they are made of thin leather, painted with gold and with various figures, like these ones which you see hanging here, which we brought with us so as to be able to show our people some examples of European adornments. The winter ones, however, are made partly of wool, partly of silk, and are decorated with gold and silver thread, and with various figures of men, animals, forests, mountains, and rivers. The work is varied, pleasing, and valuable, because of the materials, namely silk, gold, and silver, but also because of the artistry of the embroidery work, which is why the nobles generally make use of these hangings.[1] We wanted to have one to show as an example, and we were bringing with us several which the Archbishop of Évora (of whom more later) had given us as a gift; however, they were totally lost when one of the ships for India ran aground on some rocks, was wrecked, and broke up. There are other tapestries of this kind made of velvet, with gold embroidery or decorated in some similar way, ideal for adorning the walls.

Then you have the beds, made of the very best wood covered in gold and various other colours. These are spread with the softest of silk mattresses, with linen sheets, with velvet coverings, sometimes gold-embroidered, and with pillows and cushions just right for

---

[1] On tapestries as metaphors of power and propaganda as well as for their more practical use, see Tuohy, *Herculean Ferrara*, pp. 220–23; Jordan, 'Portuguese Royal Collecting', pp. 286–92. Among the presents given to Hideyoshi by Valignano during his embassy on the boys' return were four tapestries featuring animals (Fróis, *História de Japam*, V, p. 299).

supporting the head. All of these are available in both winter and summer forms, more substantial, to ward off the cold, or lighter, to tolerate the heat. Finally, the whole is covered with embroidered veils or silk canopies, and the entire furnishing and ornamentation of a bed can cost three or four thousand ducats. But the Europeans sit in high chairs as well as lying down, and the halls and chambers of their houses are embellished with very fine chairs, made of wood inlaid with ivory, and these chairs are made softer with excellently painted leather, or with silk and velvet, like the ones we have sometimes seen used by the captains of the ships that come to Japan, or the one which the Father Visitor gave in years past as a gift to Nobunaga.[1] They also use tables, which match the chairs most admirably, and these are made with the same craftsmanship, are adorned with most costly draperies, and are a notable and major embellishment for the house of a wealthy man. Add to these the cases, coffers, bookcases, sideboards, chests, and other household furniture of many kinds, which add greatly to the ornamentation of the house, all of it so skilfully and expertly made that the very chamber pots, washbasins, and similar vessels, however low their use, are kept in silk-covered boxes.

Lino: You said that the Europeans do not normally sit on the ground. How then can they treat each other with proper politeness and respect, or have they no concern at all about these things?

Michael: Forms and norms of politeness are by no means lacking in Europe, but they are not the same as those observed in Japan. The way of sitting is quite different, indeed, and the same is true of their way of life and their upbringing, so it is only to be expected that their style of politeness will also differ greatly from ours; and, since we are not accustomed to this, we regard the Portuguese who come here as barbarians who know nothing of human refinement.

Leo: We can't do otherwise than regard them as barbarians, since we see them do many things which are grossly ill-behaved. They enter temples without taking off their shoes or boots, and they often defile and pollute the straw mats which we use by spitting and blowing their noses on them, casually and unrestrainedly, and they do other similar things which seem totally incompatible with any civilized behaviour.

Michael: But in fact the reason for this is not that they are uncouth, but that they have different preconceptions and customs with regard to matters of formality and politeness. Just as we, in our ignorance of the language of the Portuguese, think that their way of pronouncing is barbarous, while they, similarly, not knowing our language, consider us hopelessly ignorant and incompetent when it comes to speaking properly, so also in matters of politeness, because we are different, each sees the other as unrefined and boorish. With regard to those things which seem totally irreconcilable with the norms of cleanliness in temples, you won't judge them to be so if you look at their way of sitting;

---

[1] During his visit to Kyoto in March 1581, Valignano gave Nobunaga a velvet and crimson gold-embellished chair of state (*cadeira de estado*). Nobunaga was carried in the chair by four men and on ceremonial occasions alighted and then ostentatiously sat down again on the chair. See Fróis, *História de Japam*, III, pp. 255–6; *Cartas*, II, f. 3v.

they sit on chairs, and don't use our mats made of straw, but just a floor made of stone, so to spit or blow their noses on to the floor doesn't seem rude to them, especially as for the most part they are circumspect and discreet about it, and generally they use handkerchiefs to catch the phlegm which comes out.[1]

Leo: Well, they may be polite in their fashion, but it still seems to me that our way of sitting is much the better; they have to have their legs hanging down from their seat, and they can't really be entirely at ease and comfortable in a chair.

Michael: Elegantly expressed, and clearly the speaker is Japanese. What is quite certain, however, is that Europeans take a very different view, and find it extremely difficult to sit with knees bent and legs tucked in. And indeed, if you consider simply what accords with nature, European chairs do seem much more appropriate; they have a certain dignity, and present no impediment to comfort, since the feet rest either on the ground or on a step which forms part of the chair, and the rest of the body reposes most comfortably. Sitting on the ground, in addition to looking undignified, is rather uncomfortable, since the body is supported to a considerable extent by the legs, as the priests of the Society can testify, since they find it very uncomfortable and troublesome to have to remain seated in our fashion.

Leo: You are so taken even with their way of sitting that it is almost as if you had given up being Japanese and become European. But I would like to know what is the custom among the other peoples and nations that you saw, as this would help us to judge.

Michael: If you judge by the customs of other nations our way of sitting will not be widely approved, with the exception of the Europeans the Chinese were the only refined and cultured people we saw, the others being very unrefined, and we saw that the Chinese sit on chairs like the Europeans, whereas all the other backward nations sit on the ground. Mind you, the floor on which we sit is more elegant, and our way of sitting more polite. But we can dispose of this kind of argument by pointing out that each nation has developed its own customs suitable for its own kingdom and region, and has brought in these customs over many years. Thus our way of sitting is appropriate for us, given our income and resources, and the European style is very well suited to their large revenues and powers, which require much more substantial spending. So in different nations there is a variety of different customs, but there are also various reasons to consider these customs good.

Leo: I like that tolerant attitude; but now I would be glad if you could say something about the clothing of the body.

Michael: You can guess something about the way Europeans adorn their bodies from the way they adorn their walls. Before I speak about this, however, a remarkable point to

---

[1] Valignano touched on these cultural differences in *Il cerimoniale*. He stressed that rooms for receiving and entertaining Japanese guests in Jesuit establishments must be kept scrupulously clean. Living like '*Nabangis*' (*nambanjin* or southern barbarians, i.e. the Portuguese who frequented Nagasaki) was completely unacceptable (*Il cerimoniale*, pp. 170–73).

note is that the Europeans do not keep always to one and the same kind of clothing, but almost every year they think up and invent different sorts of clothes, as if they were bored with constantly having to wear the same things. But all their clothes, of whatever kind, are made for the most part of very fine and very valuable woollen cloth, or of silk or velvet, with gold embroidery, and they spend very considerable sums in having this ornamentation done. They use different clothes in the privacy of their own homes, and in public places; at home they wear a full-length robe which they call a gown, made of wool, silk, or velvet, with borders skilfully embroidered with gold or silver. There are besides some types of clothes for winter, and others for summer, most of the winter ones being made from the skins of various animals, especially of a particular animal called an ermine, or, in popular parlance, a stoat. These ones are so prized that sometimes people will pay two, three, or four thousand ducats for them.

With regard to women, it would take a long time to recount all the expense they go to for gold, silver, and other ornaments for the body, and like the men they always seek out things which are new and unusual, so that in this matter it is as if they were competing with the men. And this kind of magnificence in clothing is not confined to the masters and mistresses, but extends also to their servants and followers. The more noble the men the more they take pride in the sophistication and elegance of their servants, so that sometimes the servant appears to be turned out as well as or even better than the master. The magnificence of the display of clothing, and the expenditure on it, is such that there is often a need for the excessive spending to be restrained by law; but there scarcely exist penalties or threats which can hold the Europeans back from clothing themselves in this way, especially as they are constantly and eagerly on the lookout for every possible occasion for it, a prominent wedding, for example, or various feast days.[1] At those times, not content with adorning their bodies in any ordinary way, they make a practice of having clothing made with various gems, large pearls, and other similar things, with ornaments of gold and silver, with chains and necklaces of great value hanging from their necks, and on their fingers rings of superb workmanship, the pearls in which are often worth many thousands in gold; and I say nothing for the moment of the tibials, femorals, tunics, thoraxes, hats, and other articles of clothing, which, with gold and silver embroidery, and adornment of gems and pearls, offer a most notable display of beauty and splendour.

The charms of the ladies are greatly enhanced by these pieces of work fashioned of gold and silver, and they are accustomed to adorn themselves with necklaces, bracelets, belts, earrings, and many other accessories of great value; and they add to these, as we mentioned before, gems, or pearls, at almost incredible prices. We ourselves saw some of these, called diamonds and beryl,[2] which were quite small and yet were said to be worth four, six, and even ten or twenty thousand in gold. I'll restrict myself to just one example, to give you a better idea of the value of precious stones of this kind. When the most illustrious duke of Savoy and prince of Turin married the younger daughter of King Philip of Spain, while we were still in Europe, he sent to his betrothed just five pieces made of gold and adorned with jewels, and these were worth five hundred thousand ducats.[3] There were besides

---

[1] On sumptuary laws in Italy, see Fenlon, *Ceremonial City*, pp. 210–11.

[2] Original edition (p. 93) gives '*adamantes, berillosq*'.

[3] Catalina (1567–97), second daughter of Philip II and Elizabeth de Valois, married Charles Emmanuel, Duke of Savoy, on 11 March 1585 in Zaragoza.

many other items which he gave to the king, to the king's sons, and to other members of the Spanish aristocracy, and these gifts will perhaps indicate to you the scale of wealth of Europe.

Lino: What you have been telling us about precious stones, and pearls, and their price, is remarkable, so much so that, to tell you the truth, I am inclined to think it rash and stupid to spend so much on such small stones.

Michael: It would indeed be unreasonable to spend so much on such small things if it wasn't for the fact that those high prices for pearls are normal throughout Europe and much of Asia and Africa; but since those prices, as I said, are very widely accepted throughout most of the world, no one doubts the value of gems of that sort. Besides, it would seem that the nature of the object itself provides some justification, in that these gems do have a remarkable beauty and brilliance, so that some of them shine at a very great distance, and many of them have an admirable capacity to avert illness or to remedy other afflictions to which man is subject, so that it is not surprising that they are so prized by Europeans and others. If you consider our own things, then, it is much more remarkable that our people set so much store by our pieces made of earth, or clay, or iron, such as plates, and tripods, and the bowls which we use for preparing and serving hot water in our fashion, known as *chanoyu*,[1] and that ones which are famous for their antiquity or for other reasons can fetch two, four, six, ten, or fifteen thousand ducats. The same can be said of certain sheets of paper, or paper hangings, with a drawing of a single tree, or bird, or something of the sort, just in black ink;[2] the Europeans can't help being astonished when they realize how we prize all these things, since there is nothing, neither in the material, nor in the skill of the artist, nor in anything else, intrinsic or extrinsic, to justify the enormous price. All we can do, then, is leave it to the judgement and opinion of the various nations, who are at liberty to follow uncoerced their own feelings, customs, and judgment.

However, if we are to make a judgment on the basis of consideration of the things themselves, and not of the opinions or nations or peoples, there is no doubt that jewels should be esteemed highly for their beauty and brilliance, for their durability, for the unusual power which they have greatly to benefit human life, and finally, because so many nations agree about it that it is difficult to believe that all of them could be mistaken. Our

---

[1] 茶の湯 or tea ceremony which originated in China and became an essential part of Japanese culture during the Heian period (794–1185). In the 16th century the tea master Sen no Rikyū (1522–91) introduced Japanese utensils into the ceremony. Rikyū was patronized by Nobunaga and Hideyoshi until he fell out with the latter and was ordered to commit suicide. Rodrigues devotes four chapters of his *History* to tea and the importance of the tea ceremony in Japanese culture. See Álvarez-Taladriz, *Juan Rodríguez Tsuzu S.J.: Arte del cha*, passim; Cooper, *João Rodrigues's Account*, chs 32–5. Valignano ordered that tearooms should be constructed in all Jesuit houses to entertain important guests and gave instructions about how they should be staffed and maintained (*Il cerimoniale*, pp. 72, 136, 160–62, 274, 278, 294, 300). In the *Sumario*, Valignano mentions the high value placed upon tea ceremony utensils by the Japanese, especially tea bowls (茶碗 *chawan*), one of which, he was informed, was worth 14,000 ducats but which, in his opinion, was worth only one or two *maravedis*. He acknowledged that the tea bowls which the Jesuits possessed were not at all esteemed by the Japanese who prized ones made by master potters and that the Japanese had eyes as keen as jewellers in Europe for detecting the genuine from the fake (*Sumario*, pp. 43–7).

[2] Ink brush paintings (*sumi-e* 墨絵) and hanging scrolls (*kakejiku* 掛け軸). Valignano mentions ink brush paintings and the, for him, puzzling value placed on them in the *Sumario* (p. 47).

earthenware or ironware pieces, however, are not very highly esteemed anywhere except here in Japan. It is not difficult to believe that one people could be wrong in their judgment, but the judgment of many seems likely to be right.

Leo: That may be so, but given the choice I would prefer any of our artefacts, including earthenware, to the gems and pearls of that other world.

Michael: I would agree, if it was only a question of exchanging, or buying, or selling those things in Japan. But since the Portuguese prize little stones of that kind so highly, if this region of ours produced many of them, it would be possible to sell them and then buy quantities of our pottery.[1]

Leo: In other words the Portuguese are not aware of the value and the excellence of the artefacts. Very well, let each nation keep to its own opinion. But tell us whether there are great numbers of those little stones.

Michael: In Europe there are indeed many. To that most famous region of the world things of great value are brought from Africa and Asia, and in Europe we saw articles of great price brought from those places. But to conclude this question of European clothing, from the examples which we have brought, of such different kinds of cloth, of silk, and with gold together with the colour, you can easily imagine what their other clothing is like.

Lino: Certainly, with regard to your clothes, we are all greatly struck by their variety, their value, and their workmanship, and there was no other way for us to come to have real knowledge about European clothing and how very fine it is, other than by these evidences, so to speak, which you have brought us.[2]

Michael: What will you say when you have heard about the way horses are adorned, and about horsemanship? I leave this subject, since it is one in which we Japanese take great pleasure, for tomorrow, when I shall also be speaking about servants and about European customs with regard to service. But first let the night now bring an end to this colloquium, and let us devote some time to rest.

Leo: Agreed.

---

[1] In the following century Japanese pottery, in particular porcelain, became for a while a much-prized commodity in Europe. The Dutch exported large amounts to satisfy European demand. See Volcker, *Porcelain and the Dutch East India Company*; idem, *Japanese Porcelain Trade*; Nishida, 'History of Japanese Porcelain', pp. 60–70.

[2] This comment suggests that the Portuguese clothes available in Macao, which were fashionable in Japan, were not of the highest quality. When the boys met Hideyoshi in Kyoto in 1591 they were richly dressed in the European clothes which they had received from the pope and Cardinal Albert. See Fróis, *Historia*, V, p. 300; Cooper, *Rodrigues the Interpreter*, p. 76.

COLLOQUIUM X

Of the multitude of servants and the pomp which the princes of Europe use at home and abroad

Leo: We enjoyed yesterday's talk about the culture and character of the Europeans very much, and we are looking forward eagerly now to today's colloquium on the servants who attend them.

Michael: I am aware of the difficulty of the task which I have undertaken of explaining to you in detail all about Europe, but since I have undertaken it I am not now going to decline to do it. To move on, then. I would ask you to note, first, that service, in Europe, is fixed and stable; the servants and attendants perform a definite task, and do not easily change their place or position, as does often happen here in Japan. Those who minister to our *yakata*, or other leading lords, are not always in the one place, nor are they maintained by wages from the lords, nor does each of them have a fixed task to attend to; but all of them are as it were circling round, with a constant succession of different people providing service at different times. The custom in Europe is very different, for people are not bound by any law to the service of a ruler simply because they are in his territory or under his jurisdiction; their obligation is merely to pay the accustomed taxes. So the nobles themselves always have in or close to their palaces attendants to serve them, and these are either hired, for pay, or they are constrained to work by the hope of some major benefit which may accrue to them.

Two advantages follow from this, the first that the house of a prince or ruler is never short of courtiers; on the contrary, there is a plentiful supply, each of them always ready to carry out his function. The second advantage is that there is an incredible mutual bond of love between masters and servants; since many of the servants have been brought up from their youth within the walls of the lord's own house they cannot but be loved by their lords as by their own parents, and they in turn love them as if they were their parents, and accordingly they obey them with full measure of love and willingness, and they receive from them no small reward for their labour. From this you can understand what diligence they show in their service, what assiduity in their attendance, what commitment in all things. Nor should it be thought that these servants are of obscure or low birth, but as there are distinctions between the various lords, so also there are different ranks of servants ministering to them, and the princes and highest nobility have in their service none but men of noble birth. In addition to these they are always guarded by a retinue and escort, and thus accompanied they go forth in public with great pomp.

Lino: Perhaps they fear treason by some rival, and it is for this reason that they are always aware of danger imminent and employ these guards.

Michael: Not at all. That is not the reason, and in fact they live without any fear of treason. What they are doing is following an ancient custom, which has been in force for many years, and it is not only the kings, but viceroys too, and castle lords and ships' captains. All of these always employ a retinue of guards in a display of ceremony and dignity; and in this and other matters related to how they are served and attended I find it almost impossible to describe for you the pomp and magnificence of the Europeans.[1]

Leo: These arrangements about servants seem to me admirable; but I would like to know whether they also have banquets, and what ceremonies they use in them.[2]

Michael: Why bring up now the question of banquets, something which deserves a colloquium all to itself? For if we are to treat of feasts and of the food at banquets, all is lavish, elegant, exquisite, and prepared with a variety of seasonings, and there are, moreover, so many of them that their leading men seem to be giving them constantly; and most of them, even the private ones, are so grand and so expensive that they cost four hundred or five hundred ducats, or even more; to say nothing of others which are public and more solemnly celebrated, especially for weddings or similar occasions, and it is hard to imagine what these might cost. Princes usually invite others of their own rank to banquets of this sort, since it is customary for the kings, and those who have none of comparable rank in the same place or jurisdiction, to sit alone with others standing in attendance. With regard to the contents of the sideboards, these are filled with a remarkable array of vessels and ornate receptacles, together with plates, saucers, goblets, cups, and an almost infinite number of other dishes for use at table, and all of these are made of admirably engraved gold or silver. We once even saw the bowl in which these things are usually washed made of silver. But among the nobles of whatever rank it is normal for the jugs and bowls for washing the hands, as well as spoons, forks, salt cellars, candlesticks, and other such items to be of silver; the quantity of gold and silver in Europe is so great that it was only natural for us to be astonished both at the abundance of it, and at the lavish and unstinting way they spend it.

Leo: Your account has astonished us, since we see the Portuguese who come here for trade behaving very differently with regard to food and the way they are served. At table they do not seem to observe the norms of cleanliness, and they have no choice in their food, but always eat beef, or pork, or other similar meat, which is abhorrent to us; and they handle it in a disgusting way with their own hands instead of with chopsticks, and they do other things of this sort, things from which our nature and custom recoils. Besides, we see certain Ethiopians, or other men black in colour, to whom civilized behaviour seems wholly alien, serving them at table. And yet you, in your words, extol them as being the acme of elegance and fashion.

---

[1] The retinues of guards provided for the boys during their travels were not just for ceremony and dignity but to protect them.

[2] Jesuit observers found Japanese banquets rather stiff and formal and, in comparison with Europe, frugal. See Fróis, *História de Japam*, V, pp. 306–7; Cooper, *João Rodrigues's Account*, ch.30. Richard Cocks, the head of the English factory in Japan 1613–23, enjoyed Japanese-style banquets, admittedly in informal surroundings, together with the pleasures of the *caboques* (kabuki), or 'dancing bears' (prostitutes) as Cocks called them, who were not, of course, procured for the Jesuit guests of the Japanese (Massarella, *A World Elsewhere*, pp. 234–5).

Michael: It is not surprising if Japanese who have never been outside Japan hold that opinion, and there is no lack of good reasons inclining them to that view. Since the only ones they know are those who have come to Japan, they base their judgment of others on these, using the same measuring rod for all, and this is a very serious error. For those men who come here to Japan, apart from the captains and a few merchants, are for the most part merchants' agents, who are not very familiar with polite society, and who fall easily into certain faults and mistakes in etiquette.[1] It happens sometimes that those brought here to Japan in the ships cannot easily bring with them the things which they normally use in their own homes, and act from necessity rather than following the custom and etiquette of their own country. That being the case it is the more remarkable that men of this kind are so liberal in their attitude to spending, seeming to have no regard for money, and it is certain that in their own homes they behave in a more refined and civilized manner.

With regard to the food that they eat, and our aversion to the taste and the smell of it, the Portuguese are similarly taken aback by our food. In this matter there is no question of right or wrong, but simply of use and custom. However, if we turn our eyes away from custom and look to nature itself, it does seem to me that European food is much better for supporting the body and much more pleasing to the appetite, for their meals are prepared sometimes from meats of various kinds from domestic fowls, from wild animals, from birds which they catch, and sometimes from carefully selected fish, all of these marvellously seasoned, together with a remarkable variety of desserts. But, to try to deal with the whole question of food in a single sentence, I think Japanese food is well adapted to our poor and scanty soil, whereas European food is appropriate to rich and fertile land. And that's all I'm going to say on the whole subject of food.

Leo: I'm not going to deny that our food is less costly, but I totally reject the idea that it is inferior in taste.

Michael: You admit that their food costs more, and that leaves almost no room for doubt about the taste, since the whole question of taste depends on use and habit, and habit is second nature, according to a well-known proverb.[2] Now with regard to what you said earlier about the Portuguese handling meat and other food with their hands, we observed in Europe that this is not customary among more refined people; they normally take their food with silver forks and spoons, and if the Portuguese do sometimes touch meat with their hands, that is perhaps excusable, as they make use of cloths and napkins, and when they sit down at table and again when they rise they wash their hands and dry them on towels, and allow no trace of a disagreeable smell to remain on them. In fact the handling of meat with the hands seems to derive from military life, which is the normal life in India, and in military life the concern is more with speed and necessity than with good manners. And as a final point let me say something about their servants: those that

---

[1] In Europe the fork was first used in Italy as a personal eating utensil and then only by the upper classes before spreading elsewhere. Its use remained limited to those classes until the late 17th century (Elias, *History of Manners*, pp. 68–9). Valignano probably had in mind Erasmus's description, and condemnation, of prevailing eating habits and table manners in *De civilitate morvm puerilivm* (1530) when he wrote about the need for the Jesuits to distinguish themselves from the supposedly uncouth Portuguese in Japan, a constant refrain in *Il cerimoniale* (esp. pp. 152, 172). See also Elias, *History of Manners*, pp. 53–8.

[2] '*Consuetudo quasi altera natura effici*' (Cicero, *De finibus bonorum et malorum*, V: 25).

are brought to Japan are usually procured in India, or in other countries outside Europe, either for a price or by some other method,[1] but those whom they use in Europe are free men, educated as such and well brought up. So from now on you ought to think of the Portuguese as highly civilized.

Leo: We'll make it our business to set aside the opinion which we have held of them up to now, and to adopt a different and much more favourable view. But now that you have spoken about the question of servants I would very much like to hear something from you about horsemanship.

Michael: With regard to horses, it is hard to describe what and how elegant is their form, how great their agility in running and in every movement of their bodies, with their nature quick to obey the reins and the spur. The horsemen are also trained in practice and theory, so that it is most impressive to see the ease with which the horse is controlled and made to wheel more or less in a circle, with just one of the rider's hands on the reins. Please don't think I am exaggerating: we ourselves saw horses in a circular enclosure performing to order turns, circuits, and figures, without ever transgressing, be it never so slightly, the set line, something which we would have found difficult to believe if we had not seen it for ourselves. And as well as running and turning in a circle they also sometimes trot, sometimes jump, and perform other movements, showing clearly how well trained they are in everything that pertains to masterful horsemanship. And what am I to say of the trappings and adornments of the horses? Breast band, crupper, girth, saddle, and all the other parts of the harness, are rich with silk and gold, no less adorned than are the persons of their masters. A truly outstanding example of this is the equestrian accoutrements which the most glorious King Sebastião of Portugal had made, at a cost of five hundred thousand ducats.

Leo: Everything that you have told us, and not least these things to do with horses, leave us wonderstruck, and we only wish that, as well as hearing about them, we could have seen them with our own eyes. For although we make such a profession of the art of horsemanship, we have never yet mastered the knack of controlling our horses with one hand, and yet you say that is a normal thing. This means, I take it, that in Europe they can also fight their enemies on horseback.

Michael: You are right: for in battle the horsemen play a very important part, and they are used to great effect in fighting and in horsemanship. You can see a lightly equipped horseman on a very fast horse wielding his sword or spear with the one hand and his small shield with the other, which also manipulates the reins so rapidly and skilfully that at the will of the rider the horse runs, jumps, stands still, runs back, and performs other necessary actions so impressively that nothing, I think, will give more pleasure to a horseman or to anyone devoted to the military arts than to watch European riders on horseback, and to see them exercising in mock combat.

---

[1] By this time the enslavement of European Christians in Western Europe, with a few very minor exceptions, had disappeared (Blackburn, *Making of New World Slavery*, p. 62). Slave trafficking was a separate issue. There is a further discussion of slavery below (pp. 167–8, 184–7).

Leo: I certainly agree. What greater pleasure than to see and have fast horses ready for a gallop, but obedient to the rein, and outstanding in all else needed for equestrianism. But as I said, I do wish we ourselves could have seen these things.

Michael: You have to admit, though, that the real thing, which you want, is available to you in large part when you look at the two horses which we ourselves with much importunity persuaded the Father Visitor to bring, even though there were many who thought it impossible to bring them in the ship to such faraway lands, because of the many and various difficulties which presented themselves; but all of these were overcome by the strength of the Father Visitor's determination to favour Japan and us.[1] These horses are Arab, not European, and are not to be compared with European horses; nevertheless, in many ways they themselves, and also their beautifully made harness, illustrate to some extent what I have just been saying about European horses and their equipment.

Lino: I agree with you about that. If we had not seen those horses brought from India we would have found it hard to grasp just how powerful European horses are, and how well trained in running and fighting.[2] But there are two things which occur to me that I would like to ask about: one is why those horses have such a variety of equipment, and the other how it is that they have iron shoes on the bottom of their feet, attached with nails, but without affecting either the health of the horses or their speed of foot.

Michael: With regard to the variety of equipment, that goes back to the different styles of horsemanship. The Europeans have two different styles of equestrianism, one with the stirrup straps shortened, suitable for galloping, the other with the straps let out, good for walking, and for each style, galloping or walking, there are appropriate saddles and other equipment; whereas we use only the one style. It is hardly surprising if the European way of equipping horses differs from what we are accustomed to see here. And your surprise at their iron horseshoes is also because of their unfamiliarity or novelty; in Europe shoes fashioned of iron are fixed to the horses' feet so that they leave a firmer hoof print, and so that constant running does not wear the horseshoes out so quickly. And it does not harm the horses' hooves, for the nails used to fix those shoes on do not damage the flesh at all, but only go into insensitive tissue, so that without pain or bleeding the horses are equipped with a kind of shoes, and this makes it easier for them to run about here and there even in mountains and forests. This work demands remarkable skill on the part of the European craftsmen. We know nothing of this, and can provide only shoes of straw to protect the feet of our horses. The Europeans do better than this. They are good at learning ways of doing things from one another, and are more than happy to master others' techniques and discoveries, nor is there any shame involved in taking things in this way from one another. In our nation it is regarded as somehow shameful for nations to take

---

[1] On these horses see below, p. 399.

[2] On Japanese horses, which were smaller but still impressive, and elaborately furnished, see also Saris (*Voyage*, pp. 125–6), who described them as 'very full of mettle, in my opinion farre excelling the Spanish Iennet in pride and stomacke', and Cooper (*João Rodrigues's Account*, p. 109).

anything from one another, and the unfortunate idea is very prevalent that we should accept only what we have ourselves discovered.[1]

Leo: As a native yourself and at home here you have very neatly picked out a vice of our race. But explain to us how noble matrons travel, for we can't believe that they make long journeys on foot.

Michael: Indeed; for although in Europe the men have total control of the administration of the family, they make much of their wives, and are diligent in providing them with their clothing and accessories; so noble women do not journey on foot outside of their houses. They travel in very suitable chairs or litters, and sometimes also on horses or mules, with cushions set on the backs of the animals. For the most part, however, they use coaches, which are as it were miniature houses made of wood, covered with a kind of arched roof, and enclosed in these noble women are conveyed, either lying down or sitting on cushions. These carriages are usually pulled by two or four horses; so sometimes two horses are attached to these vehicles and sometimes four, as you can see from this sketch. And it is not only important ladies, but also noble and dignified men, and sometimes priests and prelates, who use coaches and litters.

Leo: Yes, we can see from this sketch how comfortable these litters are, and that a noble man or woman could very well make a journey in them, sitting, or lying down, or reclining, with six or eight companions; it is not clear, though, how four horses together could be controlled and directed.

Michael: There is no difficulty at all about that. European horses are very docile, and very well trained to make journeys, and when they are accustomed to these carriages they will complete the journey at a gallop, a trot, or a walk. There is besides the skill and knowledge of the drivers, who sit on the coachman's seat manipulating the reins with one hand and the whip with the other, managing the horses admirably. They normally choose two or four good-looking horses, of similar size and colour, so that you can hardly tell one from another, and decked out with blankets of a different type from other horses. The carriages themselves are covered with silk tapestries and draperies interwoven with gold, and with velvet, and the interiors are so magnificently and so elegantly decorated that you could ask nothing more of the interior of a house.

Lino: Is there a great number of these carriages in Europe?

Michael: Yes, a truly remarkable number, since there is an almost infinite number of horses in Europe, very fine horses, especially the Spanish, the Neapolitan, and the

---

[1] The Japanese were highly accomplished in horsemanship (*bajutsu* 馬術). Of particular note was *yabusame* 流鏑馬 the firing of arrows from galloping horses, a skill that continues to impress spectators. On the question of learning from others, the Japanese had, of course, learned and acquired much from China and more recently they had learned about European firearms from the Portuguese. These they copied, manufactured and employed highly effectively in battle. Far from being a vice, acquiring and adapting new technology was very much a virtue in Japan.

Mantuan horses, which are renowned above all others for beauty and for speed. There are also countless noble men and ladies, and they have most ample income for expenditure of this kind; so it will be clear what sort of numbers there are of carriages. We were told that in Rome alone there are about three thousand. This is the usual method of making a journey employed by the nobility of Europe. And since many things remain to be said about the customs of Europe, and we have already been at this colloquium for a long time, let us leave the next part for tomorrow.

Leo: I agree, even though every time you leave off from your discourse you interrupt the delightful flow of our pleasure.

COLLOQUIUM XI

About the agreeable and honourable exercises which the nobles of Europe engage in, and of the noble education of their children

Lino: Last night you told us about the servants of the patricians and nobles of Europe, so you should also treat of the exercises in which they engage, since it cannot be that men of such prudence while away their time to no purpose.

Michael: It is indeed as you would expect of their prudence, and the leading men of Europe take care not to allow time to pass them by without engaging in some proper activity. These activities are of various kinds, and I'll deal with the principal ones for you today. I'll begin by saying that the Europeans educate their children admirably; they hand them over to teachers to have them trained in all the proper fields of study. Their main care, however, is that they should be brought up, whether by themselves or by these teachers, in Christian piety, with the fear of God and the observance of His commandments impressed on their souls; so that after having been steeped in this primary colour they may then proceed to instruction in manners and learning, for each of them always makes a thorough study of the bearing and qualities appropriate to his position. All of them learn to read, to write, and to have some understanding of the Latin language; and with this foundation laid down, those who are to be initiated into holy things, and those who are to devote themselves to public office, make a long and serious study of many other fields of learning. But I shall treat of the exercises of those nobles who follow the secular way of life which is appropriate to both the equestrian and the senatorial order.

First therefore is the exercise of arms, the various sorts of which they are accustomed to wield with the utmost speed and dexterity, partly for the enjoyment of it, and as a relaxation from other labours, but partly also to make them more expert and more fit for battle and fighting. Next follows the study of horsemanship, which they practise most diligently, training the horses in every kind of running and walking, for they consider that valuable whether in war or in peace. They learn besides to play various musical instruments, to which they add the harmony of most sweet voices, and the delightful art of dancing and treading a measure. And they hold in no less esteem hunting, fowling, and other pleasures of the countryside, and to these too they are greatly addicted.

Leo: You have lumped all these exercises together, but Lino and I would like you to take up each one separately and explain it more fully, so that we can learn by hearing about things which we never had the chance of seeing, and may enjoy to the full the pleasure of listening to your account of them.

Michael: We are happy to comply with your wish, to rehearse in memory and to declare in speech what we saw, and as the speaker I look forward with pleasure to doing this. But I shall be leaving to another time the question of how they wage war and engage in battle, and also the use of weapons for sport within private walls (which takes many forms, with sword and dagger, sword and buckler, or two swords; sometimes just with a double-edged axe or a spear; and there are other similar styles); I shall go out from domestic and sheltered exercises to the field and the dust of public contests. These are sporting events, but the Europeans put enormous effort and industry into them. I shall not be dealing with all of them, however, for that would be a very long story, but shall only be giving an outline of the main items.

Leo: I am very confident that, however long this story, we will never tire of it.

Michael: With regard to these public sporting events, most of them are equestrian, European horses, with their great speed and agility, being particularly suited to them. Now the most notable events, and they are very famous, are those commonly known as tournaments, in which mail-clad horsemen take the field with lance in one hand, shield in the other. Two of them charge at each other and attack each other violently with their lances, which break with the impact. And the more brilliant the blow struck, for example if one scores a hit on the other's forehead, the greater the renown he gains.

Leo: Rather than pleasures of life these contests can surely be called instruments of most certain death. There will be danger, it seems to me, for two reasons; firstly, since the horses are very powerful, and the horsemen charge at each other, it could easily happen that they not only suffered injury, but could be completely torn to pieces; secondly, the blows they receive from the lances could often be lethal and mortal.

Michael: There is no worthwhile and useful sport without some element of risk, but against each of the two dangers you mention there is adequate protection; in the first case because in the arena they normally place a kind of barrier, commonly known as a fence, between the horses running from the two opposite ends, so that the bodies of the horses do not touch. And if sometimes there is a contest without this barrier, they rely on the agility of the horses to avoid contact between the horses and yet allow the horsemen to come close enough to strike each other. Besides, even if the bodies of the horses themselves were to collide, all the danger from the crash would be to the horses, not the riders. And danger from the blows they receive is avoided in two ways: firstly, because the armour with which the horsemen cover themselves is so strong and stout that it can take and repel a blow not only from a spear, but also from a musket, or rather from a ball fired from a musket; secondly, because the shafts of the lances which they use, and which are tipped with blunted iron, are of a material which breaks easily. But you can see what European armour is like from the examples we brought back with us.

Lino: Yes, we have seen them, and were in admiration at their beauty and style, as well as their strength and hardness; but at the same time they seemed to us so heavy that they could not possibly be worn on a human body.

Michael: It is recorded in Sacred Scripture that the same thing happened to David when he was a youth. He was about to face the giant called Goliath, and when he was being dressed in the royal armour by King Saul he said 'I can't go thus, for I am not used to it'.[1] But Saul was accustomed to that armour, and reckoned that the weight of it was tolerable, and David himself, as time went on, became used to wearing other similar armour, and he too came round completely to the same opinion. In the same sort of way, because you are not used to it, European armour may seem to you and to others of our men heavier than Etna, as they say.[2] To the Europeans, however, because they are accustomed to wearing it, and because they are outstandingly strong, it is not so.

Leo: But for the encumbrance of the weight of it I have no doubt that those mail-clad horsemen would be without equals in a fight.

Michael: Without equals except for other mail-clad horsemen, of whom the Europeans have many. But to return to those sporting contests; it sometimes happens in them that when the horses run together swords are drawn from their scabbards and there are remarkable displays of swordsmanship. It is most entertaining to see how they assail each other, the one attacking, the other retreating or dodging, then again attacking his adversary, who avoids the blow, using his shield as protection, and then goes for his opponent, and so it goes on, with various twists and turns, and with the horses always obedient to the will of the swordsmen. Sometimes they do the same with shield or buckler and spear, a different kind of spear from the lance with which they strike each other when they charge. Sometimes the contest is fought out with canes and oranges and balls made of mud, and here too, in the same way, attacks, flight, dodging, retreating, and other similar moves provide wonderful entertainment. These horsemen also regularly compete in throwing spears at a target and smashing them to pieces; so active and agile are they in this that they often hold the spear by the point as they begin their gallop, then soon afterwards throw it in the air, catch it again by the shaft, aim it at the target and smash the spear on it. They also often compete in putting a lance through a ring suspended from a transverse cord. The lance is inserted and fixed into a reed in such a way that when the point of the lance has gone through the ring there is no more resistance, and the ring is carried away, so it does not get in the way of the galloping horse. Lastly, a goose or similar bird is sometimes suspended from a high place, and the horsemen compete to see which of them can sever the head most neatly from the body and carry it away. When they are doing this it sometimes happens that the horseman does not manage to cut through the neck of the goose at all, and he himself ends up suspended by his own hand, unseated from his galloping horse, and the butt of the spectators' ridicule. By participating enthusiastically in these and other similar exercises the Europeans hone their own equestrian skills and train their horses for battle, and these activities are at once both useful and extremely pleasurable.

Lino: I think those contests are so entertaining that I judge you were right to go to all the trouble of your voyage even just in order to see them. When I hear you talking about

---

[1] I Samuel 17:39 (Douay-Rheims version).
[2] *'Onus Aetna grauius'*, a load heavier than Etna: Cicero, *Cato Maior de Senectute*, II: 4, which alludes to Enseladus who was consumed under Mount Etna after the Olympians defeated the Giants.

them I am totally caught up in my desire to see them, and in my yearning to fly away from here in order to witness those spectacles. But do tell us what prizes are offered to the victors, and who are judges of the whole contest

Michael: There are various prizes of many different kinds, provided by the princes or rulers who are watching the contests, but for the most part they are works of gold or silver, set off with gems, or of silk, or velvet, or other precious materials. The judges or referees are other noble horsemen, expert in the same contests, who, installed at some elevated vantage point, observe the whole of the fight attentively, diligently noting blows inflicted on both sides, and errors, even slight errors, if there should be any. After taking everything into account they announce the victors, and assign the prizes to them, with great applause from all the spectators. And in order to have these solemn contests celebrated to greater renown and with more splendid attire, they usually announce two further prizes in addition to those given to the victors, namely one each for the most richly and the most elegantly dressed man to appear in public. It sometimes happens, therefore, that one and the same knight carries off three prizes, the first as victor, the second as most richly dressed, the third as most elegantly adorned; and thus decorated with prizes and with praises from all sides he draws to himself the eyes of all.

And since such a press of people, such a concourse of spectators, comes to these contests, it is easy to imagine how much they cost, and the quantity of money spent in putting on these games. We don't have the time now to speak at greater length about this, but you can read about the magnificence of these games in a variety of books, and especially in the history written about the life of the most glorious King João II of Portugal, in which there is a splendid account of the sumptuously staged contests and games at the wedding of his son prince Afonso and Isabel, the daughter of King Ferdinand of Castile.[1] But there is no need for me to rely solely on referring you to stories recorded in books, for we can tell you that when we ourselves were staying in Europe contests of this kind were staged to great acclaim at the wedding of the most illustrious duke of Savoy to the second daughter of King Philip of Spain,[2] and it was the universal opinion that these games could stand comparison with any others, however magnificent. Anyway, in order to provide the Japanese here with more information about this kind of display, and about the various types of clothing which they are accustomed to wear in Europe, we brought back from Europe a remarkable book, in which are printed very fine images of famous princes, mostly from the most ancient and noble family of King Philip of Spain.

Leo: Oh, yes. We looked through that book the other day and were very much impressed with it. Those images did not seem to be just printed; they seemed to be alive and breathing.[3] But do go on; tell us more about the equestrian exercises of the Europeans.

---

[1] Afonso (1475–91) married Isabel (1470–98) on 27 November 1490. The account of the festivities and contests referred to is Garcia de Resende, *Vida e Feitos D'El-Rey Dom João Segundo*, chs CXIV, CXVII in *Lyuro das obras de Garcia de Rese[n]de que trata da vida & grãdisimas virtudes: & bõdades magnanimo esforço: excele[n]tes costumes & manhas & muy craros feitos do christianissimo ... Rey dõ Ioão o segundo deste nome*, [Lisbon] 1545, 2nd edn 1554.

[2] See above, p. 139.

[3] On the influence of European painting and perspective in Japan at this time, see Gutiérrez, 'Survey of Nanban Art'; Vlam, 'Kings and Heroes'.

Michael: To go through all of them would take a very long time, but I will add this: the Europeans do put a great deal of effort into their horsemanship. The stables of counts, marquesses, and dukes do really contain four, five, even six or eight hundred horses, and those of kings and princes far more, and a great part of their time is taken up with exercising the horses. For the most part it is usual for the nobles to go out to the country in the morning to exercise the horses, and by galloping them until they tire and controlling them in various ways with the reins they train them for battle. Then in the evening, mounted on the same horses, they walk through the streets in the centre of the city, or through the spacious squares and open spaces which there are before the walls or in front of the magnificent houses, visible to all and presenting a very fine appearance. Thus it is that they are constantly engaged in equestrian exercises.[1]

Lino: These things which you have been relating are such that anyone eager to learn about gentlemanly pursuits must long to see them with his own eyes, for they are evidence of the extraordinary magnificence and grandeur of European men. But come, tell us whether they also engage in hunting and fowling.

Michael: With regard to hunting and fowling, I truly believe that the Europeans leave all other peoples trailing, for they diligently profess both as if they were among the noble arts. In the pursuit of them there is considerable variety in the different provinces; the people of all those provinces, however, are at one in their interest in looking out for any bird pertaining to the hawk or sea eagle species, and suitable for hawking, buying it at a high price, and taking great care of it, for there are in Europe many birds, storks, cranes, herons, and others, which can be caught by hawking, and which are either remarkably beautiful, or agreeable and varied to the taste. The Europeans also keep dogs for hunting, hunting dogs of various species, greyhounds, Molossian hounds, Corsicans, wolfhounds, and other similar kinds, and with these they hunt a variety of wild beasts, bears, boars, wolves, stags, deer, rabbits, hares, and many other animals which there are in Europe, and the kind of dog they use varies according to the kind of animal they are hunting. Some rouse the game, others tire them out with the chase and then catch them, others again struggle violently and strenuously with them, and sometimes pull and tear them apart spectacularly. All of these kinds of hunting fill the Europeans with great delight. They themselves at the same time ride their swift-moving horses in pursuit of the larger beasts, and often transfix them with their hunting spears, and return home exulting in the prime booty they bring with them.

And in all this, everything to do with both fowling and hunting, there is no doubt that the men of Europe go to great expense, and to keep these beasts more carefully it is customary for most of the nobles and patricians to have certain very extensive and spacious areas in their woods and forests surrounded by a rampart or a wall, and to keep within this area wild beasts of all kinds, and they take great delight in hunting them there whenever

---

[1] Feats of arms provided pleasure, exercise, military training and a chance for young, ambitious men to catch the eye of a future patron. Tournaments and jousting, by this time relatively safe, were indeed expensive but they provided occasions for rulers to display their wealth. See Keen, *Chivalry*, pp. 83–101, 200–212; Tuohy, *Herculean Ferrara*, pp. 246–57.

it pleases them to do so.¹ And as well as these areas they have also others, often closer to the cities, where they construct ponds, aviaries, and other similar places for pleasure, and they go there often in order to relax. I say nothing here of the delightful gardens attached to the houses themselves, as I shall be speaking about both of these later. And since we wanted to show our Japanese men all the things which we saw in Europe, we brought from Europe various books about hunting and fowling; there are pictures in them of birds and animals of various kinds, and the remarkable skill in painting and engraving them can also be seen there.

Lino: Martin showed me those books recently, and the various depictions which I saw there are so realistic that it does not appear to be a question of art imitating nature, but of a human mind having imagined all those figures. I don't believe they are imaginary, however; from the birds and animals which we have in Japan I suppose that in Europe they do have those other ones.

Michael: It is quite certain that there is nothing imaginary there, since those books were made for the use of the Europeans themselves, and not for people from outside Europe, who could possibly be deceived. The same goes for the other books, in which there are pictures of buildings, kingdoms, cities, or provinces.

Leo: There is no doubt that we should believe them, since you offer such proofs and arguments, and you yourselves, most certain witnesses, are present here. But let us hear about other kinds of enjoyable pastimes.

Michael: It would take too long to go through all the others, but besides those I have already mentioned, there are also the arts of singing, playing musical instruments, and dancing.

Leo: Do the Europeans have many musical instruments?

Michael: They do, and very agreeable ones, such as the *nablia* or psaltery, the lute, the lyre, the zither, to say nothing of those of the common people, played by blowing into them, such as *tibiae* or flutes, *sambucae* or hurdy-gurdies, recorders, trumpets, and others of the same kind, which belong within an orchestra. When all of these are skilfully played they produce a most sweet harmony.²

---

¹ There was a long tradition of hunting in Japan. It was considered one of the required skills or arts for an individual to be fully accomplished in *bunbu-ryōdō* 文武両道, the literary and martial arts (Cooper, *João Rodrigues's Account*, pp. 85, 314). Foreign observers were impressed by the size of Japanese hunts: see Fróis, *História de Japam*, V, p. 532; Saris, *Voyage*, p. 125. In a letter written in 1618 by Richard Cocks to his patron Sir Thomas Wilson, Cocks estimated the hunting party of the shogun Tokugawa Hidetada at 10,000 men. The letter, which includes vivid descriptions of Edo, Kamakura and Kyoto, was dismissed by the monarch as 'the loudest lyes that ever [he] heard of' (Massarella, 'James I and Japan', pp. 377–86, esp. pp. 378, 385). On hunting as a vital part of Eurasian political culture, see Allsen, *Royal Hunt in Eurasian History*, passim.

² On these instruments, see *New Grove Dictionary of Music and Musicians*; Marcuse, *Musical Instruments*; Harich-Schneider, 'Renaissance Europe through Japanese Eyes', p. 23; Tominaga, 'On the Nomenclature', passim.

Lino: We were indeed greatly entertained last night when we listened to you playing musical instruments, but we were not aware of that sweetness which you claim.[1]

Michael: You must remember, as we said earlier, how much we are swayed by longstanding custom, or, on the other side, by unfamiliarity and inexperience, and the same is true of singing. You are not yet used to European singing and harmony, so you do not yet appreciate how sweet and pleasant it is, whereas we, since we are now accustomed to listening to it, feel that there is nothing more agreeable to the ear. But if we care to avert our minds from what is customary, and to consider the thing in itself, we find that European singing is in fact composed with remarkable skill; it does not always keep to the same note for all voices, as ours does, but some notes are higher, some lower, some intermediate, and when all of these are skilfully sung together, at the same time, they produce a certain remarkable harmony.[2] Add to these what they call falsetto voice, and those which are higher than the normal note, all of which (whether observing the rule or, sometimes, raised above it) together with the sounds of the musical instruments, are wonderfully pleasing to the ear of the listener. With this great variety in the notes and in their modulation a whole art has developed, one of the noble arts, of composing and harmonizing these notes. Europeans apply themselves diligently to learning this art from an early age, and if they make great progress in it consider it a not unworthy way of life. With our singing, since there is no diversity in the notes, but one and the same way of producing the voice, we don't yet have any art or discipline in which the rules of harmony are contained; whereas the Europeans, with their great variety of sounds, their skilful construction of instruments, and their remarkable quantity of books on music and note shapes, have hugely enriched this art.

---

[1] The boys studied music and practised on their instruments throughout the trip. See ARSI, Jap.Sin 11: II, f.192; Gualtieri, *Relationi*, p. 152; *Dai Nihon Shiryō*, XI: 2, p. 200. In Europe they were exposed to the best of Spanish and Italian music and met some of the foremost musicians of the time. They also became quite accomplished at playing various European musical instruments by the time they returned to Japan. On the way back they performed publicly in Macao on the feast of the Circumcision and in Kyoto, during the official banquet for Valignano, they entertained Hideyoshi with a musical performance. After entering the Society, they taught others to play instruments. See ARSI, Jap.Sin 11: I, f. 46v; Fróis, *História de Japam*, V, pp. 308–9, 434, 479; Harich-Schneider, 'Renaissance Europe through Japanese Eyes', pp. 19–21; Waterhouse, 'Southern Barbarian Music', p. 364; Tominaga, 'On the Nomenclature', pp. 13–14. On the musical instruments brought to Japan before the boys' return, see Harich-Schneider, *History of Japanese Music*, pp. 466–7; and esp. Waterhouse, 'Southern Barbarian Music', pp. 351–60. See also Verwilghen, 'Christian Music in Japan', pp. 1–13. Despite the extensive use and importance of music in the Jesuit mission to Japan, Loyola had strongly disapproved of music in Jesuit institutions and services. His successors were divided on the issue, opponents arguing that music was not conducive to piety and encouraged moral laxity while others appreciated its inspirational capacity. At this time there was a more tolerant attitude towards the use of music in Jesuit institutions in Asia and America than in Europe. Valignano himself favoured music in church services and music was used to attract curious Japanese to Christian services. See Wicki, 'Gesang, Tänze und Musik', pp. 15–30, repr. in *Missionskirche im Orient*, pp. 138–52, esp. p. 150; Kennedy, 'Jesuits and Music', pp. 70–95; Waterhouse, 'Southern Barbarian Music', pp. 354–9; Crook, '"A Certain Indulgence"', pp. 462–3.

[2] In Japanese music there are five tones or '*goin*' although *gagaku* or court music uses the heptatonic scale. See *Vocabvlario*, f. 354, '*goyn. Cinco toadas ou toens da voz da musica de Iapam*' (*goin*. Five tones or vocal sounds of Japanese music); Cooper, *João Rodrigues's Account*, p. 352 n. 6; Harich-Schneider, *History of Japanese Music*, p. 460; Waterhouse, 'Southern Barbarian Music', p. 353. For a general discussion of Japanese music at this time, see Malm, 'Music Cultures of Momoyama Japan', *passim*.

Lino: I am sure all these things which you say are true; for the variety of the instruments and the books which you have brought back, as well as the singing and the modulation of harmony, testify to a remarkable artistic system. Nor do I doubt that our normal expectations in listening to singing are an impediment when it comes to appreciating the beauties of European harmony. But now tell us something about the ways in which, in Europe, they dance or tread a measure.[1]

Michael: It will be enough to know that these too are many and various, according to the variety of the music from the lyres, on which all dancing depends. These styles do vary, and are appropriate to different ages and persons, so that whereas dances for the young are light-hearted, those in which men dance with men, women with women, or men with women, especially at a solemn or royal ball, present a demeanour at once grave and festive.

Leo: You say that women dance with men. This would seem greatly to detract from the gravity of the Europeans.

Michael: Not at all; the dance is performed with such maturity and modesty that it delights the heart without in any way inciting to lasciviousness. This gives me an opportunity to say something about the virtue and seriousness of European women; it is such as rightly to strike any foreign visitor with admiration, and it is customary for Europeans to consider that the highest point of their honour is to be found in the character, the refinement, the dwelling, and the whole way of life, redolent of an admirable virtue, of their women. Thus it is that there is no greater dishonour with which anyone's name can be branded than the suspicion, be it never so slight, that a wife, or a close blood relative, even if she is unmarried, has compromised her faithfulness or her virtue; and they do not hesitate to cleanse their honour of this stain, even at the cost of shedding of the blood of the women, although the law provides that this should be done not by individuals but by the officials.[2]

Leo: Is the art of dancing in Europe very different from the style that we follow, and is it totally superior to ours?

Michael: Comparisons of different peoples and their customs usually result in offence being given if some nations are preferred to others; so it was never my intention to bestow overmuch praise on European customs, nor to belittle the customs of Japan,

---

[1] The business of music printing had taken off at the start of the 16th century. Much was available at the time of the boys' stay in Europe. While music lovers were beginning to appreciate and recognize differences among composers, Europeans were only beginning to value the importance of the sound of music rather than a composer's mastery of technique (Haar, 'Value Judgements in Music of the Renaissance', pp. 15–22).

[2] In early modern patriarchal societies the sanctity and stability of marriage was considered essential for the maintenance of social order and for the acquisition and disposal of property. Nevertheless, adultery was common at all social levels. Wife murder was tolerated in order to maintain family honour, but generally not approved, particularly in view of the prevailing view that women were the weaker sex. See Hale, *Florence and the Medici*, p. 147; Carroll, *Blood and Violence*, pp. 234, 237–8. For a graphic description of the punishment meted out to the cuckold-maker by the cuckolded and his accomplices, see Hale, *Civilization of Europe*, p. 423.

except perhaps in the case of some custom disapproved of and rejected by divine law or the common consensus of all peoples. And with regard to dancing, ours could easily be said to be an imitation or copy of European dancing if certain things were taken out of it, things which in the judgment of the Europeans have nothing much to do with dancing.

Leo: What are these things which you say have nothing much to do with dancing?

Michael: Two in particular: the first is that among us those who dance often appear in public masked, either putting on the sad likeness of some woman already dead, with dishevelled hair and sorrowful face, or representing similarly the spirit already released from the body of a man; and these appear to induce sadness and lamentation rather than the gaiety and gladness proper to dancing. The other is that the dancer sometimes stops in the middle of the dance, and produces a sound as of wailing, and the others who are watching answer with the same sound, so that to the Europeans it seems more like a confused howling than a festive and joyful dance. So if the Japanese would lay aside those mournful impersonations, and would always dance in splendid finery, and if they would keep to the sound generally used in Europe, they would have a grasp of the norms of European dancing. But, let each nation keep its own customs![1]

Leo: One question remains on this subject, namely whether the Europeans use any performance or drama on solemn feasts.

Michael: In our opinion European drama excels all other drama, of any nation. Their types of drama are many and varied, with dialogue, comedy, tragedy, tragicomedy, and other similar performances, in which there are many things to admire; to say nothing of the splendour of the costumes, the works which are sometimes staged to represent some event are remarkable. Such an artfully constructed likeness is put before the spectators of a city, a citadel, or some other place, that it seems to be not a likeness of the place in question, but the very city or citadel itself. And those who take the parts of the men or women who speak accommodate their voices to the subject, so that they can be joyful or doleful, sometimes solemn, sometimes more cheerful, in fact moving through all the moods in such a way that the variations seem not to spring from any artifice but to be entirely natural. They do not raise their voices as if singing, as is usual with our performers. There are, however, most beautiful songs which occur in the course of each performance; there are also certain interludes, as they call them, witty or comical, and these give a balance to the totality of the performance, so that though it be long it is seldom boring, even if it continues with the people watching for many hours. And from all this you can appreciate the expense involved in putting on these plays, which is often reckoned to be four or five thousand ducats.

---

[1] *Nō* 能 remains a difficult art form for non-Japanese to appreciate easily. Fróis described the *gagaku* 雅楽 or court music which was performed during the ceremonial visit of the emperor Go-Yōzei and the retired emperor Ōgimachi in 1588 as 'dissonant and little pleasing' (Fróis, *História de Japam*, V, p. 70). Elsewhere, Valignano described Japanese music as 'tormenting the hearing' (Valignano, *História*, p. 143).

Leo: I declare that all things European are admirable, for since so much money is expended on them that there is nothing impossible to obtain, it is evident that there is nothing, no matter how difficult, which the Europeans do not bring to a successful conclusion.

Lino: I would like to ask if there are other games which you have not yet told us about.

Michael: There is certainly no shortage of other games for relaxation of the mind among those noble and wealthy nations living in such peace and tranquillity. Most common of all is a ball game, which the Europeans regularly play in a large court,[1] and with this game not only do they refresh their minds, spending their time innocently and by no means idly, but they also attend to their health, getting rid, with exercise and sweat, of the bad humours which their rich and varied food tends to produce, and leaving their bodies agile and fit for work. There are other games as well, for example chess (something like our chess, indeed, but also differing in a number of points),[2] draughts,[3] dice, cards,[4] and some of these are in use among us too. But now that, while we have been giving an account of these pleasant exercises, a great deal of time has slipped past almost without our noticing, let us break off our narration to interpose some rest, and leave until tomorrow our next topic, namely government.

---

[1] Tennis.

[2] 将棋 *shōgi* Japanese chess, which like its Western counterpart originated in India and reached Japan via China in the Nara period (710–94).

[3] *go* 碁.

[4] *karuta* カルタ playing cards, from the Portuguese *carta*, introduced by the Portuguese and which sparked a gambling craze.

COLLOQUIUM XII

The arrangements and customs of Europeans with regard to the administration of kingdoms and republics

Leo: We have been eagerly awaiting today's meeting, to hear you speak about the way of governing in use among the Europeans, and the wait of one day has seemed long indeed.

Michael: I shall be glad to deal with this subject, to prepare the way for another most pleasing to you, namely the order in which an army is led into the field, since peaceful government comes before the conventions of engaging in battle. The first thing to note about administration in Europe is that the target set and, so to say, the basic foundation laid for kings and governors of republics, is that the leading men, who have the governance of the kingdom, the people, or the republic, must serve not their private but the public interest, and must see to it that the entire people be kept in complete peace and tranquillity, that rewards be distributed according to merit and virtue, and, in fine, that in everything the principle applied should be true and genuine justice, with all laws, institutes, and decrees being directed to this end. For this reason the kings and principal men take contributions and taxes from the whole population, in order to return an equal favour to them by sustaining and protecting the people according to the laws of right and justice. For it is not only the light of nature which urges kings to maintain their people in peace and justice; the divine law itself, handed down by Christ the supreme teacher, admonishes men about the same thing, teaching clearly that the more that is committed to the care of any person, the more severely that person will be called to account for it, as can be seen in the parable of the talents in the Gospel.[1] Thus those who govern to satisfy their own unbridled appetites, and not for the good of the people, who mete out violence rather than justice, are called not true kings or princes, but Tyrants.[2]

Now, to go through the various types of European government one by one: it is certain that in the philosophy which deals with customs, there are three ways of governing a multitude. The first is when just one prince holds the supreme governance of the whole multitude; and this way of governing, if the prince rules the people according to law, is called Monarchy,[3] and this is like what we call the Tenka, which is to say, the universal administration. But if his rule is by power and violence, and not by law and justice, the philosophers usually refer to it as tyranny. The second is when the one government is

---

[1] Matthew 25:14–30.
[2] Original edition (p. 114), *Tyrani*.
[3] Ibid., *Monarchia*.

managed by many; this government is called a constitutional government[1] if it is constituted by law, but a Democracy[2] if it is occupied by force. The third is when the whole administration of the multitude depends on a few; if these are men outstanding in virtue and observant of justice and the laws, this way of governing is usually known as Aristocracy;[3] but if they are men who pervert justice it is referred to as Oligarchy.[4] Thus in each of the ways of governing both good and bad administration can be found; good when its concern is for justice and law, but bad when its eyes are on force, power, and private greed.[5]

The European kings and princes act according to the first way, rightly administered. Certain free republics follow the second way, rightly, however, and justly, obeying no king or prince; an example is the most illustrious Republic of the Venetians, which I mentioned briefly already, and shall have more to say about later. The kingdoms and republics of Europe, however, are administered not only according to the common law, drawn from nature itself, and interpreted by the laws of Caesar and the Ancients, but also according to the particular rules of the various kingdoms, provinces, and republics, and these from time to time moderate the common law, and adapt it to the needs of different places, provinces, and nations. And in order that every place in the entire kingdom or republic might participate in just administration not only are there the magistrates of highest rank established in the principal city or metropolis of the kingdom or republic to administer justice for the citizens; there are also others of lesser rank distributed throughout all the cities and towns, magistrates, judges, sheriffs, commissioners, superintendents, and other similar officials, each of whom diligently examines the cases (different according to the different office of each) brought before him, hears and considers the reasons adduced by both sides, and brings an end to the dispute or quarrel. And in addition to these to whom belongs the administration of justice, there are other counsellors, to whom other graver negotiations are referred: with regard to the waging of war, for example, or concluding alliances, pardoning crimes, rewarding the deserving, and finally, with regard to the safekeeping and augmenting of the income of the kingdom.[6]

---

[1] Ibid., *Politia*.
[2] Ibid., *Democratia*.
[3] Ibid., *Aristocratia*.
[4] Ibid., *Oligarchiae*.
[5] The categories are taken from Aristotle's *Politics* (Book III: 7).
[6] Here and in what follows Valignano gives an idealized account of the political, juridical and social structures of contemporary Europe. Nevertheless, the account reflects a number of common assumptions in Jesuit political thought. Firstly, 'the people' were the authors of the *leges regiae* or fundamental laws of a polity. Laws were not imposed by a ruler and the ruler was not above the laws. Nor were the laws derived from God directly. Secondly, while recognizing the diversity of political institutions in states, the Jesuits had a preference for monarchy, but not, of course, unfettered monarchy or tyranny. Monarchy was the most efficient agency through which to apply and enforce laws. Thirdly, the Jesuits believed in hierarchy, the preservation of which helped ensure stability and a well-functioning polity. Fourthly, while the Jesuits were unique in taking a fourth vow, one of obedience to the pope, this did not mean that they unswervingly exalted the power of the papacy above that of the secular rulers, although, obversely, as becomes clear later in the colloquium, they held that the papacy enjoyed a *potestas indirecta* in temporal affairs. In reality, the Jesuits trod a fine line in their dealings with the secular and papal powers. To have supported the papacy too overtly, as some Jesuit commentators favoured, would have fatally undermined their ability to continue their activities which depended greatly on the support of secular authorities. The point was made by Loyola: 'All members of the body participate in the welfare of the head, and all subjects in the

Leo: These arrangements for the administration of justice seem to me excellent, but I would like you to explain to us in more detail the procedure which is followed in a trial.

Michael: I can only tell you what I heard, for we never had the chance to be present at any trials. Firstly, therefore, whenever there is a dispute between two people about the law with regard to something which they want to have, a day is set on which he who is called to trial must present himself before a judge. The person who is the plaintiff bringing the suit against him presents his petition, and the accused puts the case for rejecting it; the plaintiff then impugns the reasons advanced by the accused with further documentation, and the accused is afforded the opportunity to reply. With the two sides of it being put in this way the judge has a much better appreciation of the difficulties of the case. They proceed then to give evidence supporting the points made; there is an appeal to witnesses on both sides, with a written record of their testimony, and if any particular witness is suspected of hiding or exaggerating or playing down the truth, the disputants can, with the permission of the judge, exclude him. After testimony has been brought by both sides to shed light on the dispute, accused and accuser are again given the opportunity to argue their case at the end of the process. The judge considers long and earnestly all of this, duly recorded; he then gives his decision, and when it has been written out, signed and sealed, he promulgates it in court.

After this promulgation, if it is a matter of minor importance, after a certain number of days which are allowed for objections, if no plea is brought forward, the judge's decision can be carried out, and that puts an end to the whole process. If the matter is of greater importance, however, either the plaintiff or the defendant is at liberty to appeal to a higher magistrate, and he, after a conference with his associates or assessors, has the power either to confirm and ratify the judgement pronounced by the lower judge, or to rescind it entirely. By the observing of this order of things all have the assurance of the fullness of justice; patricians and nobles cannot bring force to bear on the common people, but all live under the same law, and each is given his due.

Lino: This way of doing things which you have described is perfectly in accordance with reason, so long as it does not provide an occasion for men of inferior condition to think less of men of knightly or senatorial class.

Michael: There is no danger of that, for the gentry are always held in honour by the people. If a dispute arises an action is brought against them, but without any point of the

---

welfare of the prince, and so we ought to esteem the spiritual assistance that we give to these [princes] more highly than the assistance that we provide others' (quoted in Bireley, *Jesuits and the Thirty Years War*, p. 27, see also p. 273). Fifthly, the Society did not have an official policy advocating tyrannicide, although there could be circumstances under which it was warranted, but only with regard to Christian rulers who were, by definition, within the church. Some of these assumptions were reflected in Valignano's and other Jesuits' thinking about Japan, an obviously hierarchical society in which, after years of warfare, strong 'monarchical' rulers (Nobunaga, Hideyoshi and, later, Tokugawa Ieyasu) were emerging. Alas, because of the deficiency of the laws, in the Jesuit assessment these rulers, became tyrants rather than Japanese avatars of the idealized Renaissance prince pictured in *De Missione*. On the complexity of Jesuit political thought, see Höpfl, *Jesuit Political Thought*, esp. pp. 225–7, 347–51, 358, 363–5, 371–6. On the flexibility of Jesuit political thought in practice, see Bireley, *Jesuits and the Thirty Years War*, passim.

veneration and reverence due to them as gentry being affected; and they do not themselves appear in court, the action being conducted by advocates and agents, except in the case of very grave crime, which we shall be speaking of shortly.

Mancio: You should not be surprised, dear Lino, that in Europe the nobles too can be taken to court, even by the common people, for the kings themselves are also subject to the same law. Whenever it happens that any person finds that his interests have been harmed by the king or prince it is open to him to take to court the name of the king, a name so revered among the Europeans, and this in no way stains the dignity of the king. For this reason there is in every kingdom someone appointed as royal advocate, who can be taken to court in the name of the king, and who can bring before the judges anyone who diminishes or misappropriates royal property; and it is by their judgment, and not merely by the will of the king, that cases concerning him are concluded. The European kings are most just; they do not wish anyone to be unjustly harassed by themselves, nor do they wish their own property to be eroded or stolen by any criminal; therefore all disputes and cases with which the kings are connected are decided not by their unbridled desires, but by most just laws and ancient right.

Martin: There is another point I should like to add about the royal justice. Whenever someone has deserved well of the royal majesty either in war or in some employment, and deserves that the king add honours to his fortune, or grant him some payment, this deserving man is at liberty to petition the king for an increase of the honour or the payment, with documentation and evidence of his achievements and his work, taking his claim to the officials of the king; and they decide what reward or remuneration he deserves, and arrange for it to be given to him by the king. And further, if a man of this kind, who has deserved well, is conscious that the treatment he has received is less than his just due, he can still take his complaint to the officials, and expostulate with them about the inadequacy of the reward or stipend, until he succeeds in obtaining the position, the reward, or the payment which he deserves.

Leo: That order of procedure cannot be seen as other than admirable, and if it is followed it is certain that there will no longer be any offence or injustice with regard to punishment or remuneration.

Julian: The procedure followed by European kings in all things is indeed wonderful, not only in the things which have been mentioned, but also in all their other duties of every kind; for they take account of the place and rank of each one, and deal with nobles and other men in such a way as to omit no part, however small, of their duty.

Michael: I shall say something besides about cases concerning crimes; these are brought either by accusation, or by denunciation, or by investigation by a judge. In all of these, as has already been said, arguments are offered and evidence produced on both sides; and if these provide some indication that a crime has been committed the defendant is thrown into prison, or held in custody in some other place, according to the dignity of each, so that his crime may be more safely discussed, for no one is condemned to death rashly, without much long and mature consideration. Accordingly, since Europeans know that they will be treated justly under the law, they allow themselves to be put in jail without undue upset, for they see that some are brought from jail to suffer their punishment, but others leave unpunished and free, depending on the merits of each, which will have been properly examined by the judges.

Leo: Our Japanese are by no means as calm about this as the Europeans, who, as you say, do not take it so hard when they are put in prison; our Japanese men, by contrast, are so proud that they often redeem a stay of even one day in prison with their blood and their lives.

Michael: It is not surprising if our men do that, since here in Japan in the government of kingdoms and the administration of justice the European order of procedure is not observed. Our Japanese, knowing that those summoned to imprisonment are going to certain death, and that a death sentence has already been passed on them, do not hesitate to anticipate the threat to their lives, and to repel by force of arms the violence to be visited on them, so as not themselves to have to undergo the disregard for right and justice which they have witnessed in a variety of cases of others condemned to an undeserved death or cruelly killed.[1]

Mancio: That is certainly the reason why the Japanese are so indignantly opposed to being imprisoned; our rulers and lords and other leading figures, following not justice or law but the movements and perturbations of their own spirits, and fearing that other men may play them false, disgorge on to them the poison of their own bitterness, and inflict dreadful punishment on the innocent.

Leo: It is indeed true that the blame lies to some extent with the rulers and princes, but the other men who are subject to the princes must also take their share of it; for their

---

[1] Although embroiled in civil wars, Japan was not lawless. Domains had their own House Laws (家法 *kahō*). In the *Sumario*, Valignano noted the frequency of wars between the daimyo but claimed that within the domains themselves people live 'more peacefully than among us in Europe because they do not have so many fights and stabbings as are usual in Europe'. According to custom, he continued, those who wounded or killed someone, other than their own servants or vassals, were sentenced to death (pp. 13–14). Fróis described this as the 'absolute and obligatory law of Japan' (*História de Japam*, I, p. 118). See also Katsumata, 'Development of Sengoku Law', pp. 101–24. Later, in the *Principio*, Valignano described Japan as being governed by military law, in the same manner as armies in Europe were. However, with the ascendance of Nobunaga, and more so Hideyoshi, the lord of the Tenka had acquired absolute power, so much so that Valignano quoted a Japanese saying, of Chinese origin, that there is not a span of land in the country over which the lord is not sovereign. Within their respective domains, Valignano suggested, the daimyo had '*mero y mixto imperio*', that is jurisdiction over civil and criminal matters, including life and death, but they were subject to attainder at any time should the lord of the Tenka so order. While conceding that this seemingly arbitrary power was 'fearful and terrifying', Valignano, echoing some of the assertions in Machiavelli's *Art of War* (1521), argued that such governance, which had parallels in the military institutions of Europe, was not so harsh nor unreasonable for it had provided peace and order and there was less violence in Japan than in other polities which had more laws and a greater propensity towards legal proceedings. A further advantage, he suggested, was that, as estates were subject to attainder, the daimyo were not attached to material things and could easily accept their loss, and those who had become Christian could see such loss as beneficial for the well-being of their souls. See Valignano, *Principio*, ch. 5, printed in *Adiciones*, p. 404, and ch. 6, printed in *Sumario*, pp. 318–30 esp. pp. 318, 325–8. In practice the centre did not dominate the Japanese polity to the extent Valignano and others imagined. This would become clearer under the Tokugawa shogunate; on this point see Ravina, *Land and Lordship*, esp. pp. 40–45.

tendency is to defect from their own prince to another as soon as the slightest suspicion arises in their minds that in some way they are going to be punished. Thus it is hardly surprising if, after quick and secret inquiry into capital matters, the princes, when they know of crimes committed, inflict severe punishment on men within their jurisdiction.

Michael: I do not take the view that conspirators minded to foment rebellion are to be excused, but I am convinced that the whole overall cause of all the disorder arises from a distortion of the right administration of justice; for if the princes, in judging cases, kept to justice and the law, men living under their jurisdiction would easily allow themselves to be bound by the law, knowing that if penalties were imposed on them it would be by due process of law, and not at the whim of troubled kings. But when they see that they will have no chance to refute or disprove the charge against them, nor to impugn the reliability of suspect evidence, nor indeed any opportunity to prove their own innocence, they defend themselves by force of arms against the violence and injustice with which they are confronted.

Lino: It seems to me, all the same, judging by what you have told us, that in Europe too the whole question of punishment depends on the rulers and the kings, since all cases are ultimately referred to them, as to the supreme judges.

Michael: Europe is entirely different from Japan in this matter. In Europe, as I said before, the kings have constituted and designated magistrates, all of them expert in the law, who deal diligently with all cases, both capital cases and what are called civil cases, after hearing the arguments and testimony adduced by both sides. Thus everything is done with due process of law, and without any regard to the anger or rage of the kings; and therefore the kings do not normally impose the death penalty, nor exile, nor confiscation of property, nor any other similar punishment, on anyone, unless the punishment is approved by the judges or magistrates, even if the prisoners themselves are accused of conspiracy to kill the king and take over the kingdom. With regard to the question of what evidence justifies what penalty, this does not depend simply on the judgment of the magistrates, but is prescribed by the sanctions of ancient law, which the judges must keep to, honestly and impartially. And besides, the actual penalties appropriate to each crime are set out in the laws and in the institutes of their forefathers.

Leo: This order which you set before us must be judged not only congruent with reason, but also divine and heavenly. But I would ask further whether the kings are so bound by the laws that they can never contravene them so as to kill men without reference to the magistrates.

Michael: They can indeed do that, if they are willing to abandon the role of king, and take on the very different character of Tyrant. This title, as I said before, denotes those who have no regard for the law, and govern according to their unrestrained appetites. But any kings who should wish to govern their kingdoms in violation of the laws would not only be accepting the hated name of Tyrant, but would also lay themselves open to rebuke for their crime, with great shame and dishonour, by the priests who hear their private confession of sins, and by the bishops and archbishops to whom belongs the sacred administration of their entire kingdoms. It could be that they would take things to such an extreme as to alienate the whole people and rouse them to opposition and even to take arms against them; and they could even go so far that the Supreme Pontiff might abrogate their power and authority. Thus there are many constraints in Europe on even the most powerful of kings in the exercise of their office.

Lino: All this is fine, provided it does not diminish or dilute the reverence or veneration of subjects for their kings.

Michael: There is nothing there that can detract from the veneration of kings, and much indeed that in every way promotes this respect and reverence. The Divine Law commands it, and also the majesty and power of the kings themselves; finally the love which Europeans have in their souls for their kings, especially when they see that they are governed with such benevolence and love; all these things move the Europeans powerfully towards reverence for their kings. But if you wish to have some knowledge of how great the good will of Europeans is towards their rulers, you can have a clear it understanding of it by considering the things which happen in Japan, for opposites are often best studied in comparison with each other.[1]

In Japan we see here or there lords killed by their servants, princes and rulers driven and expelled from their domains by those who are under their jurisdiction, and all too frequent conspiracy and sedition.[2] In Europe, on the other hand, things are very different: those who are under the jurisdiction of some prince afford him a most loving respect, as to a parent, and there is no one thinking of conspiracy or faction. The rulers themselves are so pleasant in their manner that they treat their subjects with indulgence, as if they were their children, and they lie in such security and tranquillity of spirit that they never fear that there is anyone so wicked as to plot treason against them; and individuals and the common people have no fear that the rulers may suddenly have them killed, for they know that if they have committed any crime a case has to be brought against them with due process of law, and only then, if it is right, are they to be cast into prison, and from there every one of them is permitted to make his defence, or even to be in free custody, and to present himself before the judges. And if there is something which prisoners and criminals fear, it is the length of the imprisonment, the trouble involved in clearing up the crime, and finally death itself, which although it may come entirely justly, nevertheless is wont to afflict men with very great fear.[3] But here in Japan, by contrast, neither rulers nor those subject to their jurisdiction live secure: the princes fear some perfidious machination, and

---

[1] The subject matter of Fróis's *Tratado*.

[2] A reference to the subversion of established hierarchies during the *sengoku* wars when the phenomenon of *gekokujō* 下剋上, the toppling of lords by their inferiors, turned the social order upside down. The expression was included in the *Vocabvlario* (f. 115v.). The *sengoku* period was also the age of the *nariagari* 成上り or upstart, the most striking example of whom was Hideyoshi. In the *Adiciones*, written after his return to Japan in 1590, Valignano praised Hideyoshi for his 'vigour, prudence and great government', qualities that had transformed Japan into 'a perfect monarchy', peaceful and law abiding (pp. 366–9, esp. p. 366). In the *Principio*, he acknowledged that while no one was secure in their estate the country enjoyed peace and security (printed in Valignano, *Sumario*, pp. 329–30).

[3] As a student Valignano himself had languished in a Venetian prison for more than a year after a sword fighting incident. He was freed thanks to the intervention of the papal nuncio. See *Sumario*, p. 5*; Schütte, *Valignano's Mission Principles*, 1: 1, p. 32 and n. 106.

the subjects fear that some punishment will be unjustly inflicted on them either by the harshness of an irate ruler, or because of the calumny of their enemies. Thus even in the middle of a banquet there is often a copious spilling of blood, and song and concert turns to wailing and lamentation.[1]

Mancio: It is so, indeed, in all things, so that when I recollect that peace and security of Europe I cannot but marvel; but when I consider the ways of our people, I see plainly that our people care little for love, for faith, for friendship. Thus it is that there is no place, no position, no family which is not in great danger, and such are the changes of positions and of families that position and power hardly ever survive from great-grandfather and great-great-grandfather to grandchild and great-grandchild; whereas in Europe power and position of honour are often handed down over centuries from ancestor to ultimate descendant, continuing without any intermission.

Leo: O how blessed that land, how happy that region, where peace, tranquillity, and security flourish so; how happy too the rulers who have such men under their jurisdiction, and the people, who are governed with such love and benevolence by their rulers! But I should like to know how European judges proceed whenever crimes are not clearly known but are merely suspected and under investigation.

Michael: In all these cases, and in others there are certain norms which have been handed down, prisoners are dealt with in one way when the evidence is clear, in another when information about the crime is unclear, in another again when there are only slight suspicions to go on. But in addition to the evidence there is sometimes also a confession of the crime either proffered by the criminal of his own will, or extorted from him by torture; and if the men in question are such that torture cannot be used, some lighter punishment is imposed in accordance with the gravity of the suspicions and the evidence.

Lino: Would that we had the same order of things here in Japan, instead of having innocent people condemned to death or exile at the merest hint of a suspicion of crime. But tell us whether those condemned to death in Europe are put on a cross as is done

---

[1] The House Laws outlawed the resort to violence as a way of settling scores or affronts to honour (Katsumata, 'Development of Sengoku Law', pp. 104–8, 117). Violence was also far more common in Europe than *De Missione* alleges, as Valignano conceded in the *Sumario* (see above, p. 163 n. 1). In France, churches were among the most common places for settling scores, especially during or after services when the intended victim would be most likely to let down his guard. In Italy, churches were preferred locations for the assassination of princes. In Japan, on the other hand, Fróis noted, Christians removed their swords on entering a church, retaining only their single-edged short sword or *wakizaki*, as a mark of respect and to defy anyone intent on disrupting the services (Valignano, *Sumario*, p. 13, n. 61). Violent crime and the resort to violence to settle disputes was endemic in Rome when the boys visited the city. The citizens armed themselves accordingly, resisting attempts by the papal authorities to curb violence by outlawing arms. Violence could be gruesome. In May 1585, while the boys were in Italy, a bread riot took place in Naples. One of the town councillors whom the poor blamed for the rising price of bread was seized by the rebels, tortured, castrated, mutilated and finally killed. Some of the rebels bit into the victim's raw flesh and sucked the blood. The boys had to cancel their visit to Naples because of these disturbances. See Burckhardt, *Civilization of the Renaissance*, p. 32; Muir, *Ritual in Early Modern Europe*, p. 120; Carroll, *Blood and Violence*, pp. 118–25; Blastenbrei, 'Violence, Arms and Criminal Justice', pp, 68–87.

here, or boiled in a cauldron, or, for the sake of testing the blade of a sword, cut to pieces?[1]

Michael: Since in Europe it is a question not of passion or anger but of justice, persons condemned to death are treated by the rulers and magistrates with complete humanity. They are not suddenly carried off to death, but first are benevolently informed by a priest that they are to be punished by death for the crime they have committed; they are therefore advised that they ought to cleanse their souls by confession, and beseech God for pardon for their sins, and implore all the saints to intercede for them. Encouraged by these words they listen patiently to the sentence pronounced on them, and then are taken from the prison with a great concourse of people, with some religious, to the place of execution, which we call the gallows, and there are hanged, or beheaded, or put to death in some other way, differing with the various provinces and persons, but without any sign of cruelty. They are not boiled in cauldrons, nor are they crucified, for the cross is the sign of our salvation, and therefore is revered by all as holy and sacred. Nor is it lawful to try the edge of a sword on the body of anyone, living or dead; indeed the bodies of the dead are handed over, even by enemies, for pious burial.[2]

Leo: It occurs to me to ask besides how the magistrates deal with the children and wives of men condemned to death. In Europe do they too suffer the penalty of death, of forfeiture of property, and of slavery, as normally happens here in Japan?

Michael: With regard to the children and wives of the condemned, they cannot be punished with the penalty of death or of slavery for the crimes of their parents, and there is no confiscation of property, except where treason or some other particularly atrocious crime has been committed. In the case of such a crime, the wife still retains some part of the property, but that part which belonged to the husband is taken into the royal treasury; for the Europeans do not consider it just that a wife, who was not privy to any crime,

---

[1] Valignano describes Japanese punishments, including crucifixion, or more accurately 'stringing up' (磔 *haritsuke*), which dated from the 12th century, in the *Sumario*, pp. 14–19. Boiling alive (釜煎り *kamairi*) was a more recent invention. See also Schmidt, *Capital Punishment in Japan*; Botsman, *Punishment and Power*, pp. 14, 16–17.

[2] This assertion does not square with the facts. Torture and executions in Europe were often cruel and bloodthirsty. Montaigne, for example, believed that executions should be simple and speedy. Anything other than that would be cruel because care must be taken to ensure that the soul departs the body in a state of grace which would be unlikely after an individual had endured lengthy torments. He also abhorred the unbridled cruelty unleashed by the Wars of Religion and the sheer pleasure men derived from killing. See *Essais*, II, bk 2, ch. 11, pp. 109–11; Muir, *Ritual in Early Modern Europe*, p. 118; Hale, *Civilization of Europe*, p. 425. As has been mentioned, Valignano wrote that, despite the prevalence of civil war, within each domain there was more peace and order than in Europe because there were fewer fights and stabbings (above p. 163 n. 1), but he also alleged that the Japanese were disposed to cruelty and easily killed people, even simply to try out their swords (*Sumario*, pp. 30–31). Later, in the *Principio*, he changed his mind and denied that the Japanese were inherently cruel or barbarian. Deaths, he said, occurred in battle or in the course of carrying out the lawful commands of their lords and the testing of swords (試し斬り *tameshigiri*) on people was a rare occurrence (*Principio*, ch. 8, printed in Üçerler, 'Sacred Historiography', II, pp. 51–2). Christian sources suggest that the testing of swords was common. In the Edo period, however, sword testing was practised in the grounds of the prisons on the corpses of those just executed, which is what Kaempfer reported. See *Sumario*, p. 31 n. 44; Bodart-Bailey, *Kaempfer's Japan*, p. 223; Botsman, *Punishment and Power*, p. 20.

should undergo the same punishment as her criminal husband. The reason for passing laws, after all, is to do away with crime, not to provide rulers with opportunities for the exercise of cruelty and avarice.

Lino: All of that is entirely in accord with reason; namely that he who has committed the crime should suffer the due punishment, but that the welfare and the property of the innocent should be unaffected. But here in Japan, as we see, things are different. Here, whenever there is question of any crime, even of a minor sort, many innocent persons are put to death, their property is confiscated, and their rights are violated.[1]

Mancio: It is hardly surprising if that is the notion of justice, or rather injustice, which the Japanese have, since they are still pagans; they are not concerned about the future, eternal, life, and they cannot be compelled by law to restore what belongs to another; nor do they govern the people for the common good, but rather for their private advantage. Let us therefore pray to God that sooner or later He may let the light of the Christian faith shine upon the Japanese, so that thus illuminated they may more easily understand the requirements of the law of nature, and what is conducive to the common good.

Leo: God grant that that may happen! For we already have considerable experience of the value of the Christian religion in the governing of the state in those princes who are numbered among the Christians, their way of governing the people being very different from that which the pagans follow. There will come a time when our people will totally abandon all customs contrary to justice, and all false religion, and Christian customs together with true piety will take deep root in Japan. But now I would like to know whether European kings ever, even when grave necessity puts them under pressure, seize possessions which are not their own; and if there happen to be certain men of the nobility who do not find favour with them, whether the kings can deprive those men of their status and replace them with others.

Michael: That would be entirely alien to European custom; for neither kings nor princes can drive anyone from his possessions if there is no crime committed or before sentence is passed on prisoners. If, however, a kingdom is threatened by some grave danger, and a great sum of money is required in order to dispel that danger, the kings convoke citizens' assemblies, and the revenue collectors of all the cities come together, and they ask the people for a subsidy. The people, through their agents and procurators, decide on the sum of money, and this is collected from each individual, quietly and in peace, without offence to anyone. It sometimes happens that the king suffers a repulse, the people judging that the danger is not so grave, or the necessity so absolute, that they should have to submit to a compulsory tax. With regard to those who are somewhat out of favour with the king, the king may treat them with less familiarity, or offer them fewer honours, or even forbid them access and audience, but if they are guilty of no crime he cannot deprive them of their goods or turn the goods over to others for their use. And thus the Europeans pass their lives in great security.

---

[1] For an account of the dispossession of Ōtomo Yoshimune for disobedience during Hideyoshi's invasion of Korea in 1592, see Fróis, *História de Japam*, V, pp. 486–90.

Leo: I marvel indeed that, in all that power which the European kings have private cupidity and individual desires have no place.

Mancio: So far are the European kings from indulging their own desires when it comes to government that they do not even order the distribution of money from their own treasury without diligent deliberation and examination of the merits of those to whom the money is to be awarded.

Leo: An excellent mode of government indeed. But now at the end of this colloquium I have a question: is the power of the kings great enough for them to be able sometimes to overrule the law, pardon those condemned to death, and set them free unpunished?

Michael: Yes. The royal prerogative does include this power, which cannot be taken from the European kings by any law. However, the kings are very observant of justice and of the law, and will not cancel the punishment imposed by the judges except after very careful consideration, perhaps, for example, sometimes when the prisoner has such gifts of nature, or such merits, that his life should be spared for the sake of the common good, or where there is other just reason for exempting him from his punishment. But if the crime committed by the prisoner is such that it involves harm to someone, the prisoner is never freed from his sentence until the harm has been put right.

Leo: It remains for me to ask whether dukes, marquesses, and counts can also punish criminals with death in the places under their jurisdiction, and to ask further whether any nobleman can impose the death penalty on a servant who has committed a crime?

Michael: With regard to dukes, marquesses, counts, or other rulers, who have some authority or jurisdiction, but who nevertheless are obedient to the kings, the procedure is that the magistrates authorized by these dukes and rulers, magistrates who must be qualified in the law, can in certain cases sentence prisoners even to death, but with provision made for appeals to the royal senate and the supreme judges, as happens in other cities which are directly subject to the kings, without being under the jurisdiction of any other rulers. On the authority of the supreme judges either the sentence is confirmed, or it is commuted, either entirely or in part, and thus they always abide by the law and follow proper legal procedure. Other men, however noble they may be, who do not exercise jurisdiction bestowed on them by the king, have no right at all to inflict the death penalty on men subject to them, but merely to apportion to them some more or less paternal punishment, without going so far as to shed their blood.

Lino: I understand from what you say that no head of a household can kill a domestic servant who has committed a crime, as is customary here in Japan.[1]

---

[1] Servants (*fudai* or *hikan*) could be executed by their masters who regarded them as their property. See Leupp, *Servants, Shophands*, pp. 13–16; also Valignano, *Historia*, pp. 128–9. Richard Cocks noted this prerogative as well in a letter to Lord Salisbury in 1614 (Farrington, *English Factory*, I, pp. 259–60).

Michael: That's right, Lino. That custom which holds sway in Japan is against all reason, for only those who hold the supreme power, or those to whom that power is delegated, can with justice sentence to death those subject to them. Others, such as heads of households, can only punish their servants' crimes with beatings or with other lesser penalties. But if the servants, in spite of these punishments, do not reform and amend their way of life, they can easily be expelled from the family and the house, and thus serve as a warning to others. It is a principle among Europeans, however, that people should be led by love rather than by fear of punishment to seek the good and practise virtue.

Mancio: I would add one last point that you should know about to this explanation of the administration of justice, and it is a point which I am sure will impress you. Whenever magistrates come to the end of their term of office, they are strictly held to account for their past administration of justice, and those who have been in any way disadvantaged have the opportunity to accuse them. When these proceedings have been completed and the evidence has been recorded, consideration is given to whether these magistrates are to be raised to higher dignity or to be punished; for the Christian kings do not want such honours to be conferred rashly or without due consultation on evil men, giving swords, as it were, to madmen; nor that these men, on the pretext of law and justice, should inflict some harm on the people.

Leo: All these arrangements with regard to government seem to us excellent, entirely in conformity with reason and with Christian piety, and they deserve to be embraced wholeheartedly by all Japanese. But I am looking forward now to your account of arms and the apparatus of war, unless perhaps you judge that this theme needs a rather lengthy treatment and should be left till tomorrow.

Michael: I think it should, indeed it must, both so that we can devote some time to resting, and lest such a weighty matter should seem to getting too cursory a treatment.

COLLOQUIUM XIII

Of the wars which are usually waged in Europe, the way of setting up an army, and land battles[1]

Leo: Now that you have treated of the administration of kingdoms, Michael, and of matters relevant to public peace and quiet, it is time for you to tell us of the order of war, and of the disposition of armies and of battle which they adopt in Europe. We look forward with joyful anticipation to hearing about this from you.

Michael: And I am particularly glad to speak about the subject because there is no doubt that the Japanese have a special interest in war, and I am confident that you will be very willing listeners. In the first place, then, a point which seems worthy of praise and commendation in Europe is that nobles, men of respectable family, even high officials cannot go to war with one another, but only kings, free princes, and independent republics, who owe obedience to no superior. Other rulers, dukes, marquesses, counts, who live under the jurisdiction of kings or states, are prohibited absolutely from taking it upon themselves, of their own will, to start a war. And here you can see clearly the difference between the Europeans and the Japanese, for among our Japanese almost all those whom we call *kunishū* or *yakata* have the power to wage war against each other; or, to be more exact, they arrogate this power to themselves. And since there is a great number of these in the whole of Japan, it is inevitable that there are frequent wars, a conflagration, so to speak, in which the country is trapped. Things are different in Europe, where there are few with the right to wage war, and they are committed to Christian piety and public order, and they embark on war only for most just cause and after long consideration.

Leo: Why is it that dukes, marquesses, and counts cannot wage war against one another, and avenge with arms and the sword injuries committed by this side or that?

Michael: You inquire after the cause, but it is clear from what was said in the last colloquium. Dukes, marquesses, and counts do not have full power of life and death over those within their jurisdiction; there can be appeals against death sentences passed by them or their magistrates, appeals to the king or the royal senate. Much less, therefore, are these rulers free to wage war against their peers or counterparts. And this is surely entirely in accordance with nature. For as in the human body it is from the head, where the power of the senses and the intellect is strongest, that other members derive their

---

[1] The influence of Machiavelli's dialogue, *The Art of War*, is apparent in this colloquium.

movement or restraint, so also it is right that in kingdoms, where the king takes the place of the head, it is from the king that all the administration of war or peace is delegated to other leaders. Thus, if it should happen that leaders of this sort wrong each other, they have recourse to the king as their ultimate protector and avenger, but no battle is fought to resolve their personal enmity. From this it follows that other than kings, supreme princes, and free republics, no rulers, unless they be given command and commission to do so, can maintain an army, fortify a citadel, or have a garrison of soldiers; and if they do indeed do so they normally do it not as independent masters, but as leaders designated by the kings, supreme princes, or republics. And from this custom comes the advantage that, without those occasions which so frequently serve as the torch to set fire to unbridled natural desires, it is not easy for rulers to defect from or rebel against their kings. Here in Japan, however, things are entirely different; for the *tono* have soldiers in their garrisons, they fortify their citadels in their own names, and they readily embark on war or stir up sedition against the *yakata*, so that we cannot enjoy peace but are constantly troubled by conspiracies and the tumult of wars, with the *tono* frequently under suspicion of treachery, and the *yakata* never confident of their security.

Lino: That is true, indeed; for even the lords of our whole world here, the Tenka, as we call it, have very often tried, in order to avoid being obliged so frequently to engage in wars, to bring these *tono*, and other lower rulers, under their control, and to deprive them of their garrisons and their citadels; but they have never been completely successful, and this deplorable custom according to which the *tono* jealously guard their personal forts and citadels is now long established in Japan.

Michael: For my part I am persuaded that this custom dates from the time when the proper and legitimate king of Japan, whom we call the *dairi*, was cast out from what was his from ancient times by the *kubō*, the Genji and the Heike, who were fighting among themselves to gain possession of the Japanese empire, and so many and such various jurisdictions were introduced.[1] That is how it came about that for the past five hundred years we have been tossed about in this universal confusion and disorder.[2] In Europe, however, it is not so; for the most part the kings succeed their fathers by right of heredity, their royal sway is firm and stable, and their power is such that it is almost impossible for them to be toppled from their seat by any kind of ruler.

---

[1] The Taira-Minamoto War or Gempei War (1180–85), ostensibly a power struggle between two families, the Taira (Heishi or Heike) in central Japan, who enjoyed power in Kyoto, and the Minamoto (Genji) in eastern Japan, who were excluded from power at court. The Minamoto emerged victorious and the political, social and economic order of Japan was altered irrevocably. Warrior government replaced government controlled by the court nobility and the era of shogunal rule that survived until the Meiji Restoration was established. The struggle is recorded in the *Heike Monogatari* or *Tale of the Heike*, a rousing account and source for later writers on the ultimate futility of human ambition. A condensed version of the *Heike Monogatari* was published in Roman letters by the Jesuit mission press in Japan in 1593 (although dated 1592) along with Aesop's fables (*Nifon No Cotoba to Historia uo narai xiran to Fossvrv Fito No Tameni Xeva Ni Yavaragvetaru Feiqe no Monogatari*, Amakusa, 1592, *Esopo No Fabvlas*, Amakusa, 1593). The former was intended for use as a history textbook for European missionaries and the latter as an accessible lesson in Christian morality (Laures, *Kirishitan Bunko*, pp. 46–9). See also Satow, *Jesuit Mission Press*, pp. 12–20.

[2] In fact the first Europeans reached Japan towards the end of the *sengoku* wars which had started in 1467.

Mancio: When I consider the causes of the disorder here in Japan it seems to me that there are three main reasons why rulers are so ready to take it upon themselves to decide to start a war. Firstly, because in the governing of the people and directing of warfare our *tono* are not as dependent on the *yakata* as European rulers are on their kings. Secondly, because the European people who live under the jurisdiction of counts, marquesses, or dukes do indeed respect and obey them, but they have a much greater reverence for the lord of all of them, that is, for the king himself. This means that they would not follow their rulers if these were to turn against the king; in fact they would hold them in the utmost abhorrence for their violation of the fealty they owe to their king. Here in Japan, by contrast, the people who are subject to the *tono* or other similar lords are so submissive to them that they conform themselves totally to their will, and they are much more dependent on them both for their goods and in the administration of justice. Accordingly, if their *tono* rebel against other *yakata* the people will also certainly rebel. Thirdly, the European rulers who are subject to their kings cherish the honour which was given by those same kings and as it were handed down by their forebears, and besides, when these dignities are first conferred on them they swear a personal oath of loyalty to the king, and thus religiously bound they believe that nothing could be more contemptible than to rebel and conspire against the king. Our *tono*, on the other hand, whether their subjection to the *yakata* is a matter of ancient law and origin, or whether they freely chose to put themselves in subjection, are not bound by any religious oath. If they judge it to be to their advantage they can without further ado start a conflict, or defect to other *yakata*, and they do not think that this will in any way redound to their dishonour or shame.[1]

Leo: All this is true. But now could you speak about European strongholds and their defences.

Michael: Since there is a great difference between the European and the Japanese way of building it is not difficult to appreciate the disparity there is when it comes to building and fortifying strongholds. Our strongholds are fortified more by nature than by art,[2] but in Europe they are strengthened by great structures and contrivances built with marvellous skill, and with these their cities are very well defended, the heaviest attack with artillery can be withstood, and the enemy in turn are attacked and suffer very great losses. Nor indeed is there any other way for the Europeans to defend their cities against artillery attack, for the guns are so large, and made of such materials, namely bronze and other metals, and when they fire balls and sulphurous powder it is with such weight and force that only the most massively solid of buildings can stand up to and repel such violence. These artillery pieces are sometimes transported on a certain kind of vehicle, and set up in so many different places, and they cause the walls of the cities to shake with such force and so much noise, that it seems as if the sky was

---

[1] In Europe alliances were easily broken as well, contributing to protracted warfare (Hale, *Civilization of Europe*, pp. 104–5).

[2] Nobunaga's castle in Azuchi and Hideyoshi's in Osaka impressed Fróis and other Jesuits. See *Cartas*, II, ff. 160v–161, 176v–177v; Fróis, *História de Japam*, III, pp. 256–9; IV, pp. 168–70, 229–30; Cooper, *João Rodrigues's Account*, p. 323; idem, *They Came to Japan*, pp. 134–8.

splitting, the earth quaking, and the whole world tottering.[1] It follows that cities, if they are not to be overwhelmed by heavy bombardment from such artillery, have to be girded round with massive walls, towers, ramparts, and bulwarks. And in addition to walls, ramparts, and the most impregnable of fortifications, they usually also have a very lofty citadel, the principal defence of the city, like what we call in Japanese the *tenshu*,[2] though very different in construction. In these citadels there are soldiers constantly armed and on guard, taking turns to keep watch day and night, with just as much care and diligence as if the cities were under siege, even when no immediate danger threatens.

Leo: What is the purpose of all the diligence in keeping watch and the combat readiness of the soldiers in the citadels, when the European princes have no fear of plots to overthrow them, their kingdoms are not threatened by enemy incursion, and the soldiery cannot be maintained without heavy cost?

Michael: The European princes want the very best of military skill to flourish in their kingdoms so that their soldiers may not lapse into idleness and sloth, but may always be on their toes and ready for battle; so they rejoice when the military arts are practised in their kingdoms as if danger was always impending and never absent.[3] They are persuaded, and rightly, that those who cease to train for war as long as they can enjoy the benefits of peace, cannot easily, when war returns, reaccustom themselves to arms. No one can master the other good arts in a short time either, nor can they (witness St Jerome)[4] become experts all at once; and in the same way no one can excel in matters of war without long and hard practice, especially as inactivity, which they avoid so sedulously in Europe, can sap and enervate the spirits of the young.

Leo: If that is the training that they have in Europe, the inhabitants of that region will indeed be good soldiers. I would like to know, however, whether, when war is declared, all the people, commoners or gentry, are obliged to take up arms and follow the king or a leader appointed by the king?

---

[1] While the Japanese were quick to take up the gun, manufacturing and utilizing copies of Portuguese muskets, they did not develop the art of casting ordnance, although, according to Father Organtino, Oda Nobunaga succeeded in fitting the seven large ships he used in Osaka Bay in 1578 with three pieces of heavy ordnance each (and plenty of large muskets) which the father found amazing, for with the exception of some small pieces of cannon cast by the Jesuits for Ōtomo Yoshishige, 'we know for sure that there are no others in the whole of Japan' (*Cartas*, II, f. 415v; Lamers, *Japonius Tyrannus*, p. 155). Regardless of Organtino's surprise, the Japanese had no need to develop ordnance for with the establishment of Tokugawa rule after 1600 the civil wars ended and made redundant the need for cannon to reduce enemy fortifications. See Boxer, *Jan Compagnie*, ch. 2 *passim*; Parker, *Military Revolution*, pp. 140–45; Chase, *Firearms*, pp. 175–86.

[2] 天守, *Vocabvlario*, f. 255v, '*Tenxu*' or *donjon*, the multi-storeyed tower constructed from wood in Japanese castles. See Cooper, *João Rodrigues's Account*, p. 323.

[3] Machiavelli's point, made at the beginning of the *Art of War* (p. 10 and pp. 79, 80–81, 209). On the admiration of warfare and the perception of war as a purifying process in Italy, see Hale, 'War and Public Opinion', pp. 94–122 *passim*.

[4] Eusebius Hieronymus Sophronius.

Michael: Among the Europeans no one is forced to take up arms.[1] The gentry and nobles have their own revenue, and are obliged to pay only annual dues to the king; apart from that they are free, and are bound by no obligation. The common people too are divided according to their occupations, and everyone is at liberty to use his skills to make a living. The nobles therefore, especially those who are usually called members of the royal family, can be assigned and called to arms by the kings themselves in certain circumstances, when very grave danger threatens, and particularly if the king himself is setting off for war. In the general tumult of war, however, when the signal is given, only those take up arms who want a soldier's pay; for they live not on their own income, but on the pay given to each one according to his rank by the king. European soldiers, therefore, do not easily abandon their arms, nor do they seek to return to their homes for any minor reason, as so often happens here in Japan; on the contrary, they continue long at the same task, the more so because they not only receive their pay, but also, if they have given a good account of themselves in war, many honours come their way. Even if the war lasts ten or fifteen years, they persevere in their commitment to waging war, and though they may have begun as recruits they end as veterans and experts. From being veterans they come to be discharged as deserving ex-soldiers, and can pass their declining years in their homes, paid as long as they live.[2]

Leo: There is no doubt that if soldiers are exercised in the art of war in that way they will be advanced in both the theory and the practice of matters military. But how is it possible for the kings to maintain great armies over a long period of time from their own treasuries?

Michael: The European kings can do this with ease because of the abundance of their revenues, and of the gold and silver overflowing their treasuries; and thus they have, for years on end, a huge number of soldiers under arms and on martial service.[3]

---

[1] Forced recruitment was common and much resented, and many eligible men tried to avoid the draft. See Thompson, *War and Government*, pp. 103–23; Vassberg, *Village and the Outside World*, pp. 110–14; Hale, *Civilization of Europe*, pp. 457–8.

[2] This description is more appropriate for mercenaries on whom all European states depended to fight their wars in the 16th century and beyond (Mallett and Hale, *Military Organization*, pp. 485–6). War-wounded veterans were viewed indifferently by society (Hale, *Civilization of Europe*, p. 129). Machiavelli described Italian soldiers as 'a parcel of intemperate, licentious and drunken fellows' (*Art of War*, p. 168).

[3] In the case of Spain, the huge influx of New World bullion, which is alluded to here, did not enrich Spain under Philip II, nor did it enable him to finance his military ambitions. Financial problems consistently undermined his grand strategy, most spectacularly in 1576 when troops in the Army of Flanders either mutinied or deserted over pay arrears, one of many such mutinies over the years until 1607. See Thompson, *War and Government, passim*; *idem*, 'Impact of War', p. 283 n. 101; Parker, *Grand Strategy*, pp. 88, 130, 136, 165. During Philip II's reign the Castilian treasury defaulted four times (ibid., pp. 87–8). In Venice, the cost of wars – and they were frequent in the 16th century – caused budgetary problems necessitating a number of ad hoc measures including increased tolls and taxes, lotteries, and even the sale of offices. It was only in 1584 that Venice created a war reserve to ease the financing of future wars (Mallett and Hale, *Military Organization*, ch. 16 *passim*). In England, the cost of war during Elizabeth's reign stretched government finances almost to breaking point (Outhwaite, 'Dearth, the English Crown', pp. 24–7). Early modern standing armies were a far cry from the professional, well-trained and well-paid forces that *De Missione* suggests. See Mallett and Hale, *Military Organization*, p. 485.

Lino: We would like to know how many soldiers there usually are in an army, and how they are paid.

Michael: There is no fixed figure for the number of soldiers in an army; depending on the threat which the war poses, and on the power of the opposing kings, an army may have fifteen thousand men, and sometimes twenty, thirty, and even fifty or a hundred thousand.[1] These are foot soldiers, you understand, but there are also squadrons of cavalry, their numbers varying with the numbers of infantry, containing two, three, six, eight, ten thousand horsemen, or even more. Now these cavalry and infantry are all suitably armed, so the spectacle offered by an army drawn up in proper formation is a brilliant display and a joy to behold. You can judge the quality of these soldiers from the very careful way in which they are chosen; it is not the feeble and ignorant who are chosen, but strong men with some acquaintance with arms. It is usual to have someone chosen first of all as supreme commander of the army, and he is always of noble and illustrious birth; then other subordinate officers, and it would be tedious to list all their titles. Some of these are then sent through all parts of the kingdom, charged with the task of recruiting soldiers, and they appoint certain principal soldiers, paying them immediately a part of their stipend, and direct them to assemble at a certain designated place.[2] These soldiers have been paid, and if they now go into hiding, or look for an occasion to abscond or desert, which they have no right to do, they will pay for it with their lives. Among these soldiers there are various grades and ranks, for as well as the distinction between horse and foot soldiers, some use muskets, others spears, or double-edged axes, or javelins; others again bows, or weapons of some other sort, to say nothing of the armour which is for the defence of the body, leather or metal helmets, iron breastplates, cuirasses beautifully fashioned of very fine chain mail, and other similar items. The cavalry include skirmishers, who are lightly armed, and the heavily armed or cataphracts: the former have just one horse, but the latter have two horses each, and use both, changing frequently from the one to the other; the former use lighter and the latter heavier spears, and after they have launched the spears at the enemy they close to fight with swords, and there is very fierce hand to hand fighting with the different types of sword.

Now since among these soldiers there are various ranks, and various kinds of arms, there is also a different stipend specific to each of these ranks. Spearmen rank above common soldiers, musketeers above spearmen, skirmishers above musketeers, cataphracts above skirmishers, but everyone receives a stipend of not less than three ducats every month, and some, namely the heavily armed cavalry, have a stipend of as much as ten ducats a month. As well as this stipend paid to each individual, the commandant of each cohort, whose

---

[1] The Duke of Alba commanded 70,000 troops during his invasion of the Netherlands in the spring of 1568 to crush the revolt which had started in 1566. In 1574, during Count Louis of Nassau's invasion of Flanders, the army was nominally 86,000 strong (Parker, *Grand Strategy*, p. 122; *idem*, *Dutch Revolt*, p. 165). The invasion force assembled for the enterprise against England in 1588 was 27,000 men (*idem*, *Grand Strategy*, pp. 235–6). On the size of Venetian armies during the 16th century, see Mallett and Hale, *Military Organization*, pp. 213, 473, 477. Muster rolls were frequently inflated to defraud the government (ibid., pp. 281–3). Machiavelli believed 24,000 was the right size for an army (*Art of War*, p. 92).

[2] On the recruitment process in Spain, which was both inefficient and corrupt, and unable to meet the government's needs for its ambitious foreign policy, see Thompson, *War and Government*, ch. 4, *passim*; Vassberg, *Village and the Outside World*, pp. 110–14.

stipend is much larger, is given two or three hundred ducats to distribute among his soldiers by way of merit awards.[1] Nor are the kings content just with these awards; they also confer great honours on the generals and commandants, and allow them most generous incomes, which motivates others to aspire to arms and battle honours.[2]

Lino: Deal now, Michael, with ranks and offices in the army.

Michael: With regard to the ranks of the soldiers, these correspond exactly to their regiments, battalions, divisions, and companies, each of which has its own commander; there are, besides, adjutants and standard-bearers or ensigns, and in each battalion these rank next to the commander. In addition there are others who are in command of several battalions, and above them there is one who commands the infantry, and another who commands the cavalry, light or heavy, and each of these is deferred to according to his rank, his judgment, and his authority. There are two more besides these, namely the camp measurer, as he is known, and the paymaster: the first selects the site where the camp is to be set up, and fortifies it with ramparts and palisades where necessary; the second is in charge of the paying of wages. Above all of these, each of whom has his proper rank, is the supreme commander. He is pre-eminent by virtue of his blood, his valour, and his other gifts, and he represents the king's majesty, so he wields supreme authority over all other officers. But all the soldiers display towards their battalion commanders, divisional commanders, and the other officers whom I have mentioned, and they towards the supreme commander, a degree of respect and obedience difficult to express in words, both because all those committed to military matters consider it essential to their rank and honour to show this kind of respect and attention, and because fear of most certain punishment deters from even the least transgression those who, lacking something in nobility of spirit, have no great fear of being labelled dishonourable; for military discipline is so strict among the Europeans that any soldier who fails in his duty or leaves his post will incur severe and weighty punishment. Whether in camp, therefore, or on the march, or finally in attacking and engaging with the enemy, the order and discipline maintained is extraordinary; and the key to this is the attention and the energy of the camp measurer, or camp master, who, following the directions of the supreme commander, orders each man to his particular station, and does not permit any soldier to take it upon himself to abandon his post.[3]

---

[1] Payment was neither regular nor generous. It was commonly in arrears, often irredeemably so. At the time of the 1576 mutiny, pay for Spanish forces was two years in arrears. The cost of the army was 1,200,000 florins per month (more than the combined income from Castile and the Indies). The Military Treasury was lucky if it received a quarter of this amount to pay its way. Mutiny, desertion, deprivation and rampage were disastrous for Spanish policy in the Low Countries and elsewhere, and contributed to the rise of the Black Legend (Parker, *Dutch Revolt*, pp. 164–5, 172, 222; Thompson, *War and Government*, pp. 73–6). In Venice, pay and conditions for the common soldiers were inferior to those of unskilled labourers (Mallett and Hale, *Military Organization*, p. 496).

[2] In the case of Spain, the nobility were no longer interested in a career in arms or in serving in military engagements in far-off places. By the end of the 16th century a career in arms was looked down upon. There was no large pool of Castilian officers to command the army, although this changed in the 17th century as Spain itself was surrounded by enemies. In other parts of the Spanish empire, however, there was less reluctance to pursue a military career (Thompson, *War and Government*, pp. 146–59; Kamen, *Spain's Road to Empire*, pp. 390–92).

[3] The serial mutinies in the army of Flanders disprove this assertion.

Leo: Move on now, Michael, to the European way of drawing up the line of battle.

Michael: With regard to the line of battle and the arrangement of the whole army, although the custom varies in different provinces and kingdoms, for the most part the armies are usually arranged in a half-moon formation,[1] with the two horns equipped with squadrons of cavalry, and the infantry in the centre, with order strictly maintained. The army as a whole, however, is divided into three, namely the front, rear, and middle sections. The first has the cavalry at both extremes, and itself brings up the artillery. In the middle section the commander of the whole army, and the king if he is present, have their station, together with all the principal nobles. The rear section, which also contains a great force of soldiers, includes the things necessary for the support of the army. The number and variety of things transported in order to feed and equip an army, especially a large army, is remarkable, as is the number of merchants who travel with the army in order to sell their wares, so much so that you would think it was a fair or a public market rather than part of an army; and the stalls are set out in such a way that the place seems more like some noble town than a military camp.[2] And what am I to say of the whole army and its display of so many different kinds of tents, all so skilfully constructed. The one we brought with us, which you saw the other day and so commended and admired, was an example.[3] There are besides, and they add not a little to the beauty and decoration of the army, various flags and standards, carried by the different battalions, by which the soldiers recognize their own standard-bearer and position; the splendid armour shining in the sunlight, and the costly garments which, for further adornment, many wear over their armour.[4]

Lino: All this that you have recounted is most agreeable to hear; but come now, give an account of how they join battle and engage in combat.

Michael: When armies come together and battle is to be joined, the first thing that happens, before all else, is that the supreme commander exhorts the soldiers to give

---

[1] Naval battle formations, such as at Lepanto, were half-moon; the battle formations of armies were flatter. See Machiavelli, *Art of War*, pp. 87–92. In Japan the half-moon or *engetsu* was known as a 'back to the wall' formation, when an army was on the defensive (Turnbull, *Samurai Armies*, pp. 10–12).

[2] In the words of I. A. A. Thompson: 'The coming of a company of soldiers was awaited with the same kind of trepidation as a hurricane.' Soldiers lived off the land and the peasants had to provide for them (Thompson, *War and Government*, pp. 113–16, esp. p. 113; Vassberg, *Village and the Outside World*, pp. 105–10). In the 1590s, the army in Flanders faced an additional enemy besides the Dutch: starvation (Parker, *Dutch Revolt*, p. 232). In 1571 the Venetian governor-general in Dalmatia, Giulio Savorgnan, commenting on the inadequacy of a soldier's pay to purchase basic foodstuff in the local market, wrote to the doge, 'What soldier ... would leave Italy for Dalmatia knowing that he would not be able to feed himself, let alone buy shoes and other necessities, nor match, powder and lead for his arquebus?' (quoted in Mallett and Hale, *Military Organization*, p. 386). On the miserable conditions of the English garrison at Berwick, of the English conscript army in Ireland in the 1590s and of destitute sailors in the Spanish galleys in the mid-1590s, see Outhwaite, 'Dearth and the English Crown', pp. 30–33; Thompson, *War and Government*, p. 179.

[3] The field tent, described as 'very beautiful', was one of the gifts presented to Hideyoshi by Valignano on behalf of the viceroy (Fróis, *História de Japam*, V, p. 299).

[4] Cf. the ironic comment made by a doctor with the imperial forces during the siege of Metz in 1552–3 who noted that his wounded patients insisted on dying 'notwithstanding that each soldier had his field-bed, and a tester strewn with glittering stars more bright than fine gold' (quoted in Hale, *Civilization of Europe*, pp. 127–8).

themselves bravely and vigorously to the fight, with the hope of victory held before them, and calling to mind the divine glory, which Christian men fighting with enemies of the name of Christ keep always before their eyes. With the soldiers now roused for the fight battle commences with the artillery, balls of remarkable size are fired, and the lines of the enemy are scattered; then the horns of the front line, that is, the cavalry on both wings, make a strong charge at the enemy, attacking them with their spears, and slaughtering as many of them as possible; next come the infantry, using their muskets, and firing iron bullets at the enemy until they are so close that swords are drawn and it comes down to hand-to-hand combat. Meanwhile the supreme commander is more on the lookout than anyone else, watching vigilantly for any place in need of help, and ready to send soldiers to assist as required: he orders reinforcements to go now here, now there; and thus the battle continues till all the forces on both sides are committed and engaged in action, and it becomes possible to judge which will emerge victorious. I leave out of account certain things which contribute to the solemnity of the battle, such as the repeated sounding of bugles, trumpets, drums, and other similar instruments, the constant playing of which has a powerful effect in inciting the soldiers to fight. I say nothing either of the various challenges and private contests in which soldiers frequently engage to make trial of their military prowess. And, finally, I make no mention of the order which is maintained when retreat is sounded, and all return to their stations. In all of this, skill and assiduous training are clearly in evidence.

Leo: Admirable indeed is this form of conflict, and I would say that those are men of iron and adamant rather than of nerve and muscle who do not hesitate to confront the full force of artillery and cannonball for the sake of winning praise and gaining victory.

Michael: But much more admirable, without doubt, are the attacks on citadels, and in capturing them the loss of blood and life is much greater. It is impossible not to admire men so brave, so careless of death, that they will launch an assault on a walled and fortified citadel, defended by cannon, bristling with soldiers. They know they are facing almost certain death, yet have no hesitation in bursting through gates, bringing up ladders, and using any method to open the way to the citadel. Meanwhile there is nothing sluggish or weak about those on the inside; they put all their effort and strength into repelling the enemy attack with cannon, muskets, and other arms, and there is no doubt that much blood will be spilt in the battle, and that the way to the citadel and victory will be lined with corpses.[1] These citadels are particularly well defended because the garrison within the walls is made up not of just any soldiers, but of very specially chosen troops. For if there is war between Christians, only those citadels and cities which can withstand an enemy

---

[1] In reality, castles and cities at this time were highly fortified in what was known as the 'modern style' in Italy and the 'Italian style' elsewhere. These fortifications included thick walls, star-shaped bastions and moats designed to keep the enemy at a distance while giving the defenders the opportunity to fire at his siege works. Albrecht Dürer's treatise, *Etliche Underricht zu Befestigung der Stett, Schloss und Flecken* (1527, Latin trans. 1535), made them well-known throughout Europe. See Mallett, *Mercenaries and their Masters*, pp. 165–8; Parker, *Grand Strategy*, pp. 111–12; Bury, 'Italian Contribution', pp. 77–85. In his political testament, Charles V, who had ordered construction of such fortifications in the Habsburg possessions in Italy, urged Philip to maintain them no matter the expense as their strategic value was immense (Bury, pp. 83–4). For Machiavelli's advocacy of robust fortifications, see *Art of War*, pp. 183–7.

attack are garrisoned. Other towns which are not defended in that way surrender, without any defection or betrayal, and this does not endanger the liberty or lives of their inhabitants, for even amidst the tumult of wars, which sometimes, for various reasons, cannot be avoided, there shine out remarkable manifestations of mutual charity and Christian brotherhood.[1]

Leo: I have to acknowledge the magnanimity of Europeans, who can withstand such harsh sieges and attack cities with such force. But tell me, do those sieges usually last a long time?

Michael: Since the citadels are so well fortified, and the soldiers so brave and so loyal to their kings, the struggles cannot but be long-drawn-out; especially as they do not follow our Japanese custom of having all sorts of men and women within the citadel, but only soldiers of the first rank, as I said, picked out from among the best and strongest. That is why here in Japan they are quick to abandon the defence of a citadel when the food runs out, though when there is no such shortage they often hold out very well for a long time. But now, if you don't mind, let us take some rest. We'll sleep tonight, and tomorrow I'll move on to naval battles.

Lino: Agreed.

---

[1] Manifestations of Christian charity and brotherhood were not the norm. When the town of Naarden in Holland refused to surrender to Alba in 1572, the duke, applying his policy of what Parker has called 'selective brutality' aimed at pacification, reported that '[t]he Spanish infantry gained the walls and massacred citizens and soldiers. Not a mother's son escaped' (*Grand Strategy*, p.127). The policy was applied selectively because a number of towns had erected the Italian-style defences mentioned here and were not amenable to easy attack (ibid., p. 129). An English witness writing in 1588 noted, 'I observed in our journey from Ostend to Burbourghe all round about … for ye space of 40 miles in length, and somewhat more, that ye villages were desolated, and raysed in a manner to the grounde, noe inhabitante to be founde in them, scarcely any houses but here and there scattered standinghe to dwelle in' (quoted in ibid., p. 236). As J. R. Hale has put it, 'this was not a humanitarian age'. Italians were shocked by the invasion in 1484 not so much because of the cruel, indiscriminate violence inflicted on them but because of the realization that they had not been capable of fighting back as ruthlessly. See Hale, 'War and Public Opinion', pp. 111–14; *idem*, *Civilization of Europe*, pp. 127–9, esp. p. 129. The voices of those horrified by the human cost of warfare were few; Montaigne was one of the few. See *Essais*, II, p. 111.

COLLOQUIUM XIV

Of the naval battles in which they usually engage in Europe

Lino: The account which you gave us yesterday of the battles in which they usually engage in Europe caused us no little astonishment; but since you said that these engagements take place both on land and at sea, we are looking forward most eagerly to the account you are going to give us today of the naval battles.

Michael: I'm happy to proceed with my story, and to speak of what pertains to naval battles. In the first place I should mention that as Europe is washed partly by the ocean and partly by the Mediterranean Sea, both of which are frequently plagued by either pirate or enemy fleets, the European kings and princes are obliged to maintain their own very heavily armed fleets, to repel attacks by their enemies, and to punish the bold temerity of marauding pirates. So the ships which carry merchandise hither and thither, and are called cargo ships, are of a different kind from those which are used to engage in battle or combat. The latter too are not all the same, and generally take two different forms. Some of them are very tall, long and beaked, and suitable only for sailing, and these the Europeans commonly refer to as galleons. Ships of this kind usually carry a large number of guns, a very large number; in years past one ship of this type, built in the time of the most celebrated King Sebastião of Portugal, was very famous indeed, and usually carried as many guns as there are days in a year.

Lino: Dear God! Can there be any fleet great enough to overpower or to sink one of those ships?

Michael: Our ships, because their structure is so feeble and fragile, certainly could not do it, but the European ships are so strongly built that they can overpower and repel any force, even if they cannot match it for size.[1]

---

[1] The age of the *shuinsen* or 'vermillion seal ship' voyages (i.e. ships officially licensed to sail for south-east Asian ports, first by Hideyoshi, then by the early Tokugawa shoguns), was barely underway in 1590. Between 1604 and 1635, the year in which the voyages were banned, 356 *shuinsen* voyages are recorded. Most of the ships were built in Japan. They ranged from 70 to 800 tons, with an average of 300 tons. Ieyasu was well aware of Japan's deficit in shipbuilding and long-distance maritime skills. He requested Philip III to send shipwrights from New Spain to help Japan develop its maritime technology, a request the Spanish turned down on grounds of national security. Japanese craftsmen did construct a small number of ships which successfully managed to cross the Pacific. One, which had been built under the supervision of William Adams, was put at the disposal of the interim governor of the Philippines, Rodrigo de Vivero, whose own ship had been wrecked off Japan, in order for him to continue his voyage to Acapulco. Another was built under Spanish supervision in 1613 for

Mancio: According to what we have heard, that beaked ship of King Sebastião was indeed of a remarkable size, but one which the most famous Republic of the Venetians ordered to be made, and which was said to carry 500 guns, was much larger.[1]

Leo: That must have been an incredibly large ship; even large cities, after all, do not have as many guns as that.

Michael: What Mancio said is absolutely true, but you should not think that all the beaked ships are of similar size. There are others which are smaller, and most of them carry thirty or fifty guns, but sometimes some are built on that tremendous scale, so as to strike terror in the enemy. The other type of fighting ship is those long ones, not so tall, in which they use not only sail but also oars, so many oars that they have twenty-five or more on each side, each of them moved and driven by three or four rowers, so that the ships themselves are called triremes or quadriremes, and vessels of this sort are very well adapted to combat. Those taller ships are entirely dependent on their sails, so whenever the wind drops, and there is a calm at sea, those ships are useless for attacking the enemy; whereas the triremes or quadriremes, even if there is no wind blowing, can be powered by the oars so sometimes they bear down on the enemy and attack them with their guns, and sometimes retreat and take to flight; in short, they can move about quickly, coming and going here and there. For this reason the Europeans use these ships in very large numbers when they engage in battle, and, depending on the requirements of the situation, a European ruler sometimes has ten, twenty, thirty, sixty, or even more triremes in a state of perfect readiness to defend the coast of his kingdom.[2]

Nineteen years ago there was a great battle with these ships, and at that time King Philip of Spain and the Venetian Republic, together with the pope, entered into a solemn alliance against the Saracens, the most dangerous enemies of the Christian name, and they provided two hundred and ten triremes.[3] Commander of all this tremendous fleet, and this was a condition of the alliance itself, was the most famous John of Austria, brother of King Philip.[4] His second-in-command was the most illustrious duke

---

Date Masamune's embassy to Rome, which was led by Hasekura Tsunenaga, known as the second Japanese embassy to Europe or the Keichō Embassy. Chinese as well as Europeans provided knowledge of shipbuilding. See Vivero, *Du Japon et du bon gouvernement de l'Espagne et des Indes*, pp. 18, 22, 64, 66; Farrington, *English Factory*, I, p. 72; *Documentos para la historia de la demarcación*, pp. 899, 971, 993; Scipione Amati, *Historia del regno di Voxù*, Rome, 1615, reprinted in *Dai Nihon Shiryō*, XII:12, pp. 8–9; Iwao, *Shuinsen bōeki-shi*, pp. 127, 130–48.

[1] A Venetian round ship or *barza*, a precursor of the galleon or beaked ship mentioned here, built in 1497 carried more than 400 guns. The ship, whose departure on her maiden voyage was viewed by the ambassadors of the states participating in the alliance against Charles VIII of France, was described by the Venetian diarist Marino Sanuto as 'one of the most beautiful things which has now for many a year been on the sea' and the captain said it was well suited for heavy ordinance (Lane, *Venetian Ships*, p. 60). The *Botafogo*, a Portuguese galleon employed by Charles V in his attack on Tunis in 1535, reportedly had 366 mounted guns (Diffie and Winius, *Foundations*, p. 218).

[2] The discussion here refers to the Mediterranean world not the northern European one. See Lane, *Venetian Ships*, chs 1 and 2.

[3] Frederic Lane gives the figure as 208, with other sources differing by one or two. Venice provided 52 per cent of the galleys at Lepanto. See Lane, *Venice*, p. 369; Guilmartin, *Gunpowder & Galleys*, p. 254.

[4] 1545–78, illegitimate son of Charles V.

Marcoantonio Colonna, commander of the papal triremes,[1] and Sebastiano Veniero, a most noble man, admiral of the Venetian fleet, who later, because of that famous battle, was made doge of the Republic of Venice.[2] The Saracens had a much larger number of triremes, but with Christ as leader (and Christ always comes to our aid, unless thwarted by our sins) the Christians won a victory worthy of eternal memory. They captured 170 of the enemy's triremes and twenty of his galleys, sank a further forty triremes, killed 30,000 Saracens and put about 4,000 in chains, restored to liberty 15,000 Christians captured by the enemy in various regions, and returned to their country loaded with excellent booty. It was a victory worthy of comparison with the greatest of victories recorded from the past. Anyone who reads the written account of it cannot but marvel at the numbers of the triremes, the military equipment on display, the havoc wrought on the enemy, and the other amazing things that took place in that battle, most notably that so many of the enemy were killed, and so few of the Christians; only 5,000, with just one of our triremes sunk, and these numbers were easily made good from the many thousands of captives freed from slavery to the enemy, and the many triremes taken over by the Christians.[3]

Leo: That naval battle must have been amazing. When we see just one merchant ship approaching, and hear the roar of its guns, we marvel. What would it be, then, to see a battle involving more than 400 triremes? But we want to know who these Saracens are whom you have spoken about.

Michael: They are a barbarous and cruel race, living in a part of Asia and of Africa. At one time they were subject to the Roman emperor, but in the course of a whole sequence of events they became independent after the decline of the Roman Empire, and had as their leader Mahomet, a most pestilential man, whose followers are called Mahometans. In order the more easily to lead this backward and ignorant people into error he pretended

---

[1] Marcoantonio Colonna 1535–84, afterwards viceroy of Sicily.

[2] Sebastiano Veniero c. 1496–1578, doge 1577–8, painted by Tintoretto.

[3] For a highly informed discussion of the battle of Lepanto, see Guilmartin, *Gunpowder & Galleys*, pp. 235–64. Some 30,000 Turks were killed or captured, 9,000 Christians killed, 15,000 Christian galley slaves freed, 117 Turkish galleys (out of a total of 288) seized and 8 Venetian galleys sunk (Lane, *Venice*, p. 372; Guilmartin, *Gunpowder & Galleys*, pp. 257–8, 262, 267 n. 59). The propaganda and morale boost given to Catholic Europe by the victory at Lepanto should not be underestimated. The victory was commemorated in numerous paintings. In the *Sala Regia* in the Vatican the boys would have seen Giorgio Vasari's frescos, commissioned by Gregory XIII, depicting the battle. Other paintings of the battle, copied from European originals, were produced by Japanese Christian artists. The geopolitical consequences of the battle were another matter. An attempt to salvage something from the collapse of Christendom by creating what, under the prevailing circumstances, was the next best thing to a crusade, the Holy League, did not outlast the victory. The division of Europe along religious and political fault lines and the economic self-interest of the participants themselves shattered the temporary unity the Holy League had provided. Spain and the papacy became closer. Venice, which had come late to the alliance, but given the league victory, continued to pursue its own interests after Lepanto. Mallett and Hale describe this policy as 'planning for war and negotiating for peace', which was concluded with the Turks in 1573. Even the Papal States, in contravention of papal orders, traded weaponry with the Turks. At the military level, Lepanto was one of the last hurrahs of the war galley in Mediterranean naval warfare. The galley fleets were too big and too costly to secure victory for either side. See Lane, *Venice*, pp. 372–3; Mallett and Hale, *Military Organization*, pp. 233–41, esp. p. 240; Prodi, *Papal Prince*, pp. 176–7; Parker, *Grand Strategy*, pp. 100–101; Guilmartin, *Gunpowder & Galleys*, p. 264; Dandelet, *Spanish Rome*, pp. 70–72.

he was a man sent by God, and he invented a false sect, taking some part of our truth and corrupting it with many errors, combining a life of licence with certain external rites, and perversely mixing the three conflicting laws, the Christian, the pagan, and the Judaic, as handed down to the Jews. He represented God according to his own ideas, and attributed to him many things which were false and imaginary. Since the followers of this sect defected from the Roman Empire and are enemies of the name of Christian, the Christians are continuously at war with them.[1]

Leo: If that race mixes such different religions together and makes them into one, and if it links together some part of the truth with falsity and errors, then I would judge it to be pestilential indeed, and wicked.[2] But I would like to know if there is also war between Christian rulers and other peoples?

Michael: The war which is common to all the Christian kings and in which they are constantly engaged, is against the Saracens, not only because they are inimical to the Christian religion, but also because they commit acts of brigandage by both land and sea, and live off the plunder.[3] Besides, they are given to other most depraved customs, so much so that in the perversity of their customs they outdo even the pagans themselves, for all their worship of false gods. There are however also other wars which sometimes break out among the Christian princes themselves for certain just causes. Careful consideration is given to these causes, however, and unless, after mature deliberation, they are judged to be sufficiently weighty, the princes do not resort to arms.

Leo: At this point perhaps I can ask what happens to those who are captured or give themselves up. Are they condemned to death or to perpetual slavery, as is usual here in Japan?[4]

Michael: Those who are captured or who are obliged to give themselves up in a war waged between Christians are not subject to either of these fates, for all of them are either

---

[1] Latin Christianity and Islam, both introduced into Asia at about the same time were competitors for people's spiritual allegiance (Reid, *Southeast Asia in the Age of Commerce*, pp. 132–5,143–50). In the Malay archipelago Islam came out ahead (*Cambridge History of Southeast Asia*, pp. 518–26).

[2] Establishing orthodoxy was central to the Counter-Reformation. In Japan, the Jesuits, aware from the early days of the mission of the division of Buddhism into sects, were on their guard against any manifestation of schism or syncretism. In 1572 in Amakusa, an interpreter who had worked with one of the European *irmão* had asked the Jesuit superior in Japan, Francisco Cabral, for permission to leave his post. This was granted but, to the horror of the Jesuits, the disciple created a breakaway movement numbering more than 1,500 Christians in Amakusa. The lord of Amakusa, himself a Christian, forbade the former interpreter to preach in his domain and he moved elsewhere. See Schütte, *Valignano's Mission Principles*, I: 1, p. 221. The need to present Christianity as a single entity in order to distinguish it from a divided Buddhism, and to ensure that the Japanese understood that Christianity was not just some exotic branch of Buddhism, a difficult task, was one of the reasons why Valignano insisted on excluding the mendicants from Japan.

[3] War against Islam was not, of course, a strategy favoured by all Christian rulers. Francis I of France signed a treaty with the Ottomans in 1536 shattering forever the idea of a united Christian foreign policy. Relations between Christians and Muslims as presented here is highly coloured by the Ibero-Luso experience of *reconquista*.

[4] *Nuhi* 奴婢 slaves. See *Vocabvlario*, f. 188 '*nusumidaxi*'. For discussions of slavery in Japan, see Álvarez-Taladriz, 'Apuntes sobre el Cristianismo' in Valignano, *Adiciones*, pp. 498–511; Nelson, 'Slavery in Medieval Japan', pp. 463–92.

exchanged for other captives, if there are any, or set free, or, finally, they may purchase their freedom for some sum of money. There is an ancient custom in Europe, a custom with the force of law, that no Christian captured in war should be forced into slavery.[1] With Mohammedans or Saracens, however, things are different. Since they are barbarians, and enemies of Christianity, they remain in perpetual slavery if they are taken prisoner after a battle.

Leo: So there is no Christian who is legally held as a slave among Christians because he has been captured in war?

Michael: Absolutely no one is deprived of his rights in that way, and, as I said, there is a definite and ancient custom to that effect. The Portuguese indeed, and all the Europeans, marvel to see our people so avaricious, so greedily intent on amassing money, that they sell each other, and sully the name of Japan with a mark of infamy. We ourselves often, at various points in our journey, saw Japanese men who had been sold and condemned to slavery, and found ourselves unable to contain a deep and burning anger against our own people who, for such a vile price, heartlessly hand over their countrymen, though of the same blood and language, as if they were cattle or beasts of burden.

Mancio: Michael is entirely justified in complaining about our people. In other respects they are concerned about refinement and humanity, but in this matter they seem to abandon all humanity, manners, and refinement, and to make a proclamation of their greed to almost all peoples.

Martin: That indeed is how it is; for who is not moved to pity, seeing so many of our people, men, women, boys, and girls, snatched away for such a small price and dispersed to so many different parts of the world, suffering the misery of slavery? And they are not sold only to the Portuguese. That would be easier to tolerate, since the Portuguese nation treats its slaves with consideration and kindness, and instructs them in the precepts of Christian doctrine. But who can bear to see our people dispersed among such diverse kingdoms, where people are of the lowest kind and given to false religion, there not only to suffer the misery of slavery among men barbarous and black in colour, but also to be fed with false and erroneous teaching?[2]

---

[1] Historically the Venetians had not been averse to enslaving Orthodox Christians who at times were considered heretics and infidels (Lane, *Venice*, p. 7). As Lane remarks, during the War of Cyprus in 1570 the Venetians, desperately short of men, appear to have resorted to techniques that were indistinguishable from Turkish slave raids (ibid., p. 369). In the 16th century, Protestants could be seized in the New World for example and sent to the galleys. For a detailed discussion of slavery in Portugal's maritime empire, see Godinho, *Os descobrimentos*, IV, ch. 9 *passim*.

[2] The Jesuits consistently opposed human trafficking and Portuguese involvement in it in Japan. Japanese, and Chinese, slaves were greatly appreciated by the Portuguese because they were highly intelligent and industrious. However, the Portuguese were not alone in trading humans. The Japanese bought African and Malabar Coast slaves from the Portuguese and they brought Korean and Chinese slaves from the continent during Hideyoshi's invasions in the 1590s, some of whom were sold to the Portuguese. The Christian daimyo and other Japanese Christians kept slaves but were encouraged by the Jesuits to manumit them. The sale of Japanese to foreigners

Leo: Well said, indeed. In Japan we regularly condemn the custom of selling Japanese in this way, but some put the blame for it entirely on the Portuguese and the fathers of the Society; on the Portuguese because they are so eager to buy Japanese, and on the Jesuits because they do not use their authority to put a stop to purchases of this kind.

Michael: It is not the Portuguese who are at fault. They are merchants, so they cannot be blamed if they buy our people with the hope of gain, and later make a profit by selling them in India and other places. It is entirely our people who are at fault, who for a small payment so easily allow even their own children, whom they ought dearly to cherish, to be torn from their mother's bosom. With regard to the fathers of the Society, if you are to understand how strongly opposed they are to this kind of selling and buying, you should also know with what care and diligence they obtained from the king of Portugal a royal letter prohibiting any merchant, under severe penalty, from coming to Japan and buying a Japanese slave.[1] But what effect can the severity of this edict have, when the cupidity of our people is such that they bring their brothers, their relatives, their comrades, and others, seized by force or guile, secretly and under cover to the ships of the Portuguese, and persuade those Portuguese, partly with their pleas, partly by offering them at low prices, to buy them as slaves. The main excuse the Portuguese give to cover their violation of the law is that they are put under pressure by the importunity of the Japanese themselves. And in fact the Portuguese do not treat our people badly. They learn Christian doctrine, and besides, they are treated with great kindness, as if they were free, and after a few years they are set free. Not that this lessens the blame attaching to our people who

---

offended Japanese sensibilities. In July 1587 Hideyoshi complained to the vice-provincial, Gaspar Coelho, that the Portuguese, Chinese and Cambodians (presumably overseas Chinese) came to Japan, bought Japanese and took them overseas never to see their homeland again (some ended up in the New World). Coelho agreed that it was an outrage and reiterated that the fathers had opposed such activity but said it would be necessary for the Japanese to pass a law forbidding it in order to stop it. Hideyoshi obliged. In addition to his decree expelling the missionaries that year, he issued another decree which included a clause forbidding the sale of Japanese to foreigners and outlawing the trade in human beings within Japan. The decree was not enforced. Examples were made, but the traffic did not cease and in 1616 the Tokugawa shogunate issued a new decree banning human trafficking. Even so the practice continued within Japan, although subject to new restrictions, while in 1621 the Europeans trading with Japan were forbidden to carry any Japanese on their ships whether bought for money or hired for wages. See Fróis, *História de Japam*, IV, pp. 402–3; Farrington, *English Factory*, I, p. 140; Boxer, *Christian Century*, pp. 226–7; idem, *Fidalgos*, pp. 222–34; Elison, *Deus Destroyed*, p. 118; Massarella, 'Ticklish Points', p. 46; Álvarez-Taladriz, 'Apuntes sobre el Cristianismo', in Valignano, *Adiciones*, pp. 505–7, 511; Godinho, *Os descobrimentos*, IV, p. 199; Leupp, *Servants, Shophands*, pp. 17–25; idem, 'Images of Black People', pp. 2–3. On Jesuit attitudes towards slavery elsewhere in the Indies and in Europe at this time, where they were far more accommodating to the institution and practice than in Japan, and for developments in Brazil in the following century where the Society became 'the pre-eminent slaveholders in colonial Brazil', see Alden, *Making of an Enterprise*, pp. 506–27, esp. p. 526, although the brief discussion of Japan (p. 509) is somewhat misleading.

[1] '*Provisão para os portuguezes não possam regatar nem captivar japão algum e para que os que foram ao Japão comprar e vender por um mesmo peso e balanço*', 20 September 1570. See Okamoto, *Porutogaru o tazuneru*, pp. 217–18; Álvarez-Taladriz, 'Apuntes sobre el Cristianismo', in Valignano, *Adiciones*, p. 504. Boxer (*Fidalgos*, p. 231) gives the date as March 1571.

promote slavery of this kind, and all those among us guilty of this crime should be severely punished.

Leo: Not least among the laws laid down by Quambaquundono, ruler of all Japan, is the one forbidding the sale of Japanese.

Michael: It would indeed be a most excellent law if the subordinate rulers, who are responsible for its observance, did not connive at the continuation of these practices, and did not allow those who sell people to go unpunished. It is necessary, therefore, for the authorities themselves to see to it that the law is very strictly observed, and for the rulers, and the lords of the ports to which the ships come, to insist on obedience in this matter, with very severe penalties for any transgression.[1]

Leo: It is right that you should put this to our rulers and princes as useful and necessary for Japan.

Michael: We shall take care to put it to them and impress it on them, but I am afraid that the hope of private advantage may count for more among our people than concern for the common good. The Europeans, because they always have the common good before their eyes, never permit these vicious customs to be introduced in their kingdoms. But let us revert to the theme of our talk.

Lino: We were dealing with the effects of naval battles. Their scale is such that, whether the battles are at sea or on land, even a very large kingdom can quite easily collapse and be ruined in one battle.

Michael: That is not at all likely, for the whole resources of a kingdom are not committed to putting together and setting up an army and then starting a battle; a large part also goes to fortifying their strongholds. Since these fortresses are many and are very strong, it is usual for kings and princes not to take part in the battle but to repair to the fortresses, to stay there, out of danger, for a long time, and to make peace, on just conditions, with their foes. This is especially so when, if the struggle is between Christians, the pope interposes his authority, to which, more than to any other, the kings submit themselves, reconciles them, and cuts a way through the whole disagreement.

Leo: But surely it must be difficult, extremely difficult, to supply from the royal resources the wherewithal to cover the enormous expense of war whether at sea or on land.

Michael: The expense is indeed great, but nevertheless the kings are so wealthy, so opulent, that they do have the resources; for on each of their triremes, each year, they spend five thousand ducats, and from this you can see how much a great fleet of triremes

---

[1] The point made by Coelho. See Fróis, *História de Japam*, IV, p. 403.

will cost; and the cost of equipping the beaked galleons, and other ships of equal size, is even greater.[1]

Mancio: And what are we to say of the sums which they also spend on their armouries, replete with every kind of war equipment? So well supplied are they with military things that it seems as if the European princes are always ready for war. We ourselves are witnesses who have seen the extraordinary quantity and abundance of these things, for we were shown some stores of arms so well supplied with the materials of war that we judged that they could arm fifty thousand men, and perhaps more.

Lino: When I think about the wealth required to cover such enormous expenses I can't get over my astonishment.

Michael: As our colloquia proceed we'll be explaining to you at greater length many things about the magnificently liberal spending of the Europeans, and their abundance in the things pertaining to warfare, which Mancio mentioned briefly just now.

Leo: Come then. Tell us how the kings treat their soldiers when the wars are finished and over, and what payment or reward they give them by way of remuneration.

Michael: They reward them with the liberality befitting a European prince, especially if the soldiers are veterans who have earned their pay over a long period, for they give them an annual stipend after they have served their time, and compensate them in whatever way they can for the labour and hardship which they accepted in war.[2] But there is no one who does not benefit from the generosity of the king. And if this is how they treat their soldiers you will easily appreciate what their beneficence will be towards their nobles, knights, and other illustrious men. It is so great, indeed, that it is most certain that the status of the counts and other rulers had its beginning and origin in the favour and benevolence of the kings towards men who distinguished themselves in war.

---

[1] Many of the galleys in the Spanish king's service were neither built, owned nor operated directly by the Spanish crown (*administración por cuenta de Su Majestad*). Most belonged to private entrepreneurs who contracted their galleys to the crown (*asiento*). After the defeat of the Armada against England in 1588, Philip II created a Spanish royal navy and many galleons were built by *administración*, although contracted galleons made up for insufficiencies. The privatization of the means of war was a controversial policy. The cost of contracting out was similarly controversial. Critics of the *asiento* alleged that costs were higher; supporters, the contrary. Either way, figures for the cost of a galley per year (and throughout the century operating costs were on an upward path) varied between over 6,600 to more than 10,000 ducats. By 1590 the debate was irrelevant for by then the galley as an instrument of war in the Mediterranean was finished. They were too expensive and no match in either cost or effectiveness for the heavily armed sailing ships of the northern Europeans who were making their presence felt in the Mediterranean. The cost of a contracted galleon per annum was put at 17,821 ducats in 1594. In Venice the cost of a light galley c. 1580 was 4,806 ducats and that of a galleon c. 1560 was 32,822 ducats. See Lane, *Venetian Ships*, pp. 264–5; Thompson, *War and Government*, pp. 32–3, 174–5, 178–9, 191–7, 268–9; Parker, *Grand Strategy*, pp. 271–2; Guilmartin, *Gunpowder & Galleys*, pp. 39–46, 235–40, 287–8.

[2] Some welfare policies and institutions for the care of veterans did exist. See Mey, 'La asistencia social a la invalidez militar', pp. 598–605.

Leo: Since you have spoken about retired soldiers we would like to know whether in Europe too the kings and other rulers, who have performed their duties, abdicate and hand over the administration of the kingdom to their sons, as usually happens here in Japan.[1]

Michael: This custom, observed among our people, does not exist in Europe, for they do not consider it right that a king, after some years taken up with the administration of his kingdom, when he has had some experience of events, dealings, and negotiations, and is fully informed, should abandon his royal functions and give the helm of his kingdom to an adolescent, naive, and inexperienced son. Indeed if we care to enquire into the causes of the wars we have here in Japan, we shall find that not the least of them is this: that the kings and rulers who have the authority to which their age and experience entitles them live in retirement, and the young men now at the helm of their kingdoms have not yet attained to maturity of judgement or practical experience, and they throw everything into confusion and disorder.

Leo: I find your argument most convincing, but that European custom does leave me doubtful and uneasy about one point, namely that it would seem to offer to the sons of the kings an opportunity to plot treason and seize power for themselves, and since, as is well known, young men, especially those born to such a noble and exalted position, are naturally disinclined to submit to the yoke of obedience, and have an urgent desire to have the highest place, it can easily happen that they foment sedition against their parents and perpetrate the ultimate crime in order to remove them.

Michael: If you were thoroughly familiar with European things you would know that there is absolutely no danger of that sort of villainy. In the first place, as we have already said and shall be saying again from time to time, the love of children for their parents and the kindness of parents towards their children is so great that no suspicion of any such crime affects behaviour in Europe, as you can see from an example handed down to us in the books of the Portuguese. When Afonso, king of Portugal, the fifth of that name, was now almost fifty years old, and, wearied by the very important war which he had undertaken and by the administration of his kingdom, resolved to go on pilgrimage to the holy sepulchre of Christ in Jerusalem, he left the governing of his kingdom to his son João, a young man rich in prudence and in other gifts of nature, intending to spend the years of life left to him piously and holily in that region famous for the footsteps of Christ when once he lived on earth. He was called back however, from the road on which he

---

[1] *Inkyo* 隠居 or retirement, the custom whereby the head of a household nominally relinquished power to his successor and moved to different living quarters. In 1579 Ōtomo Yoshishige 'retired' in favour of his son Yoshimune and the practice was used most effectively by the first two Tokugawa shoguns, who became nominally *ōgosho* or retired shoguns in 1606 and 1623, to secure the succession. See *Vocabvlario*, f. 132 '*Inquio*'; Valignano, *Sumario*, pp. 49–50, esp. n. 137, 315; Álvarez-Taladriz, *Juan Rodríguez Tsuzu*, pp. 25–6; Cooper, *João Rodrigues's Account*, pp. 167, 184, 202–3, 283–4. The references to *inkyo* in *De Missione* are inconsistent. Here it is criticized; below (p. 240) it is mentioned favourably, although in relation to Christian daimyo. The custom was known in Europe. The retirement of Charles V in favour of Philip II is also mentioned positively (below, p. 236) and in 1564 Cosimo de' Medici abdicated in favour of his son Francesco but remained active in affairs of state behind the scenes (Hale, *Florence*, p. 139).

had set out, by the entreaties of almost all the kings of Europe, and of the Supreme Pontiff, and with that there began a courteous and deeply affectionate argument between the father and the son, the father wishing to live in retirement in the kingdom under the administration of his son, the son by contrast flatly refusing to exercise the royal office while his father was alive, and the entreaties of the son were so vehement that they forced the father, reluctant though he was, to take his royal seat again. From this you can see how alien to the European mind is the crime of sedition.[1]

Moreover the princes, sons of kings, are treated by their parents with the utmost love and honour, so that after they have grown up they have their own residences and their own court officials, and command ample revenues, and they are called by their parents to take a share of the responsibilities and to participate in the governing council, and they gain experience for the full power of governing which is to be theirs. And thus they live with great love for their parents, and with the good will and veneration of the people.

Leo: What you have told us gives us great joy; but explain, I beseech you, how the sons of kings succeed to their deceased fathers' position.

Michael: There would be an opportunity here for me to speak of the customs which are observed, when the kings are gravely ill and close to breathing their last, of the distractions by which the sufferings of their illness are alleviated, of the various kinds of medicaments, of the splendid and magnificent funerals in which their dead bodies are borne to the grave, of the prayers offered to God for them by the whole populace, of the sombre mourning attire which all men affect at their death, of the grandeur of the sepulchres erected for the perpetual preservation of their memories. But rather than extend my narrative unduly, I pass over these things in silence. Some part of them you will understand, however, from certain pictures which we have brought back with us, in which the funeral of the Emperor Charles V, father of King Philip II of Spain, made and celebrated by the son for the father, is marvellously depicted.[2] From these, as from an example, you can imagine the splendour and the trappings of European funerals. But since some of the things which have been mentioned here only briefly and in passing will be dealt with in the colloquia to come, I will say only that the applause of the people, and the general celebration, when the princes, sons of the kings, are proclaimed king through the cities and town after the death of their fathers, and all the assembled people pray that they may long live and reign, is extraordinary. But these things too you will understand for the most part from what we have yet to say; and now I shall move on to the splendour of these same cities and towns, but first we must break off our narration in order to rest this night.

Leo: We wish you, who have such an agreeable story to tell, good night and a good rest.

---

[1] Afonso V, the African (r. 1432–81), involved himself in the dynastic struggles in Castile. He sought the help of Louis XI of France but was rebuffed and attempted to abdicate in favour of his son; however, he died before the *cortes* could meet to ratify his decision.

[2] *Magnifique et Somptueuse Pompe Funèbre faite aux obsèques et funérailles du très victorieus empereur Charles V. Célébrée en la ville de Bruxelles*, Antwerp, Cristoph Plantin, 1559, illustrated with woodcuts by the brothers Jan [Johannes] and Lucas van Doetechum from drawings by Hieronymous Cock, Plantin-Moretus Museum, Antwerp. See Pinson, 'Imperial Ideology', pp. 205–32, esp. pp. 222–4.

COLLOQUIUM XV

Of the size of the cities, the splendour of the churches, and the magnificence of other buildings

Leo: We have seen the pictures in which the funeral of the Emperor Charles V is excellently represented, and from them we can easily imagine how the Europeans spare no expense to honour the death of their princes, and from that it is also clear enough how weighty and ample is their spending on the protecting and conserving of life. We would be very glad, though, to hear something from you of the grandeur of the cities, churches, and other buildings in Europe, for we surmise that this is something equally remarkable.

Michael: When I am faced with the prospect of discoursing on this so important subject, the example comes to mind of Timante, a most famous painter, an example transmitted to us in the books of the Europeans. Timante was depicting, in a painting, the death of a certain most noble woman, Iphigenia by name, daughter of Agamemnon king of Argos, and had portrayed her relatives standing around, very sad and lamenting; but when he came to the father he judged that he would be unable to do justice with his brush to his sorrow and sadness, so he at once artfully and prudently covered his face with a veil, and by thus concealing him succeeded in revealing much of his grief and sorrow.[1] In the same way when I come before you to speak of the cities and the edifices of Europe, built with such wonderful skill and variety, I am convinced that I cannot convey to you any notion of their beauty, their splendour, their elegance, and that, if you permitted it, it would be better to draw a veil of taciturnity or silence over all these things.

However, since I have begun to speak of the things of Europe I have to make bold to proceed further, and to say something of the greatness of their buildings. To a considerable extent the books which we brought back about the European buildings and cities, some parts of which we saw and some heard about, in which the nobility and magnificence of the European buildings is demonstrated to the extent that the art of printing can represent it, will make up for the poverty and inadequacy of my account. Now I'll leave more detailed points till later in my story, and begin with some general points. There is a very great difference between the kinds of dwelling normally used by the Europeans and the Japanese, for our Japanese, especially the nobles, do not live in such numbers in the cities and towns; for the most part they will choose a place among their own fields and estates, and they prefer and find it more agreeable to live there. The European nobles, however, follow a very different custom where their residences are concerned, for although they

---

[1] 'Sacrifice of Iphigenia from the House of the Tragic Poet', by Timante (5th–4th century BCE), Museo Archeologico, Naples.

do from time to time enjoy the rustic peace of a country habitation, so as to be able to relax and relieve their spirits of the troublesome pressure of affairs, their usual and general residences are in the cities, so they are accustomed to expend just as much energy on building houses in the cities as on their rustic retreats for pleasure and delight. The result of this is that, since the nobility and the rulers are so concerned about their urban residences, the cities are not only full of common people and merchants, as with our Japanese cities, but are adorned also with a most noble throng of rulers and leaders, so that not only those cities where the kings live, but also the other cities dispersed throughout the whole kingdom are truly famous and populous. And since in this matter the nobles are accustomed to compete with one another, with some degree of rivalry and envy, the scale of the construction of the buildings, which usually are of two or three storeys, is astonishing, and means that the cities themselves are not only renowned for the great number of houses, but are also of very beautiful appearance.

Adding to the nobility of the European cities is the multitude of religious houses, and their astonishing size. In many cities you can count fifty, a hundred, and even two hundred churches, and in lesser towns you will find ten, twenty, or thirty. And you should not think that churches of this kind have just the one holy house where prayers are to be said, but since they are inhabited by religious men and women they contain many rooms and cells appropriate for them to live in, and you can imagine how many of these there are and what they are like from the number of these same religious. In the one monastery or college there are sometimes living a hundred or even two hundred men, and the number of holy virgins, who are enclosed in convents, is no less great. Since there are these great numbers of them and many, both men and women, come from the nobility, and have large incomes and alms to live on, you will easily understand what the structure of these buildings is like. And as well as these monasteries there are also other churches, which are as it were the heads of the city parishes, where priests of the order of St Peter, as they call them,[1] are accustomed to recite the divine prayers. Head of all of these is the bishop, or pontiff, who has his seat in the leading church. And this is why there are in the cities so very many men dedicated to religion.

Leo: I find this number of religious and of churches astonishing, and it seems to me that a whole city could consist solely of those people and places.

Michael: You have witnesses here present of this and of the other things, and they will not allow me to go beyond the truth in what I say.

Mancio: We do indeed confirm it with our testimony, and add besides that the magnificence of those religious houses is such that, unless you are entirely convinced that in our narration we are above all presenting you with the truth, it will be almost impossible to persuade you to give credence to our account of it; for there are many monasteries in Europe which undoubtedly cost a hundred or two hundred thousand ducats to build. And there are even some, built by kings and popes, which cost as much as a hundred or two hundred million sesterces.[2]

---

[1] I.e. the secular clergy.
[2] I.e. 2.5 million and 5 million ducats. The Escorial cost more than 5 million ducats.

Lino: When I hear you counting money in that way it really is as if you were reckoning the number of grains of rice, and I think this can only have come from the abundance of European riches, which you have seen with your own eyes.

Michael: You put it very neatly when you say that when we reckon the total outgoings of the Europeans we are as it were counting grains of rice; and yet it is no more than the truth, as is confirmed by another point already made, namely that it is perfectly clear that the houses even of private persons can often be valued at thirty or even sixty thousand ducats. From this you can make your own judgement about the royal palaces, and will not be so astonished to hear that such sums of money are used on the churches which the Europeans care for so religiously.

As well as churches, and houses sacred and secular, there are also others designated for the use of various societies; when I say societies I mean associations of pious people, who although they are not in religious life, dedicate themselves to performing works of piety for the poor and the unfortunate. Some of these societies distribute money to persons who are in need, but who are of respectable family and ashamed to live by begging for alms; others give themselves to visiting the sick and helping relieve their sufferings; others again to bringing out the bodies of the dead and burying them with solemn ceremony. Not a few dedicate themselves to arranging marriages for girls of respectable but needy families, lest their reputation or virtue be endangered, and every year they give in marriage twenty, thirty, or more of these to men of virtue and honour. Others besides give themselves diligently to other works of piety, in accordance with their various institutes.[1] There are also certain other societies, especially in Italy, which are commonly known as *Montes Pietatis*, which are concerned mainly with lending money to the indigent; and this is arranged with security for the loan, so that there is no danger of the money not coming back to the *Mons Pietatis*; and they take in addition seven per cent per year, which pays for the assistants who busy themselves with this work. And since the money taken in over and above the amount of the loan is to cover normal costs and is not for the loan itself, no danger of usury arises. A number of these societies have temples or other similar places, and on certain days all who are joined in a kind of brotherhood assemble there, and have most useful meetings concerning the business of their associations. And from this you can appreciate how famous are the places for which the European cities are celebrated.[2]

---

[1] The Marian Congregations or *sodales* set up by the Jesuits in the 16th century to counter heresy and reform manners. They spread from Italy to other European countries. Such congregations had been encouraged by Loyola and the Marian congregations were championed by Aquaviva (Chatellier, *Europe of the Devout*, pp. 3–46 and *passim*). Marian Congregations made their first appearance in Japan in the 1590s (Cieslik, 'Laienarbeitin der alten Japanmission', pp. 179–81).

[2] The first *mons pietatis* was established by the Franciscans in Perugia in 1462 to break the Jewish monopoly over moneylending. It offered small loans to the poor using pawns for security at a rate of around 5 per cent, charged from when the loan was made. The *montes* spread throughout Italy but were controversial. Their critics charged them with condoning usury. The *montes* were legitimized by Leo X at the Fifth Lateran Council in 1515. See Pullan, *Rich and Poor*, pt 3, *passim*; Wood, *Medieval Economic Thought*, pp. 202–5. Valignano had a high opinion of the *montes pietates* and favoured introducing them in Japan (*Sumario*, pp. 340–44). Only one was established in Nagasaki (Cieslik, 'Laienarbeiten der alten Japanmission', pp. 178–9).

There are besides in those cities many other residences which certainly deserve to be brought to your attention. Some are called *xenodochia*,[1] and they are specifically for strangers, who are to be received in a friendly manner and treated most hospitably; and there persons from other places can spend some days restoring their strength and recovering from the hardships of their long journeys. Others are called *nosocomia*,[2] and there those who are afflicted with any disease are diligently cured, and have ready access to all medicines and other remedies without any payment. And since there are various kinds of illnesses there are also various kinds of hospitals, or hospitals with different separate buildings, in which the most careful attention is paid to order, cleanliness, and the curing of the sick. These residences, all set out in good order, ready for those suffering from illnesses, and able to accommodate a great number of people, present a most impressive spectacle to any stranger visiting. There are others called *brephotrophia*,[3] in which babies abandoned by their mothers, whether because of poverty or for some other reason, are taken in and cared for, and handed over for feeding to various wet-nurses; and this kind of work of mercy is of special importance, since babes of that tender age are so vulnerable to danger. There are, finally, others which, not deserving the title of nunnery, can be referred to generally as houses of women. Many women ask permission to resort to these, after years spent living less modestly; they commit themselves to a better way of life, and pass their lives imitating holy virgins in praising God and in other works.[4]

Leo: It seems to me that all those places are extremely valuable, since they mean that so many evils which are common here in Japan can be avoided; such as the ravishing of virgins, bawdy houses of lewd women, wretched abortions procured with herbs or other pestiferous medicaments, the atrocious killing of tender babes by their own mothers by suffocation or some other form of cruelty, and finally, the unconcern, which flies in the face of all humanity, at the sick or otherwise afflicted here and there around them dying of want. In comparison with these evils the good things of Europe point to the truth of the Christian religion.[5]

---

[1] *Xenodochia* were hospices set up by the church during the reign of Constantine to provide care for the elderly, sick or indigent and accommodation for travellers.

[2] From the Greek *noskomeion*, a hospital.

[3] Foundling hospitals or asylums for abandoned infants mentioned in Justinian's laws.

[4] The Casa Pia, founded by Pius IV in 1563 to receive repentant prostitutes, superseding the earlier Casa di Santa Marta founded by Loyola in 1541–2 as a refuge for marginalized women, in particular reformed prostitutes and women who had suffered abuse. See O'Malley, *First Jesuits*, pp. 178–88; Lazar, *Working in the Vineyard*, pp. 37–70.

[5] On abortion and infanticide in Japan, which the Jesuits condemned, ascribing it to poverty, excommunicating those involved in the practice, see Valignano, *Historia*, p. 141, and the extensive references in *Sumario*, pp. 31 esp. nn. 49 and 53, 340 esp. n. 4. See also *Vocabvlario*, f. 387v: '*Vminagaxi [uminagashi], Mouer, ou lançar a criança morta antes do tempo*', to crush or eject a dead child before term. Richard Cocks described infanticide as 'the most horriblest thing of all' (Farrington, *English Factory*, I, p. 259). In 16th-century Rome, the ratio of men to women was abnormally high, thanks to the large number of celibate clergy and the number of prostitutes as a percentage of the female population was remarkably high. The prostitutes were divided into two categories: 'honest courtesans' (rich ones) and 'courtesans of the candle' (poor ones). Various efforts were made throughout the century, especially under popes Pius V and Sixtus V, to regulate the trade (including unsuccessful attempts to confine them to a ghetto). Around 1542 Loyola established the Compagnia delle Vergini Miserabli di Santa Catarina which accepted the daughters of prostitutes aged between nine and twelve, educated them in Christian virtues and domestic skills before providing them with a dowry and marrying them off. The institution

Michael: You do well indeed to compare the two cases, and you seem to be gathering not a little fruit from our colloquia, and to be weighing matters European in an accurate balance. But there are other places in European cities, generally known now as academies,[1] which I should not omit. It is usual for these to be built in various kingdoms of Europe, and in their principal cities. These academies are exceedingly spacious residences and palaces designated for the teaching and education of studious youths. The Europeans cultivate not only military discipline, essential though that is when it comes to waging war; they also teach many other liberal arts directed to governing the people, maintaining peace, and upholding justice; so these most famous places are open to large numbers of those same studious adolescents who devote themselves to the liberal arts.[2] From all quarters they come, and they study the teachings of all the disciplines, starting from the first elements. The buildings of these academies are extremely large and very splendid, and in them, as well as the spacious quadrangles and vestibules, there are most beautiful halls, extremely impressive to behold, which can comfortably accommodate the great number of pupils who assemble there. There are benches to sit on, and desks to write at, all set out in perfect order, and there are elevated chairs suitably positioned, where the masters teach, and all listen to them.[3]

Leo: What is it that those masters teach their disciples?

Michael: You are right to ask, Leo, and you offer me an opportunity to say something to you, in the brief time available, about the noble arts cultivated so diligently and studiously by the Europeans. This is a subject which deserves at least one whole colloquium to itself, but we shall have to make do with inserting it here, since what we are primarily concerned with is our journey, and we cannot offer more than a rather summary account of all the rest. Before I say something about the liberal arts, however, I shall preface it with a little about the letters of Europe, which are the first and certain foundation of the liberal arts, and which children learn diligently from an early age. These characters were most ingeniously invented by the ancestors of the Europeans and first inhabitants of Europe. It is not as with the Chinese and ourselves, where for the most part it has been normal to have as many figures or letters for things as there are things themselves. This was

---

remained under Jesuit control until 1544. See Montaigne, *Journal*, p. 224; Delumeau, *Vie économique et sociale de Rome*, pp. 416–32, *passim*; Lazar, *Working in the Vineyard*, pp. 71–98, which is more reliable than Delumeau on Jesuit activity. Given the openness of prostitution in Rome, and elsewhere in Italy, it is not surprising that Valignano's instructions on how the boys were to be chaperoned emphasized that whatever was bad in Europe was to be screened from their view (Abranches Pinto and Bernard, 'Les instructions', p. 393; Álvarez-Taladriz, 'En el IV centenario de la embajada', p. 137).

[1] Original edition (p. 148) '*Academiae*' or universities.

[2] Original edition (p. 148) *bonis artibus*, the second half of the motto of the Roman College, '*Religioni et bonis artibus*'.

[3] The Jesuit curriculum in schools and colleges was modelled on that of Paris (*modus et ordo Parisiensis*) where Loyola and his companions had studied. See Farrell, *Jesuit Code of Liberal Education*, pp. 32–3; Grendler, *Schooling in Renaissance Italy*, p. 377. On the rapid expansion of Jesuit education after the opening of the first Jesuit school in Messina in 1548, see Farrell, *Jesuit Code of Liberal Education*, p. 25; Grendler, *Schooling in Renaissance Italy*, pp. 363–81. The increase in Jesuit schools in Italy owed much to Spanish patronage, for which they were criticized (Brizzi, 'Les jésuites et l'école en Italie', pp. 46–7).

a system easy to devise, but extremely laborious for those who learn our or the Chinese letters; so much so that it takes many years to learn to read and write them even moderately well, unless we happen to want to use those syllables which we call *kana*; but more educated people do not normally use this way of writing. The Europeans, on the other hand, have only twenty-three letters, and those are simple.[1] They combine and join them together so cleverly and ingeniously that with them they can make first the syllables, and then all the words and expressions for things. This means that when they know these letters they can read and write much more easily in their fashion.

Lino: You are right, for I have heard that some of our boys in the seminaries have been found to have learned to read and to form the European elements in one or two months. But for the more numerous Japanese and Chinese characters a very long time is required, so it would be excellent for us if the European letters were taught to us by the fathers of the Society, since they are so easy to learn, provided that our Japanese language was correctly expressed by those letters.

Michael: That is a very important point that you have raised, for the curriculum of the Japanese and Chinese letters is so long that it leaves no time for the other arts and disciplines which the fathers are eager to teach us. There is, however, in our letters an advantage not to be despised, in that they represent properly and without any ambiguity many of our words which are ambiguous because of the similarity of the sound.

Lino: Do you mean that our words which are similar and ambiguous in their sound cannot be represented by those European letters?

Michael: I admit that it is a little difficult for words which have an ambiguous sound to be represented or expressed with those letters. But the fathers are working towards this by introducing various accents and marks, and I have no doubt they will succeed.[2] But let us move on from letters to the liberal arts.

Leo: I have been looking forward to that, and I would be glad if you would tell us about the number of those European arts.

Michael: It is a subject which, as I said, would require an entire colloquium, if not more, to itself, but for your sake I shall speak about all the arts together, in a sort of brief

---

[1] Classical Latin had 23 letters.

[2] The Jesuits eventually succeeded in replacing Chinese characters with the Roman alphabet not in Japan but in Vietnam thanks to the efforts of Alexandre de Rhodes in the 17th century. João Rodrigues discusses the Japanese language more fully. See Cooper, *João Rodrigues's Account*, pp. 330–42. For the efforts by the Jesuits and others to master Japanese and to provide accessible texts for language study, see Schurhammer, *Kirchliche Sprachproblem*; Doi, 'Sprachstudium der Gesellschaft Jesu'. The crowning achievement of these efforts was the *Vocabvlario* and Rodrigues's *Arte de Lingoa de Iapam*, both printed in Roman letters. Valignano himself, despite serious efforts, and his insistence that mastery of local languages was a requirement for missionary success, never became proficient in Japanese or in any Asian language. According to Mesquita, he always needed the services of an interpreter. See *Documenta Indica*, XV, pp. 326–7; Schütte, *Valignano's Mission Principles*, I: 1, p. 43; I: 2, p. 65.

summary, to let you see the multiplicity of the Europeans' studies. They divide the arts into two very broad categories, including in the one those which deal with language, and in the other those which treat of things. In the first category they put Grammar, Rhetoric, Dialectics, and some other arts which are concerned with language.[1] The second category is larger still, and wider; it contains many more arts which, for the sake of brevity and clarity, can be divided into three parts: the first dealing with nature, the second with illnesses, and the third with things raised above nature. All the disciplines which consider and contemplate the nature of things solely by the light of reason belong to the part which deals with nature. (Allow me here to take in this way the arts which deal with nature.) To this order belong, in the first place the four which are called Mathematics, namely Geometry, Arithmetic, Music, and Astrology:[2] the first of these is concerned with magnitude, the second with numbers, the third with sounds, the fourth with those things which are observed in the sky. Now if you join those with the three which deal with language, namely Grammar, Rhetoric, and Dialectics, they make up the *septenarium* of those arts which are appropriate for the free man, and which are therefore generally referred to as the liberal arts.[3]

In the same way add to this order Philosophy, which reflects deeply on things consisting of form and matter, and that other philosophy called *Prima Philosophia*, or, to use the common term, Metaphysics, which claims for itself things dissociated from all bodily materiality. Add further the art of healing, which treats of the types of illnesses and the variety of medicine. Now, to come to the part which is concerned with conduct, it comprises not only that Philosophy which is called moral by most people, together with political and economic philosophy, but also that pre-eminent discipline dealing with both sets of law, namely Roman and canon,[4] and it is customary for the Europeans to devote many years of assiduous effort to both, for the sake of the government of the state. Among all these doctrines and disciplines the one which holds the principal place is that which looks in the light of faith at the things which are set above nature, and it is mostly those who profess the religious life who, after the curricula of philosophy, make this their study.

Lino: Say something of the order of learning, and the time devoted to the curricula of these arts.

Michael: After the letters, of which I spoke, there follows the study of those arts which are concerned with language. After that, and depending on whether they are inclined to this or that kind of life, the scholars either give themselves to Roman and canon law, or, after completing the curriculum of philosophy, they study theology, prince of all the arts, or, finally, if that is what they wish, they dedicate themselves to the art of healing. In the study of these arts, after establishing the base of Latin grammar, the Europeans spend five,

---

[1] The *trivium*.

[2] The *quadrivium*.

[3] On the liberal arts as a subject of study appropriate for a free man, see Seneca, *Epistles*, 88. The most influential pedagogical text of Renaissance humanism, whose influence can be easily detected in *De Missione*, is Pier Paulo Vergerio, *De ingenuis moribus et liberalibus studiis adulescentiae* (1402 or 1403). See Grendler, *Schooling in Renaissance Italy*, pp. 117–19.

[4] Original edition (p. 150) gives '*Caesarei uidelicet et Pontificii*'.

six, or ten years, and sometimes even longer. Finally, after an examination and testing of their erudition, they receive *summa cum laude* their laurels, i.e. their three degrees, lower, medium, and highest, the highest being called doctor or master, and we shall sometimes mention this later on. They then take on and discharge various public offices, either sacred or secular, according to the abilities and status of the person, and to their different studies in arts. Now, brief though it has been, let this suffice about the liberal arts until we come to the more famous places among the European cities.

Lino: We were very much taken with your listing of all those liberal arts which the Europeans master before, enlightened also with the light of faith, they give an admirable account of themselves in the administration of kingdoms and republics. Nor is it surprising that our people, deprived as they are of all these advantages, err so greatly in matters concerning government and the knowledge of nature.

Michael: It is remarkable, on the contrary, that our people, even though lacking help of both these kinds, have nevertheless attained to such a degree of nobility and urbanity that in this matter we judge them to be the most similar to the Europeans of all the peoples we have seen.

Leo: For us that is a most gratifying judgement. There is another thing that it occurs to me to ask, however, namely whether those cities also have numerous workshops for artisans, who usually provide very fine adornments for such communities.

Michael: You seem to be wanting me to speak to you here, Leo, about craftsmanship and other manual arts. There is indeed no lack of these in the European cities; in fact, it is a most agreeable spectacle to see, in their famous cities, so many streets given over to such a variety of craftsmen. In these streets some work diligently with gold, others with silver, others again with colours, leather, stones, cloth, iron, and any other material of which works are made. All of them strive to excel in their arts, for outstanding craftsmen, especially those who practise the nobler arts, are held in high regard by the kings and princes. I could tell you many things now about the art of weaving, about the military, nautical, and agrarian arts, or about working in wool, but I feel that I have already talked too much. Let us come back now to public works.

Leo: The things you have told us about the buildings and the most famous places in the cities of Europe are indeed wonderful, for it is certain not only that they make the cities populous and noble, but also that they afford the maximum of utility to their citizens, while supplying the needs of so many people. But I would like to know with what funding, public or private, these works are constructed.

Michael: The works I have spoken of are constructed with funding from various sources, pontifical, royal, sometimes public and sometimes private, from aristocratic and noble men. For since, as I said already, the ranks in Europe, both sacred and secular, are so various, the incomes attached to them very generous, and the treasuries of the princes extremely rich, there is enough money to spare for the building of these most magnificent works.

Leo: I attribute the magnificence of those buildings not only to the opulence of Europe, but also to its tranquillity. Would that our Japan had remained in that state in which it began, and that the most eminent power of the king of all, whom we call the *dairi*, had not been divided up among so many members. Then not only would our ancient buildings (and they too were famous) have been preserved in good condition; they would have increased day by day. But with Japan in an unquiet condition it is not to be wondered at if most of them have gone to rack and ruin, and we now feel the lack of the ancient splendour and magnificence of Japanese buildings. But the ruins left after the fires of so many wars show clearly enough the greatness of soul of our Japanese who erected the great structures of those buildings and set up with such outstanding skill those temples of outworn superstition.[1]

Michael: Oh that not only that tranquillity, which was once ours, may be restored to us, but also that the Christian religion may come to pervade all the parts and members of Japan, for then, if we could bring together the greatness of soul which made those buildings, and piety, there is no doubt that we would come close to the fame of the Europeans. But we should now come on to the question of sacred splendour, and keep for another place what remains of this subject. I find no better way of explaining the sacred splendour than to have us recall to mind the magnificence of the kings and other princes, which I spoke about before. If we compare the two it will be scarcely possible to discern which outdoes the other in grandeur and abundance. Besides the Supreme Pontiff, and those who are numbered among the cardinals, there are many archbishops, bishops, canons, and other similar priests, no less in number than the secular rulers, and with revenues not less abundant, so it is hardly possible to judge which of them live in greater wealth and splendour. Add to these the furnishings of the temples and monasteries, which are generally in use in religious services, in which so much gold, silver, silk and other precious stuffs are consumed that in this so magnificent ornamentation the truth of the Christian religion is in some sense splendidly manifest. For although these external things in themselves add nothing to the solid truth, that truth shines out in them as in signs, just as we say that the power and the beauty of God shines forth in created things. Thus it is that, just as, according to the testimony of learned men, it is necessary for anyone who looks steadfastly at the fabric of all this round world to acknowledge God as its governor, so also he who has contemplated the services regularly offered to God in the churches of the Christians, the great number and the piety of the people, the frequency of the sacrifices, the richness of the sacred vestments, and in all these things the singular propriety which is always observed, cannot but confess that this is the cult of the true and living God. But there will be another occasion to treat of those things which pertain to the divine and the sacred, so, now that these points about the things of Europe have been in some way presented to you, let us come back tomorrow at more leisure to proceeding with our account of our journey.

---

[1] In the *Adiciones* (p. 363), Valignano praised Hideyoshi's extensive rebuilding projects in Kyoto such that the capital had never been 'so great nor so sumptuous' under any emperor. See also Berry, *Hideyoshi*, pp. 193–203.

COLLOQUIUM XVI

Reverting to the account of the journey, with a description of Lisbon, capital of the kingdom of Portugal

Leo: What you have told us so far, Michael, brief though it has been, about the things of Europe, has greatly enlightened our minds so as to enable us to understand them. But now do please move on and give us an account of your journey as far as the Roman curia, though without leaving out, as far as the brevity of these colloquia permits, anything which pertains to the nobility of the cities and the notable things in them. And to bring you back to the same place where you left off, let me remind you that you were in Lisbon, that most celebrated port, enjoying most welcome hospitality at the house of the professed fathers of the Society of Jesus.

Michael: I'll be glad to go back to the point from which was diverted by your questions about the things of Europe in general. But our digression should not be regarded as merely of minor importance, for we have laid the necessary foundations, without which nothing can be brought to a proper conclusion, for everything that is to follow. It will also help you to understand what we shall be saying later, when we deal separately with the various European cities, to look at those books which we showed you some days ago about the towns and the buildings of Europe.

Leo: We liked those books very much, and we understood from them that the people of Europe are notable for their concern with elegance, for their abilities, and for their manual skill and dexterity; for they not only construct most magnificent buildings, but also depict them in remarkable printed reproductions. But come now to the account, which we have been eagerly awaiting, of the things of Lisbon.[1]

Michael: You lay a very heavy burden on me, asking me to expound in such a brief address things which would require a whole book to themselves. What arouses and encourages me, however, is that that most famous city, which has deserved well of all the Orient, is worthy of whatever labour it requires of me. For it is the capital of the Portuguese kingdom, from which, as from a most abundant source, the Christian religion has spread through all these regions of the East. Therefore, and rightly, immortal is the memory of the Portuguese kings, who not only, to great acclaim, banished the Mahometan people, enemies of the Christian name, from the territories of their kingdom, but who sent their fleets to the most remote lands to take to them the signs of our salvation. And to the first of

---

[1] The boys arrived in Lisbon on 11 August and left on 5 September (see above, p. 93 n. 2).

them, Don Afonso Henriques, invincible king, Lisbon owes much more than to Ulysses, most ancient leader of the Greeks, who, according to the tradition of the Ancients, was her founder. For he it was who rescued her when she was oppressed and almost annihilated by the Saracens, and restored her to the liberty and light of Christianity.[1] Those who succeeded him on that royal throne followed in his footsteps, and to honour them I now name them: Sancho, his son; Afonso II; Sancho II; Afonso III; Dinis whose wife was Isabel, numbered among the saints; Afonso IV, his son, famed for his celebrated victory over the Moors at the Salado river;[2] Pedro, most concerned for justice; Fernando, of singular mildness; João I, who was also the first to go over to Africa, and who captured by force of arms the heavily fortified city of Ceuta;[3] Duarte famous for his illustrious posterity;[4] Afonso V, who crossed to Africa three times, and added many towns to his possessions;[5] João II, admirable for his strength and fortitude of mind, and for his equally great prudence and holiness;[6] Manuel, more illustrious than any of his predecessors for his good fortune;[7] João III, outstanding in religion;[8] Sebastião, a king of most invincible spirit, who, in zeal to propagate his kingdom and the Christian faith, went to a most valiant death on the very field of battle;[9] and finally Henrique, rich in every kind of virtue.[10] Lisbon acknowledges all of these, and rightly indeed, as its illustrious progenitors and benefactors.

Now given that these kings, blessed with perfect peace, have enriched and ennobled the kingdom of Portugal, which has been established for five hundred years, and the city of Lisbon, capital of the entire kingdom, it is easy to understand how noble, how large, and how populous is the city of Lisbon, where the kings of Portugal have so long had their seat.[11] Also contributing to its nobility is the outstanding site of the city, for it is

---

[1] Afonso I Henriques (r. 1139–85) became king of Portugal in July 1139 and in 1147 seized Santarém and Lisbon. In the 16th century it was believed that Ulysses had founded Lisbon (Olissipo). See Góis, *Lisbon in the Renaissance*, p. 8; Camões, *Os Lusíadas*, VIII-5: 1–4.

[2] Afonso IV (r. 1325–57) joined forces with the Castilians and defeated the armies of the Magrib and Granada at the battle of the Salado river in October 1340.

[3] João I (r. 1385–1433) conquered Ceuta in 1415.

[4] Duarte (r. 1433–8) *o eloquente*, the eloquent, or *rei-filósofo*, philosopher-king.

[5] Afonso V (r. 1438–81) *o Africano*, the African, seized Ksar el-Kebir (in present-day Morocco) in 1458, failed to take control of Tangier in 1463–4, but conquered Arzilla in 1471.

[6] João II (r. 1481–95) *o Príncipe perfeito*, the perfect prince.

[7] Manuel I (r. 1495–1521) *o venturoso*, the fortunate, under whose rule Portugal established her maritime empire in Asia.

[8] João III (r. 1521–57), *o piedoso*, the pious.

[9] Sebastião (r. 1557–78), defeated and killed in battle at Ksar el-Kebir, also known as the 'Battle of the Three Kings', on 4 August 1578. His death gave rise to the cult of Sebastianism. A number of impostors claimed to be the dead king.

[10] Henrique (r. 1578–80), *o cardeal-rei*, the cardinal king, younger son of Manuel and brother of João III, successively archbishop of Braga, archbishop of Évora, cardinal and Grand Inquisitor and patron of the Jesuits in Portugal. His death prompted rival dynastic claims to the vacant throne resulting in Philip II of Spain's invasion in 1580 and Philip II's election as Filipe I of Portugal on 25 March 1581.

[11] Most of what the young Japanese saw in Lisbon was destroyed in the great earthquake of 1755. The following description is, therefore, an invaluable guide to Lisbon before the earthquake struck. It is much more detailed than Góis's *Urbis Olisiponis descriptio* (1554). This lengthy colloquium undoubtedly represents de Sande's contribution. Valignano had been in Lisbon for only a few weeks before taking ship for the Indies. The most famous engraving of Lisbon around this time is in the 1598 volume of Braun's *Civitates orbis terrarum* which identifies 140 of the city's most famous buildings by number. A different illustration of the city appears in the 1572 volume.

in the middle of the maritime coast of Spain,[1] in the area where the Tagus, a famous river, after irrigating a very long stretch of Spain with its waters, flows through a most ample bed, with a great abundance of water, into the ocean, making the port of Lisbon most celebrated, and frequented by almost all the peoples of Europe. Germans, Belgians, French, Cantabrians, Asturians, Italians, especially Genoese and Venetians, to say nothing of the fleets from the Indies and others from the Eastern ocean, flow into Lisbon, such a multitude of people bringing or coming to purchase merchandise that some of them have set up their own special chapels where they take part in divine worship; the Belgians have their chapel and sodality in the parish of St Julian,[2] the Germans in the monastery of St Dominic,[3] the Italians in the parish of the Blessed Virgin of Loreto,[4] and finally all the Spaniards from outside Portugal have their own chapel in the monastery of St Francis,[5] and there they recite the divine prayers with their own singing. And these same foreign peoples, since there are so many of them, have their own special magistrates, by whom their lawsuits are judged. The numbers of these foreigners increased greatly after the kingdom of Portugal came into the hands of King Philip, because commerce with other parts of the world became much more open and was greatly amplified. So although there are in Europe many most outstanding cities, and some are more notable than others in certain respects, this one has in such abundance all those things for which a city can be famed, that it yields to none, and takes the palm over most cities however celebrated.[6]

Cities are usually famed for their site, their antiquity, their fortifications, their population, and for how abundantly supplied and how agreeable they are. To these add, if you will, religion and divine worship, the most important thing of all. Now this most flourishing of cities is abundantly adorned with all of these things, and you will readily appreciate just how abundantly from what I shall tell you. To begin with the most general points, it includes in a sense two very considerable cities, with their fortifications, walls, and ramparts, with a total of thirty-eight gates and seventy-seven towers. It has more than a hundred and thirty churches, of which almost forty belong to parishes, and the rest are attached either to monasteries of religious men, to convents of holy virgins, or to the houses of similar congregations or societies.[7] It contains besides six royal palaces of the utmost magnificence, two of them built by the sea shore, and the other four in inland

---

[1] The original edition (p. 155) gives: '*post longissimum Hispaniae spatium*'. During the late Middle Ages the Christian kingdoms of the Iberian Peninsula (the Five Kingdoms, viz. Portugal, Leon, Castile, Aragon and Navarre) called themselves *Hispaniae*, after the Spanish provinces of the Roman Empire. After the union of Aragon and Castile in 1479 and, disregarding Portuguese protests, the joint monarchy's appropriation of the name Spain for the unified kingdoms, the Portuguese began to style themselves Lusitanians, after the Roman province Lusitania (which was not, however, the same as modern Portugal). See Livermore, *New History of Portugal*, p. 9, n. 1; Kamen, *Spain's Road to Empire*, pp. 10–11; Disney, *History of Portugal*, I, p. 31.

[2] São Gião.

[3] Mosteiro de São Domingos.

[4] Nossa Senhora do Loreto.

[5] There were two Franciscan monasteries, São Francisco da Cidade and São Francisco de Xabregas; the former is meant. See Brandão, *Grandeza e abastança*, p. 115; Rodrigues de Oliveira, *Lisboa em 1551*, pp. 76–8, 82–3.

[6] Brandão claimed that Lisbon surpassed Venice, Cairo, Babylon and Paris (*Grandeza e abastança*, p. 24). See also Camões, *Os Lusíadas*, III: 57, 1–2; VI: 7.2.

[7] Cf. Góis, *Lisbon in the Renaissance*, p. 32, and Brandão, *Grandeza e abastança*, pp. 113–38, which has a list of the religious institutions of Lisbon.

locations.[1] With regard to the houses of the nobles, it is hardly possible to number them precisely. All the nobles who exercise jurisdiction in different parts of Portugal usually go to great pains and expense to erect houses in that city which is the capital of the kingdom, and where the climate is most agreeable and salubrious, especially since in the time of the kings of Portugal they seldom left their side. The city contains seven hospitals,[2] and I shall shortly be speaking of the largest of these, and a number of other places built at public or royal expense and designated for various purposes useful to the state. All of these things make this city remarkably famous, noble, and populous, so that it was with justice that a certain queen of Portugal said, so we are told, that a king who was master just of that city could be numbered among the most powerful of kings.

And now, since this is the first European city which I have undertaken to describe, I'll show you, as succinctly as I can, the form it takes, so that you can more easily have an idea of the scale, the variety, and the number of the buildings, and of the other most notable things in this city and also in the other noble cities of the whole of Europe.

Lino: It will be most pleasing to us, Michael, if you can impress on our minds an image of that first city, whose name we have so often heard mentioned by the fathers, so that from what you say about it we may the more easily be able to form judgements about other cities.

Michael: I shall do as you ask, and I shall deal first with the most celebrated estuary of the Tagus, which is right in front of the city, flowing to the west, and guarded on either side by two very heavily armed forts, the one that of São Sebastião, the other that of Belém.[3] Of these two the fort of Belém, which is on the near side, in the Lisbon area, is of very remarkable construction, with its foundations set in the sea itself, and so well defended on all sides that what with the number of guns and the diligent garrison of soldiers which it has it keeps that shore safe and free from any hostile incursion.[4] Every ship, Portuguese or foreign, coming into the port acknowledges that citadel as master of all the sea, by signalling with its guns, by lowering its sails, or even by sending a boat with some sailors to the fort. If it did otherwise it would suffer for it and would immediately be sunk by cannonballs fired from the fort.

Not far from that fort is situated the very famous monastery of the religious of the family of St Jerome, which is dedicated to the Blessed Virgin of Bethlehem, from which the fortress too gets its name, and this can be said to hold first place among all the religious buildings of Lisbon. This monastery was established by the most illustrious King Manuel, and was magnificently extended by his son João III. For when, as I said before, after many famous victories produced in Africa by earlier kings, Manuel, most powerful of kings, put his mind to the expedition to India, and when India was opened up in his most auspicious time, his first priority was to erect that monastery at the first entrance to the port of Lisbon as a most sacred shrine of holiness and religion, in which all those who were setting

---

[1] The Alcáçova, Estáus, Real de Santos (or Velho), Santo Eloí, Ribeira and Xabregas palaces. For a full discussion of the palaces of Lisbon, see Holanda, *Da fábrica que falece à cidade de Lisboa*, pp. 78–85.

[2] Cf. Brandão, *Grandeza e abastança*, pp. 123–32.

[3] São Sebastião is at Caparica, on the opposite side of the Tagus from Lisbon and Belém.

[4] One of the most famous monuments in Lisbon, the Belém tower, designed by Francisco de Arruda, was constructed under Manuel I between 1514 and 1521.

out from there for various parts of the world should make an auspicious beginning to their voyages with divine services performed and prayers offered up to God.[1]

There are many things which make this monastery outstandingly famous. In the first place the priests' rooms are very large, and they have a corridor so long that, no matter how acute your sight, you cannot recognize from the entrance to it a man standing at the far end of it. The cloister of this monastery has such a vault, rests on such columns, has such paving, and is decorated with such paintings, presenting a multiple image of Christ suffering for us, that it is a manifest tribute to the nobility of the king. And what am I to say of the church of the same monastery, each part of which deserves a whole colloquium to itself. Particularly outstanding is the main chapel, dedicated from when this monastery was first built to the tombs of the kings of Portugal. All of it is of stone of Paros so highly polished that every part of it shines and glints like jasper. In it there are four tombs of the kings and queens, each of them supported with wonderful artifice by two elephants made from the same precious stone, and ingeniously fitted with tusks of ivory; and the coverings of the tombs are adorned with royal crowns in gold, of strikingly fine workmanship. The same monastery is rich in the possession of many sacred relics, especially the heads of three of the eleven thousand virgins,[2] and many other relics brought to that place by the diligence and labour of the kings. And the vessels of gold and silver, the sacred vestments with their silk and embroidery work, are such as befit the munificence of the kings buried there. Most precious of all these sacred works is one particular chalice, admirable in the ingenious workmanship of its carving, made by command of King Manuel from the first gold brought from the Orient, as it were the first fruit of the India voyages, and offered by the same king to the Blessed Virgin.[3]

I'll move on now to a description of the city. Imagine it as taking the form of a bow and arrow, if the buildings of both the city itself and of its surroundings are included. The maritime shore is stretched out like the string, with the central part of the city extending like the arrow, and the sides, which contain two very large hills, taking the form of the bow. Let us now make as it were a three-day journey (three days being the minimum time required to take in the famous places), and see with what splendid buildings the city is adorned. If we start from the coast, a mile along from the monastery of Belém is the first entrance to the suburbs of Lisbon, with a church dedicated to St Maurus.[4] From there on churches and well-known places gradually appear, but it will be better to refrain from

---

[1] The Jerónimos monastery, founded by Manuel I to honour Portuguese overseas voyages and to serve as a mausoleum for Manuel and his spouse, Maria. The foundation stone was laid in 1501 and the structure, using local stone, *pedra lioz*, was largely complete by 1551. Work on the interior stopped after the union of the crowns in 1581 when funds were diverted to the construction of the Escorial. The building survived the great earthquake in 1755 but was much restored in the 19th century. In addition to Manuel and his wife, João III, his wife Catarina, Vasco da Gama and Luís de Camões are interred in the monastery.

[2] Ursula and her 11,000 virgins were allegedly martyred near Cologne by the Huns in 383. The order of the Ursulines was founded in 1535. The story of Ursula and her virgins is now considered a fabrication and Ursula was removed from the canon of saints in 1969. Ursula figured prominently in Portuguese and Spanish overseas expansion. The Jesuits were important in spreading and encouraging the cult overseas. See Osswald, 'Society of Jesus'.

[3] The monstrance of Belém, made in 1506 by the celebrated writer and goldsmith Gil Vicente with the first gold brought back from Mozambique.

[4] The church of São Amaro, dedicated to the first disciple of St Benedict.

describing these and proceed to the docks area which is next to the royal palace.¹ This is a very large area, bounded partly by the city wall, partly by the royal buildings, which extends right down to the sea, and in which are constructed ships of all kinds, but especially those enormous vessels by which the voyage to India was first opened and has since continued without intermission, with ships dispatched every year; and it is said that each of these ships costs twenty thousand ducats to build.² The abundance there of everything required for equipping the fleet is a sight to see. The quantity of masts and sail-yards, the great length and thickness of the ropes, the types of pitch and tar, the ways of making iron and steel pliable, the machines and contrivances for lifting weights; all of these leave nothing to be desired. In all these things, whether invented in Portugal or brought in from elsewhere, this city abounds.

I come now to the royal palace, which is so outstanding in its amplitude, its magnificence, and the appropriateness of its site, that the kings of Portugal have always been accustomed to live there.³ In the first place, its grounds border the seashore, and are so spacious that they offer a most opportune place for the Portuguese gentry and nobility, who come in their carriages, to stroll and be at their ease; and all find them particularly inviting in the summer season, when an agreeable breeze comes from the sea, and the grounds are daily sprinkled with water brought there in carts. But what am I to say of the royal residence? It has doors, halls, colonnades, terraces, bedchambers of every kind, and very many other rooms, so that it can accommodate the king and queen and their extensive household, their royal brothers, and their children. It is also much embellished by a heavily defended fortress, which extends to the seashore, and is fully equipped with cannon and all the engines of war. It also benefits from a delightful garden, not only sown with trees and with plants most pleasing in their perfume, but also boasting various pathways very skilfully paved with mosaics of different colours. It has besides a chapel for divine worship, with a large number of important priests, most of whom are subject to a bishop of high rank, and there the sacred prayers are recited with such good order, with such sweetness in the singing, and with such a variety of musical instruments that you could say that it was no chapel but some very great church.

Close to the royal palace there are other very famous places, chief among them the royal armoury, in which all the equipment belonging to warfare is most carefully kept.⁴

---

¹ The area is called the Ribeira das Naus.

² At this time the *Estado da Índia* provided the ships fully equipped for a voyage but the voyages themselves were made by a syndicate of merchants who contracted with the *Estado* for five years. At the end of the contract, the merchants returned the ships to the *Estado* and indemnified it for depreciation costs. By the early 17th century, however, the *Estado* was also contracting out shipbuilding. See Godinho, *Os descobrimentos*, III, pp. 51, 55–6. In the 1580s, the cost of arming, freighting and provisioning a ship, which averaged 600 tons, although some were between 1,500 and 2,000 tons, was around 16,000 *cruzados*. See ibid., p. 56; idem, 'Portuguese and the "Carreira da India"', p. 15; Boxer, *Portuguese Seaborne Empire*, pp. 207–10; and, for comparison, Phillips, *Six Galleons*, p. 107. The actual cost of ship construction is difficult to determine. The cost of building a 480 ton merchantman in Venice, an order of 1570 limiting them to a maximum of 450 tons notwithstanding, was 32,250 Venetian ducats. The cost of building a Spanish galleon of about 443 *toneladas* in 1617 for royal service in the Atlantic was about 13,292 ducats. See Lane, *Venetian Ships*, pp. 264–5; Phillips, *Six Galleons*, pp. 60–61, 78–9, 229.

³ The Paço Real da Ribeira, built by Manuel I, completed c. 1511, destroyed in the great earthquake.

⁴ The Arsenal de Guerra. See Góis, *Crónica de Dom Emanuel*, p. 600; idem, *Lisbon in the Renaissance*, pp. 30–31.

There you can see some enormous cannon, forged from the best of metals, and some of them were seized from enemies, and are on display in commemoration of victories; others were made at the royal expense, and are in a state of complete readiness for any outbreak of war. There various store-rooms for different kinds of arms can be seen, muskets in some, spears in others, swords in others, and all kinds of equipment, heavy and light, offensive and defensive, is held there. There are striking and remarkable statues there of knights in armour, set on wooden horses, and formed in such lifelike fashion that they could be taken for men armed and ready for a real battle. To sum up, those places are so filled with the royal arms that it is most reliably reported that, in past years at least, an army containing seventy thousand men was able to be equipped for battle and supplied with arms there. The place is therefore very celebrated among the Portuguese, and with reason, for we can affirm that it was from it, and from that city, as from the Trojan horse, that the glorious conquerors of all the Orient set out armed; and what is more admirable is that still today almost three thousand Portuguese leave the port of Lisbon every year, sent to India, Brazil, and the other Portuguese colonies, leaving aside the African expedition, so that what was brought to birth by their ancestors is preserved, to universal praise.[1] Linked to this same armoury there is a certain building, known as India House,[2] to which all the merchandise and spices brought from the whole of the Orient on the ships are carried with the greatest care, and when they have been exported to Belgium, France, Germany, and other parts of Europe, and sold, they greatly enrich the royal treasury.[3]

In the same royal palace can be seen many rooms set apart for various assemblies of senators. For one of these many men expert in justice and law, known as court senators, come together, and they diligently discuss and come to decisions in the name of the king regarding certain grave matters to do with justice and the law, concerning, for example, the pardoning of crimes and the rewarding of merit. For another there are other men, no less outstanding in jurisprudence and knowledge of the law, who come together to deal with and unravel matters to do with the three most famous military orders,[4] the leading orders of Portugal, entrusted to the king himself as their supreme master, and with all other particular matters about which the royal conscience might be troubled; and the king approves their judgement and deliberation, and thus he discharges better and more

[1] At this time the average annual number of sailings for the East Indies was five. Unless military requirements in the Indies dictated otherwise, in which case there would be additional numbers of soldiers, each vessel carried up to 500 people, mostly soldiers, plus a crew of 120 men and boys. Very few women sailed for Asia. Those who did were mainly *órfãs d'El-Rei* or Orphans of the Crown. A small number of prostitutes found their way aboard as well. Boxer suggests a figure of 4,000 people, not all of whom were Portuguese, sailing from Lisbon overseas during the 16th century. See Boxer, *Portuguese Seaborne Empire*, pp. 52–3; Godinho, 'Portuguese and the "Carreira da India"', pp. 40–43; Godinho, *A Carreira da Índia*, pp. 51–3.

[2] The *Casa da Índia* which grew out of the *Casa de Ceuta* (1415) and *Casa de Guiné* (mid-15th century). The *Casa de Guiné* was moved from Lagos to Lisbon around 1480 and became known as the *Casa de Guiné e Mina*, and after 1499 as the *Casa da Índia*. It was an imposing building, rebuilt in the mid-16th century and flattened by the great earthquake. The *Casa*, under the control of a factor appointed by the king, was in essence the headquarters of Portugal's overseas trade. See Góis, *Lisbon in the Renaissance*, p. 30; Brandão, *Grandeza e abastança*, pp. 168–72; Lach, *Asia in the Making*, I: 1, pp. 92–3, 120–21; Diffie and Winius, *Foundations*, pp, 316–17.

[3] At this time the *Estado da Índia* was profitable (Matos, 'Financial Situation', pp. 92–3).

[4] The Orders of Christ, Avis and Santiago. The masterships of these orders were annexed by the crown between 1550 and 1551. See Livermore, *New History of Portugal*, p. 132; Sá, 'Ecclesiastical Structures and Religious Action', pp. 257–8; Disney, *History of Portugal*, I, p. 160.

securely the duties of his office. The third assembly is made up of three very famous and distinguished men, together with many other magistrates, to whose care is committed and entrusted the royal income, taxes, monies, and all the royal resources; they deliberate carefully about how these are to be augmented, invested, exacted, and distributed, and decide what is to be done. The supreme council, the most highly regarded of all, is the one called the royal council, which comprises the most grave of nobles and the most learned of priests; kings presided over it in the past, but now that the kings are no more, the most illustrious Cardinal Albert, representing the person of King Philip of Spain, presides, and at that council the most careful consideration is given to the affairs of the whole kingdom, the state, and the Portuguese jurisdiction, and they apply themselves most diligently to providing for Africa, India, and the other provinces.[1]

Beyond the royal palace and its grounds many other most magnificent dwellings can be seen, and in front of these there are a great number of markets, set up in various neighbourhoods and streets, in which they sell an almost infinite number of vegetables and fruits (and the Lisbon district is outstandingly good at producing these), animals both tame and taken in the hunt, birds both domestic and caught, various kinds of foods made from milk, in which the Europeans take great pleasure, everyday desserts of many different types and tastes, and all the other things related to food, in extraordinary variety and abundance. The supply of meat is so copious that it fills three very large markets, set up in different parts of the city. And the quantity and variety of fish, whether fresh or salted, is so great, and its taste so very pleasing, that it is not only transported to many inland towns in Portugal, but also exported by land and sea to as many as possible of the cities of Europe.[2]

Let us move on now to the storehouse of grain, which indeed can be said to be the granary for the whole of Portugal.[3] There the corn is stored, corn not only from many

---

[1] This description of the government of Portugal after the union of the crowns is muddled and inaccurate. Philip II of Spain, who became Philip or Filipe I of Portugal in 1581, was determined from the outset of his rule that Portugal should remain '*siempre um reino de por sí*' (always a kingdom by and for itself). The key institutional structures to achieve this were agreed at the *cortes* of Tomar in 1581 and by subsequent enactments in the early 1580s. The provisions of this settlement included the establishment of a Council of Portugal (*Conselho de Portugal*), composed of six individuals, all Portuguese, residing at Philip's court, which after 1583 was located in Spain (the old *Conselho de estado* or Council of State was maintained in Lisbon but much diminished); the creation of the post of viceroy, a relation of the king, who would reside in Portugal to represent the monarch and see that his instructions were carried out, the first incumbent being Albert of Austria, who held the office until 1593 and whose three advisors were Portuguese; the confirmation of all existing offices, rights and privileges. The military orders of Santiago and Avis had three *ouvidorias* or special magistrates responsible for their affairs, two for Santiago and one for Avis. Nevertheless, change and reform occurred both in government and in the administration of justice after the union of the crowns. After all, Portugal had suffered from the convulsions of civil war, invasion and the decimation of the ruling class at the battle of Ksar el-Kebir in 1578. As for the administration of the affairs of Portugal's overseas possessions, responsibilities were divided according to the various jurisdictions. The East Indies had a magistrate-general presiding over a tribunal, a chancellor, a magistrate for crown affairs, and various other legal and administrative offices. In 1591 a Treasury Council was established to administer domestic and overseas finances. For a comprehensive discussion of Portuguese government after the union, see Elliot, 'Spanish Monarchy and the Kingdom of Portugal', esp. pp. 51–2; Bouza, *D. Filipe I*, pp. 180–250, esp. pp. 186–7, 196, 207, 209–10, 242, 244; Disney, *History of Portugal*, I, pp. 154–9, 200–204.

[2] On food and drink consumption in Lisbon, which was estimated to be worth 1.6 million *cruzados* in the middle of the 16th century, see Góis, *Lisbon in the Renaissance*, p. 29; Brandão, *Grandeza e abastança*, pp. 25–35; Godinho, *Os descobrimentos*, IV, pp. 12–14.

[3] The Terreiro do Trigo. Cf. Góis, *Lisbon in the Renaissance*, p. 28.

parts of Portugal, especially those beyond the Tagus, but also from many other provinces; and it must be understood that, just as we live on rice, the Europeans live on bread made from kneaded wheat flour, and in Lisbon the bread is made by the most skilful and expert bakers in all Spain, and is delicious. Not far from here, across a street, the eye of the beholder confronts the church and famous house of that sodality popularly known as the Society of Mercy,[1] for it devotes itself most diligently to works of piety such as relieving the needs of the poor with alms, providing the sick with medicines, burying the bodies of the dead, paying to ransom captives, arranging the marriages of virgin orphans, and seeing to all the other things which pertain to the offices of piety. This Lisbon sodality is as it were the mother of all the others which are spread over the whole realm of Portugal and its cities and towns. I say nothing further of the structure of the church and house, which is indeed regal, but it should be pointed out that not only common people but also certain most noble persons are selected to perform the duties of that house, especially the person who takes on the role of director general and is chosen each year by a majority of votes, and this person is usually a noble or son of a noble. And it is truly remarkable how that sodality, which does not and indeed by its constitution cannot have any annual income whatever, nevertheless possesses such ample funds, either bequeathed to it by the wills of persons deceased or otherwise acquired, that every year it distributes thirty, forty, or even sixty thousand gold ducats to the poor, to widows, virgin orphans, travellers, and various others suffering from poverty and want. And the members and house of this sodality are held in such regard that there are many who earnestly and persistently entreat them (rather than their own friends and relatives) to see to and act as executors of their wills, and who consider themselves most fortunate if the sodality agrees to undertake this task.

And that same shoreline, as it bends to the east, is adorned with many other most splendid buildings, such as that hall or royal house to the lower part of which all merchandise is brought to be taxed, except for the merchandise from India, which has a separate hall of its own.[2] And since this port of Lisbon is thronged with so many people from Europe, the number of merchants that flock to it is extraordinary, as is the contribution which these taxes make to the royal income.[3] The upper part of this building

[1] The Santa Casa da Misericórdia was founded in 1498 under the patronage of Manuel I. Most of the building was destroyed in the great earthquake. Branches of the *Misericórdia* were established throughout Portugal's maritime empire. The *Senado da Camara* and the *Misericórdia* were the most important institutions in the empire. The first *Misericórdia* in Japan was established in 1555; the Nagasaki one in 1583. The latter was governed according to the statutes of the *Misericórdia* in Macao and had a hospital and a leprosarium, distinct from the one run by the Jesuits. The impetus for the creation of the Nagasaki *Misericórdia* came from two Japanese Christians from Sakai, Justino and his wife Justa, and Japanese Christians were actively involved in running the *Misericórdia* in Japan. See *Vocabvlario*, f. 141v, 'Iifiya. Casa de Misericordia, ou hospital', from the Buddhist notion of *jihi* 慈悲 mercy or charity; Fróis, *História de Japam*, IV, p. 122; V, p. 228; Schütte, *Monumenta Historica Japoniae I*, p. 520 n. 12; Ruiz-de-Medina, *Documentos del Japón 1558–1562*, pp. 662–78; Góis, *Crónica de Dom Emanuel*, p. 599; idem, *Lisbon in the Renaissance*, p. 24; Brandão, *Grandeza e abastança*, pp. 117–23; Boxer, *Portuguese Seaborne Empire*, pp. 273, 286–95; idem, *Fidalgos*, pp. 217–20; Subrahmanyan, *Portuguese Empire in Asia*, pp. 226–7; Cieslik, 'Laienarbeiten der alten Japanmission', pp. 176–8; Braga, 'Poor Relief in Counter-Reformation Portugal', pp. 201–14; Costa, 'The *Misericórdias*', pp. 67–79; Disney, *History of Portugal*, I, pp. 162–3.

[2] The Alfândega Nova or New Custom House, destroyed in the great earthquake. Imports from Asia were handled at the Casa da Índia. See also Góis, *Lisbon in the Renaissance*, p. 28.

[3] Brandão claims that 1,500 vessels from all parts of Christendom visited Lisbon each year (*Grandeza e abastança*, p. 111).

was formerly devoted to the administering of justice, but is now occupied by the royal paymasters and prefects of the treasury, who daily keep account and compile a reliable and authoritative record of income and outgoings; and many very considerable men are appointed to occupations dealing with these financial matters.

Leo: I cannot restrain myself, Michael, from interrupting your account, which is giving me the greatest pleasure, to express my admiration for those things which you have related to us so far. No one could but be astonished to hear of these things, and no one could fail to appreciate that in this most noble city which you describe three excellent things shine especially bright, namely ingenuity, prudence, and piety, together with the utmost magnificence and abundance of everything. The ingenuity is clear to me from their diligence in procuring arms and food, the prudence from the many committees intent on dealing wisely with every kind of matter, and finally the piety from that so famous sodality of which you have just been speaking.

Michael: Your inference is excellent, Leo, and your reasoning most judicious. But you will be able to draw your conclusions about all these things, and about many other similar and equally admirable things, as our narrative continues.

Lino: For my part too I can say that I now see in your description of this city, as in a perfectly clear mirror, sharply and in detail, the things which you told us in general terms about the cities of Europe. If the other European cities observe the same order and course, this should be seen not as a human invention but as a gift from heaven.

Michael: Most certainly they do observe it, and you are right to say that this order is something heaven-given, because all these advantages and embellishments in this and other cities flow, as from a most bounteous spring, from the Christian religion, which is from heaven. But let us complete the remainder of this first journey. I come therefore to the public fountains, and especially to the one known as the King's Fountain, constructed of marble with workmanship of superb artistry, which receives water which gushes out not far away (there is water in great abundance in that area), and it flows out through very broad and skilfully worked orifices, to be collected by an almost infinite number of slaves or servants, even at dead of night (such is the multitude of the population there). Not only is that water extremely abundant, but its quality is such that it is particularly good for health, especially if kept for some time in the house.[1] There are plenty of other excellent fountains in the suburbs of Lisbon, however, notably one other one, close by, and not so copious, which generally provides the supply of water for the various voyages which are setting out.[2]

Beyond this place other very famous places follow one after another, and it would be tedious to list them all, but especially notable is that part of the city frequented by the fishermen, who have their own parish church dedicated to St Stephen.[3] And although

---

[1] Chafariz d'El-Rei. Góis also remarks on the purity of the water from this fountain. In fact Lisbon's water supply was poor in both in quality and quantity. See Góis, *Lisbon in the Renaissance*, pp. xxv, 23; Brandão, *Grandeza e abastança*, pp. 103–6.

[2] The Chafariz dos Cavalos. See Brandão, *Grandeza e abastança*, p. 103.

[3] Santo Estêvão. For a description of the fish market, see Góis, *Lisbon in the Renaissance*, p. 29.

they pay out no small amount in taxes to the king they are so rich, and have so much money, that their annual festival, held on the day on which the most holy body of Christ is remembered and honoured, competes on equal terms with the city's own festival, for those men devoted to fishing do not hesitate to contribute very substantial sums of money for that day.[1] I say nothing of those places in which timber from every species of tree is sold, and others where cannon for war are forged, and other similar places filled with crowds of people.[2] I leave out of account also the monasteries and convents close to that shore, especially one particularly famous one in which noble virgins live, and the holy relics of Saints Verissimo, Julia, and Maxima, martyrs of Lisbon, are kept with all veneration,[3] and another, dedicated to the Mother of God, in which the rule of St Francis is most strictly observed by holy virgins.[4] I shall add only that the furthest end of that shore is ennobled by another most magnificent royal palace, which João III ordered to be built with no expense spared, to serve the kings of Portugal as a suitable refuge whenever they were oppressed with the heavy burden of affairs of state, and wished to lift and restore their spirits.[5] It would indeed be a great pleasure for you if I were able to describe to you so that you were able to see in your minds all the works of that palace; then you would be able to comprehend the magnificence of the buildings of the palace, the liberality of the kings in paying for them, and finally the skill of the craftsmen. But since there were in Lisbon so many things so deserving of our attention, we were almost overwhelmed by the scale and the multiplicity of things, and did not have the time to examine every single building, nor to commit the details to memory.

Beyond this royal palace are two more most noble monasteries, the one dedicated to St Francis,[6] the other to St Benedict.[7] There is besides, a little further away, a convent, the most famous for its antiquity of all those in Lisbon, popularly known as the convent of Chelas, which formerly, in the time of pagan superstition, was inhabited by vestal virgins, or so the story goes.[8] It was there that Achilles, one of the most valiant men of antiquity, when he was yet a boy, was once hidden, dressed as a girl, by his mother, so that he should not find out about a certain very important war which was then being waged against the Trojans, but Ulysses, founder of the city of Lisbon, was clever enough to uncover the

---

[1] The festival is held on 13 June, the feast day of St Anthony of Padua, who was born in Lisbon in 1195.

[2] The Casa de Madeira and the Casa da Fundiçao de Artilharia. On the latter see Brandão, *Grandeza e abastança*, p. 165.

[3] At the time of the boys' visit the relics of the three legendary martyrs were housed in the Convento das Comendadeiras de Santiago de Espada. Previously they had been kept in the Santos-o-Velho palace. They were subsequently moved to the Mosteiro de Santos-o-Novo which was built during the 17th century. The monastery was dissolved in 1895 but the relics remain in the Igreja do Mosteiro de Santos-o-Novo or Church of Santos-o-Novo. See *Lisbon in the Renaissance*, p. 20; http://coromaterdei.no.sapo.pt/santos.htm.

[4] Convento de Madre de Deus founded in 1509 by Queen Leonor (1458–1525), wife of João II. She was instrumental in bringing the relics of St Auta, one of Ursula's followers, to the convent from Cologne. They were installed amidst great ceremony. The convent was famous for its religious music. See Góis, *Crónica de Dom Emanuel*, p. 500; Lowe, 'Rainha D. Leonor', esp. pp. 231, 237.

[5] The Xabregas palace, built in the 16th century near the site of an earlier palace. See Gomes, *Making of a Court Society*, p. 325.

[6] Mosteiro de São Francisco de Xabregas. See Brandão, *Grandeza e abastança*, p. 115; Oliveira, *Lisboa em 1551*, pp. 76–8.

[7] Convento de Saõ Bento de Xabregas. See Oliveira, *Lisboa em 1551*, pp. 81–2.

[8] Mosteiro de Chelas (Brandão, *Grandeza e abastança*, p. 116). On the alleged association with Ulysses, see Sande, *Embaixadores Japoneses*, I, p. 394 n. 108.

protective ruse of the mother. Now since that Trojan war was at least a thousand years before the birth of Christ the Lord, the Portuguese can calculate how much more ancient Lisbon is than the other European cities. And that, brief though it is, is what it occurs to me to say, given the restrictions on our time, about the shore of the river at Lisbon, crowded with buildings as it is, and extending for six miles.

Lino: It seems to me that this seashore, which you have run along so rapidly, is of a most pleasing aspect. But come, now you are going to lay out the whole interior of the city for us.

Michael: To attempt the whole interior, if everything is to be explained in detail, is to be drawn into a most profound abyss. But within the time available let us make our second journey, and let us go through in a straight line all that space which previously I likened to the arrow. We go back, then, to the royal square, and pass through the walls and gates of the city, beyond which the busiest streets of all come into view.[1] The first one, called Rua Nova,[2] is notable above all the others for its breadth, its length, and the number of many-storeyed buildings in it. In a part of this street separated off by iron grilles (which shows just how wide this street is) all the merchants assemble who carry on trade in various parts of Europe and do business with other merchants, especially merchants from Seville, Burgos, Valladolid, Medina, Venice, Genoa, and many others who live in other European cities and markets. It is extraordinary how rich the shops of the merchants in this street are; in them not only is there the greatest possible variety of every kind of cloth made of wool, and very valuable, but the quantity of clothing of many kinds made of silk, velvet, damascene, and embroidery work, is such that the range of goods set out for sale by all those merchants is worth several hundred million sesterces or, as they commonly say, several million ducats. Apart from other things there are in this street very fine houses with so many floors and so many people lodging in them that some can be found who do not know any of the others, whether by face or by name.

The second street is the street of the goldsmiths,[3] in which most precious works in gold are shaped with craft and artistry, and a variety of pearls are polished, either to be sold or to be inserted into the gold work. It is scarcely possible to say which is the greatest, the art, the abundance of gold and gems, or the number of the craftsmen, nor could I easily say which of these two streets excels the other in the price and the abundance of goods for sale. The third street too is no less busy, frequented by engravers, sculptors, men working in bronze and producing carvings in relief. But I said I would proceed by the direct way, so I shall not delay to speak about the other streets however remarkable; if I were to mention them, however, you would be moved to no little surprise, especially the street in which they sell things made of sugar. For every year an immense quantity of pure white sugar is imported from the island of São Tomé, a thousand leagues distant, and also from many ports of Brazil, from the Canary Islands, and from those called Madeira, and is brought into the port of Lisbon in many ships, and in that one street so many things to

---

[1] The Cidade Baixa.
[2] The Rua Nova dos Mercadores (Góis, *Lisbon in the Renaissance*, p. 27; Brandão, *Grandeza e abastança*, pp. 97–100).
[3] The Rua Nova d'El-Rei (Góis, *Lisbon in the Renaissance*, p. 27).

eat are made from the sugar that they not only suffice to satisfy the people of Lisbon but are also transported for sale in many cities of Europe.¹

You would marvel no less if I were to make my way through the workers in silver, in linen, and in wool, for there are three other streets given over to these, but there would be almost no limit to the time it would take to give an account of the workers of every kind, all in their proper streets and places, so let us proceed directly to that most famous site, almost square in shape, in the centre of the city.² It is surrounded by most impressive buildings, two of which are particularly outstanding.

The first of these is the royal hospital, dedicated to All Saints, a notable building paid for by King Manuel, and provided with all the income necessary, but then given a great increase both to the structure of the building and to the adequacy of its income by King João III.³ The church of the hospital is supported on the vaults of the arches below, arches through which runs a broad passageway, vaults so elevated that that the way up to the doors of the church is a staircase of twenty or more steps, made of the finest stone. In this chapel, which has just the one roof and single interior area, both the ceiling, which is splendidly carved from Sarmatic wood, and the walls themselves, are adorned with many fine figures, especially of the Portuguese kings whom I listed above, carved in relief, and these are of such value that they are covered with veils on ordinary days and are exposed to view only on feast days. Now the high altar of the main chapel is so sited, with windows fitted on three sides, that when the priest immolates the sacred host he can be seen by almost all the sick lying in their beds. And not only is there Mass every day, but also holy prayers are recited by the many priests who belong to that church, and on feast days sung by a great number of cantors, accompanied by musical instruments. With regard to the galleries of the hospital, there are three in particular, very long, and pointing, as I said, towards the high altar; in one of them wounds and other ailments belonging to surgery are treated; in the second are lying men brought low with fevers, and in the third women with the same illnesses. There are two other galleries besides these, for those suffering from contagious maladies.

Beneath the floors with these galleries there is a very spacious dwelling, which properly should be called a hostel, where there is very convenient accommodation for all the poor, whether local people or strangers. There is another hall which is properly a nursery, in which new-born infants who have been left out abandoned, or who are in some other such circumstance, and who are helpless and in need, are fed by hired wet-nurses, and afterwards, when they are older, are handed over to various men and women to be instructed in some honourable occupation. There is another house besides set aside for the care of those who are mentally abnormal, so that they can be restored to sanity. And there is also a residence for men of the nobility who cannot conveniently be cared for in their own homes, and there all medication is supplied to them in abundance, on the understanding, however,

---

¹ On the re-export trade and the prosperity of Lisbon, see Godinho, *Os descobrimentos*, IV, chs 6 and 7; Disney, *History of Portugal*, I, pp. 147–8.

² The Praça do Rossio.

³ The Hospital Real de Todos-os-Santos, built between 1492 and 1504 on the Rossio square and mostly destroyed during the great earthquake. See Góis, *Crónica de Dom Emanuel*, p. 600; idem, *Lisbon in the Renaissance*, p. 25; Brandão, *Grandeza e abastança*, pp. 123–32. There were two annexes, Nossa Senhora da Vitória and Hospital de Santana, for people with incurable diseases – in the case of the latter, veneral disease (Brandão, *Grandeza e abastança*, pp. 126–7).

that if they have the means they should afterwards repay the cost, so that the goods available for the poor should be in no way diminished. Besides these there is another separate area for those suffering from incurable diseases, and there, until their final departure from life, the necessities of life are administered to them. Finally, a special place is provided for religious men, especially those who follow the stricter rule of St Francis, where in seclusion from the mass of other people they apply themselves to health and healing.

What can one say about the arrangements for caring for all of the sick? They are truly remarkable, with men to look after men, women after women, and the sick assigned to different rooms in such a way as to allow the bodies of the dying to be taken out through a secret door, lest the fear of death cause those who remain and are in danger to lose heart. With regard to the doctors, surgeons, and those whom they call apothecaries, all of them are highly paid employees, selected as being the best in the whole city. The expenses of the whole of this vast house are covered by the income attached to it by kings Manuel and João, and in everything the abundance, the cleanliness, the equipment, and other things befitting a royal house are in evidence.

Next to this royal hospital, and very much worthy of mention, is a monastery of religious of the family of St Dominic which can stand comparison with the greatest monasteries of Lisbon for the scale of its building, the number of priests outstanding for virtue and letters, and the crowds of people who come there.[1] To give you rather more detail, the study of philosophy and theology is flourishing in that monastery, so much so that there are many doctors or masters, as they call them, of theology, and a very large number of preachers, who spread out through the whole city and district of Lisbon. Taking together all those from that family their number comes to a hundred and twenty, who were adorned at that time by the presence of Luis de Granada, a very religious man, whom we visited, noted all over the world for the sanctity of his life, the erudition of his books, and the power of his preaching.[2] The sacred furnishings of the church are very splendid, and include, among other things, twenty-two silver lamps, forty chalices, and fifteen candelabra, also of silver.

Another side of the same square boasts a most sumptuous royal palace, with most delightful gardens attached, but it would take too long to describe its magnificence and its beauties. This palace was built by the most glorious prince Pedro, son of João I, to accommodate all foreign ambassadors conveniently and with full hospitality, and it is numbered among the seven principal buildings of Lisbon.[3] The royal stables were usually attached to this palace, and contained a great number of horses, corresponding to its resources and opulence.

There is another thing which I should not omit, which adds very greatly to the renown of the square and surroundings which I have been speaking about. This is a market which

---

[1] Convento de São Domingos in front of which the sentences of the Inquisition were proclaimed, destroyed in the great earthquake (Brandão, *Grandeza e abastança*, p. 115).

[2] 1504–88, Spanish Dominican, theologian and author of Christian tracts. The boys presented him with Japanese translations of some of his writings in manuscript form with which he was said to be well pleased. Abridged translations of some of his works, including the famous *Guía de Pecadores* (1556), were later printed in Japan. See Fróis, *Première ambassade*, p. 36; Laures, *Kirishitan Bunko*, pp. 43–4, 60–62; Cooper, *Japanese Mission*, p. 47.

[3] Paço dos Estaus, originally built to lodge foreign ambassadors but since 1536 the seat of the Inquisition. It was destroyed in the great earthquake (Góis, *Lisbon in the Renaissance*, p. 26).

is held once a week, on Tuesdays, with such a press of people, with stalls so arranged, and with such an enormous quantity and variety of items for sale, that you would think it was set up not for a day but for a month or indeed a year; and not only the common people and the upper classes too, but ladies of the nobility go there also, and without their train of servants, and it is even said that the queen, desiring to see it, went there once.[1]

If we proceed further we find, outside the walls of the city, several very flourishing convents, most notably the one dedicated to the Annunciation of the Blessed Virgin.[2] This was originally founded by a private individual, but with the course of time it has grown so much that now it takes certain very noble virgins, and there are signs in it of extraordinary sanctity, which, however, since it is not for us to praise the living, I leave to others to record later and to commit to print. Beyond this place there is a very long street, in which the houses are country-style rather than urban, and are truly magnificent because of their delightful gardens, and because of the villas, full of attractive things, which many of the nobility build here, where the density of buildings is less of a problem. But let us come now to the point of the arrow which I spoke of earlier, at which there is a most noble monastery of the Fathers who are called priests of the Order of Christ, built not long ago, and now extended with new buildings paid for by the most illustrious princess Maria, daughter of King Manuel; she died twelve years ago, a virgin sixty years of age, rich in many gifts of nature and of soul, and in outward wealth.[3] This journey which we are making is four miles or one and a third leagues in length, and takes us in a straight line through Lisbon to the interior regions.

Leo: Michael, you seem to have described two cities already, and such cities that you have aroused in us a great interest in how they look.

Michael: I am not surprised to hear you say that, since Lisbon is indeed like several cities. I'll tell you now about the third part of it, which, as you'll see, is a much larger part, although, because of lack of time, my account of it may be shorter than it ought to be. This third journey which we are going to make will be uphill, and it also twists and turns, and is the longest yet. We begin again from the shoreline and travel through the inland regions in an arc, and the distance to be covered in the curve of this journey can be gathered from what we have already said, with the bowstring along the maritime shore being six miles long and the arrow four. Picture to yourselves, then, the space between the monastery of Belém and the area of the Royal Palace. There there are nuns living in a convent dedicated to Our Lady of Hope,[4] and from there a road leads upward to inland areas and the hills which encircle Lisbon, a road which we are to travel in spirit.

---

[1] The Feira de Ladra, held every eight days at the Rossio (Brandão, *Grandeza e abastança*, pp. 90–95).

[2] Convento de Anunciado, founded in 1519 (*História dos mosteiros, conventos e casas religiosas de Lisboa*, vol. I, pp. 362–4). The signs of extraordinary sanctity allude to one of the nuns claiming to have the stigmata of Christ's passion on her body at the time of the boys visit. In December 1588 the claim was officially proclaimed fraudulent (Sande, *Embaixadores Japoneses*, I, p. 394 n. 113).

[3] 1521–77 (and therefore 56), daughter of Manuel I and Eleanor of Habsburg. Maria was patroness of the buildings which were built on the site of a former hermitage and were largely destroyed in the great earthquake. She was buried in the Igreja de Nossa Senhora da Luz which still stands (Sande, *Embaixadores Japoneses*, I, p. 394 n. 113).

[4] Nossa Senhora de Esperança, destroyed in the great earthquake.

Now it is certain that Lisbon is surrounded by a number of hills, and you can read different accounts as to how many there are, but there are three or four principal ones which extend to several other summits in various places.[1] When we have climbed up the first thing that presents itself to our eyes is a monastery of the fathers of the order of St Benedict, an order which has flourished so greatly in Portugal that in just one province, namely the Interamnense Province, meaning the province between the Rivers Douro and Minho, this family of religious has forty-eight monasteries, with very ample income.[2] Now if we proceed from this monastery to a most famous gate of the city, called after St Catherine, and then little by little move up to the top of this hill, the splendid professed house of the Society of Jesus, consecrated to São Roque, comes into view.[3] There, as I said earlier, we were welcomed with most generous hospitality, and the longer we stayed there the more things we became aware of which I should tell you about.

Living there are upwards of seventy fathers and brothers of the Society, gathered from the flower of all Portugal, with regard both to the maturity of their years, and to their wisdom and their religious practice. Therefore they work most zealously in preaching, hearing confessions, assisting those condemned to prison, to the galleys, or to death, and in performing other works of piety, and for that reason they have always been high in favour with the Portuguese people, nobility, and kings, with whose help they have built this magnificently constructed house. If you look at the residence of those fathers the cloister is so spacious, the corridors so many, and the rooms so large, that it could easily accommodate an even larger number; and if you turn your eyes to the church you will realize what an admirable building that is. It is all just one nave, but that so broad that because of the difficulty of constructing the arch of slate or stone it was made, and made very well indeed, from beams which, on account of the length required, were brought at great expense all the way from north Germany,[4] and adorned with such panelling that you have no desire for stone vaulting or brick arches. The church is also embellished with many excellently finished chapels, in which a wonderful treasury of relics is now kept,[5] and I shall be able to treat of them in their proper place as we proceed. And the sacred

---

[1] Góis gives five. Others preferred seven, as in Rome. See Góis, *Lisbon in the Renaissance*, p. 22.

[2] The Benedictines established themselves in Portugal in 1567. Their first monastery in Lisbon was founded in 1572, the Mosteiro de Nossa Senhora da Estrela. This was later found to be too small and too far from the city. In 1581 it was decided to build a new monastery and work commenced in 1588. The new monastery was called the Mosteiro de São Bento da Saúde. After the government order disbanding of all religious houses and the confiscation of their property in 1834, the government took over the buildings and the site of the former monastery is now occupied by the Portuguese parliament. See Oliveira, *Lisboa em 1551*, pp. 81–2; http://www.parlamento.pt/Parlamento/Paginas/HistoriaMosteiroSaoBentoSaude.aspx.

[3] St Catherine's gate no longer exists. São Roque was originally the Hermitage of São Roque, founded in 1506. The site was given to the Jesuits in October 1553. In 1565 the Jesuits began work on a bigger church, designed by the royal architect Afonso Álvares, modelled on the Gesù in Rome. The church opened for services in 1573 and was expanded and better furnished after the union of the crowns. It was damaged in the great earthquake. The attached buildings, which once included the Jesuit professed house, are now part of the Misericórdia. The tower was destroyed in the great earthquake. See Fróis, *Première ambassade*, p. 31 n. 113; Lopes, *Roteiro historico*, p. 25; Kowall, 'Innovation and Assimilation', pp. 486–7.

[4] Original edition (p. 170) '*Cimbrica cheroneso*', northern Germany.

[5] The collection of relics acquired by Juan de Borja, the second son of St Francisco de Borja, rivalled those in the Escorial. See Livermore, *New History of Portugal*, p. 165; Osswald, 'Society of Jesus', pp. 603–4; below, p. 245. For a full description of the relics, see *História dos mosteiros, conventos e casas religiosas de Lisboa*, vol. I, pp. 238–52.

furnishings are so opulent that they seem to belong to people who live not by soliciting alms, but from a most ample income. Attached to the church is a strikingly high tower which offers a delightful prospect of almost the whole city, and which contains splendidly forged bells, at the sound of which, or so it is reliably reported, as many as five thousand people gather to listen to sermons.

Among other wonderful benefits which the fathers from this house provide for the people of Lisbon is teaching and instruction to the children of the whole city in all those things which belong to the rudiments of Christian doctrine. The fathers of the Society have indeed taken on that responsibility all over the world, but nevertheless in this house there is a special commitment to it, so that children are regularly called together throughout the city, not only in the church of São Roque, but also in the parish churches and the public squares, and are taught, and presented with laurels and honours and gifts, and spurred on to a perfect understanding of those rudiments in so far as the capacity of their age allows; and in this cause the fathers in their diligence and piety have composed certain little books in the form of numerous questions and answers, with Portuguese verses suitable for singing. We were told that at an early date another house, which they call the house of the novices, was to be built close to the wall of this house of the professed, with the cost covered by a certain noble man who decided to spend a large part of the fifty thousand ducats which he had amassed here in the Orient on the building of that house, and despising all human things to give himself to the Society.[1]

Now let us leave this place, lest I should seem to be trying to favour our hosts unduly, and move on to other similar places of which we have yet to give an account. If you go down a little from there you will come to a monastery of that religious family which names itself after the Most Holy Trinity,[2] and which, in addition to other matters pertaining to the worship of God, has devoted itself specifically to the ransoming of those pitiable persons held captive by the Saracens. Thus not only have these religious men earned the deep gratitude of the Christian populace, but also they have free access and entry even to the lands of the Saracens, and every year they liberate a great multitude of people from the yoke of slavery.

If from here you go forward a little and pass by the parish churches of the Virgin of Loreto[3] and of the Martyrs,[4] you will come to the great monastery of the family of St Francis,[5] where you will be hard put to it to decide which to admire more, the massive buildings, the spaciousness of the church, or the abundance of the alms daily collected. Leaving aside other considerations, it has more than two hundred religious men, and the

---

[1] In addition to the Jesuit college (see below, pp. 219–20) the Society governed and administered a number of other educational and charitable institutions in Lisbon such as the Colégio dos Meninos Órfãos (the College for Orphan Boys). Some of the orphans taught Christian doctrine and sang in the streets of Lisbon and elsewhere and some served with the Jesuits overseas (there was a similar house for female orphans). Another Jesuit-administered institution was the Colégio Real dos Catecúmenos, founded in 1579 for Muslims seeking admission to the Catholic faith. See Rodrigues, *História da Companhia de Jesus na Assistência de Portugal*, I: 1, pp. 677–707; Lopes, *Roteiro historico*, pp. 47–58.

[2] Trinitarians or 'Ordo S. Trinitatis et de redemptione captivorum', founded by St John of Matha at the end of the 12th century.

[3] Nossa Senhora do Loreto (Brandão, *Grandeza e abastança*, p. 114).

[4] Nossa Senhora dos Mártires (ibid., p. 114).

[5] São Francisco da Cidade (Oliveira, *Lisboa em 1551*, pp. 76–8; Brandão, *Grandeza e abastança*, p. 115).

size of the church, with its three separate aisles, is such that Lisbon has none more capacious. It contains many splendidly rich chapels, among them, besides the main chapel, which is an outstanding work, a famous one, covered all round in gold, built by Martim Afonso de Sousa, who was at one time governor of the whole of India.[1]

But let us move over to another part of the same mountain, where we find the remarkable monastery of the religious family which dedicates itself to Our Lady of Mount Carmel. The buildings of this monastery, in addition to being of an immense size, outdo all other buildings in Lisbon, the Cathedral alone excepted, in antiquity. Its founder was a most illustrious nobleman, Nuno Álvares Pereira,[2] a name most celebrated among the Portuguese, from whom the dukes of Bragança, of whom we shall be speaking later, are in part descended. He proved himself a most faithful ally to King João, first of that name, in many important wars waged both at home and abroad, and participated with him in his great victories and glory. In old age he renounced all human things and at his own expense and only with the utmost effort and greatest difficulty built this monastery. For we are told that more than once the foundations were shifting, and a huge quantity of iron had to be put in to secure them. But when the building was almost complete that same most celebrated nobleman lived there piously and religiously in that monastery until he breathed his last.

From there let us travel to other hilly places further to the east, and go up to the place where there is a church and a convent dedicated to Saint Anne, mother of the Blessed Virgin, whose feast day is celebrated by the people of Lisbon with a great concourse of people and variety of activities, largely because the place is particularly elevated and extremely spacious, so that it offers an ideal site for spectacles of all kinds.[3] Not far from here can be seen the hippodrome or stadium where the nobles and patricians of Lisbon are accustomed to exercise themselves in equestrianism on all feast days.[4] The number of both horses and spectators there is extraordinary, and the degree of competition for first place among the nobles and patricians themselves is incredible. On expeditions to Africa, and Lisbon is the main source of these expeditions, there is a great need for horses and horsemanship, so the people of Lisbon, who very frequently cross over to Africa in order to wage war with the Saracens, make a great point of exercising themselves in equestrianism. To develop their dexterity in this, sometimes one of them acts the part of a Saracen and another of a Christian fighting with him, and with each of them attacking the other, taking to flight, twisting and turning, and exercising other forms of horsemanship, they increase their own and their horses' skill and readiness for real combat.

---

[1] 1500–64, governor of India 1542–45, immortalized in *Os Lusíadas*, X: 63-7. The monastery is São Francisco da Cidade, founded in 1217 and destroyed in the great earthquake. See Oliveira, *Lisboa em 1551*, pp. 76–8.

[2] 1360–1431, a key figure in Portugal's struggle for independence from Castile, called the 'scourge of the Castilian monarchs' in *Os Lusíadas*, IV: 24. The Carmo convent or Convento do Ordem do Carmo was founded in 1389 by Pereira who himself joined the order, dying in the convent in 1431. The remains of the convent are now occupied by the National Guard and the impressive remains of the church, largely destroyed in the great earthquake, are a Lisbon landmark. See Góis, *Lisbon in the Renaissance*, p. 27; *História dos mosteiros, conventos e casas religiosas de Lisboa*, vol. I, pp. 165–91.

[3] The Convento de Santa Ana, the remaining structures of which are now part of the Faculty of Medicine of Lisbon University. The nearby Campo de Santana was used, among other things, for bullfights before it was transformed into the Campo Mártires da Pátria in 1879.

[4] The Campo Grande, now a large park.

Now let us head for the high places which follow, but without ignoring a valley which there is in between, and which is known for certain things. We can see firstly a very large enclosure to which all the animals which are regularly slaughtered for food in Lisbon are brought, from the Lisbon area and other places.[1] You will get a good idea of the numbers if I tell you that of sheep alone there are five thousand killed every day and taken to the three markets which I have already mentioned. In this place it is a very entertaining spectacle to watch highly trained dogs attacking bulls, which are sometimes extremely ferocious, and holding on to their ears with their teeth in such a way that do what they will the bulls cannot escape death, though they do sometimes throw the less powerful of the dogs up into the air with their horns and inflict mortal wounds on them. Situated in the same valley is the hospital for those suffering from leprosy, the disease of Saint Lazarus as it is commonly known, because it is the opinion of some doctors that the ulcers from which the beggar Lazarus in the holy Gospel suffered come from that disease. So in this place any sufferers from this disease are most diligently cared for, nor does the disease, so abhorrent to fastidious human nature, prevent them being supplied with everything with the utmost piety and charity.[2]

But let us return to the high places, and without speaking of the place where there is a church dedicated to Our Lady of the Mount,[3] for it is some distance further away, or of the great variety of pottery most artistically fashioned at the foot of that hill, and the Lisbon clay is ideal for vessels of that sort, I come to the hill which is famous for the monastery of the Augustinian order, a tremendous structure which can stand comparison with the other principal holy places of Lisbon; for not only does it have a very large church, under three roofs, and with many splendid chapels, but also the cloister is a work of such craftsmanship that just a quarter of it, with its upper storey, cost twenty-five thousand ducats.[4] The room for the sacred vestments and furnishings has such cabinets, is embellished with such figures and images, and is paved with such varied mosaic work that every visitor reacts with delight and admiration, especially as its greatest adornment is a chapel in which is buried a most noble virgin, granddaughter of King João II. With regard to the fathers of that order, there are a hundred and twenty of them, they are abundantly provided for with thirteen thousand ducats,[5] and courses in Latin language, philosophy, and theology are provided there, with high praise from both learners and teachers, as well as talks which are very well received by the people. In this monastery there is a sodality specially devoted to the resurrected Christ, and which has regularly numbered among its members all the most noble and distinguished persons. The services of the day consecrated to the triumph of Christ over death are so lavishly and

---

[1] On the abattoirs of Lisbon, see Brandão, *Grandeza e abastança*, p. 78.

[2] Leprosy had been on the wane in Europe, except for Scandinavia, since the 13th century. Its symptoms were similar to those of a relatively new disease, syphilis (Pullan, 'Counter-Reformation, Medical Care', p. 22). It was common in Japan in the early modern period and both Jesuits and mendicants set up leprosaria.

[3] Nossa Senhora do Monte, originally built in 1147 (Brandão, *Grandeza e abastança*, p. 115).

[4] The Convento dos Reverendos Padres eremitas de Sancto Agostinho, known commonly as Nossa Senhora da Graça, founded 1271. The convent and church were destroyed in the great earthquake but rebuilt. The place is now known as Convento do Graça and commands a fine view over the old city. See *História dos mosteiros, conventos e casas religiosas de Lisboa*, vol. I, pp. 109–43, which has a full description of the old convent's treasures.

[5] The original edition (p. 173) gives '*triginta*', 30,000, but the errata list corrects this to 13,000.

magnificently performed, and the extraordinary variety of lamps and torches is so especially striking, that the entire population of Lisbon is drawn to that celebration.

From here those who proceed along the curve are confronted with that celebrated rock on which is built the most heavily fortified of all the fortresses in Lisbon, popularly known as the castle.[1] On it can be seen many ramparts and fortifications, and many lofty towers, most notably the one at the very top of which can still be observed that most ancient sword which was covered with a great quantity of enemy blood in the slaughter of the Saracens which occurred when Lisbon was recaptured by King Afonso I.[2] In the same place is sited the fourth royal palace,[3] which for magnificence has no superior, and in its antiquity and its far-reaching prospect over all that maritime shore and the far bank of the Tagus, with the many towns sited in those areas, is far and away superior to all the others. Within that same castle there is a house which we can call the Royal Archive,[4] in which all the original documents containing the histories and ancient deeds of the kingdom, as most certain records of the truth, are preserved, and everyone is at liberty to extract from there anything connected with any ancient possession, any royal grant, any evidence in law.

At the foot of this rock, to the north, stands the college of the Society of Jesus dedicated to St Anthony the Abbot.[5] Sixty of the Society live there, and they teach the humanities in public schooling to the youth of Lisbon. The whole student body is divided into eight classes, and the total number of those attending exceeds one thousand. There are besides upwards of two hundred men who have been initiated into sacred things, who apply themselves to learning moral theology from two fathers who are expert in this. This college can claim a special pre-eminence as the origin and seedbed of all the others which have been established throughout Portugal, Brazil, and India, and in antiquity it yields only to the house of the professed in Rome, for it was founded by the most glorious King João III, when he first implored and persuaded Ignatius, that most holy man, father and founder of the Society, to send those two outstanding fathers, Francis Xavier and Simão Rodrigues, to propagate the Society throughout Portugal and India. And when Francis Xavier, eminent and widely famed for his sanctity, had sailed for India, Simão Rodrigues remained in Portugal and set up that first house of the Society, which gradually acquired the name and the site of the college. This college was established by the same João III, and was afterwards provided with increased income by King Henrique. This king, when he was dying, was so generous towards the college that he left a legacy of two thousand five hundred ducats to the fathers to erect a new building in a more convenient place, and

---

[1] Castelo de São Jorge, which still dominates the Lisbon skyline, was, until the early 16th century, the principal royal residence. Cf. Góis, *Lisbon in the Renaissance*, p. 24.

[2] In 1147.

[3] The Alcáçova.

[4] Housed in the Torre do Tombo until the great earthquake.

[5] The Colégio de Santo Antão. The first Jesuit house in Lisbon, indeed the first in the world, established by Simão Rodrigues in 1542, located in the Mouraira district, was a building known as Santo Antão-o-Velho, previously belonging to the Dominicans, and originally a mosque. Work on the new college, known as Santo Antão-o-Novo, began in 1579 and continued into the 17th century. It was almost completely destroyed during the great earthquake. The Jesuits opened the first college for lay students in February 1553 at Santo Antão-o-Velho and it remained there until 1594 when the Jesuits sold the property to the Augustinians. The students transferred to Santo Antão-o-Novo. See Rodrigues, *História da Companhia de Jesus na Assistência de Portugal*, I: 1, pp. 282–5; Lopes, *Roteiro historico*, pp. 15–18.

he assigned to them a good part of the wall and three towers which were to be used for the building on a somewhat sloping part of the hill of Santa Ana.

Let us make our way down now from the rock of that supreme citadel to the square of St Andrew, where can be seen the fifth and most magnificent royal palace, where formerly the kings of Portugal resided, and which later was occupied by the University of Lisbon. Eventually the university moved to a more appropriate city, namely Coimbra,[1] with which we shall be dealing, and the palace came to be used for the perpetual custody of those convicted of offences against religion. From here we come after a short space to two notable monasteries, the one, of the Order of St Eloi,[2] known not only for its own buildings but also because of its proximity to the sixth royal palace;[3] the other,[4] again of the order of St Augustine, that is, of those fathers known to the people as Canons Regular. The magnificence of their buildings, the number of the religious fathers, the richness of their sacred vestments, and all their other embellishments, leave nothing to be desired. Their principal adornment, however, is a complete arm of St Sebastião, whom the Europeans invoke as a special patron to ward off the evil of the plague.

Let us proceed now to a place a little lower down, where the public prison, a very large prison, is located. On its upper storey are most spacious halls given over to the administration of justice. Here there come together every day most grave and learned senators. With absolute rectitude they process the more important cases sent from all over the country by lower-order magistrates, and they impose sentences of death or exile, or other penalties, on the criminals.[5] But there is another, pre-eminent in the nobility of his lineage and in prudence, who in the name of the king takes precedence over all these most learned men. He is popularly known as the regent, and he sits in the supreme tribunal and prescribes what is to be done by the senators, and he is held in almost the same honour as the king himself would be if he were present.

Let us move on further to the cathedral of Lisbon,[6] an edifice most magnificent and ancient, the huge church being marked off by three tall towers, two of them at the sides of the main door, the third at the back of the main chapel. The church is provided with

---

[1] The university was founded in 1290 and was, after a number of displacements, moved permanently to Coimbra in 1537. The original location of the Escolas Gerais was near a building which had variously been the royal mint and a royal palace and which later became the Limoeiro prison (see below, n. 5). See Góis, *Crónica de Dom Emanuel*, p. 600; *idem, Lisbon in the Renaissance*, p. 21.

[2] Santo Elói. See Brandão, *Grandeza e abastança*, p. 135; *História dos mosteiros, conventos e casas religiosas de Lisboa*, vol. I, pp. 200–201.

[3] Paço Santo Elói.

[4] Mosteiro São Vicente de Fora, founded 1147 by Afonso Henriques to commemorate his victory over the Moors. The church, construction of which began in 1582, was originally intended to honour São Sebastião but Philip II, fearing it might become a focus for the cult of the memory of the late king Sebastião, ordered the church to be dedicated to St Vincent. See *História dos mosteiros, conventos e casas religiosas de Lisboa*, vol. I, pp. 1–47.

[5] The Limoeiro Prison, which was the city prison, a royal prison and a court house. Situated near the cathedral, it had been a royal palace and the royal mint. The Limoeiro remained a prison until the revolution in 1974. It is now the Centro de Estudos Judiciários. See Góis, *Crónica de Dom Emanuel*, p. 601; Brandão, *Grandeza e abastança*, p. 163.

[6] Santa Maria Maior de Lisboa or Sé de Lisboa, started 1150, on the site of the main mosque of the Moslem city. The cathedral was damaged during the great earthquake. See also Góis, *Lisbon in the Renaissance*, pp. 15–16.

many and very splendid chapels, and in the main chapel is preserved with all veneration the most holy body of St Vincent the Martyr, which was brought from the sacred promontory to Lisbon.[1] And since it was not without a miracle that his holy body, borne in a small boat and with crows for company, came from Valencia, where he earned the palm of martyrdom, to that promontory, the people of Lisbon took him for their patron, and display the image of a boat and crows in his coat of arms.[2] I could speak of the income of the archbishop of Lisbon and of the whole chapter of canons, as they are called, also of the sacred vestments and furnishings of this cathedral, but from the magnificence of the whole city and of the other churches these can easily be imagined. Let us come therefore to the church of that saint who more than any other is the glory of Lisbon, namely St Anthony, flower and ornament of the Franciscan order. His church, no mean structure,[3] is built in the very house in which the father of St Anthony, and at one time St Anthony himself, actually lived, so it is held in very great veneration by all the people of Lisbon. The back part of that house is occupied by those whom we can call the triumvirs, who, together with other magistrates, carefully administer those matters which have to do with the common good of the city and the people.[4] I would be saying more about St Anthony, born and brought up in Lisbon, but for the fact that there will be another opportunity to do so elsewhere, namely when I speak of Padua, where he died a most blessed death.[5] I know that I have passed over in silence many things of no small fame, especially convents and the palaces, very many of them, of the nobles, but the brevity of the colloquia, the lack of time, and many other things which remain to be covered as we proceed, have made me keep my account shorter than it should have been.

Leo: These journeys have been such a pleasure that we are left not tired, not bored, but on the contrary filled with, steeped in a wonderful sweetness, and in an eager anticipation to hear more. But now it is only fair to allow our Michael some rest.

Lino: I think he deserves rest but also praise for giving so very pleasing an account.

---

[1] The Promontório Sacro also known as Cape St Vincent. See Camões, *Os Lusíadas*, III: 74.
[2] St Vincent of Zaragoza, patron saint of Lisbon, martyred in 304. Other European cities also claim to have the relics.
[3] The church of Santo António de Padua (1195–1231), near the cathedral, on the site of the house where he was born. The church was destroyed in the great earthquake and rebuilt (Góis, *Lisbon in the Renaissance*, p. 16).
[4] Góis also mentions this location of the municipal government (ibid., p. 16). After the union of the crowns the structure of the municipal government of Lisbon was changed (Bouza, *D. Filipe I*, pp. 208–9).
[5] See below, p. 362.

COLLOQUIUM XVII

Which gives an account of the things which took place in Lisbon, and then in Évora and Vila Viçosa, and then proceeds into the kingdom of Castile, to Toledo and to Mantua Carpetana or Madrid

Leo: Last night, Michael, you presented us with such a vivid picture of Lisbon that waking or sleeping I seemed to be seeing it with my own eyes; but proceed now and tell us more, and have no fear of any weariness in your audience, but rather every confidence that they are avid to hear more.

Michael: I have no fear whatever that you will be bored, but I am held back and inhibited by the magnitude of the subject and my inadequacy to expound it. Anyway, I'll add something about the countryside in the Lisbon area, which is so healthful and so fruitful in all the products necessary to life that it is in no way inferior to other places of Europe, be they never so delightful and fertile.[1] Just how great a variety of fruit there is can perhaps be gathered from the fact, recorded in a most trustworthy book, that in a single orchard there were found no less than seventy-six different types of pear. In this countryside of Lisbon, therefore, so many noble men have their villas that it is scarcely possible to count them. The perimeter of this area stretches for thirty leagues, and within it are found very many villages and towns belonging to the jurisdiction of Lisbon. It is renowned especially for certain places which the kings of Portugal have chosen to alleviate the weight of their responsibilities, and as a most opportune setting for their pleasures and delights. Most celebrated among these are the towns of Almeirim, Peralonga, and Sintra, in which can be seen, and a wonderful spectacle they are, magnificent palaces for their habitation, most spacious enclosures for the hunting of wild animals of every kind, aviaries filled with an almost infinite number of birds, ponds overflowing with innumerable fish, continual and abundant fountains of cool water, and all other things conducive to delight. It is my intention, however, to distribute the description of these remarkable things, in which Europe is rich, among various kingdoms and provinces. Whatever I say from now, therefore, about remarkable villas designed for the pleasures of the country, should be taken to apply more or less to those places too, for from any one place or thing of a particular kind, and without intending offence to anyone, I would like the magnificence of all the others to be appreciated.

---

[1] The fertility of the land had been noted by Strabo (*Geography*, III: 3, 1, 4) and by later writers. See Góis, *Lisbon in the Renaissance*, pp. 33–4, 35; Bertini, 'Marriage of Alessandro Farnese', p. 54. During Portugal's golden age agriculture was expanding and becoming more market-oriented (Disney, *History of Portugal*, I, p. 146).

Lino: It is prudent of you, Michael, to wish to give satisfaction to all, according to their merits, and to avoid the ill-will of any. And now we are waiting eagerly to hear what you did in Lisbon.

Michael: I said earlier that we went to see the most noble Cardinal Albert who in the name of King Philip administers the whole of Portugal and all those places which are under its jurisdiction. Now hear something about him, and the benevolence with which he received us. It is this most noble cardinal, son of the Emperor Maximilian, brother of Rudolph, who is still alive, and nephew of Philip, king of all Spain, through his sister, whom his uncle himself placed at the head of the entire jurisdiction of Portugal when he was not yet an adult, but was endowed with an extraordinary prudence, and with other gifts of nature and virtue. This prince therefore, as was fitting for one endowed with such nobility and dignity, both sacred and secular, received us with all kindness and generosity, and although, as I said, he governs the whole of Portugal, and has a household and train of servants such as formerly the kings of Portugal were accustomed to have, his friendliness and benevolence towards us were such that in the three times that we visited him in the space of the month or thereabouts that we stayed in Lisbon he always treated us with the utmost love, and he would not suffer us to kiss his sacred hand, a custom and rite of veneration observed by all the nobles and lords. And he not only treated us with such courtesy, but also, among other things, he frequently ordered that his own coach, in which he was normally borne through the city, should be put at our disposal, and we rode through the famous places of Lisbon in that coach. And we were received by him and by the other lords of Europe in a way that left no doubt about the love which they bear the Japanese nation.

Lino: The Europeans love our people? But I thought they had hardly even heard of Japan.

Michael: You are much mistaken, most dear Lino. You should realize that the fathers of the Society, by means of the letters which they regularly send, arouse in the minds of people in Europe that same love for our people which you believe the fathers have in their souls. In those letters they so commend our nation, and they so extol our courtesy, our discipline in military matters, and above all our inclination towards the Christian faith, that, notwithstanding the enormous distance that separates us from them, we are wonderfully loved by Europeans whom we have never seen.[1]

Leo: We are greatly relieved and consoled to hear what you say. Since we knew that the fathers of the Society living among us did not always have a high opinion of our customs we were inclined to think that the letters the fathers sent to Europe might be more likely

---

[1] The first book of 'Indian letters' in which Japan was mentioned was published in Rome in 1553. The first collection of Japan letters was published at Coimbra in Spanish in 1565. The first collection of Japan letters in Portuguese appeared in Coimbra in 1570. Thereafter, many editions of Japan letters came off the presses in Portugal, Spain, Italy and northern Europe, one of the most important printed in Évora in 1598 under the auspices of the archbishop of Évora, Teotónio de Bragança. See Lach, *Asia in the Making of Europe*, 1: 1, pp. 318–21, 325–6; José Manuel Garcia, introduction to *Cartas*, I, pp. 18–20.

to arouse an aversion to us than to win us esteem; but you assert that the opposite is the case.

Mancio: It is exactly as Michael says: towards us the fathers of the Society act as parents and masters, and whenever they are dealing with us they are concerned for our good, and they censure as vicious not the customs concerned with political life, but those which are contrary to the divine law and to the light of nature, and they argue against them as best they can. But when they send letters to Europeans about Japanese things they are conscious of their paternal love for us, and they give an account to them of the gifts of nature and of industry which we possess, and are inclined to say nothing about or to conceal our vices. The result is that from their letters carried to Europe no shame redounds to our name, but rather glory and most high praise.

Martin: Indeed from all of our things of which word had reached Europe we realized that the fathers of the Society loved us greatly, and as a result commended our things so much that they attributed to them more brilliance and splendour than they actually possess; and it is easy to appreciate this from the fame of the Japanese rulers which is spread through all of Europe. In particular the exploits of Nobunaga[1] in war and in peace have become so well known among the Europeans that no other man of our nation has been able to achieve such extraordinary renown with them.

Julian: What then can be said of the celebrity and fame of Quambaquundono,[2] who could find no heralds or trumpeters of his praises more prominent than the fathers of the Society, by means of whose letters his fame and glory know no narrower bounds than the sun itself in its course. If only he knew of this there is no doubt that he would load the fathers with many favours and rewards, instead of being so ready to listen to false rumours about them spread by malevolent men.

Michael: My companions are right in what they say, and they speak as persons who have experienced in truth and in practice the love towards us of the Europeans, and especially the love, like the love of a parent, of the fathers. But (to take up the thread of our discourse) when we disembarked from the ship the fathers of the house of the professed in Lisbon treated us exactly as if they were greeting beloved and long awaited sons returning safe and sound from most grave danger on the heaving seas. We stayed in Lisbon for twenty-five days, and would have stayed much longer had not care for our duty

---

[1] Oda Nobunaga, 1534–82, the first of Japan's three unifiers or hegemons. Nobunaga appeared to have good relations with the Jesuits who expressed hopes that he might become a Christian. Valignano met Nobunaga at the latter's impressive new castle at Azuchi in 1581. He obtained a valuable gift from Nobunaga, a series of folding screens or *byōbu* depicting the castle which Nobunaga had previously shown to the emperor. Valignano had it packed with care and sent to Europe with the boys. It was presented to Gregory XIII. Unfortunately, the screens, the only known source to depict Azuchi, which was burnt to the ground in 1582, have disappeared. Eventually, the Jesuits in Japan became disillusioned with Nobunaga, describing him as vainglorious and diabolical, a tyrant seeking to be worshipped as a deity. See Fróis, *História de Japam*, III, pp. 191–3, 197–8, 202–3, 259–60, 331–2, 361–2; idem, *Première ambassade*, p. 184 n. 659; *Dai Nihon Shiryō*, XI: 1, p. 176; Cooper, *Japanese Mission*, pp. 203–8; McKelway, *Cityscapes*, pp. 165–7. See also below, p. 301. On Nobunaga more generally, see Lamers, *Japonius Tyrannus*.

[2] The *kampaku*, i.e. Toyotomi Hideyoshi.

urged us on to visit the king and to kiss the most sacred feet of the supreme pontiff Gregory XIII.[1] Having obtained the permission of Cardinal Albert, therefore, and taken leave of the fathers, and with Father Nuno Rodrigues having gone on ahead on business,[2] we set out on the fifth of September, together with our teacher, Father Diogo de Mesquita, on the road to Rome, and to meet on the way King Philip of Spain, who lived in Madrid. The reverend Father Sebastião de Morais, superior of the Portuguese province of the Society of Jesus, decided to come with us as far as the border of Portugal. As I said earlier, he was later consecrated Bishop of Japan, but lost his life on the journey to India. So we crossed the river Tagus (from Lisbon to the far bank where we landed is a distance of three leagues), and journeyed for some days through the Portuguese province of Alentejo, very fertile with wheat and oil, till we reached a town called Montemór, where there were many Portuguese gentlemen. Already waiting for us in that town was a steward of the most illustrious archbishop of Évora,[3] who had been told that we were coming and had sent his steward ahead to meet us there and to offer us the best possible welcome, with a carriage and other domestic equipment. The steward did as he thought the archbishop would wish, the archbishop who showed us the utmost benevolence, and we set out with him on the following day and came to Évora, which was five leagues away.

This town is one of the three most important, after Lisbon, in Portugal. It boasts as its first founder Sertorius, an illustrious Roman general,[4] and is distinguished by its many very ancient buildings and some other new ones. I don't propose to describe every part of it, for we did that with the first city, and that should suffice. I shouldn't fail to mention, however, that this city is notable for its abundant supply of water, which they call the silver water, brought in a long way, from more than two leagues outside the city, by aqueducts.[5] These aqueducts are of extraordinary construction, hidden under the earth for a league and a half, and then gradually rising for the remaining half league. By means of these such a quantity of water is brought into the city that it can be dispersed and apportioned most copiously through four very artistically finished fountains, set up in public places, each with many mouths, and the same water is provided in abundance to all the monasteries of religious men and the convents of virgins, which have their own individual fountains in their cloisters. The same city has the honour of being the place of

---

[1] For further details of their stay in Lisbon, including a visit to Sintra, see Fróis, *Première ambassade*, ch. 3; Cooper, *Japanese Mission*, pp. 45–8.

[2] In Goa, in November 1583, Rodrigues had been appointed procurator to represent the province of India and the vice-province of Japan at the forthcoming conference of Jesuit procurators scheduled to begin in Rome on 15 November 1584. Valignano's instructions to him emphasize that this assignment was to take precedence over accompanying the boys. In addition, Rodrigues carried numerous letters and documents relating to the Jesuit mission in India and Japan including *Il Cerimoniale*, the *Sumario* and the minutes of the various consultations held in Japan during Valignano's visit. See *Documenta Indica*, XII, pp. 888–9; Abranches Pinto and Bernard, 'Les instructions', pp. 392, 400; Álvarez-Taladriz, 'En el IV centenario de la embajada', pp. 137, 141.

[3] Teotónio de Bragança (1530–1602), son of D. Jaime, the fourth duke of Bragança, archbishop of Évora since 1578. He had been a Jesuit from 1549 to 1555 when he left the order. He was especially interested in the missions in the East Indies, and was an important patron of the Jesuit mission in Japan, and corresponded with Valignano. His reception of the four young Japanese is described in Agostinho, *Relaçam*, ff. 62–4. The copy of *De Missione* in the Oliveira Lima Library (Catholic University of America), call no. RBK 976 1590 is dedicated to Bragança.

[4] Quintus Sertorius, c. 123–72 BCE, Roman general who established a power base in Hispania and rebelled against Rome. He was much admired by the Lusitanian tribes. Mentioned in *Os Lusíadas*, III-63: 2; IV-33: 1; VIII-7-8.

[5] The Aqueduto da Água de Prata, constructed between 1531 and 1537 by the architect Francisco de Arruda and described in *Os Lusíadas*, III-63: 3–4. It is still standing.

birth of certain saints, most notably of St Vincent and his two sisters,[1] and also of St Mancius the martyr,[2] to whom there still stands a famous memorial, namely the column to which it is said he was bound, before he was subjected by a cruel tyrant to whipping and other tortures, and thus obtained the palm of heavenly victory. There is also in a certain convent of holy virgins a statue, mostly ingeniously wrought, in which the form of Christ the Lord when he was yet an infant is represented, and this statue is held in the highest veneration by the people, because when prayers have been offered before it to God in a religious spirit, God Himself has often answered the prayers and wishes of the suppliants by bringing about many miracles, freeing some from most grievous illnesses, and snatching others from other dangers to life; and there is witness of all these amazing facts very precisely recorded.[3] In this city can also be seen magnificent and outstanding buildings, of which there are many, both secular, because of the large number of leading Portuguese who have their residence in that city, and also sacred, of religious men and women.

But I shall speak only of the College of the Society, which was also our residence.[4] From its very beginnings it was built with the utmost magnificence by order of the most holy King Henrique, while he held the position of Archbishop of Évora. When King João III of Portugal, his eldest brother, and many other brothers, were still alive, this King, a man of outstanding sanctity, committed himself to sacred things, and was created archbishop first of Braga, then of Évora, and finally cardinal. But then João III died, and his grandson Sebastião died without children, and the crown of Portugal came to Henrique, and after him, by right of heredity, to Philip the most powerful king of Spain. Now when the most illustrious Henry held the position of archbishop of Évora, since he had a very high regard for the fathers of the Society, he had this college, dedicated to the Holy Spirit, built with no expense spared. There are many things about it which certainly should be mentioned, and I shall deal with them briefly. In the first place, it is not just a college of the Society but also a public academy, one of the two in Portugal, in which many excellent arts and doctrines are taught by the fathers to the youth who converge there from all parts: in particular, in addition to the Latin language, the study of philosophy and of both kinds of theology, namely the theology concerned with divine things and the theology which deals with morality, flourishes exceedingly. And in order to increase the number of students and their commitment to the study of arts, this same most illustrious Henry

---

[1] Igreja de S. Vincente, dedicated to three local saints, St Vincent and his sisters Sabina and Cristeta. See Barata, *Évora antiga*, p. 36.

[2] According to legend the first bishop of Évora, martyred in Évora in the 5th century. Mancio Itō was his namesake. His feast day is 15 March.

[3] An ivory statue, of the Virgin holding the infant Jesus, famous and much venerated in its time, was in the Convento de Nossa Senhora do Parásio, founded in the early 15th century. The convent is no longer extant. See Quemado, *Alentejo glorioso*, pp. 142–5. Another famous, and greatly venerated, image of Jesus was the Menino Jesus de Santa Mónica in the Convento de Santa Mónica. The convent is no longer extant but the image is now in Évora cathedral (Moniz, *Dominicais Eboreneses*, p. 137).

[4] The Colégio do Espírito Santo founded in February 1553. By papal bull the college became a university in April 1559 and was inaugurated as such the following November. During its existence it rivalled Coimbra as a seat of learning. With the outlawing of the Jesuit order in 1759 and the subsequent closure of the university, the books from the library were dispersed to various libraries in Portugal, including the Biblioteca Pública de Évora which acquired a copy of *De Missione*, still among its holdings. The university was re-established in 1973 and the buildings, with modification, remain much as the boys saw them. See Mendeiros, *Roteiro histórico*, pp. 13, 16–17, 36, 45, 62; Moniz, *Dominicais Eboreneses*, pp. 154–60, 186.

established residences, with permanent income assigned and guaranteed to them, in which no small number of young men, dedicated to the study either of philosophy or of one or other of the branches of theology, are splendidly, indeed magnificently, supported. And that adds not a little to the renown of this academy, and greatly encourages those studious young men to apply themselves more zealously and with more exact attention to mastering the humanities.

The structure of the college itself can truly be called regal, for it boasts many remarkable architectural and artistic features. It has first of all a most spacious quadrangle, with a fountain in the centre, in which can be seen, besides the large number of columns of polished marble, very capacious lecture halls, in which various students assemble in great numbers. The church too is of very fine construction,[1] and not only embellished with many chapels on both sides, but also adorned with many figures and images of the saints excellently depicted on both the left and the right wall. These paintings, being very valuable, are not always displayed; on ordinary days they are covered with cloths, but on festive and solemn days they can been seen, and it is a delight to see them. The sacred furnishings too are perfectly appropriate, being of the same magnificent craftsmanship, whether you consider the vessels of gold and silver or the great variety of most precious vestments. What am I to say of the interior of the fathers' living quarters? There too can be found another no less magnificent quadrangle, corridors with very comfortable living rooms, abundant running water in many places, a refectory of no inconsiderable size and elegance, and all other facilities necessary for the life of religious men. The fathers number more than a hundred and twenty, they have fully adequate income provided by the same King Henrique, and all that large number of them not only instruct the youth there and the whole city in Christian piety and knowledge of divine things, but also devote themselves to preaching and other exercises concerned with the salvation of souls throughout all that Alentejo region.

When we entered that college in the company of the Father Provincial of Portugal we were delighted to see the college and the fathers, but in addition to that we were very happy to find Archbishop Teótonio himself present there. He, being of the royal family, and uncle of the duke of Bragança, has most ample and abundant resources, with fully fifty thousand ducats a year in income, but he considered nothing more important than to call on us immediately, and to offer us a most joyful welcome, and during the seven days we were in Évora he had an abundance of food sent to us daily. In addition to all this, on the day dedicated to the exaltation of the Holy Cross[2] he invited us to celebrate that feast in the cathedral and to a banquet in his house.[3] It was a day of most wonderful solemnity; there was a public procession, then the archbishop himself officiated at the solemn Mass, and a sermon was preached by the inquisitor of crimes against the faith. In the course of his sermon he took the opportunity to digress from the victory of the cross to treat of the things of Japan and to celebrate our arrival so appropriately as to bring great joy to the minds of all present. And what am I to say of the courtesy with which the most

---

[1] Igreja do Espírito Santo, built 1567–74. Work started before that on the Gesù in Rome (1568), and São Roque in Lisbon (Mendeiros, *Roteiro histórico*, p. 40).

[2] 14 September.

[3] The archbishop's residence is now the Museu de Évora. During the visit to the cathedral, Mancio and Michael played what was then the only three-manual organ in Portugal. See Fróis, *Première ambassade*, 43–4; Waterhouse, 'Southern Barbarian Music', p. 361.

illustrious archbishop, when the Mass was over, conducted us to the banquet, or of the magnificence of that banquet, worthy of such a prince, or of the concern of the same archbishop for the poor. For when he sits down at table it is his custom, and he observed it on that day, to invite twelve poor persons to another table, and there everything is supplied to them in abundance by his attendants. What he is doing in this is imitating those ancient pontiffs of the Christian religion who made a point of showing great solicitude for the poor, especially Pope Gregory the Great, whose custom it was most courteously to invite poor people to dinner, and who is said sometimes to have entertained the angels themselves, and occasionally even the lord of the angels concealed in the guise of a pauper.

At the beginning of the banquet the same archbishop took us to see his chapel, which in addition to its elegance of craftsmanship and ornamentation, is graced with relics of famous saints, beautifully mounted, and all of these he said he would give as a gift to Japan, and that he would keep them and then hand them over to us on our way back, as indeed he did. He also gave us four tapestries woven of silk and gold with wonderful skill, and these manifested a truly royal splendour, and they could have provided our people with excellent evidence of the grandeur of Europe, had we not lost them when one of the ships for India was wrecked on the rocks.[1] He provided in addition two hundred and fifty ducats for the journey, and presented us with a further thousand ducats on our return, to allow us buy some beautiful and elegant European things to take back as presents for our families and kinsmen. Such, indeed, was the beneficence of this archbishop towards us that I can justly say that his memory is engraved deep in our hearts, and can assure you that all our country of Japan owes a debt of gratitude to that most worthy prince for his zeal and solicitude for the things of Japan.[2]

I come now to another city, distinguished as the domain and by the presence of the duke of Bragança, called Vila Viçosa, which in Portuguese means pleasant and delightful. We left Évora for Vila Viçosa on 15 September,[3] in the archbishop's own coach, on our way to visit the duke,[4] who is the archbishop's nephew, son of his brother. This duke of Bragança is greatly celebrated in Spain because of the ties of blood which link him on both sides with the kings of Portugal. On his father's side he is a descendant of King João I of Portugal, but on his mother's side he comes even closer to the royal line, for his mother Catarina is granddaughter of King Manuel of Portugal, and is first cousin on their fathers' side to King Philip of Spain.[5] As well as this nobility of blood this duke has a very rich patrimony, providing most abundant income, which has come down to him from his ancestors of long ago, and which has been increased and maintained, so that the annual income which comes to him is estimated at one hundred thousand ducats or more. And so elegant are the furnishings of his house, to which his ancestors always devoted the

---

[1] See above, p. 136.

[2] For more detail on the boys' stay in Évora, the archbishop's care for their welfare and his generosity, see also Agostinho, *Relaçam*, ff. 62–4; Manuel Fialho, *Évora illvstrada*, vol. II, MS CXXX/1-9 in Biblioteca Pública de Évora, printed in Moura, 'Notícias', pp. 40–42; Fróis, *Première ambassade*, pp. 40–46.

[3] The original edition (p. 184) gives '*decimo octauo calendas Octobris*', i.e. 14 September, but Agostinho (*Relaçam*, f. 63v) and Fróis (*Première ambassade*, p. 47) give the 15th.

[4] Don Teodósio (1568–1630), the seventh duke, then aged 16. He had been present with Sebastião at the Battle of Ksar el-kebir in 1578.

[5] Catarina de Bragança (1540–1614), who had been a claimant to the Portuguese throne on Sebastião's death.

utmost care, and such is his retinue of servitors, that he appears to behave not as a duke subject to a king, but as if completely free and totally independent; thus he is so outstanding in all the marks of distinction which I have mentioned that he is counted as holding the first place of all the lords of Portugal.[1]

This duke therefore, when messengers had given him notice of our coming, followed the example of his uncle in sending a carriage to convey us to the city. As soon as we entered it we made for a church where the duke himself awaited us with all the assembly of nobles. He came to the door of the church, welcomed us most courteously, and most respectfully invited us in to the Mass which was about to be solemnly celebrated.[2] How can I describe to you the sweetness and the melody of the singing at that Mass, or the variety of the musical instruments, or the costly ornamentation of the sacred vestments, all of these displaying not merely a ducal but a regal magnificence? And what am I to say of the lavish, indeed sumptuous welcome extended to us within the duke's palace after the Mass was ended?[3] Our first visit there, since the duke wished it so, was to the mother of the duke, the most illustrious princess Catarina, granddaughter of King Manuel, who received us with no less love than she would have shown if it had been her own four sons, come from some far distant place, who hastened to meet her. Afterwards the duke himself introduced us to a most sumptuous and magnificent banquet, where we were moved to the utmost admiration by the various dishes, the gold and silver plate, and the other most costly furnishings. I say no more of the other evidences of a magnificence truly regal, but even the basin in which the silver tableware was washed was itself made of the best quality silver. In the afternoon, after various other delights and entertainments, Catarina the mother of the duke wished to see us again in Japanese dress, and then to spend part of the evening in informal conversation with us. She took particular pleasure in examining the Japanese garments and in hearing about Japanese things, and we could almost read in her face the ardent desire of her heart that the whole of our Japan should be led to the Christian religion. And a notable indication of her inclination towards Japanese things was that she ordered our clothes to be brought to her, and with them as the model she had other most elegant clothes made for her second son, Duarte, and on the following day invited us most kindly to see a certain young Japanese noble. When we were present, behold, her son Duarte made his appearance, strikingly dressed in Japanese clothes, to the delight of all who saw it.

In addition the duke wanted to entertain us with rustic sport, and he took us, together with a company of a hundred and fifty horsemen, to a very large enclosure which he has,[4] filled with various wild animals, and there we very much enjoyed not only hunting the beasts, and the most pleasing spoils of the hunt, but also an equestrian game with oranges, and watching the extraordinary agility of the horses. After these and other similar

---

[1] The 'premier grande' in both rank and wealth (Disney, *History of Portugal*, I, p. 155).

[2] In the Mosteiro de Santo Agostinho opposite the ducal palace (Fróis, *Première ambassade*, p. 48).

[3] At the time, the palace, originally built in 1501, was being remodelled by the architect Nicolau de Frias. Work on the facade started in 1583 and was completed in 1601.

[4] The Tapada Real, near the palace, immortalized by Lope de Vega in *La Filomena* (1621), 'Descripción de la Tapada, insigne monte y recreacíon del excelentísimo señor duque de Berganza', in *Obras completas*, pp. 138–59. Lope de Vega was also the author of two works about Christian martyrs in Japan: one in prose, *Triunfo de la fee en los Reynos del Japón por los años de 1614 y 1615* (1618), and a play, *Los primeros mártires del Japón* (c. 1621). See Cummins, 'Dominican Mission', *passim*.

demonstrations of their love we said farewell to the duke, his mother, and all their family, and we received from him two hundred ducats towards the expenses of our journey, and other gifts which manifested his love, and we declare that we are bound to these two lords, the archbishop and the duke, by a chain of obligation for the favours they have done to us.[1]

We departed from Vila Viçosa on 18 September, passed through the Portuguese town of Elvas, and through Pax Augusta, Badajoz in the vernacular, a Spanish city, in the region of Mérida, and after five days, which is to say on 23 September, were glad to reach the renowned monastery of the order of St Jerome, where the church is dedicated to the Virgin of Guadalupe.[2] Now this monastery is famed in Spain for many reasons, for its great buildings, for its large income, but most of all for the frequency of the miracles which God the most great and good deigns to bring about in that place through the prayers of the Blessed Virgin; and these are not only confirmed by the testimony of many people, but also since times long past are proclaimed to posterity by various signs and pictures hanging in the church, and there are new miracles daily with witnesses there to see them. For this reason the kings and lords of all Spain have adorned that church with many and various gifts. Therefore the magnificence of that church and of its sacred furnishings is extraordinary, and there are fifty silver lamps always burning before the image of the Blessed Virgin.

With our souls cleansed of the stain of sin in confession here, and with the sacred ceremonies duly performed, we journeyed on and arrived at Toledo, capital of the kingdom of Toledo, or New Castile.[3] This is a very ancient city, and especially notable in various ways, and here the fathers of the Society have a house of the professed and a college of scholastics. In the city there are many and various buildings, and among them are numbered sixty or more churches of various religious orders, and eight hospitals.[4] Larger than any of them, in fact quite extraordinarily massive, is the cathedral,[5] which has five parts or areas, each with its own roof, and is besides so broad that in addition to the main chapel and another known as the royal chapel, it contains twenty chapels in different places, each of which could be said to be a fair-sized church, which will give you an idea of the vast size of the cathedral. The main chapel is on a scale appropriate to the enormous mass of this church, and the sacred retable behind its altar is illustrated and adorned with such images that we had never seen anything finer of this kind, and could well believe that a huge quantity of gold had gone into its construction. This same altar is wonderfully adorned with a tabernacle in which the Holy Eucharist is reserved, a most admirable work.

---

[1] On their stay in Vila Viçosa, including an account of the palace written in Portuguese by Constantino Dourado, see also Fróis, *Première ambassade*, pp. 48–56, esp. pp. 50–53.

[2] The royal monastery of Nuestra Señora de Guadalupe, founded 1340, where in 1486 Columbus sought financial support from Ferdinand and Isabella for his projected voyage and to which he made a pilgrimage of thanks after returning from his first voyage. For a more detailed description of the visit to the monastery, see Fróis, *Première ambassade*, pp. 57–60. The monastery was plundered by French forces during the Peninsular War in 1809 and abandoned in 1835, but since 1908 parts have been occupied by the Franciscans.

[3] There is a fuller account of their stay in Toledo in ibid., pp. 63–71, part of which (pp. 64–8) was also written by Dourado which bears a striking similarity to *De Missione*, esp. pp. 67–8.

[4] The boy's account gives 58 religious institutions and 8 hospitals (ibid., p. 64).

[5] The Cathedral of Santa Maria de Toledo, construction on which started in 1226, was built on the site of the main mosque some of whose features are retained. The cathedral, with its retable (1497–1504), Chapel of the New Monarchs (1531–4), the processional monstrance and belfry, remains an impressive structure.

Above the door of this tabernacle there is placed a statue depicting the Most Blessed Virgin with her beloved Son in her arms, and many miracles have been performed there at the invocation of her name, so that the souls of all are affected with a very deep piety towards her, and eight silver lamps burn continuously before her. Know also that all the other chapels, especially the one called the chapel of the kings, in which it was customary for the ancient kings of Castile to be buried, are of the same standard of workmanship. In this church there is also a remarkable choir which boasts a very large number of seats in which the canons sit in order to recite the sacred prayers, and these seats are so beautifully made that it is estimated that each one cost one thousand ducats, and there are seventy-four of them, all arranged in order.

What can I say to you of the sacred furnishings of that church, the chalices, the crosses, the reliquaries, and other objects made of gold and silver? Most famous among them is a monstrance in which the Holy Eucharist is carried in public processions. This monstrance is so large that it takes twenty priests to carry it in a litter, and it is encrusted all round with so many pearls large and small that it is scarcely possible to guess at its value.[1] Besides all these there is a tower of remarkable construction, seven storeys high, in which are located bells, eleven of them, made of a remarkable admixture of metals; one of these is particularly noteworthy as measuring forty-six palms round the rim. Now this cathedral of Toledo is reckoned among the most famous in the whole of Europe, and it is believed and held for certain that more than one hundred million sesterces were spent in its construction,[2] and the number of priests and sacred ministers there is so great as to beggar belief. So generous are their incomes that among those of special rank some can be found who have twenty-five thousand ducats per annum, and the archbishop himself receives two hundred thousand, and wields secular as well as sacred power over many cities. It is not surprising, therefore, that this church should be rich in so many and such precious works.

We stayed in this city of Toledo twenty days,[3] being held back by the sickness into which I myself fell, and we saw a number of other public works, among which I'll mention only two. One of them is a construction of certain remarkable aqueducts, by means of which water from the river Tagus, that most celebrated river which I mentioned when I was dealing with Lisbon, is forced, against nature, as it were, to rise to the uppermost area of the city, which is four hundred and fifty palms away from the bank of the river.[4] In the first place a very broad flight of steps extends from the edge of the river up to that area. There are beams laid down on these steps, and the bronze ducts for the water are supported by these beams, and they are shaped so that they take in the water at their wider end and then move it on into smaller tubes. They are linked by supported joints, and connected and fastened together by iron chains underneath, and so arranged that every time the lowest one, which is at the river's edge, takes in water by its own movement and sends it to the one above, the others all move in a fixed order, and transmit to those above the water taken in by those below, until it reaches the highest point. This entire mechanism is moved by two wheels, which are at the lowest point, by the river's edge,

---

[1] The processional monstrance was designed and built by Enrique de Arfe between 1517 and 1524. See also Fróis, *Première ambassade*, p. 67.

[2] I.e. 2.5 million ducats.

[3] They arrived in Toledo on 29 September and left on 19 October.

[4] The Artificio de Juanelo or Ingenio de Toledo. There were two such devices which continued in operation until 1639.

and it is roofed in so that no part of the workings of this truly royal machine can be disturbed or damaged by the weather.

The other famous work is a clock made with admirable art, which, though barely four palms in height, wonderfully imitates all the movements of the celestial orbs, with the coincidings of the wandering stars, the oppositions, eclipses, and other similar things, so that none is missing, not the contrary motions of the first sphere, nor the motion commonly called trepidation of the eighth sphere, nor the course of the seven planets with the variety of the hours of the sun and the moon, nor finally the risings and settings of the twelve signs of the Zodiac.[1] So you can see all the heavenly orbs completing their courses, the first sphere in a single day, the orb of Saturn in almost thirty years, the sun over a full year, the moon with the passing of a month, and all the others in their set times, so that there is no motion of the heavens, among those which astronomers contemplate, which is not shown most certainly and ingeniously, with its designated time, so many years, so many months, so many days; with the golden number also provided, and the dominical letter which occurs in each year. In all, this work comprises eighteen hundred small spheres, made with such skill that no two of them are exactly alike. It was twenty years in the devising, and another three and a half in the making, and those who examine it are lost in admiration at this incredible spectacle. These two, namely the aqueduct and the clock, compete with each other in the unheard of skill which has gone into them, but both were invented by a certain Italian, Gianello Turriano of Cremona,[2] hugely famed throughout Europe, and magnificently recompensed for his extremely painstaking work by an award from the Emperor Charles V and his son King Philip of Spain.

Leo: All these things which you have told us leave us deeply impressed, and easily persuade us of the remarkable ingenuity of the Europeans, and of the beauty and magnificence of their things. I wonder, though, how it can be that a craftsmen can carry through the construction of those works by the power of his thought and the application of his intelligence.

Michael: Your doubt about that would be completely removed from your mind, Leo, if you were familiar with the intelligence of Europeans, exercised in many arts, which allows them to succeed in many things which seem incredible. But the things which we shall be saying as we proceed with the colloquia will help to persuade you that this is really so. Many other things could be said about the royal city of Toledo, for it is rich in all those things which adorn all the most noble cities of Europe; but you can easily imagine what those are from what I have already said about Lisbon. I shall not, however, omit to mention here the honour and benevolence with which Juan Mendoza,[3] at that time archdeacon of the Toledo church, but now a most illustrious cardinal, treated us in all the time we were in Toledo. Not only did he visit us often and take us to various famous and

---

[1] The Cristalino, which in its time was famous throughout Europe.

[2] c. 1550–85, clockmaker, engineer and mathematician, who first arrived in Spain in 1529. He was involved in the formulation of the Gregorian calendar. This particular clock was already familiar in Japan; Father Organtino, who had arrived in Japan in 1570 and who had passed through Toledo on his way to Lisbon, described it to some Japanese daimyo who wished they could possess a similar one (Fróis, *Première ambassade*, p. 69).

[3] Juan Hurtado de Mendoza (1548–92), son of Diego Hurtado de Mendoza (1520–60), duke of Saldaña and eldest son of the fourth duke of Infantado. He became a cardinal on 18 December 1587.

remarkable places in the city, putting his coach at our disposal, but he also invited us to a family meal at his house, which he has furnished with the beauty and splendour befitting such a noble and outstanding man. For he is of the illustrious family of the dukes of Infantado, and his brother, who is now the duke,¹ is among the wealthiest and most powerful nobles of Spain. We were so very kindly treated, therefore, by this most noble man, that we declare ourselves to be bound to him by ties of perpetual obligation. Accordingly, when we were in the port of Macao and heard that he, together with certain others of whom we shall speak later, had been numbered among the cardinals by the Supreme Pontiff Pope Sixtus V, we were filled with very great joy.

Many others of the nobility and leading men of that city also came to us, with indications of the most ardent love for us, and I have no words to describe the kindness towards us of the fathers of the Society who live in the professed house there, but I acknowledge myself specially obliged to them, because when I was suffering from the very disagreeable sickness of the smallpox,² to which the Japanese usually react with revulsion, they were so kind and went to such trouble, calling most learned doctors and providing me with everything I needed, that I really could not distinguish between them and my own parents.³ In addition to the professed house there is also in the same city a college of the Society, which was built a few years ago by the most illustrious Archbishop Gaspar Quiroga of Toledo,⁴ who is also a most distinguished cardinal. And since his benevolence towards the Society is great, and he knows that the Society produces in abundance fruit from which all derive great benefit, he generously had another college built in Talavera, a town which we passed through.

After I had recovered from the sickness which I mentioned we left that city on 19 October, and on the following day reached the royal town of Madrid,⁵ in which is the most celebrated court of the most powerful King Philip of Spain. And as we approached the town many noblemen, some among them the sons of dukes and counts, came out to meet us in their carriages, and after mutual greetings one each of them, to show respect and goodwill, took one each of us into his carriage, and accompanied us to the college of the fathers of the Society, with signs of affection, just as if they and we were old and familiar friends. And as we took our leave of those noblemen and entered the church, the fathers of the Society received us most kindly as their guests. But what took place in Madrid deserves a whole colloquium to itself, so I shall end this colloquium here.

Lino: I agree with Michael. It will be entirely appropriate to begin tomorrow night with the royal town of Madrid and what happened there.

---

¹ Íñigo López de Mendoza (1536–1601), one of the most powerful men in Spain. His estates comprised 620 towns and villages and 85,000 vassals. His annual income in 1600 was 120,000 ducats, but, like most of the upper aristocracy in the late 16th century, he was heavily indebted (Elliott, *Imperial Spain*, pp. 313–14).

² The original (p. 191) gives 'bulluiarum', i.e. 'pulluiarum'. Smallpox (痘瘡 *tōsō*) killed many children in the early modern period. The disease was endemic in Japan and had been longer established there than in Europe. In the first half of the 16th century, there were several epidemics, See Janetta, *Epidemics and Mortality*, pp. 45, 68–9, 107.

³ For more on Michael's sickness, which was serious and life-threatening (2,000 children had already died that year from the disease in Toledo), see Fróis, *Première ambassade*, pp. 70–71.

⁴ 1512–94, friend of Ignatius of Loyola, appointed Inquisitor General of Spain in 1573.

⁵ The original (p. 190) gives the Latin name Mantua Carpetana, one of the legendary names of the city.

COLLOQUIUM XVIII

Of the power of King Philip of Spain, and the oath by which the nobles of the kingdom swore allegiance to his son as his successor, and of the visit which the ambassadors made to both

Lino: We have come together more eagerly than usual for this meeting, since we know you are going to deal with your arrival at the royal seat of King Philip of Spain, and with his power and majesty; and since you have said so many things about various princes who are under the jurisdiction of such a great king, of the king himself it must be expected that everything will be deserving of admiration.

Michael: So indeed it is, for whatever pertains to wealth or power and is in some way scattered among the other princes, is brought together and contained in this one most powerful king.

Lino: Is this King Philip, of whom you speak, greatest and supreme among all the kings of Europe?

Michael: With the exception of the emperor,[1] who has the highest rank of all, it is difficult to compare the kings of Europe one with another, since they all have completely free and independent jurisdiction, or to give absolute primacy to any one. But it can be said without fear of incurring odium or giving offence to anyone that King Philip has extended the jurisdiction of his kingdom further and wider than any of the other European kings. Indeed, if I leave out the Roman emperors, who brought under their empire a large part of the world, there has never been any king who carried his standard to so many and such remote provinces. For the world, as I said earlier, is divided into five principal parts, namely Europe, Africa, Asia, America, and the unknown southern land, and king Philip of whom we are speaking, has, to begin with, one of these parts, namely America, whole and entire, under his jurisdiction, and that includes the extremely rich countries of Peru and Mexico, as well as a great number of other islands and provinces; and Brazil also belongs to America. Then in Europe, the best and most fertile part of the whole world, which is made up of a great number of kingdoms, King Philip is lord of seventeen or eighteen of them. He is lord in the first place of the whole of Spain, which numbers fourteen distinct kingdoms. He is renowned as the count of Belgium, which contains the excellent provinces of Flanders, Zeeland, Holland, Brabant,

---

[1] At this time Rudolf II (r. 1576–1612).

and many other regions.[1] He is besides king of the kingdom of Naples, sited in Italy; king also of Sicily, and most powerful duke of Milan. With regard to Africa, on its maritime shore, some part of which is washed by the Mediterranean but the greater part by the ocean, he possesses many heavily fortified fortresses and towns, and in the Mediterranean areas he has many tributary and stipendiary kings. The main fortresses on the Mediterranean are Oran, Peñon de Velez, Tangier, Ceuta; and on the ocean, as well as Arzila and Mazagão, the islands of Cabo Verde and São Tomé, Congo, Angola, Sofala, and Mozambique. Next in Asia, first of all he has the kingdom of Ormuz, which comprises the island itself in which is the city of Ormuz, and other places in Persia and Arabia. Then in Nearer India he is lord of many cities which I have already spoken of to some extent, and in Further India he holds under his dominion the most famous city of Malacca. Also contained within his empire are the most celebrated islands of the Moluccas, and those which are named the Philippines, after Philip himself. Thus almost the entire navigation of the ocean is subject to him, from which you will easily understand how far and how wide his power extends.

Leo: I am astonished at the power of this king, but I would also like to know why he has not added other kingdoms to his possessions.

Michael: There are two reasons, Leo. One is that Christian kings normally enlarge their dominions by right, not by force, and the other is that other European kings are also notable for their power and for the extent of their kingdoms, so that it is not easy for one king to subjugate another.

Lino: It remains for us to ask, then, how it came about that King Philip acquired such extensive dominions in all parts of the world.

Michael: First of all it must be attributed to Divine Providence,[2] at whose will, as the sacred writings testify, kingdoms are changed, and are transferred from one people to another. Secondly, if you look to human causes, it is all to be attributed to remarkable good fortune in the hereditary succession, and I'll summarize this succession, as a full account of it is dispersed in many different books and chapters. In the first place I present to you, as the foundation of this whole realm, the kingdom of Aragon (which is a part of Spain). The son of the king of Aragon, Martin by name, married the daughter of Frederick king of Sicily, and thus the kingdom of Sicily was joined to the kingdom of Aragon [in 1469]. Then Joanna, queen of the kingdom of Naples, adopted Alfonso, prince and heir to the kingdom of Sicily and Aragon, and with this as the starting point (for the sake of brevity I omit other considerations) the kingdom of Naples came to belong to the kingdom of Aragon [in 1504]. Later Ferdinand, heir to the kingdoms of Sicily, Naples, and Aragon, married Isabella, princess of both Castiles, and thus [in 1479] took control of the kingdom of the whole of Spain (with the single exception of Portugal). This

---

[1] Since 1565 the Low Countries had been in revolt against Spanish rule and from 1568 the revolt was transformed into the Eighty Years' War, finally settled in 1648 with ratification of the division of the Low Countries into the United Provinces and the Spanish Netherlands.

[2] Something in which Philip believed fervently (Parker, *Grand Strategy*, pp. 97–109).

Ferdinand gave his daughter, who was his only surviving heir, in marriage to King Philip, the illustrious count of Belgium, son of the Emperor Maximilian, and when he died [in 1516] his son Charles inherited all the kingdoms listed so far, and also Belgium. This Charles was declared emperor by the votes of all the electors, and in his time the land of America, one fifth of the world, which had been discovered in the time of his grandfather, was brought wholly within his empire; and because this emperor had deserved very well of Francesco Sforza, duke of Milan, he was named, by the duke who was dying without an heir, successor to the dukedom of Milan [in 1535].[1] Charles' son Philip, second of that name, about whom we are now speaking, auspiciously obtained the whole of Portugal [in 1580], and the parts of Africa and Asia which belonged to the dominion of Portugal, when King Henrique of Portugal, who was Philip's uncle, departed this life; and now that his realm extends so far and so wide, into so many kingdoms and provinces, and he is sovereign over such vast possessions, it is fitting that we pray God that he continue to rule for many years yet. It is now the thirty-fourth year since this most glorious king took over the helm of his kingdoms, while his father Charles was still alive, Charles who after winning the highest praise for his many victories over his enemies, and for his outstanding conduct of affairs both at home and on the field of battle, partly because he was afflicted with many illnesses, partly because of his confidence in the prudence and authority of his son, put the key to all the affairs of the kingdom in his hands [in 1556]. Then, in order to pass the remainder of his life in piety and holiness, having cast off all human cares, he committed himself to a certain monastery, and there, thirty-two years ago, he gloriously exchanged this wretched and calamitous life for the life eternal [in 1558].

Leo: That joining up of so many kingdoms by right of heredity and without any force is indeed admirable.[2] But we would very much like to know at how much the annually collected income of that most powerful king is reckoned.

Michael: It is difficult to count up the total, but we have been told that his annual income is reckoned to be sixty million sesterces, or more.[3]

Lino: Great God! Sixty million sesterces! How can such an amount be collected by one king, unless taxes are exacted with great harshness and indeed injustice to the people?

Michael: The richness of his revenues comes not from the harshness to which you object, Lino, but from the number, the wealth, and the extent of his kingdoms, and if you consider these that enormous sum is perfectly credible; for from America alone, which includes Peru and New Spain, he gets thirty million sesterces,[4] so you can imagine the amount that will accrue to him from so many kingdoms and provinces. But the expenses

---

[1] Francesco died in 1535 and Charles inherited Milan, but the French refused to accept the succession and the issue became a part of the larger Habsburg–Valois struggle. Spanish sovereignty over the duchy was confirmed in the treaty of Cateau-Cambrésis in 1559.

[2] The Portuguese throne was, of course, acquired by force.

[3] I.e. 15 million ducats. The income of Castile is estimated to have been 9.49 million ducats in 1588 and 11.9 million ducats in 1594 (Thompson, *War and Government*, p. 288).

[4] I.e. 7.5 million ducats. Income from silver imports from the New World is estimated at 2 million ducats in 1588. The best that was achieved was around 3 million ducats in the following decade (ibid., pp. 68, 288).

he incurs each year clearly indicate the same thing, and anyone who calculates the number of ships, galleys, military garrisons, and other similar things, which are maintained at this king's expense, and how many kingdoms and provinces he defends from the incursions of enemies, will readily appreciate that he must have an immense weight of gold as income. This richest and most powerful of kings, therefore, chose as his royal seat this town, commonly called Madrid, but which formerly belonged to the Carpetan people.[1] He chose it not with an eye to the comforts of an agreeable life, but considering the common good, and set this place, which is just about in the centre of the whole of Spain, and can be easily reached from all points, above other cities however populous and noble. In addition, the climate of this place is salubrious, the soil is notably well cultivated, and the outcome is that what was formerly a small town has now attained to great fame. The reason for the increase in population, however, is not that the king has compelled the nobles from all his kingdoms to build houses there, as the lords of all Japan have sometimes been accustomed to do,[2] thus bringing a very large population to a city which they are founding. On the contrary, all of this is left to the free will and choice of people who tend, most willingly and without any coercion, to congregate in the royal town.

Now during the time that we were in Madrid there took place the solemn swearing of an oath by which all the nobles of Spain bound themselves to recognize Prince Philip, son of King Philip, as heir to all the kingdoms, so it will not be inappropriate to give you an account now of the pomp and magnificence of that ceremony, and indeed I have purposely reserved this subject matter for this place. It is customary, then, for European kings, whenever they want their sons to be acknowledged by all, by means of an oath, as their heirs, to summon the nobles and the people, or their representatives; and if it is difficult to have all the people from all the kingdoms come together in one place, this solemn day of the swearing of the oath is celebrated separately in each country. And since King Philip could not make the people of all his countries come together at the same time and in the one place to pledge themselves to his son, he invited only the people and nobles of the two Castiles to take part in this ceremony. There were present, therefore, the flower of the rulers and nobles, the representatives of the cities, the bishops and archbishops and other very important priests, when the day for the oath to be taken was proclaimed, and it was 11 November, which is the day dedicated to St Martin. The place was also announced, and it was of course a famous church, outside the suburbs of the town, where religious of the order of St Jerome live.[3] When the day dawned for which all had been waiting, behold, the walls of the church were covered with tapestries of a wondrous variety, the floor was laid with the best of carpets, the adornment of the high altar was

---

[1] The early history of Madrid is conjectural. It was settled by Arabs before the end of the first millennium. Philip II moved the capital there in 1561. Most visitors were unimpressed by the city and overwhelmed by the stench in the streets. See Hillgarth, *Mirror of Spain*, pp. 92–5.

[2] In October 1580 Lourenço Mexia wrote to Aquaviva that Nobunaga intended that all the principal lords of Japan should build imposing residences at Azuchi. He judged the policy to be highly beneficial to the Jesuits (*Cartas*, I, f. 476; Fróis, *História de Japam*, III, pp. 191–2). Hideyoshi followed the precedent, ordering all the lords of territories he had conquered to build residences in his new stronghold of Osaka, and under the Tokugawa the practice of *sankin kōtai* 参勤交代 or alternate attendance in Edo (where they left their families) and in their own domains was institutionalized. See *Cartas*, II, f. 100; Valignano, *Adiciones*, p. 364; Berry, *Hideyoshi*, p. 142; Vaporis, *Tour of Duty*, *passim*.

[3] The monastery of San Jerónimo el Real.

splendidly woven of gold and silk, and indeed everything was perfectly prepared for the ceremonies of the festive day. In the chancel there were two tabernacles, one on the right, the other on the left. The tabernacle to the right was covered with a canopy of richest cloth, and in it sat King Philip himself on a most magnificent throne, accompanied by Philip his son and heir,[1] his sister, who was the wife of the emperor, and his two daughters Isabella and Catarina. The king and his son were attended by youths from the flower of all the nobility of Castile, who stood to either side of them, and behind his sister and daughters were young girls, they too most noble, and excellently attired. Next to the royal youths and their attendants stood the presidents of the royal councils and other most noble men. In the other tabernacle, to the left, there were sitting, on most ornate seats, various legates of foreign kings and princes, especially of the Supreme Pontiff, of the emperor, and of the Venetian Republic. Near the high altar, in special seats adorned with velvet, sat two most illustrious cardinals; the cardinal of Toledo in the centre,[2] and Cardinal Granvelle[3] on one side of him; on the other side eight prelates or bishops occupied splendidly decorated seats. Outside the chancel there were sitting two rows of nobles: on the right, on sumptuous and beautiful benches, those who in the kingdoms of Castile are specially referred to as 'grandees'; on the left fifteen other marquesses and counts who, although most noble, are nevertheless not distinguished with the title of 'grandee'. And finally, after these, the multitude of noble men which filled that vast church was almost infinite.

In the walls of the chancel there were two windows with their alcoves, and the king himself assigned to us one of these, the one which was opposite the royal tabernacle, so that we could see from a convenient place the enactment of the whole of that ceremony, in the company of most noble persons, among whom was Cristóvão de Moura, a most distinguished Portuguese man,[4] whom the king holds in particular esteem. All therefore being present, with ears and minds attentive, the cardinal archbishop of Toledo celebrated the Holy Sacrifice with such a variety of voices and musical instruments, and such sweet harmonies, that it is scarcely possible to imagine it, let alone find words to describe it. When the sacred ceremony had been duly and solemnly enacted, a table covered with most precious cloth was set before the high altar, and on it a book containing the holy gospels, and an image of Christ crucified, of wonderful workmanship. The cardinal of Toledo was seated at the table, ready to put the oath to each of those who came forward. A magistrate, similar to those whom the Romans used to call *patres patrati*,[5] read out the documents indicating what was to be done, and a prefect of the royal council gave an eloquent explanation of the form of the oath. Then the empress, King Philip's sister, was

---

[1] The future Philip III (r. 1598–1621). For a fuller accounts of the proceedings, see Sepúlveda, 'Sucesos del reinado de Felipe II', pp. 492–4; Fróis, *Première ambassade*, pp. 75–82.

[2] Gaspar de Quiroga y Vela (1512–94), Inquisitor General and member of the Council of State (1573). Later he became archbishop of Toledo (1577), and a cardinal from 1578. As Inquisitor General he issued, in 1583 and 1584, the Index of prohibited and expurgated books known as the Quiroga Index (Kamen, *Spanish Inquisition*, pp. 113–14).

[3] Antoine Perrenot de Granvelle (1517–86), minister of Philip II in the Netherlands, Italy and Spain, who was instrumental in securing Philip's accession to the Portuguese crown in 1580–81.

[4] 1538–1613, Philip's envoy to Portugal 1578–80, helped secure the Portuguese crown for Philip and was later a member of the Council of Portugal, and chamberlain to Philip with responsibilities which included dressing the monarch and massaging his feet (Parker, *Grand Strategy*, p. 177).

[5] Officials who read out the text of a treaty.

the first of all to come up to the set place in order to bind herself with the oath, and she came not as wife of the emperor but as in a sense the first among the principal women of Castile. When she rose the king also stood up, and he accompanied her, with head uncovered, as she went and as she returned, thus gladly conceding to his sister, as wife of the emperor, the highest possible honour. The king's two daughters also went with her,[1] and thus the three most illustrious women of all Spain, in due order, with the empress first, followed by the older and then the younger daughter of the king, bound themselves by an oath, acknowledging Philip, a boy not yet six years old, son of King Philip, as prince and heir of all the kingdoms. Then, coming back to the place where the prince himself was sitting, the empress wished to kiss the hand of the prince in veneration and reverence. When he most courteously refused to have this, and instead himself took the hand of his beloved aunt, she embraced him fondly; and when the other two, the sisters of the prince, also bent to kiss his hand, and the sisters and the prince were striving to outdo each other in courtesies, finally, at a sign from the king, the prince allowed his sisters to kiss his hand in reverence. After these three illustrious women had taken the oath, first Cardinal Granvelle, then the bishops in order of rank, then those who have the illustrious name of grandee, afterwards those who are marquesses and counts, and finally the representatives of the cities, all did the same.[2]

You will perhaps understand the degree to which in Europe, in all these things, regard is had to order and rank, from the following example. In Europe there is an ancient dispute between the two famous cities of Burgos and Toledo with regard to their relative rank and antiquity, and whenever kings arrange a convention or assembly of this sort, to make sure that no disturbance arises because of this dispute, and to remove the possibility of any offence being taken, it has been prudently ordained by the kings of Castile that in summoning these cities the king should use these words: 'Let those of Burgos approach, for I know full well that those of Toledo will obey us.' With these words neither city is accorded the primacy, and all occasion of offence is removed. In this assembly, therefore, the procedure was that those of Burgos were the first to bind themselves with the oath, while the king affirmed his confidence that those of Toledo would do as they were commanded.[3] The representatives of the other cities followed those of Burgos, but those of Toledo were separately summoned, in the name of the king, by the count of Fonte Oliva,[4] and took the oath, considering that in this way no less honour was accorded to them than to those of Burgos. From this you will appreciate how much attention the kings of Europe pay to distinctions of rank and degrees of antiquity. This ceremony was such a tremendous occasion and such an enjoyable spectacle, that the five hours which it took up seemed only the briefest moment of time. There was such a multitude of people flocking together there that it would have been extremely difficult to make a way through the densely packed crowds to the other side. Finally, the beneficence that day of the king and

---

[1] Isabella Clara Eugenia (1566–1633), who married Albert, archduke of Austria; and Catalina Micaela (1567–93), who married Charles, duke of Savoy.

[2] A list is given in Fróis, *Première ambassade*, pp. 80–82.

[3] On the dispute between Toledo and Burgos over precedence, which was resolved in this manner by Alfonso XI of Castile (1311–50), see Góis, *Crónica de Dom Emanuel*, p. 32, on which the account given here is based.

[4] Original edition (p. 197) '*Fontis oliuae*'. Pedro López de Ayala (1537–99), fourth count of Fuensalida, literally 'where the spring sprouts' (L. '*fons*' '*salire*'). Fuensalida called on the representatives of Toledo in the name of the king to take the oath. See Fróis, *Première ambassade*, p. 82.

the prince towards their people, and the way they distributed rewards, was such that it was easy to see their benevolence, and their inclination and wish not so much to command them as to deserve well of them. This is customary with the European kings when they bind their people with an oath acknowledging them or the princes their sons.

Leo: This custom, generally followed by the European kings whenever a king or prince is proclaimed heir to the kingdom, is most pleasing to us, and, if you remember, it is a custom not unfamiliar to us Japanese.[1] For whenever a king announces that he is giving up the exercise of power and administration, and withdrawing to private life, he hands over to his son his sword, that is, his power over the life and death of his people, and then commits to his care all the documents in which the records of the kingdom and the lineage of the royal family are contained. And once the son has been proclaimed king all the nobles come with reverence to pay him homage as their lord. And other rulers observe the same custom whenever they relinquish their power and right to rule to their sons.

Michael: This custom of ours is also laudable, and if, after Christian piety is introduced, two other things are added, namely the holy sacrifice duly celebrated and the oath as religious ceremony, without any doubt it will be able to be judged perfect in all respects. But now I shall give you an account of our entry to the king. The following day, namely 12 November,[2] was appointed as the day when, by order of King Philip, we were to be introduced to him. We were carried to the palace in coaches which the king himself uses, and the crowds of people thronging the streets and squares were so great that we barely managed to find a way through them. And when we did make our way to the king, the multitude of people there was so dense that the attendants of the royal officials could scarcely open a way for us. The king had already been briefed by the fathers of the Society about the reasons for our journey, and who the Christian princes were in whose names we were visiting the king and, especially, the pope; and he was therefore willing to receive us with honour as the emissaries of most noble princes, especially as we had come from the extreme limits of the east to the furthest boundaries of the west, on the longest voyage so far discovered. The king, then, received us most kindly and merrily, standing, as is his custom when dealing with ambassadors, together with his son and heir and his daughters, in the inmost quarters of his residence, which we reached only after passing through twelve splendidly furnished halls and rooms. He did not suffer us to kiss his royal hands, but embraced us most warmly, and his son and heir and his daughters did the same. Then

---

[1] On this custom, see Lewis, 'Anticipatory Association' *passim*. Shortly before his death in September 1598 Hideyoshi ordered the most powerful daimyo to pledge their allegiance once more to his son and chosen successor, Hideyori. The first three Tokugawa shoguns retired from office in favour of their heirs to secure the succession. See Berry, *Hideyoshi*, pp. 234–5; Toby, *State and Diplomacy*, pp. 34–5, 72–5. See also above, p. 189.

[2] The audience took place on 14 November (see Fig. 8). The boys wore Japanese clothes which are described in detail in Guzman, *Historia*, II, p. 236; Cooper, *Japanese Mission*, p. 60. On the 12th, the king's chamberlain and trusted councillor, Cristóbal de Moura, went to the Jesuit house to discuss the arrangements for the audience (Guzman, *Historia*, II, pp. 235–6; Fróis, *Première ambassade*, p. 85; Cooper, *Japanese Mission*, pp. 59–60). The palace which they visited, the Antiguo Alcázar or Old Castle, was destroyed by fire in 1734, and the present palace was built between 1738 and 1755.

Figure 8. Audience with King Philip II, engraving by Abraham van Diepenbeeck, in Cornelius Hazart, *Kerckelycke historie van de gheheele wereldt*, vol. I, Antwerp, 1667, facing p. 64.
By permission of Professor Tominaga Michio.

we presented to him the letters sent by the kings of Bungo and Arima and the prince of Ōmura, and gave him the message with which we had been entrusted, namely that our kings of Bungo and Arima, and prince of Ōmura, imbued with Christian piety, held nothing to be more important than that in their name we should visit the Supreme Pontiff the Vicar of Christ, and should humbly present ourselves to honour and revere King Philip himself, famed and celebrated throughout the whole world, and should declare, with all the fervour of which we were capable, how truly devoted our kings and princes were to him.[1]

He, when he had heard the letters read out in both Japanese and Spanish, answered the messages with a glad countenance, saying that he held the Japanese kings and princes of the same religion to be allied to him by law, joined to him by a new bond of brotherhood, and imprinted and engraved on his breast; that he was delighted that they had sent him, as witnesses of their mutual benevolence, such fine and noble young men, and that he hoped that in the future this most pleasing custom would come to be followed more and more often.[2] After that he treated us with even greater familiarity, asking many questions about Japanese things, examining our clothing most studiously, drawing our Japanese swords, which we were wearing at our sides, from their scabbards, paying close attention even to our shoes and their form, and finally accepting most graciously certain gifts which we presented to him in our own name, praising their beauty and elegance with many words. In all of this his warmth and affability was such that even the nobles and the servants who best know his normal grave bearing were surprised at his friendliness and kindness, and said that they had very rarely seen the king deign to be so relaxed and gay. The children who, as I said, were present, followed his example, and thus we found that royal and illustrious family extremely kind to us in all things.

There were many other most noble ladies extremely eager to see us, among them a most distinguished lady, daughter of the duke of Aveiro,[3] who stands out among the nobility of Portugal for the illustriousness of his lineage, so that he need not yield to any, no matter how noble. The king therefore, wishing to satisfy these ladies, asked if we would like to hear vespers sung in his chapel. When we said that nothing could be more agreeable to us we went there, and the prayers were recited with such sweetness in the singing, and such melody from the organs, that we were convinced that we were listening to something heavenly and divine rather than something composed by human artifice. When the solemn prayers were at an end those most noble ladies, together with some gentlemen of

---

[1] The letters, in Portuguese, are printed in Frόis, *Première ambassade*, pp. 90–92. An English translation of the letter from Ōtomo Yoshishige is printed in Cooper, *Japanese Mission*, pp. 62–3, who alleges that they were not 'personally composed' by the daimyo, presumably meaning they were not authorized by the daimyo. No evidence is cited for this assertion. The Spanish translations are in RAHM, MS 09-02663, ff. 323, 324v, 326. See also Introduction, pp. 11–12.

[2] Original edition (p. 199) '*quotidie magis ac magis*', literally 'daily more and more'.

[3] This is either Doña Madalena d'Aveiro, daughter of Don Juan Tellez de Giron, count of Urena, and widow of the second duke of Aveiro, Jorge de Lancastre, who died in 1578 at the battle of Ksar el-Kebir, or her daughter Doña Juliana de Lancastre who married her cousin the third duke of Aveiro in 1588. As the original edition (p. 199) gives '*filia*', the latter is probably meant; but cf. Frόis, *Première ambassade*, p. 78 n. 285, where the editors misname Doña Madalena as Juliana and suggest that the person mentioned is the former.

high rank who were present, enjoyed a spectacle which pleased them greatly, studying us eagerly, and taking note of everything about us.[1]

It remained for us to visit the sister of King Philip, wife of the dead emperor, but because of the dense crowds of people and the lack of time we left that for another day. From there, with night coming on, we made for the college of the fathers of the Society, with such a concourse of people that it seemed as if the entire city had come together there, eager to see us. And so many illustrious women rushed to the church of that college, wanting to see us and our clothing, that it seemed necessary to go into the church and satisfy their wish; and they were all very eager to look at us, and seemed extraordinarily pleased, and wished the fathers of the Society, and us, and the situation of Japan, all success and good fortune. And in the house an equally large number of noble men awaited us, among them two most important bishops, of Plasencia[2] and Salamanca,[3] and all of these studied us and everything about us with the keenest interest, and through an interpreter exchanged most familiar conversation with us.[4] And since with that a day most happily occupied came to an end, let us put an end also to this our colloquium, so as to come back the more willingly tomorrow night to what follows.

Leo: We are content, dear Michael, to have you end your talk in this way, but I would like you to know that your narration leaves our minds athirst and eager rather than tired or bored in any way.

---

[1] On the visit to Philip II, see also Fróis, *Première ambassade*, pp. 85–93; *Dai Nihon Shiryō*, XI: 1, pp. 128–30; Boncompagni-Ludovisi, *Le prime due ambasciate*, pp. 1–2; Cooper, *Japanese Mission*, pp. 59–63. The presents given to Philip included a bamboo writing desk and some lacquerware. Philip noted the difference between these Japanese artefacts and those of China. The king also showed an interest in the Japanese custom of drinking hot water. In all, the audience lasted three-quarters of an hour. See Fróis, *Première ambassade*, p. 88; Boncompagni-Ludovisi, *Le prime due ambasciate*, p. 2; Cooper, *Japanese Mission*, p. 62.

[2] Andres de Noronha (d. 1586), appointed 1581.

[3] Jerónimo Manrique Figueroa (d. 1593), appointed 1579.

[4] Guzman (*Historia*, II, pp. 236–7) prints an anonymous description of the boys which clearly originates from one of those who met them.

COLLOQUIUM XIX

Of various works built by King Philip, especially the work of the Escorial, and of how we came to the city of Alón or Alicante

Leo: The things which you told us about King Philip in the last colloquium were many and remarkable, but my mind is held in a sort of avid anticipation of hearing yet more, and if you do relate more things it can never tire of hearing them.

Michael: If I were to enumerate all the things which we noted in the royal capital I would have to hold forth for a very long time. Since Philip is the most powerful of kings and has the largest jurisdiction, there are new things to be seen daily in his royal capital, with the new arrival of various princes and nobles to visit him, and with the wonderful variety of the many things brought to the one place. But it is not my job to attempt to describe everything; what I have to do is give an account of the principal things, so as to put before the eyes of your minds the state of things in Europe.

To return to my account, then, we considered that on the following day[1] it was our duty to pay a visit to the king's sister, the empress. She knew we were coming, and she sent us two carriages which she uses, and King Philip himself sent us two more of his, and in these four carriages we were conveyed to the palace of the empress. And in this matter the love of the king and of his sister for us is evident and manifest, for they would not have us transported in the carriages, and there are any number of them, of any other duke or noble, but deigned to offer us their own, which they themselves use. The empress was surrounded by a crowd of most noble girls and ladies, among whom the first was Leonor Mascarenhas, a most noble Portuguese lady of that same family to which belongs, as I said, the viceroy of India whom we visited.[2] King Philip, when he was only a child, was instructed and educated by her, and for that reason, but also for her singular prudence, she is held in high regard by the king and his sister. The empress received us with the same benevolence as her brother King Philip; she would not permit us to kiss her august hand, but embraced us most familiarly, and engaged us most pleasantly in conversation about various matters. The other ladies around her imitated her manifestation of love, and listened most eagerly when we spoke of Japanese things.

---

[1] 15 November.

[2] By this time Leonor had retreated to the convent of Nuestra Señora de los Maria de los Ángeles which she had founded in 1563 as the convent of Santa María de los Ángeles. On this foundation, see Triguero, 'Fundación y dote', pp. 41–56. Leonor, an exemplar of pious chastity, never married. She is misidentified in Fróis, *Première ambassade*, p. 76 n. 273, as the wife of João de Mascarenhas, the captain of Diu during the second siege in 1546.

After this, and with the permission of the empress, we were conducted by her grand chamberlain, Juan de Borja,[1] son of the duke of Gandía, as a sign of his affection, to his own palace. This duke of Gandía was the same who, repudiating all human things, was received into the Society, and when he left this life was Superior General of the Society, as I related earlier. Borja therefore took us into his chapel, which we can justly call a treasury of sacred relics. There he showed us twenty-eight heads of saints in containers of silver and gold, and six arms preserved in the same way, one of them an arm of St Mary Magdalen; one of the thorns from the crown of Christ the Lord, kept in a precious box, and finally a cross two and a half palms long, in which relics of the twelve Apostles were inserted in a remarkable manner, and many other most precious works of this kind. This spectacle seemed to us so very much remarkable, that in no other private house of any noble did we see its like. After we reached the port of Macao in China we learned from a letter that all these holy relics had been given as a gift by the same Borja to the house of the professed fathers in Lisbon, and had been received with extraordinary popular acclamation and a great celebratory procession; and this example of generosity and magnanimity should be judged worthy to be remembered in perpetuity.[2]

Great were the signs of affection for us which this most illustrious man clearly showed, and João de Bragança, a most noble man,[3] son of the count of Tentúgal[4] and a close blood relative of the duke of Bragança, did the same. At that time he was living at the court of King Philip, he was always at our disposal with unfailing kindness and generosity, and of him also we cherish the most happy memory. The ambassador of the most powerful King Henry of France[5] showed himself no less well disposed towards us, and he urged us with the utmost entreaties to pass through France on our way to Rome, so as to pay a visit to his king. But that would have meant a considerable detour, so we expressed our profound gratitude to the ambassador and told him, but without making any commitment, that if time allowed we would be delighted to do that. This king of France is, after King Philip, more powerful than any other, and his kingdom is outstanding for the antiquity of the Christian religion there, for its discipline in military matters, for its study of arts and letters, and for other most honourable marks of distinction, but as we did not go there there is no need for us to dwell on it or give any further account of it. After that day we paid visits also to other leading men, especially those two illustrious cardinals, the cardinal of Toledo and Cardinal Granvelle, and the love and kindness with which they welcomed us is almost beyond the power of words to describe.

And King Philip, not yet satisfied with the many proofs and demonstrations of his benevolence towards us, wanted us to be shown things which we would like to see, for he was sure that after such a long voyage this would lift our spirits considerably. King Philip has many very well-known places close to Madrid for leisure, among them Aranjuez,

---

[1] Duke of Ficallo and Mayalde (1533–1606), he was the second son of St Francisco de Borja. On his life see García Mahíques, *Empresas morales*.
[2] They were given to the church of São Roque in 1588. For a list of the relics, see Carvalho 'Os recebimentos de relíquias em S. Roque', pp. 95–155, esp. pp. 151–4.
[3] d. 1609.
[4] Francisco de Melo (1520–88), second marquess of Ferreira and second count of Tentúgal.
[5] Henry III (r. 1574–89). On the French ambassador, see below p. 302 n. 3.

which is four leagues from Madrid, and is famously agreeable and elegant.[1] There is another place called the Pardo,[2] which is ideal for hunting, and the forest of Segovia is also excellent for hunting. In all of these are to be found many buildings of royal magnificence, many delights and opportunities for pleasure, and finally a marvellous variety of beasts for hunting. Above all other places, however, the one called Escorial is fixed in our minds, and for good reason, for it contains one of the most magnificent buildings in all Europe.[3] For the past twenty-four years King Philip has been devoting extraordinary efforts to building it, with two thousand men constantly at work on it, and with two hundred and eighty million sesterces having been spent on it.[4] The principal part of this work is a magnificent monastery of religious men of the order of St Jerome, which King Philip greatly favours. The church of this monastery is indeed magnificent, manifesting the royal splendour. In the vestibule of the church are six folding doors, three to the right and three to the left, each of them twenty-four palms in height, executed with remarkable craftsmanship in highly polished stone, and representing, almost to the life, six of the most ancient kings of the Old Testament, with Solomon, Josaphat, and Manasseh on this side, and David, Josias, and Ezechias on that. The size of the church is indeed extraordinary, for it includes forty chapels, all of them adorned with sacred pictures, beautifully painted. In the middle part of the church are two musical instruments, commonly called organs, one on the right and one on the left, impressively large and elegant, and there are two more set up in the choir. The choir, like the whole structure of the church, is constructed of stone cut to fit and excellently finished, and in it there are, for those who sing the divine prayers, seventy-six seats fashioned with the most consummate skill.

This church is also enriched by an almost infinite number of relics of the saints, and there is a special chapel for these next to the entrance to the church. There are in particular twenty-four heads of the holy virgins, nine thorns from the crown which was fixed on the sacred head of Christ the Lord, and whole arms of many saints, all of these most beautifully enclosed and preserved in silver and gold. There are besides eleven chests of the same material filled with the bones and other relics of the saints. And what can I say of the sacred furnishings, the gold and silver chalices, and of the revenues of this monastery, which are estimated at fifty thousand ducats? There is also another room in

---

[1] The Palacio Real de Aranjuez, started by Philip II using the architects of the Escorial, Juan Bautista de Toledo and Juan de Herrera, and completed during the reign of Ferdinand VI.

[2] The Palacio Real de El Pardo, originally a royal hunting lodge and in modern times the residence of Francisco Franco. It is now used to accommodate visiting heads of state.

[3] Known as San Lorenzo de El Escorial, named after Philip's victory over the French at St Quentin on 10 August 1557 (St Lawrence's day), the Escorial was modelled on Solomon's Temple of the Mount in Jerusalem. The palace/monastery was a powerful metaphor of Philip's majesty and of his self-image as a new Solomon. The cornerstone was laid on 23 April 1563 and the building completed on 13 September 1584. Jerónimo de Sepúlveda called it 'the eighth wonder of the world' (Sepúlveda, 'Sucesos', p. 490). On the Escorial as a projection of Philip's majesty, see Lazure, 'Perceptions of the Temple', pp. 165–73. For a detailed description of the Escorial, see Quevedo, *Historia*, pp. 263–349.

[4] I.e. 7 million ducats. The building costs from 4 April 1562 until the end of 1601 were calculated by Fray José de Sigüenza in 1602 and are printed in Kubler, *Building the Escorial*, app. 5. Sigüenza gives a total of 5,701,955 ducats (ibid., pp. 147, 153), but there are discrepancies in his calculations, and also in Kubler's (ibid., pp. 146, 152) which, when corrected, produce a figure of 6,101,956 ducats, 82 *maravedís*, almost 170,000 ducats per annum.

the same monastery where, in addition to the ordinary furnishings, there are other items of extraordinary value, and many relics of saints, among them one of the six water jars of which the water was turned into wine by Christ, as is recorded in the sacred scriptures.[1] That same place is decorated with more than sixty sacred pictures, in which many mysteries pertaining to the life of Christ are exactly depicted, and with other images which show the Blessed Virgin, the apostles, various saints, and many popes, cardinals, and other distinguished men. No less remarkable is a certain book, in which are contained the prayers usually recited in the sacred ceremonies. The letters in it are written by hand, but with such skill and artifice, in such a variety of gold and colours, with the outside of it covered and adorned with gold and silver, together with most brilliant pearls, that the value of this book is almost beyond calculation. There are besides, as well as many other vestments, two sets of sacred vestments for the priest and the deacon and sub-deacon who officiate with him at Mass, the one set of red silk with gold embroidery, inlaid with many pearls small and large, so that it is extraordinarily valuable; the other woven in such a way, with gold embossing, that its value can be no less.

With regard to the fabric of the monastery, that is also most magnificent and, except for the part designated for royal habitation, is square in shape. Within this quadrangular space there are fourteen courtyards or cloisters, two of them very large, the others of smaller size, all of them graced with various fountains playing most agreeably. It is a strikingly tall building, for it is six storeys high, with an elevation of twenty and in some places even of thirty palms from one storey to the next. The whole is girt about with nine most lofty towers, the roofs of which are adorned with globes of gilded bronze, each of them large enough for eight or even ten men to sit in it. One of these towers contains forty-two bells of various sizes, and these, when set in motion with the hands and the feet, give out a most sweet sound in multiple harmony. The number of rooms in the whole residence of the Escorial is so large as to be almost incredible. Many say that there are eleven thousand doors and windows, and from this, with a very simple calculation, one can work out how many rooms there are. The same monastery boasts a very fine double library, one part of which contains books concerned with various arts and languages, beautifully and expensively bound, and the other part books to do with the art of music, and these books are many and of unusual size, adorned with wonderful colouring and with gold; and the value of this library is put at fifty thousand ducats.[2] The part of that residence which is exclusively royal is of a striking magnificence, not only in the palace building itself and its beauty, but also in the number of most delightful gardens and of fountains from which admirable art has water constantly flowing, and the hunting enclosures replete with a multitude of wild beasts. The superior of the monastery, whom they call the prior,[3] received us with the utmost kindness, for the king, in letters given to us and sent to him, had indicated that he would be most gratified if the prior would make

---

[1] According to Quevedo, there were 7,422 relics in the Escorial (*Historia*, p. 233). The heads of the holy virgins were from among Ursula's 11,000.

[2] The curator of the library was Benito Arias Montano (1527–98), biblical scholar and humanist, editor-in-chief of the Antwerp polyglot bible *Biblia sacra, hebraice chaldaice, graece et latine*, 8 vols, Antwerp, 1569–73. He was appointed in 1576, remaining in the post for ten years. He was no friend of the Jesuits. See Rekers, *Benito Arias Montano*, pp. 9, 105–17; Cárcel, 'Las relaciones de la monarquía de Felipe II', pp. 233–4. For a description of the library, see Quevedo, *Historia*, pp. 328–37.

[3] Miguel de la Alaejos, the fifth prior.

sure that we experienced his unstinting hospitality in every way. He set about doing so with all diligence, showing us all the most pleasing features of the whole place, which I have just summarized for you.

Leo: When I heard you in previous colloquia giving an account of the expense incurred by the Europeans, and speaking of so many thousands of ducats, I couldn't help thinking that this was something unbelievable, but now, when you have listed one by one these works which you saw with your own eyes, all doubt is plucked from my mind, since these works would appear to require just as much gold and silver as the sum you mentioned earlier.

Michael: Marvellous indeed are the European works, and their cost, and it is not only you who marvel as you hear about them now; we too found them a marvel when we beheld them then. But I shall mention besides two further things which we saw in that same place, which showed a marvellous elegance and ingenuity. The first was a work made of glass, five palms high and three wide, and so cunningly constructed that it provided an almost infinite number of reflections. The other was a square work of wonderful writing which formed a cross with four equal arms, with the letters written in such a way that the component members of that square narrowed towards the centre, in the form of a pyramid; but the arrangement of the letters was so ingenious that whether you went from each of the arms towards the centre part, or from the centre out towards the arms, or finally right across the centre, you found the same order of letters and the same sense in the words. But enough! We don't have time to go into detail about anything else.[1] Let us return now to Madrid, and after taking our leave of the religious of that most celebrated monastery and of the prior we did indeed go back to Madrid, where there were many things which we had yet to see.

After our return, then, we saw first a royal stable and then a royal armoury, both of them in the same building, with the horses in the lower part, and the upper storey given over to arms.[2] This royal stable had, besides other things, seventy specially selected horses, some specially trained in the art of jumping, others for racing; some outstanding for their fighting power, others for their bodily form and singular beauty in walking; all of them standing out for their size, some of them especially so; all of them, finally,

---

[1] The visit to the Escorial lasted two days. Fróis incorporates a description of the building and of their activities in Madrid after their return said to be written by the boys themselves (Fróis, *Première ambassade*, pp. 99–106). The description notes that in the library there were books in many languages, including Chinese, but nothing in Japanese. As a result, the party left a short testimonial of their visit written in Japanese on Japanese paper saying that they had come from Japan to see 'the things of Europe' and had been sent to see the Escorial by Philip and that they were amazed and happy to view such a magnificent and marvellous building the sight of which had made their hazardous journey from Japan worthwhile. See ibid., p. 104; San Jerónimo, *Memorias*, pp. 395–6; Cooper, *Japanese Mission*, pp. 67–8. According to Sepúlveda, Mesquita was quizzed by his and the boys' hosts about Japan and whether there were such magnificent buildings there. He said there were not and added that even if the Japanese wished to build one, the materials would have to brought from afar (presumably to Kyoto) and that even if this were not the case he thought they would be unable to construct anything similar anyway. Mesquita was also asked about the Japan mission. He attributed the lack of progress there to the fact that the Japanese were a cruel and bellicose people who did not enjoy a day of peace and that those who are not Christian attack those who are (Sepúlveda, 'Sucesos', pp. 497–9)

[2] The armoury, including a number of the pieces described here, is housed in the royal palace.

brought from various provinces and chosen from the flower and breeding of the noblest of horses. With regard to the armoury which, as we said, is of the same size as the stable, it was completely full of very beautiful armaments, and right at the entrance, for the eternal memory of all, were placed the arms, pertaining both to the defence of the body and the attack on the enemy, used by the Emperor Charles V, father of King Philip, a man most celebrated among the Europeans for his military glory, whose memory is preserved by the present generation, nor will it be forgotten in all the years to come. There were besides, placed all over the armoury, fifteen cabinets containing different kinds of arms for the protection of the body. The space between each cabinet and the next was full of various kinds of offensive weapons, such as spears, swords, double-edged axes, muskets, crossbows, bows. Other armaments, specially suited to horsemen, were also set out in excellent order above the cabinets, and there too were three most precious spears sent by King Sebastião of Portugal as a present to King Philip, and another notable spear, connected with two muskets in such a way that when the spear is thrown balls are also fired from the musket. At the far end of this armoury there were six wooden horses with sheets of copper round them in the form of armour. All in all, this armoury is notable for many reasons, and although in the size of the place and the multitude of arms it does not equal the Lisbon one, it nevertheless deserves to be numbered among the most magnificent of armouries.

We saw also the royal storehouse, with four separate rooms. In the first of them there were contained in twenty great chests all the things to do with the sacred vestments and the equipment and ornamentation for divine worship, all of them of such magnificence and price that whenever the royal chapel is adorned with them it merits comparison with the most celebrated churches. In the second chamber are kept all the royal jewels, diamonds, beryls, emeralds, sapphires, and other gems of this kind, which are so valuable, as I said before, that there are some reckoned to be worth twenty thousand ducats, and others thirty, forty, and fifty thousand. All these precious stones, together with the pearls kept there, constitute a treasure of the utmost opulence. There were almost forty other chests there holding all the gold and silver plate for the royal table.

In the same place we saw, as it were, relics preserved from the ancient treasure of the Portuguese kings, that most precious equestrian apparatus which King Sebastião ordered to be made for himself in India, and which is reckoned to be worth five hundred thousand ducats. There were almost sixty standards hanging all around over this room, and their appearance provided an effect of extraordinary grace and gaiety. In the third room there were many other items of gold and silver, hidden there as in a treasury. They were all shown to us one by one, but I can't give a detailed account of them. Among them, however, was a special box in which was enclosed an arm of St James the Apostle, patron of all Spain and held in the highest honour by the Spaniards.[1] There is also another box containing a garment of the Blessed Virgin between two pieces, of a considerable size, of the cross to which Christ the Lord was fastened. On each of these boxes there was a cross with the image of Christ depicted on it, a cross half a palm in size, which the tradition tells us was cut out and carved by St Jerome, one of the doctors of the Church, from the very wood of the Holy Cross. Underneath was placed one of the sacred nails with which Christ the

---

[1] St James was martyred in Judea in 44 CE. According to tradition he preached the gospel in Spain and, allegedly, his relics lie in the cathedral of Santiago de Compostela.

Lord was fastened to the Cross, and all the surrounding parts were adorned with precious stones and pearls.

The last room which we saw is the king's private treasury, with six huge chests containing coins, and each said to hold four hundred thousand ducats. Besides these we saw a further six boxes, holding a very great sum of marked gold, and these are kept untouched against any grave necessity. These are the things which seemed to me to need saying about the wealth of King Philip, and it is hardly possible for anyone who has not seen with his own eyes the riches at his disposal to understand or calculate their price or value. There were other things which we were very glad to see in that same royal court, but they were so many that I can't list them all, for fear that you might find yourselves bored with the length of my narration. Let me add, however, that in that same place we saw two animals of, as it were, a prodigious nature, namely an elephant and a rhinoceros, which have been brought from India to Portugal and thence to Madrid, and which are kept there because of their enormous bulk of body and extraordinary shape, so that all can view them as sort of prodigies of nature.[1]

Lino: When we hear you giving an account of these things they cannot but arouse in our minds a certain degree of envy and a desire to emulate you, when we see you come back to our own country imbued with knowledge of so many things.

Michael: You will see the flames of that envy which you feel flare up daily more and more whenever you appreciate, as we proceed with the colloquia, that more things, and things more wonderful, are being set before you. We stayed thirty-seven days in Madrid,[2] both because of the many and various things which were to be seen there, and because of the grave and dangerous illness with which Martin was afflicted, and from which he recovered, after he had been suffering from it and had been in danger for twenty days, having had the best, in fact the royal doctors in attendance, and having been cared for by the fathers of the Society, whose guests we were.[3] On the last day we spent in Madrid, which was 25 November, the feast of St Catherine, we were very happy to see the king, attended by many nobles and notables, coming to the college of the Society, and we understood that we should regard this as a great favour to us, that the king with his royal train should seek out the place where we were, and from which we would be leaving the following day.

Having received presents from the royal bounty, then, among them seven hundred ducats to cover the expenses of the journey, with a coach, and a carriage to transport the baggage, we left Madrid, and the king sent various letters commending us both to the authorities in the maritime ports and to the Count of Olivares, his ambassador in

---

[1] For another description of the elephant and its trainer, and of the rhinoceros which was described as 'melancholy and sad' and ungrateful to the humans caring for it, see San Jerónimo, *Memorias*, pp. 368–9. Blinded and with its horn sawn off, the rhinoceros long remained a tourist attraction (Lach, *Asia in the Making of Europe*, II: 1, p. 169).

[2] 20 October–26 November.

[3] Martin's illness included bouts of high fever which the royal physicians attempted to cure with various remedies including the standard procedure phlebotomy. In a letter to Aquaviva, the Jesuit provincial described Martin's condition as 'grave and dangerous', but he made a full recovery. See Boncompagni-Ludovisi, *Le prime due ambasciate*, p. 1; Fróis, *Première ambassade*, pp. 73–4.

Rome.[1] On the same day we reached Alcalá,[2] a town which is very famous in Spain for its fine university, which cultivates all the good arts, and which was founded there by Francisco Jiménez, cardinal and archbishop of Toledo,[3] who for that and many other reasons is most worthy to be remembered for ever. The number of students who come together there to study the arts comes to four thousand, and for the same reason there is also a large college of the fathers of the Society, where a hundred of the Society live. They were not expecting us to come that day, because it was raining very heavily. Nevertheless, a very large crowd of men gathered at the college of the Society, among them the rector of the whole university, a man outstanding for his nobility and his rank.

The next day there were disputations in the school of theology of the college, with many very important men present, among them Iñigo de Mendoza, son of the marquess of Mondejar, one of the most important of the nobles of Spain.[4] The day after that we were invited to another literary ceremony being performed in the university, in which a certain philosopher was to be presented with the insignia of master of that art. There was a very great concourse of people there, and when we had made our way there the rector of the university, with the doctors and masters of the college and their associates, came out to the doors to meet and receive us, this being an honour accorded only to great princes by the professors of the university. He took us first, with the accompaniment of most sweet singing in harmony, to the church and to see the relics of the saints; then to the library, which it was a great pleasure to see, on account of the large number and excellent arrangement of the books. Finally we proceeded to the theatre, where it was no mean spectacle for us to see the doctors, masters, and graduates placed in order and in their designated positions, and surrounded by the multitude of students adorned with all their decorations. The chancellor then gave an oration, in the course of which he moved to speaking of us, as we sat there in the seat of honour, proper to princes, with such power of eloquence and such an effect on the emotions, especially when treating of things Japanese and of the propagation of the Christian republic, that he not only wept himself but also brought many of his audience to tears. After the oration the candidate was invested with the insignia, and presents were distributed among the doctors, masters, and graduates. Nor were we excluded from this generosity, but were most kindly presented with most elegant

---

[1] Don Enrique de Guzmán (1540–1607), second count of Olivares, Spanish ambassador to Rome 1582–91, father of Gaspar de Guzmán, third duke of Olivares (1587–1645), Philip IV's first minister. For Philip's letters, see Fróis, *Première ambassade*, pp. 109–10. Philip also provided the boys with a royal passport (ibid., p. 108). For further details of the journey from Madrid to Alicante, see ibid., chs 12 and 13.

[2] Or Alcalá de Henares.

[3] Francisco Cardinal Jiménez de Cisneros (1436–1517), archbishop of Toledo from 1495, and one of the most important statesmen in Spanish history. Cisneros founded the university at Alcalá in 1499 and it became the centre of humanist studies in Spain. Loyola studied there in 1526 until the summer of 1527, as did two of his companions, Diego Laínez and Alfonso Salmerón (O'Malley, *First Jesuits*, pp. 27–8, 30–31). The university was removed to Madrid in 1836 and is now known as the Complutense University (Complutum being the Latin name for Alcalá). The present university in Alcalá dates from 1977. Amongst other things, Cisneros advocated a policy of forced conversions of the Moriscos and crusades in North Africa. He was also responsible for initiating the project which resulted in the publication of the trilingual Complutensian Bible in 1517. During his stay in Alcalá, Loyola was accused of heresy, immoral conduct with women and Judaizing, and spent time in prison. Any mention of these processes is excised from one of the manuscript versions of Loyola's autobiography, as it is from *De Missione*. See Munitiz and Endean, *Saint Ignatius of Loyola*, pp. 40–44.

[4] Iñigo Lopez de Mendoza, named after his father, the third marquess of Mondéjar.

gloves, offered to us on a silver salver, in a token of love not normally given by the professors except to those of noble family. We also visited the church dedicated to the most celebrated martyrs Justus and Pastor, which is very fine and splendidly decorated.[1] There we were most generously treated by the distinguished canons who are the priests of that church, and were shown various things which we were very glad to see.

In the end, after three days spent most happily in that town, we left it on the 29 November and on 1 December came to Villarejo, a town seventeen leagues distant from Alcalá. There too there is a college of the Society, where seventy fathers and brothers live, and having lodged very comfortably there we headed for Belmonte, another town, which is four leagues further on. In that town also there is a college of the Society,[2] and the foundress of that college, the illustrious lady Francisca de León,[3] sent the steward of her household with her carriage to meet us. After him came the mayor of the town, with many horsemen, and the prior of the cathedral with the canons, to say nothing of the innumerable multitude of other people who hastened out to meet us as we approached. At our entrance there was a tremendous noise of many guns firing, and many fireworks made of paper and powdered sulphur were set off, particularly in the college itself, where, after a speech and a musical performance, we were welcomed in the cloister with a display of multiple pyrotechnics, notably two very skilfully fashioned, one of them representing a trireme propelled by many oars, the other a sea beast attacking it, and the clash between the two presenting a remarkable picture of a battle. Though we were anxious to go on without delay, we were detained for two days in this town, where we were most kindly received by the illustrious lady Francisca de León, whom we visited, and most generously treated; and we were really delighted by the students, who put on a performance representing our expedition, at which we were exposed for the first time to the charm, beauty, wit, and humour of European theatre.

From here we departed for Murcia, a city forty leagues from Belmonte, and we entered it six days later, on 10 December. The mayor of the city knew from a letter which he had received from the king that we would be coming, and as well as ordering a splendid meal to be ready for us in a nearby village called Torrespinaldo, he came out to meet us with a hundred and fifty horsemen, together with canons and distinguished men of ecclesiastical rank, and the people turned out in great numbers, so that not only the road but the windows and even the roofs were full of them. Our coming was celebrated not only with trumpets and fifes and other musical instruments, but also with ringing of the bells of the churches themselves, and with the acclamation of all the people. In Murcia there is a college of the Society, which provided us with ideal accommodation, for the building and structure are such that it seems that it can stand comparison with the principal residences of the fathers in Spain.[4] It has a very impressive church, sacred pictures most ably painted,

---

[1] Catedral de los Santos Niños Justo y Pastor de Alcalá de Henares The saints were martyred at Alcalá around 304 CE and are the patron saints of Alcalá de Henares.

[2] The rector at the time was Luis de Guzman whose two-volume history of the Jesuits in Asia (Guzman, *Historia*) provides some additional details about the boys' travels, although in general his account of their mission is based largely on Fróis. See also Cooper, *Japanese Mission*, p. 72.

[3] Francisca Ponce de León. The college was founded in 1558 and was endowed in 1582 by Doña Francisca (Nalle, *God in La Mancha*, pp. 87–8).

[4] San Esteban, built between 1555 and 1582, the third Jesuit establishment in Spain, now houses the government of Murcia (Selfa, *La primera embajada*, p. 105).

and also delightful gardens, no less delightful than the gardens of the city itself. After we had spent two days in meetings here and there with the principal men of that city, we withdrew to a villa belonging to the fathers, and there we had time to ourselves, and were able to recover from the fatigue of the journey. We also wrote letters to be sent shortly to Portugal, and thence to India and Japan. On the vigil of the day on which Christ the Lord was born we returned to the city to spend the solemn following day with the fathers, and finally, after the day dedicated to the Holy Innocents, we went to various churches and famous places in the city, and in particular to the cathedral, which in its form and in the structure of the building seems similar to the cathedral of Toledo.[1]

Leo: I find it very surprising that you foreigners were received in all those various towns and cities with such gladness and acclamation.

Michael: You must bear in mind, dearest Leo, that the Europeans are most zealous in their cultivation of Christian charity and of good manners, and were also aware of many things about our journey: firstly of the princes by whom we were sent, then of King Philip, who had written to commend us to them, and finally of the fathers of the Society, who are held in the highest esteem by all the Europeans. But you will learn much more about this as we go on with our story. On 1 January, the feast of the circumcision of the Lord, we had an invitation from the leading men of the city, who asked if we would care to be present at the equestrian game of the reeds. Since there was the same dexterity with the horses, the same agility from the horses, and in everything they did the same skill which I described for you in an earlier colloquium, I think I may refrain from spending further words recording it again.

After spending twenty-three days in Murcia, waiting for news about the voyage to Italy, on 3 January 1585 we moved on from there to another city called Orihuela, and there we were similarly received into the city with horsemen coming out to meet us, with a variety of musical instruments, and with crowds of people. There is no college of the Society here, but we stayed in the monastery of the religious of the order of St Dominic,[2] and at night very much enjoyed watching an equestrian game in which riders with torches in their hands vie with each other in galloping hither and thither, making the night at once joyful and solemn. On the following day we made for another town called Elche, and there again many horsemen came out to meet us, and they accompanied us, fifty or even more of them, bearing lighted candles, to the house of Bernardo Perpinhão, a noble and distinguished man, who is the brother of Father Luís Perpinhão,[3] who was with us from Portugal to Madrid, and at his house we were given splendid and sumptuous hospitality. I say nothing of the great number of cannons and muskets which were discharged to celebrate our arrival in this town, nor of the tremendous noise which resulted.[4]

---

[1] The Iglesia Catedral de Santa María en Murcia.

[2] The Convento de Santo Domingo which later became a university and remained so until it was suppressed in 1824. Ironically, the convent then became a Jesuit boarding school.

[3] Luís Perpinhão, a native of Elche, was a renowned humanist who accompanied the boys from Lisbon to Madrid. They would meet him again at Coimbra on their return from Rome (Fróis, *Première ambassade*, pp. 39, 83, 258). Luís appears to have been a kinsman of Bernardo rather than his brother (Selfa, *La primera embajada*, pp. 91–2).

[4] The cost of these displays, as noted in an official record, was borne by the town (Selfa, *La primera embajada*,, p. 92.

On the following day we came at last to the port of Alo or Alicante, on the Mediterranean Sea, where our advent was similarly celebrated with horsemen coming out to meet us to the sound of cannon, trumpet, and fife. King Philip had sent instructions to the governor and the prefect of this city about provisions for our journey to Rome, and that they should see that we were abundantly supplied with everything necessary, and they followed his instructions with all diligence. They had accordingly prepared magnificent and most suitable quarters for us in a very stout ship bound for Italy, with a generous supply of provisions sufficient for a very long voyage.[1] For that reason, and because of the kindness with which they treated us throughout the time that we stayed there, we felt ourselves greatly obliged to them.[2] But since we now have to give an account of our voyage, let us leave off now for a day, and take up the story again tomorrow night.

---

[1] Fróis (*Première ambassade*, p. 123) says the ship was 'de sinco mil, e tantas toneladas' or more than 5,000 *toneladas* with 34 pieces of artillery. This is clearly a mistake, deliberate or not. A Spanish galleon of 550 *toneladas* was above average and galleons carried between 20 and 24 cannon. Portuguese *nau* of the *Carreira da Índia*, at this time, were supposed to be between 300 and 450 tons and, according to an order of 1604, were supposed to have at least 28 cannon, a number they failed to reach. See Pérez-Mallaína, *Spain's Men of the Sea*, p. 134; Phillips, *Six Galleons*, pp. 228–9; Boxer, 'The Carreira da Índia', pp. 35–6; Godinho, *A Carreira da Índia*, p. 49.

[2] During their stay in Alicante the boys wrote letters of thanks to the various Jesuit institutions which had hosted them and to the prominent individuals who had entertained them. Each received letters from the archbishop of Évora, expressing his love for them and urging them to return quickly from Rome for it was desirable that they should not delay their return to Japan (Fróis, *Première ambassade*, pp. 123–4).

COLLOQUIUM XX

The voyage from Spain to Italy, the visit to the grand duke of Tuscany, and things noted in Pisa and Florence

Lino: We meet today with a keener anticipation than usual, to hear you speak of your voyage to Italy and your landing in that province, whose renown you have so often mentioned.

Michael: That anticipation is certainly neither vain nor misplaced, as you will appreciate when you come to have a full understanding of the things of Italy which I am going to recount for you. So we left Alicante after fourteen days and put out to sea on 18 January, but the wind being against us we came back twice to that same port, and then set sail again on 7 February. We had to contend with waves and adverse winds for some days, but in the end we were borne to the Balearic Islands, and reached the port of Alcudia in Mallorca, one of those islands. The governor of the city, learning of our arrival, came to visit us, and on the Sunday, when we left the ship in order to attend Mass, he accompanied us with four hundred soldiers armed with muskets, and ordered that our entry into the city be celebrated with musket and cannon fire, and afterwards he again attended us as we returned to the ship. Then the magistrates of another city in the interior, which is the capital,[1] were informed about this and they came on horseback to visit us, and four fathers of the Society came from the college in the same place, and they brought with them many things to eat and drink, to relieve the tedium for us. This island is of a considerable size, with thirty or more towns in addition to those two cities, besides the villages and minor castles, so that with us it could be regarded as a substantial kingdom.

The ship left that port on 19 February, and fulfilled our wishes by completing the voyage to Italy and landing at the port of Livorno on 1 March. And there is good reason to believe that it was because of the special providence of God that the winds were against us, for we learned afterwards that that delay most certainly saved us from the hands of Saracen pirates, who were there on the lookout with many triremes, so that, had we not been held back by that contrary wind, we would have been put under the yoke of wretched slavery.[2] I give thanks then unceasingly to God, and move on now to treat of matters Italian.

---

[1] Palma.

[2] This was no exaggeration as Barbary pirates, based in Tripoli and Algiers, were active and much feared in the Mediterranean at this time. Unmentioned are the equally fearful and ruthless activities of Christian pirates and privateers in the eastern Mediterranean. See Braudel, *Mediterranean*, II, pp. 865–91; Davis, *Christian Slaves, Muslim Masters*, *passim*.

Italy, then, is the most famous of all the provinces of Europe, and is situated in the middle of it, and almost surrounded by the two seas, the Tuscan and the Adriatic. Its principal adornment is the most illustrious city of Rome, formerly capital of the Roman Empire, and now permanent seat of the Supreme Pontiffs. Thus not only does the bishop of Rome himself hold the most extensive dominion there, but also the many rulers among whose jurisdictions Italy is divided recognize the Supreme Pontiff as their true lord, and pay an annual tribute to him. In Italy, besides those princes and rulers whom I have mentioned as having their own jurisdiction, and the papal states and the kingdom of Naples, there are three free and exempt republics, namely Venice, Genoa, and Lucca, and of these Venice stands out for its antiquity and its size.

Among the principal rulers of Italy must be numbered the duke of Tuscany,[1] to whose jurisdiction belongs that port where we landed. Because of the extent of his dominions, the number of cities and towns, and his resources of wealth and power, he could rightly be called a king, as indeed the lords of Tuscany once were. His annual income is more than forty million sesterces,[2] and his treasury contains, or so it is commonly said, eight hundred million sesterces,[3] and there is hardly any king that possesses such a sum of money, so that, even if not a king, he is at least called the Grand Duke.

Lino: From the riches of this duke alone we can readily appreciate how great is the wealth of the European kings.

Michael: It is scarcely possible for you, being so far away from it, to understand it, but by hearing about so many things you will at least grasp it to some extent. To return to the port, then; we had very suitable accommodation there, prepared for us by order of the grand duke. I'll say nothing of various things which we saw in that port, in particular the heavily armed fortress, and a remarkable bronze lamp, set in a very high tower constructed in the sea, with thirty wicks which shine far and wide in the night, and with all their light guide sailors to the port.[4] Instead I shall begin to speak of the benignity shown to us by this duke, who, by means of a knight of his own family who came to the port, urged us insistently to make for the city of Pisa, where he then was.[5] This is also a city of Tuscany, the second city after the metropolis which is called Florence. On the following day therefore, at the request of the duke, we set out for Pisa and reached it at lunch time, and we were received there by many nobles who came to meet us, and had most courteous

---

[1] At this time Francesco I de' Medici (1541–87), second grand duke of Tuscany. His daughter, Maria, married Henry IV of France. The Medici sought to maintain their interests by balancing them against those of other powers, the Habsburgs, the papacy and the French. The title 'grand duke' was granted by the papacy to Cosimo I de' Medici against the wishes of the Emperor Maximilian. The grant was a reminder that Spanish power and influence in Italy had its limits. See Levin, *Agents of Empire*, pp. 5, 89–93.

[2] I.e. 1 million ducats.

[3] I.e. 20 million ducats.

[4] The fortifications of the port of Livorno were designed by Bernardo Buontalenti who also designed several other architectural adornments to the city including the grotto in the Boboli Gardens. The lighthouse was built in 1304, destroyed in 1944 and rebuilt in 1956.

[5] The grand duke gave instructions for the boys to receive the same honours they had been accorded at the Spanish court. See Boncompagni-Ludovisi, *Le prime due ambasciate*, p. 4; Fróis, *Première ambassade*, p. 126; *Dai Nihon Shiryō*, XI: 1, p. 133.

visits first from the governor of the city, and then from Pietro de' Medici, brother of the duke.[1]

In the afternoon we ourselves went to the duke, conveyed in his carriages and honoured by being accompanied by a crowd of nobles and their servants. He received us most graciously, descending halfway down the staircase of his palace with his brother and others of the nobility, and expressing in words which did us great honour his satisfaction at our arrival, and then conducted us to the most illustrious princess his wife[2] who had many most noble young girls pressing round her. All were delighted with that gathering, what with the sweetness of the singing and harmony, with the varied talk on this side and that, and with their pleasure in seeing the Japanese clothes. It was our intention to head for Rome without delay, but the duke urged us to stay in Pisa for some days, and it would have been discourteous to refuse. Nor did these days pass without excellent entertainment, for we were invited once by the duke to go fowling. I have spoken already of this kind of recreation, so I shall say only that it was a very great pleasure for us to watch the ferocious struggle between the hawks and various other birds, and the not inconsiderable booty which they brought back. Back at the house we were invited to a solemn dance, and we found it quite remarkably enjoyable. The wife of the duke announced that it was to be held in her palace, and all the most noble young ladies of the family assembled there, dressed and adorned with the utmost elegance. The duke himself and an entourage of nobles took part, and we were seated next to him in a position of honour. The variety of the measures at that most lively dance was remarkable, for after the men and the women had danced together with gravity and grace they embarked on a kind of dance in which one man takes the lead, and invites to dance whatever woman he chooses, and then she is left on the floor and brings on the man of her choice, and with this interchange of persons the dance is of continuing interest. First of all, then, the brother of the duke, the leader in this dance, invited the duke's wife to dance, then she chose our Mancio, he chose another noble lady, and finally that lady chose me to be her partner.

Leo: I suppose it must have been a very embarrassing experience for you, since you were unaccustomed to it and had to perform before highly skilled experts.

Mancio: I was indeed troubled not a little by embarrassment at not knowing the procedure, and also by some natural timidity, given the respect in which I held such a great lady, but at an event so public I had to be bold, to summon all my courage and strength so as not to appear boorish. There is also some kind of similarity between the European style of dancing and our own, and that helped a good deal.

Martin: Mancio and Miguel were the first to face that ordeal, and that would have mitigated the embarrassment for us who came after, if Julian, who was the last to have to choose a partner, had not opted for a certain elderly woman who happened to be there among the spectators. It made everyone laugh when he chose her.

---

[1] 1554–1604, youngest child of the first duke, Cosimo, by his first wife, a spendthrift and rake who had recently returned from Spain to implore his brothers to cover his debts. He had murdered his wife, whom he accused of adultery, in 1576.

[2] Bianca Capello de' Medici (1548–87), Francesco's second wife. Both she and her husband died on the same day under mysterious circumstances.

Julian: What if I did it deliberately, so that the embarrassment of that poor old woman would go some way to covering my embarrassment, and in order to transfer the laughter of the spectators from me and my clumsiness to her, she being even less of a dancer than me?

Lino: That was very neatly done, then, getting her to take a share of your embarrassment, so that the spectators were presented with the boy, as you then were, on the one side, and the elderly lady on the other.[1]

Michael: That is indeed what happened. But let us move on now to other matters. In the days which followed we saw in that city various things well worth viewing, notably the cathedral, built at vast expense, and also the monastery of those known as the Knights of St Stephen.[2] For a better understanding of their purpose you must know that there are in Europe certain societies of knights, founded with the most prudent counsel of kings and princes, and dedicated to military matters, rather like those societies committed to divine worship. Most of these societies wear on their breasts the sign of the cross in different distinguishing colours. Some of them lead a celibate life, and the others, though they are married, nevertheless observe the rules of their order, and are at all times in a state of total readiness for war. And since the insignia of these societies are both very honourable and very profitable, for they have attached to them income of many thousands of ducats, all the most noble men aspire to obtain them. And for that reason they are constantly and vigorously engaged in military matters. These military societies are led either by the kings themselves or by others of the rulers of Europe, and they have the title of masters of these orders and hold the position of highest honour in them.

    Coming back then to the order of the Knights of St Stephen: it was the illustrious duke of Tuscany, father of the present duke, who founded it, and obtained for it from the pope the income of the highest of priesthoods, and confirmation of the whole order, and thus notably increased the wealth and renown of his state. So the duke, wishing to do everything possible for the gratification of us his guests, took us to the church of St Stephen on the first day of Lent, the day when it is the custom in Christendom, as a reminder of death, to have ashes set on your head. All those knights were assembled there, wearing their distinctive dress, to receive the blessed ashes according to the custom. The distinctive dress of these knights is a white garment down to the feet, with long sleeves which can be drawn back elegantly behind them, and with a long extended cloak making a most majestic impression. On the breast is embroidered an image of the cross, purple in colour, and their whole appearance in this dress provides a display both beautiful and solemn. For this ceremony, then, the duke was seated on a raised throne, and opposite him there was a chair assigned to each of us. Within the chancel, on both sides, eighty

---

[1] The Jesuit Francisco Rodrigues mentions the dance in his report to the rector of the Jesuit College in Madrid on the boys' journey. The report may well be the source of the account given here. See RAHM, MS 09-02663, f. 441r–v.

[2] The Sacro Militare Ordine di Santo Stefano Papa e Martire, founded by Cosimo de' Medici in 1561 to fight the Turks and pirates, although some of their activities were themselves piratical (Braudel, *Mediterranean*, II, pp. 877–9). They followed the Benedictine rule. Their church was Santo Stefano di Cavalieri, which contains banners captured from the Turks at Lepanto, and their headquarters the Palazzo della Carovana on the Piazza dei Cavalieri.

knights of that order occupied ornate seats. The remainder, a much larger number, were away in various places on military business. All of these, before the ceremony began, performed an act of solemn veneration of the duke as the master of their order, first genuflecting before the high altar, then bowing to us, then reverently kissing the hand of the duke himself. After that the sacred ashes were placed on the heads of all, of the duke first, then of us, then of the others who came forward to the holy altar and genuflected in supplication. Lastly there was Mass with solemn singing, which brought the whole ceremony to a conclusion.

This order of the Knights of St Stephen has four triremes, which keep the Tuscan or Tyrrhenian Sea, which would otherwise be infested with Turkish and Moorish pirates, safe and free of all danger. These ships are so fast and so well armed with everything necessary for battle that they are feared by many other enemy ships and triremes, and have often had notable victories over them, as is shown by the hundred and more standards seized from enemies and hung on the walls of the church as a reminder to posterity. The structure both of the church and of the house of this order is remarkable. We saw there many sacred relics, an extremely rich treasury, and an armoury crammed with every kind of weapon. I shan't give you a detailed description of them, because other similar ones have already been dealt with more than once, so you already know about them. I find it difficult to describe the honours which this grand duke and his wife accorded us throughout the time we stayed in Pisa. He appointed most noble boys and men from his palace and his family to look after us, and treated us with the utmost generosity, demonstrating towards us such benignity that we really ought to acknowledge and pay tribute to it for the remainder of our lives. When it was time for us to travel to Florence, as he himself urged us to do, he sent us men to take care of all our needs and to show us in detail everything delightful in Florence.

We took our leave, then, of the grand duke, his wife, and his brothers, departed from Pisa, and made our way to Florence, the chief city and capital of all Tuscany,[1] deservedly and for many reasons numbered among the most famous cities in the whole of Europe. The river Arno flows through it, irrigating it and making it most agreeable, and there are four very beautiful bridges, made of brick and stone, so that it is very easy to cross the river. The streets are so straight, broad, and well paved, and graced with so many famous buildings, that it looks as if it had all been constructed and measured with the utmost precision, so that its claim to be the most beautiful of all Italian cities is justified. Its citizens are very wealthy, partly because of their most ample incomes, partly because of their most flourishing commerce. This city also has churches outstanding for their architecture and their size, and in beauty and fame it leaves nothing to be desired. Many horsemen from all the noble families came out to meet us as we reached the city, and we were accompanied by the servants of the grand duke from our first entry through the gates right up to his palace. Our intention had been to lodge with the fathers of the Society, but the duke insisted that we should go to his palace.

We rested briefly after the journey, and then visited the cardinal archbishop of Florence,[2] who received us most courteously, coming halfway down the staircase, and

---

[1] They left Pisa on 7 March and stayed in Florence until 13 March.
[2] Alessandro Ottaviano de' Medici (1535–1605), later the short-lived pope Leo XI (10–27 April 1605). The duke sent the cardinal a letter urging that the boys be treated with full honours (*Dai Nihon Shiryō*, XI: 1, p. 152).

among other gifts which he gave us as a token of his great love for us he presented us with an image of Christ crucified, beautifully carved from ivory. We also paid a visit to the nuncio or legate of the Supreme Pontiff. We were treated with the utmost kindness by both the archbishop and the nuncio,[1] and were then taken to view the principal places in the city in a great company of many most noble men, and especially of Virginio Orsini,[2] son of Paolo Giordano Orsini, the most illustrious duke of Bracciano, and nephew, by his mother,[3] of the grand duke.

If I were to list for you the notable buildings of this city it would take a very long time, for each of the houses in it is like a magnificent palace, and there is a very large number of public buildings both sacred and secular, among them about fifty parish churches, more than seventy convents of religious men and women, about thirty other pious institutes such as hostels, hospitals, and nurseries, nine colleges for boys, and I make no mention of the numerous other associations which there are. I'll say something, however, of the palace of the duke himself, which is such, and so well arranged, that is fully the equal of the royal palaces of the other European kings.[4]

To begin with it is situated in an extremely spacious setting, and has in front of it a most ingenious fountain,[5] a quite remarkable piece of work, the whole being square in shape and with representations of various figures constructed in marble and bronze. In the centre sits a giant, of enormous proportions, in stone, in a four-horse carriage, and the horses have their forelegs extended out over the water in such a way that it is as if they are trying to rear themselves away from that abyss. In each of the four sides of the pool there is a nymph made of bronze, with a satyr lying at her feet, and from various parts of the bodies of all of these statues water springs most delightfully, continuously filling the pool. Proceeding further towards the palace you come across two giants of polished stone, each of them supported by a pillar, who with clubs raised high threaten to kill two men, almost as large, who are prostrate at their feet.[6] After that there are two more statues, of a man and a woman looking at each other.[7] One is holding out a chain to the other, and sometimes, when required, this chain can be stretched across so as to block that whole entrance. In the entrance court of the palace are the duke's guards and also ten cannon

---

[1] The nuncio was Valerio da Corbara. He wrote three letters about the boys' stay in Florence. See Boncompagni-Ludovisi, *Le prime due ambasciate*, pp. 5–6; *Dai Nihon Shiryō*, XI: 1, pp. 153–6.

[2] 1572–1615.

[3] The original edition (p. 219) gives '*ex sorore nepote*'. This is a mistake for 'by his mother', who was Isabella de' Medici-Orsini (1542–76), daughter of Cosimo I de' Medici. On Paolo Giordano Orsini, see below, pp. 304, 330 n. 1.

[4] The Palazzo Pitti, bought by the Medici in 1550 and used as the official residence of the main branch of the Medici. The palace was connected to the Palazzo Vecchio, facing the Piazza della Signoria and now the town hall of Florence, by the Corridoio Vascariano in 1565.

[5] The Fountain of Neptune, by Bartolomeo Ammanati, commissioned by Cosimo in 1565 to commemorate Francesco's marriage to his first wife, Johanna von Habsburg of Austria, and intended to demonstrate Tuscan command of the sea. This paragraph closely resembles the account in Fróis, *Première ambassade*, p. 135.

[6] A not very accurate description of Hercules and Cacus by Bartolommeo (or Bachio) Bandinelli (1534), intended to symbolize the Medici vanquishing the republicans, and a refutation of Michelangelo's symbol of republican virtue, David (1504).

[7] Baucis and Philemon by Bandinelli, carved from a huge marble block originally allocated for Michelangelo's use, were intended to hold an iron chain. See Hare, *Florence*, p. 47. The description in Fróis, *Première ambassade* (p. 135), mentions statues of a man and an armless woman which the editors suggest was Judith and Holopherne by Donatello (c. 1460), moved to the piazza in 1495. This seems unlikely as Judith is beheading Holopherne.

mounted on their carriages, and various arms are hanging on the walls, ready for use by the watch and the guard. The vestibule or peristylium is supported on eight gilded columns, and from it you ascend to the great hall, so spacious, so high, and built with such art, that it struck us as very remarkable. It is eighty paces long and thirty wide, and is fifty cubits in height, but in addition on the ceiling, which has different sections, there are depicted most artistically, and presented with the utmost skill, in gold and various colours, stories to do with the Medici family. At the far end of the hall you go down seven steps to two sort of chapels in which there are, carved from marble of Paros, statues of two popes, namely Leo X and Clement VII,[1] both born of that same most illustrious Medici family. After this most famous great hall there are so many rooms and dwellings, adorned with pictures, statues, and most costly furnishings, that whoever sees them cannot but acknowledge in them a truly regal magnificence, and we experienced this not only in the way everything looked, but also in the splendidly ornate guest chambers.

The whole building is adorned with two extremely long porticos, one on either side of it, extending two hundred paces, constructed of polished stone, and these make it one of the busiest parts of the city. The walls of one of these porticos have, in their upper part, a hundred and fifty square mosaics in which are to be found the images of an equal number of emperors, kings, and rulers famous for their deeds; in the lower part there are various statues, each in its niche, ingeniously carved from marble, and many of the rooms are also adorned with statues in either marble of bronze, and show to great effect the admirable skill of the sculptors. Along the walls of the other portico there are set various trees, in large earthenware jars, with enough earth to allow them to put out roots and produce fruit, and at the far end of that portico there are hanging gardens, their construction an extraordinary achievement, which, though they really are elevated, are nevertheless most ingeniously irrigated by water flowing from fountains. As well as these two porticos there is also, leading off from one of them, a third and very long portico, which stretches for a quarter of a league, and is the way to a delightful garden known as the Pitti garden,[2] to which the duke of Florence is accustomed frequently to repair in order to refresh his spirit, and it would mean a long speech indeed if I were to give an account of each of the pleasures of this most beautifully tended garden.

The structure of the residence is truly magnificent, rising to an impressive height with many storeys. It is notable for its many and various statues, is embellished with doors, entrances, and other similar places made of porphyry or ophite, and is filled with extraordinary, indeed regal furniture. I say nothing of the gold and silver objects, nor of the items of clothing in silk, velvet, and embroidery, but the twenty-four draperies which cover the duke's pack horses when he travels, woven with the same gold and other embroidery and finely engraved with his insignia, were certainly a joy to behold. I make no mention either of the beautifully fashioned beds and their coverings, of the priceless chairs, the tables, the tapestries, for the outstandingly fine collection which that house had of all these things contributed not a little to its splendour. I pass over besides the delights of the garden sown with innumerable trees and its multitude of copious fountains, as I shall soon be speaking of similar matters.

[1] Giovanni de' Medici (1475–1521), second son of Lorenzo the Magnificent, Leo X from 1513; Giulio de' Medici (1478–1534), son of Giuliani de' Medici, brother of Lorenzo the Magnificent, Clement VII from 1523.
[2] The Boboli Gardens.

Mancio: There is one point which we would like you to appreciate, namely that although Michael here is doing his best to match his words to the greatness of European things, he does not entirely succeed, so you have to take all the things he is saying as imperfect indications and not as a perfect representation of the magnificence of Europe.

Leo: What you say makes us even more amazed, for if we are so astonished at hearing what you say are imperfect indications, how would it be if we could take in with our own eyes and minds the European things themselves in all their splendour and magnificence. The things which Michael describes for us are so great, so rich, so brilliant, that when we hear him speaking of the fabric of some palace or temple it seems to us that nothing can be added to its value or its beauty; but when, not much later, he portrays another one in words as if he was painting it with a brush, and setting it before our eyes, the earlier one seems to yield to the later, and the same thing happens whenever he describes the pleasures of gardens, the delights of villas in the country, and the beauty and elegance of other things of this kind.

Lino: From what you have said, Michael, I gather that the wealth of the Europeans is very great indeed, and that there exist things much too great for you to relate or us to grasp.

Michael: That is the plain truth, for we are unable to express in speech the image of European things which we have graven on our minds. For you yourselves to conceive of it you would have to have the things present to you, if that were possible, so as to be able to exercise your senses on them. But since our narration has made a start to supplying what is missing because of the immense distance involved, let us proceed to the many other things which remain, and which you will hear the more eagerly and gladly if we interpose a day's rest as usual.

Leo: Your suggestion of rest is timely, and I assure you it will be the sweeter because we know from you that we can look forward to hearing new things.

COLLOQUIUM XXI

Of the delights and pleasures of the Pratolino villa of the duke of Tuscany, and of things observed at Siena, Viterbo, and on the remainder of the journey to Rome

Michael: Of this colloquium also, which you have joined so eagerly, matters concerning the Grand Duke of Tuscany must take up a good part, since it is not possible to do justice in one colloquium to the regal magnificence of his wealth and resources. Today, therefore, I shall continue first with the time we spent in the country at a remarkable villa, known as the Pratolino,[1] of the same duke, then with other things which we saw in Florence when we had returned there, and finally I'll deal with our journey all the way to Rome. Well then, among other very famous places most suitable for recreation and relaxation which the duke has there is that villa which I referred to as the Pratolino, which is rightly regarded as superior to the other places dedicated to enjoyment in its delights, its artistry, and its amenities of all kinds. The villa is on a particularly pleasing site, one league from Florence, and possesses in great abundance everything to delight the senses. It has, to begin with, two palaces, one standing in a higher place, the other in a lower, the first designated mainly as comfortable accommodation for guests, the second built mainly for various delights and pleasures of the body. The former is of a great height, five storeys high in fact, and on each floor fourteen rooms can be seen, so lavish in the decor, and furnished in such a way, so nobly, that nothing more sumptuous can be found even in the richest of royal palaces. The ceiling panels are decorated with various paintings done in gold and in diverse colours, and the walls are adorned with most artistically woven tapestries and hangings. On some of these various images of men and various stories from history are depicted; on others all kinds of animals, trees, forests, and other similar things are represented. This residence is further enhanced by couches arranged in every place, with coverings and other accoutrements, in gold, silk, velvet and linen, which I can scarcely find words to describe.

Lino: I marvel when I consider what must be the value of such a variety of furnishings, and I find it hard to see from where such a quantity of gold and silver can have come.

---

[1] The Pratolino Villa and gardens, built between 1568 and 1586 by Francesco for his mistress and future wife, Bianca, and designed by Bernardo Buontalenti, were demolished in the early 19th century. For descriptions of the garden, see Smith, 'Pratolino', and, comprehensively, Brunon, 'Pratolino'. Montaigne gives a, briefer, description of the villa, grotto, fountains and aviary, where he spent two or three hours, all of which impressed him (Montaigne, *Journal de voyage*, pp. 175–7). The boys' enchantment with the garden was mentioned by their chaperon for the day, Raffaello de' Medici (Brown, 'Courtiers and Christians', p. 895).

Michael: My companions who are here are my witnesses that in speaking of the richness of European furnishings I am not in any way exaggerating, and you will get a good idea of the expense and the splendour from my description of the other palace. The palace which is on the lower level, as I said, is entirely equipped for recreation for the spirit and pleasure for the body, especially in the summer, when the excessive heat is not merely tempered but totally cancelled out by the continuous and multiple flow of bubbling waters. You find there water flowing delightfully from every side from such a number of fountains, springing out in such abundance, that nowhere are you troubled by the heat, and there is every occasion for well-being and delectation. When you enter a certain hall, excellently lined with bricks, scarcely have you put foot to floor when you find yourself surrounded on all sides by, so to speak, lancing jets of water coming at you from many different outlets. If you try to seek refuge and protection in some corner, and indeed there are various nooks and crannies there, you will straight away find yourself tricked and deceived, ambushed, as it were, by the outlets discharging the water. If, however, you flee from this refuge to another house which at first sight seems safer, you will be assaulted by a rain which falls with the greatest force as if from the heavens, leaving no place where you can escape the force of the water; and some find it so slippery, and the force of the water so strong, that when it suddenly strikes them on the chest they are forced to the ground or spun round in a most entertaining way.

Leo: That house can indeed be called a house of pleasure; but I don't see how the water can be produced so easily, since elsewhere it is necessary to keep it stored under lock and key, as it were, to stop it from flowing all over the place.

Michael: The whole artifice of the thing consists in precisely the point you are asking about, for the stoppers or covers which keep the water in are so simple, and yet so cleverly constructed that they open at the slightest foot pressure, and the water flows out to the various places. But come, let us move on to describe the other fountains at this villa, and the artifice which has water gushing from them. They are made of steel or of very highly polished stone, and present such a variety of figures to the observer that anyone seeing them might think he was watching a performance on the stage or in the theatre. To take some of the more ingeniously contrived of these spectacles, there is, first, at one of these fountains a wide pond, and at the far end of it a large receptacle with folding doors and another door above them. When the water is released a Triton, formerly known as Neptune's trumpeter, suddenly appears, blows on his trumpet or bugle with puffed out cheeks, and produces a loud sound. At this sound the folding doors open wide and a goddess called Galatea, formerly regarded by the pagans as the goddess of the sea, comes forth into the pond mounted on the back of a sea beast, and as she comes forward into view other doors open on either side and two sea nymphs come out and accompany her as if they were ladies in waiting. In their company she proceeds round the pond, studying what is going on in it as if it were her kingdom. Then she retraces her steps and goes back little by little into her house; the nymphs also return to their boxes, the gates close, and the spectacle is at an end.[1]

---

[1] A remarkably similar description of this grotto appears in Francesco de'Vieri's famous description of the gardens, *Delle marauigliose opere di Pratolino* (Florence, 1586), quoted in Smith, 'Pratolino', p. 158.

Lino: What seems particularly remarkable to me is this: those statues have no motion whatever of their own, so I find it hard to understand what power it is that causes them to act, so that they go out, cover a certain distance, and come back again.

Michael: All this movement of the statues, their progress and regress, is to be attributed to the cleverly controlled flow of water, together with certain wheels and some cords or wires made of copper, which are set in motion by the force of the water, and bring about all that movement. We may have more to say later about cleverly contrived movements of this kind. In another fountain there is an equally entertaining spectacle, where one can see a certain sort of sylvan man, whom the Ancients called a satyr and conceived of as being a man down to the navel but in his lower parts ending up as a beast. This satyr is in a kneeling position in the fountain, and has in his hand some tubes like those of the instrument called an organ, made up of seven pipes. On the other side a nymph, with the upper part of her body protruding from the water, joins him as if as his companion. When the water is released the satyr rises and plays his pipes, producing a pleasant harmony. At this immediately two boys and two girls, who are standing above his head in another place, do various cheerful dances, fitting their dance movements to the sounds sent up by the satyr so well, that they seem to be alive and not just artificial statues. Again in another place a new sight presents itself to the eyes: a person in the form of an angel plays a trumpet when the water is released; at the sound what the pagans called a faun (this too is a man of the forests) lifts a jar, and when it is full of water offers it as a drinking cup to a serpent which is nearby, and then once, and again, and indeed many times refills it when it is empty, until the spectators are satisfied; all this to the life, so much so that they can be reckoned to be not just effigies but the things themselves. In another a huge lizard flees at high speed the great rush of flowing water as if there were danger of death, and takes refuge in some artfully constructed rocks or wild beasts' lair. In another there is a boy with a ball in his hand, and he tosses it this way and that, and squirts out, both from the ball and from various parts of his body, water which two geese drink up as if they were extremely thirsty. In another a huge goose lowers its neck into the water, takes up some water with its beak and its mouth, and sprays it pleasingly on the bystanders. I omit mention of other figures of similar artifice which we saw in various fountains of this villa, which offered no little delight to the eyes and affected the mind with astonishment.

Leo: When you tell us these things you seem to be doing it for entertainment and indeed in jest, wanting to make us believe that the flow of the water brings about all those movements and gesticulations of the statues.

Michael: My dear Leo, believe me, what you are hearing is serious and no jest These colloquia are not concerned with trifles or jests, and even if I had any inclination to bring in stories or old wives' tales my companions, who are here present, would not permit it.

Mancio: How odd of Leo here to suspect that what Michael was saying about the fountains of the Villa Pratolino was a joke, given that these colloquia were arranged in order to deal with serious and solemn matters.

Lino: Since you say these things are entirely true and certain, provide some explanation of all those movements.

Michael: I'll explain them to you by taking various similar cases. Those who give puppet shows, for example, are skilful in making images and figures, of cardboard or some other similar material, move very rapidly, so as to present some action or drama to the audience, with wheels turning and setting other wheels in motion, making the figures which are otherwise inert advance and recede. Similarly it is possible for certain mechanisms to be put in place and then set in motion by water so that these or those figures are activated and spectators see them moving. Something rather similar can be seen in the clocks which the fathers of the Society of Jesus bring to us,[1] in which one wheel, turned by an iron weight, imparts movement to other wheels, with the result that at fixed intervals of time the correct hours are marked by a bell. What is effected in the one case by an iron weight is achieved in the other by the force of water. But something much more admirable can be seen in that Toledo clock which I mentioned earlier, in which so many revolutions of the spheres are represented by means of so many wheels made to turn, and it is certain that all of this is made according to most definite proofs and rules of arithmetic and geometry; and in the same way very many other spectacles are produced by the flow of water, controlled and diverted in various ways.

Leo: From these parallels which you have put to us we can get some idea of the cause of so much activity, and we can readily appreciate that the subtlety of intellect of the Europeans rivals their wealth.

Michael: I omit mention of the many other figures to be found in the fountains, fearing to bore you, adding only that the water is distributed and sent round in that villa through so many aqueducts, pipes, tubes, and apertures, that it seems like a banquet with an almost infinite number of courses. There are so many outlets to the fountains that in all, somewhere, there are fifteen hundred of them; and the figures represented are so various that they even include Apollo himself, formerly believed by the pagans to be the god of music, together with the nine muses playing different musical instruments, the sound issuing from them imitating the harmony of the best performers on the cithara. But let us leave the fountains now, and move on to other things.

This villa also has, in addition to the plantations, orchards, and landscaped gardens, of which I'll say nothing, an aviary filled with almost innumerable birds, and it is so large, and fenced in so cleverly with such fine iron threads that the birds themselves seem not to be enclosed, but to enjoy the open sky and rove freely without any sort of custody.

---

[1] A mechanical clock was among the objects 'never before seen in these parts' that Xavier presented to Ōuchi Yoshitaka, one of the most powerful daimyo in western Japan, in Yamaguchi in April 1551. See Fróis, *História de Japam*, I, p. 39; Schurhammer, *Xaveriana*, p. 586. Fróis gave a small alarm clock to Oda Nobunaga in 1569 and used other clocks, which he describes as 'rare and pleasing' in Japan, to impress the then shogun, Ashikaga Yoshiaki, and to help counter the influence of the Buddhist priest Nichijō Shōnin, an enemy of the missionaries (Fróis, *História de Japam*, II, pp. 277, 295–6, 344). A clock, brought back from Europe, was among the presents Valignano gave to Hideyoshi in 1591 and João Rodrigues presented a clock, made in Nagasaki, to Tokugawa Ieyasu in 1606. See Fróis, *História de Japam*, V, pp. 281, 317; Cooper, *Rodrigues the Interpreter*, pp. 210–11, 216. In temples, the Japanese, like the Chinese, used fire-clocks. See Cooper, *João Rodrigues's Account*, p. 393.

There is besides a most copious spring and a most delightful stream, on whose banks, as it were, birdsong can be heard all around; and in the same place there are so many trees that the birds can easily settle there, build their nests, and bring up their young. And now that I have spoken of this aviary I shall return to Florence and say something of an enclosure for wild animals, first noting, however, so as not to have to retrace my steps, that this villa which I have been describing is so abundant in everything relating to pleasure and enjoyment that we did not see any other place more delightful or better accommodated to relaxation of the spirit.

Back in Florence, then, we saw a remarkable enclosure in which, as something to be proud of and boast about, many huge wild animals, brought together here with great labour and at great expense, are kept under guard. Ten lions can be seen there, animals which, besides being very ferocious, can be found only very rarely and with great difficulty; also four tigers, four bears, and two deer wolves, which imitate the form of a panther. All of these beasts are kept in their own different places, in such a way that they can produce offspring, and very considerable expense is necessary to provide them constantly with food, but the grand duke willingly pays the expense in order to provide a very pleasing and unfamiliar spectacle for visitors from outside and for the citizens.[1]

But let us say something of the holy things, very much worth viewing, which we saw in Florence, and firstly of that most celebrated image of the Blessed Virgin, which portrays her receiving the heavenly message from the mouth of the Angel Gabriel, and which is held in such veneration by all that it is opened to public view only once a year. To tell you of its first beginnings, which were not without a miracle, they say that there was once a certain very famous painter who was vehemently moved in spirit to paint a picture of this kind. He had begun with the lower parts of the body, and when he came to the face, fearing that he would not be able to achieve the proper degree of beauty with his brush, nor to express the lineaments of that heavenly face, he took refuge in holy prayers and divine assistance, purifying his soul of the stain of sin in confession and receiving the Holy Eucharist, and then determined to set to work once again. When the day destined for that work dawned he found that the whole picture had been completed, by angelic power, or so it is believed, and that what he himself did not dare to supply with human hands had been provided by divine art. And it is not for nothing that there is this belief, for so many miracles and prodigies have subsequently taken place as a result of pious contemplation of this picture, together with prayers, that they witness clearly to the touch of the divine hand on that work. So we went three times in order to see this most celebrated picture, and twice we were blocked by the multitude of the people flocking there, but then the third time we gained entrance to the church before dawn, and were very greatly consoled to be able to see throughout the Mass that image which sets before the gaze of the viewer a beauty truly divine.[2]

---

[1] The visit to the zoo is mentioned by Corbara (Boncompagni-Ludovisi, *Le prime due ambasciate*, p. 5).

[2] The fresco of the Annunciation is in the Basilica dela Santissima Anunziata and was the focus of a cult and only shown when important dignitaries were in town or at times of tribulation (Brown, 'Courtiers and Christians', p. 896). The visit did indeed cause a commotion. The boys asked to see the painting again before their departure from Florence, but the duke's Guardaroba, Giovanbattista di Cerreto, stubbornly rejected the request as unprecedented (ibid., pp. 896–8). The boys' piety was similarly aroused on their visits to the Basilica di San Lorenzo and the Duomo where they adored and kissed the religious relics much to the edification of observers. See *Dai Nihon Shiryō*, XI: 1, p. 135; Brown, 'Courtiers and Christians', p. 893.

What am I to say of the structure of the cathedral, which is all of marble, and adorned all round with so many statues, embellished with such a vestibule, and with, on the sanctuary, such a magnificent dome, which they call a cupola, with a height of five hundred and sixty-nine steps, that its cost has been justly reckoned as two hundred million sesterces.[1] I say nothing of the roof of this dome, built of copper, nor of the tower of the same height of stone of Paros, holding many bells, and other similar works which would take too long to list

I return again to the possessions of the duke, so as to mention a few further items before leaving Florence. We viewed with much pleasure the armoury and the storehouse of the grand duke, both of them of royal proportions, for in the armoury we saw more than five thousand instruments of heavy armament, not to mention innumerable other kinds of offensive and defensive arms, enough to equip a very large army. And so as not to leave out anything which we might like to see, the wife of the duke himself ordered her private possessions to be shown to us, and these included so many works of gold and silver, so many gems and pearls, so many exquisite pieces of work of every kind, that you could call them the treasure and the possessions of a most illustrious queen. This illustrious princess, as well as being of extremely hospitable and benevolent character, was so splendidly generous that we were offered the chance to choose and receive, in her name, whatever piece should be most pleasing to us. This choice was managed gracefully and without any breach of etiquette, for Mancio here, by chance and without consultation, came upon a picture of the princess herself, and said that that work pleased him above all the others, and that if there were others of the same type he would very much like to have one of them. This judgement about her picture pleased the princess, and since that one was, she said, not completely finished, she ordered another to be made immediately to give as a gift to Mancio.[2]

But now let us leave Florence and head for Siena, the next place after Florence on that road.[3] This city, which we reached on 13 March, also belongs to the jurisdiction of the duke of Tuscany, and is by no means the least of the noble cities of Italy. In it, by order of the same duke, having been welcomed by the governors of the city who had come to meet us, we made for a certain magnificently furnished house. There was no lack of things which we were very glad to view in that city, in particular the cathedral, which, whether you consider the work or the materials, can compare with the most magnificent; for the whole of it is built of marble, and not only the roof but also the floor is adorned with mosaic figures representing various stories, with such art that even the highly polished

---

[1] I.e. 5 million ducats.

[2] This request is also mentioned by Antonio Inglese, who had accompanied the boys from Livorno. He adds that Mancio wanted to have a picture 'so that in his country the women may see how much these [women] exceed them in beauty and style' (quoted in Brown, 'Courtiers and Christians', p. 895).

[3] The grand duke ordered a heightened security guard for the boys and their entourage as they left the city to protect them from beggars who 'most impudently', importuned them for money and because 'word has already spread that they [the Japanese] are laden with precious stones and jewels' (quoted in Brown, 'Courtiers and Christians', p. 892). Indeed, when they were about to leave Siena a Spaniard stole a case containing some valuable objects and attempted to make for Florence but was arrested and the case returned. See Sanesi, 'I principi Giapponesi', p. 128; Fróis, Première ambassade, p. 142 n. 522. When they entered the Papal States, in which banditry was endemic, they were accompanied to Rome by a papal escort (Boncompagni-Ludovisi, Le prime due ambasciate, p. 7; Fróis, Première ambassade, p. 142).

stones themselves seem to provide a variety of colours. In this church and in many others we viewed various relics of saints ingeniously enclosed in casings of both gold and silver, and we judged the religious ornamentation to be not inferior to the magnificent display in the other most noble cities. We went also to the college of the fathers of the Society, and experienced in many things their charity and benevolence, and that of other religious men.[1]

We left this city on 17 March and came to a town called San Quiricio,[2] and there the pope himself sent a messenger to us to say that he would be glad if we would make haste, so as to satisfy as soon as possible the most eager expectation with which he awaited us. In fact that most holy pope had a presage of the brevity of the time which remained to him before his death, and he was anxious to enjoy being able to see us, which he believed would be a great joy to him, for as long as possible. Accordingly we made what haste we could, and came to a town called Acquapendente, which was within the jurisdiction of the pope himself. There the governor, accompanied by two hundred musketeers, came most courteously to meet us.

From there we passed through Bolsena and arrived at Viterbo, and before we entered we were met by the leading nobles together with two hundred guards, and were most kindly admitted to the city, and installed in splendidly equipped quarters.[3] We stayed a full day in that city in order to see some of its buildings. We went first to the cathedral, and after we had attended a solemn Mass many holy relics beautifully mounted in gold were shown to us; above all one of those thorns by which the sacred head of Christ our Redeemer was pierced; also the jaw-bone of St John the Precursor, and many other relics which time does not permit us to enumerate. Later we were taken to a convent of holy

---

[1] For details of their stay in Siena, see Sanesi, 'I principi Giapponesi', pp. 124–30, which is a contemporaneous letter from Marcantonio Tolomei to his brother-in-law Alemano Marescotti, concerning the boys and their visit. Tolomei describes them, unflatteringly, as of medium height, olive-skinned, with a Moorish profile, small, with greyish eyes which appeared to be incapable of looking at heights, thick-lipped, and for the rest very ugly (ibid., pp. 127–8). An anonymous account of their stay in Rome describes them as aged between 15 and 18, sallow with very rustic faces (Boncompagni-Ludovisi, *Le prime due ambasciate*, p. 7). Gualtieri describes them as small of stature, olive-skinned (as a result of the journey, he conjectures), with small but acute eyes, aquiline noses, in short individuals of noble and ingenuous appearance (*Relationi*, p. 150; *Dai Nihon Shiryō*, XI: 2, p. 198). This depiction was echoed by Alessandro Benacci, who adds that 'there is nothing barbarian' about them and admired their civility, courtesy, modesty and intelligence (*Avisi*, pp. 152–3). The fullest description of the boys is by the Milanese cartographer Urbano Monte, who met them in Milan and drew the only extant portraits of them (see Figs 3–6). He described them as below average in height, olive-complexioned, with small eyes, large eyelids and wide noses. They had an ingenuous and noble countenance with nothing barbaric about them. They were civil, courteous and modest He described their Japanese clothes, their swords ('well tempered and sharp') and their use of chopsticks when eating. They were intelligent and mature and had manners such as one might believe them to have been brought up in Italy. They spoke Portuguese well, Spanish poorly, Latin 'in great part' and understood Italian well (Gutierrez, *La Prima ambascierta Giapponese*, pp. 67–8; Cooper, *Japanese Mission*, pp. 126–7). Tolomei noted that at a banquet in their honour the boys were afraid of the two Jesuit priests who accompanied them and dared not so much as raise their eyes without seeking their permission. He also noted that at the banquet they drank only water and in the morning 'hot water' (Sanesi, 'I principi Giapponesi', p. 126; *Avisi*, p. 153).

[2] San Quiricio d'Orcia.

[3] Gregory XIII had written to his vice legate, monsignor Horatio Celso, that the boys were to be so received (Fróis, *Première ambassade*, p. 144). The honour guard was provided for reasons of protocol and security.

virgins, where we saw the venerable body of a certain saint called Rosa.[1] Although four hundred years have passed since her death her body has remained incorrupt, preserved by the divine power. And outside the walls of the city we saw a church dedicated to the Blessed Virgin of the Oak Tree. The origin of the name is this: a certain poor man was in grave danger of losing his life; he invoked the Blessed Virgin, and when he raised his eyes to an oak tree he saw there an image of the same Virgin bringing him succour. The citizens were moved by this miracle and prodigy to build a church for the most holy Virgin, and to enclose the same oak tree, with the image itself, in a very large chapel in it, so that the miracle would be forever remembered.[2] And the many other miracles which have since been performed, with the divine assistance, and which are accomplished even in this present time, mean that that church, and the monastery of religious of the Order of St Dominic, are extremely famous.[3]

We also went to a place called Bagnaia, constructed by Cardinal Gambara for pleasure and delight,[4] where we were presented with just as many opportunities for enjoyment and entertainment as at the Villa Pratolino of the duke of Tuscany; and although the place is relatively small it has an enclosure very well arranged for hunting, and there, using hunting dogs, which are used a great deal in Europe, we raised and then hunted down some wild animals. I omit mention of the gardens, fountains, and other testimonies to the amenities of this place, which can easily be imagined from what has already been said, and shall speak only of a certain musical instrument which they call the clavicimbalum[5] and which had us deservedly captivated and deeply impressed. It is six palms in length, four in width, one in height, and the covers of the holes it has for taking in air are so arranged that by a simple movement of them, when the same keys are struck the sounds and voices of several different instruments are produced, so that with the air being drawn in different ways more than a hundred kinds of notes are most sweetly emitted. And if you wish to hear each instrument on its own, your ears can easily receive the sweet sound, now of the cithara, now of the lyre, sometimes of the organ, sometimes of the pipes, or again of trumpets, and finally of the harp, the lute, the mandolin, the psalterium, and any other musical instrument. This instrument of which we speak is a work of such ingenuity that whether you wish to hear many sounds at once or these or those sounds separately you can achieve what you wish, and with a minimum

---

[1] St Rosa of Viterbo (1235–52), who stood up for papal power in the strife between the papacy and the emperor. Her feast is celebrated on 4 September and on the preceding day the Macchina di S. Rosa, an enormous illuminated bell tower, is paraded through the town.

[2] The sanctuary of Santa Maria della Quercia which possesses an image of the Virgin and child painted on a tile. The tile had originally been hung by a peasant on an oak tree in 1417 and became the object of a cult. The sanctuary was built between 1470 and 1525 on the site of the tree and was finally consecrated in 1577.

[3] The Convento di Santa Maria in Gradi di Viterbo, founded in 1215, now a part of the Università degli Studi della Tuscia.

[4] The Villa Lante, commissioned in 1566 by Cardinal Gianfrancesco Gambara (1533–87), cardinal from 1561. Montaigne considered the fountains in the gardens superior to those of the Pratolino and the Tivoli (*Journal de voyage*, pp. 346–7).

[5] The original edition (p. 230) gives '*clavicymbalum*', an early quilled keyboard instrument (Marcuse, *Musical Instruments*, Clavicimbalum). Eta Harich-Schneider says it was an organ (*History of Japanese Music*, p. 470) but this is debateable. Frois (*Première ambassade*, pp. 137–8) places the demonstration in Florence on 10 March.

of labour, and this was invented and worked out by a certain Venetian artificer, a man of genius. As well as this instrument there is a certain box like a water tank which has eight receptacles on this side and that, and whenever that instrument emits the sound which they call the signal to attack, those receptacles are opened by air, cleverly constructed triremes descend to do battle, trumpets sound, oars are swung and held, cannon are fired, and in fine a remarkable scene of battle and struggle is presented to your sight, and all of this is effected by a controlled flow of air, as it was by water in the case described earlier.

Leo: With every day that passes you tell us more extraordinary things, and I no longer doubt that Europeans outdo all others in their abilities; and yet if we had not had you and your companions as most trustworthy witnesses we would have regarded all these things as fiction and thought nothing of them.

Mancio: There is no reason for doubt, since we are Japanese men, above any suspicion of falsehood, and what we are putting before you are things which we have, so to speak, handled with our own hands.

Michael: We left Viterbo on 21 March, though Julian here was tired from the journey and somewhat ailing, and arrived at a villa called Caprarola, belonging to the most illustrious Cardinal Alessandro Farnese, of the most famous family of the dukes of Parma.[1] Were it not that I would be boring you by repeating many things I ought to describe this villa to you in detail, for it is in no way inferior to those which I described previously, neither in the structure of the building, nor the dwelling containing a hundred and fifty halls and rooms, nor in its grandeur and the variety of its gorgeous and costly furnishings; it is in fact such as befits that most powerful and wealthy of prelates, whose name is most celebrated throughout the whole of Christendom. I leave aside, therefore, the splendidly green plantations, the springs of water flowing along most beautifully constructed aqueducts, the enclosures abounding in wild beasts, the cellar crammed with about a hundred barrels of wine and many other things for the entertaining of guests, the stables containing a hundred and twenty horses, and many other things which it took a full twenty-four years to bring to the state in which they now are. Let us, then, leave out all these things and hasten on at last to Rome, towards which we had striven with such zeal and longing. The pope had decreed that we were to be received with crowds of people and public acclaim, but first of all we entered the city privately and almost without spectators, and were welcomed most kindly, with a

---

[1] 1520–89, cardinal from 1534, dean of the Sacred College of Cardinals from 1580. Farnese was the grandson of Paul III, to whom he and his family owed its rise. Like his grandfather, under whose auspices the Jesuit order was established, he was an important patron of the Society and during his lifetime one of the most important patrons of the visual arts in Rome. See Robertson, '*Il Gran Cardinale*', passim. The pentagonal-shaped building was commissioned by Farnese and designed by Vignola and his successors. Construction began in 1556 and was largely completed by 1573. The interior decorations were mainly designed by Taddeo Zuccaro. Montaigne was greatly impressed by the Caprarola considering it incomparable among the beauties of Italy and St Carlo Borromeo was led to wonder if Paradise could exceed it. See Montaigne, *Journal*, pp. 347–8; Robertson, '*Il Gran Cardinale*', pp. 74–130, esp. p. 129. There is a slightly longer description of the Caprarola in Fróis, *Première ambassade*, pp. 144–5.

fond embrace, like beloved sons coming from a faraway region, by Father Claudio Aquaviva, Superior General of the Society of Jesus and father to all its members.[1] But since our public entrance into the city needs a new colloquium, let us renew our strength with a night's rest, and begin to speak of Rome, capital of the whole world, tomorrow.

---

[1] They arrived in Rome on 22 March to a deliberately low-key reception in keeping with protocol. Outside the city they had been met by representatives of Philip II and had been reunited with Father Nuno Rodrigues. They went straight to their lodgings in the professed house of the Jesuits. See Fróis, *Première ambassade*, pp. 146–7; Cooper, *Japanese Mission*, p. 84.

COLLOQUIUM XXII

Of the entrance into the celebrated city of Rome, the audience with the Supreme Pontiff Gregory XIII, and of the sacred palace and the most august church of St Peter

Leo: With what eagerness and avidity of mind we come to this colloquium you yourselves can judge, you who, when up till now you have made mention of the cities of Europe, have spoken of Rome as the head and as it were the queen and ruler of all the others;[1] so that although we have been delighted to hear all about the other cities, as we wait to hear you speak now we are very conscious of a new ardour and an unaccustomed avidity.

Michael: It is only right that the expectation of hearing a description of the city of Rome should arouse a new degree of ardour and eagerness in your minds, since the greatness, the sanctity, and the religion of that city are such that it not only moves those who are present there to a most intense love of it, but it also arouses in the minds of those who are not there an extraordinary desire to see it. This is most clearly acknowledged not only by you, who have been promised such an account of it, but also by the other men of Christendom, so that whoever has not seen Rome confesses that he has been deprived of the most pleasing of all sights. Oh for a new river and rich flow of language to add to my poor and almost exhausted powers of speech, so that in the presence of such majesty all that I have already said about other cities could be considered insignificant and inferior. But let us come to the subject itself, remembering always that no description could do justice to the magnificence of so great a subject.

In order to speak about our solemn entrance into the city I should first say something about the mind of the pope in receiving us. The pope was well aware, thanks to most reliable messengers and letters, that we were coming from Japan, the furthest place in the world, and were making for Rome in order humbly and reverently to acknowledge him as the Vicar of Christ, in the names of the kings of Bungo and Arima and the prince of Ōmura, who had recently adopted the Christian religion. He therefore judged that the most fitting thing would be for him as pope to receive us, as legates of kings, with pomp and festivity, even though the fathers of the Society, because of the humility which they profess, and given that this was their concern and responsibility, did their best to play down the occasion, and tried hard to arrange that our reception by the pope should be just private. The pope, however, deeming this to be a matter which concerned the whole of

---

[1] Cervantes's character Tomás Rodaja describes Rome in similar words as 'queen of cities and mistress of the world' (*Novelas ejemplares: El licenciado vidriera*, in Cervantes, *Obras completas*, II, p. 130).

Christendom in common, judged it most fitting to treat this new progeny of Christ, propagated in the utmost parts of the earth, with every possible sign and testimony of love and benevolence, and gladly to accord to us the same honour which is accorded in the Roman curia to the legates of other kings and princes. Therefore on the day set for our entry [23 March] we were taken to a certain villa of the pope's[1] which is regularly used as a most convenient lodging where the legates of kings can rest from their journeys to the city of Rome.

I would have to spend many words on the description of this extremely well-appointed villa, if I were not called away by weightier matters, and if I had not already said enough and more about similar places, presenting some cases to serve as examples, on the basis of which a judgement could be made about the others. Suffice it to say, therefore, that in its appointments, in the structure of the buildings, and in the richness and variety of the furnishings, the villa is worthy of the greatest of popes. We stayed only a few hours in that place, just long enough for the preparations for our reception to be made, for Pope Gregory, as it were foreseeing how short a span of life remained to him, was unwilling to allow any procrastination or diminution of the very great joy which he conceived that our coming would bring. When all was prepared, then, we began to approach the walls of that most holy of cities, with the order and ceremony which I shall now describe.[2]

First in line were all those knights whose commission it is to guard the pope, a hundred and more in number, fully armed as if going into battle. Following them came the Swiss with their double-edged axes, part of the pope's infantry guard, in their many-coloured and richly textured uniforms. After these came the insignia of the cardinals, borne by their servants riding on mules, and with the red hats of their masters on their backs, representing the absent cardinals, for at that time the cardinals themselves attend the waiting pope, and it is through their messengers that they congratulate legates on their arrival. After these there were also the attendants of the other ambassadors who are normally sent to Rome by kings and princes. Also making the journey were people playing musical instruments, mostly trumpeters, horn-blowers, and others like that, who with the various sounds which they produced put on a splendid performance. After these came the head chamberlains of the pope, carried on horseback, and other palatine magistrates in long red cloaks, and shortly afterwards many most dignified priests and prelates, and those who are called clerics of the chamber. Following these was our Mancio, representing Francisco king of Bungo, and accompanied by two archbishops, one on either side of him. I came after that, together with two bishops, and then Martin, with other men of high rank. Only Julian was missing, for he was ill at the time and unable to appear. We, however, were carried on horses richly

---

[1] The Villa Giulia built by Julius II and designed by Vignola, located near the Porta Flaminia (now the Porta del Popolo), historically the main entrance to the city and the one through which protocol dictated embassies should make their formal entry after spending the night outside the gates. The entry into Rome and the procession to the Vatican echoed the imagined pomp and ceremony of the Roman triumph. For a description of the entry and procession of the Portuguese ambassador to Leo X in 1514, see Bedini, *Pope's Elephant*, pp. 44–52. One of the observers of that procession mentioned that the exotic quality of the foreign legation and its gifts reminded him of the descriptions of Marco Polo (ibid., p. 48).

[2] For a more detailed description of the procession to the Vatican and their welcome there, see RAHM, MS 09-02663, ff. 441v–4; Fróis, *Première ambassade*, pp. 151–4; Boncompagni-Ludovisi, *Le prime due ambasciate*, pp. 12–13. The procession was not without hitches. At one stage some of the horses got out of control (RAHM, MS 09-02663, f. 442v).

Figure 9. Audience with Gregory XIII, engraving by Abraham van Diepenbeeck, in Cornelius Hazart, *Kerckelycke historie van de gheheele wereldt*, vol. I, Antwerp, 1667, facing p. 68.
By permission of Professor Tominaga Michio.

caparisoned, their coats of black velvet with added gold thread reaching almost to the ground, and there followed at our heels an almost infinite number of Roman knights, of all the nobility of the city, such a multitude of them that the whole train stretched for almost half a league, making a show befitting the fame of Rome. And what am I to say of those unable for whatever reason to leave their houses, and of the women who, for the sake of modesty, do not usually appear in public; there were so many of these watching from windows, and the walls and windows were so decorated, that they presented a most agreeable spectacle, especially as all those Roman matrons were extremely pleased, and with great acclamation wished us prosperity and happiness on our arrival.

Proceeding in this order we reached a very beautiful and most famous bridge which crosses the river Tiber in front of the Castel Sant'Angelo, and our arrival was splendidly celebrated from that fortress, first with the sound of various instruments in harmony, and then with the multiple and impressive sound of cannon and muskets.[1] From here we were taken by a most noble and much decorated street to the sacred palace, and there the sound of musket and cannon fire started up again, most impressively. As we entered the palace and the hall known as the Sala Regia it was a great joy to us to see the most grave seated assembly of all the cardinals and of other prelates and most noble men with whom that most ample hall was filled. But what moved our minds deeply and in an unwonted and more than human way, and drew us to an extraordinary piety, was the inexpressible majesty of the Supreme Pontiff, seated alone on his most august throne, representing to the life Christ whose supreme power fills the temples of heaven, and moving our souls to love entirely what is divine, and to despise what is earthly and human. Yet for all his great dignity he was not lacking in a singular and incredible humanity, so that when he first saw us making for his feet he embraced us with the warmth of a most loving father, and favoured us, unworthy though we were, with the most sacred kiss of peace; and his whole soul being moved he could not avoid showing the depth of his feeling with an abundance of tears.

These demonstrations of his love helped us to recover somewhat from a certain fear which we naturally felt when face to face with such majesty, and we presented the letters and messages from the kings of Bungo and Arima, and the lord of Ōmura, in which it said, to summarize, that those kings and princes had been called by divine inspiration from the false worship of idols to Christian piety, and conscious of the fullness of authority which was his as Vicar of Christ on earth, considered that there was nothing more important, nothing more worthwhile, than to send us, in their name and from the most remote parts of the world, to kiss his most sacred feet and, for the sake of religion, to put our heads beneath his feet.[2] All of this was expressed in our Japanese language, and

---

[1] In 1581 Montaigne mentions the cannons firing and the festive atmosphere, 'la pompe espagnole', when the Portuguese ambassador proceeded to the Vatican to make obeisance to the pope (*Journal de voyage*, p 220), a ceremony, he notes, that failed to impress Ivan IV's envoy, perhaps out of pique over his own treatment in Rome. In 1582 the pomp surrounding Olivares's entry into Rome, especially the extraordinary salute from the Castel San'Angelo, caused the French to complain that other ambassadors were not shown similar respect (ibid., pp. 220–21; Dandelet, *Spanish Rome*, p. 76).

[2] The letters were printed in Latin in the official proceedings *Acta Consistorii Publice Exhibiti A S.D.N. Gregorio Papa XIII Regvm Iaponiorvm Legatis Romae, Die XXIII Martii MDLXXXV*, Rome, 1585. See Boscaro, *Sixteenth Century European Printed Works*, p. 4. The *Acta* were printed in other European cities including Dusseldorf and Prague (ibid., pp. 8–21). Spanish translations are in RAHM, MS 09-02663, ff. 323v, 325v, 327v; and Portuguese translations of two of them in Fróis, *Première ambassade*, pp. 173–4.

explained in Italian by Father Diogo de Mesquita, acting as interpreter, and then the pope himself gave an answer worthy of his dignity and his humanity, expressing clearly his most ardent love and more than paternal benevolence towards us. Then the master of ceremonies[1] took us to the place assigned to ambassadors, and we stood there, bareheaded and reverently, while the letters which we had presented to the pope were read out publicly in the Italian language.[2]

When this had been completed a certain priest of the Society of Jesus called Gaspar Gonçalves made a speech,[3] as is customary at such ceremonies and assemblies, a most elegant oration, about the same matter, namely our coming and the reasons for it. It was printed later, and now it is read with great pleasure by all. We have brought it with us, so you will be able to see for yourselves how well he spoke about it; but the witness to how his audience reacted to and were moved by his presentation is the abundance of tears shed by those most dignified priests and most illustrious cardinals, and also by the pope himself. Those tears were manifest witness to the great joy and enthusiasm with which all present there welcomed the bearers of the happy news of the spread of Christendom, and to the great love with which the new disciples of Christ were embraced. When the oration was finished a man of distinguished rank[4] answered in the name of the pope, making a shorter but very impressive speech, saying that the pope was truly delighted at our coming, that he accepted under his guardianship and protection the named kings and rulers who were now part of the Christian flock, as well as us and all Japanese who had declared themselves for Christ, and that from now on he would always be concerned for the things of Japan, and would not be lacking in effort and diligence in promoting and providing for them. Then we approached the throne of the pope, kissed his feet once more, and were most kindly received by the most eminent cardinals who surrounded us, and who, as it were, took us to their inmost hearts in a demonstration of their love for us.[5]

When all this had been done and the pope was about to withdraw he conferred a further and different honour on us; he had Mancio and me take the train of his sacred vestment in our hands and accompany him, this being a privilege normally granted to the

---

[1] Francesco Mucanzio.

[2] This is described more fully in Boncompagni-Ludovisi, *Le prime due ambasciate,* pp. 13–14. See also Fróis, *Première ambassade,* p. 156. Montaigne alleges that in 1581 Ivan IV's envoy, Ivan Thomas Schwerigin, pointedly refused to kiss the pope's feet, kissing only his right hand (*Journal de voyage,* p. 211). Out of consideration for the friendly relations the papacy enjoyed with Poland at the time, the envoy was not treated as an ambassador but merely as the bearer of a letter from Muscovy and was, therefore, refused a public audience and other marks of respect. See Pastor, *History of the Popes,* XX, pp. 435–6.

[3] Gonçalves was a professor of humanities and proficient in Latin, Greek and Hebrew. See Fróis, *Première ambassade,* p. 157 n. 577. His speech (printed in ibid., pp. 163–72) hailed the Jesuit achievements in Japan as Gregory's own and compared the pope to his namesake, Gregory the Great, during whose reign the British nation had been converted, although now, alas, that island was in revolt against the church. Fortunately, the present pope had ensured that that the loss of one island had been compensated for by the admission of other islands (Japan) into the church (ibid., p. 169). Gregory was, of course, a fierce opponent of Elizabeth I and of Protestantism in general. Gonçalves's speech was printed in the *Acta Consistorii* and in separate editions (Boscaro, *Sixteenth Century European Printed Works,* p. 38).

[4] Monsignor Antonio Boccapaduli, papal secretary, scholar and orator. See Pastor, *History of the Popes,* XIX, pp. 11, 54n, 259, 514, 527. His speech is printed in Fróis, *Première ambassade,* pp. 172–3.

[5] The consistory and speeches are described by Purchas (*Purchas his Pilgrims,* XII, pp. 254–6). An engraving depicting the boys kissing the papal feet was included in Ciappi, *Compendio.* It is reproduced in Fróis, *Première ambassade,* facing p. 163. A more striking depiction is that by Diepenbeeck (see Fig. 9).

legates of the emperors, who outrank all others. After the pope had retired to his residence we were invited by his nephew, the most illustrious Cardinal of San Sisto,[1] to a banquet at which were present his cousins Cardinal Vastavillano[2] and the duke of Sora, Giacomo Boncompagni.[3] There is nothing for me to say about the magnificence and splendour of the banquet, since it can be readily understood from what I have said already about the custom of the princes of Europe in conducting a banquet, and certain things which I have described. Everything, whether with regard to the variety of the food or the costliness of the furnishings, was of regal magnificence. After the banquet the pope invited us again to talk privately with him, and I am scarcely able to explain with words the humanity and affability with which he treated us, but you can imagine it for yourselves if you picture a most fond father in conversation with his beloved sons. And when we considered the kindness of the pope towards us and at the same time the greatness of his majesty we saw clearly that that sublimity and greatness was not attained by human effort but was a gift of God, a sublimity which does not make a man haughty and arrogant, but rather, and even though his power is great indeed, an imitator of the benignity and gentleness of Christ.[4]

Leo: You have spoken, Michael, of the wonderful humanity shown to you by the pope, but there are other things we want to hear about, and in more detail. What finery does he use, what clothing does he wear, and how does it differ from the apparel of the cardinals and other prelates? To hear about these and other similar things would be a pleasure for us who are so far distant from them.

Michael: I think it would be wiser not to try to explain all those details, since it would take a long time, and could not be done without some treatment of the various rites and customs of the see of Rome. I'll say only that the pope's attire varies greatly according to the various seasons, but that whatever it is it always displays the utmost majesty and gravity, and in its form it differs very much from the dress of the cardinals.[5] But since it is customary, for the sake of religion, for all, of whatever rank, to kiss his feet, he normally wears a cross on the top of his red velvet shoes, so that the kiss is offered to the cross rather

---

[1] Filippo Boncompagni (1548–86), nephew of Gregory XIII, cardinal from 1572 with the title of San Sisto. At the urging of the curia he had been appointed Cardinal Nephew but he was rather ineffective in this role. See Pastor, *History of the Popes*, XIX, pp. 30–31; Ippolito, 'Secretariat of State', p. 142.

[2] Filippo Guastavillani (1541–87), cardinal from 1574, and nephew of Gregory XIII on his mother's side (Pastor, *History of the Popes*, XIX, p. 32).

[3] 1548–1612, illegitimate son of Gregory XIII, born ten years before Gregory took holy orders, amongst other things, commandant of the papal troops and general of the church. Gregory was proud of his son but took pains to counter suggestions of nepotism by not bestowing undue favours on Giacomo or other relatives. See Pastor, *History of the Popes*, XIX, pp. 33–7. Fróis (*Première ambassade*, pp. 160, 187) styles him the pope's nephew, a euphemism for the illegitimate offspring of the clergy.

[4] For more detail, see Boncompagni-Ludovisi, *Le prime due ambasciate,* pp. 13–15, and Fróis, *Première ambassade*, pp. 155–61.

[5] Shortly before the consistory, the pope robed in the Sala dei Paramenti and then proceeded to the Sala Regia. See Boncompagni-Ludovisi, *Le prime due ambasciate,* p. 13; Fróis, *Première ambassade*, p. 154 n. 571. The boys wore Japanese clothes. The pope's attire included the scarlet mantle, the scarlet shoes and the papal tiara, all of which emphasized 'his function as an emperor-monarch' (Ullmann, *Growth of Papal Government*, p. 318), the status accorded him in what follows.

than to the shoes themselves. As for the cardinals and their dress, it is distinguished from that of other prelates only by its colour; they use scarlet or, at the time of the Lenten fast and the advent of the Lord, purple. So much for normal clothing. With regard to sacred vestments, these are many and various, both for the pope and for the others, for the various seasons. There are many books about these, and we have brought them back with us, so it will be easy for you to read through them.

Now I must say something about the pope's most magnificent palace,[1] and about the church dedicated to St Peter, prince of the Apostles, the most celebrated in Rome. First of all I must point out that nothing that I say is going to do justice to the majesty and magnificence of these two buildings. All I can do is to draw attention to certain things and then leave it to you, who have already heard descriptions of other buildings, to form your own judgement about these two, which far excel all others. What am I to say, first of all, about the most august palace of the Supreme Pontiff, which far surpasses the royal and august residences of all kings and emperors? Many centuries ago the popes, moved by a divine instinct, fixed their seat in this most famous city of Rome, and always, as they succeeded one another, they enlarged and embellished this building, adding lustre to it and leaving it for posterity as a memorial to their names, so that the size to which that most ancient structure has grown, and the way in which it has been renewed and extended, is extraordinary. Almost too many to count, therefore, are its cloisters, corridors, halls, dining-rooms, apartments, and an almost infinite number of other rooms. Just how many there are is indicated by the fact that the palace contains no less than seventeen hundred fireplaces and chimneys, and the size of the buildings is fully matched by the cost and the workmanship that has gone into it. Every kind of work, whether relief, or inlay, or of whatever other ancient kind, can be found in the floor, the walls, the ceilings of this palace. Everything is so adorned with gold, colours, figures, images, that it deserves to be considered the best in all the countries of the world, and all, whether Romans or from other places, will find there a feast for the eyes and the mind. And in this most perfect of palaces the pleasure of the gardens and orchards, the delight of the fountains, watercourses, and ponds, the enjoyment of the menagerie, leave nothing to be desired. Whatever is to be found of art, of pleasure, of delight in the other most celebrated villas which I have described, is contained, all of it, with a higher degree of art and in greater perfection, as if in the highest and most ornate of all buildings, in this one palace of the Supreme Pontiff. And the scale and grandeur of the building is such that it is possible to ride on horseback up almost all the staircases leading to the interior of the palace.

But to come now to a more specific account of some of the chambers of this building, within it is that most famous room in which all the cardinals assemble, when the Supreme Pontiff leaves this life for a better one, in order to provide another prelate to replace the deceased.[2] There also are certain most spacious halls in which the cardinals, summoned by the pope, customarily convene for meetings public or private. The public ones are those at which it is customary for the ambassadors of the emperor, the kings, or the republics to be received with solemn applause from that most illustrious assembly; the private those to which the pope calls the cardinals, as he frequently does, to consult about most grave

---

[1] The Apostolic Palace.

[2] The Sistine Chapel which was used in 1565 for papal conclaves. Previously it had served as a dormitory for the cardinals during the conclaves (Stinger, *Renaissance in Rome*, p. 354 n. 1).

matters concerning the common good of Christendom. There are besides in the same palace two papal chapels,[1] which can be said to be churches of no inconsiderable size, in which, on set days and with all the most illustrious cardinals assisting, the pope celebrates the divine services; and I say nothing here of certain feast days on which he celebrates the Holy Sacrifice in the church of Saint Peter or in other churches. Between those two chapels stands that most famous hall which is generally known as the Sala Regia, since that is where the kings who come out of reverence for the pope, or the ambassadors sent by the kings, are received by the Roman Pontiff in a full assembly of the great and good, both sacred and secular; and in all that could be wished for by way of artistic workmanship this hall far surpasses all the other parts of this palace, indeed of any building. The base of the walls of this hall rests on certain squares of most precious stone of different colours, fixed together with marvellous skill, and the surface higher up is covered with gold-surrounded reliefs of wonderful artistry, in which can be seen various stories and figures skilfully depicted. Finally, the panels of the vaulted ceiling are decorated with the same ornamentation of gold, and colours, and figures, and offer a most delightful spectacle to the eyes of the beholder. It was in this chamber that the pope did us the honour of receiving us, amid public congratulation and general rejoicing, as soon as we came to him in the name of the Japanese kings and princes.

Mancio: I can see that you are getting out of your depth, Michael, in trying to find words to describe the scale, the beauty, the size, the wealth of that august papal palace. Perhaps it will be better, now that you have made some mention of those things, to leave the rest to the imagination and judgement of your audience.

Michael: You were right to come to my rescue, dear Mancio, when my discourse was labouring along like a mere raft out on the vast ocean and fearful of shipwreck; but I am in fear of rocks no less dangerous when I see that I now have to deal with that most celebrated of all churches, the one in Rome dedicated to St Peter. But following your advice and shortening the sail of my discourse I shall keep to the safer shores of the coast, and do no more than point out the area which my oratory does not dare to enter. I trust you will excuse this preamble to what I am going to say about the most magnificent and never sufficiently praised building of that church. I would have you know, therefore, beloved hearers, that as the city of Rome is the head of all Christianity and the holy house where people come in search of answers, as from an oracle, when various doubtful things happen, so the truth of this is as it were presented to our eyes in an external sign, namely this most holy church, which is pre-eminent for its size, its abundance of religious things, and the sanctity of its religious observance. There is no doubt, therefore, that everything splendid, everything richly and skilfully made, everything of expert workmanship, indeed everything so far invented by human genius, is to be found in this church.

The excellence of a work tends to be reckoned according to its price, especially in the minds of those to whom it is not present, and the cost of this work is such that not only has a very large sum been set aside for it annually for centuries past, but also there have been papal letters promulgated and alms gathered throughout Europe, amounting

---

[1] The Sistine Chapel, and the Cappella Paolina, the parish church of the Vatican. The Sala Regia lies between them.

sometimes to two hundred thousand ducats, sometimes to three hundred thousand. In addition huge disbursements have been made by the Christian kings themselves, from their treasuries, with the result that, although eighty years have now elapsed since the first foundations were laid and the work is not yet even half finished,[1] three hundred million sesterces have already been swallowed up, a sum equivalent to seven and a half million ducats, which indicates clearly the incredible magnificence of the church.[2] Now I don't want to be carried away out into the ocean of different things which could be described, so I leave it to you to imagine what this fabulous church is like, saying only that just three chapels of this church, and the part called the sanctuary, were almost eighty years in the making. Each of them, however, is so large that it can be regarded as a church of no small dimensions, and the skill and the expense that have gone into building them on that sumptuous scale are such as to provide a full explanation for the long years it took.

I can't refrain from saying something about the very high roof of the sanctuary, commonly called the cupola, which, although it is round, is so large and raised to such an altitude that it is scarcely possible to conceive of the ingenuity by which it was finally put in place. The foundations which support and the walls which carry the tremendous height of it are a matter for wonder, but they are so big that within the width of them there is a staircase constructed which reaches almost to the top of the roof and can take two beasts of burden, and whatever can be carried by these beasts is taken up almost to the highest point of the roof. Other heavier weights are lifted up as easily as could be to that extreme altitude by a very clever wheel which is turned by the power of just one horse, or by another instrument revolved by just two men. I am overwhelmed by the magnitude of the subject and don't dare to say any more about it, except to add that the magnificence of those three chapels can be inferred from another smaller one built by the most holy Pope Gregory XIII, which is sited beneath the sanctuary of the church and which cost about three hundred thousand ducats.[3] Suffice it to say, therefore, that although there are many most magnificent buildings in Europe, which we have dealt with or shall be dealing with in these colloquia, these two, namely the sacred palace and the church of St Peter, must be counted as holding pride of place.

Leo: As we listen to you we cannot but be astounded at the pre-eminence of the things of Rome which you have so far described above all others; but together with this unusual wonderment there also continues a burning eagerness to hear more from you about things in Rome, about the form which those meetings take at which the cardinals come together to elect the pope, about the acclamation and the multitude of people when the new pope is announced, about the rites and ceremonies with which he celebrates the holy sacrifice, about the relics of the saints for which that most famous city is renowned. For all these

---

[1] Work on the new St Peter's began in 1506 and the basilica was completed in 1626. The cupola, begun by Michelangelo, was almost finished when the boys were in Rome. It was completed between 1588 and 1590 by Giacomo della Porta, who also designed the Gesù.

[2] The cost of building St Peter's is unknown but is estimated to be 1.5 million gold *scudi*. See Pastor, *History of the Popes*, XX, pp. 565–8; Delumeau, *Vie économique et sociale de Rome*, pp. 763–4; Partner, 'Papal Financial Policy', p. 55.

[3] Cf. Delumeau, *Vie économique et sociale de Rome*, p. 764, who gives costs of 80,000 and 100,000 silver *scudi*.

things I can see that new meetings and new colloquia are needed, for I think you have laboured enough, and more than enough, with your description of your first entry into the city of Rome, and of the sacred palace and the church of St Peter.

Michael: I'll gladly take up all those things later, particularly as you are aware of the need to interpose some rest, and your minds are by no means sated even with the narration of so many things.

COLLOQUIUM XXIII

Continues with things noted at the pope's solemn Masses and elsewhere

Lino: Now, dear Michael, do please continue with things which you and your companions were glad to see and to record in the city of Rome, theatre of all the world,[1] for we find that the more we hear of that city the greater is the desire aroused in our minds and the more vehement our avidity to hear still more.

Michael: I shall indeed continue what I have begun, beloved Lino, though I feel that my words are inadequate and that whatever power of speech I may have had so far is drying up as the days go past. Returning then to matters Roman, I cannot possibly move on without speaking further of the most holy Pope Gregory.[2] Such was his benevolence towards us that on the day after our visit to him he had an emissary visit us, and he sent us stuffs of silk and velvet of various kinds, so that not only we but also our attendants and servants could fit ourselves out in the Roman style. The variety and the worth of these materials were so great that we could not but be amazed at the liberality and generosity of the pope, as if of a most loving father, towards us. So from that most ample supply of cloths we chose the portion that seemed sufficient to allow clothes to be made for us; and although we used due moderation in this, those presents offered to us were so costly that even just the portion we selected was worth three thousand ducats.[3]

Leo: Good God! The portion you accepted was reckoned to be worth three thousand ducats?

Michael: Yes, it was. The whole of what was offered to us was worth perhaps ten or twelve thousand ducats. It seemed right to us, however, not to reject the benignity of the pope towards us, but to fulfil our duty rather than satisfy our greed. And that was not the only matter in which the supreme father manifested his generosity to us, for he also sent one thousand ducats to the Father General of the Society to be spent on treating us sumptuously and splendidly.

---

[1] The same expression was used by Ludovico Ludovisi, cardinal-nephew of Gregory XV, in a letter to Duke Maximilian of Bavaria thanking him for the donation of the Palatine Library to the Vatican in 1623 (Rosa, 'The "World's Theatre"', p. 78). See also Montaigne's judgement that Rome was a city in which national difference matters least and everyone there feels as if at home (*Journal de voyage*, p. 231), and Hyde, 'Medieval Descriptions of Cities', p. 322.

[2] For Montaigne's description and assessment of Gregory and his rule, see *Journal de voyage*, pp. 194–5.

[3] ARSI, Jap.Sin 33, ff. 40–42, lists the clothes made on the pope's orders.

Lino: From these considerations and others which you have noted I see clearly how great is the wealth and the generosity of the European princes who, as it were, pour out gifts and presents with such bounty even on those to whom they are not bound by any ties of family or friendship.

Michael: Let us move on now from this place and explain what else was done and noted. By the same messenger the pope invited us to be present the next day at a solemn ceremony which would take place in the church of the religious of the Dominican order commonly known as the church of Minerva.[1] It is customary for the pope to celebrate that feast day, which is dedicated to the angelic Annunciation to the Blessed Virgin, in that monastery, with many other events and also with the contracting of the marriages of many orphan girls to respectable men, all at the expense of the pope himself. The following day, therefore, in the morning, we put on Japanese dress, totally different from our attire of the previous day,[2] and set out to accompany the pope, who was surrounded by an innumerable throng of the aristocracy both sacred and secular, as he made his way on horseback to the Dominican church; and in this most noble company, by order of the pope himself, the most honourable place was reserved for us, for all the other secular nobles went ahead of him, and we rode at their heels, which is to say close to the Supreme Pontiff, carried on horses richly caparisoned. All the cardinals, two by two, followed the pope, and when we entered the church he honoured Mancio and me by having us hold the hem of his vestment. And since that was the first occasion for us to see the rite followed at a solemn papal Mass it is not alien to my purpose briefly to put before your eyes that event, so famed and so majestic.

It should be noted, firstly, that solemn Mass is celebrated by the pope in person, together with the cardinals, not on any day, but on certain more festive days; on other days he either says Mass privately or attends Mass. Whenever a papal Mass is to be celebrated, then, either in one of the chapels of the sacred palace or in another church dedicated to the saint whose feast day it is, all the cardinals head for the sacred palace in order to accompany the pope, and as they cross the bridge of Castel Sant'Angelo they are greeted by the festive boom of the cannon of the castle, pleasing harmonies on the pipes, and a joyous blaring of trumpets. Since these most illustrious cardinals have most ample annual incomes and a very great retinue not only of servants but also of prelates and nobles, the crowd of people that assembles at the sacred palace at those times is extraordinary. When the Supreme Pontiff comes out all the cardinals do him reverence with a deep bow, and he receives them with a joyful and gratified countenance, but

---

[1] Santa Maria sopra Minerva. See also Boncompagni-Ludovisi, *Le prime due ambasciate*, pp. 7–8. Montaigne saw the same procession and ceremony in 1581 which he called 'la cérémonie de l'aumône', the ceremony of the alms for the maidens (*Journal de voyage*, pp. 230–31).

[2] In fact they wore Japanese clothes and European hats and swords during their official reception into the city and the consistory. This contributed greatly to the theatricality of the occasion and, as was intended, gave the proceedings an exotic quality. See Boncompagni-Ludovisi, *Le prime due ambasciate*, pp. 7, 10, 14; Fróis, *Première ambassade*, p. 153. Gregory's biographer, Ciappi, echoing Gualtieri, said that their clothes and bearing made them appear like the Magi coming to adore the baby Jesus and provided an illustration (*Compendio*, pp. 81–2). Cf. the reception earlier in the century of envoys from sub-Saharan Africa whom Katherine Lowe suggests were required by strict papal protocol to dress as Europeans thereby experiencing '[r]itual "Europeanisation"' ('"Representing" Africa', p. 119).

without ever uncovering his head to any of them, centuries-old custom having taught them that this is as befits the papal majesty. With this brilliant company, therefore, the pope proceeds to the place where he normally dons the pontifical and sacred vestments.[1] When he is dressed all the cardinals go before him two by two, their attendant priests bearing in their hands the hem of their vestments, and the pope is borne in the pontifical chair,[2] carried by eight men. If he wishes to journey on foot, however, two of the most important cardinals attend him, one on either side, with the most important of all the secular dignitaries following behind and holding the hem of his vestment, and this person is usually the ambassador of the emperor. And when the pope travels, all those whom he comes across kneel in humble veneration, and he, making the Sign of the Cross with his right hand, prays for heavenly and eternal blessings on them.

When they come to the sacred altar where Mass is to be celebrated, first of all the supreme prelate sits in the designated pontifical chair, which is six steps up, and then two cardinal deacons occupy the seats which are arranged on either side. Below them all the other cardinals take their seats on large benches which are one step up, the set order being that first the cardinal bishops sit, then the presbyters, and afterwards, on a different bench, the deacons. All those bishops and prelates who have not yet been honoured with the rank of cardinal are seated on benches further away. Finally, the space to the side of the pope is occupied by all the legates of the emperor and the kings, standing; and although they cannot but become very tired standing there when the Mass goes on for a very long time, they nevertheless regard their position there as a great honour, for they are there in the name of their kings and princes as guard and support, as it were, for the pope. When they have taken their seats, before the prayers and the Mass begin, all the cardinals make a solemn act of reverence, used on these days when they are in assembly, to the pope, and I'll describe briefly the form it takes. First of all the cardinal who holds the first place rises, and the second cardinal with him; they bow to each other, the second takes his seat again, and the first dons a cloak which an assistant priest has ready, and with the long train and dragging the long train which indicates solemnity and great majesty, moves majestically to the altar and bows low. He then turns to face the pope and in humble reverence makes a similar bow. Next he mounts the steps with all gravity, and bowing, approaches to kiss the hand of the pope, though the pope keeps his hand beneath his sacred vestment. This done he returns to his place with the same solemnity, and then the second follows him, and thus all the others make the same act of reverence to the pope, with the same rite and observation of ceremony, and most pleasing it is to the eyes and minds of those who see it, and of those who ponder divine things.

This ceremony complete the divine prayers and sacrifice begin, and in these things you can imagine for yourselves, from what I have said already about the splendour of divine services performed in the presence of kings, the quality and variety of the rites, the multiplicity of the ceremonies, the excellence of the harmony of instruments and voices, the beauty and incredible costliness of the sacred vestments; the pope makes use of all of these, but to a degree far and away more ornate and more splendid, so much so that there does not seem to be anything on earth that offers such a display of that heavenly sweetness, majesty, and abundance of all good things. What then am I to say to you here about the

---

[1] The Sala dei Paramenti.

[2] The *sedia gestatoria*.

sacred accoutrements of the Supreme Pontiff, the proliferation of gold plate, the variety of most precious vestments and their worth, the infinite number of gems and pearls with which these objects are replete? Suffice it to say that when we saw them they seemed to us stupendous, and no light evidence of this will be the fact that just a single sacred vestment, which was once given as a gift to Pope Leo X by the most auspicious King Manuel of Portugal, cost one hundred thousand ducats, and a certain tiara, which is an ornament for the head, containing an interconnected triple crown, cost three hundred thousand.[1] Even this one is outdone, however, by another reckoned to be worth five hundred thousand, and it would take too long to describe the artistry of these products, with their interweaving of many gems and pearls of the utmost price.

Lino: With every day that passes we are more impressed with the opulence of Europe, of which you offer so many proofs, weightier by the day. By now we are fully convinced that of all regions that is both the wealthiest and the most fortunate.

Michael: After the Holy Sacrifice had been celebrated on that day, in that same church of the blessed Virgin, in the way I have described, a marriage ceremony was conducted, with solemn pomp, between a hundred and sixty orphan girls and men of respectable family, with a certain sodality which takes its name from the Annunciation of the same Virgin providing appropriate dowries for the brides, with assistance also from the pope himself.[2] He does this every year, not without very considerable expense. And since it is customary also for the nobles and men of substance who are present there to be asked to contribute alms for the support of the same orphans, Pope Gregory, of his paternal benevolence towards us, lest in our ignorance of that custom we might not have money available, and might therefore fail to do our duty in that respect and appear to neglect the norms of generosity, ordered money to be brought and secretly given to us so that afterwards we could offer it to the collectors of alms; and so we did, thus fulfilling that duty of men of substance. In that matter the pope's solicitude and care about us, the fond concern of a true parent, was evident to us and to the others who knew of it, when in the midst of all the multitude of the cares of his office he was mindful even of such a minor thing affecting us.

Leo: I do indeed applaud and greatly admire the paternal solicitude of the pope both for you yourselves and especially for those orphaned girls, who, but for his assistance, might well have fallen into the greatest danger to both soul and reputation.

---

[1] The opulence of these gifts and others, but especially the *pièce de résistance*, Hanno the Elephant, impressed contemporaries when Manuel's ambassador presented them to the pope in 1514. One contemporary estimated the cost of the cope alone at 70,000 ducats while another claimed that the tiara was 'adorned so richly with pearls and precious stones that one of equal value had never been seen in Rome' (Bedini, *Pope's Elephant*, p. 55).

[2] In reality the girls were not married during this ceremony. They were from poor families and were accompanied by an elderly relative and, after kissing the pope's feet and receiving a benediction, they were given a promissory note which upon their marriage would be exchanged for a dowry. Montaigne said the dowry amounted to 35 *écus* plus a white gown, worth 5 *écus* which they received during the ceremony. When he viewed the ceremony, 108 girls took part. In 1600, 235 girls participated and each received a note for 100 silver *scudi*. The Sodality of the Annunziata established the ceremony and, while most of the money was provided by the popes, it is clear from the account given here that contributions from others were expected. The event was one of the measures to counter the spread of prostitution in the city. See *Journal de voyage*, pp. 230–31; Delumeau, *Vie économique et sociale de Rome*, pp. 430–31.

Michael: With regard to the beneficence of the Supreme Pontiff and shepherd towards the flock entrusted to him, you are right not just to praise but to admire him, if you consider the huge expense to which he goes, not only in diligently satisfying the needs of the Roman republic, but also in supplying the wants of many other provinces spread throughout the world, and regularly providing reliable help for the miseries and calamities which do occur.[1] The best illustration of this for you is perhaps the fact that Pope Gregory XIII alone has established in various places twenty colleges and seminaries in which boys of good family are educated.[2] And it is not just the Roman Pontiff who performs these pious and publicly useful works. The cardinals and other prelates, and the Christian princes, follow his example and put great effort and diligence into performing pious works and alleviating the needs of the poor.

Lino: From that I can clearly conceive how much Christendom differs from the heathen nations which lack the light of faith, how strongly charity and benevolence flourishes there in all men, and how brutish and monstrous is the nature of those not yet instructed in the teachings of the Christian religion.

Mancio: You are right to note that distinction. Just as trees (as the primal truth testifies) are known one from another by their fruits, good trees bringing forth good fruit and inferior trees giving fruit which is tasteless or disagreeable;[3] no less does the Christian religion, adorned with the harvest and fruit of piety and mercy, differ far and greatly from pagan superstition, which offers nothing but the briars and thorns of savagery and cruelty.

Michael: Let us proceed further, and take up the other things that there are in the city of Rome, where, whether we deal with the old or with the new, we shall be entering deep waters if we want to pursue all the different things one by one. The very ruins of their buildings and remnants of their works show plainly what ancient Rome was like, and people come from many parts of the earth to see them, and cannot but be astonished at such magnificence when they view them. There are also many books testifying to this, especially one written about the marvels of Rome, and another very famous printed

---

[1] Although papal receipts increased steadily throughout the 16th century so too did papal expenditures, notably costs relating to papal borrowing and debt servicing, subsidies to foreign Catholic rulers to advance foreign policy objectives, and outlays for construction works in Rome and elsewhere in the Papal States. In addition, the running costs of the papal palace were high even if Gregory XIII and his successor Sixtus V were more frugal than some of their predecessors. Under Sixtus V, who criticized Gregory for denuding the treasury, papal finances were restructured in such a way that papal gold reserves were effectively withdrawn from circulation, requiring the papacy to resort to other measures, such as the sale of office and the imposition of import duties to finance its activities. For discussions of 16th-century papal finances, see Ranke, *History of the Popes*, I, pp. 318–25, esp. p. 319; Delumeau, *Vie économique et sociale de Rome*, pp. 751–68, esp. pp, 757–8, 761, 763–4, 767–8; Partner, 'Papal Financial Policy', pp. 17–62 *passim*.

[2] Many, but not all, were Jesuit institutions (Pastor, *History of the Popes*, XIX, pp. 237–58; ibid., XX, pp. 585–9). In fact papal disbursements for such purposes were not so generous. The percentage of papal income spent on seminaries and colleges outside Italy and on overseas missions at this time was around 1 per cent, a little more than that spent on alms. The percentage spent on papal nepotism is estimated to be 4–5 per cent of income (Partner, 'Papal Financial Policy', pp. 51, 55–7). Valignano felt that Gregory could have been more liberal in his spending on Jesuit colleges in Japan, noting tartly that what was required for Japan was a fraction of the monies spent on the German and Roman Colleges (Valignano, *Sumario*, p. 338).

[3] A reference to Matthew 12:33.

picture of the ancient city of Rome. We have brought both of these works with us so you can easily see them.[1] A very strong proof of the fame of the ancient city is the abundance of people, recorded in the books, their number being said to have reached six million at one time,[2] and their buildings were of such astonishing size that even the remains of them seem incredible. Behind all this was the power and dominion of that most glorious city of old, which in those days ruled over the greatest and most important part of the world.

With regard to modern Rome, it is without any doubt one of the greatest and most populous cities of Europe, and if it did not have such an abundance of gardens, orchards, and enclosures, there would be no argument about its holding the first place for population and size; but with account taken of its present site and the way it is used, it does not appear to be outdone by any in population,[3] and in the magnificence of its buildings it excels all others. Besides what I have already said about the papal palace and the church of St Peter, there are also many other palaces of the pope, notably the one which takes its name from St Mark, and is most magnificent in its scale and in its cost.[4] All the cardinals, besides, have their own very grand houses, and the other prelates, and the ambassadors of kings, and other great men who have their seat in Rome; and they possess not only houses for residence, but also many others arranged for pleasure and delight. Add to these the number of monasteries, convents, and churches, as well as hostels, hospitals, and other places dedicated to works of mercy, which are said to amount to two hundred in number, but in our judgment are many more than that. It is almost beyond me to describe the magnificence of all these places, the abundance of gold and silver furnishings, the costliness of the cloths. Various rulers, princes, and cardinals have had these buildings constructed at their expense, and the work and resources which they committed to them are extraordinary.

What am I to say of the things to do with secular sights, which are no less remarkable. A great multitude of people converges on Rome for purposes of business from all parts of Europe, and there is no one who can do justice to them in describing their numbers, their equipment, and how they conduct themselves. If you take just carriages pulled by two or four horses, they number about three thousand. And since it is not only business that is brought to Rome but also messengers from all parts of the world, there is nothing that goes on anywhere in Europe, indeed in the whole world, without Rome knowing about

---

[1] The standard works were the *Mirabilia urbis Romae* and Palladio's *L'antichità di Roma*. A number of engravings of ancient Rome (or rather how it was imagined to have been) were produced during the second half of the century. These included Etienne du Pérac's *Urbis Romae Sciographica ex antiquitis monumentis accurat iss[ime] delineata* (1574) and Mario Cartaro de Viterbe's *Celeberrimae urbis antiquae fidelissima topographia* (1579). See Pastor, *History of the Popes*, XX, pp. 553–5; Delumeau, *Vie économique et sociale de Rome*, pp. 148–65, esp. p. 163; McGowan 'Impaired Vision', pp. 244–55, esp. pp. 251–2; Palladio, *Palladio's Rome*, pp. xv, xlvii; Saastamoinen, 'Use of History', *passim*.

[2] A reliable estimate for the population of Rome in the middle of the 2nd century, when the city was at its maximum, is 'a million plus' (Robinson, *Ancient Rome*, p. 8).

[3] The population of Rome in 1580 was about 80,000 and in 1600 about 105,000. In these years, the population of Naples was 212,000 and 281,000; Venice 158,000 and 139,000; Lisbon 98,000 and 100,000; Paris 130,000 and 220,000; London 80,000 and 200,000. See Vries, *European Urbanization*, pp. 270–78; Partner, 'The Papal State', p. 28.

[4] The Palazzo di San Marco now known as the Palazzo Venezia, built by Pope Paul II (1417–71), who was born in Venice. It was used by some of his successors as a summer residence. Pius IV (1499–1565) ceded it to Venice. See Rodd, *Rome of the Renaissance*, p. 181; Magnuson, *Studies in Roman Quattrocento Architecture*, pp. 245–96.

it very quickly indeed, and because of this it is commonly said to be the theatre of the world.[1] Besides, because the Roman Pontiff is as it were the greatest of all, and presides supreme over all orders of priests and religious, there are so many of these men, in that category, that their number strains credulity; there are thought to be close to six thousand priests of the order of St Peter in Rome, and almost as many of those known as regular clergy. And you can grasp how many residences they have from this one piece of evidence: it is scarcely fifty years since the Society of Jesus was founded, but it has eight full residences in Rome.

Leo: Can there be eight residences of one religious order in one city?

Michael: That is how many there are, and I'll list them briefly for you. The first residence is the one called the House of the Professed, where the Superior General of the whole Society lives, together with his counsellors, assistants, and others, the number coming to seventy in all, and all of these live on alms got by begging. This professed house has an extraordinary church,[2] built with funds from the most illustrious Cardinal Alessandro Farnese, and it is a fact that a hundred and twenty thousand ducats were spent on the construction of this building. This church is large, covered with just one roof, but furnished with many chapels on both sides, and especially with a most artistic top, or cupola, as they call it, to the sanctuary. After we left we heard that the construction of the chapels which there are on both sides of that church is going to be paid for and looked after by most illustrious cardinals, each chapel by one cardinal; and since those cardinals have the most ample resources it is easy to see how outstanding and magnificent all the finished work of that church is going to be. Currently the part designated as the fathers' residence is put together, but not particularly well, from many old houses joined together, but the fathers hope that it will soon be rebuilt through the generosity of the same most illustrious cardinal, or through the resources of another similar leading man.

The second residence of the fathers is the Roman College, whose originator and principal founder was the supreme pontiff Gregory XIII.[3] When that most holy pope understood what abundant fruit would be produced from that college not only for the

---

[1] On Rome as perhaps the most important information hub in Europe, see Delumeau, *Vie économique et sociale de Rome*, ch. 2 *passim*. In the jubilee year of 1575 the number of pilgrims flocking to the city was around 400,000, many put up by confraternities (ibid., p. 171).

[2] The Gesù, near the Palazzo San Marco, built under the generous patronage of Alessandro Farnese (with contributions from Gregory XIII) and reflecting his architectural vision rather than the simpler design the Jesuits favoured, notably by choosing a vault instead of a flat ceiling. Farnese had set a budget limit of 25,000 *scudi* for the building costs but these were later estimated at 100,000 *scudi*. It was one of the most impressive churches in Rome, designed by Jacopo Barozzi da Vignola, with a facade by Giacomo della Porta. Its interior has been much altered since the boys' visit. The cornerstone was laid on 26 June 1568 and the church was consecrated on 24 November 1584. See Pastor, *History of the Popes*, XX, pp. 576–80; Robertson, '*Il Gran Cardinale*', pp. 181–96; Bailey, *Between Renaissance and Baroque*, pp. 191–4.

[3] The Collegio Romano, founded by Loyola in 1551, the cornerstone of the new building was laid on 11 January 1582. Gregory XIII donated generously to the high cost of the project, estimated at 400,000 *scudi*. The design is traditionally attributed to Bartolomeo Ammannati, but is more likely the work of the Jesuit architect Giuseppe Valeriano. The college was intended to be an outstanding international centre to promote Catholic orthodoxy and extirpate heresy. The new building was inaugurated on 28 October 1584. Since 1873 the college has been known as the Pontifical Gregorian University. See Pastor, *History of the Popes*, XIX, pp. 250–54; XX, pp. 586–9; O'Malley, *First Jesuits*, pp. 232–4; Bailey, *Between Renaissance and Baroque*, pp. 111–12, 118.

citizens of Rome but also for the whole of Christendom, and also appreciated that there was no sufficient income from anywhere, nor any building suitable for a residence, he resolved of his great benignity to provide for both. With regard to the building he spent a hundred and thirty thousand ducats on the construction of the schools and the first part of the residence, and from that you will appreciate that, when the roof is in place, the building will be one of the most sumptuous in the city. He then increased its revenues, so that the annual income of this college is now estimated to be twelve thousand ducats, and in it a hundred and fifty of the Society are provided for, and this number is to rise to three hundred when with the completion of the building this becomes possible; and thus from this nursery of the Society many other colonies may be propagated throughout the world,[1] and once planted may see an increase in the number and authority of the members of the Society there. And in the community of members of the Society now living in that college it is a very remarkable and joyful thing to see so many brothers from so many nations merge into one body, so that when some cardinals are invited to dinner, in the private and domestic conversation which usually takes place over meals, eighteen or even twenty different languages can be heard, but the whole multitude is joined together by such a bond of charity that the college really seems to be the residence of the indwelling Holy Spirit.

The third house of the Society is the one known as the House of Probation, or the novitiate,[2] in which brothers as yet uninstructed and but recently come from the turbulence of the world are exercised in the practice of virtue and purity of spirit. At that time there were seventy of them there, as well as ten others more senior, who have charge of the house and its business. The foundress of that house was the duchess, wife of the duke of Paliano, a most distinguished lady, born of the blood of the kings of Aragon, and mother of Marcantonio Colonna, most illustrious duke and Roman noble.[3]

The fourth house is the one commonly known as the House of Penance.[4] It is situated in the suburb next to Saint Peter's, and thirty of the Society are provided for there, and they hear the confessions of various men who come to Rome as to a sacred fountain, converging there in order to expiate their sins, and to be treated with most opportune remedies for the most grave wounds on their souls. Pope Pius V entrusted the Society with this most important task, and Pope Gregory XIII greatly increased the income of that house.

The fifth residence of the Society in Rome is the college called the Germanicum, which was established in the time of Pope Julius III by the industry and care of Father Ignatius,

---

[1] Original edition (p. 249) '*coloniae*'. The term '*colonia*' with the same meaning is used by Juan Alfonso de Polanco, Loyola's secretary, in his chronicle of the Society. See Polanco, *Vita Ignatii Loiolae*, II, p. 166; O'Malley, *First Jesuits*, p. 234.

[2] San Andrea al Quirinale. For descriptions of the pre-1610 paintings in the novitiate, none of which survive, but which included pictures of Xavier being received by the daimyo of Bungo, Ōtomo Yoshishige, see Bailey, *Between Renaissance and Baroque*, chs 2 and 3, esp. pp. 57, 63–4.

[3] The Errata list gives the foundress as '*Ioanna Aragonia*' and indicates '*Aragoniorum*' should be changed to '*Neapolitanorum*'. The person in question was Giovanna d'Aragona (1502–75) who had married Ascanio Colonna, duke of Paliano (1500–57). Their son, Marcoantonio (1535–84), was one of the protagonists at Lepanto.

[4] The Palazzo dei Penitenzieri, built between 1480 and 1490 by cardinal Domenico della Rovere and originally known as the Palazzo Della Rovere. Today the building is the headquarters of the Equestrian Order of the Holy Sepulchre of Jerusalem.

first founder of the Society, so that German youths could be educated there, in order to provide good teaching and rescue the province of Germany from near disaster, for at that time it was struggling desperately, and restore it to a happier condition.[1] When Pope Gregory XIII had seen and approved the impressive beginnings of this enterprise he gave the college added income of twenty thousand ducats, and with that there is now a community of two hundred living there, and twenty-five of the Society, who govern all that family. They invite carefully chosen youths from the whole of Germany to be educated there, and afterwards, when they have been instructed in learning and virtue and are invited by many different prelates of that region to assume many and honourable positions there, they send them back to their own country with the highest recommendation.

The sixth house is the Roman Seminary, set up by decree of the Council of Trent and authority of the pope, for the benefit and advantage of the diocese of Rome, and the same has been done in the other dioceses of Europe, with youths being schooled in common seminaries in piety and the good arts. In the Roman Seminary at that time there were sixty who were being educated, and who were to be ordained when they reached a mature age, as well as many others in addition to this number, who have been permitted, at the request and entreaty of the Roman aristocracy, to live with the community there, but supported from their own resources, not from the common income of the seminary. At that time they were a hundred and fifty in number.[2]

The seventh house of the Society is the English College,[3] dedicated to the benefit and advantage of the kingdom of England. England is a certain most noble island situated in the ocean to the north of the region of France, forming a very large kingdom, whose queen, infected with the perverse errors of the heretics, has drawn that people for the most part into the same perversity. Therefore when the pope learned that religion was in a troubled condition in that island, he wished to have English youths of outstanding ability and religious integrity educated in that seminary, so that imbued with learning and virtue they should return to their country, root out the errors from the souls of their

---

[1] The Collegium Germanicum or German College was established in 1552 to train clergy from Germany and northern Europe to return home and battle Protestantism. This lofty ambition was not fully realized until Gregory XIII provided financial and moral support. It then became the model for the various other national colleges engaged in clerical training. See Pastor, *History of the Popes*, XIX, pp. 237–41; O'Malley, *First Jesuits*, pp. 234–6. The Collegium Hungaricum, founded 1578, merged with the Germanicum in 1580 (Pastor, *History of the Popes*, XIX, pp. 241–2).

[2] The Seminario Romano presumably gets short shrift because the Society had been reluctant to run this kind of episcopal seminary envisaged by the Council of Trent. The Roman seminary had disciplinary problems far greater than the German College before the reforms made possible by Gregory's support. In 1570 the Jesuit rector described some of the students as 'liars, cheats, ingrates ... corrupters of the few good among them' (O'Malley, *First Jesuits*, pp. 236–38). Valignano's awareness and experience of these problems lies behind his order that the boys were not to be lodged in the colleges or seminaries during their travels, only at the houses of the professed.

[3] The English College grew out of St Thomas's hospice, a lodging for English pilgrims visiting Rome founded in 1362. In 1576 Gregory supported the foundation of a college to train English clergy. The college was handed over to the Jesuits in 1579 after a dispute between Welsh and English students over charges of favouritism by the Welsh rector of the college, Mairice Clenocke or Morus Clynnog, caused a mutiny among the English students. The English Jesuit Robert Persons served as temporary rector until Alphonso Agazzari was appointed permanent rector on 23 April 1579. See Munday, *English Roman Life*, pp. 22, 79–94; Pastor, *History of the Popes*, XIX, pp. 243–4. Munday, a Protestant, was a participant in the mutiny.

fellow citizens, and put their lives in danger of all kinds for the glory of God and to defend Christian truth. And that is what some have actually done, having before their eyes the fresh and outstanding example of Father Edmund Campion[1] and others of the Society, who recently shed their blood for Christ in that province, and not only gained immortal glory for themselves, but also shed much lustre on the Society itself. So the pope assigned this seminary a place in the church of St Stephen of the Rotunda,[2] and gave it six thousand ducats a year, and in it there was already, in addition to those of the Society who looked after the seminary, a community of fifty.

The eighth and last house is the College of the Maronites,[3] who are some of them Greeks, some of them Chaldeans, from the lands subject to the Turkish jurisdiction but nevertheless of Christian birth, and they are accustomed to come to the city of Rome to devote themselves to a better knowledge of the truth, and when they have been nourished in this seminary they can greatly benefit the people of their own nation. These too the pope has committed to the care and vigilance of the Society, so that they can make all possible progress in knowledge and virtue.

Leo: As I understand it then, the Society must have great authority with the pope, since he commits matters so various and of such moment to the care and direction of the fathers.

Michael: What would you think, then, if you had heard Popes Gregory XIII and Sixtus V calling the Society one of the pillars and bulwarks of the Church?

Lino: Happy city of Rome, adorned with so many holy and divine things, but also having the crowning happiness of possessing so many residences of the fathers; whereas our condition is far inferior and it is our lot sometimes to have hardly a single priest in many towns and districts.

Michael: Our condition should not be considered so unhappy, but rather fortunate, since we have the advantage of having a hundred and fifty fathers of the Society dispersed all over Japan,[4] and we hope that from now on their number will increase, and that with the solicitude of the fathers all this land of ours and all its people will embrace the Christian religion, and also that the vast kingdom of China will be added to the number of Christian kingdoms. But to come back to my story, we ourselves visited all these houses of the Society, and I can't tell you in detail how warmly we were received, in what honour we were held, and what excellent hospitality we enjoyed in each of them. Specially fixed

---

[1] 1540–81, who along with Robert Persons and the lay brother, Ralph Emerson, led the first Jesuit mission to England in 1580. He was canonized in 1970.

[2] This is a mistake. The English College was assigned to San Tommaso di Canterbury in the via Monserrato (Pastor, *History of the Popes*, XX, p. 585). Santo Stefano Rotondo, consecrated in the 5th century, is part of the German College thanks to the merger with the Hungaricum. The English College quickly attained a reputation for producing martyrs. An annual St Stephen's day sermon on the subject of martyrdom was given and, like Santo Stefano Rotondo, the college church has graphic paintings on the subject of martyrdom by Niccolò Pomerancio. For a detailed description of life in the English College, see Munday, *English Roman Life*, ch. 3.

[3] Founded in 1584, on the Quirinal (Pastor, *History of the Popes*, XX, p. 585).

[4] In 1590 there were 142 Jesuits in Japan, of whom 71 were Japanese (Costa, 'Os Jesuítas no Japão', pp. 306–7, 329, 330).

in our minds, however, as firmly as a nail hammered into a beam, is the benefit we received from the hospitality of the professed house, and the memory of that most religious residence, where we were treated both by the reverend Father General and by the other most distinguished fathers of the Society with a love and kindness that will never be forgotten. This professed house is the mother house of all the other colleges and houses of the Society, and is as it were the head from which is derived all the power and the control of the other members of the Society. The first founder of this house was the most holy Father Ignatius, first author and establisher of the Society, and he lived there, with the highest reputation for sanctity and piety, for sixteen years after the establishment and confirming of the Society, passed his last day there in all holiness, and left there the deathless imprint and memory of his virtues. His blessed body is kept there, preserved in the main chapel, to the great joy of the fathers.[1]

The same house is the fixed seat of the Superior Generals, who have governed the Society admirably till the present day, one succeeding another when death intervenes. The second, following Ignatius, was Father Diego Lainez,[2] a man outstanding not only for virtue but also for learning. The third, Father Francisco de Borja, whom I mentioned earlier, combined the highest sanctity with illustrious nobility. The fourth, Father Everard Mercurian,[3] was of singular prudence in governing the Society and in bringing together matters pertaining to its Institute. Finally, the fifth is Father Claudio Aquaviva, in whom the virtues of all the others come together and shine out most brilliantly, who also received us with the greatest kindness when we came to Rome, and embraced us with paternal love. There too the four counsellors, who are generally called the Assistants, have their place, and the Superior General takes counsel with them about all matters of great weight and moment, and after they have been considered appropriately, determines what is to be done about them. Here is held the congregation of the whole Society, when a Superior General dies, the provincial superior and two electors coming from each of the provinces of Europe. Since there are nineteen provinces of the Society in Europe it is easy to see what a large and splendid assembly of professed fathers comes together for that election. There also the procurators of all the provinces convene once every three years, and there is a meeting with the Superior General and a discussion of all doubtful and difficult matters.[4]

And since it is the custom of the Society that every father or brother should communicate as much as possible with superiors, and especially with the general, as members with their head, and that this should be by means of frequent letters and messages, the number of letters arriving at that house from the whole Society is extraordinary, as is the volume of business to be dealt with and the diligence combined with tranquillity in expediting it, and the number of letters and answers sent to the various provinces. And for the expediting of all these things the Superior General has in his confidence another very experienced father who deals with all matters pertaining to the

---

[1] His remains now lie in a bronze urn in the chapel of St Ignatius in the left transept of the Gesù.

[2] 1512–65, Spanish, General 1558–65.

[3] 1514–80, Belgian, General 1573–80.

[4] For discussions of the organization and governance of the Society, codified in the *Constitutions* in 1558, which, with a few revisions, applied until the dissolution of the order in 1773, see Demoustier, 'La distinction des fonctions', pp. 3–33; Alden, *Making of an Enterprise*, pp. 8–10, 229–54, 298–318; Harris, 'Mapping Jesuit Science', esp. pp. 217–22.

records and who, with other helpers, sees that all the letters get written, so that there is no delay or procrastination where business is concerned.[1] As a result the Superior General has a precise knowledge of all the things going on in the Society, and there is no one, not even a novice recently co-opted into the Society, whose name, with information on his character and his virtue, escapes his notice. And he is so attentive in scrutinizing and dealing with all the most distant things, such as our Japanese affairs, that it is as if he was present there himself to all of them.[2]

It was not without reason, therefore, that we were very much struck by the order and the administration in that house. And it is not only those who deal with the general government of the Society who live in that house, but also many other very learned and religious fathers, who perform a great service for the people of Rome by hearing confessions, giving sermons, explaining the sacred texts from the pulpit, and finally alleviating the distress of people in affliction, and therefore they are held in great favour and veneration by the pope himself, the cardinals, the nobility of Rome, and everyone else.

We were also very glad to see the Roman College, because of the size of the building, the multitude of colleagues living in harmony, and the great variety of teaching of the arts, which requires such a large community that we heard, as I said, that there will be provision for three hundred of the Society in that college when it is completed.[3] Besides the fact that it is the principal seminary of the Society, so many arts are taught to the pupils that a large number of masters is also required; for besides the Latin language, students of which are divided into various classes, the precepts of the disciplines of rhetoric, dialectics, philosophy, and mathematics, and of the Greek and Hebrew languages, are expounded. There is also interpretation of Sacred Scripture and treatments of controversies against heretics, and finally the whole of the teaching which is known as cases of conscience, which includes moral philosophy and a good part of both kinds of law, is dealt with thoroughly and appropriately, together with speculative theology.[4] The number of auditors eager to study these arts comes to almost two thousand, among whom, in addition to other worthy undertakings, there exists a certain fraternal sodality named after the Annunciation of the Blessed Virgin.[5] Many privileges have been conferred on it by the pope, and from it have come not only many priests, but also prelates, and there are

---

[1] The secretary. The first holder of this office was Juan Alfonso Polanco (1517–76), appointed by Loyola (O'Malley, *First Jesuits*, pp. 6–7, 10–11). At the time of the boys' visit the secretary was Niccolò Orlandini, the Jesuit historiographer.

[2] As the Society expanded its activities it was impossible for the Jesuit general to have such precise and accurate knowledge. See Valignano, *Historia*, pp. 22*–31*; Alden, *Making of an Enterprise*, pp. 229–30. Nevertheless, the sheer volume of information sent to Rome about the Society's activities is impressive. The character references concerning Jesuits in Japan are brief, usually limited to nationality, age, health, proficiency in Japanese and scholastic achievement. For examples, including one about Valignano written by Valignano himself, see Schütte, *Monumenta Historica Japoniae I*, pp. 306–25.

[3] The Roman College, designed by Bartolomeo Ammannati, was opened in October 1584.

[4] This curriculum was modelled on that of the University of Paris. For a broader discussion of Jesuit pedagogy, see O'Malley, *First Jesuits*, pp. 215–16, and ch. 6 *passim*.

[5] Founded in 1564, it served as a model for the other Jesuit Marian congregations (see above, p. 193 n. 1). The primacy of the Roman College's congregation of the Annunciation was established in a papal bull by Gregory in 1584, the other Marian congregations becoming its branches. Central control was tightened by a further bull in 1587 (Chatellier, *Europe of the Devout*, pp. 9–10).

many other sodalities, devoted to good works, set up in other academies in imitation of it. Of the college buildings, I'll say only that what gave us the most satisfaction was a very large hall where scholastic exercises are held, whose walls are adorned with very fine paintings of all the colleges and seminaries founded by the most holy Pope Gregory XIII, which preserve the memory of the same most meritorious founder with this splendid memorial. Among these pictures we were especially happy to see those of our own Japanese ones, whose likeness we recognized depicted there.[1]

What shall I say to you of the other things with which this most famous city is adorned. If I were to list them there would be no end, especially if I dealt with relics of the saints. Since Rome is as it were the head of the Christian religion, and the seat chosen by God for the Supreme Pontiff, He also willed that it should be adorned with all the most celebrated relics of Christ and the saints. The diligence of the Supreme Pontiffs also helped to bring this about, for they most diligently sought out and brought to that most famous theatre of the world all the monuments of the Christian religion, so that the city has always had these riches in abundance. It has taken from this treasure many and most precious gifts, and has distributed them to almost all other cities, and yet still keeps an exceedingly ample store.[2]

Firstly, with regard to the insignia of Christ, they have in Rome the manger which Christ sanctified with his divine body when He had been born of the Virgin Mary; some small swaddling cloths in which He was first wrapped by his most holy mother; a shirt which He wore; the column on which He leant when He spoke in the temple of Jerusalem, which still retains such great and divinely given power that all those seized by some evil spirit are easily freed if they touch it. In the same city is that table at which Christ shared the Last Supper with his apostles, the cloth with which he washed their feet, one of the thirty denarii, the desire for which led disloyal Judas to betray his Lord and Master; the pillar to which he was tied and beaten with whips for us; some thorns from that cruel diadem which was placed on his sacred head; the purple garment splashed with his blood; the reed with which his reverend head was struck; the staircase of twenty-eight steps by which he went up to the hall of Pontius Pilate,[3] stained with drops of blood that fell from his sacred body; the towel on which an image of his face wet with blood is imprinted; many pieces of that sacred wood on which he hung for us; one of the nails by which he

---

[1] The original paintings no longer exist but there is another description of them from the previous year (1584), which also mentions the three Japan colleges (Bailey, *Between Renaissance and Baroque*, p. 119). Woodcut illustrations depicting the colleges established by Gregory, including the professed house in Usuki, the college in Funai and the seminaries in Arima and Azuchi, were published in Ciappi's *Compendio*. The depictions are of European buildings rather than Japanese ones and would not have been recognizable as Japanese buildings to the boys. For modern reproductions, see Boncompagni-Ludovisi, *Le prime due ambasciate*, facing p. xxxviii; McCall, 'Early Jesuit Art in the Far East V', p. 53. See also Bailey, *Between Renaissance and Baroque*, p. 120.

[2] Most of the relics mentioned in what follows are located in the seven pilgrim churches listed below (p. 297) as 'the seven most celebrated churches' The churches and their relics were part of the standard pilgrim itinerary in Rome. See Palladio, *Descritione de le chiese, stationi, indulgenze & reliquie de Corpi Sancto che sono in la città de Roma*, 1554 (trans. in Palladio, *Palladio's Rome*), which lists their relics and the indulgences pilgrims could accrue. It is as respectful and credulous as the account given here. The boys visited all seven churches (Fróis, *Première ambassade*, pp. 185–6). So too did Anthony Munday, whose description of what he termed 'the egregious follies and devilish drifts, whereby God is despised, and men too much wilfully blinded' provides a counterpoint to Palladio's and the boys' description (*English Roman Life*, pp. 45–59, esp. p. 59).

[3] The Scala Sacra in St John Lateran.

was transfixed; the inscription attached to the top of the cross in Hebrew, Greek and Latin letters, declaring him to be King of the Jews; the sponge soaked in gall and vinegar which was offered for him to suck; the iron of the spear by which his sacred breast was transfixed; some fragments from the sacred tomb which received the most holy body of Christ, and the pillar split into two parts when Christ on the Cross breathed his last.

All these relics of his most bitter torments and pledges of our salvation are kept in various churches with the utmost veneration, and we saw them and were profoundly moved by them. The devotion of the Christians to all of these is so great that although the sacred staircase, which I referred to, is made of extremely hard marble, its steps are for the most part worn away, such is the number of the devotees who ascend it on their knees. There too can be seen a drop of blood, covered with an iron grill, on which fingers have so often been pressed that it has made a considerable hollow in the stone itself, but without the colour of the blood being lost.

What shall I say of the relics of the saints, which also greatly ennoble the same city? In it the bodies of the holy apostles Peter and Paul are guarded with piety and reverence, and the churches of the same apostles and of St John Lateran are adorned with their venerable trunks and heads. No less famous are the places in which they met a glorious death. At the place where St Peter was raised on his cross there is a church of the Franciscan order, dedicated to the same apostle, which has taken the name of Montorio from the hill on which it is situated.[1] At the place where St Paul was beheaded can be seen, in addition to a very fine church, the three famous fountains which still flow from the three places touched by his head as it jumped in an amazing way.[2] The water from these fountains is good for health of mind and body, and we drank some and took some away with us. There too are the bodies of the apostles Simon, Jude, Philip, James the Less, and Bartholomew, the heads of the apostles Andrew and James the Greater, and of Luke the Evangelist, the bodies also of Saints Stephen Protomartyr, Laurence, and Timothy, and of the Pope Saints, Leo I and Gregory the Great, as well as of St Jerome, St John Chrysostom,[3] and of other most holy pontiffs and confessors of Christian truth.[4] But what shall I say of the martyrs?

When in times past the city of Rome was the capital of the Roman empire, and the emperors, with pagan superstition still remaining, always lived there, and most of them subjected Christianity to severe persecution, the havoc which they caused was frightful, but also extraordinary is the amount of evidence which still exists of the cruelty of the pagans and the fortitude of the Christians, namely the holy bodies and bones, whether complete or divided up into parts, of many martyrs who, either thrown into the flames, or cut to pieces by the sword, or torn with iron hooks, or subjected to other kinds of torments, gave their lives and souls to Christ. Witnesses to the same thing are many places of the same martyrs, still steeped in their holy blood, especially certain pits in which Christian men and women reverently hid the bodies and, where they could collect it, the

---

[1] San Pietro in Montorio.

[2] San Paulo alle Tre Fontana, the old Roman spring known as Aquæ Salviæ. Munday records this story as well (*English Roman Life*, p. 48).

[3] His relics, part of the pillage from the Fourth Crusade in 1204, were brought to Rome but were returned to Greece in 2004.

[4] Not all of the remains listed are in St Peter's, let alone in Rome: for example, St Luke's body is thought to be in Padua rather than in Rome. The list owes more to legend than to fact.

blood of the same martyrs. There are, besides, certain crypts which still exist and which offer further testimony to the same.[1] Very holy men took refuge in these, so as not to be seen by the tyrants, and lived out their lives there in the darkness and the dirt for the sake of Christ. From this multitude of relics an extraordinary piety flows out into the souls of the citizens of Rome and beyond, for though there are so many churches and religious shrines, the multitudes thronging these religious places are so great, especially when the things to see are shown to the people, that they can hardly fit into the churches. The same devotion is shown to those wax images which display the form of the divine Lamb, that is Christ, which are made when the pope begins his pontificate and every seven years thereafter, which are eagerly desired and sought after by all.[2] The same goes for sacred or expiatory bulls, which are always avidly desired.

Besides all these there is the publicizing of numberless miracles which God of his infinite power and goodness often provides, to be seen and viewed, sometimes through sacred relics together with the divine power, sometimes also when He sees the piety and devotion of Christians; and books, and the voices of the people, and the whole of Christendom are full of these. Thus it is that these things which I have spoken of, together with the authority and the sanctity of life of the pope, the cardinals, and the prelates and religious men of whom Rome is full, provide by their testimony most certain confirmation of the truth of Christianity, and we, having seen so many things, have it firmly fixed in our minds and are bringing it back to our fatherland.

Leo: Happy are you who have not only achieved such firmness of faith by seeing these things with your own eyes, but have also brought it about that in our minds too, as we listen to you, faith is very much strengthened.

Michael: Indeed. But what shall I say now about the seven most celebrated churches, which all are accustomed to visit in order to obtain pardon for their sins? They are dedicated to St Peter, St Paul, St John Lateran, St Mary Major, St Laurence outside the Walls, St Sebastian, and the Holy Cross of Jerusalem,[3] and it would be almost impossible to describe the kindness with which we were treated when we visited them by the priests and religious living there. Add to those another most famous church, St Mary of the Rotunda,[4] which is extremely large, a hundred and seventy palms in length and in height, to be precise, and which is covered by a vault in the form of a perfect semicircle at the summit of which is a transparent sphere which diffuses light throughout the whole of the church. The chapels and altars of this church are adorned with most elegant columns, the walls are decorated with many precious stones of various kinds, and the roof, formerly of

---

[1] The catacombs had been venerated by pilgrims until the 9th century and after that largely forgotten, although some were still visited. The discovery of an impressive catacomb on the Via Salaria in 1578 caused a sensation and reminded people that there had been a previous long history of church persecution and martyrdom. The discovery was exploited to foster a renewal of religious life. See Pastor, *History of the Popes*, XIX, pp. 262–4, 266–9. For Munday's account of the catacombs, see *English Roman Life*, pp. 60–69.

[2] *Agnus dei* which were much sought after by visitors to Rome.

[3] Excluding St Peter's, the other churches are known as San Paolo, Santa Maria Maggiore, San Lorenzo Fuori le Mura, San Sebastiano and Santa Croce in Gerusaleme.

[4] Santa Maria Rotonda, more commonly known as the Pantheon, consecrated in the 7th century. Montaigne was also greatly impressed but his description is extremely brief (*Journal de voyage*, p. 228).

silver tiles, is now very well made of tiles of lead. The vestibule, finally, is excellently furnished with thirteen columns each made from one piece of stone, so thick that it is eighteen palms in circumference, and remarkably tall, and with huge beams of gilded bronze; and I say nothing of the bronze doors, of most beautiful artistry, and other things which greatly ennoble the precinct of the church.

What purpose would it serve to describe for you in detail the pagan and ancient buildings, for example the Coliseum, where formerly spectacles were regularly staged for the people, and the baths of Diocletian and Antoninus, where once they washed in hot water brought long distances by means of most ingenious aqueducts. Then there are the columns of the Emperors Antoninus Pius[1] and Trajan. You ascend the first of these, which is a hundred and seventy six feet high, by an interior spiral staircase of a hundred and forty steps, and lest it should be in any way short of light there are a hundred and six windows to let it in, and all around it is adorned with figures illustrating the victories and triumphs of the Emperor Antoninus. The other column is a hundred and twenty-three feet high, and boasts a spiral staircase with a hundred and fifteen steps and forty-five windows, with the triumphs of the Emperor Trajan depicted there. Why, besides, should I mention the obelisk or needle of Caesar, which is just one stone in the form of a pyramid, every bit as tall as the columns just referred to, with the ashes of Julius Caesar contained in a sphere at the top. Pope Sixtus V, however, has now had this needle transferred, at great expense, to St Peter's Square, and he has got rid of Caesar's ashes and has placed a cross at the apex.[2]

Why again should I spend time describing the Castel Sant'Angelo for you?[3] In it is the very famous structure known as Hadrian's Mole, all of it solid, and made of stone fixed with lime, in which the ashes of the Emperor Hadrian were formerly preserved. Its summit was closed off by a bronze pine tree, of extraordinary size, and provided with an abundance of pine cones to match. We saw one of them, which still exists in Saint Peter's Square, and is an ell and a half in height, so you can imagine how big the tree itself was. In that place, then, where formerly there was just the Mound of Hadrian, there was built this citadel dedicated to the Archangel Michael, which is chiefly the main defence of the sacred palace, and contains numerous noble apartments and rooms. It is joined to it by an extremely long corridor, extending for a quarter of a league, with very artistic work, which stretches out all the way to the sacred palace. I can't justify extending my account further by mentioning and describing in detail these and other buildings, since the city of Rome

---

[1] A mistake for the Column of Marcus Aurelius in the Piazza Colonna, which, like the column of Trajan in Trajan's Forum, can be ascended by stairs. The Column of Antoninus Pius was mostly buried underground before it was excavated in 1703. It is now in the Vatican.

[2] The obelisk, mentioned by Pliny the Elder, was brought to Rome from Egypt by Caligula in 37 CE and adorned his circus, later renamed after Nero. It was removed the short distance from its previous location to its existing one in the centre of St Peter's Square, a major undertaking, between April and September 1586, after the boys had left Rome, although such a move had long been planned. It was already well-known that the sphere at the top did not contain Caesar's ashes and had nothing to do with him. See Delumeau, *Vie économique et sociale de Rome*, p. 304; Curran et al., 'A Fifteenth Century Site Report', pp. 235, 241 n. 30, 242 n. 33. For a description of the move with illustrations, see Fontana, *Della trasportatione dell'obelisco Vaticano*.

[3] Originally built between 135 and 139 CE, Hadrian's ashes were interred in the mausoleum a year after his death in 138 CE. The mausoleum was crowned with a garden of cypress trees. Later, it became a fortress. The corridor, or Passetto di Borgo, was built by Nicholas II and the fortress was used as a refuge by Clement VII during the Sack of Rome in 1527.

is adorned with an almost infinite number of palaces and magnificent houses. And it is not only Rome within the city walls that is ennobled with these buildings, for the whole district of Rome is as it were embellished with other places dedicated to pleasure and relaxation, and each of these certainly stands comparison with other such places which I have spoken of earlier.

One example is the villa of the Medici cardinal,[1] another that of Cardinal Arestino, and there are many similar, constructed with such ingenuity and art that in one of them, built at Tivoli by the cardinal of Ferrara,[2] we heard a musical instrument, commonly called an organ, played by water power as skilfully as if by a master organist, with the most sweet song of the nightingale or Philomel brought to our ears by the cleverly controlled movement of the water. We also saw many other admirable fountain designs at the same villa, particularly one producing various bird-warblings, first very loud, then reduced as the sound of a nightingale comes in, then picking up again as the nightingale song dies away. But enough! The delights of Rome can't easily be set out in words, nor can the imagination of anyone not present there do justice to them.

---

[1] Ferdinando de' Medici (1549–1609), cardinal from 1562, succeeded his brother Francesco as grand duke of Tuscany in 1587 and remained a cardinal until he married Christine of Lorraine in 1589. He bought the villa in 1576 and made it a symbol of Medici power in Rome. He was an astute observer of papal politics. See Guarini, '"Rome Workshop of all the Practices of the World"', pp. 53–77.

[2] Ippolito d'Este (1509–72), archbishop of Milan, cardinal from 1538, known as the cardinal of Ferrara. He commissioned the Villa d'Este at Tivoli. His grand-nephew, Luigi d'Este (1538–86), bishop of Ferrara 1550, cardinal from 1561, governor of Tivoli from 1572, was staying at the Tivoli at the time of the boys' stay in Rome. A number of letters concerning them are addressed to him (*Dai Nihon Shiryō*, XI: 1, pp. 243–55). Montaigne noted that he had not carried out any work on the place; he also noted the organ-like sound created by the water (*Journal de voyage*, pp. 233–4). As for Cardinal Arestini, or Arestino, no such individual has been identified. It is possible that Arestini and either Ippolito or Luigi d'Este are one and the same. The latter was born in Arezzo. Pietro Aretino, the celebrated author, was also born illegitimately in Arezzo and used the name Aretino, i.e. 'of Arezzo'. The cardinal mentioned could also be of or from Arezzo where, in fact, Ippolito d'Este was born.

COLLOQUIUM XXIV

Of what took place in Rome up until the death of Pope Gregory XIII[1]

Leo: So far, Michael, you have spoken about the buildings of Rome. Now we are no less eager to hear from you what else you did in Rome in all the time you were there, for that must also be of no little importance.

Michael: Everything that happened in Rome is certainly worth remembering and recounting. I'll continue with it, then, no less diligently than before, and I'll bring the story back again to Pope Gregory XIII. To remember him and to speak of him reanimates me, for the more than paternal love with which he embraced us when we were staying in Rome, right up till his death, is unforgettable. He sent messengers every day to inquire after us, and showered us with gifts. He was so concerned for Julian who was in bed ill that he put him in the hands of six expert doctors, and ordered them to visit him twice a day, and when he himself was at his last gasp, like a parent mindful of his children rather than himself, he asked most lovingly whether Julian was well.[2] What more shall I say? When that most holy pope, weakened by age and a brief illness, rendered his life to nature and his soul to God on the eighteenth day after our arrival at Rome,[3] it was widely rumoured that the Supreme Pontiff had died of joy at our arrival. He was in sound health for almost eighteen days after our arrival, so the story was popular rather than true; nevertheless, the signs of benevolence which he daily exhibited towards us provided the whole people with ample occasion to spread that rumour.

After the feast day of the angelic Annunciation to the Blessed Virgin, then, the same pontiff again instructed that we be invited for the solemnities to be celebrated in St Peter's church on 29 March, and when we arrived to accompany him and he saw us in our new clothing in the Roman style, of black velvet with fine gold trimmings, he was delighted, and cordially commented that the outfits suited us extremely well, but that for the Easter season which would soon be upon us they should be changed for others more festive and richer. Then, taking the same place that I described earlier, we accompanied him, together with a large concourse of cardinals, to the church of St Peter, and proceeded reverently into the palace, and we were most kindly conducted into the inner chambers which are

---

[1] In the original edition (pp. 259–68), all of Colloquium XXIV and the first two pages of Colloquium XXV are mispaginated as pp. 255–64.

[2] Julian was seriously ill with malaria and was attended by Alfonso Cataneo, the cardinal d'Este's personal physician, who reported regularly to his patron on the patient's health and treatment. See Fróis, *Première ambassade*, p. 183 n. 654; *Dai Nihon Shiryō*, XI: 1, pp. 177–8, 237, 249, 251–6.

[3] 10 April.

completely closed to other externs.¹ Again on the following Sunday, 31 March, which was the fourth Sunday of Lent,² we accompanied the pope to his chapel. On this day, by ancient custom, a golden rose is blessed and sent as a present to some Christian queen or princess. So we attended the Mass and the sacred ceremonies which it is customary to celebrate on that day, and we saw the new Roman senator, that is, supreme magistrate, together with the conservators and other lower magistrates, taking the oath of fidelity and submission, as ancient custom requires, before the Supreme Pontiff. For as I said before, the Supreme Pontiff holds secular as well as sacred power and jurisdiction over the city of Rome and many other cities.³

The pope reserved the following Thursday, which was 4 April,⁴ for an intimate conversation with us because before then, on account of the many religious ceremonies, he had had no free time. In that private conversation he spoke in a most loving and familiar way about many things, and asked a number of questions about matters to do with Japan, inquiring for example about the number of Christians in the islands of Japan, of churches built and consecrated to God and the saints, and of European priests living there. He asked besides about how the divine services were conducted, what hopes there were of fruit becoming daily more abundant, and other similar things; and as we answered each of his queries he, the common father of the whole Christian people, was delighted, his demeanour showing how pleased he was. On that same day we offered to him, as tokens of homage, some presents which we had brought from our country, among them certain panels given to the Father Visitor by Nobunaga as a gift, on which there were paintings of the most magnificent walls of the city of Azuchiyama, founded by the same Nobunaga.⁵

The pope showed himself very much pleased with these gifts we offered, even though they fell far short of his great majesty, and immediately after that he conducted us most kindly to the inner chambers of the palace, and to his museum, the place dedicated to literary study. It was a place, indeed, most admirable to behold, embellished everywhere with various figures painted with great skill, adorned with a great many expensively bound books, and all in all of a magnificence befitting such majesty and grandeur. From there we were taken to a certain loggia known as the Galeria, by which the pope has private access to a most agreeable garden called the Belvedere, thus named, of course,

---

¹ See also Boncompagni-Ludovisi, *Le prime due ambasciate*, p. 16, which is essential for dating these events.

² Also known as Rose Sunday when the pope blesses a golden rose which is occasionally given as a mark of esteem to monarchs, governments or people in recognition of their devotion to the Holy See. The ceremony is performed in the pope's private chapel (ibid, p. 8).

³ Ibid., loc cit. The government of the free commune of Rome had come to an end in 1398. Thereafter the Senator and other officials were papal appointees devoid of real power. Ceremony and ritual were essential ingredients in the assertion of papal power vis-à-vis the Roman magistracy. See Prodi, *Papal Prince*, pp. 49–51; Partner 'The Papal State', p. 34; Fosi, 'Court and City', pp. 31–52; Nussdorfer, 'Vacant See', pp. 176–8.

⁴ Original edition (p. 260) gives '*Diem Iovis sequente, qui fuit Nonis Aprilis*', or Thursday 5 April. The previous Sunday was 31 March, so the Thursday was 4 April. Fróis (*Première ambassade*, p. 184) gives Wednesday 3 April.

⁵ The screens or *byōbu*, possibly painted by Kanō Eitoku, had been given to Valignano personally by Nobunaga at Azuchi in 1581. According to Fróis, Nobunaga's generous gift caused surprise in and around Kyoto and was deemed a rare honour, with many people coming to view the screens at the Jesuit church in Kyoto. The other gifts included an ebony writing-desk. See Berchet, 'Documenti', pp. 153–4; Boncompagni-Ludovisi, *Le prime due ambasciate*, p. 8; *Dai Nihon Shiryō*, XI: 1, pp. 175–7; *Cartas*, II, ff. 39r–v; Fróis, *História*, III, pp. 260–61; Cooper, *Japanese Mission*, pp. 203–8. The screens were last seen by Philips van Winghe sometime between 1589 and 1592. He incorporated one of the towers and gateways of Azuchi into sketches which were later reproduced as prints in Vicenzo Cartari's *Imagini delli dei de gl'antichi* (1647).

for the extraordinarily fine view which it offers. Who could describe in words the magnificence of this loggia, the manifold mosaics attached to the walls, and the walls themselves, clothed in gold and a variety of colours? You yourselves must use your imaginations to work out, from the power of the pope, the things which I pass over in silence, but it was in that loggia, so ornate, that the pope commanded that those panels with the depiction of Azuchiyama were to be placed, thus showing that our gift was to be numbered among those held in high esteem.[1] After that he asked us, when we came back to him, which Roman and European things we would be most glad to take back with us to our country, and he instructed that a list of all those things should be written out and that we ourselves should hand it to him, for he, the supreme father, wanted to gratify us, as his most dear sons, in everything, and wanted it done without any delay, lest his death should unexpectedly intervene. On the following Sunday we were present when Mass was solemnly celebrated in the presence of the pope, then as always among the ambassadors, Mancio and I standing on either side of him; of our other companions one, namely Julian, was still ill, and the other, Martin, was seated close to feet of the pontiff.

Leo: Why was he sitting when you were standing?

Michael: Because it is proper for ambassadors (and that is what we were) to be at the pope's side, as his most faithful guards, so that position, though less comfortable, is more honorific. You yourselves may imagine how often, in all of the period I have been talking about so far, we had to visit the most illustrious cardinals and others of the nobility of Rome, and how often we had to receive them on their frequent visits to us. Lest this constant running about hither and thither, or the frequently repeated invitations to banquets, should harm our health, the pope, like a most vigilant father, ordained that we were not to attend any banquet except with his approval; he could not withhold it, however, when the legates of the kings persistently importuned him, so we did in fact attend sumptuously prepared banquets with each of them, and were invited, in the names of the kings and princes themselves, to visit their kingdoms and courts on our way back to our own country. The legates of the most august emperor,[2] of the most Christian king of France,[3] and of the duke of Savoy[4] proposed this and pressed it on us with vehemence, but it would have been so far out of our way that it was not possible to accede to their request. The legate of the republic of Venice made the same request,[5] however, and in this case, given that the city and republic were not far away, it would not have been possible to refuse without a dereliction of our duty,[6] and I shall be dealing with our journey there

---

[1] The Galeria, decorated by the Dominican Egnazio Danti with maps of Italy, would have been a fitting place to display the screens. The Belvedere is a courtyard rather than a garden.

[2] Gian Federico Madruzzo (1531–86), brother of Cardinal Ludovico Madruzzo (1532–1600) (Hübner, *Sisto Quinto*, vol. I, p. 111).

[3] The new ambassador, Jean de Vivonne, marquess de Pisany (1530–99), arrived on 18 April. Until then Henry III's affairs were handled by the Cardinal d'Este (ibid., loc. cit.).

[4] Unknown.

[5] Lorenzo Priuli. For his letters concerning the boys' stay in Rome, see *Dai Nihon Shiryō*, XI: 1, pp. 257–63.

[6] Original edition (p. 262) gives '*saluo efficio*' which must be a misprint for '*saluo officio*', i.e *salvo officio*, a quotation from Cicero's oration *Pro Sex. Roscio Amerino* (I: 4).

Figure 10.   Commemorative medal struck by Gregory XIII to mark the embassy.
By permission of Biblioteca Apostolica Vaticana, with all rights reserved.

as we proceed. Let me sum up then by saying finally that all the nobles of Rome visited us most honourably, and that we are particularly grateful to two very illustrious and famous men, Giacomo Boncompagni, duke of Sora, and Paolo Giordano Orsini, duke of Bracciano,[1] for the special love which they showed for us. Among the legates we remember very particularly the most illustrious count de Olivares, who was the legate acting in the name of King Philip of Spain. He frequently visited us, sent us presents, and provided services of all kinds for us, doing all that could be asked and more to represent the person of the Catholic King, and showing love and benevolence to the new offspring of the republic of Christendom.

But since up till now I have been speaking of private persons who came in contact with us, it will not be out of place to make mention here of the public welcome and extraordinary expression of love which we received from the senate and people of Rome. A few days after our entry into Rome the supreme magistrate, who is called the senator, and who holds the topmost rank in that republic, came to visit us, together with three others known as the conservators, and with all the others who perform important functions in that republic. They all came to us with the same pomp and display which they are accustomed to use at their public ceremonies. The senator came wearing a very long embroidered cloak with gold interweaving, the other conservators similarly in black velvet, and the remaining magistrates also in togas of the same silk. Preceding them came twenty-four lictors with gilded staffs in their hands, in ornate dress partly red, partly saffron-coloured. Following them and bringing up the rear were many noble Roman citizens, very expensively dressed, and many of them with their breasts adorned with the sign of the Cross, denoting a special rank in a military order, and a great throng of the people. And the order and gravity which they displayed in their progress, and the magnificence in all other things, were such that we could justly contemplate the Roman republic in those magistrates, as in its head. All these who came to us we received with the courtesy which was their due, and from what they said we learned of the great joy and happiness which had spread all through the people of Rome on our arrival, when we came from the most distant of regions to visit the pope. And they not only honoured us with their felicitations, but later, through a messenger, made a highly important addition, namely that that it pleased the Senate and People of Rome to bestow on us, as a further mark of their esteem, Roman citizenship (something rarely granted, and normally only to very important and especially deserving men), and to count us among not just any citizens, but among their noble patrician citizens.

We first of all expressed our thanks, through a messenger, for the great honour done to us, and then, on the designated day, which was before the feast of the Lord's Ascension, we proceeded to the Senate to offer our thanks in person and also to have that honour conferred on us. The senator and the other magistrates received us with the honour which they are accustomed to accord to kings and leading men, and when we were honourably seated an orator made a speech on behalf of the whole senate, the burden of which was that the people of Rome were overwhelmed with joy at seeing,

---

[1] 1541–85. He had strangled his wife, Isabella de' Medici, in 1576, after accusing her of infidelity. He later ordered the murder of Francesco Peretti, nephew of the future pope Sixtus V, with whose wife he was having an affair. He fled with his mistress, whom he subsequently married, to northern Italy and met the boys again when they reached Venice.

with most joyous eyes and souls, noble youths from the most remote provinces of the earth who had made such a long journey and who professed the recently received faith of Christ; and that they therefore granted that the four of us be numbered among the citizens of Rome (the best and greatest sign of love that they could offer), bestowed on us the privileges enjoyed by the patrician nobles and the senators of Rome, and begged us to look favourably on this testimony of love, this pledge of benevolence. After this speech four men of good family presented to us, on four silver salvers, four parchments, decorated with gold and various different designs and adorned with the insignia of our families and with gold seals, on which those privileges were set out. We very gladly accepted these most welcome evidences of their love for us, and in answer told them that we would never forget so great a favour. Then, accompanied again by trumpets, flutes, and the singing of a whole choir, we returned to our usual quarters in the house of the Society.[1] From this, then, you can see how great Christian love is towards those whom Christ deigns to accept into his family.

Leo: In these deeds and works we can see, as in a most clear mirror, that charity which, as I have already learned, is the best known aspect of Christianity, according to what Christ himself said: 'By this shall all men know ... etc'.[2] So I can easily see that all those who give their name to Christ take on this form and face, as it were, and that is why they are so loving to one another and so bound by ties of brotherhood.

Lino: What our Leo says can be confirmed not only by the example of the Europeans, with their ancestral faith, accepted centuries ago by their forebears, but by the very recent testimony of our own Japanese, who, when they are first initiated into Christian teaching, simultaneously imbibe that love towards others of the same Christian faith, so much so that they love those Christians more than their own blood relatives.

Mancio: This in fact is why it has happened that some pagans in some places have formed the wrong opinion, and have unreasonably persuaded themselves, that the fathers of the Society and other Japanese, bound to one another by a most ardent bond of love, might easily think of seizing power over the whole of Japan.[3]

---

[1] The ceremony took place after Gregory's death but before the installation of the new pope, Sixtus V, on 26 May. For additional details of the ceremony, the handsomely decorated diplomas granting the boys Roman citizenship, dated 10 May, and the related deliberations of the Roman senate, see Berchet, 'Le antiche', pp. 264–5; idem, 'Documenti', pp. 162–4; Boncompagni-Ludovisi, *Le Prime due ambasciate*, pp. 17–19; Fróis, *Première ambassade*, pp. 198–9; *Dai Nihon Shiryō*, XI: 1, pp. 304–10. On behalf of the others, Mancio delivered a short speech of thanks noting that in the past Rome had been born to be mistress of the world extending its empire first by force of arms, but now thanks to the holiness of religion its reach extended to Japan (*Dai Nihon Shiryō*, XI: 1, pp. 280–81, 285). Montaigne had to pull strings to get his diploma of citizenship (*Journal de voyage*, p. 232). He included the diploma of citizenship in the *Essais*, in the chapter on vanity, commenting that he found it inane and vapid (*Essais*, III, ch. 9, pp. 240–42). Hasekura Tsunenaga, the envoy of Date Masamune, daimyo of Sendai, to Spain and Rome in 1614–15, also received a diploma of Roman citizenship (*Dai Nihon Shiryō*, XII: 12, pp. 298–9).

[2] John 13:35.

[3] Valignano was determined to counter such opinions. He had strongly condemned the plan advocated by his fellow Jesuit, Alonso Sánchez, for a conquest of China to advance Christianity when he learned of it in Macao in 1582, and he similarly condemned as highly irresponsible and dangerous the request of some of his colleagues

Michael: As if the Christian law commended loyalty and charity towards princes any less than towards men linked by the same religion. Indeed, if they wished to reason correctly, since Christians love each other so much, no better means of keeping Japan in peace and tranquillity could be devised than that all should embrace the Christian religion. For with all Japanese, whether princes or subjects, linked together in this way, there would be no question of taking up arms, or shedding blood, or failing to abide by the commitment given to kings, nor finally of inciting disturbance of any kind, and all their thinking would be directed to maintaining and extending peace throughout the land.

Leo: Please God all the pagans may come round to this most salutary idea, and eventually at some point may escape from the error in which they now dwell, and that affairs in Japan, labouring now under such afflictions, may with the favour of the divinity be resolved and healed. But let us return to Roman matters.

Michael: The Roman matters which I now have to record are such that the mind shudders at the memory and shrinks from the sorrow of them.

Leo: What matters are these, so sad and sorrowful?

Michael: The almost totally sudden and unexpected death of Gregory XIII, of whose more than paternal benevolence towards us we had so much experience and so many proofs. From the time when we entered Rome everything had gone so very well for us, but in the course of human affairs such happiness and joy must needs be tempered with some sorrow. The more unexpected the darts are the more harm they do, so the departure of the pope from this life, so unexpected that we knew of his death before we even heard that he had fallen ill, delivered a great shock to our minds. For on 9 April the pope, despite the weight of years on him, was so well that he celebrated Mass freely and promptly; but then on the next day, when we were travelling by coach through some places in Rome, the most illustrious Cardinal of San Sisto informed us by a messenger of the unexpected death of the pope. With the coach covered, therefore, we made our way home, giving ourselves over wholly to mourning and tears, and in the house we found the fathers similarly grief-stricken at the loss of such a father.

This kind of death was indeed unexpected and unforeseen, but could certainly not be called a sudden or abrupt death, which rarely happens to the upright and virtuous. For on the previous night he had begun to be afflicted by a cold and a high temperature, and since he was in his eighty-fourth year his very debilitated condition was unable to resist

---

in Japan for military assistance from Manila to counter Hideyoshi's persecution when he learned about it on his return to Macao in 1588. Nevertheless, Valignano had accepted Ōmura Sumitada's and his son's cession of Nagasaki to the Jesuits in 1580 on the grounds that it would provide a defensive and secure refuge for Christians endangered by persecution and the civil wars raging in Kyushu. In February 1582 Coelho described the Jesuit properties in Nagasaki as 'very beautiful and secure', surrounded by a solid mud wall. He even called it 'the fortress of Nagasaki' (ARSI, Jap.Sin 46, f. 62). Not surprisingly, after his successful pacification of Kyushu, Hideyoshi cancelled the agreement between Ōmura and the Jesuits over Nagasaki and placed the port under his own jurisdiction.

the illness, and on the following day he was advised by the doctors that his life was in very great danger. Then he was wholly unconcerned about matters human and mortal, and considered nothing more important to him than to wash away in confession any stains on his soul, and to fortify himself with the other defences instituted by Christ for the last struggle with the enemy of the human race. He did all these things, therefore, with no thought in his mind except of immortality, and he gave back to God his creator that most holy soul, adorned with so many virtues and accompanied by so many good works, obtaining immortal glory for himself, but leaving the whole Christian population sadly mourning his loss. Nor was it without good reason that his departure brought deep sorrow to all, for what with his benignity, his charity, and his benevolence he could be regarded as father of all rather than as supreme ruler. And if the whole Christian people, linked to him by the many favours they had received from him, found his loss very hard to bear; if the fathers of the Society, to whom he was especially devoted, and of whose services he had made use in enterprises of such moment, were in such sorrow at having him snatched from them, you can imagine the grief and sadness into which we were cast, we who were sent from places so distant in order to visit him, and who had found him nothing less than a most loving father to us in Rome.

Leo: I don't doubt that the sorrow you speak of must have been profound, when in such a short time all that rejoicing and happiness was reduced to grief and tears. Even just hearing about it we too have been very much moved.

Lino: Indeed it has been all I can do to refrain from weeping at hearing how afflicted you were at the loss of so illustrious a father.

Michael: You are right to speak as you do. However, the incredible weight of our grief was considerably lightened when the Father General consoled us by pointing out that another pope would soon replace him, with the same position and rank, and that without doubt we should find in him the same fullness of paternal benevolence towards us. A consolatory messenger also arrived from the whole Sacred College of Cardinals, and did much to relieve our great sorrow, for when they assembled to perform the customary funerary ceremonies for the deceased pope, they deigned to send a certain prelate to us, and in their name he told us that whichever of them was the replacement for Pope Gregory would have no less care and solicitude for things concerning Japan than he had. We should therefore be of good heart, sustained with the firm hope that the unease of the current situation would soon be resolved; and in the meantime if there was anything we needed it would be supplied in abundance from their resources. We were greatly encouraged and honoured by this message of consolation, for we understood how concerned the whole College of Cardinals was for us and for Japan, and such a clear sign was set before our eyes of the good which we could hope for from the next pope. After that, almost all the days which followed right up until the feast of Easter were taken up with the celebration of the funeral exequies of the deceased pope, for the cardinals themselves all came together to celebrate them with all due solemnity, and the men of each of the religious orders performed the services and rites proper for such a beloved parent in their own churches. The fathers of the Society, who were so greatly obliged to him for the many benefits received, were the most diligent among them, the Superior General saying Mass, with all the others of the Society, and us too, in mourning dress, assembled in the church of the professed house. But since the events pertaining to the exequies of the deceased pope and the election of his successor certainly deserve to be related, and I believe this will not be displeasing to you, and since those things need to be treated at greater length, let us leave them to the next colloquium.[1]

---

[1] On the final illness and death of Gregory XIII, see Pastor, *History of the Popes*, XX, pp. 635–6; Fróis, *Première ambassade*, pp. 186–9.

COLLOQUIUM XXV

How the funeral of a pope is carried out, and the way in which another pope is chosen, and to what great and universal applause Sixtus V was proclaimed pope

Lino: At today's meeting, Michael, we look forward very eagerly to two things which you have to tell us about, one of them the form observed in carrying out the exequies or funeral of a pope who has died, the other the procedure followed in choosing a new Supreme Pontiff.

Michael: I shall deal with both of those Lino, as I promised, and meantime you must all be sure to note the remarkable order which shines out in all European things, for the progress of all this narration is directed to that. Know then in the first place that it is fixed by custom that when the pope is near to death he summons all the cardinals and addresses them, first of all saying in a spirit of humility that as a man subject to human frailty and wretchedness he has erred not a little in the performance of his office, and that accordingly it is for them, as his most dear brothers, bearing in mind the mutability of human affairs, to remove completely any animosity which they may have towards him in their hearts, and to help him with their prayers as he labours in the final struggle. He then commends to them the whole Christian republic, and diligently urges them to choose as pope, after he has departed this life, one who will discharge in full the most heavy responsibilities of the office committed to him. Finally he bids farewell for the last time to all, not without much grieving and tears on the part of those listening to those last words of the Pontiff. Three cardinals are then chosen, and together with one other who holds the office of chamberlain they deal diligently with things necessary for the pope who is breathing his last, and matters concerning the care of the sacred palace, and assiduously prepare all the things required for the exequies. Meanwhile the assembly of cardinals is vigilant in providing for the city of Rome and the whole ecclesiastical state, so that all is in order in the city and in the papal jurisdiction.[1]

After the spirit of the pope is released from the chains of the body, and after many solemn prayers for him offered to God by the cardinals, his venerable corpse is washed by servants who are present with sweet-smelling water, embalmed with most precious unguents and balsam, and then attired in pontifical vestments, as if he were alive. Finally he is taken on a most ornately covered bier to the pontifical chapel. There immediately all

---

[1] Transitions imposed strains on papal finances amongst other things because of fears of disorder. See Delumeau, *Vie économique et sociale de Rome*, pp. 758–9; Nussdorfer, 'Vacant See', *passim*.

the priests and men from all the religious orders come together, and they chant, according to the custom, many and various prayers, and they attend his dead body with the other customary ceremonies. Afterwards it is taken by the canons to the church of St Peter with all pomp and magnificence, and there once again prayers and entreaties are offered anew and with great fervour by the same and other priests, and then the venerable body of the supreme father is left, duly attended, in the church, with permission for it to be seen, reverenced, and kissed by the whole population. Wonderful indeed are the crowds of people at that time, come to see with their eyes and pay respect with their souls and inmost senses to the body of the supreme father, and thronging round to embrace and kiss his feet, worthy of the utmost veneration. Finally, after some days taken up with these acts of piety and devotion by the people, the dead body, adorned with the pontifical insignia, is put away in a most magnificent tomb, not without the tears of all.[1]

Then begin the solemn exequies, of which I'll give you a brief description. First of all, in the same church, which is everywhere adorned with the insignia of the dead pontiff, a cenotaph is constructed, of wondrous size and height, in the shape sometimes of a pyramid, sometimes of a quadrangle or an octagon, all of it covered in silk, and with white candles everywhere, from the lowest point right up to the very top. The bier is enclosed within this or (there is more than one way of doing it) placed on top of it, at the apex, as it were, as you can see from the painting of the cenotaph of the Emperor Charles V which we brought with us. Round this empty tomb, if I may thus allude to etymology,[2] stand all those of the pope's household and the palace, and the civil magistrates, in cloak and mourning dress, and all the others who are present, cardinals, ambassadors, nobles, and common citizens, hold in their hands torches made of pure white wax, countless numbers of which are distributed throughout all the nine days on which the exequies take place. Also distributed is a great deal of money, most generously donated to the convents and sodalities of men and women. For as long as the funeral rites for the pope are being celebrated in this way each of the cardinals celebrates Mass at the high altar, and meanwhile a very large number of other priests offer the Holy Sacrifice at the seventy or more other altars. You can gather from this the amounts of money spent on these exequies, for everything necessary is supplied in great abundance.[3] On the first day of the exequies some prelate to whom this task is assigned gives a funeral oration on the life and laudable merits of the deceased pontiff;[4] and the last day ends very appropriately, after the accustomed Mass for the dead pope, with another Mass to ask the special favour of the Holy Spirit, and another sermon about the creation of a new pope. This is, in brief, what I think should be said about the funeral rites. You can imagine for yourselves the pomp, the enormous expense, the crowds of people, the magnificence of it, and all the other things omitted in my account.[5]

---

[1] Gregory's body lay in state for three days (Fróis, *Première ambassade*, pp. 189–90; Pastor, *History of the Popes*, XX, p. 637).

[2] I.e. of the word 'cenotaph'.

[3] On such costs, see Fróis, *Première ambassade*, p. 192; Delumeau, *Vie économique et sociale de Rome*, pp. 758–9.

[4] Gregory's funeral oration was given by the Jesuit Stefano Tucci on 17 April. In it he referred to Japan and the embassy on two occasions, praising Gregory's care for the universal church (Fróis, *Première ambassade*, p. 191 n. 681).

[5] The exequies lasted until 17 April (ibid., p. 191).

Leo: Certainly no one could fail to approve of that order and splendour in the burial and the funeral rites of the pope, which serves also as a strong commendation of the way things are in Europe.

Lino: It seems to me that it not only gives a very good impression of European things, but deserves to move all minds, even those most averse to Europeans, to love and enthusiasm for them.

Leo: Now then, Michael, move on and tell us about the way the new pope is chosen, which I have no doubt is equally in accord with reason.

Michael: Note first then, with regard to this matter, that they go to great pains and are extremely careful to ensure that in the process of proclaiming the new pope there should be no room for ambition, for conferring beforehand, for corruption in the voting, and that the new pope should be elected with all speed.[1] Accordingly they are enclosed in a conclave, as it were in a cloister, with the cubicles assigned to each of them separated only by linen curtains, and all the windows blocked with bricks and lime, with no more than small gaps left to let in some light. The doors are closed in the same way, with the exception of just one entrance, to be used for necessities; but this door is closed with five keys, and these keys are handed over to five men of great authority. As long as the cardinals are inside they cannot come out, nor can they bring anyone in, nor call anyone to speak to them privately. With each cardinal, however, just two servants are enclosed, who are their attendants for necessities, and they are allowed not luxurious but moderate food, prescribed by ancient law, which each of them eats by himself. This means that they are living very simply and uncomfortably for men of such wealth and state, and find it hard to accept the limitations of that accommodation, and thus bring all diligence to bear on the business of electing the Supreme Pontiff. Such is the vigilance in rejecting and turning away anything brought from outside which might influence the minds of the cardinals that even the daily food which is normally brought to each of them from their own houses is diligently searched, lest anything written should be sent to them hidden under the guise of food, which might corrupt or pervert the minds of the electors.

And to secure the assembly of the cardinals totally from any disturbance of the people or any force of the powerful, many guards from among the most important nobles and

---

[1] The account of the conclave which follows is idealized. At the conclave in 1572, which resulted in the election of Gregory XIII, the Spanish, in the person of Cardinal Granvelle, had lobbied hard in association with the Medici, to ensure that Alessandro Farnese, the Jesuits' patron, would not become pope, and that the successful candidate would be *papabile* (electable) to the Spanish monarch. In the 1585 conclave, in which national, international and family interests and calculations again figured prominently, Spanish lobbying was more restrained but was certainly not in support of Farnese, and while not Philip's first choice, Cardinal Montalto, the future Sixtus V, proved acceptable to Spain. See Hübner, *Sisto Quinto*, pp. 101–96; Pastor, *History of the Popes*, XXI, pp. 7–22; Guarini, "'Rome Workshop of all the Practices of the World'", pp. 74–5. Regardless of the dependency of the Papal States on Spain for grain imports from southern Italy, and on Spanish military might, which reduced the papal military budget considerably, relations between Philip II and Sixtus V, especially over France, were far from harmonious. See Pastor, *History of the Popes*, XXI, pp. 262–73; Delumeau, *Vie économique et sociale de Rome*, pp. 619–22; Dandelet, *Spanish Rome*, pp. 76–8, 83–7. On conclaves more generally, see Wright, *Early Modern Papacy*, pp. 47–52.

prelates are brought into the sacred palace. Firstly a certain nobleman, with a garrison of soldiers, guards the first door; then a magistrate of the city with an appropriate mass of citizens guards the second door; the legates of the kings and princes, with an abundance of guards and servants, look to the third, and finally, the most important prelates, enjoying total trust and authority, guard the last door, the one closest to the cardinals. After the cardinals have made their way into St Peter's church, then, and from there, two by two, into the conclave, all the guards swear an oath before the cardinal bishop, the first of all, promising not to fall short in any way in guarding the palace and providing protection and security for the cardinals; and the last of them, that is to say those guarding the door nearest to the cardinals, add that they will take care not to allow in anything which could in any way disturb the minds of the voters. Then that last door is closed with five keys, which are distributed some among the guards, some among certain priests who have charge of the ceremonies and who remain within.

Then that first cardinal bishop fraternally and lovingly admonishes the cardinals, who are now shut in, to consider carefully the greatness of the matter now entrusted to them, and to elect with their votes him whom all may acknowledge as truly the father of Christendom. Now he can be proclaimed pope in either of two ways, by agreement of at least two thirds of the secretly cast votes, or alternatively by universal consent and acclaim, which is not at all unusual. Each time there is to be a vote, after Mass has been piously and religiously celebrated, all the necessary preparations are made, a sacred chalice with a lid is set on the high altar, and the votes, in writing, are placed in this chalice. The first cardinal bishop sits, then, at the altar, and the first priest and the first deacon, who are also cardinals, accompany him, with all their other brethren occupying lower seats in their proper order, and it is in that order that the voting begins. The procedure in voting is that each one has to announce his name clearly, state that he chooses as Supreme Pontiff the most eminent Cardinal So-and-So, and sign his vote with his seal. When the votes have been put in writing that cardinal bishop who is first in rank kneels before the altar, prays for a short time, then reverently casts his vote into the chalice, the first cardinal deacon opening the chalice for him and then immediately closing it; and each one then performs the same duty as the others insert their votes in the same way. After all the votes have been collected in the chalice the first cardinal bishop takes each of them out and hands it over to the cardinal priest. He in turn gives it to the cardinal deacon who reads all of it out in a loud voice. All the cardinals have in their hands a list of their fellow cardinals, and they put a note beside the name of the one for whom the vote has been cast, to make it easier to be sure of the number of votes, and, as I said, whoever receives the votes of at least two thirds of the cardinals is nominated as pope. But if on the first vote no one candidate garners the necessary two thirds of the votes, another vote is taken, and another, until the number I mentioned is attained.

When that designated number is reached, therefore, by acclamation or by the votes, and the one who has been accorded the acclamation or for whom the votes have been cast confirms it with his assent, he is proclaimed pope by the first cardinal bishop. No words can express the joy then of all the cardinals, and the universal rejoicing and celebration when the cardinal deacon opens the little window which is designated for that purpose and makes the following most joyful proclamation: 'I announce to you a great joy: we have a pope, the most illustrious Cardinal So-and-So, who, with his new office, has taken the new name of Such-and-Such'. Immediately, therefore, the doors of the conclave are opened, and the pope is led to St Peter's church, with the maximum possible congratulation from everyone.

Leo: We are indeed most satisfied with this procedure in the election of the new pope, and how could it be otherwise, for we see that it bars the way to all those evils which human perversity can introduce into similar proceedings.

Michael: Daily experience confirms the same thing, and for the most part we see raised to the supreme position of pope men who are outstanding for their wisdom, virtue, and other gifts, both those with which nature has endowed them and those which they have laboured to acquire. Thus after the death of Pope Gregory XIII and the performance of his funeral rites, almost fifty cardinals came together in order to provide a new pope to replace him. Their first meeting was held on 21 April, and on the twenty-fourth of the same month,[1] to the great joy of all, the most illustrious Cardinal Montalto,[2] a man most advanced in the study and practice of virtue of every kind and of arts and letters, who had previously been a member of the Franciscan order, was proclaimed pope by general acclamation, and decided to be known by the name of Sixtus V. A point which gives particularly strong support to this most worthy choice is that when Pope Gregory XIII was still living and was considering who might succeed him, those who were round him raised the names of certain cardinals, among them the most illustrious Cardinal Montalto, and the pope passed over the others and indicated that he was the one who would become pope.[3]

This Pope Sixtus is of Italian birth, from the lands of Piceno, now commonly known as the Marches of Ancona. Though born of humble parents he was endowed by nature with high intelligence and great abilities; he gave himself to arts and letters, progressed gradually in the study of wisdom and in virtue, and was received into the Order of St Francis, in which he held many posts with distinction, and eventually became Minister General of the whole order. In this capacity he so pleased Pope Pius V that he first made him a bishop, and later chose to number him among the cardinals. The city of Rome greeted the proclamation of his election with a great celebration: the mighty boom of the cannon of Castel Sant'Angelo sounded time and again, many most ingenious kinds of fireworks could be viewed, all through the city torches, candles, and various different kinds of lamps with fire in them could be seen, and the light of all of these shining at the same time in the hours of darkness lent an extraordinary beauty to the night. And what am I to say of us, to whom it seemed that a new light had risen, for we felt, and with reason, that a very dear father had been restored with great joy to his sons. Nor was it only the city of Rome that received this most welcome announcement, for the same glad news was spread with all speed throughout almost all the provinces of Europe, by messengers

---

[1] The original (p. 272) gives '*sexto Calendas eiusdem* [i.e. May]', or 26 April, a mistake.

[2] Felice Peretti Montalto (1521–90), born at Grottammare near Montalto, although his ancestors were from Dalmatia, cardinal from 1570, Apostolic President of the Franciscans from 1567.

[3] Cardinal Montalto and Gregory did not enjoy good relations. Gregory is alleged to have remarked to his inner circle that 'they should beware of that great charnel-box of a gray friar'. The antipathy was mutual. See Ranke, *History of the Popes*, 1, p. 307 n. 4; Pastor, *History of the Popes*, XXI, pp. 39–41; Fosi, 'Justice and its Image', pp. 79, 82.

sent to its various parts; and the kings and princes sent legates to convey their humble expression of homage to him.

After Sixtus V had been declared pope, then, he was carried, as is the custom, to St Peter's church, and then set on an altar as the Vicar of Christ. There all the cardinals reverently kissed his hands and his feet, and the other prelates and secular nobles followed, bowing down in veneration at his feet. All the while musical instruments and the beautiful voices of the cantors provided wonderful harmonies, and finally the pope himself, making the sign of the Cross, invoked blessings and prosperity on all. On the following Saturday[1] we too went to the pope to congratulate him most joyfully on that supreme rank to which, by the divine will, he had been raised, and, in the name of the Japanese kings and princes, to do him the homage due to him. He received us with gladness and joy, as if he was Gregory XIII raised from the dead, and when we manifested our joy at his election he assured us, with many and most benevolent words, that he would be no less loving and diligent in caring for the things of Japan, and that we need not in any way regret the absence of Gregory XIII. He also charged the fathers to take great care that we be provided with everything necessary, and to lay before him anything that would be helpful and fitting in all matters to do with Japan, and he gave a firm promise that he would never be found wanting in anything. These words were evidence of his very great love, and they were fully borne out in deed and reality, for as long as we were in Rome nothing was lacking, as far as we were concerned, of the benevolence and liberality of Gregory XIII, nor of his care and solicitude for the things of Japan.[2]

On the first of May we were invited by the pope to the festive celebration of his consecration, for after the pope is elected by the votes of the cardinals the custom is that a certain day be designated for him to be consecrated with a solemn rite and anointed with holy oil. When that festive day dawned, therefore, he came out from the interior of his residence and, with a concourse of cardinals, prelates, and nobles around him, made his way to the hall called the Pappagallo to don the papal vestments.[3] From there the pope was carried in a procession to St Peter's, with the cardinals in front, two by two, and the whole throng of the nobles coming behind, and when he entered the vestibule all the canons and priests of that church did him humble reverence, and bent down to kiss his feet. All then immediately went into a chapel dedicated to St Andrew, the pope was seated on a throne, and all the cardinals came to do him the customary reverence. Then, after the performance of many rites and ceremonies which it would take too long to describe, the pope was anointed with holy oil and consecrated by the most illustrious Cardinal Farnese,

---

[1] 27 April.

[2] During this meeting, which occurred the day after Aquaviva and his assistant for Portuguese affairs, Manoel Reiz, had performed obeisance to the new pope and pledged loyalty on behalf of the Society, the boys were used as 'living letters'. Mancio Itō, speaking through Mesquita, who was described as their 'maestro' and interpreter, declared that the pope was not only the sacred, universal father of the church but also the father of the church in Japan. Mesquita himself then made a pitch concerning Japan. He requested the pope to place the mission under his personal protection and beseeched him to hear from Aquaviva about Valignano's proposals for the mission (ARSI, Ital. 159, f. 9; ARSI, Jap.Sin 11: II, f. 290; Sacchini, *Historiae Societatis Iesv Pars Qvinta*, p. 229). A few months later, after his third audience with the new pope in July, Aquaviva wrote to all Jesuit provincials to reassure them about future relations between Sixtus V and the Society (ARSI, Instit 40, f. 98). This is a copy of the letter. The fact that it follows immediately after the account of the boys' meeting with Sixtus V on 27 April suggests that in the general's opinion the boys had performed well as 'living letters'.

[3] The Sala del Pappagallo adjoining the Sala dei Paramenti.

Dean of the Sacred College, and two other bishops who, by ancient custom, hold this office. After that our Mancio here poured water for him to wash his sacred hands (this is considered a great honour, given to the most distinguished men present, kings or princes), and two other nobles, who were on either side of him, proffered the towel for him to dry them. After that the cardinals, patriarchs, archbishops, and bishops, dressed in sacred and pontifical vestments, and the other priests and sacred officials, clothed in white, accompanied the pope as, seated on the pontifical chair and carried on the shoulders of the Roman magistrates, he moved to the main chapel of St Peter's to say Mass.

I must make mention here of one custom worthy of note which is observed as he progresses. The official known as the master of ceremonies holds in one hand a stick with a thread hanging from it, and in the other hand a wax taper, lighted and inserted into a stick. He lights the thread with the taper, and when it suddenly catches fire and burns he turns to the pope and says 'Holy Father, *sic transit gloria mundi*' (thus passes the glory of the world). And when that official said that three times, as is customary, we saw Pope Sixtus reflecting deeply and nodding his bowed head in evident agreement, and indeed one can believe that, with that image fixed in his mind, far from priding himself on the supreme honour done to him, he will have maintained the same even tenor of mind whatever fortune befell him. When the main chapel was reached, and the cardinals had all taken their places, and the deacon and sub-deacon theirs, the pope celebrated a Mass full of grave and solemn religion, wonderful in its rites and ceremonies, so many and so various that I cannot possibly find words to describe them.[1]

After the Mass the pope, with the same throng of cardinals, nobles, officials, and people, made his way to a very ornate stage set up in the vestibule of the church, in front of the square, to be crowned with the pontifical diadem. The place is extremely broad and spacious, and an extraordinary multitude of people of every condition had come to see the spectacle, so that not only the whole square, and the windows, doors, and colonnades, but even the very roofs of the dwellings were packed with crowds of people, and when the Pope, accompanied by the assembly of cardinals and the other nobles, was moving along a raised balcony, it was all the palatine magistrates could do to open a way for him. When the pope took his seat under a very ornate canopy which was set up above the stage, the cardinals being already seated, Cardinal Farnese and some others with him recited certain sacred prayers, after which one of the cardinal deacons, sitting on the left of the pope, removed the usual skullcap from the head of the Supreme Pontiff, and another cardinal deacon, who was on his right, reverently set on the same sacred head the extremely ornate tiara, topped with a triple crown, and laden with extremely precious gems and pearls. Then followed the acclamation of the people, wishing Pope Sixtus V a most long and

---

[1] The Mass was celebrated on 1 May. Three of the boys (Julian was still recovering from illness) played a more prominent part in the proceedings than is suggested here, helping to carry the papal canopy along with other dignitaries whose number included the French and Venetian ambassadors. The latter, shocked to find that he had been placed behind the Japanese with the French legate in front of them, protested that this was an insult to Venetian prestige and insisted that even if the boys were ambassadors, unlike Venice, they represented unknown and little esteemed rulers. As a result of the protest, Priuli was placed beside the French ambassador and the Japanese behind him. His masters were pleased that a diplomatic insult had been avoided. See Boncompagni-Ludovisi, *Le Prime due ambasciate*, p. 17; Fróis, *Première ambassade*, pp. 196–7; Boscaro, 'First Japanese Ambassadors', pp. 16–17; Cooper, *Japanese Mission*, pp. 99–100.

happy life, together with the joyous sound of trumpet and fife, and soon after, again and again, the salute from the cannon of the citadel, with such enthusiasm that all were roused to a great exhilaration and permeated with a new joy, and with this wonderful celebration the new pope was inaugurated. But since we not only took part in that most celebrated event, but have now spent a long time remembering and recounting it, it seems right, with your agreement, that we should take our usual rest.

COLLOQUIUM XXVI

The cavalcade with which the pope made his way to the church of St John Lateran, and the ambassadors, invested with the insignia of knighthood, departed the city; and of the most noble city of Naples, and the church of the Blessed Virgin of Loreto

Leo: I cannot find words, most dear Michael, to explain how delighted we have been with your account of the things of Rome, and if you have more to tell us of those things our eagerness to hear it is undiminished.

Michael: Before finishing with Rome I shall recount what remains, with no fear that you will be bored or sated, and shall then move on, today, to our return journey. And since I think you take special pleasure in hearing of things pertaining to the Roman pontiff I shall start by describing in all its nobility the cavalcade with which the pope is accustomed to visit the church of St John Lateran, in order to take possession of that cathedral, as is due and proper to his papal office.[1] This will give you an understanding of the majesty of the pope when he makes a public appearance. Picture the order of this cavalcade, then, and of any other similar one, as follows: first come the horsemen designated as the papal guard, advancing two by two (and you should know that all that follow them also proceed two by two), armed and equipped as if going into battle, but also adorned with outer garments of velvet. Following them come the keepers of the wardrobes of the cardinals, bearing their lords' clothing in bags of scarlet cloth, on horseback, and each of them accompanied by men of their household. Next in the procession are those responsible for the papal robes, with all the others of the same station, and along with them come all the other men of good family who do not hold a rank which would entitle them to any special place. After them comes one of the papal grooms, leading a white horse, most elegantly adorned and beautifully bedecked, which carries a certain silk-covered wooden ladder used by the pope, according to ancient custom, when he mounts

---

[1] The procession and ceremony, known as the *possesso*, took place on 5 May. Unlike more recent ones, Sixtus's *possesso* was an austere affair. There was a food shortage in Rome. Moreover, there was always a danger that the *possesso* would degenerate into lawlessness and violence. According to Sixtus's Master of Ceremonies, in order to avoid the customary throwing of coins in the piazza from becoming 'a prodigal waste, since the vagabonds, and tricksters, who put on a show of being poor, and are of robust body, join with violence in the fray, and collect all the money, and the true poor, weak, ill, lame, and old get none of this profusion of money', the new pope ordered that the money was to be distributed through charitable institutions. Pastor, *History of the Popes*, XXI, p. 75; Stinger, *Renaissance in Rome*, pp. 53–7; Fosi, 'Court and City', pp. 48–51, esp. p. 50. The mural depicting Sixtus's procession is in the Vatican Library where the Japanese are visible (see Fig. 11, right, middle two rows).

Figure 11. Mural in the Vatican Library of Sixtus V's procession to St John Lateran, 5 May 1585. By permission of Nagasaki Bunkensha.

a horse. Next come those known as the papal 'cursors', carrying twelve banners, to the eternal memory of the victories which the twelve apostles of Christ gained over the most foul enemy of the human race; and immediately after them thirteen bearers of banners representing, or so it seems, the thirteen regions of the city of Rome.

No less distinguished are the five standard-bearers who follow them. The first carries the Roman eagles, insignia of the senate and people of Rome; the second the insignia of the Teutonic Order; the third that of the Order of St John of Jerusalem; the fourth the pope's own special insignia; and finally the fifth carries the standards and genealogical tree of the whole of Christendom. And as they advance their armament and the elegance of their clothing are a sight to see. They are followed by twelve richly arrayed horses, for the use of the pope, led by grooms dressed in scarlet, and then by four more horses, these carrying four papal hats of scarlet silk. After these come the clerics of the Apostolic Camera,[1] and the prelates of the assembly called the Rota;[2] then all the nobility, namely the counts, marquesses, and dukes, who are under the jurisdiction of the pope; then the ambassadors of the kings and princes, and at the same time the Roman senator, who takes the first place after the ambassador of the emperor. When these have all passed it is the turn of those who hold a sacred rank, first of the Apostolic subdeacons, one of them holding the pontifical cross, who are accompanied by the master ushers bearing in their hands rods encased in red silk. Also carried at this point, on a horse both marvellously adorned and remarkably meek, is a sacred case, all covered with silk and gold, in which is kept the most holy body of Christ, and it is attended by twelve priests, on foot, carrying lighted torches, and two more priests from the pope's chapel, on horseback, and also carrying fire, but enclosed in silver lanterns, so that there is no chance that it will go out; and the sacred case is covered over with a canopy or tent embroidered in gold, carried by eight most noble men, their heads uncovered. Thus whenever the pope is to go in solemn procession, on horseback, he has with him the most holy body of Christ as his most certain defence and the source of all his honour; and with this sign he emphatically indicates that the supreme honour paid by the whole people is paid not so much to himself as to Him whose vicar on earth he is. Next after this come the guards of the sacred palace, and then the bishops, archbishops, patriarchs, and cardinals in their pontifical robes, all wearing on their heads most costly mitres. After all of these comes the Supreme Pontiff, manifesting the utmost majesty, riding either on a very submissive horse, or in a most ornate litter with eight carriers, and with a silken covering or sunshade, also held by eight men of the nobility.

As I already said in an earlier colloquium, when he travels on horseback there is an established custom that the emperor, or a king, or some other principal ruler who is there, supports his feet as the pope mounts the horse, and then holds the reins in his hands for some distance until the pope bids him mount his own horse. If he is being conveyed in the litter, that too is carried for a short distance by kings and supreme rulers if they are present, again until they are given the signal to mount. It has always been customary for them, with this show of honour, to reverence the pope as the Vicar of Christ on earth, in his presence to set at nought even the highest marks of distinction, and to take the part of a servant. The place at the pope's back is occupied by the commandant of the military

---

[1] *Camera Apostolica*, in charge of papal finances.
[2] The *Sacra Romana Rota*, a tribunal.

guard, with the soldiers themselves lightly armed and in perfect formation. The crowds of people that follow after the procession through all the streets where it passes are so great that in order in some degree to hold back the throngs of people surging towards the pope it is necessary for a papal magistrate to scatter silver coins for them to scramble for. The procession on horseback is so very long that, although the distance from the church of St Peter to St John Lateran's is almost a league, when the first riders are almost at St John Lateran's the last have not yet left St Peter's. This procession takes place in this way whenever the Bishop of Rome, after receiving the pontifical diadem with solemn ceremony, and adorned also with the papal vestments, makes his way to the church of St John Lateran. But when Pope Sixtus V celebrated this solemn ceremony the procession to St John Lateran's was postponed till another day, and some things were changed. The pope did not wear the papal vestments, the cardinals followed after him, as is usual, and we ourselves were among the ambassadors preceding him. As far as the ceremony of receiving him in the basilica of St John Lateran is concerned, I think you should learn about it from the books written about this matter rather than from my account of it.

Leo: The things you tell us about the Roman court, and about the authority of the pope, are extraordinary, and they show clearly that he is worshipped and adored by all as the Vicar of Christ.

Michael: All the things of Europe are indeed most impressive and splendid, especially in the courts of the kings and princes, but there is nothing to compare with the majesty which astounded our eyes and our souls as we contemplated it in the papal court in Rome.

Lino: How lucky you are, how fortunate, to be the first to have been able to sail from our less refined world to that other world which is so splendid and magnificent. But now give us an account, please, of what transpired with regard to your affairs before you left Rome.

Michael: The Supreme Pontiff Sixtus V elected to engage with us very frequently and most familiarly, like a true parent, but the multitude of commitments and matters of business at the commencement of his pontificate was such that even a young man in full vigour, never mind an elderly man worn out by his labours, as he was, might well have been overwhelmed by the mass of it and might have sunk under its weight. Nevertheless he, vigorous in mind rather than in body, saw to everything so well that one could truly recognize the divine power present there. He sent emissaries to visit us several times, giving a clear indication of his benevolence, and on one occasion he decreed that we be invited by bishop Alifi,[1] at that time major-domo of the sacred palace, to attend a banquet being held in the pontifical villa. This we gladly did, and we were brought there in coaches, were greeted there by twenty-four prefects of the papal chamber, and were provided with sumptuous hospitality by the same bishop in the name of the Roman pontiff. Then on the 27 May we were again called by the pope to join in a public procession arranged by a

---

[1] Gualtieri (*Relationi*, p. 91; *Dai Nihon Shiryō*, XI: 1, p. 283) describes him as 'Monsignor' Alifi.

convent of Franciscan fathers known as Santa Maria in Aracoeli,[1] and the pope himself graced it with his presence, together with a most distinguished assembly of cardinals. This procession had no less magnificence and splendour than the equestrian procession which I described above.

And lastly, when the date of our return journey to Lisbon was already close, the pope wished personally to invest us with the insignia of chivalry, something considered a mark of high honour, customarily conferred not on just anyone, but on men of the highest distinction and merit. On the day prior to the date set for the ceremony, which was the vigil of the Ascension of the Lord,[2] the prefect of ceremonies was sent to us by the pope to instruct us about the rites to be observed on that occasion; and on the following day, when the prayers for the vespers of the Ascension of the Lord were solemnly sung, we were present, dressed most ornately, in short toga and sword, as knights to be. The prayers finished, with all the cardinals and bishops present, and with us kneeling, the pope duly blessed four unsheathed swords and four golden spurs, and handed the swords over to us, addressing the following words to each of us: 'Take this sword in the name of the Father, and of the Son, and of the Holy Spirit, in order to use it in your defence, in defence of God's Holy Church, for the confusion of the enemies of Christ and of the Christian Faith and, as far as human frailty permits, in such away as not to harm anyone unjustly; and may He vouchsafe to grant you this who lives and reigns, with the Father and the Holy Spirit, for ever and ever. Amen.' Then we placed the swords in their scabbards, and the principal dignitaries who were present, namely the ambassadors of the most illustrious king of France and of the Venetian Republic, and the marquess Altemps,[3] who was at that time governor of the Roman suburbs, girded on us the swords thus sheathed, the ambassadors doing this for Mancio and me, and the marquess for Martin and Julian, who had recovered from his illness. Meanwhile the pope addressed each of us with these words: 'Be armed most powerfully with your sword at your side, in the name of the Father of Our Lord Jesus Christ, yet remember that the saints conquered kingdoms not by the sword but by faith.' We then rose, drew the swords from the scabbards, brandished them on high three times, as is the custom, stabbed the ground three times with the points of the swords, wiped them on the sleeves of our right arms, and replaced them in their scabbards; signifying with this rite that at the pope's command we would not hesitate to draw those swords in order to defend the Christian faith and the majesty of God and of Our Lord, and at the pope's order to lay them down again, without harming anyone unjustly. Four military commandants then put our spurs on our feet, and the pope kissed us, not without tears of joy, an indication of his paternal love for us, wished us peace with all happiness, and with the utmost benevolence put golden chains, with his own image stamped on them, round the neck of each of us. Then, taking our swords in his hands, he touched the back of each of us three times, saying, 'Be a soldier peaceful, vigorous, faithful, and devoted to God.' And, striking our faces lightly with his hand, he added, 'Wake from the sleep of evil, and watch in the faith of Christ and in laudable fame.' With the insignia

---

[1] The church, on the Capitoline, was given to the Franciscans by Innocent IV in 1250. The original edition (p. 279) gives: *'nomine Ara caeli, ad Sanctam Mariam maiorem habitae'*.

[2] 29 May.

[3] Mark Sittich von Hohenems or Altemps (1533–95). His mother, Chiara de' Medici, was the sister of Pius IV who made him a cardinal in 1561, and an important figure in papal politics and administration.

of knighthood thus conferred upon us we kissed the feet of the pope, in profound gratitude for such an honour, and all present congratulated us on our elevation to this high rank.

And now the time for us to set off was approaching, and the Superior General of the Society saw to the arrangements with the pope about our concerns; and he was so effective in explaining the needs of the Japanese church and the dangers it faced that, on the recommendation of the most eminent Cardinal Antonio Carafa,[1] a great friend of the Society, the pope decided not only that the income of four thousand ducats, granted to the church of Japan for twenty years by Gregory XIII, should be approved and guaranteed, but that it should be increased by a further two thousand and paid in perpetuity. In addition he gave three sets of most precious vestments as a gift for the fathers working in Japan, and he also wrote letters filled with love to the kings and the prince whose legates we were. To each of the kings he sent a sword enclosed in a scabbard of silver worked with gold, a royal skullcap, and a case in the form of a cross with a considerable number of relics of the real true cross of Christ; and to the prince of Ōmura he also sent a sword and another similar case. Gifts of this kind are always very highly prized by all Christian kings and princes, both in themselves and for the prestige of the giver, so it is not surprising that King Protasio of Arima here was seized with an unexampled joy on receiving those presents; and that we were greatly upset by the death of King Francisco of Bungo and of prince Bartolomeu of Ōmura, both of whom had deserved so very well of the Japanese church, knowing as we did that the greater part of the general joy and congratulation at our arrival belonged to them. We are consoled, however, by the well-founded hope that their sons will be most worthy heirs not only of their fathers' possessions but also of those gifts and of that great joy, born of Christian piety.[2]

But with regard to the generosity of the pope, he ordered that we be given a further three thousand ducats as provision for our journey, yet still with excuses for what he persuaded himself was his ungenerous and inadequate treatment of us, due to the newness of his pontificate and his lack so far of a clear and explicit understanding of his

---

[1] Or Caraffa (1538–91), cardinal from 1568. He was born in Naples to a family which provided a large number of cardinals from the 15th to the 19th centuries and was a nephew of Gianpietro Carrafa, Paul IV, who, like Valignano, was born in Chieti. Valignano corresponded with Carrafa, notifying him of the boys' return and the success of the visit, and Arima Harunobu wrote to him in 1590 thanking him for his reception of Michael and the others. Ōmura Yoshiaki wrote similarly as did Michael, informing him of the situation in Japan and the joyous welcome he had received on his return (ARSI, Jap.Sin 33, ff. 61–4; 11: II, ff. 210–11v, 218–21v).

[2] Ōmura Sumitada died on 25 May 1587 and was succeeded by his son Yoshiaki who was baptized as Sancho. Ōtomo Yoshishige died on 28 June 1587 and was succeeded by his son Yoshimune who had been baptized as Constantino the previous April. Following Hideyoshi's anti-Christian edict of 1587, Yoshimune apostatized and, according to the Jesuits, under the influence of his mother, whom the Jesuits styled Jezebel, began to persecute Christians. On the boys' return from Europe, he was reconciled with the church thanks to Mancio's tactful mediation (Fróis, *História de Japam*, V, pp. 179–81, 281–4). He was disenfeoffed following his poor performance during Hideyoshi's first invasion of Korea in 1592. In an apostolic brief, Sixtus elevated Ōmura Sumitada to the ranks of the Most Christian Kings. For a pope who quickly acquired a reputation for frugality, his presents to the Japanese daimyo, and his outlays for the boys' onward journey were very generous. See RAHM, MS 09-02663, ff. 445r–v; Fróis, *Première ambassade*, pp. 201–2. For Sixtus's letters to the three daimyo, see Berchet, 'Documenti', pp. 158–62, and for a description of the presentation of the letters and gifts after the boys' return, see Fróis, *História de Japam*, V, pp. 334–6.

household and his treasury; all this despite the great generosity with which he had in fact treated us. He also wrote a commendatory letter to Philip, most powerful king of Spain, telling him to order that everything necessary for our return to Japan was to be provided for us in abundance, and indeed King Philip did so, and splendidly.[1] There was one thing above all others, however, which the pope did for us, which showed his extraordinary love for us, his greatest favour, the crown, as it were, of all the others. Before our departure from Rome for such a long journey he said Mass privately for us in his chapel, and with his own hands gave us the most holy Eucharist. We were profoundly affected, and moved both to piety and to a more ardent devotion to the pope himself. When all arrangements had been made, then, and we had taken our leave of the leading Romans both sacred and secular, we went on 4 July, a Sunday, to the pope, to ask a blessing on our journey and a final farewell from his sacred lips. He, like a most loving father, gave us further proof of his love and benevolence, and assured us with wonderful words of the concern he would have for the things of Japan; and he granted to us, by the power which he has from Christ, with many bulls, many very great privileges with regard to the remitting of the punishment of sins. When we left him, therefore, we took back with us to our homeland an image of a supreme father, imprinted in our minds and never to be entirely erased.

Leo: It is a real delight for me, Michael, to hear you say such things, for it is seemly for noble men, when they cannot repay with thanks so many benefits received, to preserve the memory of them in perpetuity.

Michael: My dear Leo, there are indeed no words for me to convey the benevolence, the charity, and the generosity towards us of both popes. Suffice it to say that we found in each of them a father wonderfully indulgent towards his cherished sons. And this is to omit mention of the admiration and extreme reverence which the majesty and magnificence of their supreme rank impressed indelibly and forever on our souls. What am I to say, besides, of the most illustrious cardinals, whose prestige and distinction I have already mentioned a number of times? We visited all of them one by one, found them most courteous in returning our greetings, and could not but marvel at their grandeur, conjoined as it was with a singular piety and affability. They gave us such open and clear indications of their love and benevolence towards us and our people that we confess that we are permanently linked to them, and especially to Cardinals San Sisto, Carafa, and Rusticucci.[2] What am I to add, finally, about the fathers of the Society, and among them about the reverend Superior General, whose paternal care for us we recognized in everything, and from whom we could not be torn away without grief and many tears on both sides? And we observed how all the fathers of the Society, however distant they were from one another, were of one mind in their love for the Japanese nation.

After leaving the city of Rome we were supposed to visit another most noble city by the name of Naples, which is about forty leagues to the east of Rome, but it would have been

---

[1] The pope's letter to Philip is printed in Boncompagni-Ludovisi, *Le Prime due ambasciate*, p. 20. Sixtus wrote similar letters to Cardinal Albert in Portugal and to the authorities in Venice, Genoa and elsewhere on the boys' route (ibid., pp. 20–21; Fróis, *Première ambasse*, pp. 202–3).

[2] Girolamo Rusticucci (1537–1603), papal administrator, cardinal from 1570.

dangerous to travel there because of the weather, which in the summer is inhospitable to visitors, so we were unable to do as we and many others wished.[1] However, I'll say something about it from what we learned from its reputation and from what we heard, especially as so many people had told us how celebrated it was. As I said, then, this city of Naples is established in the kingdom of Naples, which takes its name from the city. This kingdom belongs to the jurisdiction of King Philip, as a fief, as it is commonly called, and it pays an annual tribute to the pope as its proper lord. Now Naples is counted among the most noble of European cities; it is inferior to none, and outdoes all others in the agreeableness of its situation and the number of its nobles. For with regard to nobles and most illustrious men, their number is extraordinary, there being in that kingdom thirteen princes, twenty-eight dukes, about the same number of marquesses and just as many counts, and the number of lords with noble titles, taking them all together, is about a hundred. And since almost all of these have their seat in Naples, where the viceroy is, who governs all that kingdom in the name of King Philip, it is incredibly populous and splendid; for all those nobles, with their train of servants and their multitude of horses and carriages, proceed with such splendour that an army of knights seems almost always to be moving all through the city and its excellently paved streets. And all that multitude is in clothes so costly, fashioned of silk, velvet, finest wool, and other similar material, that because of the elegance and grace of its citizens Naples has appropriated to itself the title of elegant and gracious.

Conjoined with this elegance is the splendour of the buildings, which whether sacred or profane are most magnificent in structure and very many in number, for every one of the nobles has a most spacious palace, and there are men of all the religious orders living in splendid religious houses, so much so that in the number of its churches this city yields only to Rome. There are three houses of the fathers of the Society there, namely a house of the professed, a college, and a novitiate house, with about two hundred members of the order living there, their residences being very appropriate buildings; and among these the church of the professed house, now under construction, is a very fine building.

The administration of the city, as I said, and of the whole kingdom of Naples, is in the hands of a viceroy from a most noble Spanish family,[2] who, since that city is filled with a multitude of nobles, conducts himself with no less majesty than a most powerful king in his court. For these reasons, and others which for brevity's sake I omit, Naples is famous, and without a doubt we would have gone there had we not been prevented by the consideration which I referred to above. And indeed if we had taken the trouble to go, so as to satisfy the many people who had asked us to come to Naples, it would not have been in vain, and they said that in not being able to see how delightful it is, because of the unfavourable weather, we had suffered no small loss.

---

[1] The reason for not visiting Naples had nothing to do with the weather but with the security situation prompted by bread riots. See above, p. 166 n. 1; Boncompagni-Ludovisi, *Le Prime due ambasciate*, pp. 21–2; Muir, *Ritual in Early Modern Europe*, p. 120. Danger existed along the route taken from Rome as well. On 3 June, Nuno Rodrigues wrote to Aquaviva from Civita Castellana that no escort was waiting for them on the journey onwards and he requested that one be sent from Rome. See ARSI, Ital. 159, f. 18; Yūki, 'Shinshiryō', p. 98; *Dai Nihon Shiryō*, XI: 2, pp. 4–5. Unsettling and dangerous conditions forced Cervantes's character Tomás Rodoja some 20 years later to travel by sea to Naples, a city which he described as 'the best in Europe and even in the whole world' (*Novelas ejemplares: El licenciado vidriera*, in Cervantes, *Obras completas*, II, p. 131).

[2] At this time Pedro Téllez-Girón y de la Cueva, first duke of Osuna (1537–90).

The journey to Naples was abandoned, then, and on 3 June we headed by the direct route for the church of the Virgin of Loreto, which is situated in a town called Loreto. In the course of this journey we entered many cities belonging to the particular jurisdiction of the pope, notably Narni, Terni, Spoleto, Foligno, Assisi, and Perugia, and in all of these we were welcomed with great honour by the assembled citizens, to the repeated sounding of bells and cannon, and were most splendidly treated by the governors and magistrates of these cities.[1] They had been ordered to do this by letters from the pope, and did it so diligently that in some cases the keys of the cities themselves were presented to us as if to their own lords. In all of these places we saw many things both sacred and secular which deserve to be described, but I omit mention of them lest I should seem to be always repeating the same things. It would not be right, however, for me to say nothing at all about St Francis of Assisi, whose admirable sanctity is proclaimed throughout the whole of Christendom by many most certain testimonies, and is evident in the very great religious order which he founded, in which men so illustrious and outstanding in religion have flourished; and since the books are full of their deeds there is no need for me to recount them here. The holy body of St Francis is there, and remains as if alive, or so many say, for there is no opportunity now to see it;[2] and it still keeps fresh those stigmata which Christ of His love willed should be imprinted on his hands, feet, and side, so as to make His most faithful servant as like as possible to Himself. Some memorials of him can be seen, however, namely the hair shirt with which he mortified his flesh, the book from which he recited the sacred prayers and other similar things, and it is very moving to see these things. Also in the same city is the venerable body of St Clare, who, following the same discipline of St Francis, united many most virtuous virgins with their heavenly spouse, and was the founder of many convents in which the same rule of life is carried on to the utmost glory of Christ and benefit and praise of Christendom.[3]

On the same journey we passed through a town called Montefalco, where we rejoiced exceedingly to see the sacred body of another St Clare, who takes her surname from the same town.[4] Not only is her venerable body still there, whole and incorrupt, but her heart is also marked by images of Christ fixed to the Cross and of other mysteries. On the same heart are also to be found three balls exactly the same in size and form, and they have besides a more than natural power which makes the weight of all three

---

[1] The journey from Rome to Loreto took nine days. It was a hectic schedule and it created stress. One of the Jesuits who accompanied them, Alessandro Leni, wrote that he was greatly worried about the toll on the boys' health. They were sleeping for around four hours a night and the food they were given on formal occasions at banquets and civic receptions was not agreeable to them. See ARSI, Ital. 159, ff. 55r–v; Yūki, 'Shinshiryō', pp. 123–4. Account records from Ferrara give an indication of the rich food provided at banquets, and the cost. See *Dai Nihon Shiryō*, XI: 2, pp. 36–57. On their reception in Loreto, see also ARSI, Ital. 159, ff. 36–7v; Yūki, 'Shinshiryō', pp. 120–22. During their stay in Loreto, Mancio wrote to Aquaviva thanking him for his fatherly love and all that he had done for the boys. See ARSI, Ital. 159, ff. 38r–v; Yūki, 'Shinshiryō', pp. 125–6.

[2] The body had been buried under the high altar of the church, the Basilica of St Francis of Assisi, erected in the saint's honour, construction of which began in 1228. The coffin was rediscovered in 1818.

[3] St Clare of Assisi (1194–1253) founded the order of the Poor Clares in 1212. Her remains are in the Basilica di Santa Chiara in Assisi.

[4] St Clare of Montefalco (c. 1268–1308). Her remains are in the Chiesa di Santa Chiara, Montefalco. For Munday's description of the remains, see *English Roman Life*, pp. 72–3.

together, and of each of them taken separately, exactly the same, so that it makes no difference whether you put one in one balance and two in the other, or again all three in one balance. And in this we recognized that a manifest sign of the most holy Trinity was on display, in which each person separately or again all three persons together have the same nature, power, and majesty, and this saint venerated above all in her mind this most holy mystery of our faith.

In Perugia, which is also a noble city, we had no option but to remain three days, for the benevolence of the citizens of Perugia towards us, and the evidence of their love for us was such that they even sent representatives to Rome and through them begged us not to pass through Perugia without engaging in greetings to the city. Words cannot easily describe the generosity and magnificence of their hospitality to us. There too we experienced the very great benignity and courtesy of the most illustrious Cardinal Spinola,[1] legate of the pope, who, in addition to other demonstrations of his love, welcomed us to a most splendid banquet at his house. Nor was our welcome from the fathers of the Society, in whose college we were accommodated, any less friendly, and we enjoyed seeing many other things which they showed us, but which, as we are hastening to the house of Loreto, it will be prudent for me to omit.[2] On the same journey we passed through Camerino, Tolentino, Macerata,[3] and Recanati. These cities too are under the jurisdiction of the pope, and we were greatly struck by the fact that there are in Italy such famous and populous cities, and in all of them we met with kindness from the citizens and a most welcoming attitude towards us; this especially on the part of the most illustrious Cardinal Gesualdo,[4] the pontifical legate, who invited us to lavish and splendid banquets in the cities of Camerino and Tolentino, and treated us with every kind of solicitude and love.

On 12 June we reached the town of the Most Blessed Virgin of Loreto, and its most celebrated church,[5] which is deservedly renowned throughout Christendom, for in that church is preserved that most august and holy house in which the most chaste Virgin Mary dwelt and, while she was living in the town of Galilee called Nazareth, received the salutation from the Archangel Gabriel and, after this happy annunciation, conceived the divine offspring, that is, the eternal Father's Son, who thus bound human nature to himself with a wondrous bond. Now it has been passed down to us on most certain testimony that after the Most Blessed Virgin ascended to heaven this house was carried by angels, with

---

[1] Filippo Spinola (1535–93), cardinal from 1583, and, at this time, papal legate in Perugia and Umbria. His nephew Carlo, a Jesuit who served in Brazil, was captured by privateers returning from New Spain and taken to London. He returned to Lisbon in 1598 and the following year was able to fulfil his ambition to serve in the East Indies. He arrived in Japan in 1602, stayed on after the proscription of Christianity, and was martyred in Nagasaki on 10 September 1622 (Schütte, *Monumenta Historica Japoniae I*, pp. 1301–2).

[2] The rector of the Jesuit college tried to have the celebrations toned down but was unsuccessful and the boys were given a triumphal reception. On their reception in Perugia and for more details of the trip to Loreto, see ARSI, Ital. 159, ff. 51r–v; Yūki, 'Shinshiryō', pp. 136–38; Gualtieri, *Relationi*, pp. 97–9; *Dai Nihon Shiryō*, XI: 2, pp. 7–9; Fróis, *Première ambassade*, p. 211 n. 740; Cooper, *Japanese Mission*, p. 108.

[3] Birthplace of Matteo Ricci, whom the boys had met in Macao in 1582, and whom they would meet again on their return.

[4] Alfonso Gesualdo (1540–1603), cardinal from 1561, at this time papal legate in Marche.

[5] The Basilica della Santa Casa. According to tradition, the house was conveyed by angels to Illyria in 1291 and three years later to Loreto. For Munday's account of the house, which he describes as 'an old little brick room', see *English Roman Life*, pp. 70–72. The boys arrived in Loreto on 12 June.

walls and roof intact, a most amazing thing, first to Illyria, a province of Europe, and then to Italy. And when it had been for some time not far from the place where it is now most religiously venerated, because of discord between two brothers who quarrelled over the profits from the alms, of which there was a great quantity there, it was eventually carried over by the same angels to the town of Loreto. For these reasons this, of all the churches of the most pure Virgin, is held in the highest veneration, above all others, by the Christian people, and has the largest number of visitors.

The little holy house is built of bricks in keeping with the poverty in which the Virgin lived while she was among mortals. Now, however, it is adorned with an exterior structure most skilfully fashioned of marble, but in such a way that the new architecture, however precious, has never been able to merge into one with the old. With the passing of time and the steady advance of religion a most noble church was erected, with that holy house or chapel preserved in the centre of its sanctuary, and covered by a most beautifully wrought cupola which hangs over the highest part of its roof. In the same chapel there is an altar which has been granted many indulgences by the popes. Behind the altar can still be seen the fireplace with its brazier, in which the Blessed Virgin would light a fire and prepare food for her beloved son, and no Christian can behold it without being deeply moved. The same altar holds a likeness of the Blessed Virgin, by St Luke, or so it is believed, very artistically made, and on the far side is a door by which the Angel Gabriel is said to have entered her holy room. The trophies of victories, planks from shipwrecks, chains from captives, and the variety of other memorials of miracles which adorn the walls of the church are such as can scarcely be believed.[1]

What am I to say of the size of its income, reckoned at thirty thousand ducats, not to mention the daily contributions which bring in as much again every year? What of the numbers of priests and cantors, and the solemn rite with which the divine prayers are recited? What of the most precious equipment in use in the sacred ceremonies, whether you take the vestments, or the altar vessels and other instruments? What finally of the tremendous number of people washing away the stains of their sins? In order to deal with these more expeditiously there are always present, in addition to the many priests of St Peter assigned to the same church, twenty-four of the Society, equal in their powers to those known as penitentiaries in Rome, from the college in the same town, where forty of the Society are provided for out of the revenues of the same church.

Leo: Up till now I have called you happy for many reasons, but it must be regarded as by no means the least part of your happiness to have seen with your own eyes so many remains of ancient religion, and so many relics, so piously preserved and so celebrated for their miracles, of the Blessed Virgin and other saints.

Michael: You are entirely justified in calling happy the eyes which, in the course of such a long journey, have had the opportunity to see such things, especially as there was hardly

---

[1] Cervantes's character Tomás Rodaja was also impressed by 'the crutches, shrouds, chains, fetters, handcuffs, wigs, innumerable waxen figures paintings and altarpieces' cluttering the room, a testimony, he believed, to the intercessionary powers of the Virgin (*Novelas ejemplares: El licenciado vidriera*, in Cervantes, *Obras completas*, II, p. 131).

any city in which the relics of some saint, whether man or woman, were not venerated. There are other things which I recall which you would be glad to hear, but lest I drag out my tale at too great length I intend to pass over in silence many things, but these things can easily be learned from the books which we have brought back with us. Permit me then to deal with the remaining part of our journey in just a few colloquia more, and let us call a halt here, for our usual repose, to today's colloquium.

COLLOQUIUM XXVII

The journey through other cities, especially Ancona, Bologna, Ferrara, and Venice, and the things seen there

Leo: Anyone of sound mind must surely be astounded to hear of the great crowds of people who welcomed you all through Europe, and must surely grant that the people of Europe have delightful customs, incredible refinement, and a singular degree of charity to all. I say nothing of the pope's more than paternal love for you, and the joy that possessed him as he manifested it, but who would not marvel at the glad welcome which you always received from all the people, cities, and princes through whose lands you made your journey.

Michael: Certainly we came to the conclusion that if, as the common proverb has it, the unanimous voice of the people is to be taken as the voice of God, the welcome which all extended to us was so great that it must be a divine instinct and not mere human enthusiasm which moved those throngs of people to gather to see us. I'll move on, therefore, and tell you, as briefly as I can, of the joy with which the citizens of many others cities greeted us. We left the town of Loreto, therefore, though we would have liked not merely to prolong our stay but, had it been possible, to spend our lives there without ever being torn away from the sight of that most religious church, and set ourselves to head for Bologna, and from there to make our way to the most famous city of Venice.[1] Many towns worth seeing presented themselves to us in the four days of that journey, and many cities so famous that even a cursory account of each of them would require an entire colloquium. But since I have decided to make a point of being brief in my account of our return journey, I have to ask you to allow me to leave some things out.

On this road, then, we saw the famous city of Ancona, the metropolis of the Piceno district, and because of it the whole district is also known as the Marches of Ancona.[2] It comes under the jurisdiction of the pope, and its citizens gave every sign of pleasure and joy in welcoming us, leaving nothing to be desired whether in their parade and display of instruments of war, their musical performance, or finally their splendid hospitality. And there were abundant spectacles for us to contemplate, buildings secular and sacred, relics of saints, and other things. On the following day we saw three other cities, Senigallia, Fano, and Pesaro, the second of these belonging to the papal jurisdiction, the other two to the duke of Urbino,[3] who is subject to no king, but who nevertheless pays an annual

---

[1] Again the pace was hectic. The journey from Loreto to Venice lasted twelve days, 14–26 June.

[2] Sixtus V was born near Ancona.

[3] Francesco Maria II della Rovere (1549–1631), the last duke, upon whose death the duchy was annexed by the Papal States.

tribute to the pope. We passed through Senigallia and Fano, to a great show of enthusiasm on the part of their citizens, and spent the night in Pesaro. There a relative of the duke of Urbino, namely the marquess della Rovere, came out in a cavalcade to meet us in the name of the duke himself, and conducted us to the duke's palace, where the duke, returning from hunting, treated us with the utmost politeness and honour, and most courteously put at our disposal himself and all that he had. But since we found that he was busy offering hospitality to the duke of Brescia we left on the following day and went to three other cities, namely Rimini, Cesena, and Forli.[1] I omit mention of the rejoicing with which our arrival in each of these cities was greeted, but the last of them has a college of the Society, and there we had a very good time. The next day we passed through Imola, another city of not inconsiderable fame, but I had better continue without speaking of the enthusiasm with which they greeted our arrival. All these cities, when they saw us, were so exultantly joyful that it seemed as if the very cities themselves, with their walls, wanted to rise from their seats and advance to meet us.[2]

On 18 June we entered Bologna,[3] a famous city and the capital of the province of Emilia. Since it is the first and principal city of that province its citizens wanted to outdo the inhabitants of other cities of the same province in their numbers and their acclamation, to which not a little was contributed by the presence of the two illustrious cardinals Paleotti[4] and Salviati,[5] the one the archbishop of Bologna, the other the papal legate, as they and their retinues, as well as many knights from the city, came out in procession to meet us. The numbers of those welcoming us on our entry was so great that in addition to the horses a hundred carriages were counted, which will give you some idea of the magnificence of this city. We were invited by retainers of each of the cardinals, in their names, to accept the hospitality of their palaces, but not wishing to offend either of them we made straight for the college which the Society has in that city. The cardinal legate, however, was not wanting in liberality, for he represented the person of the pope in that city, and wished to imitate his customary generosity, and he provided us most abundantly, for as long as we were in that city, with everything required for our support. Cardinal Paleotti the archbishop showed his love for us no less clearly, and we were also invited to dinner by him, a dinner, however, which was not sumptuous and splendid but rather modest and frugal, such as he himself normally has. He is a man greatly endowed with virtue and humanity, and among the other proofs of holiness which he provides as an example to all, his custom of eating with his domestic household at a common table, as religious do, shines out especially. We were much struck, and rightly so, with his benevolence and his holiness of life.

---

[1] The duke was also meeting with Paulo Giordano Orsini whom the boys had already met in Rome. After the election of the new pope he had fled the Papal States with his new wife, the widow of the pope's nephew whom Orsini had had murdered. See Gualtieri, *Relationi*, p. 104; *Dai Nihon Shiryō*, XI: 2, pp. 12–13; Pastor, *History of the Popes*, XXI, pp. 75, 96.

[2] Gualtieri provides extra details of their reception in these cities which was similar to those described elsewhere. See Gualtieri, *Relationi*, pp. 105–6; *Dai Nihon Shiryō*, XI: 2, pp. 13–14. In Imola the boys left a brief note in Japanese for posterity recording their stay (Gualtieri, *Relationi*, p. 106; *Dai Nihon Shiryō*, XI: 2, p. 14). The note is published in Hamada, *Tenshō kenō shisetsu-ki*, pp. 393–4.

[3] The editors of Fróis, *Première ambassade*, p. 216, give 19 June.

[4] Gabriele Paleotti (1522–97), cardinal from 1565.

[5] Antonmaria Salviati (1537–1602), cardinal from 1583.

We also took part in a procession which was taking place at that time, in which the memory of the most holy Body of Christ is honoured with devotion, and we could see that its pomp and splendour lacked nothing in regard to magnificence, variety, and Christian piety.[1] Among other things the legate himself carried the pyx with the Blessed Sacrament, and for a while we held the poles on which the canopy covering the sacred receptacle and the priest is supported. We handed them over after a short while to other nobles and, taking our places on either side of the cardinal archbishop, made our way with that splendid procession to the designated place. In that city we saw magnificent buildings, especially sacred ones, and many relics of saints. We saw besides the holy and incorrupt body of St Catherine of Bologna,[2] although it is already two hundred years since her death; and what is even more astonishing is that it is sitting and, so they say, it still has power in its nerves so that the hands and feet imitate wonderfully the movement of someone living.

On 22 June we left that city and headed for the noble city of Ferrara, which belongs to the jurisdiction of the duke of Ferrara.[3] The duke of Ferrara is one of those who exercise independent power, free of subjection to any king, but he pays tribute to the pope. When this duke knew that we were approaching he ordered the count of Bevilacqua,[4] a subject of his, to go out to meet us, and he was accompanied by fifty knights. There were besides five excellently appointed carriages, followed by company after company of light infantry. As we approached the walls, Alfonso d'Este, uncle of the duke and a man of the highest authority, came to meet us, joined us in our carriage in the most friendly way, and accompanied us to the palace of the duke. Thus we entered within the walls, accompanied by knights and by the carriages of many nobles, as if by an army ready for action, and we were conducted to the palace of the duke, who himself came down and met us most cordially in the entrance courtyard. After he had expressed, in many courteous words, the gladness that he felt at our arrival, he led us to most magnificently appointed guest chambers, where not many years previously he had received the king of France himself,[5] so that we could rest after our tiring journey.

We found in this duke an affability and sweetness of manner no less impressive than his power and nobility. All this is greatly enhanced by his extraordinary wealth, the splendour of his possessions and furnishings, the size of his palace and the workmanship of its construction. We were in admiration at all of these things, and realized that he is almost the equal of the European kings. It is consistently reported that he has annual income of

---

[1] The feast of Corpus Christi.

[2] 1413–63, Poor Clare, mystical writer and patron saint of artists. Her incorrupt body remains on display in the chapel of St Catherine in the Monastero Corpus Domini in Bologna.

[3] Alfonso II d'Este (1533–97). Alfonso died without issue and the princely house of Este came to an end. Ferrara was then incorporated into the Papal States. Burckhardt called Ferrara 'the first really modern city in Europe'. Ferrara and its ducal palace, the Palazzo del Corte, now the Palazzo Comunale, were the crowning achievement of Ercole I d'Este (1471–1505) who intended to impress visitors to the city with a show of wealth, power and status to match that of a rapidly expanding Venice. In 1570 many of the buildings were destroyed or damaged by an earthquake. The Castel Vecchio, which remains today, was altered by Alfonso II whereas Alfonso I had abandoned many of his father's building projects. See Burckhardt, *Civilization of the Renaissance*, p. 27; Tuohy, *Herculean Ferrara*, pp. 2, 20, 25, 119, 312, and ch. 3 *passim*, for a full description of the Palazzo del Corte. Ercole's use of architecture to project ducal power is similar to the architectural ambitions of Oda Nobunaga in Azuchi and Toyotomi Hideyoshi in Osaka.

[4] The Bevilacqua were a courtier family of the d'Este (Tuohy, *Herculean Ferrara*, pp. 28, 129, 250).

[5] Henry III who visited Italy in 1574. Honoured visitors were put up in the Camere Dorate (ibid., pp. 75–9).

700,000 ducats, and that he holds in his treasury five hundred million sesterces or even more,[1] the same as we reported of the grand duke of Tuscany. He also has remarkable statues of Christ and the twelve apostles, made of solid gold, and an extraordinary cabinet, which we ourselves saw, filled with so many gold and silver dishes, that nothing more splendid could be desired, even for kings. In one very large hall there is a cabinet stretching the whole length of the room, with shelves at many different levels right up to the ceiling, full of pieces too many to count and of outstanding workmanship, of gold and silver. Among these works five fountains occupied the first place, nearest to the floor. They were fashioned with wonderful skill of silver inlaid with gold, with craftsmanship which seemed fully worthy of these materials. All the works contained in this cabinet were not meant for general use – there were many others designated for that purpose – but as a display of majesty and magnificence.[2] The splendour of the house and its furnishings is fully matched by the duke's household and servants, which are on an almost regal scale, as is clear not only from the noble servitors he has in his palace, but also from the fact that under his authority, which is extremely extensive, he has counts and marquesses. We stayed for three days in this city, during which we had several happy and friendly meetings with the duke, and also visited his wife,[3] a most illustrious lady, and his sister, wife of the duke of Urbino.[4] They were wonderfully pleased to see us, and treated us with the utmost honour and civility.

We also went out into the country, to a most agreeable villa belonging to the same duke and abounding in everything which could be desired for pleasure and delight. There is no need for you to ask me for a description of it, for you can readily imagine it from the many others that you have already been told about, but the one I am speaking about now deserves to be thought of as in no way inferior to those other places. On the way there we saw the duke's very extensive stables, containing a hundred and fifty horses, some suitable for walking, others for war, some proficient at jumping, and many trained to perform, and others of other kinds, selected from various provinces and kingdoms.[5] Besides these places we were also taken by the duke himself to others which were excellent for hunting, one of them called the Barco[6] and another generally known as Montagnola,[7] and there

---

[1] I.e. 12.5 million ducats. Borso d'Este, the first duke, 'who always rode in the country clothed in cloth of gold and silk' bedecked with chains worth 70,000 ducats each, is reported to have left money worth 500,000 ducats at his death in 1471 (ibid., p. 52).

[2] The duke's Guaradaroba was responsible for the purchase and maintenance of precious objects and works of art and for their display before visiting dignitaries, whom, it was intended, should be suitably impressed. On such visits the Estense treasures were displayed on the *credenza* in the Sala Grande. The Estense art collection was dispersed after 1598 (ibid., pp. 228–31).

[3] His third, Margherita Gonzaga (1564–1618), some 30 years his junior, was patroness of the *balleto delle donne* which often performed for visiting dignitaries and did so for the Japanese guests (*Dai Nihon Shiryō*, XI: 2, pp. 33, 35).

[4] Lucrezia d'Este (1535–98).

[5] Borso d'Este, was reported to have had a stable of 700 horses procured by his agents from many places. The horses won frequently in races but by the end of the 15th century the Estense stable had been eclipsed by that of the Gonzaga (Tuohy, *Herculean Ferrara*, p. 241).

[6] The ducal hunting ground. The original edition (p. 292) gives '*Parcus*'. On Estense hunting and the renown of the Barco, see ibid., pp. 124, 244–5, 343.

[7] The Montagnola is mentioned by Leni in his account of the boys' reception in Ferrara. See ARSI, Ital. 159, f. 72v; and *Dai Nihon Shiryō*, XI: 2, p. 33. The Montagnola is described in *Descrittione della Porta di San Benedetto della città di Ferrara, de' luoghi delitiosi, che erano attorno le mura di essa, e del residuo de giardini ducali*, Padua, 1671, online at http://www.castelloestense.it/ita/castello/delizie/penna.html

everything was provided that we could have wished for, forests of deep shade, wild beasts of many kinds, and every opportunity to hunt. In almost all of these places we were met a number of times by the duke's wife, accompanied by noble girls and ladies, who of her great kindness towards us had taken the trouble to come by another route, and who treated us with the utmost courtesy. I should not fail to mention the pleasure we felt at the sight of a chapel built within the duke's palace, which seemed to us outstanding for the expense of its construction, for the many relics of saints there, for the ornamentation of the sacred vestments, and for the admirable paintings, especially one depicting Christ our Saviour.[1] Finally I must add that the combination of perfect courtesy and great eminence in this duke bound us very firmly to him, so that the memory of his spirit, at once magnificent and extremely welcoming, is still with us even now. In that same city we saw many very fine churches, and among them the college of the Society, but the duke himself made it his pleasure to offer us hospitality, and did not permit us to stay in the college.[2]

When we viewed the city as a whole we realized that it is one of the most heavily fortified of all the cities of Italy. Not only is it surrounded by walls, towers, and many fortifications, but its site is such that a whole league of territory right round it can easily be swamped and covered by the waters and estuaries of the river Po, and this makes it almost impregnable, given that it also has an almost infinite number of cannon and other weapons of war.[3] We took our leave of the duke, his wife, and others of the nobility of Ferrara on 25 June, and headed directly for Venice by the famous river known as the Po or Eridano, travelling most comfortably in a beautifully made ship belonging to the duke himself and called a *bucintoro*.[4] Such care had been expended in the making of this ship that it seemed more like a well-built house than a ship, for above the decks and the seats of the rowers it had another level containing quite a large hall and two bedrooms, adorned with gold, paintings, coverings, and luxurious furnishings, in which voyagers could take their ease or divert themselves with some agreeable pastime, without in any way distracting the oarsmen from their task. This ship was followed by three others, the first carrying

---

[1] The chapel, only the shell of which remains and which had one of the best choirs in Europe, had been used by Alfonso II's mother, Renée of France, among whose childhood friends was numbered Anne Boleyn, and whose Protestant sympathies aroused the ire of Rome. Jean Calvin was one of a number of Protestant guests at her court. She returned to France after her husband's death and provided support to the Protestant cause. On the chapel, see Tuohy, *Herculean Ferrara*, pp. 90–95.

[2] On behalf of the boys, Mancio Itō wrote a letter of thanks to the duke and his wife for their hospitality, and in turn received a reply from the duke (*Dai Nihon Shiryō*, XI: 2, pp. 110–12).

[3] One of the many cannon in the arsenal, *il gran diavolo*, was immortalized by Ludovico Ariosto in his poem *Orlando Furioso*. Montaigne was also impressed by the arsenal (*Journal de voyage*, p. 171). On the fortifications of Ferrara more generally, see Tuohy, *Herculean Ferrara*, pp. 124–7. During the stay in Ferrara Julian had a fever and was attended by the duke's physicians. The boys presented a set of their Japanese clothes and a sword belonging to the daimyo of Bungo. In return, the duke gave them a gold chain and his wife gave them silver and gold flowers for their mothers. For these and additional details about their stay in Ferrara, see Gualtieri, *Relationi*, pp. 110–14; *Dai Nihon Shiryō*, XI: 2, pp. 29–36; Guzman, *Historia*, II, pp. 274–6; Fróis, *Première ambassade*, pp. 218–20; Cooper, *Japanese Mission*, pp. 110–11.

[4] This *bucintoro*, the rival of its Venetian namesake in which the doge performed the *sensa* or marriage of the sea, was built for Margherita (Montaigne, *Journal de voyage*, p. 171). Julian was still unwell and continued to be attended by the ducal physician on the way to Venice (Fróis, *Première ambassade*, p. 220). For earlier Estense *bucintori*, a description of their rich decoration and furnishings, and an estimate of their cost, see Tuohy, *Herculean Ferrara*, pp. 154–60.

soldiers, cannon, and a considerable number of musical instruments, the second all necessary provisions, and the third bearing everything needed for cooking. When the time for dinner approached these last two were carefully manoeuvred alongside our ship, and there was provided for us, by the duke's servants, a banquet no less elegant and sumptuous than could have been laid before us if we had still been dwelling in his palace. No wonder in speaking to you we dwell so often and at such length on the splendour of Europe.

After a brief and agreeable voyage on this delightful river we came to a city named Chioggia, or Fossas Clodias, situated in the area within the jurisdiction of Venice. The governor of the city[1] came out a full league beyond the city gate to meet us, borne in a little ship covered in silk, and formally bade us welcome. And as if in a happy and auspicious advance pledge of generous hospitality he respectfully invited us, in the name of the Venetian senate, to embark on his ship. The bishop of the city came to meet us with no less benevolence,[2] accompanied by a great number of priests and churchmen of rank, and attended by all of these we made our way to the gate of the city. We disembarked from the ship, were welcomed by the acclamation of crowds of people, the celebratory firing of musket and cannon, and the jubilant sound of drum and trumpet in unison, and immediately, in the first open area of the city, were wonderfully entertained by various fireworks compounded of sulphur which were promptly and adroitly set alight. When we reached the public palace the bishop himself, by way of celebration, gave a splendid oration on the subject of our arrival, the joy of the citizens, and also the recognition due to the fathers of the Society at whose bidding we had undertaken this journey. We stayed that night in that palace, with everything to do with supper and sleeping accommodation perfectly arranged.

The next day[3] we set out for Venice, accompanied by the same bishop, the governor, and other nobles, and before our entry into the city we were greeted at a certain island dedicated to St George[4] by repeated cannon fire, and by the applause of the soldiers who were in galleys. Further on, at an island with the emblem of the Holy Spirit,[5] we were met by forty noble Venetians from the solemn council known as the Pregadi,[6] dressed in long robes of velvet and pure silk, scarlet in colour. First among them was a patrician of the noble family of the Lippomani,[7] and he congratulated us on our arrival in the name of the whole Venetian senate and in most honorific language. These nobles were transported in

---

[1] Filippo Capello (*Dai Nihon Shiryō*, XI: 2, pp. 58, 65). He had been ordered by his Venetian master to treat the boys with the appropriate level of courtesy and honour (Boscaro, 'Manoscritto inedito', p. 33 n. 48; *idem*, 'First Japanese Ambassadors', p. 16).

[2] Gabriello Fiamma, a renowned orator who died from a malignant fever which was said to have been brought on by the force with which he delivered his splendid oration for the boys. See *Dai Nihon Shiryō*, XI: 2, pp. 59, 65; Boscaro, 'Manoscritto inedito', p. 34 n. 49.

[3] 26 June.

[4] San Giorgio in Alga (between Giudecca and Fusina), on which there was a monastery belonging to the canon regulars of San Giorgio in Alga. The island is now abandoned. See Sansovino, *Venetia città nobilissima*, p. 240.

[5] The island of Santo Spirito, now abandoned, on which there was a monastery at the time of the boys' visit (ibid., p. 229).

[6] The *Quarantia*, or Forty, and the *Consiglio dei Pregadi*, or Senate.

[7] Hieronimo Lippomano. See Boscaro 'Manoscritto inedito', p. 33. The following year Lippomano became Venetian ambassador to Spain 1586–89 and he is an important source of information about the Spanish Armada.

boats of a kind which they call *piatta*.¹ They are covered over with many costly tapestries, and they are specifically for the reception of important and distinguished guests. In their company, then, and with them leading the way, we joyfully entered the city of Venice, so celebrated in Europe, by the Grand Gate and Canal, as they call them, and made our way through the middle of the same city, which was filled with an extraordinary number of people and citizens; and when we saw the magnificence of the buildings and the majesty of the whole city it was easy to understand how well-deserved was the fame in which it is held throughout Europe.² We were conducted by those noble men to the professed house which the Society of Jesus has in the city, and were welcomed most eagerly and joyfully by the Jesuits; and during the ten days we spent in that city we were treated with splendid liberality at the expense of the Republic.³

Leo: We have been told or have had reported many things about the city and republic of Venice to which we judged that we should not give entire credence. It seemed scarcely credible, in particular, that the huge foundations of the city were actually resting in the sea itself, that one travelled in its long streets not on foot but by boat, and finally that the city with its splendid buildings is also renowned for its most spacious squares.

Michael: You have heard a great deal, I think, about the fame of this city, but it seems to me that no words can in any way do justice to the excellence of the thing itself. I would have you bear in mind, therefore, that whatever I say will fall far short of the merits of the

---

[1] Original edition (p. 294) gives '*Piattas*'. *Piatta* or *peàta* were used for carrying cargo.

[2] The manner of the reception of the boys, who, like all important visitors, approached the city from the sea, was decided according to precedent and politics. While not usually described as 'ambassadors' but more often as 'these Japanese Gentlemen' in official Venetian documents, the boys were received in the city with great honour and ceremony befitting ambassadors. The Venetians had strict rules about ceremony and at this time political considerations mattered as well. The manner of the reception of the French king, Henry III, in 1574 was influenced by the conflict between the *giovani* and the *vechi* which rocked Venetian politics in the late 16th century. The former were anti-Spanish, anti-papal and highly suspicious of the Jesuits. With the recent accession of Sixtus V, the *vechi*'s preference for restraint in dealing with the papacy would have been a factor in deciding how to welcome the boys. See Lane, *Venice*, p. 393ff.; Boscaro, 'First Japanese Ambassadors', p. 16; Muir, *Civic Ritual*, pp. 232–7; Fenlon, *Ceremonial City*, pp. 194, 306–7.

[3] Venice had played an important role in the formation of the Jesuits and it is surprising that this is not mentioned in the text. It was in Venice that Loyola and his companions from Paris, intent on taking ship for the Holy Land, held their rendezvous and it was there that they fortified themselves spiritually while tending to the sick, many with syphilis, in the hospitals of the Incurabili and Santi Giovani e Paolo. It was in Venice too that Loyola and six others, including Xavier, were ordained. Like the boys, the companions had witnessed a Venetian procession, on Corpus Christi, and been presented to the doge. However, Venice never warmed to the Jesuits. There was no Jesuit college in the city and the Venetians were uninterested in Jesuit education, preferring to have their offspring acquire a business education rather than one grounded in the humanities. Later, the Jesuits did not endear themselves to the city state with their loyalty to the papacy and their withdrawal from the city during the Interdict of 1606–7. However, in 1585, after the death of Gregory XIII, with whom relations had been strained particularly after Venice's peace treaty with the Turks in 1573, and with the accession of a new pope, the Venetian Republic was interested in improving relations with the Holy See. The boys became the focus of a Venetian charm offensive. According to one report, the 'Sigri Giaponesi' were welcomed to the Republic 'in the manner in which Princes and Dukes are received'. See ARSI, Ital. 159, f. 61; Schurhammer, *Francis Xavier*, I, pp. 297–310, 338–44, 347–8; Boscaro, 'First Japanese Ambassadors', p. 16; *idem*, 'Manoscritto inedito', p. 13; Pullan, *Rich and Poor in Renaissance Venice*, pp. 57–8, 264–5, 405–6; O'Malley, *First Jesuits*, pp. 32–3; Munitiz and Endean, *Saint Ignatius of Loyola*, pp. 31–3, 58–60, 144–7.

city itself and the republic. Especially wonderful is the point that you mentioned, namely that the foundations of this city are set not on any hill or rock but in the very water of the sea, so that not only all the walls are washed by the sea, but also the houses built on this side and that, and arranged as if by rule and line, with the sea between, form really long and straight streets. Having this site means that the city is not only astonishing and famous, but also extremely secure and totally inaccessible to its enemies.

Leo: Well then Michael, explain how it was possible for this city to be built in the sea itself, without the structures or buildings being destroyed by the force of the water.

Michael: The thing itself is wonderful and a joy to see, but to explain it is rather difficult. However, I'll describe to you as best I can the shape of the city, and let you see how it is laid out. Picture in your minds, then, the mainland on this side, extending in a semicircle or like a bow, and on that side shallows or a sandbank corresponding to the bowstring, but you must realize that the space in between is very large and contains a great number of islands. In the middle of that area of water, some of it shallow and some quite deep, bounded on the one side by the mainland and on the other by the sandbank, this noble city was built in a wonderful manner. It is five miles distant from the mainland and two miles from the sandbank that I mentioned. Seven rivers from the mainland flow into this gulf of the sea, and they maintain their flow and open up seven gateways through that sandbank out to the expanse of the open sea; and in those gateways human ingenuity, with no little help from the power of nature, has fashioned seven gates, as it were, for ships to come in to land and for ingress and egress to and from the city. From this you can easily see how secure and impregnable the city is, though it is enclosed by no walls other than the shallows on the mainland side and those sandbanks extending across on the sea side. Add to these the fortifications which guard those gates and doors, fortifications so strong that no ship can evade their defences and their cannon. From this it can be plainly seen how convenient this city is, and how it abounds in all the necessities and the refinements of life, all of which can be brought to this most famous market either from the mainland on the seven rivers, or from other faraway kingdoms and provinces. Thus it is that many European peoples and nations, Mediterranean or from beyond the seas, come together in great numbers to Venice, drawn by its convenience.[1]

What shall I say of the administration, which gives this city and republic pride of place among others? This is a republic entirely free, owing tribute to none, subject to no king. It has under its power many and various provinces, cities, and towns, and its administration of all of this is so excellent that, if compared with kings, it must be said to be in no way inferior. Indeed, if we look back briefly at antiquity we find that this most illustrious republic has in the past for various reasons waged major wars against many very powerful kings, has beaten and overthrown them, and has always managed to maintain its own most prosperous condition. The same republic has subdued and held back the savage tyrants of the Turks and Moors who with huge armies threatened to devastate and destroy Christendom, has extended far and wide the bounds of its own jurisdiction, and has preserved its own dominion for a very long time in the midst of barbarous peoples. A point

---

[1] Venice was, and remains, a source of wonder to visitors. On the creation of the city and its relationship to its environment, see Crouzet-Pavan, *Venice Triumphant*, pp. 1–18, 36–45.

which I should mention which is special to the administration of this republic is that it belongs entirely to the patricians and nobles, no one from the common people being accepted into it; and in this way it has always been most prudently governed, for the last twelve hundred years. The patricians who take care of the administration are almost three thousand in number. Everything of any importance is discussed among them, and they hold offices and magistracies in that city and in other places.

The assembly of all these patricians is divided into three categories. The first contains all those who have completed their twenty-fifth year (though sometimes there is a place in the assembly for some before that age), and after mature deliberation this assembly assigns the offices and magistracies. The second, more restricted, is known as the Senate of the Pregadi. There are more than two hundred in it, and it deals with matters of greater weight and moment, whether concerning peace or war. The third, finally, is known as the College, and is made up of the chief magistrates and counsellors, seventeen in number, and they have supreme authority in this republic. Above and ruling over all these leading members of the Republic is a most illustrious doge, who in this republic takes the place of a prince, and it is in his name that business is conducted and coinage is minted, and, in short, all administrative power is in his hands. However, although this doge wields such great power, he differs from a king in that he can do almost nothing of any importance on the basis of his own judgement and decision, but faithfully refers everything to the senators of those three assemblies, and settles all weighty matters together with them. With regard to the veneration in which he is held by all, his rank is not inferior to that of a king. In addition to this threefold order of which I have spoken there are many official posts and offices which are assigned to various nobles with a gradual progression from lower to higher. Those who perform honourably in the role assigned to them have further honours laid on them, but those who are negligent or corrupt in their performance pay a heavy penalty for their misdeeds. Among these nobles the use of long black clothing is customary, but some officials holding certain positions wear garments of red or violet silk or velvet cloth, and there are some who wear purple.

Besides this customary refinement in dress, indicative of their dignity and maturity, they have another custom, of walking unaccompanied through the city, taking no pleasure in any retinue of servants such as I have previously spoken of as being normal. This is because they fear that if they were to allow a multitude of accompanying servants there might be jealousy and contention among the nobles themselves, and that equability which they cultivate as equal members of the republic might gradually come to be lost Thus the illustrious admiral or commander who has led a large army in a major war against kings and princes may be seen, when the post-war arrangements have been concluded, walking alone through the city like others of the same rank, without any train of attendants. This thriving republic has kept these and other honourable customs and practices and has flourished mightily for twelve hundred years, its power and glory increasing steadily and greatly with the passing of the days and the years.[1]

---

[1] The government of the Venetian Republic, much-admired in Europe, was complex. The city state was governed by individuals whose family members accounted for between 6 per cent and 7 per cent of the republic's population. The government of the republic comprised a series of interlocking councils which were not separated into legislative, executive and judicial functions. The summary of the government apparatus in *De Missione* is generally accurate and reflects what has become known as the 'myth of Venice'. Male members of the nobility, with the exception of clerics, became members of the Great Council, the republic's sovereign body, at the age of

Leo: We cannot but be greatly pleased with the government of that city, especially as its constancy and stability over a very long time indicates to us the admirable prudence of its citizens. But I should like to know in more detail about everything to do with the city, including private matters.

Michael: I would have been satisfied just to speak in that general way, so as not to be overwhelmed by the quantity of things, if it weren't that I think I have a duty to deal with your question. But who could go through, in detail, everything to do with that city? Its site, as I said, is admirable, its buildings and structures extraordinarily sumptuous and magnificent, its churches wonderfully large, and the quantity of sacred relics amazing. To put it briefly, the perimeter of this city is eight miles, which comes to four of our leagues, and it is divided into seventy parishes, which with their churches and priests come under the patriarch. It has fifty-nine religious houses, with religious men living in thirty-one of these, and twenty-eight of them belonging to holy virgins. There are also other minor chapels, and the houses of various sodalities, so that the total number of churches comes to a hundred and fifty.[1] The city also has fourteen hospitals, in which, as I said earlier, those suffering from illness of any kind are given medical treatment. All of these buildings, especially the religious one, are embellished with superb workmanship, and particularly with eighty-seven very high towers which present a striking spectacle; among them the one sited in front of the very famous church of St Mark stands out. What am I to say of the holy relics? This city alone keeps the intact bodies of forty saints, with all reverence and veneration; and the churches are so well equipped that they contain a hundred and fifteen of the musical instruments which the Europeans call 'organs', in cases most artistically adorned with gold and silver. What, again, can I say about the sacred vestments and furnishings? The city has an overwhelming abundance of works of gold and silver, and of garments embroidered or covered with gold leaf, all of these things made there with wonderful art.

With regard to the common utilities of the city, and how conveniently available they are, the city is built in that bay of the sea which I spoke about, so in order to allow easy passage everywhere on land four hundred and fifty bridges have been constructed, with

---

25 if not before. The Great Council was too large to conduct routine government business or to formulate policy (in 1500 it numbered 2,500) and the senate or *Consiglio dei Pregadi* took over such responsibilities. The doge, his councillors, the three heads of the Forty (the court of appeals which also had some legislative functions over finance) were known collectively as the *Signoria* and were responsible for the overall running of the Venetian government. They were assisted by three groups of *savii* or ministers whose remit included senate affairs, war, the mainland, commerce, ceremonial affairs and colonies overseas. When these *savii* met collectively, they were known as the *Pieno Collegio*, or full college. The college could submit its proposals either to the Senate or to the Council of Ten, established in 1310 to oversee internal security but which during the course of the 16th century (until 1588 when its powers were clipped), became prominent in matters of national security. As for the doge, the visible face of the Venetian Republic, the nature of his office has been much scrutinized. He was *primus inter pares*, sacral prince, the source of legitimacy, and yet remained a crucial voice in decision-making in the Republic. See Lane, *Venice*, pp. 95–8, 116–17, 252–73; Mallett and Hale, *Military Organization*, pp. 248–62; Muir, *Civic Ritual*, pp. 19–21, 44–55; Crouzet-Pavan, *Venice Triumphant*, ch. 5 *passim*; Fenlon, *Ceremonial City*, ch. 4 *passim*. On dress, see Lane, *Venice*, p. 253, and on the administration of justice, see Muir, *Civic Ritual*, pp. 245–9.

[1] On the importance of the parishes and monastic churches in Venetian history and society, see Lane, *Venice*, pp. 11–12; Crouzet-Pavan, *Venice Triumphant*, pp. 33–5, 255–9.

arches high enough for boats to be able to pass beneath them as they move hither and thither through the districts. The boats, of the kind commonly known as gondolas, are remarkably well adapted to sailing and making their way to all the various places. In their central part they have as it were little houses, neatly covered, which will take six passengers whether sitting or lying. They are notably fast, for just two sailors, or even just one, can handle them and steer them anywhere like swift horses. The number of these boats in the city is very considerable, and is said to be as high as ten thousand, some of them belonging to the citizens and some being for hire and available at various places.

With regard to the buildings, I'll say briefly that besides the general structure of the houses, which is excellent, there are almost a hundred palaces, which stand out as far and away superior to other dwellings, and in the magnificence of the architecture and the style with which they are furnished are such that any one of them would make a suitable residence for a king. And although this city has its foundations on the bed of the sea, it is large enough to include a hundred and seven delightful gardens, constructed and planted by the most noble patricians of the city; also fifty-three piazzas, all of them beautifully tiled, and in various places a hundred and thirty-five wells for the use of all the people. The statues positioned in public places or in churches number a hundred and sixty of marble and twenty-three of bronze, plus nine equestrian statues, beautifully made of bronze with gold inlay, and these monuments preserve the memory of illustrious and celebrated men who have deserved well of the Republic. In the churches the tombs, of marble of Paros and many other kinds of costly stone, are of extraordinary magnificence, with statues of noble and famous men who adorned and enriched their country with their many outstanding merits and glorious deeds, and who themselves have thus received no small reward for their labours with these distinctions and marks of honour passed down for the memory of those who come after them. This will have to serve as a summary of the main points about the magnificent city of Venice, all of which will indicate very clearly to you just how celebrated it is.

Leo: The summary which you have provided of these things does not quench or satisfy our avid thirst, but rather kindles in us greater ardour and eagerness to know about them, so Lino and I are very keen to have you proceed to explain all these different things at greater length.

Mancio: Leo's request is reasonable, for things in Venice are such that it is not enough just to summarize the main points.

Lino: It might be enough if this city was just the same as the others which have been described, but since it is totally different from the others in its site and in many other things, it is only fair, Michael, that you should accede to Leo's request

Martin: That is an excellent point that Lino makes, especially as the great difference in those things means that there is no chance that your audience will be bored.

Julian: I think you will have done enough for our brothers here, Michael, if you speak first about the three most celebrated places in Venice, namely the palace of the doges, the church of St Mark, and the square, and after that about the harbour, and about how honourably we were treated by that most famous Republic.

Michael: That is no light task, Julian, but I'll gladly take it on, provided I'm allowed the usual day in between.

Leo: As you request, Michael. It's yours.

COLLOQUIUM XXVIII

Gives an account of notable things observed in Venice, and of the honour with which the Japanese ambassadors were treated by its august Senate

Lino: It's time now, Michael, for you to fulfil the undertaking you gave to us yesterday, and to tell us at today's meeting at somewhat greater length about all those so famous places in the city of Venice.

Michael: You seem very determined, Lino, to exact what I promised, but I'll gladly supply it, so as in some degree to satisfy your tremendous eagerness to learn, and do all I can to fix the appearance of those places in your eyes and your minds. I'll deal now with the very famous doge's palace, the most noble church of St Mark, and the great and most spacious piazza of the city. To begin with this last, picture in your minds a very large area, which we ourselves saw, consisting of a quadruple esplanade, and there is none that we ever saw or heard of to compare with it for beauty or for the multitude and the artistry of its buildings. Of this whole area one part, which faces the front of the palace, borders the sea; the second part stretches from two columns set beside the sea to the clock tower, and runs along one side of the palace and the basilica of St Mark; the third, which is directly in front of St Mark's, covers a large space and extends all the way to San Geminiano's;[1] and finally the fourth takes up the space on the far side of the basilica. The one between the columns and the clock is five hundred feet long and a hundred and twenty feet wide, the one in front of the basilica of St Mark four hundred and seventy feet long and of similar width to the other one, the one at the front of the palace and extending to the sea is more or less two hundred feet square, and the one on the far side of the basilica is almost the same in both length and width. The area which comprises this quadruple esplanade is so fine, so beautiful, that the Italian poet Petrarch was right to say that he doubted if there was any other to compare with it in the whole world.[2]

But let us now list the principal buildings which are to be found in this area, and speak first of the tower, meant for bells, which on one side overlooks the largest square and on

---

[1] San Geminiano was demolished during the French occupation of Venice, which began in 1797, to make way for the addition of a ballroom to the Procuratie Nuove, Napoleon's palace.

[2] Petrarch's observation is made in *Epistolae Seniles*, IV: 3, 10 August 1364. His laudation of Venice is frequently quoted as a key text in the propagation of the myth of Venice. See, for example, Fenlon, *Ceremonial City*, pp. 39, 325.

the other the square of the basilica. This tower is a most remarkable work.[1] To begin with, it is constructed of very white stone, like marble; next, it rises to the great height of three hundred and sixty feet, a height which one can only wonder at; finally, set at its apex it has a statue, of bronze inlaid with gold, of an angel indicating with his hand the peace and happiness for which men long; and this statue is sixteen feet high. The tower itself is square and has five columns on each side, which protrude from the solid structure, with spaces between them, and excellently adorn the whole structure, right up to the canopy over the compartment where the bells are located, and where this part of the tower ends with a most beautifully made crown. This compartment, in which are the most excellently forged bells, is most pleasing to see, and of very fine workmanship. On it can be seen the admirably constructed canopy, supported by four columns at the four corners, with, in addition, five highly polished pillars on each side, which leaves the compartment open, so that the sound of the bells travels far and wide. Above the canopy the tower keeps the same square shape, but is somewhat narrower, and at that point it has colonnades on two floors, with columns on the lower of marble and on the upper of bronze, the height of the human body. The sides of the level above these are occupied by four lions made of marble, of extraordinary size and beauty. From that point the tower rises in a pyramid, the apex of which is splendidly set off by that statue of the angel which I mentioned. Flights of stairs, ingeniously constructed, allow one to climb the tower. They curve round inside the four sides of the tower, and at regular intervals, after the last step, there is a landing and a small room, ideal for resting in, excellently lit from a great window which admits the sunlight; and this is so arranged that there are many large windows, one above another, on each of the sides of the tower, with the result that it is full of light and most pleasing to the eye. These particular stairways consist not of separate steps but of continuous inclined paving, such that horses or other beasts of burden can easily climb them. This tower is outstanding for its fortification and its workmanship, but besides that it is visible, because of its great height, from far away, and can be picked out even from ships thirty-five leagues distant from it.

Beyond the tower and bordering the same side of the square I already mentioned is a magnificent building commonly known as the Procuratie of San Marco;[2] and the procurators are the most important magistrates, holding the highest rank after the doge in the Venetian Republic. Their building is beautifully constructed on two floors on which can be seen two galleries, one above the other, supported by a graceful arrangement of columns, the base, elevation, and crown of each of them displaying marvellous artistry. Within it has three spacious residences, one for each of the three committees of procurators.[3] These are

---

[1] Originally built in the second half of the 12th century, the top of the campanile had been modified after an earthquake in 1511. The present tower, 98.6 m or 325.5 ft tall, is a replica completed in 1912 after the original one collapsed in 1902. The figure at the top is of the archangel Gabriel. See Sansovino, *Venetia città nobilissima*, pp. 294–5.

[2] The Procuratie Vecchie, built in the 1490s, now attributed to Pietro Bon, which housed the offices and rooms of the procurators. The Procuratie Nuove was started in 1586 after the boys' visit. See Fenlon, *Ceremonial City*, pp. 91–3. The title and office of procurator was largely honorific but much sought after as a source of patronage and because of the influence of the procurators over the arts and architecture of the city. There were nine procurators, all elderly, established individuals. See Lane, *Venice*, p. 98; Fenlon, *Ceremonial City*, pp. 94–7.

[3] One committee was responsible for the original task of the procurators, the management of St Mark's, another was responsible for the St Mark's side of the Grand Canal and the third for the opposite side of the canal (ibid., p. 94).

commonly known as the upper, the nearer, and the further residence, and access to them is by a splendid stone staircase with a vaulted ceiling of consummate artistry. The walls of these three residences are adorned with very pleasing portraits of procurators and of those of the same order who attained to the title of doge.

Further along in the same square and facing that building is another, no less magnificent, which closes off that side of the piazza, and at the end of it is another very celebrated tower, which boasts the public clock,[1] made with such expertise and craftsmanship that one may well wonder if there is another clock to compare with it, apart from the one in Toledo about which I have already spoken. This tower is supported on the arch over a very large door, above which there is a square, splendidly made, and within this is enclosed an ornate circle depicting the rays of the sun and the signs of the hours. Below that can be seen the twelve signs of the zodiac, and with them the stations and oppositions of the sun and the moon in a space decorated with purple and gold. Above this square is another with a depiction of the Most Blessed Virgin, and extending in front of her is a room like a balcony, with a door at each side. Whenever the hour is to be indicated by the striking of a bell the folding doors open and a statue, with the form of an angel and blowing a trumpet, comes out, followed by the three Magi looking as if they were alive. All of them bow their heads before the Blessed Virgin, and then move on and go through the other door at the other side, and then the bell is rung. This entire spectacle is brought about by the remarkable turning of various wheels (we already described a similar case in another place). Above that again there is another square, in which is the carved figure of a lion, representing St Mark, one of the writers of the holy gospel, with the doge of the Venetian Republic kneeling in front of it. In the last place, finally, the bell is situated between two statues of bronze representing men, and when the angel and the Magi cross over, as I said, at the sign of each hour, these two strike opposite sides of the bell with hammers in such a way that they really appear to be living men. This work of art was made by a certain Gian Carlo Rinaldi,[2] an Italian, and an extremely talented man.

Leo: Admirable indeed are the works of Europe, and the invention of this clock should rank as one of those most worthy of admiration.

Lino: That is certainly so, since with their skill and ingenuity they make statues of wood and bronze imitate human movement and gesture so closely.

Michael: As I have already often said, dear cousins, European works display such skill and such magnificence as to be almost incredible to those who have not witnessed them. But let us come back to describing those works: as well as the building for the three committees which I described earlier I'll mention three other edifices occupying that side

---

[1] The Torre dell'Orologio, built between 1496 and 1499 and often attributed by Mauro Codussi, houses the clock which was completed in 1499. The clock was designed and built by Gian Paolo Rainieri and his son, Gian Carlo, of Reggio Emilia. It has been restored many times. The description here follows Sansovino (*Venetia città nobilissima*, p. 317). For a full description of the Torre and clock, both of which were conscious displays of Venetian civic pride, see Goy, *Building Renaissance Venice*, pp. 233–45.

[2] Original edition (p. 303) '*Ioanne Carolo Rinaldi*', following Sansovino, *Venetia città nobilissima*, p. 317. But see n. 1 above.

(of the square). First is a sun terrace,[1] where the leading men of Venice used to congregate for recreation, but where nowadays the procurators of San Marco with their attendants act as a guard whenever on a Sunday there is a general assembly of the leading men. Four statues carved of fine Corinthian bronze, of Pallas, Apollo, Mercury, and Peace, occupy the facade of this terrace, and they represent the wisdom, eloquence, concord, and peace of that most illustrious senate. Above these there are three squares enclosing, in their central part, many other relief figures, and these too are remarkable works of art. Within this terrace, above the place where the supreme magistrates sit, there is another enclosure containing full-figure statues of the Blessed Virgin, of the most holy Child Jesus, and of St John the Baptist, highly regarded as works of art by all experts. The vault of this terrace is adorned with excellent paintings in gold and various colours.

Next after this terrace is the library known as the Libreria di San Marco,[2] and sited opposite the palace. It can be numbered among the most celebrated of buildings for its architecture both external and internal. To begin with, its facade is adorned in Doric and Ionic style with various columns and a multiple coronis above. The lower gallery rests on so many columns that from them sixteen arches are formed, and within these there are many beautiful statues. On the facing of the arches themselves are heads in turn of lions, men, and women, so that each arch has one, and the coronis panel which is above these arches is decorated with squares in which small sculpted relief figures can be seen. Above this panel is another gallery, enhanced by beautifully worked small pillars; in addition it has sixteen windows, each of them supported by four columns. Protruding from the angles of the windows can be seen statues of winged women, and in the vault, at intervals, those heads which I already mentioned. Above these windows rises another panel adorned with a further sixteen small oval-shaped windows corresponding to the arches and windows below; and above that again there extends another gallery, supported by small pillars of the same kind, and in the pediment above it are positioned sixteen statues, made with remarkable artistry. The whole building, being the work of outstanding craftsmen, is strikingly embellished with many different kinds of coils, knots, and flowers of marble which boys hold in their hands.

And when we come to the interior of this building the artwork is no less admirable. The ceiling of the lower gallery is made of tiny pieces of stone and is divided into squares depicting various figures. The door you go through to ascend to the floor above has on either side statues of women bearing the vault of the door on their shoulders, and

---

[1] The Loggetta at the base of the Campanile designed by Jacopo Sansovino (1486–1570) and built between 1537 and 1540. Originally designed to surround the Campanile, only one side was built. It was intended to continue an earlier tradition as a shelter and informal meeting place for patricians and was used by the procurators for official business concerning the shops and markets in the square. It has been called 'the most complete surviving visual representation of the Myth of Venice' (Fenlon, *Ceremonial City*, pp. 104–10, esp. p. 108). Another traveller, Thomas Coryate, describes it as 'a most glorious little room' (*Coryat's Crudities*, pp. 185–6).

[2] Now known as the Biblioteca Nazionale Marciana, the library was designed by Sansovino and completed, with five additional arches, by Vincenzo Scamozzi after 1588. It was built to house the remarkable collection of books and manuscripts collected by Cardinal Basilios Bessarion. Work began in 1537. Unfortunately, the roof over the main hall collapsed in 1545 and Sansovino was thrown into prison and released only after the intercession of, amongst others, Titian. He had to foot the bill himself for the rebuilding of the roof. From the late 1550s, the library housed the Accademia Venetiana della Fama which embodied 'the Venetian ideal of learning and religion allied in the service of the Republic'. See Lane, *Venice*, pp. 441–2; Fenlon, *Ceremonial City*, pp. 100–103, esp. p. 103. The description in *De Missione* is based on Sansovino, *Venetia città nobilissima*, pp. 308–12.

appearing to find it so heavy that they can hardly hold it up. The staircase leading to the upper part of the building is splendidly ornate, with an extraordinary ceiling wonderfully painted in gold and various colours, and also various pillars which have an extraordinary lustre, like the brilliance of precious stones. This staircase gives access to a very large hall, notable for its beautiful marble, fine cut stone, and excellent sculpted figures. Here, with the Venetian senate bearing the cost, teachers instruct the youth of the whole city in Greek and Latin letters and the other humanities. From this hall one can proceed to another which contains a library and which is also of very fine workmanship, with columns of various colours and also a square in which are written the names of the doge and the magistrates who commissioned this building. This is something very well worth seeing. The walls of this very large room are covered with shelves holding an infinite multitude of excellently bound books. In charge of this hall, known, as I said, as the library, is a certain learned and noble man, who holds this post by commission of the Senate. To give a detailed account of the cost of the books and the building would be a long task, since the roof of the whole library is vaulted and adorned with very fine stone and with gold and colours, and contains four levels of squares, making up a total of twenty-one.

After this building there is another assigned to the minting of the coinage, and it is celebrated for the remarkable architecture and fortifications of the structure.[1] So that nothing in it can catch fire it is entirely constructed of natural stone. It has a courtyard at the sides of which are residences for those who mint the coins; and in the middle is an octagonal well in which can be seen a beautifully sculpted statue of Apollo, with golden rods in his hands. Two magnificent staircases lead to the upper floor, and there are built halls and rooms of most ample dimensions for the accommodation of the magistrates of the Mint and the guarding of the coinage.

Leo: These buildings you speak of seem to me most noble; but I would like an explanation of the minting of coins.

Michael: The way in which gold, silver, and copper is used in Europe is very different from the way they are used here in Japan or in China. We weigh silver on the scales, and pay out a greater or a lesser weight according to the value of the thing bought; but in Europe when dealing with gold or silver it is a question not of weights but of coins, and these coins are minted stamped with the insignia of the kings or of the free republics.[2]

---

[1] The Zecca or mint, another fine Sansovino design which is now part of the Marciana library. Sansovino (*Venetia città nobilissima*, p. 215) describes the building as fortress-like. See also Fenlon, *Ceremonial City*, pp. 98–100.

[2] At this time Japan was a major supplier of silver in the nascent global economy. Most of Japan's output supplied China's insatiable demand for silver. The silk-silver trade between Macao and Nagasaki, which was, amongst other things, an indispensable source of finance for the Jesuit mission in Japan, was the highly profitable heart of Portugal's carrying trade with Japan. Under Nobunaga and Hideyoshi, Japan took its first steps towards the creation of a standardized national coinage. (Until then Japan had depended upon imported Chinese coinage, although some domestically minted coins also circulated.) This policy was greatly advanced under the Tokugawa. Most exports of silver were ingots rather than coin and the servants of the English East India Company, while they traded in Japan from 1613 to 1623, complained frequently about the high copper content of these silver ingots. In Asian trade the Spanish real was very highly valued. See Massarella, *A World Elsewhere*, pp. 243–5; idem, 'What was Happening in East Asia Around 1600?', pp. 17–21; *Cambridge History of Japan Volume 4*, pp. 60–62, 104–5; von Glahn, *Fountain of Fortune*, pp. 131–41. See also below, p. 421 n. 1.

The coins are made by order of the kings or the republics, the more precious ones of gold or silver, the more base of copper, and the Europeans make use of these various coins in their sales and purchases. Therefore since the Venetian Republic is independent and free it has the power to mint money like other kings, and that is why it has designated this splendid building for this purpose.

Lino: I suppose those coins, so beautifully stamped, must look very pleasing, so I would love to see some.

Michael: That will not be difficult, Lino. We wanted you to have as much pleasure as possible from our return, so we brought with us coins of each kind. But now let us go back to the piazza. On the opposite side, facing the buildings we have described, are St Mark's church and the doge's palace, and we shall shortly be describing them. The part of the square which borders the sea is not occupied by any tall buildings except for two notable columns, separated by a considerable space; notable, I say, for their thickness, their height, and finally because the shaft of each of them is one piece, a quite remarkable thing. These two columns together with a third are said to have been brought from Constantinople, and when they were being taken from the ships to the land that third one fell into the sea. The sea at that point is shallow, not deep at all, but the column with its great weight had pressed down and buried itself so firmly that it was impossible to pull it out. The other two were hauled up on to the land, and they lay there on the shore for a long time, for there was no one with the skill and daring to raise them and set them up, until many years later a most famous man was found who with marvellous skill did erect them. And it is indeed extraordinary that those two huge columns stand there intact and straight, with no support whatever other than the bases on which they rest. A statue representing St Theodore,[1] who is also patron of the Venetians, occupies the architrave of one of them, and shows him armed to fight for the Republic; and a magnificent winged lion, symbolizing St Mark, stands on the capital of the other. It is usually in the space between these two columns that the death penalty is exacted of those condemned to death.[2]

Leo: The way you have described that square, Michael, has convinced me that it must be one of the most beautiful in the whole world, and that from now on I should regard European works with a much greater sense of admiration.

Michael: Your admiration would be much greater, Leo, if you had seen those works with your own eyes, for it is very difficult for thought alone to grasp what the keenness of the eye can perceive. But now that we have been all round the piazza let us head for the church of St Mark.[3] With regard to size, some churches indeed will be found which are

---

[1] St Teodaro of Amasea or San Tòdaro, the first patron saint of Venice (Muir, *Civic Ritual*, pp. 93–5).

[2] The columns, symbolizing saints from the Byzantine and Latin traditions, served as the ceremonial gateway to the city as well as the site for the execution of justice. See ibid., pp. 245–9; Fenlon, *Ceremonial City*, pp. 12–13, 113. The description of the provenance of the columns and the fate of the third follows Sansovino, *Venetia città nobilissima*, pp. 316–17.

[3] The description of St Mark's that follows is a condensed, and at times verbatim, version of Sansovino (*Venetia città nobilissima*, pp. 92–106).

larger; this one after all, was built as a chapel for the Venetian senate, even though it must be reckoned to be pretty large. But if the comparison is with others of the same size, this church excels all others in Italy in magnificence. In the first place, it is made of the purest marble, which, leaving aside the price, can be brought to a fine polish only with very great difficulty. It has, besides, so much sculpture and relief work, so many statues, so many columns, and such art in all of them, that the sums spent on this church are almost beyond reckoning. But to deal more in detail with each of these: with regard to columns, there are eight extremely costly columns of porphyry which make the main entrance to the church very beautiful. Above these are set various statues of marble and bronze, in ornately worked niches, and the rest of the frontage is adorned with mosaic work, which the Europeans hold in high regard. There are besides four bronze horses, sculptures dating back to the time of Nero, and fashioned with such skill that they are among the rarest examples of the sculptor's art.[1] Up on the roof of this church there is a dome with five cupolas in the form of a cross, covered with tiles of lead which make them very beautiful, and with the spaces between them very well protected with bronze pipes which catch and get rid of the rain.

But let us now enter the church itself. The roof has a remarkable dome, the surface of which is of mosaic work beautifully depicting various persons and exploits recorded in the sacred books; and the floor is finely decorated with pictures of trees, animals, and birds, in inlay work, most pleasing to the eye. And since in all of this building a great quantity of gold can be seen, it is popularly called the Golden Church. This church is also distinguished by the many and various tombs of the doges whose bodies are buried there, these tombs being embellished by the precious material, namely marble, of which they are made, but also by the names and insignia, beautifully carved, of those entombed there.[2] We come now to the main chapel, which is notable for its vault of ophite stone, supported by four columns of highly polished marble with carvings in relief, in which the relief figures, upwards of a palm in magnitude, graphically illustrate events recorded in annals ancient and modern. Admirable above all else is the sacred decoration which closes off the view, in place of a sacred retable, and which is commonly known as the Pala.[3] The whole of it is of gold leaf, with images which to some degree stand out, occupying recesses separated from one another by adamant, beryl, emeralds, and other precious stones. The front of the main altar itself is made of silver, and again it has various images standing out in their places, separated by columns, and these with their remarkable beauty complete that work of great price. Four bronze statues of the four evangelists adorn that same high altar, remarkable works of art which show the Gospel writers seated.[4] It is said that this

---

[1] The famous horses, like the columns of marble used for external decoration, were part of the plunder from the sack of Constantinople during the Fourth Crusade. The horses were sent to Venice in 1204 and erected on the terrace of St Mark's in 1254. In Constantinople they had adorned the Hippodrome and, according to Sansovino, they had previously adorned an arch in Rome built by Nero to celebrate a victory against the Parthians. *De Missione* does not support the assertion of some 16th-century travellers that they were gilded. See Sansovino, *Venetia città nobilissima*, p. 94; Lane, *Venice*, p. 41; Fenlon, *Ceremonial City*, pp. 19, 22–3.

[2] The last doge to be buried in St Mark's was Andrea Dandolo (d. 1354). See Fenlon, *Ceremonial City*, pp. 137–8.

[3] The Pala d'Oro above the tomb of St Mark, which is decorated with 187 emerald plaques and 1,927 gems (ibid., pp. 24–5).

[4] The evangelists were designed by Sansovino during his renovation of the basilica in the 1530s (ibid., p. 59).

high altar contains the holy body of St Mark,¹ whom all Venetians acknowledge as their special patron, and for that reason they have on their standards and their arms his symbol, namely the winged lion, the name and image of which refers to St Mark in Sacred Scripture. I should certainly not omit mention also of the holy tabernacle the doors of which are beautifully decorated with various figures, and with four pillars made of extremely costly alabaster or onyx.²

On the left-hand side of this chapel is the entrance to the room where the sacred furnishings are kept. The doors of this room are most skilfully fashioned of bronze, with many relief carvings representing the deeds of Christ and the apostles, with art so singular that, so we are told, the work took twenty years to complete.³ Next we should say something about the choir which is constructed in front of the high altar. It has seats decorated with ivory and ebony, and above all these a most beautiful throne in which the doge sits whenever prayers are to be chanted with solemn ceremony on festive days. Three staircases lead to this choir, the central one more costly and more beautiful than the others, and the other parts are taken up by a wall made of porphyry and ophite, highly polished stone. The upper part of this wall, which is adorned with columns, is finished with a most artistic cornice of the same material, which holds fourteen marble statues of the fourteen apostles and, in the centre, displays a very beautiful cross of solid silver.⁴ To sum up, in a word, about this church, there is nothing in it which is not beautiful and costly, and it is said that this is largely because when it was being built it was established by public decree that sailors or voyagers through the various parts of the world should bring to Venice whatever they might find of value and contribute it for the embellishment of the fabric of this church. And since this city can truly be said to be the mother of all craftsmen who produce works from gold, silver, silk, and other similar material, the sacred furnishings match the church in magnificence.⁵

After viewing this church we saw another building commonly known as the Sanctuary,⁶ in which have been kept, from long ago, holy relics and also all the most precious objects of gold, silver, and so on. With regard to the holy relics, they are celebrated not only for their number and for the greatness and fame of those saints, but also for a miracle divinely performed in the year twelve hundred and thirty. For when that building happened to catch fire, and the fire gradually took hold, and the whole building burned down, the holy relics alone survived unharmed.⁷ Not only is this a matter of public record; it is also confirmed by the testimony of the Supreme Pontiff. Now what am I to say of the precious objects? Those who view them cannot tear their eyes away. There one can see many golden

---

¹ The tomb has been called 'the most important site of Venetian collective memory' (ibid., p. 61). According to legend, the saint's remains were brought to Venice in 827 or 828 but were subsequently lost, only to be discovered in 1094 when the present church was consecrated. On the importance of the *translatio*, or removal of the remains, to Venice, in shaping the Venetian state, see Muir, *Civic Ritual*, pp. 78–92; Fenlon, *Ceremonial City*, pp. 11–18, 23, 26–33, 46–7.

² The tabernacle door was designed by Sansovino (ibid., pp. 59–60).

³ The door to the sacristy, designed by Sansovino, has been described as 'the great masterpiece of Venetian bronze-relief casting of the High Renaissance' (ibid., pp. 59–60, esp. p. 59).

⁴ The choir, as described here, was altered in the 19th century (ibid., p. 60).

⁵ The treasures of St Mark's, including religious relics, were greatly enhanced by the booty from the Fourth Crusade and from later adventures (Lane, *Venice*, pp. 41–2, 206).

⁶ The description paraphrases Sansovino, *Venetia città nobilissima*, pp. 102–3.

⁷ See ibid., p. 102.

diadems, and girdles adorned with diamonds, emeralds, topazes, beryls, chrysolites, and many other great gems; two horns of the unicorn, a most rare animal, each of them seven palms in length; some cups partly of gold and partly of solid pearls; two carbuncles as large as eggs; and a tablet of gold, also adorned all over with jewels, which it is customary to show to the people at Masses to pray for peace. Among other jewels is a beryl of great size, which Cardinal Grimaldi,[1] a Venetian, bequeathed to the Venetian Republic, and another diamond set in gold, which Henry the powerful king of France gave to the doge as a gift;[2] and I say nothing of the candelabras, cups, goblets, plates, and many other pieces in gold and silver. Finally there is also a doge's crown covered with so many pearls that it is reckoned to be worth a hundred and fifty thousand ducats. All these things together make up a treasure so great that it is said that no other of such value can be found. Now, to say something of the ministers of sacred things, this same church has many important ones, namely twenty-four canons plus deacons and subdeacons, whose leader is known as the *primicerio*;[3] add to these a very big choir, who sing the sacred prayers most sweetly, to the accompaniment of musical instruments.

Leo: From what you have been saying it seems that the opulence of the famous Republic of Venice is incredible.

Michael: It is indeed incredible, and you will see this clearly from what I have yet to say as well as what has been said. I am now going to speak of the Palace of the Doge,[4] also called the Palace of St Mark, in which the doge, or prince, of the Republic lives, and where many other meetings of the magistrates take place. This palace is such a building as to deserve to be preferred to the most noble and sumptuous buildings of all Italy. There are two sides to this palace, both of them very large, the one connected to the church of St Mark, the other facing the sea, and each of them extending for two hundred feet.[5] There is a double gallery in it, the lower and the higher, both of them supported on fine columns topped with notable architraves and embellished with work of different kinds. Above the upper gallery there is a third, on which are to be found very spacious halls and rooms adorned with a great number of windows. Finally, at the top, the outer walls are protected by strikingly worked crenellations and rise to an impressive height. The palace has two

---

[1] Original edition (p. 309) '*cardinalis Grimaldus*', but Sansovino (*Venetia città nobilissima*, p. 103) gives the Venetian, Domenico Grimani (1461–1523), cardinal from 1493.

[2] Henri III visited Venice in 1574 en route from Cracow to Lyons. Venetians recalled the elaborate ceremonies held to mark the occasion as the highpoint of the city's ceremonials during the entire 16th century. As a token of appreciation, Henry gave the doge a ring estimated to have been worth 10,000 ducats. See Fenlon, *Ceremonial City*, pp. 193–215, esp. p. 214.

[3] An administrative term used in the later Roman empire and by the early church to denote the clergy responsible for regulating the lower clerics in ecclesiastical schools and cathedral churches. It was later applied to the individual responsible for directing the liturgy and the chant. In Venice the *primercio* was appointed by the doge and was the senior cleric of St Mark's. See Sansovino, *Venetia città nobilissima*, p. 104; Fenlon, *Ceremonial City*, pp. 68–9.

[4] The Palazzo Ducale dates from the 14th century and was designed as a replica of a Byzantine palace. It was badly damaged by fire in 1574 and again in 1577, viewed by some as a sign of divine displeasure with the Republic. It was rebuilt, despite the objections of many, including Palladio, in the original style. See Fenlon, *Ceremonial City*, pp. 228–9, 316.

[5] The Piazzetta wing and the Molo wing.

courtyards, one of them square and very large indeed, and the other rooms are correspondingly large, so that with the exception of the sacred palace of the pope, which is very different in structure and form, this palace which we are now describing exceeds all others, as I said, in the whole of Italy, in its size and its elegance.

In it can be seen sixteen most spacious halls, used for meetings of the magistrates, constructed with such masterly skill that it seems that human ingenuity could scarcely progress further. All these halls are finished in fine plaster, with gold intermixed for decoration, and besides, the walls as well as the ceilings are divided into squares, in all of which there are finely executed pictures, and in some of them excellently crafted statues, splendid illustrations of ancient accounts of triumphs and other similar exploits; and in these the deeds of this most celebrated republic, praised in so many books, can in some way be seen with the eyes, and images can be viewed of its princes and senators, looking as if they were alive. What can I say about the size of those halls, which is really amazing, and especially the size of the one known as the Hall of the Great Council,[1] which is so vast that it is seventy-four feet wide and a hundred and fifty feet long, and accommodates not only the doge and the other officials, but also the more than fifteen hundred patricians seated below in ten rows of chairs. Not much inferior to this hall in size and in the quality of the work is the one called the Hall of the Pregadi, in which can be seen eleven statues representing to the life, and most artistically, the same number of emperors. The other halls, dello Scrutinio, della Cancelleria, del Collegio, dell' Anticollegio, del Consiglio dei Dieci, della Quarantia Civil Vecchia, and those of other tribunals, rival one another for quality of building, for size, and for magnificence of structure, and all of them have an abundance of statues, pictures, reliefs, and other works of art.

What am I to say, besides, about the armouries, in which are kept the arms of the nobles only?[2] There are four of them, crammed with many kinds of armaments pertaining to both offence and defence, proper to infantry, to cavalry, and to armoured horses. On show are innumerable breastplates, cuirasses, lances, bows, muskets of many kinds, and other similar instruments of war, not only well made, but also decked with gold and glittering bright. Some among them there are of such size and weight that it looks as if they must have been wielded not by men of normal stature but by giants, and thus are kept not for use but as a memorial to antiquity. These halls are adorned not only with marble statues but also with trophies and spoils taken from captured enemies, and I doubt if there is another armoury, no matter of what king or prince, that can match this one of the Republic of Venice for the variety of all the things there and the value of the arms.

But let us come now to the benevolence with which the Venetian senators treated us. The day after we arrived in Venice we called on the doge and the chief magistrates,[3] who were awaiting us in the palace, having first done us the honour of sending many senators of the order of the Pregadi, decked out in the same apparel and borne in the same boats as when they had first received us, to guide and attend us. When we disembarked from the boats to the land such a multitude of people hastened to meet us as we passed through the

---

[1] The Sala del Maggior Consiglio which could accommodate up to 3,000 people and which had been badly damaged in the fire of 1577.

[2] The armoury consisted of five rooms which only a few privileged visitors were allowed to view.

[3] The audience was on 28 June. See Fróis, *Première ambassade*, p. 226; Boscaro, 'Manoscritto inedito', p. 34; idem, 'La visita a Venezia', pp. 28–30, which prints the official record of the reception, dated 28 June. At this time the doge was Nicolò da Ponte (1491–1585), doge 1578–85, who died, shortly after the boys left Venice, on 30 July.

piazza, the portico, the courtyard, and the halls of the palace that, although they made way most politely for us, it was scarcely possible to move forward.[1] But after we had reached the prince's hall,[2] not without difficulty, the prince, who was seated in a most ornate chair, in garments embroidered with gold and surrounded by the most grave of the senators, rose with those senators as we entered, with the utmost respect and politeness drew us into conversation, and invited us to be seated in the chairs prepared for us, two on either side of him. We then expressed to him, in the most courteous language we could, our profound gratitude for the honour and generosity with which we had been treated during our journey through the Venetian jurisdiction, and indicated to him how happy we were to be visiting this most august senate.[3] In answer, with a serene and tranquil countenance, he not only made clear his joy at our coming, but also declared, showing at once love and prudence, that all that we had been given was due to noble youths who, in the cause of country and religion, had been sent from a place so distant to the Roman Curia; and besides, that what had been done so far was not yet enough to fulfil his duty.

After some further speech on his side and ours we took our leave of the prince and the magistrates and departed from them, greatly impressed. Nowhere else, after the majesty which we had observed in the Supreme Pontiff and the College of Cardinals, majesty to be looked up to, as it were, from a lowly place; nowhere else, ever, had we seen such gravity, arising from the combination of advanced age, maturity of speech, and the multitude of senators, especially when we saw the prince, surrounded by the magistrates and senators, who make up the whole body of the republic, present at the divine sacrifice of the Eucharist in the church of St Mark. And since we knew that some small presents from us would be acceptable to the same prince we gave him, as a gift, Japanese apparel together with sword and dagger, and he most gladly accepted these signs of love, and said that they would be kept forever in memory of us, and preserved as a treasured memorial.[4] After taking our leave of the prince we were taken by some very important men to various places which I mentioned before in the palace and the church, and then, to our great pleasure, conducted through the whole piazza to view the streets of the city.

We passed, therefore, through the door and archway which supports the clock tower, and came to the street which takes its name from the merchandise on sale there.[5] By express order of the senate the shops were decorated so as to lay out all the most precious things on

---

[1] After disembarking at the Molo, the boys would have proceeded, as did other distinguished visitors, into St Mark's square and entered the palace precincts through the Porta della Carta and the interior via the Scala dei Giganti. On the iconography and symbolism of these entrances to the palace, see Goy, *Building Renaissance Venice*, pp. 109–15, 221–5.

[2] The Sala dei Collegio, where important visitors were received.

[3] Their expressions of gratitude were translated into Italian by Mesquita. See Berchet, 'Documenti', p. 172; Fróis, *Première ambassade*, p. 227; Boscaro, 'La visita a Venezia', p. 29.

[4] The sword, and some of the other presents, were still in the armoury of the Council of Ten, where they had been deposited by order of the senate, in 1773. They disappeared during the turmoil following the collapse of the Republic in 1797. The sword was signed by Mancio, Martin and one of the other boys. See Berchet, 'Le antiche', p. 268; Boncompagni-Ludovisi, *Le prime due Ambasciate*, p. 27; *Dai Nihon Shiryō*, XI: 2, pp. 100–101. For a detailed account of the reception and list of the presents given by the boys, see Boscaro, 'La visita a Venezia', pp. 28–30.

[5] The area is known as the Mercerie. The Venetian chronicler, Marino Sanudo, described it as 'lined with shops on both sides ... Here is all the merchandise you can think of, and whatever you ask for is there' (quoted in Goy, *Building Renaissance Venice*, p. 233).

sale for us to view, things so precious that it would be almost impossible to estimate their worth. Taking just the shops selling gloves, perfumes, and liquids pressed from various sweet-smelling flowers, it was reliably said that most of them held merchandise worth ten or twelve thousand ducats; and from that you can judge what could be said of the other shops where embroidered apparel, or cloth embellished with gold or silver leaf, and other such costly garments were on display. The quantity, the ornamentation, and the almost infinite variety of it, taking up all the space from St Mark's church as far as the Rialto bridge, left us absolutely stupefied. And since I have mentioned this bridge I shall say something about its magnificence and its architecture. To understand this you have to remember that this whole city of Venice is washed by a shallow sea, as I said before, with many canals, of which the most celebrated is the largest, which like a winding serpent envelops the city, and has the shape of the European letter S. Since this canal is very wide just this one bridge, called the Rialto, has been built to cross it; and although it is constructed of wood it is of extraordinary magnificence.[1] It is so broad that it has shops set on either side of it, like a street, but the middle part of it is so made that it can sometimes be removed so as to make way for larger ships to pass, but at other times can block their passage. But there is no shortage of boats for crossing this canal; indeed, as I said before, they are available for hire in great numbers. Those who come to this bridge can see a notable palace, which was once used by the Venetian senate, but is now assigned to the Germans and their merchandise, and accordingly also takes its name from them.[2] Such a quantity of merchandise is brought there from Germany that from it very great tax revenues accrue to the Venetian Republic. This palace is so large that its rooms and halls number more than two hundred. The interior of most of these rooms, but also the exterior of the whole palace, is adorned with extraordinary and most precious paintings of remarkable beauty.

Lino: Are you saying that even the external walls are decorated with paintings? But how can they remain undamaged by rough weather, rain and wind?

Michael: You mustn't think, Lino, that those paintings are done on paper or any other fragile material, as happens with us. They are painted on the walls themselves, after these have been smeared with lime; and the colours are not just any mixture of paint, but combined with the juices of various fruits in such a way that they can remain there a very long time, and if some part should be damaged they can be restored.

When you cross the bridge of which I am speaking you come to open space called the Rialto,[3] which is very famous on account of the great number of merchants who flock to

---

[1] The bridge, as the boys saw it with the shops and drawbridge, was constructed in 1458. Plans to replace the wooden bridge, which needed frequent repairs, with a stone structure were seriously discussed in 1551 but funds were not made available. The present bridge, designed by Antonio da Ponte, was completed in 1591. See Crouzet-Pavan, *Venice Triumphant*, p. 153; Goy, *Building Renaissance Venice*, pp. 44–5.

[2] The Fondaco dei Tedeschi, built originally in 1228 and rebuilt, between 1505 and 1508, after a fire in 1505. The new facade was decorated by Titian and Giorgione but the paintings have disappeared. See Crouzet-Pavan, *Venice Triumphant*, pp. 120–22, 163; Goy, *Building Renaissance Venice*, pp. 45–7.

[3] The Rialto Vecchio. The Rialto was the financial and commercial hub of the city, and, like the more imposing Piazza San Marco, a religious and ceremonial centre as well. It was redeveloped after a fire in 1514. See Crouzet-Pavan, *Venice Triumphant*, pp. 150–62; Goy, *Building Renaissance Venice*, p. 14; Fenlon, *Ceremonial City*, pp. 117–20, 182–3.

it, especially those who are engaged in lending money at a fair rate of interest, contracting with merchants from many other cities, receiving money from some, paying out money to others. This business of lending money makes the place very crowded, and links the men of this city with those of other most noble cities in many kinds of association and commerce. The spacious buildings which surround this piazza add lustre to it, and one can see the magnificent porticos where senators and merchants come together for purposes of business, to deal with various matters to do with trade both among themselves and with any others who assemble there. At the end of the bridge we are talking about there is sited a church which is the most celebrated of all the churches of Venice for its antiquity;[1] and next to it a treasury of singular construction, made entirely of Istrian stone, which takes its name from the Camerlenghi,[2] and contains splendid halls and rooms with various most artistic paintings featuring gold and colours. In that palace there is a certain place in which the Republic of Venice keeps a vast quantity of silver and ducats, and such is the integrity of the magistrates, the security of the place, and the vigilance of the Republic, that princes from other places, from various kingdoms and provinces outside Venice, eagerly desire and earnestly request that their own money, which they are not using, be kept there in that same treasury, for they are persuaded that that strongroom is safer than their own.

If you go on through the rest of this piazza you will find many buildings for merchants, the lower porticos of which are filled with clothing for sale, mostly of precious stuffs, silk, velvet, and so on, for the covering and adornment of the body; and the value of all these things can hold its own against the price of the things for sale in the merchandise street, which I mentioned before. At the far end of this piazza is another, occupied on one side by goldsmiths and on the other by jewellers. The quantity of gold which the former engrave and sculpt, and the multitude of pearls which the latter polish and refine, is such that the great cost and variety of the work in both gold and gems induces, in all outsiders who see it, admiration and indeed stupefaction. The wealth of the Venetian Republic and of the city, accordingly, is almost beyond the conception or grasp of anyone not actually there to see it.[3]

But to give you a clearer idea of its opulence I am going to end this colloquium by adding one further item of proof or evidence, by offering you a partial description of a certain procession which took place when we were present. It is the custom in this city, as in others, that the memory of that day when Christ our Redeemer, already preparing for the death He was to suffer for us, instituted the Holy Eucharist, should be reverently and solemnly honoured with a public procession.[4] Now the nobles of Venice, having learned of our arrival, postponed the procession until 29 June, the feast of Saints Peter and Paul, for they wished to soothe our spirits when we were tired by the discomforts of the journey with something joyous, and to offer to the men come from afar the spectacle of

---

[1] San Giacomo de Rialto, the oldest church in Venice, said to have been consecrated in 421. See Crouzet-Pavan, *Venice Triumphant*, p. 158; Fenlon, *Ceremonial City*, pp. 182–3.

[2] The Palazzo dei Camerlenghi, begun 1488, completed 1525. About one-half of the paintings which decorated the interior, many by Tintoretto and his studio, have survived (Fenlon, *Ceremonial City*, p. 119).

[3] Sanudo described the Rialto as 'the richest spot in the world' (quoted in Crouzet-Pavan, *Venice Triumphant*, p. 150).

[4] The festival of the *apparitio* or apparition of St Mark, held on 25 June to celebrate the discovery of the saint's lost remains in 1094.

that most religious procession, which on our account has been considerably delayed. On the appointed day, therefore, we made our way, in the company of a number of nobles, to the church of St Mark, and occupied the places prepared for us with most ornate chairs, cushions, and footstools, in the upper choir. There we not only attended at the celebration of holy Mass, but also had the great pleasure of witnessing that most impressive assembly of two hundred and fifty of the most senior senators. After the immolation of the sacred host, with beautiful singing and other most solemn ceremonies, we were conducted by the same noblemen to a certain palace from which we were able to view to our hearts' content that public procession of the whole people of Venice, a great thronging concourse of them. I really don't know where I should start in describing this spectacle for you, whether with the multitude of citizens, conjoined in religion, or their order and correct disposal, or again with the great and wonderful value of the things they carried. But I shall say something about how the procession is normally conducted, to give you some idea of it.

Of the many religious sodalities which there are in Venice six stand out as the principal ones, and because of the great number of their members, the magnificence of their buildings, and their assiduity in the performance of works of piety, they are known as the *Scholae Maiores*.[1] The members of these sodalities walk two by two, in proper order, carrying very large candles decorated with gold and various colours, and we have kept and brought back with us, as a memento and in gratitude, some of these candles which were generously given to us by one of these sodalities, which registered us as honorary members. After these sodality members, in order as described, comes the choir singing the prayers and with it the standard of the same sodality, followed by all the other sodalists, carrying candles in the same way and keeping the same order. As these companies of sodalists advanced there were also, carried along at intervals, floats or sacred conveyances of three sorts: the first sort was made up of various works of gold and silver, boasted a likeness of something like a tower, and included whatever there was of value in the city. The second was made from various most artistically fashioned reliquaries, which presented a great abundance of both gems and pearls. The third sort, finally, contained various most beautiful statues and pictures, which illustrated the multiple mysteries of the Christian religion, and the distinguishing palms obtained by the martyrs with their many sufferings. Then, in the last of these floats, the embassy of the four of us from Japan to the pope, to obtain his favour and benevolence, was excellently portrayed. The floats of these three sorts, placed at regular intervals, numbered upwards of a hundred and forty, and they were covered in awnings partly of silk, partly interwoven with gold embroidery, all of which made these sacred conveyances so precious that all the works contained in them were said to have a possible value of four hundred million sesterces.[2] And the fact that

---

[1] The six Scuole Grandi. The members included both nobility and commoners and their activities were regulated by the Council of Ten. The clergy had no influence over the Scuole. Originally the members flagellated themselves during processions but by the mid-16th century this was no longer a regular feature of the processions, having given way to the practice of carrying religious relics encased in jewels. See Pullan, *Rich and Poor in Renaissance Venice*, pp. 33–62; Muir, 'Images of Power', pp. 38–40. The boys visited the Scuola Grande di Santa Maria della Carità to venerate some relics in the Scuola's oratory. Their names were enrolled 'che i nomi dei loro Re' (on behalf of their kings, i.e. daimyo). The Guardian Grande of the Scuola hoped that a similar institution might be founded in Japan. A commemorative plaque was made to mark the visit. It is located in the courtyard of the Seminario Patriarcale. See Hamada, *Tenshō kenō shisetsu-ki*, facing p. 176; Berchet, 'L'antiche', p. 268; Boscaro, 'Manoscritto inedito', pp. 38–9; *Dai Nihon Shiryō*, XI: 2, p. 108.

[2] I.e. 10 million ducats.

such a quantity of gold and silver is brought together for just one public procession is manifest evidence of the wealth of Venice.[1]

After these sodalities it is the turn of all the male religious, and there were a very great number of those, for the city of Venice has a hundred and fifty churches and monasteries. After the male religious comes the archbishop and patriarch of Venice with all solemnity, and the family of the prince follows him. After that come the priests attached to the church of St Mark, and they carry a most precious conveyance and the sacred box with the most holy Eucharist. Then comes the doge himself, with all the ambassadors of the kings and princes, who always reside in Venice, and after them all the magistrates and the Pregadi senators, two by two, in their long robes of scarlet silk; then the remaining nobles, and lastly all the men of the people, and since these are innumerable, and carry torches of the purest white wax, it makes a wonderful display. The doge was not present on that day because of his age and infirmity (he was ninety-five years old),[2] but nevertheless this procession had so many senators and citizens taking part, with such a quantity of most precious adornments, and distinguished with so many works of art and inventive ingenuity, and besides, continued for such a long time (it took a full three hours to cross St Mark's square), that I really don't think it is possible for you to imagine how splendid it was.[3]

Leo: I don't know how this city of Venice can have reached such a degree of opulence in everything, but this procession gives us clear evidence and certain proof of it.

Michael: There are many things in the city conducing to the wealth and power which it has in abundance, for example its status as a free republic, its jurisdiction which extends far and wide, the concourse there of merchants and negotiators; but there is one thing above all else which seems to me to have made it pre-eminent, namely the good fortune which by divine favour it has enjoyed for so very many years. God the immortal has granted to that city that right from its beginnings (and more than a thousand years have intervened between that time and this) it has never been subjected to invasion or pillage by enemies,[4] and thus that whatever has been acquired over such a long period of time, obtained through so many victories, or brought together in such a variety of works of art,

---

[1] For more detailed contemporary descriptions of the procession, see Sansovino, *Venetia città nobilissima*, pp. 457–65, partly printed in Boscaro, 'La visita a Venezia', pp. 30–31, and *idem*, 'Manoscritto inedito', pp. 34–7. See also Fróis, *Première ambassade*, pp. 228–9. The following year the Guardians of the Scuole Grandi, complaining about the heavy financial burdens they were expected to bear, reminded the Heads of the Ten of services they performed for the Venetian state such as 'in many honourable processions for the arrival of many Princes, and most recently in the procession ordered by mandate of Your Most Illustrious Lordships for the visit of the Prince Ambassadors of Japan' (quoted in Pullan, *Rich and Poor in Renaissance Venice*, p. 54).

[2] Meaning in his ninety-fifth year.

[3] For an analysis of the importance of processions in projecting the power and hierarchical order of the Venetian state and their contribution to the 'myth of Venice', see Muir, *Civic Ritual*, pp. 189-250; Fenlon, *Ceremonial City*, pp. 87–8, 120–27, 320–22. On the costs of processions, see Pullan, *Rich and Poor in Renaissance Venice*, pp. 127–9. The Corpus Christi procession in 1506 took more than five hours to pass (Muir, *Civic Ritual*, p. 224).

[4] The bleakest time for Venice was the War of Chiogga (1378–81), the climax of the struggle with Genoa, when the city was blockaded by its enemies. The republic fought back and defeated the Genoese and their allies. See Lane, *Venice*, pp. 189–96; Crouzet-Pavan, *Venice Triumphant*, p. 74.

and stored in this city as in a treasure house, has remained there safe and sound, and is conserved there in that republic, diffused and spread among the citizens of the Republic as if through the members of a body.

Lino: I have no doubt that the preservation, intact, of this one city and republic over so many centuries, a thing never conceded, as far as I know, to any other, should be counted among the divine miracles. But how painful it is to consider the difference between that so fortunate city and our Japan, prey to the depredations of so many enemies, the fires of so many wars, the conflagrations of so many cities, so much internal discord and destruction, that it is more remarkable that anything at all has survived that unrelenting devastation than that the flower of the ancient state of Japan should have fallen.

Michael: I'll leave lamentation over these things to some other time, but indeed the nobles of Venice can be said to be fortunate and blessed in being possessed, up to this time, not only of such an abundance of things, but also of tranquillity. In this most illustrious city we stayed for ten days, days which we spent in seeing various admirable things, and in repeated mutual greetings between us and the leading figures there, especially the eminent patriarch, the pope's vicar, the legates of the emperor and of the kings of Spain and France, and other men of this rank. As our companion in our journeys and sightseeing we had a distinguished nobleman, designated by the senate, named Constantino Molino, whom I mention here to remember and honour him, and to attest to the great kindness and courtesy that he showed us.[1] There would be almost no end to it if I were to list all the other things worthy of note in this city, but there are two which I must not omit and which are very famous, namely the Arsenal, that is the citadel of the senate, where there is another armoury and a most noble dockyard for all the ships, and an island called Murano, a mile distant from the city, where they produce glasswork. But today's colloquium has been long, so with your permission I'll leave these two places for tomorrow.

Leo: The time has passed surprisingly quickly, thanks to the variety of what you have said, and the extraordinary things you have told us about. But since you ask for an intermission we shall allow our pleasure to be interrupted for a short time.

---

[1] Scion of the Molino family. Antonio Molino was an actor and poet influential in early commedia dell'arte. His brother, Armonio, was organist of St Mark's. See LaMay, *Musical Voices of Early Modern Women*, p. 377. Constantino was one of the individuals to whom Cristobal de las Casas dedicated the Venetian edition of his *Vocabulario de las dos lenguas toscana y castellana* (Venice, 1600).

COLLOQUIUM XXIX

More about things in Venice, but also dealing with the access of the ambassadors to other cities, principally Padua, Verona, Mantua, Cremona, and Milan, and the rejoicing with which they were received in them

Leo: We are here earlier than usual, Michael, because we are keen to hear about those other two most famous things in the city of Venice. Your audience is ready, then, so do begin.

Michael: I only wish, dear cousins, that it was possible somehow to go with you on swift wings to that city itself and to point out to you the things you are asking me about, rather than to have them so very far away with only my poor words to tell you more. But I have to do the best I can with such abilities as I have, and persevere in my task until the due time. With regard, therefore, to the place known as the Arsenal,[1] it is the place in which all the ships of that republic are built, and where everything which needs to be prepared or repaired for military and particularly naval expeditions is most diligently kept; and the number of the things and the magnificence of the place are so great that it provides a clear demonstration of the vast wealth and power of the republic. This place takes up almost an entire league, and it is enclosed all round by a wall and very strong towers, in such a way, however, that a way remains open for access from and back to the sea; and the shore is suited to bringing ships which have been damaged or buffeted by storms at sea up into the dry, and then drawing them down to the sea again when they have been repaired and excellently covered with pitch and bitumen. All this is arranged and done with remarkable facility. The ships there are not left in the open, at the mercy of the wind and the rain, but are covered in with admirable roofs, as if they were enclosed in housing, and usually a hundred and fifty or two hundred triremes are kept under these roofs. When we were there we saw, as well as these, another twenty-four much larger ships, which we can call octoremes,[2] and in addition large numbers of lighter vessels and many smaller boats, so many that it would be difficult to count them all.

---

[1] Originally built in 1104 and subsequently enlarged considerably, with the addition of the New Arsenal (Arsenale Nuovo), completed in 1325, and the Newest Arsenal (Arsenale Nuovissimo), completed in the early 16th century. At the time of the boys' visit, the Arsenal was the largest industrial complex in Europe and occupied 60 acres or 0.24 sq. km. Dante likened it to hell. Others, such as the boys, and Coryate, who estimated it encompassed two miles, were greatly impressed. The highpoint of its activity was in the 1560s. The boys visited the arsenal on 3 July. See Dante, *Inferno*, Canto XXI, lines 7–15; Berchet, 'Documenti', p. 173; Coryate, *Coryat's Crudities*, pp. 216–21; Lane, *Venetian Ships*, pp. 129–45 *passim*, 146; *idem*, *Venice*, pp. 163–4, 362–4. The only comparable shipyards in the world had been those of early Ming China (Needham, *Science and Civilisation*, IV: 3, pp. 479–80).

[2] Probably a great galley some of which had eight men to a bench (Lane, *Venetian Ships*, p. 32).

There too there are many places where all the things needed for the arming and readying of those galleys are kept, oars, sails, and similar tackle, and anchors, cords, ropes, cannon, and other things of this kind, all of these so arranged that all the instruments are laid out for each of the galleys, a great fleet can be got ready very easily, and the state of preparedness is such that nowhere else can anything similar be found.[1] In addition to all these galleys which are kept here there are another thirty or forty which are on the move here and there, guarding the maritime coasts, so that the Venetian Republic is considered to be the mistress and queen of the whole Adriatic Sea. And to mark this in that city there is an old custom, which has come down from ancient times, according to which the doge himself, with the senators and an infinite multitude of the people accompanying him, goes out to sea on the holy day of the ascent of Christ the Lord into heaven, and in a solemn ceremony casts a ring into the sea, and the people call this the marriage of the sea.[2]

As well as the armoury I have already spoken of, which is for the nobility, there are the general armouries, in a separate location, kept in seven halls, where arms of all kinds can be found, for infantry and cavalry, for attacking the enemy and for protecting the body, and other similar kinds, in such numbers that an army of sixty or seventy thousand soldiers can be equipped for war. In another depot there are many cannon of various types, and many cannonballs of iron and stone, so large that some of them are five palms in circumference. And there are so many of these that the number of cannon comes to two thousand five hundred, and of cannonballs to more than two hundred thousand.[3] Besides all this there is always a very great quantity of the powder which they call gunpowder kept ready in certain towers. Finally, in that republic and that place there is a wondrous abundance of everything pertaining to the arming of the fleet, and the providence of the magistrates is so great that there are always sixteen hundred workers, hired by the senate, applying themselves there to various tasks relevant to naval matters, and from this you can easily get an idea of the annual expense involved.[4]

Leo: The things of Europe, and especially of that Republic, are wonderful indeed; but I wonder even more why this most powerful Republic has not subjugated far more other provinces and added them to its own jurisdiction.

Michael: I gave an explanation earlier, Leo, which covers your question, basing it, if I remember rightly, on the power of the other European princes, and the norms of justice

---

[1] On the efficient outfitting of galleys, which impressed other visitors as well, see ibid., pp. 170–75, and *idem*, *Venice*, pp. 362–4; Crouzet-Pavan, *Venice Triumphant*, pp. 143–4.

[2] The *sensa* or ritual marriage of the city and the sea, performed on Ascension Day. See Muir, *Civic Ritual*, pp. 97–8, 118–34; Crouzet-Pavan, *Venice Triumphant*, pp. 48–9, 164–5; Fenlon, *Ceremonial City*, pp. 34, 43–4.

[3] On the Venetian use of cannon on sea and land, see Lane, *Venice*, pp. 356–61; Mallett and Hale, *Military Organization*, pp. 81–7. The size, barrel length and range of the artillery pieces varied (Guilmartin, *Gunpowder & Galleys*, pp. 167–83, 243–7). Improvements in the casting of iron in England and the Netherlands later in the century enabled English and Dutch ships to be fitted with heavy cannon. This changed the nature of warfare in the Mediterranean and contributed to Venetian decline. Galleys, which relied on muscle power, were no match for heavily armed sailing ships (ibid., pp. 18–21, 287–8). Coryate was also impressed by the Venetian armouries (*Coryat's Crudities*, p. 220).

[4] Coryate says that there were 'continually one thousand fiue hundred men working in it' (ibid., p. 218). Lane gives an average of 2,000 workers in the 1560s and up to 3,000 during emergencies. See Lane, *Venetian Ships*, pp. 161–3, for a list, and *idem*, *Venice*, p. 362. On the expenditure on the arsenal, see *idem*, *Venetian Ships*, pp. 151–2.

which all are careful to observe. No words of mine, however, can do justice to the greatness of that republic.

Lino: Tell us now, Michael, about that other place which you called Murano.

Michael: I am glad to move now from the apparatus of war to the pleasures and delights of that place. It is a sort of town, filled with many buildings and gardens and villas, and also with many shops and furnaces in which the glass called crystal, very ornate, and works in glass, are made. The quantity of these is such that not only that city, and all of Italy, but also many other provinces throughout the world are delighted by the splendid artefacts which they produce.[1]

Leo: What is this glass which you speak about, and what is it used for?

Michael: An excellent question, since this material is completely unknown to us.[2] Glass is a brilliant material without any darkness in it, so that light passes straight through it, made from a kind of sand or gravel together with a type of grass. It is extremely fragile, so that if any items made of it happen to fall or are dropped they break into tiny fragments; therefore every year a very great quantity of it is purchased and consumed in everyday use. And these works of glass are not made just from that material. Gold is also added with great skill, and this means that the utensils are of no small value, as you can see from the things we have brought with us, for among other gifts which we were given by that Republic there were two cases filled entirely with glass vessels. They make not just vessels but also many other items of glasswork, such as window panes, which are excellent in admitting light but keeping out rain and wind, and are used in churches, palaces, and other similar buildings. They also make excellent mirrors, such as the ones we were given by the same Republic and have brought back with us. As well as these they fabricate towers, organs, and other works most pleasing to see, skilfully made and beautiful, and the patricians and nobles often have cabinets full of these. And for the most part all these things are exported from that place for sale in various regions.

Now the procedure that the craftsmen use in producing these works is very remarkable. First they bring the material to the fire and soften it, then they pick it up with the hooked end of hollow iron instruments which they use. These instruments are hollow, and they blow into them in such a way as to extend the material and stretch it out, keeping the inside of it empty, especially if it is cups or similar vessels that they are making. Afterwards

---

[1] In 1291 all glassworks in Venice were ordered to close and transfer to Murano, about 1.6 km to the north of Venice, as a precaution against fire. It remains the home of Venetian glass production.

[2] Glass beads were first imported into Japan from China during the Yayoi period (c. 300 BCE–300 CE). They were used for religious and decorative purposes. Japanese glass bead production began during the Kofun period (c. 300–710) and flourished until the Heian period (794–1185) when it began to decline. By the time the Portuguese arrived in 1543, glass manufacture had virtually disappeared and was a lost craft. Some glassware continued to be imported from China but Portuguese imports of blown-glassware introduced what appeared to be a new, rare product into Japan, hence the lengthy description here. Attempts to make glass locally soon began and during the Edo period Japanese glass production was reborn and was particularly successful in the Satsuma domain (present-day Kagoshima) in the 19th century. See Blair, *History of Glass in Japan*, esp. pp. 151–9, 176–93.

they smooth and polish the same material with other instruments like malleable wax, and adapt it to various uses, and they add gold and various colours to it. The finished vessels are left to harden in an appropriate place, and thus they turn out horses, lions, men, and various other shapes.

But now time is pressing, and we must move away from this city in which, because of the greatness and the number of the things in it, we have lingered. We'll mention just two of the favours done to us by that Republic, and then bring our treatment of it to an end. The first was their concern to ensure that we would not be forgotten, and with this intention those most distinguished senators decreed that the story of our embassy, with very realistic portraits of us, was to be depicted by outstanding artists, as our most certain memorial, in the Hall of the Great Council,[1] among the other great achievements of the Republic; and the cost of this work, as we heard later, was two thousand ducats.[2] The other favour was a present sent to us comprising two huge chests filled with more than five hundred pieces of glassware, plus a great deal of cloth, velvet, damascene, sheer and also undulating silk, and gold-embroidered, and finally eight very large mirrors, four of them ebony-framed and four surrounded with pictures painted in gold.[3] This gift was so

---

[1] Sala del Maggior Consiglio.

[2] The painter commissioned to do the portraits was Jacopo Tintoretto, whose workshop specialized in such official commissions. He was to be paid 2,000 ducats. The portraits were to be hung in the Sale dei Pregadi and the boys were expected to autograph them. Only the portrait of Mancio Itō was completed. The others were sketched. On 17 October the senate passed a resolution urging the artist, then 67, to complete them. Alas, the whereabouts of Tintoretto's efforts are unknown. It was also intended to add a short description in Japanese and Italian describing the individuals and their reason for coming to Venice. A copy of the description, written in Japanese on Japanese paper and signed by the boys, is extant in the Vatican Library. The best representation of the boys, and of Mesquita, was done, rather crudely, by Urbano Monte in a manuscript chronicling their visit to Milan (see Figs 3–7). Monte saw them several times during their stay, drew the sketches and described their appearance. His portraits were used on a handbill printed in Augsburg in 1586 and much reproduced since then (see Fig. 13). See *Dai Nihon Shiryō*, XI: 2, pp. 102–3; Berchet, 'Le antiche', p. 269; *idem*, 'Documenti', p. 170; Gutierrez, *La prima ambascieria Giapponese*, pp. 49, 67–8; Satow, 'Origin of Spanish and Portuguese Rivalry in Japan', pp. 136–41; Boscaro, 'First Ambassadors', pp. 13–15; Ridolfi, *Life of Tintoretto*, pp. 77–8; Cooper, *Japanese Mission*, p. 116, Fenlon, *Ceremonial City*, p. 96. Otherwise, the boys are represented in a fresco at the Teatro Olimpico in Vicenza, which they visited, and they are identifiable in the fresco depicting Sixtus V's *possessio* in Rome (see Fig. 11). For an illustration of the Olimpico fresco, see Fróis, *Première ambassade*, p. 233, and Lach, *Asia in the Making of Europe*, I: 2, following p. 656. Alessandro Benacci's *Breve Ragvaglio Dell'Isola Del Giappone* (Bologna, 1585) and his *Avisi Venvti Novamente Da Roma Delli XXIII Di Marzo M D LXXXV* (Bologna, 1585) include an identical drawing of one of the boys, appearing more European than Japanese, in a long gown. The latter booklet includes a short description of the boys and their Japanese clothes (Boscaro, *Sixteenth Century*, pp. 42–5, 74–5). On the inscription, see ARSI, Ital. 159, f. 77v; Yūki, 'Shinshiryō', p. 171.

[3] On 29 June the members of the Collegio had voted to spend 500 ducats on custom-made tabernacles containing religious relics as presents for the boys. The following day, however, the senate vetoed the resolution declaring that it was inappropriate to deprive the city of relics which earlier Venetians had expended so much effort and sweat to obtain. Instead, it was decided to spend 1,000 ducats on silks and damasks, although, the boys received fabrics as well as glassware and mirrors. See Fróis, *Première ambassade*, p. 231; Boscaro, 'Manoscritto inedito', pp. 37–8; *idem*, 'First Ambassadors', pp. 18–19; Yūki, 'Atarshiku hakken', p. 17. The presents were bulky and filled two large boxes. Nuno Rodrigues wrote to Aquaviva from Lisbon on 18 October asking the general to make arrangements to have the boxes forwarded to Lisbon (*Documenta Indica*, XIV, p. 56). The decision to deny the boys relics was not a slight. Venice, which rivalled Rome in the volume of relics it contained, jealously guarded its collection. Both the Venetian oligarchy and populace venerated the relics and believed they could intercede with the Divinity in times of crises such as during the recent outbreak of bubonic plague in 1575–7. On Venice and relics, see Muir, *Civic Ritual*, pp. 92–7; Fenlon, *Ceremonial City*, pp. 319–20.

magnificent that it would have befitted even the most powerful of princes. Besides all this the senate issued an edict to the prefects of the cities within the jurisdiction of Venice, to which we were about to travel, that we were to be received with honour by all their people, and to be provided with whatever we needed. By these gifts, then, and many other signs of benevolence and love, we were bound to that Republic.

We said our farewells to the prince, to the magistrates and senators, and finally to the fathers of the Society, who had treated us with great kindness, as beloved sons, and on 6 July we embarked on two ships, with the memory of that most glorious republic deeply impressed on our minds.[1] Many senators accompanied us as far as the church of San Giorgio in Alga, and there, with those same men, we joined in a most lavish banquet prepared for us. At the end of the banquet, which we greatly enjoyed, we departed for another city called Padua, which we reached on the same day. The journey was most agreeable, for we were drawn smoothly along a delightful river called the Brenta by horses moving along the bank and pulling on the ropes of the ship, and were able to enjoy the view of the beautiful buildings which occupied both banks of the river.[2]

In this river we saw two remarkable inventions. One of them is in the place commonly known as Lizza Fusina,[3] and it is as follows: to prevent this river from flowing too powerfully from the inland areas and flooding and clogging up the canals running through Venice, it has been carefully diverted elsewhere by the use of high banks and ramparts, and thus a short spur of land has been built up between the river and those shallows of the bay of Venice. And so that this will not be a bar to navigation a kind of curved bridge, stretching from the shallows to the river, has been developed, and boats, even heavily laden boats, are transported across it from the shallows to the river on a contraption of

---

[1] On 4 July the boys paid a courtesy call on the doge and left a letter of thanks for the hospitality they had received during their stay (Berchet, 'Antiche', p. 269; Boscaro, 'Manoscritto inedito', p. 38). In the letter, another contribution to the 'myth of Venice', they mentioned that they had not wanted to return home without first seeing 'the marvellous and indomitable' city of Venice the sight of which had 'surpassed their expectations' and added that on their return home they would spread word of its renown throughout Japan. A copy in Italian was placed in the Venetian State Archives and is printed in Berchet, 'Documenti', p. 171, and *Dai Nihon Shiryō*, XI: 2, p. 109. The original letter, in Japanese and Italian, is in the Vatican Archives and is printed in Satow, 'Origin of Spanish and Portuguese Rivalry', pp. 136–9; Hamada, *Tenshō kenō shisetsu-ki*, facing p. 178; Boscaro, 'Manoscritto inedito', illustration 5. Satow speculates (wrongly) that this document was the intended inscription with autographs for the Tintoretto paintings ('Origin of Spanish and Portuguese Rivalry', pp. 140–41).

[2] Montaigne was similarly impressed, while Coryate, travelling in the opposite direction to the boys on his way to Venice, took seven hours to do the 25-mile journey. Henry III was carried in a gilded barge and stopped over at the Villa Foscari and Federico Contarini's villa at Mira, which numbered among the many beautiful buildings along the river. See Montaigne, *Journal de voyage*, p. 161; Coryate, *Coryat's Crudities*, p. 157; Fenlon, *Ceremonial City*, p. 214.

[3] Or Lizzafusina, where a dam was built in 1437 to protect the lagoon from silting, a great danger at the time. Boats in wheeled cradles, the *carro*, were hauled up the inclined plane by horses. See Jeffery, 'Shakespeare's Venice', pp. 30, 33–4. Montaigne made the journey from Padua to Venice in reverse and describes Lizza Fusina (*Journal de voyage*, pp. 161–2); so too did Coryate (*Coryat's Crudities*, p. 157). Similar methods for hauling boats up inclined planes had long been in use in China. See Needham, *Science and Civilisation*, IV: 3, pp. 363–5. As the boat in which the boys were transported up the Brenta to Padua included Jesuits among its passengers, there was no danger of a mishap for, according to Fynes Moryson, who travelled the route in 1594, 'a local proverb saith, that the boat shall be drowned, when it carries neither Monke, nor Student, nor Curtesan (they love them too well to call them whores) the passengers being for the most part of these kindes' (quoted in Jeffery, 'Shakespeare's Venice', p. 33).

wheels, across that tract of land, by a winch or pulley, the pulley-wheel being turned by a horse.

The other invention is also a work of great ingenuity. When somewhere along the river there is a place where it rises steeply or suddenly, so as to impede the movement of the ship, they have made a kind of container for the water, with its own doors, and they can either keep the water in this or let it out, as the case requires. When ships come to that point from below they are admitted into that container. The doors are shut, and the water in the container is then increased little by little till it reaches the height of the top of the rise, and the ship can then sail away on a level course. And if a ship comes from the upper end it enters the full container, the gates are then opened, the water gradually escapes, the ship descends, so to speak, and when the water levels are the same it moves out into the stream. Thus a natural problem is solved by extraordinary ingenuity.[1]

The officials of the city of Padua were awaiting our arrival, together with other knights and patricians. They invited us into their carriages, and took us to the city and to the college of the Society, where we were treated with splendid hospitality. We stayed for two days in that city, where there are a number of different things which it is a great pleasure to see. First of all we saw the convent of St Anthony, the church of which is known in that city, by antonomasia, as 'the church of the Saint'. 'The Saint' is that most blessed Anthony,[2] the glory and ornament of the Franciscan order, about whom I already said something when I was dealing with the city of Lisbon. St Anthony was indeed born and brought up in Lisbon, and he entered the monastery of St Vincent, which is in that city. Later, however, he was received into the Franciscan order, he crossed into Italy, and after he had spent many years there his most holy soul was eventually released from his body in Padua and, with many miracles performed, went up to heaven. Devotion to this saint in Portugal, in Italy, and especially among the inhabitants of Padua has always been remarkable, so much so that they built a very famous church for him, and it is outstanding not only for the magnificence of the building, but also for the costliness of the vestments and of the gold and silver furnishings, valued at a hundred thousand ducats.[3]

In the same city there are many other very fine buildings, among which I would place first a certain public hall where the magistrates meet, which has a great variety of most artistic paintings and a roof of most unusual structure, covered with lead tiles, and is so very large that it seems that no other single building can compare with it.[4] In the same city there is also a famous university, nurse of all the arts, to which a great number of people, eager for knowledge, come not only from Italy but also from many other provinces, and

---

[1] A reference to the lock basin connecting Padua with the River Brenta. Lock technology was, of course, highly advanced in China (Needham, *Science and Civilisation*, IV: 3, pp. 344–65, esp. p, 351). In Japan, with its mountainous topography, the principal commercial and transport hubs were close to the sea, the major transport route. Canals and locks were not necessary.

[2] St Anthony of Padua (1195–1231).

[3] Il Santo, begun in the 1230s, to which the saint's remains were translated in 1263. Montaigne gives a brief description and Coryate mentions its rich possessions and was saddened by the unprepossessing coffin of Edward Courtney, earl of Devonshire (Montaigne, *Journal de voyage*, pp. 160–61; Coryate, *Coryat's Crudities*, pp. 142–4).

[4] The Salone in the Palazzo della Ragione which has one of the largest unsupported roofs in Europe. Built between 1172 and 1219, there were originally three chambers with three roofs but after a fire in 1420 the partitions were removed to form one large hall. Montaigne was also impressed by the huge roof (*Journal de voyage*, p. 161).

this contributes much to the fame of the city.¹ Also in this city a college of the Society has been built, and is flourishing greatly because of the building and its most pleasing site on the bank of a river. There the fathers accorded us most kind and welcome hospitality.

We saw in the same city a celebrated garden, planted at public expense, where the Republic of Venice is assiduous in the cultivation and conservation of all the herbs used in various medicines, and this is for the benefit of all. In charge of this garden was Melchior Ghilandino,² a distinguished man, learned in the arts, and I have good reason to number him among those to whom we owe a debt of gratitude, for besides many other signs of his love he presented us with four remarkable volumes. In the first of them is contained the 'Theatrum Orbis' of Abraham Ortelius,³ and the other three comprise the most notable cities of the whole world, drawn and engraved by extremely talented artists.⁴ This gift, as well as being valued at a hundred ducats, was given to us with generous liberality, without any expectation of repayment, and is a good demonstration of his Christian attitude and his benevolence towards these new green shoots of Japan.

We left Padua on 10 July and headed for Vicenza, another town not far away belonging to the jurisdiction of Venice, and there too we had a great welcome from the citizens and appreciated their friendly attitude towards us. Many distinguished citizens came out to meet us, and they accompanied us as we arrived with all possible gladness of soul and body. There is not time to tell everything in the detail which our due gratitude requires, but I cannot let pass without mention the singular delight which we felt at the assembling and the appearance of almost all the nobility, men and women, who came together to a certain theatre⁵ where it is the custom for certain learned men, known as academicians, to put on tragedies, comedies, and other dramas of that kind, sumptuous and ornate, for the people to see. We were received with honour in that place and heard a most pleasing and varied concert, delightful to our spirits, and from what we saw here and in other places we were deeply impressed by the excellence, the variety, and the remarkable harmony of

---

¹ The university was founded in 1222 and soon became one of the most famous in Europe.

² Melchior Wieland (1520–89), German physician and botanist, from 1561 director of the Orto Botanico or botanical gardens in Padua (founded in 1545). For Coryate's description of the gardens 'famoused ouer most places of Christendome', see Coryate, *Coryats Crudities*, pp. 148–9.

³ Abraham Ortelius, *Theatrum Orbis Terrarum*, first edition Antwerp, 1570. Twenty-five editions in various languages appeared before Ortelius's death in 1598 and several afterwards. The *Additamentum Theatri Orbis Terrarum* appeared in 1573 and four more supplements subsequently. The four volumes were valued at 500 scudi (ARSI, Ital. 159, f. 63). See also Valignano, *Adiciones*, p. 377 n. 8.

⁴ Georg Braun and Frans Hogenberg, *Civitates orbis terrarum*, VI vols, Cologne, 1572–1617. The third volume appeared in 1581. These volumes, together with Ortelius's work, were important in shaping Japanese knowledge of European cartography. The influence of Ortelius's work can be seen on three surviving Japanese painted screens portraying cities of the world. See Cooper, *Japanese Mission*, pp. 209–11. Conversely, the boys' visit was instrumental in stimulating European cartographical interest in Japan. The visit inspired Urbano Monte's map of Japan, produced in 1589. The map is quite inaccurate. See Guttierrez, *La prima ambascieria Giapponese*, pp. 75–80. On the Portuguese cartographical contribution to European knowledge of Japan, see Marques, *A cartogafia, passim*.

⁵ The Olimpico, designed by Andrea Palladio, built between 1580 and 1584, inaugurated on 3 March, shortly before the boys' arrival, with a performance of *Oedipus Rex* by Sophocles. As has been mentioned, their visit is commemorated in a fresco. Coryate mentions that the Russian ambassadors to Rome were entertained in the theatre and that 'after them certaine young Noblemen of that farre remote region in the East called Iapan or Iapona, being descended of the bloud royall of the Country, were receiued here with great state, at what time *Liuius Paiellus* a singular Orator pronounced an eloquent Oration in praise of them' (*Coryat's Crudities*, p. 299).

the instruments belonging to the art of music, which are widely used among the Europeans; and this is to say nothing of the elegant public oration which one of those academicians gave, in Italian, in celebration of our coming and in praise of the things of Japan.

From there we went on to another very famous city called Verona, whose citizens invited us firstly to a splendid lunch in a certain villa before the city itself. Then, before our entry into the city, fifty knights on horseback with a hundred armed infantry met us, and the numbers of nobles and soldiers who gradually appeared was so great, the sound of cannon so loud, and the military exercises so varied, with battle lines drawn up and manoeuvres carried out, that it was as if we were in a military camp. The college of the Society was just beginning to be built and was not really suitable for us, so we were taken to the bishop's guest accommodation, which left nothing to be desired as to diligence on the part of those caring for us, variety of musical instruments, or anything else that generosity could provide. We stayed two whole days in this city, and passed them very happily in viewing various things. We saw first of all the cathedral,[1] sumptuously constructed, and secondly the ancient theatre formerly built by the Romans in that city.[2] Being so ancient it was largely a ruin, but it has been rebuilt at public expense by the city, and is a demonstration of the art and the power of ancient Rome in making buildings. Lastly we were invited by Count Bevilacqua to see his house,[3] and viewing it gave us great pleasure and at the same time filled us with admiration. First we entered a hall filled with musical instruments, which soothed our ears with the wonderful sweetness of the various sounds they produced. We went then into another very splendid room with a large number of different marble statues, and many paintings, and finally with images of all the Roman emperors, set with great artistry in ebony cases. This spectacle was a remarkable representation of the long years of antiquity, and displayed not just a princely but a royal magnificence. Lastly we saw his library, filled with books in such numbers, and so well bound, that it was only natural for us to wish for one like it in Japan. We were greatly taken with the beauty of this city, and for the costliness of its buildings, the splendour of its nobility, and also for the charm of the river Adige, we judged it to be one of the finest cities of Italy.[4]

We departed from Verona on 14 July, and about midday we reached a town called Villafranca. This town is on the border between the jurisdictions of Venice and Mantua,

---

[1] Dating from the early 12th century.

[2] The Arena, the third largest in Italy, restored on numerous occasions. For Montaigne's description, see *Journal de voyage*, p. 158, and for Coryate's longer appreciation, see *Coryat's Crudities*, pp. 311–17.

[3] Mario Bevilacqua (1536–93), Venetian ambassador to the Porte 1579. He was a noted patron and connoisseur of music and amassed an outstanding collection of musical instruments which he bequeathed to the Accademia Filarmonica in Verona. See Castellani, 'A 1593 Veronese Inventory', pp. 15–24. He was also a collector of sculptures, books and paintings. Coryate gained admission to the palace, 'but not without some fauor', and was greatly impressed by the paintings (*Coryat's Crudities*, pp. 372–3). The boys had already met the count when he accompanied them from Bologna to Ferrara (Fróis, *Première ambassade*, p. 217).

[4] In the catalogue of Francesco Calceolari's collection of curiosities in Verona, published in 1622, there is a reference to a visit to Calceolari's cabinet by the 'most liberal Japanese princes, Martinus and Michael ... having been sent to Rome to offer allegiance to Pope Gregory XIII'. They are said to have given the cabinet 'a dress of differently coloured feathers of Indian birds' and a feather head-dress 'commonly used by Indian kings'. While it is possible that the boys visited this attraction, there is no likelihood that they presented such items which suggest an American not a Japanese provenance (Lightbown, 'Oriental Art', pp. 234–5).

so Muzio Gonzaga, a most noble man and a relative of the duke of Mantua, met us there in the name of the duke himself. This duke of Mantua is one of the greatest of the princes of Italy and one of those not subject to the jurisdiction of any king, and he had pressed us by letter, when we were in Venice, to come to Mantua.[1] I have no words to describe the honour with which this duke of Mantua and the prince his son treated us. For besides this man of such high rank sent to the border with two carriages, after we had advanced a short distance into the territory of the duke we had six more carriages come to meet us, one the duke's own carriage, covered in red velvet, and we were immediately taken into it. Later a squadron of cavalry came to meet us, magnificently armed and adorned with most costly apparel, and afterwards another squadron, of light-armed infantry, in similarly striking finery. At last, two leagues before our entry into the city, came the prince himself, son of the duke, his beauty at age twenty-one rivalling his urbanity, riding in a golden carriage drawn by four horses, and accompanied by some fifty more two- and four-horse carriages and a hundred knights exhibiting velvet dress, collars, beautiful ostrich feathers, and golden escutcheons. As soon as he reached us, after a most honorific mutual greeting, he got into the carriage in which we were riding and sat with us, taking the lowest place out of courtesy and in order to honour us.

As we came close to the city many cannon were fired from two fortresses, with a most festive and impressive sound. Equally impressive were the many soldiers at the entrance to the city, of whom there were two cohorts, the one with muskets, the other with halberds. In the outskirts of the city the illustrious Scipione Gonzaga, a relative of the duke,[2] came most courteously to meet us, conveying the duke's excuses for his absence, as indeed the prince already had, the duke himself being somewhat unwell. This was the same Scipione who was made Patriarch of Jerusalem, with very great honour, and a little later, to universal applause, was created cardinal by Sixtus V. We were taken first by the prince to a palace very splendid in its buildings and pictures, but also with a great number of statues; so splendid that we heard that eight thousand ducats had been spent only a few days before on the room where our Mancio was accommodated.[3] In the same place a splendid and most lavish banquet, with every possible adornment, was laid on for us.

The city of Mantua is among the most beautiful, the most agreeable, and the most heavily fortified of all Italy. With regard to the fortifications it has those two fortresses I mentioned, fully equipped for war. In addition it is sited in the middle of a navigable lake, with certain doors which can be cleverly opened so as to flood all the area of the Mantuan

---

[1] The duke was Guglielmo Gonzaga (1538–87). Under his rule, Mantua was at the peak of its economic and political power. Amongst other things, Guglielmo was a composer and noted patron of music. He was not so friendly to the Jesuits, whose austere approach to church architecture and the liturgy did not appeal to him. Vincenzo (1562–1612), his son and heir, also a patron of music, was 23 when the boys met him. Unlike his father, a pious man, Vincenzo was a roué but, nevertheless, popular. He was involved in the murder of his father's favourite, the Scot James Crichton (the Admirable Crichton), in 1582. Father and son, and their respective wives, were painted by Rubens in *The Gonzaga in Adoration of the Holy Trinity* in the ducal palace of Mantua. The boys are reported to have been 'treated like sovereigns' during their stay. See Brinton, *Gonzaga Lords*, pp. 180–89; Fenlon, *Music and Patronage*, I, p. 4; Haar, 'Value Judgements in Music of the Renaissance', pp. 19–20.

[2] Scipione Gonzaga (1542–93), elected patriarch of Jerusalem 23 September 1585, cardinal from 1587.

[3] The Palazzo Ducale, designed by Giulio Romano, was built between 1536 and 1538. Its paintings included eleven portraits of Roman emperors by Titian. Many of the paintings collected by the Gonzaga were sold to Charles I. Other works of art in the collection were dispersed throughout Europe after the War of Succession (1628–31).

plain, as we described in the case of the city of Ferrara. With this in mind you can imagine also the magnificence of the buildings, the beauty of the city, and how agreeable it is. The following day the duke, although still not entirely well, directed that he be brought in a chair to visit us with all the nobility accompanying him, and when we met him in this way we were very conscious of his courtesy and affability. There were some speeches from both sides, and then the duke invited us to attend a solemn Mass in the church of Santa Barbara, which is attached to the palace itself.[1] This most illustrious duke, in addition to other gifts both natural and cultivated, is a notably good singer, and there is nothing which he values or loves more than to have Mass celebrated in this church with singing in sweet harmony and other customary ceremonies.[2] This was done, with all due observance, on that day, and to this was added nourishment for our souls, for we received the Holy Eucharist. Vespers were recited in the afternoon with the same solemnity, and we had occasion for further and very considerable joy when a Jew, one of those wise men commonly called rabbis, converted from superstitious observance of the old law to Christian truth, and whom the prince himself took as his son in the sacraments, chose to be called Michael Mancio, linking together my name and Mancio's.[3]

---

[1] The basilica was designed by Giovani Battista Bertani (1516–76), who was also responsible for alterations to the ducal palace. It was built between 1561 and 1572, with an interruption in 1568 when Bertani was incarcerated by the Inquisition for several months. A crypt under the high altar is alleged to contain some of Christ's blood. See *Dai Nihon Shiryō*, XI: 2, p. 165; Brinton, *Gonzaga Lords*, p. 7; Fenlon, *Music and Culture*, pp. 185–96.

[2] In 1571 Guglielmo had secured a papal bull granting permission for Santa Barbara to use its own liturgy, missal and breviary. In 1583 the breviary and chants were published. The boys would not have been aware that the 'sweet harmony and other customary ceremonies' which they heard and witnessed were a special privilege at a time when the church was seeking to impose uniformity in the liturgy (Fenlon, *Music and Culture*, pp. 189–90).

[3] Beginning with the expulsion of the Jews from Spain in 1492 (and subsequently from Spanish possessions in Italy), and the ultimatum to Portuguese Jewry in 1496 to convert or leave, the 16th century was one of persecution and acute discrimination against Jews in the European Mediterranean world. In Italy, Jews were confined to ghettoes and were forced to wear a yellow badge. Anti-Jewish prejudice was encouraged by the anti-Jewish theology and policies of popes Paul IV and Pius V, yet tempered by commercial self-interest (Jewish banking services and the importance of Jews as intermediaries in the Levant trade made them indispensable, especially in the case of Venice). In the face of strong ecclesiastical disapproval and pressure, the more tolerant policies of northern Italian rulers, such as Guglielmo Gonzaga, prevailed only for a while. In 1571, the Venetian senate passed a resolution to expel the Jews from Venice and its dependent territories but it was never implemented. It would have been financially and commercially ruinous to the city state. In Mantua, where the Jesuit church was located next to the synagogue, Guglielmo resisted the harsh anti-Jewish measures the church sought to impose throughout Italy. Jews contributed greatly to the artistic life of the city state, especially in the theatre and in music. There were a number of New Christians among the Jesuits, including the upper echelons of the Society. Loyola's immediate successor, Diego Laínez, was one. Loyola himself had welcomed New Christians into the Society's ranks, but other Jesuits, and indeed other religious orders, especially in Spain where the *limpieza de sangre* or 'purity of the blood' laws were rigidly applied, were opposed to their admission. The early Jesuit latitude towards the admission of New Christians became a matter of controversy, within and without the order. Valignano's attitude towards New Christians is more complex than is sometimes presented. Initially, in India, he was hostile towards New Christians, less from innate prejudice, although some of his comments could be interpreted as such, than from his reluctance to cause trouble with the Portuguese authorities who were deeply prejudiced against the New Christians. Ironically, de Sande was of New Christian lineage. His maternal grandmother was a New Christian, a fact which later became known to Valignano when the question of de Sande's, and another Jesuit New Christian, Gomes Vaz's, profession of the four vows came up in 1583. Initially Valignano and other Jesuits in Goa, fearing a scandal, were inclined to delay their promotion, and that of other candidates, until he had authorization from Aquaviva that the promotions were in order. The following year,

Afterwards we were taken by the prince to see the famous places in the city and surroundings; in the former we noted the quality and elegance of the buildings, and in the latter, especially in the duke's own gardens, we observed that there was the same delight, the same magnificence, and the same perfect adaptation for all life's pleasures as in other similar cases which we described earlier. That being the case there is no need to repeat the description here. And it was not only the prince himself who gave proof of his kindness and hospitality towards us, but also his wife,[1] who chose to go out to the country on the same day, and showed such affability and courtesy that when she and the many accompanying her met us out in the open she insisted that we should pass before her carriage did.

With the approach of night we were taken by the same prince to a lake,[2] and there we boarded the prince's ship, which was adorned with red velvet and with gold both within and without, were much gratified by enthusiastic applause from six other ships and the music of various instruments, and greatly enjoyed the nocturnal view of the city. The prince had ordered that lamps and lanterns should be set up to appear at all the windows of the city and on the walls round it and the bridge leading to it, and this meant that the night seemed to shine as bright as if it was day, and delighted both eye and mind. On this lake there were also two structures like pyramids,[3] supported by two boats, and from these many fireworks made of sulphur and paper were lit and sent up in various directions. There was other material in them which kept the fire going, with the result that the fireworks not only did not go out when they reached the water, but emerged from it, jumping hither and thither, startling and splashing the bystanders in a most entertaining fashion. What with all this, together with the sounds of cannon, trumpet, and fife, the atmosphere of festivity was extraordinary. After we had enjoyed this spectacle for some time we disembarked from the boats and were met by twelve of the duke's attendants, each with a torch, and a great crowd of others with them, and together with the prince we retired to the palace.

The prince did not allow the days which followed to pass without providing something for our spirits' diversion. First of all we went on a little further and visited,

---

Valignano and the others shed their caution and decided that all the candidates should be promoted forthwith. In 1593, in a major concession to Philip II, the Society's fifth general congregation issued a decree barring anyone of Jewish or Moorish ancestry from remaining in or entering the Society without special dispensation. The most famous New Christian to become a Jesuit after the 1593 decree was Alexandre de Rhodes, who served the Society in Vietnam and Persia in the 17th century and who devised a method for the romanization of the Vietnamese language which became the basis of the Vietnamese alphabet in use today. For Jews in Venice, see Pullan, *Rich and Poor in Renaissance Venice*, pt 3 *passim*; Fenlon, *Ceremonial City*, pp. 256–9. For Mantua, see Fenlon, *Music and Patronage*, I, pp. 39-43. On the New Christians and the Jesuits, see *Documenta India*, XIII, pp. 90, 260, 444, 745, 770, 825; Brodrick, *Progress of the Jesuits*, pp. 118–21, 314–21; Boxer, *Christian Century*, p. 81 (which misrepresents Valignano's attitude to New Christians); Wicki, 'Die "Cristãos-Novos"', pp. 342–61; Burnett, 'Humanism and the Jesuit Mission', p. 427. O'Malley, *First Jesuits*, pp. 188–92; Alden, *Making of an Enterprise*, pp. 257–8; Munitiz, 'Francisco Suárez', *passim*.

[1] Eleonara de' Medici, daughter of Francesco I, grand duke of Tuscany, the prince's second wife, whom he married in April 1584. His first marriage, to Margherita Farnese, daughter of Alessandro, duke of Parma, was annulled after a year.

[2] As mentioned above, at this time Mantua was surrounded by lakes. On an island in one of the lakes was the Palazzo del Te, designed by Giulio Romano for the Gonzagas. The palazzo was evocative of ancient Rome especially the erotic frescos in the Sala di Psiche. The boys visited the Palazzo but it is unlikely they were shown the frescos (Boncompagni-Ludovisi, *Le prime due ambasciate*, p. 28).

[3] Representing the columns of Hercules. See ibid., *loc. cit.*, p. 28.

with him, a church of the Blessed Virgin which is a league and a half away from the city and which is very famous for the many miracles which take place there through the intercession of the Blessed Virgin.[1] We next visited a monastery of religious men of the Carthusian order, very flourishing in its antiquity and the severity of its discipline.[2] After we departed from there we had a most enjoyable time fishing, for many fish of various kinds. And lastly, the pleasure of that day was crowned by hunting a variety of wild beasts.[3]

On another day we travelled with the same prince to a monastery, four leagues from the city, of religious men of the Order of Saint Benedict.[4] This monastery is among the most celebrated in all Italy for the magnificence and the expense of the buildings, for the value of its revenues, and finally for the numbers of the monks, there being about a hundred and fifty of them. Prayers were said and a bronze bell rung (something done only when the visitor is a prince), and then all the monks, together with the abbot of the monastery, a man of great authority, gave us a most friendly and generous welcome. But I must not omit to mention our visit to the wife of the duke and mother of the prince, a most illustrious lady, notable for every kind of virtue. She is the daughter of the Emperor Ferdinand and first cousin of King Philip of Spain, yet she is so endowed with humility and charity that she is accustomed to visit the poor when they are ill, and not only to supply them with necessary things, but also to minister to them herself.[5] We also paid a visit to the wife of the prince, and both of these ladies, conformably with their high rank and birth, treated us with the utmost courtesy, coming out from their own private quarters to the door of the entrance hall with courtesy of a kind shown only to great princes. Then we were shown the possessions and the treasury of both families, and in both places, which were full of most precious things, we thought their magnificence worthy of their high rank. I must not omit mention here of our visit to the fathers of the Society, most dependable of hosts, but we did not stay with them, as we normally would have, as they had only recently been introduced to the city and were not yet comfortably accommodated.[6]

The two rulers, father and son, offered to us, as well as many other signs of their benevolence, most acceptable gifts of great value. The prince, firstly, gave us two complete suits of armour, of highly polished steel with gold ornamentation, and you yourselves have seen how strong, robust, and beautiful they are. He gave us in addition two ingeniously constructed muskets, which by means of a wheel could be aimed and could

---

[1] Santuario della Beate Vergine delle Grazie in Curtatone near Mantua, which also contains the tomb of Baldassare Castiglione, author of another, more famous dialogue, *Il libro del cortegiano* or *The Book of the Courtier* (1528). Only three of the boys appear to have participated in the excursion. See Frόis, *Première ambassade*, p. 239 n. 834.

[2] The Certosa of Santa Trinita.

[3] In the Bosco Fontana. In a letter to Rome written shortly after the boys left Mantua, the Jesuit, Lelio Passionei, noted that during this hunting trip Mancio displayed great fortitude while pursuing a wild boar (ARSI, Ital. 159, f. 85v; Yūki, 'Shinshiryō', p. 190).

[4] San Benedetto in Polirone, founded 1007, dissolved 1789, but still extant. A commemorative plaque to mark the visit was made in August 1586 by order of the abbot, 'Lactantius Genuensis'; it was lost at the dissolution (Berchet, 'Documenti', p. 175).

[5] Eleanor of Austria (1534–94), daughter of Emperor Ferdinand I.

[6] The Jesuit college, paid for by the Gonzaga, had been inaugurated in November 1584 (Grendler, *University of Mantua*, p. 32).

also be fired and shoot bullets; and also two swords which had guns attached to them;[1] and four clocks besides, of the kind which can be called pendant clocks, and as you have seen, they are made with wonderful skill, and remarkable in that they contain in such small dimensions everything proper to larger clocks; also a cannon, small in size but very well made, which the prince had forged with his own hands, such is his talent for works of this sort, and among them most especially for painting. That being the case he crowned all the above gifts with a most life-like portrait of himself, so well painted and so pleasing to us that every time we look at it we feel as if we were speaking to the prince. The duke also sent us other precious gifts, notably four double-edged swords, with hilts and scabbards of silver and adorned with gold, so that each of them was reckoned to be worth two hundred ducats. He sent in addition four precious containers for holy relics, each of them filled with relics of saints.[2] All of this will enable you to understand not just the wealth and affluence of these princes, but also the generosity, worthy of their high nobility, which they show to guests and foreigners.

Leo: We have had explained to us and see clearly their wealth and grandeur, in the great generosity which they showed to guests staying for such a short time, and about to sail away to such distant lands, never to be seen again.

Mancio: Indeed, Leo, it is as you say, but you must also appreciate that the princes of Europe are high-minded and noble, so that they dominate their riches and are not dominated by them.

Lino: And this is by no means the custom among the pagans; the richer they are, the more parsimonious and miserly they are in holding on to what they have acquired.

Michael: On the 18 July we left Mantua, with the prince himself and other nobles accompanying us most courteously to the gate of the city. We said our farewells to them and took the road for Milan, so as to go on from there to Genoa, where we would take ship for Spain. A large number of men were sent with us, and they came with us as far as a settlement known as Gazzuolo, which belonged to the jurisdiction of Mantua. There we were provided with hospitality as lavish and sumptuous as at Mantua. When we arrived there the illustrious Cardinal Sfondrati,[3] bishop of Cremona, sent five coaches, and as many messengers, to invite us to come via the city called Cremona where he was. The following day, therefore after thanking and taking our leave of the Mantuans, we set out

---

[1] This is a literal translation of the original edition (p. 329) '*gladios, quibus simul scloporum instrumenta adiuncta erant*', but Fróis (*Première ambassade*, p. 240) makes it clear that the arquebuses were skilfully embossed on the scabbards. The presents are also mentioned by Passionei (ARSI, Ital. 159, f. 85v; Yūki, 'Shinshiryō', p. 190).

[2] In return, the boys presented some of their Japanese clothes and a sword (Fróis, *Première ambassade*, p. 240). Passionei's list of the gifts differs slightly (ARSI, Ital. 159, f. 85v; Yūki, 'Shinshiryō', p. 190). Some of the gifts were added to those Valignano gave to Hideyoshi during his embassy to the *kampaku* in 1591 (ARSI, Jap. Sin 10: II, ff. 338v–339).

[3] Niccolò Sfondrati (1535–91), bishop of Cremona from 1560, cardinal from 1583. He was elected pope on 5 December 1590, taking the name Gregory XIV. The boys had met him in Rome where he had participated in the conclave that elected Sixtus V (Fróis, *Première ambassade*, p. 241).

with the men of Cremona and came to another villa named Suspirium,[1] where many from the family of the cardinal himself had prepared a magnificent reception for us. Further on, a full league before the entrance to the city, there came out to meet us first of all the cardinal's vicar, with many nobles and patricians, followed soon after by the chief magistrate of the city with a cohort of soldiers, and others on horseback and on foot with them, together with more than thirty carriages; and finally the illustrious cardinal himself. As we entered the city the citizens expressed their joy at our coming with repeated firing of cannon and beating of drums.

When we had come into the city the cardinal received us in his palace, and gave many indications of his wonderful benevolence towards us. He had known about us in Rome, for he was living in that city when we visited the pope, but besides that he is endowed with a holiness and piety such that he has the utmost love for Japan and things Japanese, being aware of their importance for the expansion of Christendom. He himself therefore said Mass twice with us present, once in his private chapel and once in the cathedral,[2] where we received from him the celestial nourishment of the Holy Eucharist. He said both Masses with such a profusion of tears as openly to manifest the reverence and piety with which he celebrated the memory of our salvation. Afterwards we accompanied him as he carried the most sacred body of Christ in a public and solemn procession. Among other signs of love he most kindly displayed to us, with his own hands, the sacred relics which are preserved both in his private chapel and in the cathedral; he gave each of us as a gift a golden cross containing particles of the sacred wood, and indeed did everything for us which benevolence or charity could possibly require. While we were staying in this city a certain nobleman came to us, sent by the illustrious duke of Terra Nova and governor of all the lands of Milan,[3] to conduct us in his name to Milan. When we set out the cardinal himself came with us to the gate of the city. The governor of Cremona,[4] who had just returned from Piacenza, accompanied us for two miles, and soldiers from the citadel gave us a festive send-off with trumpets and cannon of various kinds.

Having left Cremona, then, we proceeded to a town named Pizzighettone, where we were greeted by a squadron of cavalry and a cohort of infantry, and were led to the citadel with the usual demonstrations of love and joy, and there we were honoured and provided with generous hospitality by the knight who was accompanying us. From this town we journeyed to a city called Lodi, one of the principal cities belonging to the jurisdiction of Milan. The magistrate and the commandant of the fortress came out to meet us before the city with a great number of soldiers, and our arrival was given a marvellous welcome with firing of muskets and of the array of cannon in the fortress. Following them the governor of the city appeared, with many officials and nobles and a squadron of infantry, and thus we entered the city with the acclamation of a great concourse of people. Now since there

---

[1] Original edition (p. 330) gives '*castrum*', a fortified camp, which might have been the origin of the place. Villa seems a more appropriate translation.

[2] The cathedral was famous throughout Italy for its bell tower, the highest in Italy (Coryate, *Coryat's Crudities*, p. 113).

[3] Carlo d'Aragona Tagliavia (1530–99), duke of Terranova, governor of the duchy of Milan (i.e. representative of the duke of Milan, Philip II of Spain) 1583–92, viceroy of Sicily 1566–8 and 1571–7. He is referred to below, somewhat confusingly, as the duke, governor or ruler of Milan, but he was not duke of Milan which had ceased to be a duchy in 1535 upon the death of Francesco II Sforza.

[4] Rafael Manrique (Guzman, *Historia*, II, p. 283).

were instructions from the duke and the governor of Milan that we were to reach Milan on the feast day of St James,[1] we spent the next day in Lodi, and saw some of the things worth seeing in the city. We went to the cathedral,[2] where the priests, called canons, welcomed us with a procession, and the sacred host of the Eucharist was immolated with full solemnity and wonderful singing. We were shown also relics of saints and sacred vestments, all of them adorned with such a quantity of pearls and precious stones that nothing like them is to be found anywhere else in all Lombardy.[3]

After a sumptuous lunch the governor invited us to see a very pleasing display of acrobatics. There are performers who are extremely agile in their movements, whirling round spears, climbing ropes, diving through hoops like fish, and putting on other similar shows. In that spectacle we watched three women and a boy got up as a monster. At the sound of a lyre they all unsheathed their swords, performed a remarkable dance, and fought a simulated battle among themselves, producing such a noise that you would think there was a large number of soldiers there. Afterwards, to great admiration, they demonstrated various leaps, springing up and down, and performing turns and other similar movements. Lastly a fight was put on by these same performers, with puppets appearing on the stage and representing cavalry and infantry, all done so cleverly and so convincingly, with muskets and cannon also effectively used, that it almost seemed to be a real battle.

The following day, the feast of St James, we went on to Milan. We were met nine miles before the city by a large number of Milanese knights, and invited to a splendid banquet in a town called Melegnano. Two miles outside the city, the vicar of the illustrious archbishop of Milan[4] met us, and welcomed us most courteously. Further on again we were met by a man of the highest nobility, a relative of the duke,[5] at the head of a hundred horsemen, some spearmen or musketeers, others lightly armed, the former in black velvet adorned with gold, with splendid helmets, the latter in purple velvet embroidered with gold at the hems. There were also four excellently equipped horses, offered to us in the name of the duke for our entry into the city. And when we advanced on the horses the multitude of people and nobles was so great that we could see that the city was indeed the most populous in the whole of Italy. When we reached the gate on the outskirts of the city the illustrious duke, the ruler of Milan, came to meet us with his two sons[6] and the noble marquess of Avali,[7] nephew of the duke, and with him were the other magistrates and senators and five hundred gentlemen. These went before us, and we, after greetings from both sides, were each positioned at the right of one of the most important figures. Mancio was on the right of the duke himself, with all his guards and attendants; my companion was the visitor of King Philip, Martin's the head chancellor, and Julian's the chairman of

---

[1] 25 July.

[2] Built between 1158 and 1284 in the Romanesque style.

[3] The original edition (p. 331) gives '*Insubrium*'. *Insubria* is synonymous with the duchy of Milan.

[4] Gaspare Visconti, appointed archbishop of Milan on 28 November 1584. The duke had withdrawn to Vigevano following a dispute about protocol concerning the new archbishop's solemn entry into Milan on the day before the boys' arrival. See Guzman, *Historia*, II, p. 284; Boncompagni-Ludovisi, *Le prime due ambasciate*, p. 28.

[5] Don Blasco de Aragón (Guzman, *Historia*, II, p. 284).

[6] One of whom, Simeone, took holy orders and became a cardinal in 1583.

[7] Or Avalos.

the senate. Thus we were all occupied a position to the right of those four, the most important men in the city, and had around us an almost infinite number of soldiers, so that it was an entry of extraordinary pomp, added to which was the innumerable multitude of people and the famous display of shops in the streets. The merchants had been instructed to lay out the precious clothing that they had for sale, and the quantity of silk, of velvet, and of gold embroidery, also of drapery, curtains, tapestries, that our first sight of the city left us in no doubt about the splendour and wealth of Milan. There were besides spectators, men and women, in such numbers that there were many windows rented just for this spectacle, with people paying five or six ducats for them.

After two miles in this incredible multitude of people we reached the college of the Society. There, after prayers to God in the church and when we had taken our leave of the duke and the others who were with him, we were welcomed into the college by the fathers of the Society with that same generosity which we had experienced in other places. But we shall need more time to give some account of this most noble city, so if you agree I suggest we leave this subject for tomorrow.

Leo: We do agree, but we would like, today and every day, to express and put on record our gratitude to the people of Europe for the warmth with which they treated you.

COLLOQUIUM XXX

More about things noted in Milan and in Pavia, and about their entry into the city of Genoa and the voyage to Spain

Michael: I do not doubt, dear cousins, that you are gripped with a burning zeal to learn all about Milan, and to satisfy your zeal I would have you know that in Italy there is to be found a large number of populous and wealthy cities, but that among these there are four more famous than all the others, namely Rome, Naples, and Venice, which we have already dealt with, and Milan, which we are speaking about now.[1] These cities are so populous that each of them contains more than thirty thousand inhabitants, and the churches and other public buildings are so many that together with the palaces of the rulers they make these cities extremely wealthy, as is clear from previous colloquia. Among these four Rome is indeed the largest in area, but in the number of its citizens and the multitude of its people Milan is not inferior,[2] and this shows you plainly the nobility and the wealth of this city. It is also the capital of the whole of the jurisdiction which belongs to the duke of Milan, who at the present time is Philip, the most powerful king of Spain, for his father, the Emperor Charles V, took possession of it when it was bequeathed to him with right of heredity by the last duke of Milan, as has already been said.

    This city is outstanding both for its fortifications and for its pleasantness. With regard to this pleasantness, it is sited in the part of Italy which used to be called Cisalpine Gaul but is now known as Lombardy, and is without doubt the most agreeable of all the provinces of Italy. A delightful river flows through this town and makes the land beautiful with the green covering of its banks and tall trees providing excellent shade. The city is guarded with two sets of walls, the one larger and more recent, with a very wide moat; the other older, again with a moat, and both of them very strong. This city was formerly surrounded by a wall, but then its suburbs expanded greatly, and it was necessary to surround this with another wall, which made the city very large. In addition to these two walls it has a fortress, the most heavily fortified fortress that there is in all Italy.[3] It is joined to the city, but nevertheless has its own prefect and its own administration, and is surrounded by a moat and massive defences. This city is notable also for the width of the streets, the beauty of the houses, and the splendour of its buildings, and all these things make it beautiful, agreeable, and very

---

[1] The boys stayed in Milan from 25 July until 3 September.
[2] The population of Milan was 150,000 in 1500, 69,000 in 1550 and 120,000 in 1600 (Vries, *European Urbanization*, p. 275).
[3] The Castello Sforzesco. Coryate described the citadel as 'the fairest without any comparison that euer I saw, farre surpassing any one Citadell whatsoeuer in Europe' (see *Coryat's Crudities*, pp. 102–5, esp. p. 102). The new fortifications, sometimes called the Spanish bastions but now mostly destroyed, were built during the 1550s.

secure. And the fact that it has seventeen abundant lakes and sixty-four rivers contributes to the attractiveness not only of the city but of the whole district of Milan.

Moreover, this city not only has an abundance of merchants but a large number of craftsmen flourish as well about which point there is a well-known proverb which says that whoever wants to adorn Italy only needs to destroy Milan, that is because Milan is so full of every ornament and artwork that the other cities, if they took their share of her possessions, would have an abundance. In this city they make every kind of velvet, of silk, of gold embroidery, of silver leaf, and ingenious work of every other sort. There too are fashioned, from gold, silver, bronze, and marble, vases, statues, mosaics, images, and all similar things, notable for their value and their beauty. In the time that we were there in Milan we saw twenty-eight bronze statues, of the twelve apostles, the four sacred evangelists, four doctors, and several other saints, which had been made most skilfully, by order of King Philip, to be transported to the monastery of the Escorial, and each of these was said to have cost six thousand ducats. Finally, in that same city, weapons both offensive and defensive are forged with wonderful workmanship, among them those presented to us by the duke of Mantua, which you saw some days ago. Thus everything which art and skill can produce is found in abundance in this city.

Among the most noble buildings the cathedral holds first place,[1] built as it is at such expense and with such artistry that whether you consider its size, or look at it as a work of art, or think of the cost of the materials and ornamentation, there are few indeed in all Europe, with the exception of St Peter's in Rome, to compare with it. The surface of the walls both inside and out is made of the purest marble, and the whole church has such an abundance of statues of marble of Paros as to give it the greatest possible splendour and beauty. The wall of the high altar, besides, is so ornate, and the sacred reliquary such a work of art, with many pearls and precious stones together with the gold, that in costliness and beauty it is easily the equal of the others of which we have already spoken. Also in the city is a magnificent monastery of the Dominican order,[2] where among other things we judged the library to be one of the finest in all Italy. The Society of Jesus has two residences in the city, one a college, in which we were provided with most welcome hospitality, in company with the fathers and brothers, of whom there were eighty.[3] The other residence is the professed house, and although it is new, with construction not yet complete, it has already cost sixty thousand ducats. We stayed eight days in that city, a short time indeed considering the number of things to be seen there, but we could not stay longer, for a message had arrived from Genoa telling us that the ships were ready for us to embark and set out on the voyage for Spain.

In all that time we received most courteous and kind treatment from the illustrious duke, his sons and his nephew, and from his excellency the archbishop and other bishops

---

[1] Construction began on 23 May 1385 and, with restorations and remodelling, continued until the late 20th century. At the time of the boys' visit, the architectural tastes and dictates of Cardinal Carlo Borromeo, a zealous champion of the Counter-Reformation, were much in evidence. These included the huge tabernacle above the main altar, whose overwhelming emphasis on the Eucharist represented a defiant refutation of the Protestant denial of transubstantiation. Coryate was also impressed by the cathedral (*Coryat's Crudities*, pp. 98–100).

[2] The church and Dominican convent of Santa Maria delle Grazie. The convent was completed around 1469, the church later. Leonardo da Vinci's *Last Supper*, which escaped the Allied bombing in August 1943, is in the refectory.

[3] According to Nuno Rodrigues, a number of them were keen to serve in India (*Documenta Indica*, XIV, pp. 46–7).

and lords; for the bishops of Novara[1] and Tortona[2] were there, and the ambassadors of the duke of Bavaria and of the Venetian Republic, as well as the prefect of the fortress of Milan, and between them and us, as guests, no opportunity was lost for respectful greetings and meetings, all such obligations being more than fulfilled. The archbishop himself was not satisfied merely with greetings, but on the Sunday invited us to the first solemn Mass which he was about to celebrate in that diocese, and when we were there he fed us with his own hands with the most holy Body of Christ. Afterwards he conducted us to his house and there lunched with us in most friendly fashion. The duke himself was not less benevolent. All the time we were there he had food prepared for us at his expense, and he invited us most courteously to a sumptuous banquet at his house, setting Mancio at his right hand and all of us in places of honour. After lunch he had a delightful play performed for us within his own palace, and we enjoyed it very much, both the plot and the performance of the actors. In addition to this he frequently sent his sons and nephew to us in the morning and the evening, with a coach and Swiss guards, so that we could visit all the famous places in the city in their company; and he also gave each of us as a gift a sword and a dagger with gilded hilts, and with many other proofs, enough and more than enough, made his love for us visible and evident.

We also saw the very heavily fortified fortress of the city, being invited there by the commandant of the fortress, a nobleman named Sancho.[3] He came down to welcome us in the courtyard, accompanied by all the Swiss guard, and the walls were manned by five hundred soldiers, who celebrated our arrival with the sound, both deeply solemn and most joyful, of the firing of their individual muskets and of the cannon, more than five hundred guns, thus demonstrating very clearly just how secure the place was. Mass was solemnly celebrated, with us present, in the main chapel, by a priest with two ministers, namely deacon and subdeacon, and with very fine singing. When we came out afterwards there was a show of fireworks, especially of some spheres, each of which revolved a hundred times or more, over the space of a quarter of an hour, emitting a noise like a cannon. We went in after this to a most sumptuous and splendid banquet, and as soon as we were seated a soldier brought the keys of the whole fortress to the commandant, and he ordered them to be offered to Mancio, indicating by this courteous gesture that Mancio outranked him and had command of the fortress.

After lunch we were conducted by the commandant to see some of the most heavily armed places in the fortress, and we were deeply impressed by them, especially by the forty bigger cannon, many of them massive in size; also by the way they are made, for they are forged most excellently there in the citadel, and by many other kinds of defences, which are there in abundance in the fortress. And the guards are there prepared, whatever the time or place, as if faced now with imminent danger. The European kings and princes do not in any way allow their men to be inactive or grow soft, but rather keep them trained and practised in military discipline, not permitting anything to interfere with the order and organization of their way of life. We ourselves were witnesses of this, for in that place we saw a soldier, who had fired his musket sooner than he should have, ordered to be seized. At the intercession of our Mancio, however, he was released without punishment.

---

[1] Cesare Speciano (1539–1607), bishop of Novara 1584–91.
[2] Cesare Gambara, bishop of Tortona 1548–91.
[3] The governor was Don Sancho de Padilla y Guevara (Guzman, *Historia*, II, p. 285).

After that, and after visits to the house of the professed and to the seminary, in both of which a splendid banquet was provided for us, we set off from Milan on 3 August, accompanied as far as the suburbs by the sons and nephew of the duke and many other nobles. That same day we arrived about midday at the Carthusian monastery which is near Ticinum or Pavia, and is numbered among the greatest and most celebrated in all Italy.[1] It is said that the income of this monastery is reckoned to be thirty thousand ducats, and certainly the buildings are very spacious indeed, with an abundance of courtyards, gardens, and other agreeable places. Those religious men follow a particular and very severe holy rule of cloister and enclosure, so within the monastery itself they have to have a full supply of the many different things necessary for their way of life. They have a most magnificent church. The internal walls are covered with marble, and the surface of the external walls is of red tiles which produce a very beautiful effect. The vestibule too is quite remarkable, rising to a tremendous height of many many spans even before it reaches the roof. And the material of which it is made is no less striking, for it is of solid marble, with many statues of saints, each in its own niche, the skill of the artists matching the beauty of the work. An adornment of the church is the sacred tabernacle, in which the Holy Eucharist is kept, which is of inlaid work, but is also greatly embellished with gold and pearls. The whole sanctuary is of more or less the same work, and it is also adorned with the magnificent tomb of Gian Galeazzo, first duke of Milan,[2] the tomb being of marble, with a multitude of statues round it, so that the whole arrangement of the structure is by no means inferior to the tombs of kings. I say nothing of the sacred vestments of the same monastery, nor of the relics of the saints, mounted in gold and silver, which add such lustre to the monastery as fully to justify its claim to fame.

The fathers of this monastery provided us with splendid hospitality, and on the following day we headed for Pavia, another city famous in Italy. We were greeted on our arrival by the bishop, a man of great authority, who shortly afterwards was elevated to the rank of cardinal.[3] Also present was the judge of the city, a man outstanding not only for his authority as magistrate but also for the nobility of his breeding, he being the brother of the archbishop of Milan.[4] Following these came fifteen carriages, many gentlemen and nobles, and a column of light-armed cavalry, as well as a great multitude of the people. Our entry into the town was celebrated with the usual sounding of muskets and cannon, and after solemn High Mass in the church we were taken by the eminent bishop to his own magnificent house, and there were treated with every sign of hospitality and benevolence. But the following day, since the messenger from Genoa was unwilling to allow any delay, we travelled on (the bishop came with us for a full league) to a town called Voghera, and there the nobleman who had accompanied us in the name of the duke of Milan as we traversed the lands of his jurisdiction, took his leave of us with all benevolence. Another

---

[1] The Certosa di Pavia, about 8 km from Pavia, built between 1396 and 1555. Ticinum was the Roman name for Pavia.

[2] Gian Galeazzo Visconti (1351–1402). His impressive tomb is the work of Gian (or Giovanni) Cristoforo Romano, Benedetto Briosco and others.

[3] Ippolito de Rossi (1532–91), related to the Gonzaga through his mother. He was bishop coadjutor of Pavia, 1560, bishop, 1564, and cardinal from 18 December 1585.

[4] One of the Visconti family, who had ruled Pavia from the mid-14th century until 1447. The city was under Spanish rule when the boys visited.

took his place,[1] receiving us in the names of two most illustrious ladies, mother and daughter, who lived in Tortona, the former the wife of the duke of Lorraine and the latter of the duke of Brunswick;[2] and as we entered the city we were greeted with the same rejoicing and acclamation as in other cities.

On the following day we reached the territory of the jurisdiction of Genoa, where we found two messengers and noblemen of the Republic waiting to conduct us to Genoa, and after we had passed through certain towns, namely Gavi and Otagio, amid general rejoicing, on 5 August[3] we arrived at the city of Genoa, which is numbered among the noblest cities in Italy, and is distinguished by being a free and exempt republic, like Venice. Before we entered the city we were delighted to be able to view the prospect of the whole of Genoa, known for its many villas, great buildings, and most agreeable gardens. Four senators came to meet us, accompanied by many nobles and patricians. They greeted us, we mounted the four ornately caparisoned horses which they offered to us, and when we had proceeded further, we encountered four more senators, very dignified in their rich robes, many other magistrates besides, and an infinite multitude of the people. We were then taken to the residence of the fathers of the Society, where a room all decorated with embroidered curtains and tapestries was prepared for us.[4]

This city is, as I have said, one of the noblest and richest of all Italy, and in it is this most prosperous republic, with extensive jurisdiction including many cities and towns in the whole region of Liguria, as well as the famous island of Corsica. Thus although it is not quite as large as the Venetian Republic it comes close to matching it, and because of the many victories it has won in the past at sea and on land in various places it has always been held in high regard for its military prowess. It is also very powerful in wealth and abundance of all things, for its citizens are very rich, and they patrol the coastal areas with many ships, galleys, and other vessels, not only guarding the Ligurian coast from enemy incursion and thus bringing great glory to their name, but also greatly enriching their Republic by conveying many kinds of merchandise to other places or bringing them into the city.[5] The buildings too, splendid in the variety of their paintings, the architecture, and

---

[1] Fróis (*Première ambassade*, p. 249) and Cooper (*Japanese Mission*, p. 128) identify this individual as Gianandrea Doria, grand-nephew, and successor as commander of the Mediterranean fleet, of Andrea Doria (1466–1560). But, as is mentioned below, he was absent from Genoa at the time. The individual could be Stefano Doria who is mentioned in the minutes of the senate's preparations for the visit (Berchet, 'Documenti', p. 178).

[2] Christina of Denmark, duchess of Lorraine (1522–90), younger daughter of Christian II of Denmark, married by proxy in 1533 to Francesco II Sforza, duke of Milan, who died two years later. In 1541 she married François, the future duke of Lorraine who died in 1545. A portrait (1538), by Holbein, among the series of possible brides commissioned by Henry VIII, is in the National Gallery, London. Another, by Michiel Coxcie, in 1545, just after her second husband's death, is in the Allen Memorial Art Museum, Oberlin College, Ohio. Christina's youngest daughter, Dorothea of Lorraine (1545–1621), married Erich II, duke of Brunswick, who died in Pavia in 1584. By the time of the boys' visit, Christina had retired to Tortona.

[3] Fróis, *Première ambassade*, p. 249, gives 6 August.

[4] On how Nuno Rodrigues organized this reception, see *Documenta Indica*, XIV, p. 44.

[5] By this time Genoa was a satellite of Spain. The politics, economic and foreign policy of the Genoese oligarchs were in lockstep with those of Philip II. Around 80 per cent of the republic's foreign trade was conducted with Spanish possessions and about 40 per cent of the Genoese aristocracy's wealth was tied up in loans to Spain. The Spanish monarch was guarantor of the aristocracy's hold on power as manifested during the Corsican insurrection (1559–69) and the internal unrest that rocked the republic in 1574–6 during which there were fears a French intervention might reignite the Italian wars. See Parker, *Grand Strategy*, p. 82; Levin, *Agents of Empire*, pp. 108–11, 176–7.

the height of the houses, and the enormous sums of money devoted to them, are a fine sight. If the city of Venice is known for its wealth, then, Genoa is known for its magnificence. But with the galleys already prepared for the voyage to Spain we could only spend one day in that city, and the citizens were unable in such a short time to give the expression that they would have wished to their love for us.

Nevertheless, in the narrow confines of the one day which we spent, with the greatest pleasure, in Genoa, every possible courtesy was extended to us. Many of the leading men of the city and important senators came to see us. Some of these were assigned by the senate to accompany us and to take us to see the sights of the city, and when we were viewing these it seemed to us that we were seeing another Venice.[1] We saw many holy things, among them the imprint of the sacred face of Christ our Saviour left on a linen cloth;[2] also that most famous dish, made of emerald, with which Christ our Redeemer, when about to suffer death for our sake, is said to have celebrated the paschal meal with his disciples.[3] Because of that use to which it was put, and because of the size of the jewel, it is not possible to put a price on it, and among all the other gems in the whole world it justly claims pride of place. In that city we paid a visit to the duke of the whole republic,[4] and we expressed our profound thanks to him for the honour with which we had been treated throughout the territories within the jurisdiction of Genoa. He was in a most magnificent palace,[5] which can easily stand comparison with other outstanding palace buildings which we have mentioned. There were two hundred German soldiers on guard, and these raised our spirits as we arrived with the sound of instruments both of music and of war. The duke came out to the middle of the hall to receive us, with a crowd of nobles round him, and he came down as far as the staircase to see us off, the other magistrates and senators continuing as far as the courtyard.

Finally, to complete briefly my account of what happened on that one day, a present arrived for us from the senate of Genoa; no small present, for it contained abundant food of all kinds ideal for the voyage we were undertaking, adequate and more than adequate not only for us but for many others.[6] As we were just about to leave the leading men of the city called on us, among them the ambassador of King Philip, and the most noble Giannettino Spinola,[7] nephew of the illustrious prince Andrea Doria,[8] supreme admiral and, in the name of King Philip, commandant of the whole Mediterranean Sea. The prince was away at that time, and in his absence his nephew was in charge of twenty galleys which he was taking to Spain, and ordered that one of the principal galleys be prepared for us, to convey us to Spain. On that day,[9] therefore, we embarked on the ship, not without a very great nostalgia for Italy, for in that province we had been loaded with

---

[1] The senate had made preparations and budgeted in advance for the visit (Berchet, 'Documenti', pp. 177–9).

[2] The veil, a gift of the Byzantine emperor John V Palaeologus, and one of a number claiming to be the original, is in the church of San Bartolomeo degli Armeni.

[3] The *sacro catino* in the cathedral of San Lorenzo.

[4] Gerolamo Chiavari (r. 1583–5).

[5] This burnt down in 1777 and was replaced by the present neoclassical edifice.

[6] The senate reimbursed the Jesuit house for 470 *livres* for expenses incurred (Berchet, 'Documenti', p. 179).

[7] 1562–88.

[8] Gianandrea Doria (1539–1606) whose conduct at Lepanto was much criticized (Guilmartin, *Gunpowder & Galleys*, pp. 139, 261–2).

[9] 8 August.

honours by so many princes sacred and secular; and we left no less nostalgia for us in the souls of all those, so many, whether nobles, common people, and indeed cities, who had, as it were, been plucked from their seats to welcome us.

Leo: It is only right that you should make mention of that nostalgia. It strikes even us, as we listen to your account of your progress, as very remarkable, and it seems to us that even if you had been born of a most noble family in that province, and had been returning there after a long absence, you could not have been received with greater joy and acclamation.

Mancio: In fact if any criticism were to be brought against Michael's telling of the story, it would have to be that he has been too brief and concise, and not that he has been prolix or too copious, in speaking of the benevolence and benignity which we encountered in that province.

Martin: So great was the love shown to us by all that they looked on us as if we had fallen from heaven, and never tired of gazing at us, in many and various ways praying for a happy outcome to our journey, and even considering themselves blessed if they merely managed to touch our bodies.

Julian: And how moved they were to piety when they saw us expiating our faults in confession, approaching the sacred table of the Eucharist, and visiting religious places!

Lino: I feel that we ourselves as well as you are tied, as if by the closest of bonds, to the people of Europe by those many kindnesses shown to you.

Michael: In addition to all the things which I have already mentioned there are the songs, epigrams, speeches, and indeed complete books composed about our journey.[1] Every single university has published many notable records, inscriptions, and other similar documents about our journey, and has left them for posterity. But since I have come almost to the end of what I have to say about the things of Europe, and since I have already dealt at length with the things of Spain, I shall be brief in describing what we encountered on our return journey, as it was similar to what has already been described. To take up my story again, then, we left Genoa on 8 August,[2] and eight days later, on 16 August, we reached the port of Barcelona.

Barcelona is a famous city of Hispania Tarraconensis, and now it belongs to and indeed is the principal city of Catalonia or, as others call it, Gothalonia.[3] There we had the usual joyous reception from both the citizens and the fathers of the Society. But Julian was ill again, for the fourth time, so we stayed there for twenty-five days so that he could be properly looked after, and we spent the greater part of those days very agreeably at a villa,

---

[1] The most comprehensive list and description of these publications is Boscaro, *Sixteenth Century Printed Works*.

[2] They embarked on 8 August, amidst much festivity, and set sail on the 9th (Fróis, *Première ambassade*, p. 251).

[3] Land of the Goths.

restoring our bodily health and strength.[1] We did go to the city frequently, however, during that time, exchanging courtesy greetings with the nobility and making our customary visits to the sacred places. We entered the cathedral[2] with a procession, and there we venerated the holy body of St Olegario, bishop of the same city.[3] It is six hundred years since he exchanged this mortal life for life in heaven, yet his flesh appears as whole and fresh as if the spirit had left its structure only yesterday. We also saw the reliquary where the relics of saints are kept, adorned with the precious bones of the saints within, and glittering jewels without.

We left this city on 9 September for the town of Monzón in Aragon, where at that time King Philip was holding court with royal assemblies which he had summoned for the arranging of various affairs in Aragon, Catalonia, and Valencia, and so that his son might be proclaimed heir to his kingdoms, and might be offered the allegiance of the people, the same thing that had already happened earlier on in the kingdom of Castile, as we told you.[4] After leaving Barcelona, but before coming to this town, we visited the very famous church of the Blessed Virgin called Montserrat.[5] The reason for the spread of the fame of its name is the many and frequent miracles performed there by the divine power through the prayers of the Blessed Virgin. Innumerable mementos of these miracles can be seen there in the church: chains, for example, from which men have been released; the skins of serpents whose bite though lethal did not bring about death; the winding-sheets of dead persons recalled to life; and finally many wax models of various parts of the human body healed of many diseases by supernatural help. I mentioned a similar pattern to all these things when I spoke to you of the Virgin of Loreto, but I would be glad to give you an account of some of those divine deeds, but for the fact that a book has recently been written in Spanish about all of them by fathers of that same monastery, and we brought back a copy of it with us.[6]

---

[1] From Barcelona, Mancio Itō sent letters to the dukes of Ferrara and Mantua. He had written to them previously thanking them for their kindness and informing them of their journey. Not all the letters are extant, although a reply from the duke of Ferrara is. See *Dai Nihon Shiryō*, XI: 2, pp. 110–12,145, 213–15.

[2] Catedral de la Santa Cruz y Santa Eulalia.

[3] Olegario (Olegarius) Bonestruga (1060–1137), bishop of Barcelona and archbishop of Tarragona. He was canonized in 1675. His sepulchre is in the side chapel of Christ of Lepanto. The original edition (p. 341) refers to him as '*Diui Olegii*'.

[4] Philip had gone to Barcelona to see off his daughter, Catalina, who was betrothed to Duke Charles Emmanuel of Savoy. He used the occasion to summon the *cortes* of Aragon to take the oath of allegiance to his son and successor, the seven-year-old Philip. During his five-month stay at Monzón, the three *cortes* of Aragon, Catalonia and Valencia met there to address matters of legislation and supply (*Cambridge Modern History*, vol. III, p. 513).

[5] The Benedictine monastery of Santa María de Montserrat which houses the Black Madonna. After recovering from the wounds he received at Pamplona in his native town, Ignatius Loyola left for Montserrat, en route for the Holy Land. According to his autobiography, Loyola arrived at the monastery after a dispute with a Moor who had decried the Virgin birth. At a fork in the road, he decided to let his mule decide whether to proceed to Montserrat or to retrace his steps so that he could fight the Moor. The mule chose the Montserrat road. At the monastery, under the supervision of the master of novices, Loyola made a detailed list of his sins, confessed, set aside his military garb and weaponry and adopted beggar's clothes and a pilgrim's staff, symbolically casting off his earlier life. See Munitiz and Endean, *Saint Ignatius of Loyola*, pp. 18–21; Olin, *Autobiography of St Ignatius of Loyola*, pp. 31–2; O'Malley, *Early Jesuits*, p. 24. The monastery was destroyed during the Peninsular War and subsequently rebuilt.

[6] The title of this book is unknown. Guzman says the book was about the foundation of the monastery and the miracles associated with it (*Historia*, II, p. 289). A compilation of Marian miracles produced in Japan around 1591 includes Montserrat. The compilation drew upon European sources which were translated into Japanese. The book, brought back by the boys, was among those used for the compilation. See Schütte, 'Christliche Japanische Literatur', pp. 244–51.

I shall, however, say something about the site of the place, which is famous more for its natural structure than for human artifice. For nature, that remarkable craftsman, formed a certain mountain which presents to the viewer so many peaks, so many crags, so many precipitous places, that it is not only the eye that is greatly taken with it; the spirit is also easily drawn to the contemplation of the excellence of God the supreme craftsman. There are besides deep woods, shadowy glades, and secluded places ideal for the solitary life. And very religious inhabitants for those places are not lacking, men who after many years of pursuing a holy and religious life in the monastery ask permission of their abbot to seclude themselves in various chapels constructed in that mountain, as the best possible places for peace and contemplation. And we saw some of these men, followers, devotees, and imitators of the anchorites of old. But the book I mentioned deals at length with those chapels, so there is no need for me to say more about them here. In that same place there is a monastery of the order of St Benedict, very rich in its many sacred vestments, the great number of gold and silver vessels it possesses, the many cases of holy relics, and all its other ornaments. A sufficient indication of all this for you could be the fifty silver lamps, presented by various kings and princes, which burn constantly in that church before the Holy Eucharist and the Blessed Virgin. We stayed just one day at that monastery, viewing various buildings, and treating with those religious men in an atmosphere of the utmost kindness and benevolence.

From there we went on to Monzón, where King Philip bestowed on us now on our return the same friendship and favour with which he had treated us on our outward journey, and the prince his son and his daughter did likewise.[1] You can imagine all this from what has been said in earlier colloquia, so I shall not spend many more words on it here. I'll say only that King Philip, in his extraordinary generosity towards us, sent letters to the illustrious Cardinal Albert of Portugal and to the viceroy of India, charging them with full responsibility for looking after us, and as a result of his instructions in these letters we were provided in abundance with everything which could make our voyage more comfortable, as befitted the king's liberality. With the permission of the most powerful king, therefore, we began to make our way to Portugal, but on the way would be passing through various cities and notable towns in Castile.

Pride of place among these goes to Zaragoza, capital of the whole of Aragon, and one of the most flourishing cities of all Spain in the size of its buildings, the abundance of sacred things, and the numbers of its people and nobles. It has a large college of the Society. The fathers there gave ample proof of their accustomed kindness towards us, and their pupils staged a most pleasing dialogue, in which Italy, Spain, and Japan were introduced in such a way as to give honourable mention to our embassy. The citizens and the nobles of the city showed us no less benevolence, and did all they could, with a variety of entertainments, to provide recreation and refreshment for our spirits. I do intend to be brief in my account of our return journey, but I cannot omit mention of

---

[1] Both Nuno Rodrigues and Mancio reported the same to Aquaviva. See ARSI, Ital. 159, ff. 106, 108, 110r–v; Yūki, 'Shinshiryō', pp. 232–3, 235–7. The audience with Philip II was the second major occasion in which the boys were used as 'living letters' to lobby for a major policy, in this instance for the monarch to appoint a bishop for Japan. As evidence of how far Christianity had progressed in Japan, they emphasized that a bishop was needed to administer the sacrament of confirmation. See RAHM, Jesuítas 7236, f. 317v; Guzman, *Historia*, II, p. 296.

certain very remarkable holy things which there are in that city. There is the church,[1] full of sanctity and religion, which St James one of the apostles of Christ, first built for the Blessed Virgin Mary herself while she was still living, and dedicated to her. And he did this not without a divine oracle, for the Blessed Virgin herself appeared to him, accompanied by a heavenly host and standing on a pillar constructed by the power of the angels, and advised him about the place where the church was to be built. The pillar is therefore conserved even today in the main chapel as a memorial of an extraordinary miracle, and all who see it and reverently kiss it are moved to piety, so much so that both pilgrims and the citizens come in great numbers and almost continuously to visit it.

Also in the city is another image of the Blessed Virgin which the citizens venerate most piously, for on one occasion, when the guards were asleep, the Saracens made an assault on the city, and they were almost within the gates when the Blessed Virgin (who keeps that city under her special protection and patronage), accompanied by an innumerable army of the heavenly citizens, confronted the Saracen forces as they rushed into the city, and held back their onslaught with the power of heaven. As a sign of this amazing deed she left an image of herself on the very wall where a famous church is built, and the memory is reverently celebrated every year. This city also has a monastery of St Jerome, which boasts the holy body of St Engracia, a most noble Portuguese lady. She was given in marriage by her father, who was formerly a prince in Portugal, to a certain French nobleman, and on her way to France, accompanied by nineteen men of noble birth, she went in reverence to that sacred pillar of the Blessed Virgin which I have just spoken about. There she and her companions were killed by evil enemies of Christianity, with them she attained the palm of martyrdom, and the relics of all of them are held in this splendid monastery, encased in gold and silver.[2] There too can be seen the holy relics of St Lambert, martyr, who in time past was a shepherd who professed the Christian faith, and was killed by its enemies in such a way that he gave wonderful signs of his sanctity. For when he fixed his cattle prod in the ground leaves grew from the end of it as from a tree coming into leaf in the spring. Furthermore, when he had been cut down he took his severed head in his hands as if he was still alive (so wondrous is the divine power!) and went straight to the place where it was customary for Christians to be killed for the profession of their faith. He spoke with those who were buried there. He conferred with them, invited them to praise God, and began to recite the verse of Psalm 149: 'The saints shall rejoice in glory'.[3] The other saints replied to him finishing the same verse and saying: 'They shall be joyful in their beds'. Finally that venerable corpse fell on the ground, thus indicating his wish to join the others.

---

[1] The basilica of Nuestra Señora del Pilar. The present church was begun in 1681 and completed in 1685. At the time of the boys' visit, the church was a 15th-century gothic one, only parts of which remain. Mary is said to have appeared to James on 2 January 40 CE. For some additional details about the boys' stay in Zaragoza, see Guzman, *Historia*, II, pp. 289–90.

[2] The Hieronymite monastery of Santa Engracia was destroyed in the War of Independence. The crypt containing the relics of the saint and those of the other 4th-century martyrs survived and was incorporated into the present church of Santa Engracia. St Lambert's feast day is 16 April.

[3] Psalm 149 verse 5: 'The saints shall rejoice in glory: they shall be joyful in their beds' (Douay-Rheims version).

This same city is also renowned for an outstandingly excellent hospital.[1] You can appreciate something of the scale, the arrangements for care of the sick, the ample income, and the other things in which institutions of this kind excel, from my description earlier on of the hospital in Lisbon, and this one with which I am now dealing seems to be held in equally high regard.

We departed from this city, therefore, which had given us ample evidence of its benevolence towards us, and pressed on to a city of the same province named Daroca, known for a very famous miracle, the miracle of the holy cloth and the most holy Eucharist. For five hundred years ago there was an attack by many thousands of Saracens on a small number of Christians, who decided to call on divine rather than human assistance. Six of them in particular made a point of having a priest say Mass for them and intended to fortify themselves with the bread of heaven. The priest had prepared six smaller hosts, as well as the normal host for the sacrifice. These had now been consecrated, and he was ready to feed the six men with the divine nourishment. They were interrupted by the enemy, the Christians reached for their arms, the priest hurriedly hid the cloth with the sacred hosts under a stone. In response to the piety of the Christians God gave them courage, and for the most part they were victorious. They returned to the sacred table, but when the priest unfolded the cloth the heavenly bread was seen to be stained with drops of blood and adhering to the cloth. The Christians marvelled at the strangeness of this, and were much moved to religious devotion. But when the enemy replenished their forces and battle recommenced, the priest opened out the sacred cloth and set it up as a fearsome standard facing the enemy. At this the Christians, greatly heartened, once again wrought havoc among their foes. Not only was there thus a double victory, due to the divine power, but in addition to that, when some uncertainty arose as to where that holy cloth should be kept, in order to avoid any disagreement it was put in a box and set on a mule, to be carried wherever God Himself might lead. By the Divine Will it was carried to Daroca, the native place of the priest, and as soon as the animal, carrying its sacred burden, arrived there, it knelt down and breathed its last. The citizens were deeply impressed with all these miracles and have preserved with the utmost veneration this holy cloth, still now marked with the drops of the Most Precious Blood.[2]

After we had seen and venerated it we proceeded to Alcalá, where, as I said earlier, our previous journey had taken us, and now, on our return journey, we were welcomed with no less joy. We were met on our arrival by some very important men, among them Ascanio Colonna,[3] an Italian nobleman, who later was raised to the rank of cardinal, and the son of the duke, admiral of the Spanish seas. There was also the joy of the fathers of the Society, who kept us in that town for four days, with the proofs of their benevolence and hospitality as it were forming most secure bonds of love. We spent those four days very happily. We had an invitation from Ascanio Colonna to a banquet, in which we participated with him in the Roman fashion, and at which there was also a very pleasing dramatic performance staged for us. And besides, he gave us as a gift a musical instrument

---

[1] The Torreón de la Zuda.

[2] The miracle is said to have taken place over two days, 23 and 24 February 1239, and the mule wandered for twelve days after that before collapsing and dying in Daroca. The Eucharist is housed in the church of Santa María Colegiata.

[3] 1560–1608, son of Marcoantonio Colonna, duke of Paliano, who fought at Lepanto. Cardinal from 1586. Viceroy of Aragon 1602–4.

called a clavicimbalum, skilfully constructed of cedarwood, which we have kept as the greatest pledge of his love for us, and we often remember him.[1]

From there we progressed to Madrid, and there we visited the august wife of the emperor,[2] and were received by her with the same benevolence. Afterwards, taking our leave of her, and of the cardinal archbishop of Toledo,[3] who embraced us with paternal love, and of the fathers of the Society, we travelled via Oropesa, where the illustrious count[4] offered us hospitality of a nobility and magnificence worthy of his rank, directing that we be treated with the same ceremony as himself.

Afterwards, entering Portuguese territory, we hastened directly to Vila Viçosa, seat of the duke of Bragança. The courtesy of the duke,[5] and of the illustrious princess his mother,[6] of which we had previously had ample proof, left nothing to be desired; indeed we felt that it had even reached a new height, if that were possible, as we experienced their hospitality now for the second time. Thus we were obliged to spend four whole days with them, and that was scarcely enough for us to be able to satisfy their eagerness to talk to us and to treat with us with familiarity and benevolence. From there we travelled to Évora, and in that city too we enjoyed no less benevolence from the fathers of the Society and no less love from the illustrious archbishop, Teotónio of Bragança. He delayed us there for nine days, caring for our health and our pleasure with magnificent food every day, and denuding his chapel of images, paintings, reliquaries, and other precious gifts which he gave to us and to Japan; also the four very rich tapestries which I mentioned earlier, and in addition a thousand ducats, to buy various items to be taken back to our country. All these things together would be worth more than five thousand ducats, a great present indeed in itself, but little enough in comparison with his good will towards us.

In the same city was Francisco Mascarenhas, the most noble count of Vila da Horta, who was viceroy of India, as I said before at the beginning of our colloquia, when we went to India on our way to Rome. He had not forgotten his benevolence towards us in the past, and he very kindly paid us a visit to let us know that he and all he had were entirely at our disposal. We also visited him, and he treated us with great friendliness, even calling in his wife, a most noble lady, and his children to join in our meeting and talk. All the students of the academy showed us the same signs of their esteem, celebrating our return with speeches, songs, and other similar exercises, and especially with one particularly charming poem, which delighted us.[7] We left Évora, not without considerable reluctance, and, passing through the flourishing city of Alcacer do Sal, arrived at a most agreeable villa of the fathers of the Society who live in the Lisbon college, known in Portuguese as Vale do Rosal.[8] There the reverend Father Provincial[9] was eagerly expecting

---

[1] Guzman (*Historia*, II, p. 290) provides a couple of extra details, noting that the clavicymbal was inlaid with mother-of-pearl and had been brought from Rome. See also above, p. 270 n. 5.

[2] Maria of Austria.

[3] Gaspar de Quiroga y Vela (see above, p. 233).

[4] Juan Álvarez de Toledo (1550–1619), fifth count of Oropesa.

[5] Teodósio de Bragança (see above, p. 228 n. 4).

[6] Catarina (see above, p. 228 n. 5).

[7] Fróis, *Première ambassade*, pp. 254–5, provides some additional detail on the stay in Évora.

[8] In the parish of Charneca da Caparica in Almada, across from Lisbon.

[9] Sebastião de Morais (see above, p. 35 n. 1).

us, together with many others both from the professed house which is in Lisbon and from the College of St Anthony, and now that we were close to the end of our European journey, that is to Lisbon, which is two leagues from there, he received us most courteously and indulgently, with love, and we were able to enjoy several days of much needed rest together with him and the other fathers. That villa is in the area across the Tagus from Lisbon, so when we wanted to go to Lisbon after those days a royal ship was prepared and brought to us by order of the most eminent Cardinal Albert, to allow us to cross over to Lisbon.

So we crossed the Tagus, entered Lisbon, and were very comfortably accommodated at the professed house of São Roque. During our stay in Lisbon we several times called on the most eminent Cardinal Albert, who gave every possible proof of kindness and generosity towards us. For he provided fifteen hundred ducats towards the expenses of those months, as well as the sum which he added for provisions for the voyage, from which we also had made various items of clothing with gold embroidery. In that same time, when we were in Lisbon, we greatly enjoyed frequent visits to the college of Santo Antão. The extended length of time (our voyage was not until March of the following year, 1586) meant that the students were able to show their goodwill towards us in many different ways, decorating the college halls elegantly, and putting on various plays as a spectacle for us, the subject presented often being our journey and Japanese things. But since our stay in Lisbon was to be so prolonged, and we were getting many messages from the city of Coimbra, which is in the middle of Portugal, which made it clear to us that the fathers of the college of Coimbra were exceedingly eager to see us; and since we had heard much of the fame of that college, there was nothing at that time more to our liking than to satisfy the wishes of those fathers.

So in the month of December we set off on the journey, and sailed very happily along the river Tagus, which I have mentioned a number of times, coming first to the famous town of Scalabis or, in the common tongue, Santarém. It is so thronged with a multitude of both nobles and common people as to be much greater than some Portuguese cities, but the people of the town prefer to have it as the first and principal town of Portugal rather than as just one city among others. So omitting any account of the buildings of this town, which are without question the equal of many buildings in cities, it is known for four miracles, which I'll describe for you, but briefly, because time presses. In the first place, therefore, I put the mystery of the Holy Eucharist, which even to this day is made known with many and various proofs. And since it is manifested in a happening which is itself amazing, let me describe it briefly for you. There was a woman of that city who owed a certain sum of money to a Jew, who said he would let her go free, released from the debt, if she would hand over to him the Holy Eucharist, which Christians are accustomed to receive reverently in churches. She, more concerned for herself than for religion, agreed to this, approached the sacred table with wicked intention, kept the Holy Eucharist in her mouth, then took it out with impious hands, wrapped it in a cloth, and hastened to the Jew her creditor. God in His justice did not allow this dreadful crime to go unsuspected, for from the cloth within which the sacred host was hidden such a quantity of blood began to flow that it splashed on the wicked woman's body and clothes. Passers-by saw it, wondered, and gave her name to the priests. She was transfixed by fear, and hid the Holy Eucharist in an unworthy and secret place. As she was fleeing the priests and magistrates intercepted her, and they questioned her diligently to find out where she had hidden the Holy Eucharist. All then went to the place she had indicated, and there they found a container formed by divine power of a sort of crystalline material, and the heavenly bread enclosed within it. It was then carried with the utmost veneration and with a great procession to the church dedicated to St Stephen, where the container is preserved even today with all reverence.[1]

And the divine power, not satisfied with these miracles, daily produces new and unheard of ones in that same container, to the great amazement and excitement of all. For it happens that those who visit that church and gaze upon that container in a spirit of piety and devotion, see amazing spectacles divinely vouchsafed to them. Some there are who see Christ clearly, and are deeply moved to see Him, in many different astonishing forms; some see him being born in the stable, others being adored by the Magi, some preaching to the people, some praying to His heavenly Father; and more see Christ bound, scourged, pierced by the crown of thorns, carrying His Cross, fastened to the Cross, and returning to life.

Leo: These are astonishing things you are telling us, Michael, the consideration of which has a strong effect on our minds.

Mancio: That spectacle is truly such that it would seem to justify the extreme length of our voyage. It not only strengthens the minds of those who see it in the Christian faith, but also moves them to a wonderful piety and to divine love.

Michael: In the second place I put before you an admirable image of Christ crucified which there is in that same town, with the arms hanging in such a way that he appears to be assenting and agreeing. There was a man who had committed himself to marrying a certain woman, but afterwards he changed his mind and backed away from his commitment. She had no witnesses to prove that he had made it, but she had recourse to Christ the true judge, and persuaded the man to stand before Christ in the presence of many others. They went to the church, and in front of the holy image of Christ

---

[1] The Eucharistic Miracle of Santarém occurred sometime between 1247 and 1266. The details differ somewhat but do not involve a Jew. A woman discovered that her husband was having an affair. She went to a witch who advised her to steal a sacred host and mix it with other ingredients to concoct a love potion in order to restore happy marital relations. Another version says that the witch demanded that the host be brought to her. The woman received communion in her parish, Santo Estêvão, but furtively removed the host from her mouth and hid it in her headscarf. As she was making her way home, someone asked if she had injured herself because she appeared to be bleeding. Once at home, she hid the host in a trunk. Her husband returned and after dinner the couple went to bed but during the night the host began to radiate light. She confessed to her husband what she had done and for the rest of the night the couple saw visions including angels adoring the newborn Jesus. In the morning other townspeople came to see the miracle. The host was retrieved and taken in solemn procession to Santo Estêvão. The blood continued to issue for three days. In 1340 another miracle occurred. A priest went to open the tabernacle in which the relic was kept in a wax container. To his astonishment he found that the wax had liquefied and the host was now enclosed in a hermetically-sealed crystal pyx. Subsequently people have affirmed that they have seen fresh drops of blood but also visions of Christ. See http://www.culturacattolica.it/default.asp?id=72&id_n=1958. The church, rebuilt in the 16th century, is now called the church of the Santíssimo Milagre. In *De Missione*'s sanitized version one demon of the early modern imagination, the witch, is substituted for another, the Jew. Before taking passage for the Indies Xavier visited Santarém several times to teach the catechism (Schurhammer, *Francis Xavier*, I, p. 670).

hanging on the Cross the woman accused the man of the crime of breach of promise, and asked whether that man had plighted his troth to her. At that the sacred image pulled out the nails and lowered its arms, confirming that it was indeed as she said, and thus the guilty man was convicted of perfidy. And what is even more extraordinary is that the sacred image continues to have the same inclination of the body, and is most piously venerated by everyone, and a monastery of the order of St Benedict has now been built in that place.[1]

There is a third quite extraordinary thing in the Dominican monastery, namely a statue of Christ when still a child. When other children approached the altar and invited Him to their children's meal, He was several times seen coming down from the arms of the Blessed Virgin in order to join the children. When those children died happily three days later He invited them to the heavenly table.[2]

Lastly, that town is renowned for the tomb of the holy virgin and martyr Irene, which is said to have been built by divine power in the middle of the River Tagus.[3] And trustworthy authors report that the holy body of St Clement was treated by God with similar honour, and it is preserved three miles out in the sea. From this so celebrated town we set out for another which is also noble, and which is called Nabantia,[4] because of the river which flows past it. The histories bear witness that it was here that that same virgin Irene was killed for defending the integrity of her mind and her body. In that town there is a magnificent monastery of the order which takes its name from Christ, a monastery displaying in its buildings, its income, and its furnishings a regal opulence the equal of the monasteries of Lisbon. Not many years ago King Philip held a *cortes* for the whole kingdom here, and made the three estates of Portugal take the oath of fealty due to a king.[5]

We set out from that town and reached Coimbra, which we had been so eager to see. The first to come and meet us on our arrival was the most illustrious João de Bragança, son of the count of Tentúgal, whom, as I said earlier,[6] we had met at the court of King Philip when we were on our way to Rome. Soon after other magistrates arrived, and then lastly the most illustrious and reverend bishop of Coimbra, Don Afonso de Castelo Branco,[7] born of the distinguished family of that name. All of these, together with many other nobles, accompanied us to the college of the fathers of the Society, and there one of the Jesuits made a most elegant speech, in which he spoke at length and with much embellishment in praise of our kings, the kings by whom we were sent, a speech much appreciated by the audience. Afterwards there was a performance of musical instruments

---

[1] The convent of Santa Iria, now in ruins, although the church, rebuilt in the 17th century, contains a medieval image of Christ crucified, with an arm falling from the cross.

[2] One of the earliest Dominicans, Suéro Gomez, founded a monastery in Santarém.

[3] St Irene or Iria was murdered around the middle of the 7th century and her body thrown into the Tagus. Her body was retrieved by Benedictines near Scalabris and buried, and the name of the town changed to Santarém.

[4] Tomar, on the river Nabão.

[5] The magnificent Convent of Christ or Convento de Cristo, founded by the Knights Templar in the 12th century. Philip II of Spain was officially recognized as Filipe I of Portugal during a meeting of the *cortes* which began on 25 March 1581.

[6] See above, p. 245.

[7] 1522–1615, bishop of Faro 1581, bishop of Coimbra 1585.

in harmony, and many other testimonies to the general satisfaction. When we had taken our leave, therefore, of those who had accompanied us, we were extremely happy at the joy on the faces of all the fathers and the great affection with which each of them embraced us. But things in Coimbra, and other things that happened after that, need a colloquium to themselves, so let us now retire as usual.

COLLOQUIUM XXXI

Of the city of Coimbra and the famous college of the Society there, the generous treatment extended to the ambassadors in Lisbon, by order of King Philip, with regard to the voyage to India, and the reasons for the wealth of Europe

Lino: We know that the name of the city of Coimbra, which Michael mentioned at the end of the last colloquium, is often referred to in the conversation of the fathers of the Society, and that they have fond memories, often renewed, of the Coimbra college, in which many of them were educated, so we would love to be fully informed about the city and about the famous college.[1]

Michael: I'm only too pleased to tell you about it, Lino, and indeed I feel that to do so is a duty, to the fathers who live here with us, and because of the wonderful kindness which the fathers in Coimbra showed to us. The city of Coimbra, then, is famous in the first place for its antiquity, for the citizens attribute its first construction to Hercules himself. It was the first seat of the Portuguese kings,[2] at a time when their jurisdiction was very limited, much of Portugal being occupied by the Saracens. The kings broke out from there and greatly extended their territories, though they were threatened by enemy attacks from all sides. The coat of arms of the city indicates this clearly. On it is painted, on a vase, a maiden whose head is adorned with a diadem, a lion attacking her on the right and a serpent on the left.[3] This signifies that in former times when Portugal, of which Coimbra was as it were the mother, was contained within narrow boundaries, it was attacked by dreadful enemies and adversaries of the Faith, but nevertheless won a magnificent victory, and it was in this city that the crown of victory was placed on its head. Because of this the city has many memorials of its ancient kings, as will be evident to you when I describe its religious buildings.

In Coimbra, then, there is first of all a monastery of the finest workmanship, dedicated to the Holy Cross,[4] in which live canons regular professing the institute of St Augustine,

---

[1] De Sande was among those educated at Coimbra and where he taught briefly (Burnett, 'Humanism and the Jesuit Mission', pp. 427–8).

[2] Coimbra was the capital of the Portuguese kingdom from 1139 to 1255.

[3] This coat of arms was used after the city was incorporated in 1516. The modern coat was introduced in 1930. See http://web.archive.org/web/20070922042308/www.cm-coimbra.pt/530.htm.

[4] The monastery of Santa Cruz, founded 1131, redesigned and reconstructed in the early 16th century before the boys' visit.

and this monastery was built at great expense by Afonso Henriques, first and invincible king of Portugal. Both the church and the residence of the fathers can stand comparison with the most famous of those I have already described, with regard to the buildings, the sacred furnishings, and finally to wealth and income; but since I have treated of these things often and at length when dealing with other monasteries there is no need for me to give a detailed description here. This monastery is famous also for the bodies of the five holy martyrs Berard, Peter, Adjutus, Accursius, and Otho, whom St Francis himself sent into Africa to spread the law of Christ, and who were cruelly killed for professing that same law by Miramolim, the impious emperor of Morocco,[1] and are thus numbered among the holy Christian martyrs.[2] And when Pedro,[3] brother of King Afonso, second of that name,[4] of Portugal, had asked for and obtained those sacred bodies and brought them out of Africa, they were preserved with all honour in this monastery, and the saints themselves confirmed, by a famous miracle, that it was pleasing to them that their tomb should be there. The devotion of the people of Coimbra and the inhabitants of all the district round about to those saints is so great that on 16 January, the day dedicated to those martyrs, a very great number of men from the whole district of Coimbra assembles and, in their devotion, and this at the time when the cold is most severe in Portugal, they take part half-naked in a procession, piously recalling the memory of how the prayers of those saints once brought them health and safety in a time of very dangerous disease.

In the same monastery are the tombs of Afonso Henriques, first king of Portugal, and of his son Sancho,[5] who became king of Portugal on the death of his father, together with many other men and women of the same royal family. This same monastery is also distinguished by the fact that St Anthony of Lisbon once lived there,[6] for he first belonged to this religious order, but later, moved by the fame of those martyrs whom I have spoken about, he transferred to the Order of St Francis, and the room in which he lived is still preserved in the Franciscan convent which is outside the same city, and which is called after the same saint.

In that same city among many other things there is a convent of holy virgins who follow the rule of St Francis, a convent which is greatly distinguished not only by the nobility of those religious women and other things of which I say nothing, but also and especially by the tomb and the holy body of St Elizabeth, queen of Portugal, wife of King Dinis, to whose singular virtues and extraordinary sanctity many miracles bear witness, and they are recounted in so many writings that there is no need for me to retell them here.[7]

---

[1] Yusuf II, caliph 1213–24. Amīr al-Mu'minīn (Port. *miramolim*), caliph.

[2] The protomartyrs of Morocco, sent there by Francis of Assisi in 1219, died the following year after refusing to apostatize. They were canonized in 1481 and their feast day is 16 January. Their ordeal inspired St Anthony of Padua to become a Franciscan.

[3] 1187–1258, count of Urgell and lord of the Balearic Islands, born in Coimbra.

[4] Afonso II (r. 1211–23).

[5] Sancho I (r. 1185–1211).

[6] I.e. St Anthony of Padua.

[7] Dinis (r. 1279–1325) married Elizabeth of Aragon. Upon her husband's death she became a Poor Clare intending to devote the rest of her life to caring for the poor and sick. She was buried in the monastery of Santa Clara-a-Velha in Coimbra which she had founded but which was abandoned in the early 17th century because of flooding. Her remains were removed to the new Santa Clara-a-Velha monastery. She was canonized in 1625.

The city boasts a most sumptuous cathedral, and this too is said to have been built by King Afonso I.[1] It is not especially large, but stands out for the magnificence of the building. Its walls are adorned with ingeniously arranged tiling, the vestibules at both doors have their porches decorated with highly polished stone, and finally the roof of the church is set off by a dome of extraordinary height and beauty. Add to all this the attire of the ministers of that church, and the most ample income of the priests called canons, and especially of the bishop of Coimbra himself, whose revenues are higher than those of any other Portuguese bishop. Coimbra also boasts a multitude of colleges, for in this town all the religious orders have them, so that students can pursue courses in the arts in them. So many are these colleges that there is one very long and broad street, called after St Sophia,[2] in which there are hardly any houses other than these religious ones, and it is one of the most famous streets in the city.

Let us move on now to the excellence of the secular structures, and first place must be accorded to the magnificent bridge which extends to Coimbra from the far bank of the Mondego. It is hard to know which to celebrate first, its breadth, its length, the height of its arches and vaults, or finally its surface of conjoined paving in the finest stone. Its arches are of such a height that boats of no small size can easily pass under them with their masts raised and sails unfurled. This bridge, however, is supported by another older bridge which is covered up by the sand in the river.[3] In the second place we come to the citadel, which is very heavily fortified and hedged round with many towers, one of them octangular and known as the Tower of Hercules, and another with a perpetual spring of water which continuously bubbles up and contributes not a little to satisfying the thirst of those who are thrown into prison in that same citadel.[4] Third comes the splendid royal palace, said to have been built by King Dinis, and by no means inferior to the palaces in Lisbon in the spaciousness of the site, the size of the halls, the many rooms, the numerous colonnades, the remarkable view along the banks of the river Mondego, with the green fields spreading out far and wide from it, and other things conducing to magnificence. Lastly there are recently constructed aqueducts which bring the water from many fountains within the walls of the city.[5] They do not extend for any great distance, as do the ones which we spoke of in Évora, but nevertheless are outstanding for their design and construction.

But let us now speak of the university, the jewel in the crown of the city, which was moved fifty years ago from Lisbon, where it was formerly, to this city, which was judged to be a more appropriate site for it.[6] I'll describe its two principal parts to you. One part is in the palace which we have just spoken about, and it contains what are called the major

---

[1] The old cathedral of Coimbra, or Sé Velha de Coimbra, founded by Afonso I, and one of the finest Romanesque buildings in Portugal.

[2] Rua da Sofia.

[3] This bridge was demolished in the late 19th century. The present bridge across the Mondego, the Ponte de Santa Clara, one of a number of bridges now spanning the river, was built in 1954.

[4] The castle is no longer extant.

[5] The Aqueduto de São Sebastião.

[6] Founded in 1290 in Lisbon, the university first moved to Coimbra in 1308 and moved back and forth between the two cities on a number of occasions before its final move to Coimbra in 1537. The university was housed in the royal palace, leased to the university by João III. Many colleges grew up around the university transforming the appearance of the town after 1537. Coimbra has changed greatly since the boys were there.

schools. In this palace the students are taught civil law, canon law, theology, medicine, and mathematics. This major part of the university is notable for many things, and firstly for the splendour of the halls where the students assemble, for, as everyone knows, they were built at royal expense. One very spacious hall is assigned to each of the arts, and the pupils, youths who have reached the right age, come here strikingly dressed in ankle-length gowns and elegant attire. Of these halls the one most worthy of note is that to which the students of theology come, and since many come from all the religious orders spread throughout the entire kingdom they constitute a most impressive assembly. Many men outstanding for religion have acquired learning in this hall and have gone out not only to be excellent orators, but also to be raised to the episcopate and to earn the highest praise for their exercise of sacred jurisdiction all over Portugal, and also here in the vast territories of the Orient.

There is besides another celebrated hall dedicated to academic disputations, and to the conferring of various degrees on the candidates, and as well as most elaborate workmanship in its roof and extremely spacious accommodation, this hall provides a splendid spectacle whenever a scholar of one of the arts is raised to the rank of doctor or master.[1] All the doctors and masters of the various arts faculties assemble, together with others with lower degrees and a great multitude of ordinary students, all in their distinctive academic dress, with hoods of velvet, white for the theologians, saffron for the medical doctors, red for specialists in civil law, green for those in pontifical law, violet for the masters of philosophy; and all wear beautifully made caps of silk of the same colour, with silk ribbons elegantly attached to them. Then there are various speeches, the candidate is raised to the degree, many silver coins are distributed with gloves,[2] as I mentioned earlier when speaking of the University of Alcalá, and musical instruments in harmony sound all around.

The university has its own church, dedicated to St Michael,[3] and its own priests who celebrate the divine service every day, with teachers and students attending before they proceed to the study of their arts. And one of the most expert of these priests instructs those who are to become priests in the art of singing, and is rewarded for his work. Presiding over all this magnificent assembly of the university is the rector, a man of most noble family, and he becomes rector either by royal nomination or by the votes of the teachers.[4] The rector's authority, derived from his lineage and from his gifts of wisdom and prudence, is always such that he is frequently promoted from that post to a bishopric. When we were there the position of rector was held by the illustrious Nuno de Noronha,[5] son of the count of Odemira, and he had been called by the king to be appointed bishop of Viseu. That is now his position, and his administration there is accorded the highest praise. The rector has many counsellors, chosen from those most notable for erudition and

---

[1] The Sala das Capelas, originally the throne room of the royal palace.

[2] Original edition (p. 355), gives '*cu[m] chirothecis*', i.e. episcopal gloves. The modern faculties each have colours and Coimbra is famous for the student festival of the *Queima das Fitas* or the burning of the ribbons held annually in May.

[3] The Capela de Miguel.

[4] On the election of the rector and the influence of the monarch, see Fonesca, 'Social and Cultural Roles', pp. 15–16.

[5] 1540–c. 1608, rector 1578–84, bishop of Viseu from 1585. He had taken up his new duties and was not present during the boys' visit.

prudence, and together with these he diligently governs the whole university. There is also a special prefect with his own jurisdiction, who judges all cases concerning members of the university, and adjudicates their suits or disputes. The city magistrates cannot interfere in those cases, which are dealt with entirely by that one special magistrate and those under him.

What am I to say of the income of this university, so very copious that it provides a most generous living for all those professors, and not only those currently involved in teaching but also the retired. The scale of all this is perhaps best shown by the case of the most learned professor Martín de Azpilcueta Navarro,[1] famous the world over, who, after completing his career as professor of pontifical law, lived in Rome and other places for more than thirty years, and was provided annually by the university with a most ample income of a thousand ducats, which he always spent to excellent effect.[2] In addition to all that has been said this university boasts two most noble colleges, the one dedicated to St Paul and the other to St Peter, and studious men from honourable families, who have been tested for their abilities and their progress in studies, are admitted to membership of these colleges. They live there in style, and apply themselves with such diligence to the study of the arts that most of them go on from there to very prominent positions and offices in the kingdom of Portugal.[3]

Lino: You have told us many very pleasing things about the University of Coimbra and how flourishing it is. It can justly be named mother of the studious, and please God there may come a time when we have one like it here in Japan.

Michael: That will be possible, Lino, as Christianity progresses here and becomes longer established. Our people have no lack of talent and gifts of nature. Add to those diligent industry and Christianity, and it will be easy for our people to be introduced to all the refinements of culture in their thought and behaviour. But I come now to the other part of the university, which comprises the college of the Society of Jesus,[4] to which we owe a special debt of friendship and gratitude. The college is very large indeed, and as I prepare to speak about it I find that the amount of material which it offers for my

---

[1] 1493–1586, theologian, moralist and canon lawyer. He was a relative of Francis Xavier, served at the court of Philip II from 1555 to 1567, and thereafter lived and worked in Rome.

[2] The generous treatment accorded Martín de Azpilcueta was exceptional. In fact, the University of Salamanca paid more generous salaries than that of Coimbra (Ramalho, 'Aspectos da vida escolar Ibérica', p. 163).

[3] The 'secular' colleges: Colégio de S. Pedro (1543) and Colégio de S. Paulo (1550). These graduate colleges were highly exclusive and selective but were essential paths towards securing academic posts and preferment in the ecclesiastical and civil administrations and as institutions for establishing personal and social networks. See Ramalho, 'Aspectos da vida escolar Ibérica', p. 163; Fonseca, 'Social and Cultural Roles of the University of Coimbra', pp. 17–18.

[4] The original Jesuit college in Coimbra, established with royal patronage, opened in 1542. In 1547 João III established the Colégio Real or Colégio das Artes (the Royal College of Arts and Humanities) in Coimbra, modelled on the French Collège Royal, to prepare students for studies at the university. In 1555 the king entrusted administration of the college to the Jesuits. It officially became part of the university in 1561. The original Jesuit college and the College of Arts were merged at the end of the 1560s. The church, which postdates the boys' visit, became the Sé Nova or New Cathedral after the expulsion of the Jesuits from Portugal in 1759. See Rodrigues, *História da Companhia de Jesus*, II: 2, pp. 336–400; Alden, *Making of an Enterprise*, pp. 30–32.

description is no less large. I shall speak first about its beginnings, so that you may appreciate how much Japan owes to it. When King João III of Portugal, whom I wish to honour whenever I mention him in these colloquia, understood how much the work of the priests of the Society of Jesus could accomplish in bringing the pagans to Christianity, he sent priests from the house of Santo Antão in Lisbon, which with the passage of time had been granted the title of college, and their leader, Simão Rodrigues by name,[1] who was the first provincial of Portugal, to set up that college, the first in Portugal; and he endowed it with income large enough for a hundred of the Society to be able to live there, of whom he wanted twelve theologians always to be ready to be sent to India and Brazil to devote themselves totally to the conversion of the pagans to Christianity. So the greater part of the fruit of the harvest reaped in the whole of the Orient should rightly be credited to the University of Coimbra.

After some time had passed that college underwent a major expansion, for the king gave it charge of the minor schools of the university. For when the same João III learned that the instruction of studious youth in the arts, and teaching them the various disciplines together with good behaviour, was also proper to the Institute of the Society, he decided to entrust to the care of the fathers that part of the university which expounds to the students the Latin, Greek, and Hebrew languages, as well as Philosophy, and they have been carrying out this task now with great success for about thirty-five years, in all piety and wisdom developing the talents of the youth of Portugal. As a result they have not only laid excellent foundations for all the disciplines but also have caused almost all the religious orders to flourish with an intake of very talented young men. The religious orders openly acknowledge this, and give the college much of the credit due for the benefit which it has brought to Portugal.

From what I have said you can imagine how many fathers and brothers there are in that college, given that it is a seminary for preachers destined for India and Brazil, and also an institution for instructing boys in the arts, with twenty masters appointed to those duties. Eleven of them teach the Latin language, together with rhetoric and the other associated arts, to boys of good family, in eleven large schoolrooms. Four give instruction in the disciplines of philosophy, with the Greek and Hebrew languages, and three tutor in theology, and with so many masters you can imagine the number of pupils. There are about two thousand externs, and the number of members of the Society who are in the college, including the masters I have mentioned, comes to two hundred, and to more than that if you include others who are dispersed among various estates and parishes attached

---

[1] One of the original companions of Ignatius Loyola and a controversial figure in the history of the Society. He was sent by Loyola to his native Portugal in 1540, which became a province of the Society in 1546. A strong-willed, charismatic individual, Rodrigues attracted many new recruits but controversy erupted over his enthusiasm including strict penitential practices, such as fasting and public self-flagellation. Loyola feared that Rodriguez, who had become close to the king, was becoming too independent and a threat to Jesuit unity. In 1548 Rodrigues was removed from office and transferred to Aragon where he remained only temporarily before returning to Lisbon. In the meantime the Portuguese province was purged and Rodrigues recalled to Rome whither he eventually, and reluctantly, went in 1553. His challenge to the iron discipline Loyola sought to impose was broken. Chastened, he was finally permitted to return to Portugal as an old man where he wrote a history of the formative years of the Society. The effects of the controversy were felt in Goa, where some Jesuits were seen as being too much influenced by Rodrigues's ascetic practices for the good of the Society. See Alden, *Making of an Enterprise*, pp. 27–8, 36; O'Malley, *First Jesuits*, pp. 330–34; *Documenta Indica*, IV, p. 423.

to the same college. The college has annual income of at least fifteen thousand ducats, some of it from estates, some from well-endowed benefices, so some fathers are busy raising these revenues in various places outside the college.

But let us speak now of the fabric of the college itself, and it is indeed admirable and perfectly appropriate for the number of people who live in it and for its income. The building of the cloister for the classrooms has been begun but is not yet finished, and it is spacious and indeed magnificent. One side of it is complete, however, and shows how very fine the classrooms are. Almost all of the part which is the residence of the fathers is finished, consisting of very long corridors with spacious rooms on either side. Take into account also the width and the height, well worth viewing, and there will not be found in Portugal a more satisfactory religious house, nor perhaps one to equal this one, especially when the building is completely finished.

Let us come now to the kindness with which the fathers of the college treated us, kindness shown to us in all manner of things which they did for us. The college, as I said before, is especially dedicated to the spreading of Christianity, and is the seminary for the mission to Brazil and India, so it may be by some divine prompting that the fathers there seem to have a special love for, to treat as their favourites, the peoples of the East, and particularly the Japanese, and therefore most gladly treated us with all charity as a pledge of their love for the Japanese nation.

To give you a specific example of this I shall describe the splendour of our reception when we were taken in to attend the masters' classes. Each of the senior masters put on a play for us in his classroom, and to make the productions more elegant they had the walls hung with tapestries and had the students assemble in the classrooms dressed in magnificent costumes. On the day when we visited the first and highest class, a most pleasing drama, excellently representing the angels called 'Guardian Angels', was acted out for us, in which the angels guarding Japan and Europe were in conversation. The latter asked the former about how things were in Japan, and in his answer he recounted many admirable victories and exploits redounding to the praise of the Christian religion. To confirm all this Faith appeared, together with a great company of the heavenly host, and proclaimed in ringing tones the glories of the Church of Japan, finally attributing all these good things to the Sign of the Cross, which was religiously and reverently venerated. The angel guardian of Europe then explained in a lengthy speech the care he had taken to have us received with great acclaim throughout the various provinces of Europe, and to have the Supreme Pontiffs receive us with such signs of love as fathers would show to long lost sons new found. Then he committed us to the patron angel of Japan, charging him to lead us back safe and sound to our homeland. All of this was beautifully performed, in language of the utmost elegance. And during the speeches the master addressed us, comparing our arrival in the city to the most joyful return of King Afonso Henriques to the same city after a most noble victory over his enemies,[1] and he showed with an admirable choice of words how much more glorious our spoils were, for it was idolatry, which had long ruled throughout Japan, that had been vanquished.

In the second classroom they acted out a dialogue with several of the pupils telling one another how happy our arrival had made them. They encounter another young man,

---

[1] At the battle of Ourique in 1139 against the Muslims, a battle which acquired mythological status (Disney, *History of Portugal*, I, p. 75).

recently come from India and Japan, who informs them about the purpose of our embassy, and about the excellent progress that has been made in Japan with regard to the propagation of Christianity. There were others who, in various speeches among themselves, gave a fine account of all the things which had happened to us on our journey to and our return from the Roman Curia. That's a brief summary of the dialogue, which was impressively varied and which lasted several hours.

In another schoolroom again almost the same expressions were used in treating the material, but the characters introduced were different. First to appear was Asia, troubled by our absence, and lamenting it at length. Eventually she questions Ocean about us, and he answers that he had treated us gently and indulgently over a long period, that we had undergone no misfortune and had been handed over to Europe, and that she should therefore enquire of her. Accordingly Asia, still solicitous about us, goes to Europe and enquires after our welfare. Europe assures her that we are safe and sound, but in order further to reassure Asia about this she summons various provinces, Portugal, Castile, and Italy, as her daughters, to the same colloquium. Each of these gives an account of us, in so far as we concern her; of the rejoicing, that is, with which we were greeted in all her cities and towns; and in these speeches all that I have been relating so far was cleverly summarized. Asia, acknowledging these benefits conferred on her subjects as her own, offers infinite thanks to Europe and promises to be bound to her with the chain of an everlasting alliance. With great joy she welcomes us as we were restored to her, and hands us over once again to Ocean, requesting him to treat us with his accustomed indulgence and benignity. This play was very pleasing, and was notable for the skill of the actors; there was also a speech by the master himself, elegantly reviewing our whole journey and the satisfaction of the popes at our arrival in Rome.

After this happy celebration within the walls of the schoolrooms, the joy of the college burst out, as it were, into the open, and moved to the public theatre. Whenever the fathers of that college wish to celebrate the arrival of a man of special authority, they put on some particularly fine play for public viewing. And since the time of the transfer of the illustrious bishop Afonso from the see of the Algarve to that of Coimbra almost coincided with our arrival in Coimbra, it was particularly appropriate to have a most solemn tragedy to make both arrivals the more celebrated. The theme was the life of St John, the precursor of Christ, and his death so bravely faced for the sake of the truth which he had to preach. In the first act John appears as a boy five years old, who leaves his parents and the pleasures of life and takes refuge in solitude and a very severe form of life, living out his whole life in hardship until the age of thirty. In the second the people of Judea, impressed by his fame for sanctity, flow to him in great numbers, and sorrowing for their sins they are washed clean of them by him in the waters of the River Jordan. The third act is taken up with the progress of the saint to the city of Jerusalem, and his frequent warnings to King Herod, by which he attempts to deter him from his wicked incest; in the course of this act the burning love of God which consumes the mind of Saint John, and the hardening animus of the tyrant against those salutary warnings, are excellently depicted. The fourth act has him unjustly put in irons, with his patience in tolerating all adversity shining forth. The whole performance concludes with the most cruel beheading of the saint, so performed that it seems to be taking place not on the stage but in real life. Each of the parts of this tragedy was accompanied by the sweet singing of many voices. The third part in particular was notable for the virtue commonly called Penitence exhorting the angels to sing the praises of St John, which they then celebrated with splendid song. This work, which lasted about seven hours, was embellished not a little by its topography of various places, for example of the solitude in which St John mortified himself with fasting and other sufferings, and of the infernal realm from which issued furies who led the mind of impious Herod into deception and wickedness.[1]

With all this we passed the days at Coimbra very happily indeed, the fathers providing a variety of spectacles to keep us entertained. We spent the day of Our Lord's birth there in the college, just before the beginning of the year 1586, the celebration of the feast being admirably illustrated by a representation of the crib in which Christ our Saviour was born, a representation presented to our eyes with wonderful artistry, an excellent imitation, using live figures, of the grotto of Bethlehem. Added on to the history was a remarkable spectacle in which the Christian Faith was carried in a triumphal carriage borne by the four evangelists, and Francisco, king of Bungo, Protasio, king of Arima, and Bartolomeu, prince of Ōmura committed themselves wholly as clients to her patronage. Also performed was an eclogue among shepherds speaking to each other about the recent birth of Christ and the announcement by angelic oracle while piously and reverently venerating Him where he lay in the stable. We found both the variety of the subject matter and the gracefulness of the performance very pleasing.

But I come now to what we gained from our association with the bishop of Coimbra himself, who concerned himself to provide in every way for our wellbeing and our enjoyment. For as well as frequently asking after us and repeatedly sending us gifts he invited us to a private and most lavish banquet, and on the day when Christ's circumcision is remembered he not only gave a most eloquent sermon in the church of the Jesuit college, but also joined us at a banquet. He also took us to see the churches of Coimbra and all the other things which he knew would please us. We went with him, besides, on an outing to the country, on most familiar terms, not only going to his delightful villa called São Martinho,[2] but also hunting, for relaxation, and in addition visiting, with the bishop, the villa of the fathers of the Society, which is situated on the bank of the River Mondego and is fertile with fruit of many kinds. The bishop also did us the honour of inviting us on Christmas Day to the solemn Mass which he himself would be celebrating in the cathedral. He wanted us to be received by the whole chapter of canons, and assigned to us the highest ranking place on the sanctuary of the high altar, with velvet seats and cushions, with the honour of being incensed, and the kissing of the sacred tablet by which the sign of peace is given, rites both of which are granted only to great princes. For all these reasons we recognize that we are deeply indebted to this illustrious bishop. Also extremely hospitable to us was João de Bragança, that illustrious man whom I have been glad to mention several times, whose courtesy and benevolence towards us, of which we had ample evidence, left a grateful memory of him fixed in our minds. Those twenty days which we spent in Coimbra[3] passed more quickly than we anticipated, and only a few days after we left the fathers of the Society, the bishop, and

---

[1] The play, *Degolação de S. João Baptista*, was written by António de Abreu and was described as very good, devout and edifying by the Jesuit provincial (Rodrigues, *História da Companhia de Jesus*, II: 2, pp. 73–4, 469).

[2] At São Martinho do Bispo.

[3] They arrived in Coimbra on 23 December 1585 and left on 9 January 1586.

the other distinguished persons, we found that we were missing them very badly, and traces of that longing for them remain with us even now, a longing not superficial, as the shortness of the time spent there would suggest, but fixed permanently in our memories.[1]

We left Coimbra and returned to Lisbon. On the way we saw two imposing convents, the convent of Batalha, which in Portuguese means 'battle', and the convent which takes its name from the town of Alcobaça. The first is of the order of St Dominic,[2] *built by João, first of that name, invincible king of Portugal, in*[3] memory of the famous victory which he gained in combat against Juan, also the first, king of Castile. In that monastery there are many things worth seeing, the sumptuous building itself, naturally, the splendid sacred furnishings, the large number of religious, very learned men, and indeed everything befitting the royal magnificence, but since we are now hastening towards our goal I shall omit detailed description of these things. In the second monastery[4] dwell the flourishing Order of St Bernard, and this monastery was built by Afonso Henriques, first king of Portugal, to mark the famous victories he won over innumerable hordes of Saracens whom he scattered and put to flight, especially in the battles in which he took Santarém and Lisbon.[5] He provided such large revenues for this monastery that the number of religious who are said to have lived there in centuries past is scarcely credible, for it is commonly said that there were about a thousand. What is certain, however, is that the abbot of this monastery, who currently is the most illustrious Jorge de Ataíde, formerly bishop of Viseu,[6] now principal chaplain to the king of Portugal, from this richly-endowed abbacy alone receives twenty thousand ducats, so one can easily appreciate how great must be the resources of the monastery itself, which are separate.

After returning to Lisbon we again experienced the extraordinary liberality of the illustrious cardinal. For in addition to the gifts we had previously received he ordered that we be given, in the name of the king, four thousand ducats to procure provisions for the voyage to India, and the best quarters on the ship, which normally go to the captain, and that other necessary things be supplied. This must be ascribed to Divine Providence, since we did not complete the voyage in the usual six months, and what with wintering in Mozambique the whole journey took almost a year and a half, so that with the passage of all that time the food obtained in Lisbon was more than used up. The cardinal added another three thousand four hundred ducats for the priests who were to sail with us, thirty-one of them, some of whom travelled with us and some on another ship. He also wrote letters of commendation for us to the viceroy of India, and ordered that in Goa we

---

[1] Fróis, *Première ambassade*, pp. 254–62, provides additional detail about the stay in Coimbra although his account, mistakenly, suggests that the boys proceeded to Coimbra directly from Évora without first returning to Lisbon.

[2] Santa Maria da Vitória na Batalha, 10 km south of Leiria, built to commemorate the battle of Aljubarrota (1385) which secured Portugal's independence until 1580. The convent was badly damaged during the Peninsular War.

[3] The lines in italics are added from the list of errata which follows the index; they should have been included at the bottom of p. 361 in the original.

[4] The monastery of Alcobaça, founded in 1152 to commemorate the victory against the Moors at Santarém in 1147. The exterior was much altered in the 17th and 18th centuries.

[5] In 1147.

[6] He was bishop from 1568 to 1578.

should be given four fine horses,[1] and should be provided with everything else necessary for the voyage to China and Japan, and this was done, and done very well, by the viceroy. And if I put together the sum of all the presents which we received from the king and the most generous cardinal, it is certain that they would come to not less than twelve thousand ducats.

Leo: You certainly owe a great deal, as indeed we all do, to the most powerful King Philip of Spain, and to his illustrious nephew, who heaped so many gifts and honours on you. From all of this I have been able to see clearly, both now and often previously, just how rich Europe is. But now at the end of this colloquium I would be glad if you would tell us briefly the reasons for this.

Michael: From the earlier colloquia you'll have been able to deduce and to understand the causes, but I'll sum them up for you so that an appreciation of the reasons for it may make it easier for you to believe my description, so often repeated, of the wealth of Europe. Firstly, then, I attribute it to the peace and tranquillity which reigns there. Nothing is so damaging to kingdoms and provinces, nothing so brings them down, as long continued war; remove that, and it is wonderful to see how people devote themselves to increasing their fortunes and enriching themselves, and how truly peace can be said to be the mother of fortune and prosperity. Thus it is that here in Japan, since the plague and pestilence of continuous wars pervades every kingdom, the fields cannot easily be sown, nor their fruits harvested, but everywhere, whether city or country, is threatened with the tumult of war.

Lino: This is certainly a principal cause, which we learn about every day, to our cost, and needs no confirmation by proof or reasoning.

Michael: I attribute European wealth secondly to the nature of the soil and the quality of the climate. Our own temperate climate here in Japan should not be underrated, but nevertheless the climate of Europe is much to be preferred. I'll leave a longer explanation of this to the final colloquium. As a result, because rain and heat come so opportunely at their due time, the land there is much more fertile in crops and fruits, and the quantity of these is beyond belief. Among the crops they harvest not only wheat and rice, but also barley, rye, millet, spelt, and a great number of other types of vegetable, and it is really impossible to list the kinds of fruit, as they are almost infinite in number, from many different kinds of trees not found in Japan, although there are some of our trees, a very small number, which are lacking in Europe. They have besides a great multitude of

---

[1] Only one of the horses survived the trip to Japan, although two had made it to Macao. Richly adorned, the animal was used to great effect during Valignano's ambassadorial procession in Kyoto in 1591. It was then given as a present to Hideyoshi who, along with his entourage, was much impressed by the animal's appearance and stature, and declared it the finest among Valignano's presents. The horse, like the progress of Hanno the elephant to Rome, caused quite a stir. Japanese horses, which were of smaller stature, seemed paltry in comparison. The cost of transporting the horses – and the inconvenience caused to other passengers on the voyage from Goa to Macao – was used as evidence by the provincial of Goa, Francisco Cabral, Valignano's bitterest critic, as further evidence of Valignano's extravagance and pomposity. See ARSI, Jap.Sin 11: 1, f. 46; *Documenta Indica*, XVI, p. 543; Fróis, *História de Japam*, V, pp. 299, 300, 309, 317; Álvarez-Taladriz, 'Relación del P. Alejandro Valignano', p. 45; Cooper, *Rodrigues the Interpreter*, pp. 75–6; Yūki, 'A Present of Arabian Horses'.

animals, both tame and wild. From the hair and fleece of these, as I said at the beginning, expertly shorn and woven, precious wools are made, and clothing for various uses in fashioned.

The third cause of the abundance of everything in Europe is the trading the Europeans do, both among themselves and with other peoples. They do not behave as the Japanese do, who content themselves with the fertility of their own lands, without seeking anything from outside or regarding it useful for themselves. They therefore suffer from a great lack of many things in which Japan itself is poor. The Europeans on the other hand are never satisfied with the wealth of their own countries, and in order to trade they journey through all the lands and cross all the seas, pursuing every possible way to enrich their country and make it famous, so that, apart from that unknown southern land of which I spoke, the whole world now lies open to them, and they are diligently engaged in conveying merchandise here and there. Thus it is that there is nothing of value in the whole world so hidden or secret, even in the inmost veins and bowels of the earth, that they do not extract it and dig it out, so that it seems that nothing remains untouched by human industry.[1]

Lino: You have indicated the real causes, Michael, and very accurately, or so it seems to me, and I cannot but admire the industry of the Europeans.

Michael: What if you could see not only the merchants, some of whom come to us here, but also the farmers who plough and cultivate the land. You would see them leave no patch of land uncultivated or unused, with different things assigned to be sown in different places. Since, as I said, there are many kinds of planting, they sow corn and vegetables in some places, they plant orchards in others, with vines in many places and olive trees in more places again, and deep forests of other similar trees. Thus the industry of the farmers vies with the diligence of the merchants, and the experience and hard work of the artisan with both. These are in brief what seemed to me to be the reasons for the wealth of Europe, and I think you will be even more convinced of them when we come to the end of our colloquia. Now we are to move on gladly to our departure from Europe, and since that, for many and various reasons, is very well worth describing, I have no option but to put it off till tomorrow.

Leo: When you say that it is already time for you to be describing your departure from Europe, Michael, I feel a great regret, for we are all very keen to have far more and longer talk with you about that province. But very well, we'll leave things European for the time being. We'll speak about them later, when a really suitable occasion offers, and we'll keep them forever inserted into and engraved upon our minds.

---

[1] This misreading of Japan's foreign trade – the country was never uninterested in trade and was about to enjoy a substantial increase thanks to the *shuinsen* voyages – anticipates Montesquieu's similar criticism (Montesquieu, *Spirit of the Laws*, pp. 352–3).

COLLOQUIUM XXXII

The Voyage from Portugal to India, and from India to the Kingdom of China

Michael: It is time for me now, beloved cousins, after so many colloquia about Europe, to come at last to an account of our most sweet return to our own country, and of the various dangers which beset us on the way.

Leo: If the narration is to be complete, and in order to finish successfully the full course of these colloquia, we should indeed return to the point from which we set out.

Michael: When all was prepared, as I said, thanks to the splendid munificence of the king and the cardinal, and the diligence of the fathers of the Society, we said our farewells to the same fathers, with tears and ardent yearnings, and on 12 April, together with nineteen of the Society, and with the same Father Nuno Rodrigues as our leader for the journey, we boarded the Portuguese ship dedicated to Saint Philip the Apostle.[1] There were twelve more of the same Society on another ship. At that time the fleet for India had with it a number of other ships heading for various ports of Brazil, Guinea, the isle of São Thomé, the fort of São Jorge, also called the Gold Mine,[2] and other similar ones, the total number of ships being twenty-eight. The accommodation assigned to us in our ship was extremely comfortable, as I already said in the previous colloquium, being the kind which the senior officers of the ships use, for the captain had given us the use of his own quarters, as the cardinal had directed. The ships weighed anchor, the sails were hoisted, and we made our way out to sea; with a splendid wind in our favour and nothing to hold us back we sailed on until on 6 May we reached the region where the Equator or equinoctial line cuts through the middle of the sky. There the ships which were heading for various ports left us, each of them taking its own course, and we crossed the Equator a few days later, and gradually, leaving the northern sky behind us, began to observe the South.

---

[1] The *São Felipe*. They had originally put to sea at the end of March but after a day had put back to Lisbon because of bad weather. See Guzman, *Historia*, II, p 292; Fróis, *Première ambassade*, p. 264, n. 926. On its return voyage from India, the *São Felipe* was seized by Sir Francis Drake in the Azores in 1587. Hakluyt mentions that the ship had carried 'the 3. Princes of Japan, that were in Europe, into the Indies'. According to Hakluyt, the capture of the ship, the first seized on a return voyage from the Indies, was taken as a bad omen by the Portuguese, especially as the vessel bore the king's name (Hakluyt, *Principal Navigations*, VI, p. 442). The fact that Hakluyt gives three rather than four 'princes' may be attributable to Julian's absence from the audience before Gregory XIII and the coronation of Sixtus V (Cooper, *Japanese Mission*, p. 214 n. 14).

[2] São Jorge da Mina de Ouro, established in 1482, in present-day Elmina, Ghana.

As we go on I shall have to deal with the various perils which we ourselves had to face, so first of all let me set out the difficulties which affect and afflict all the Portuguese who undertake this voyage to India, so that you may at least be aware of how much we owe to the fathers of the Society, who for the sake of bringing salvation to us put up with so many trials as if it was all the most pleasant thing in the world. I say no more of the six months of enclosure, as if within a prison, which I spoke of at the beginning of these colloquia, but the storms which infest the ocean, their number and variety, almost defy description. It frequently happens that in just one day, or just one hour, everything is thrown into disorder; sometimes quite a small wind can disturb a voyage which is going well, and when that wind gets up from time to time the storms that can result are extraordinary. These storms are sometimes preceded by some sign in the sky, but sometimes arise quite unexpectedly, for no observable reason. Sometimes again no small discomfort results when there is a calm, with not the slightest breath of wind, and yet the sea heaves and swells, leaving the passengers feeling very sick. And what am I to say of the places where there are shallows and rocks? It often happens that a ship with a full head of sail smashes into them and breaks into many pieces; there is no hope of rescue for the poor men on board, who are swallowed into the bottomless abyss of the ocean. How, besides, am I to convey the threat of fire from which the ships are never free? The material of which they are constructed is dry wood smeared with pitch and some other similar types of bitumen, with tow sealing the very narrow fissures, and it is only too easy for a fire to break out and spread, and to destroy the entire ship, as has in fact happened many times. I could recount some extraordinary and piteous examples of such events, but I believe they are too well known to need retelling.[1]

Leo: I find it truly remarkable that there are men brave enough to commit themselves without hesitation to the unpredictable and stormy sea. Every time I hear about it my formerly unqualified eagerness to go to Europe and experience the things you recount to us wanes just a little.

Michael: It is extraordinary, indeed, given all this, how easily many Portuguese decide to sail for India, almost as if they were merely heading for the opposite bank of the Tagus, so much so that many of them do not bring even enough food for three days.[2] But God being provident in all things, and directing this India voyage for the salvation of many, what happens is that the Portuguese kings, far from failing in this matter, provide all that is necessary, as if their solicitude was for their own sons. They order a great quantity of salt

---

[1] According to Magalhães Godinho, around 772 ships out of 912 which had sailed from Lisbon reached the Indian Ocean between 1500 and 1635. On the return voyage about 470 of around 550 ships that made for Lisbon from the Indies arrived home during the years 1501–1635. He also suggests that insurance premiums for the voyages were favourable. Boxer, on the other hand, suggests the losses from shipwreck during 1550–1650 'were staggeringly heavy'. For one decade, the 1590s, when 44.4 per cent of returning voyages from the Indies were lost, that is a reasonable characterization. The most recent research, by Landeiro Godinho, on losses during 1550–1649, gives an annual average of 20.8 per cent. Moreover, ships were more likely to perish as a result of poor seamanship, or from enemy attack, rather than from the elements as is clear from what follows. See Godinho, *Os descobrimentos*, III, pp. 48–9; idem, 'The Carreira da India', pp. 6–7, 24; Boxer, *Tragic History*, pp. 24–7 esp. p. 24; Godinho, *A Carreira da Índia*, pp. 65, 101–102, 135–6, 160–69.

[2] Valignano describes the dangers and horrors of the outward voyage and the unpreparedness of the passengers, at times in much the same language, in his *Historia*, pp. 11–16.

meats, ship's biscuit, wine, oil, and water to be loaded on to the ships, and these are for the use of all those in good health; for those who are ill they order medicines, ointments, precious liquors, and physic of many different kinds to be prepared, and there are also doctors, surgeons, and other officials, who go to great pains to procure everything. These and all others are under the authority of captains of noble birth, who assume command of the whole ship.

Lino: I have no doubt at all that those kings go to great expense over this, but I would like to know whether all the passengers subsist on those common provisions.

Michael: On these ships there are three classes of people, namely passengers, soldiers, and those charged with some royal office. All of these are assigned daily a fixed portion of the royal provisions, a portion judged sufficient to support life; thus no one in the ship, even if he has omitted to provide for himself, need face any serious problem concerning the nourishment of the body. The nobler among them, however, have private quarters assigned to them by the king, with their own furnishings and food, and with these they live in luxury. Among the passengers too there are various classes, and some of the wealthier among them live in style and have abundant and varied food. There is besides the diligent industry of religious men, and especially of the fathers of the Society of Jesus, who come to the help of those who are ill or in want, and give a wonderful example of charity and mercy.[1]

But to come back to our voyage: on 27 May we had journeyed south and were now fourteen degrees away from the equinoctial line when the wind became so strong that it snapped the yards up on the mainmast in two, and the sail as well as part of the tackle fell into the sea. It is difficult to describe just how heavy and dangerous was the work which followed, some severing the tackle, lest the ship should go down with it, others gathering up the sail, others again clearing the decks of the fragments of the yards. When this danger was past the concern of the captain of the ship was to have new yards made by joining other pieces of wood together, but this did not mean no more sailing in the meantime, and the voyage continued, with the smaller sails unfurled and filled with wind, until on the third day the remade yards were hoisted up on high, and having traversed a great distance in our voyage, on 7 July we passed the longed for Cape of Good Hope, and another promontory not far beyond it, which is called the Cape of the Needles,[2] because at that place, for some obscure celestial reason, the navigational needles do not indicate the North so precisely, but deviate a little from it. In those waters the sea was so calm and tranquil that all were able to relax and enjoy themselves fishing for a variety of fish. We too were only too happy to do the same; with line and hook we caught more than seventy fish, and were happy indeed to have fresh fish to eat.

---

[1] The king only provided provisions for the crew and soldiers. Passengers had to bring their own provisions. Those who did not were refused passage. The king's provisions were distributed by the officers and the temptation to short measure was considerable. Surplus food could be sold off on arrival at Goa or purloined by the officers. The seamen and soldiers were responsible for cooking their own meals, unlike English and Dutch ships which had their own cooks. Those who fell sick soon became malnourished and vulnerable no matter the provision of medicine chests. Moreover, there was usually only a barber-surgeon on board rather than a qualified physician. See Linschoten, *Voyage*, I, pp. 13–14; Pyrard, *Voyage*, pp. 703–4; Boxer, *Tragic History*, pp. 15–16; *idem*, 'The Carreira da Índia', p. 51; Godinho, 'The Carreira da India', pp. 43–6.

[2] Cape Agulhas or Cabo das Agulhas, where the direction of true north and magnetic north coincide.

But the greatest calm is wont to be followed by storm and tempest, and so it was soon afterwards with us. The wind blew very strong, and we were forced to lower the mainsail and use only the topsails; but then the force of that wind increased more and more, and the sea heaved and boiled much more violently, so that the ship was thrown hither and thither by the waves, could hold its course only with extreme difficulty, and could barely be governed by the helm. New ropes were attached to the sails, and some thirty men were directed to secure them at various points, to prevent the wind getting hold of the sail in the wrong way and causing the ship to veer broadside on. There was no let up in the force of the wind, but we kept to our course, and were carried past the region which takes its name from the day of the Lord's birth,[1] since it was on that day that it was first discovered. The violence of the sea and the waves during that storm was so great, and the ship sank deep into the sea so often, that everyone was expecting shipwreck, or at least the loss of tackle; but God, who so often proved Himself our most sure guide in the voyage, preserved the ship unharmed. Time after time we had been face to face with death, but then the force of the wind began gradually to slacken, and there followed a calm which lasted no less than eighteen days.

After that we passed the rocks known as the rocks of Judea,[2] famous because of the many ships which have been wrecked there, most notably the one named *Santiago*, in which we sailed to Lisbon. That ship, as I shall shortly be explaining, tragically ran on to those rocks while on its way back to India the previous year. Now once again there was a wind, and on 9 of August we reckoned that we were almost at Mozambique, but then realized that we had been carried, not without great danger, towards the infamous Shallows of Sofala.[3] We knew this because of the turbidity and muddiness of the waters, but also by checking the depth, which was fourteen fathoms, and finally, from the aspect of the land. The ship was in very grave danger, because the water was moving with great force towards various bays on that shoreline, which offered no sort of harbour, and especially because the ship was being dragged into shallower and shallower water, so that we could make out the trees (on the shore), and from their fires we knew there were savage men there, called Kaffirs, hoping for booty if the ship was wrecked. With the sails lowered, the anchors cast, and two ropes broken by the violence of the seas, the ship was being forced gradually closer to the shore and to the shallow water. The depth was now a mere six fathoms, and we had only the one main rope, on which, humanly speaking, the hopes of all depended. Meanwhile the fears of all were increased by the total darkness of the night, the storm force of the wind, and the heavy rain which was falling, all of which appeared before us as the very image of hell itself. But I hardly need to tell you here of the weeping and wailing of the wretched passengers; it was so grievous, so mournful, that all

---

[1] Terra do Natal or Natal.

[2] Baixos da Judía or Shallows of Judea, infamous to Portuguese and other European seafarers, an atoll in the middle of the Mozambique Channel. Now called Bassas da Índia. The instructions issued to John Saris, commander of the English East India Company's Eighth Voyage which reached Japan in 1613, specifically mentioned that the Bassas were to be avoided on the voyage. See Linschoten, *Voyage*, I, p. 22; Boxer, *Tragic History*, p. 62 n. 1; Satow, *Voyage of Captain John Saris*, p. xi; Pyrard, *Voyage*, pp. 708, 949–50.

[3] The Portuguese seized control of Sofala in 1505 and murdered its ruler. It had been a major outlet for gold exports from the interior since the 7th century and much frequented by Arab traders. It was one of the places thought to be the fabled Ophir from whence Solomon procured his gold. Other locations identified as Ophir included the Golden Chersonese and Cipangu.

appeared to be facing imminent and most certain death. It was not merely a question of weeping, however, but also of the prayers, vows, and confession of sins, by which all testified to the peril confronting them. But the hope of coming out of it safe and sound always sustained me, and I am confident that each of my companions could say the same of himself.

Mancio: I can indeed say the same of myself. The danger was such that Father Nuno Rodrigues, concerned that we should be prepared for whatever might happen, was exhorting us, with words of the utmost kindness, to fortitude of mind, as the time and circumstances required, and most of the passengers were convinced that shipwreck was absolutely certain. But I was always confident, relying on Divine Providence, that nothing was going to prevent us from bringing our embassy to its completion, and rendering our account of it to our own people.

Michael: That being the state of things, with all preparing in utter despondency for shipwreck and death, the captain and the pilot[1] dedicated the anchor which was cast into the sea and our last rope with it to the Blessed Virgin, promising that they would pay the price of both (which could be reckoned to be about 500 ducats) if the ship got away safe and unharmed from those sandbanks. This vow seems to have been acceptable to the Blessed Virgin, for all that night the rope, despite all the strain the water put on it, held the ship firm, till day broke bright and serene, and hope of survival began to rise among those on board, who were persuading themselves that, even if the ship broke up, they would be able to reach the shore and make their way by land to Sofala, or else to construct a raft from the wreckage of the ship. These considerations occupied them that whole day, but meanwhile the danger was by no means at an end. The following day a light breeze began to blow from the land, and it looked as if this might take us back into deeper waters; but when the sails were up that gentle wind died away again, and we were back with the anchor down in the sea, still in grave danger. The fathers, therefore, and the passengers, decided to entrust themselves more earnestly to God for deliverance. To put this resolution into practice with more ardent piety prayers of entreaty arose all over the ship, and an altar was set up, and that most precious thorn, from the crown placed on the head of Christ our Saviour, was brought out and displayed in the place of greatest honour. During these entreaties people were greatly moved, especially when a certain priest was preaching, and invoking God with many prayers to come to our aid. With his words, but also with the tears which he could not hold back, he impelled all present to a storm of tears, so that the whole ship resounded to the wailing and crying of those who wept, and, understandably, the minds of all were turned from their sins to the true love of God.

With these signs of piety and religion the Divinity now favoured us, and on 13 August, to us a most joyful day, the wind began to blow more strongly from the land, so that all were greatly gladdened, and with the anchors raised, the sails hoisted, and God in His great kindness assisting us, we moved into deep water, sailing away from those shallow and dangerous places. On the following day, when we were moving along with the sea calmer and our minds too much more tranquil, we encountered a small Portuguese ship,

---

[1] Original edition (p. 369) gives *procurator* or manager. Pilot, the individual responsible for navigation on the *Carreira da Índia*, is meant.

which was now heading for Mozambique after spending some time for purposes of trade in the Sofala region, and which came over to us at speed. Meetings of this kind, especially after a long and dangerous voyage, are usually very joyous occasions, and for us too it was no small pleasure to be able to speak with Portuguese and tell them of all we had been through. But there was also among them a sailor who had other and longer tales to tell to us, and who gave us an account of the lamentable shipwreck of the *Santiago*.[1]

Leo: Do please recount for us, Michael, the story of that so tragic event.

Michael: I am told that there has been a whole book written about it,[2] which we shall soon have in our hands, Leo, so I'll be as brief as possible in telling you about it, passing on to you what I heard from that sailor. The ship had been driven near the area where the shallows of Judea are, but was proceeding under full sail, the master being convinced that the shallows were already behind them. In the middle of the night, when all the passengers were sound asleep, the ship suddenly ran on a rock with such violence that the keel was immediately completely torn off and left stuck there in the sandbank. The rest of the ship was shifted some little distance away by the force of wind and sea, but then was again dashed against some other rocks, and all aboard, wide awake now, found themselves aground on those sandbanks about which they had thought they need no longer concern themselves. Words cannot convey the terror which afflicted all of them that night, seeing the ship broken on those jutting rocks, and knowing that almost no hope of survival remained to them. All took refuge, therefore, in the higher parts of the prow and the poop, the parts commonly referred to as the castles, and that whole night was passed in weeping, wailing, confession of sins, and the other things usual in those who despair of life.

Things were no less confused when the day dawned, with everyone looking for some possible means of survival. The captain had the smaller skiff (which is usually the more manoeuvrable one on the ships) lowered, and taking a few others with him he began to look for any possible way to release the passengers from what seemed certain death, but when he realized that there was none, and that he would not be able to save those who were shipwrecked, he gave the order to abandon ship and to head for some port, even though it could not be less than 130 leagues distant. The larger skiff disengaged itself in an extraordinary fashion from the middle of the ship, which was broken, and some of the passengers occupied it in great haste. It was badly smashed, but they mended it as best they could, and fitted sixty men and also the priests into it; any more and the skiff itself

---

[1] The gruesome loss of the *Santiago* in 1585, with 450 on board of whom fewer than 90 survived, was shocking and a major scandal at the time, principally because of the conduct of the pilot Gaspar Gonçalves, who survived the wreck but whose arrogant behaviour was blamed for causing it. Both he and the captain, Fernão de Mendoça (later commander of the *Madre de Deus* in 1592, the ship carrying one of the printed copies of *De Missione* which was seized by the English), were among those who abandoned the ship and the other survivors to their fate. For accounts of the shipwreck and the travails of the survivors, who were dispersed into three groups, see *Documenta Indica*, XIV, pp. 363–411; Brito, *História Trágico-Marítima*, II, pp. 57–126; Linschoten, *Voyage*, II, pp. 176–83; Duffy, *Shipwreck & Empire*, pp. 115–20. A consignment of silk and gold presented by the archbishop of Évora for use in churches in Japan was also lost in the wreck (*Cartas*, II, f. 231v). For a discussion of Brito's sources for this work and his use of additional Jesuit material which reflects well on the Jesuits on board, see Boxer, 'An Introduction to the *História Trágico-Marítima*', pp. 61–4.

[2] See below, p. 407 n. 1.

would most certainly have capsized. Who could find words to evoke the piteous state of mind of those who had to suffer the indignity of being left behind, or of those others who had put some planks together in the hope of reaching some port, and were then drowned by the force of the waves? But neither was there any escape from the utmost hardship and calamity for those who were carried in one or other of the skiffs, for they were brought to the shores of the Kaffirs, savage and barbarous men, and there captured, stripped naked, and consigned to wretched slavery. Among them were six of the Society, of whom four, along with many others, because of hunger, want, or sickness, perished; or rather, they gained eternal life. The other two are still alive, and can testify now to the horror and grief of shipwreck and slavery. One of them is the Reverend Father Pedro Martins, who holds the position of Provincial Superior of the Society here in the Orient, and from him too we heard many things about this terrible tragedy.[1]

Leo: The shipwreck was, indeed, an occasion for the profoundest mourning. Your account of it makes clear to me how great and undying should be your thanks to God for snatching you from such dangers and restoring you alive to your own country.

Michael: We should indeed give thanks as long as we live. But to come back to our voyage: after taking our leave of that small merchant ship we arrived on 18 August at some islands which are called Angoche,[2] and which did cause us great anguish. These islands are thirty leagues away from Mozambique, and we were hoping to be able to cover that distance the following day, and had our minds on the port, but then we were forced back by the power of the waves till we were eighty leagues short of Mozambique. The pilot knew this, and he again ordered the anchor cast, and then he checked the

---

[1] The Jesuits' opinion of the people of this region was prejudiced by the loss of one of their own, Gonçalo de Silveira, who had been appointed provincial of India in 1556 but who was temperamentally unsuited for this responsibility. He was relieved of his position in 1559 and his successor sent him to south-east Africa to found a mission there. He achieved some success in the Mutapa kingdom but aroused the hostility of Islamic traders, who suggested to the king that Silveira was preparing a fifth column of converts to prepare the kingdom for an eventual Portuguese conquest. He was murdered on the orders of the king. The mission was a failure. Before his posting to Japan, Fróis wrote a detailed account of the incident which shocked the Jesuit community in India. See *Documenta Indica*, IV, pp. 376–81, 415, 455–6, 430, 503–4; ibid., V, pp. 333–49; Pearson, *Port Cities and Intruders*, pp. 90–91, 93. Among the passengers on the *Santiago*, were four Jesuit fathers, two *irmão* and two mendicants, one of whom was Tomás Pinto, who was proceeding to Goa to become Inquisitor and who survived the disaster. While some of the local people did attack those who made it ashore from the *Santiago*, others were friendly and helpful. The survivors were not consigned to slavery, although some were held captive temporarily, clearly in the expectation of a ransom, which was in fact paid for the release of some of the captives. See *Documenta Indica*, XIV, pp. 381–2, 390–91, 403, 406; Brito, *História Tragico-Marítima*, III, pp. 88, 91, 97. Martins went on to become bishop of Japan. In Goa he wrote an account of the wreck, dated 9 December 1586, a manuscript copy of which still exists (published in *Documenta Indica*, XIV, pp. 363–411). The account was later published in Italian (various editions, 1588, one of which is presumably the 'whole book' that Michael expects 'we shall soon have in our hands') and in French (1588 and subsequent editions), although it was not Brito's Jesuit source. See *Documenta Indica*, XIV, p. 364; Boxer, 'An Introduction to the *História Tragico-Marítima*', p. 64.

[2] A series of small islets stretching from the mouth of the Angoche river to Moma. At this time, thanks to internal strife, the sultanate of Angoche, located at the mouth of the river, was falling under Portuguese control, under which it remained until its trading value proved worthless. In 1709 the Portuguese leased it to an Indian. See Newitt, 'Early History of the Sultanate of Angoche', pp. 397–406.

depth of the water and found it to be thirty fathoms. When the sails were hoisted the next day the power of the waves soon shifted us to shallows of only six fathoms, and there we were again in grave danger of death. The smaller skiff was lowered immediately, so that all the area round about could be checked. They found that the ship would be able to make its way between an island and the mainland, through a channel eight fathoms in depth. God was invoked, we had to proceed by that way, and with the divine assistance it turned out well. A few days were taken up with this progress and regress, but on 29 August we sailed, and with a favourable wind we reached Mozambique on Sunday 31 August, and were filled with an extraordinary joy. We sent them a signal with a short burst from our two guns, and we were conducted safely into the harbour by a pilot sent from the fort who was an expert on the sandbank which is there at the entrance to Mozambique.[1]

We were three days in that harbour, days spent in restoring the body and in preparing provisions for the rest of the journey. But when we left we found that the power of the water forcing us back was great, and that because the opportune time was already past the wind was light and blew only very spasmodically, so we were forced to turn back to the same port and to wait for the appropriate time the next year. We disembarked, therefore, and determined to fulfil the vows which we had made on the sandbanks. We made our way in bare feet and with prayers of thanksgiving to the church of the Blessed Virgin of the Fortress.[2] There the sacred rites were performed, we received the Holy Eucharist, and we gave the due thanks to God. The captain-general of the fortress, the most noble Jorge de Meneses,[3] welcomed us most warmly, and throughout the time we spent in Mozambique he treated us splendidly and with honour.

Lino: Explain to us, Michael, who the inhabitants are of the fort of Mozambique.

Michael: The principal inhabitants are Portuguese, for the indigenous people are Kaffirs, who inhabit all that area of Africa, a primitive race of men, as I said earlier, rude and wild. Not far from the fort there is a very broad river, along which is the road to the celebrated kingdom of Manomotapa,[4] which is in the hinterland, and has supplies of gold in abundance. Between it and the mouth of the river there are now a number of

---

[1] The island of Mozambique, off the northern Mozambique coast, frequented by Arab traders and first visited by da Gama on his return voyage in 1498. The Portuguese seized control in 1506 and, despite its reputation for disease and its notoriety for the high mortality among transiting ships' crews, it remained the principal stopping-off point of the *Carreira da Índia* for outward voyages, although, as the text indicates, some voyages were made directly from Lisbon to Goa without stopping. A good pilot was essential to enter the port safely. See Pyrard, *Voyage*, pp. 733–4; Boxer, 'Carreira da Índia', pp. 56–8; Diffie and Winius, *Foundations*, pp. 344–5; Godinho, 'Carreira da India', pp. 29–30.

[2] Nossa Senhora de Baluarte, just outside the Fortaleza de São Sebastião.

[3] Jorge Telo de Meneses, captain-general of Mozambique 1586–9. Original edition (p. 372) gives '*praefectus*'.

[4] The Mutapa (Port. 'Manomotapa') state, or empire as it was called by the Portuguese, which thrived c. 1250–1629, was located between the Zambezi and Limpopo rivers in present-day Zimbawe and Mozambique. Mutapa was the successor state of Great Zimbabwe, famous for its stone ruins. In fact the empire was a tributary state under the ostensible control of the Mutapa ruler. The Portuguese were disappointed not to find their own El Dorado in these parts. There were no easily mined shafts of gold and the gold that the Portuguese were able to export contributed but a small fraction of global output. See Oliver and Atmore, *Medieval Africa*, pp. 199–205; Pearson, *Port Cities and Intruders*, pp. 23, 49–51, 65, 99, 120, 138–9.

Portuguese colonies, namely Tete, Sena, and others, in which the Portuguese are busy exchanging various things for gold, and they bring many of these barbarous men to true piety, after instructing them in Christian doctrine.[1]

We stayed in that fort of Mozambique until March of the following year, 1587, in considerable unease of both body and mind, because of the insalubrious weather and the great heat, but also because we knew how very concerned the Father Visitor would be about us, all the other ships having docked in the port of Goa on the same day, leaving the Father suffering sorely, longing for our ship to come. It added greatly to our distress when the ship which had brought us to Mozambique left again for Lisbon.[2] For when another ship, the *São Lourenço*, was on its way to Lisbon, before it could round the Cape of Good Hope it was damaged by so many storms and winds that those on board were forced to sail back to Mozambique in that same ship, which was so knocked about and broken up by the force of the sea that in the port of Mozambique it fell completely to pieces. So the captain of our ship and the captain of that other ship arranged that the merchandise which was being transported in the *São Lourenço* should be transferred to our ship, which would then take off for Lisbon. And with that one decision our hopes of reaching India quickly collapsed. The right time to sail for India was March or August, but the ship which remained there in Mozambique was not fit to sail, and there was very considerable uncertainty as to whether Portuguese ships could be expected to arrive in August, especially as it sometimes happens that they bypass Mozambique and head directly for India, because however much they may wish to, they cannot reach the port of Mozambique.

We had given up all hope of human things, but we relied on help from heaven, and God did not fail us, but on the contrary provided help of a remarkable kind. The Father Visitor in Goa was ceaselessly thinking of us and concerned for us, and in his solicitude he arranged with the viceroy that, since there was a real possibility that we had been wintering at Mozambique, a long, swift, light ship, what they commonly refer to as a galliot, should be sent as rapidly as possible to Mozambique (the ship was, as it happened, the property of the captain-general of Mozambique), with a letter to the governor instructing him to see to it that if we were there in the fort we should be taken to India in that same ship as soon as might be; the entire cost of providing for us throughout the winter and of everything necessary for the voyage would be supplied without stint from the royal treasury. And in this the benevolence towards us of the Father Visitor, of which we already had so many proofs, was evident to us and indubitable. He was not certain that we were staying in Mozambique, and was kept in suspense since he did not know what had become of us. Nevertheless he set about persuading the viceroy to have that ship dispatched so that we could sail in March, with full provisions and support for us provided free. Imagine the joy we felt when that ship reached the harbour of Mozambique, with a letter from the Father Visitor and many other things sent to us; and this joy was increased by the liberal and munificent attitude towards us of the captain-general, who, even without the instruction of the viceroy, had most readily offered us that same ship, if it

---

[1] They also enslaved many. Some of the slaves feature in Japanese painted screens depicting the southern barbarians.

[2] The boys wrote to Aquaviva from Mozambique informing him of their plight; the letters are no longer extant (*Documenta Indica*, XIV, p. 697).

should arrive, and had also given us 2,400 ducats from his own resources, because the king's treasury in that fortress was exhausted.[1]

We therefore prepared ourselves with all diligence for the journey to India; at the beginning of March 1587 we were ready, so on 15 March we gladly boarded the ship, and taking our leave most cordially of the captain-general, to whom we were greatly indebted, we headed for India. We were barely clear of the harbour, however, when we ran into danger graver than any already described. A furious wind got up so suddenly that there was no chance to take down the sails, the ship was leaning perilously to one side, and, with the wind getting into the sails at that angle and a great deal of water coming in through the gangways, we came close to being swamped and sinking. All attention was then concentrated on cutting the tackle so as to get the yards down as quickly as possible, and that did work, so that the ship, which had by that time been leaning over to one side at a very dangerous angle, almost sinking, for a quarter of an hour, began to come reluctantly out of the water and to right itself. Since the force of the wind also gradually eased off we were set free from that terrible fear and danger.

So we moved on and once again we crossed the equinoctial line; for in this India voyage the sailors cross twice the circle which astrologers call the equinoctial: once when they have gone 1,000 leagues from the port of Lisbon, and that is when they leave the Plough behind and begin to see the southern skies; then again about 400 leagues out from the port of Mozambique, for in that region the southern sky disappears from sight and the Plough begins to appear again. After passing the equinoctial line, then, and being carried over into the northern region, we found the sea beset with adverse winds, and the very great force of the waters drove us willy-nilly to the shores of the kingdom of Melinde, so that we came close to the city of Mogadishu in that kingdom, and were within no more than half a league of it.[2] We stayed twelve days in that area, and replenished our supply of food and provisions, but we found the long delay and the wind forcing us towards the shore very tiresome. On our way we met a small Portuguese vessel, which the captain[3] of the coast of Melinde was sending to the viceroy of India with the glad news of a victory

---

[1] Ibid., p. 425.

[2] There is some confusion here. Malinde (present-day Malindi in Kenya) is below the Equator and Mogadishu is, of course, above; nor was Mogadishu controlled by Malindi. It was an independent state. In a letter to Aquaviva, Jorge Loyola also mentions stopping close to Mogadishu and taking on provisions (*Documenta Indica*, XIV, pp. 743–4). It seems that the ship passed by Malindi and, once over the Equator, was driven close to land just off Mogadishu. The 'Victory over the Saracens' refers to the struggle between the Portuguese and the Turkish naval commander and privateer, Mir Ali Bey, who entered east African waters in 1585 and made alliances with rulers opposed to the Portuguese. Amongst other achievements, he seized a Portuguese vessel carrying a cargo valued at 150,000 cruzados. In January 1587 the Portuguese exacted revenge and attacked the African cities which had supported the Turks. In 1589 Ali Bey returned and established a fortress at Mombasa to challenge the Portuguese. The Portuguese counter-attacked with a war fleet despatched from Goa, sacked Mombasa, which was also besieged from the landward side by the Zimba, a man-eating tribe. Mir Ali Bey and some of his men surrendered to the Portuguese and were later released. Subsequently, the Portuguese failed to capture Mogadishu but they conquered Mombasa in 1593. See Boxer and Azevedo, *Fortaleza de Jesus*, pp. 21–6; Godinho, *Os descobrimentos*, 1, pp. 206--7; Pearson, *Port Cities and Intruders*, pp. 46, 70, 138, 152; Casale, 'Global Politics in the 1580s', *passim*; idem, *Ottoman Age of Exploration*, pp. 156, 158, 164–76. Chinese had visited the east coast of Africa from perhaps as early as the 8th century and Zheng He's fifth voyage (1417–19) reached Malindi. See Mills, *Ma Huan*, p. 13; Needham, *Science and Civilisation*, IV: 3, pp. 490, 495, 498. On the folk memory of the Chinese in east Africa, see Camões, *Os Lusíadas*, V: 77.

[3] Original edition (p. 375) gives '*praefectus*'.

over the Saracens. They had caused considerable damage to the Portuguese, and had now paid the proper penalty, with their towns put to fire and the sword. We gave a letter for the Father Visitor to the captain of that ship, as it was likely to (and did) reach the port of Goa much sooner than we would, and the fathers of the Society and the whole city of Goa rejoiced when they were told that we were coming.[1]

There were various other problems on the journey, however: there was a great calm on the sea for full fifteen days, with not a breath of wind from any direction, and this caused us no little anxiety, for we knew that winter time was approaching in India, when all the ports are closed because of the violence of the storms, so we were desperate to get the ship to any port, even one far from Goa, since it was already mid-May, when the rain and the storms begin in India. For that reason solemn prayers were recited by the Fathers on the solemn day dedicated to the Holy Spirit, and with ardent devotion they besought God to come to our help; the thorn which I mentioned above was also brought out and exposed with due ceremony for the passengers. God in His great mercy listened to the prayers of his own, for we had decided to let the wind take the sails and carry us to any port, whether in India or not, and had been sailing for eight days in the direction of land when at last, on 28 May, with eager eyes and inexpressible joy, we spied some rocks, commonly known as the Burnt Rocks,[2] which are twelve leagues distant from Goa. We regarded this as a great favour which God had done for us, for at that time Goa is normally already beset with dangerous rains and storms. So on the following day we entered the harbour of Goa in great gladness and amid general rejoicing; the hearts of all the Fathers, and of all the citizens of Goa, were not only released from fear and solicitude for our well-being, but also filled with a marvellous happiness. There was always someone on the watch, on the orders of the Father Visitor, for the arrival of our ship, and when word reached the same Father, from the person who was then the lookout, he came as quickly as possible, with many other Fathers, to greet us, and treating us with the love which a most fond father shows to the sons he has so longed to see, and finding us safe and sound, embraced us and led us into the city, to which we were introduced to the great applause of all, and the exultation of the viceroy of India himself.

The viceroy of India at that time was the most illustrious Duarte de Meneses,[3] born in Portugal of the most distinguished Meneses family, the head of which is the marquess of Vila Real, of whom the viceroy was a close relative. But he was distinguished not only in his noble lineage, but also for his knowledge of military matters and for his great virtue.

---

[1] On Valignano's concern for the boys' safety, especially after news of the fate of the *Santiago* reached Goa, and his stoical reactions, see *Documenta Indica*, XIV, pp. 424–5, 667, 697. The rejoicing on the receipt of the news of the boys' safety was not universal. The Florentine merchant, Filippo Sassetti, also mentioned the uncertainty about the boys, noting, tartly, that they had become too much puffed up on account of their favourable reception in Europe, but that the Almighty had humbled them by delaying them in Mozambique. The source of his information is unknown but in remarks that follow Sassetti makes it clear that he was no admirer of what he saw as the Jesuits' narrow focus on making converts in China and Japan and was critical of them for not supplying or sharing information that might be helpful to merchants such as himself (Bramanti, *Filippo Sassetti*, p. 536). See also *Documenta Indica*, XIV, p. 778, the annual letter from Goa for 1586–7; and ibid., p. 697, Valignano to Aquaviva, which state that the boys eventual arrival was greeted with joy by all the citizenry.

[2] The Vengurla Rocks or Burnt Islands (Ilhéos Queimados), to the north of Goa, a landmark for navigators making for Goa.

[3] 1537–88, viceroy of India 1584–8, great-grandson of João de Meneses, the first count of Tarouca. He fought at the battle of Ksar el-Kabir in 1578. De Meneses appointed Valignano as his ambassador to Hideyoshi, easing the way for the visitor's return to Japan. His relative was Miguel Luís de Meneses.

Figure 12. Autographs of Mancio Itō, Michael Chijiwa, Martin Hara, Julian Nakaura and Diogo de Mesquita, in Yūki Ryōgo, *Roma wo mita: Tenshō shonen shisetsu*, Nagasaki, 1982, frontispiece.
By permission of the Nihon Nijūroku Seijin Kinenkan, Nagasaki Insatsu KK and the Archivum Romanum Societatis Iesu, Rome.

Adorned with these qualities he was, before being sent by the king to India, governor of the fort of Tangier in Africa, and given command, by the most illustrious King Sebastião, of the whole army which the same king took to Africa some years ago; and then, finally, after the African disaster, he was made governor of the Algarve. His conduct of these offices was so admirable that King Philip entrusted the whole of India to him, in which province he gave such an account of himself that when his three-year tenure of the post was finished the king prolonged it for a further two years, and promoted him, with a letter according him the highest praise, to the title of Count of Tarouca, which his forebears had held. But human life is subject to various and unexpected mishaps, and before that letter reached India he was snatched from our midst by a premature death, mourned throughout India, and his soul, as we believe, taken to a better dwelling-place.

At that time, then, he was still alive, and he not only received us with great kindness, and for our entertainment ordered unusually elaborate equestrian games to be staged, but also ordered the 2,000 ducats owed by us to Jorge de Meneses, the captain-general of the fortress of Mozambique, to whom he was related, to be repaid; and he gave us four splendid horses, for our use in Goa, according to the king's written instructions, and provided us with a monthly allowance of 150 ducats for as long as we were in Goa (we were there a full eleven months). We were greatly in his debt also for many other favours, and obliged to him besides for the provisions supplied in abundance for the voyage to Japan, and for this splendid present which he is sending through us as a gift to the *kampaku*.[1]

Leo: You are right indeed to say that you are much indebted to that prince, whose great generosity you experienced. But come, tell us what you did in Goa for such a long time, since you stayed there almost a year.

Michael: We were not short of the accustomed exercises in arts and letters, and of agreeable and proper pastimes, and with these it seemed to us that the time passed quickly; for the most part we stayed in a very pleasant country house of the Fathers, but sometimes we spent time at other country places, and in the pleasure of hunting in the fields at Salsete.[2]

---

[1] On the viceroy's generosity and care for the welfare of the boys, see *Documenta Indica*, XIV, pp. 653, 669, 698. The 'splendid gift' refers to the horses (see above, p. 339 n. 1). For the other gifts presented to Hideyoshi, see below, p. 414 n. 2.

[2] During the stay in Goa, Valignano had a chance to reflect on the embassy which, as he wrote to the Jesuit assistant in Portugal, Manuel Rodrigues, had gone better than he could have wished. In this letter and in another to the archbishop of Évora he addressed criticism that had been made privately about the boys' apparent ingratitude for the hospitality they had received and their alleged indifference to what they had seen. To Valignano, such comments, a harbinger of criticism that would be made by the mendicants, undermined the favourable reviews he had been writing about Japan and the Japanese. To Rodrigues, he wrote that, while he was aware that the boys had given some people in Europe the impression that they were indifferent to what they saw, so much so that some came to believe them uncouth, the boys were, on the contrary, greatly impressed by what they had seen. As a measure of how great the abilities of the Japanese in general were, he noted that they had written diaries about their trip which were better produced than comparable ones written by Europeans. To the archbishop, he wrote that the boys would be able to do much good in Japan where they would be using their own language while in Europe they were greatly inhibited in expressing themselves because they 'did not know the language'. In a letter to Philip II, Valignano was quite upbeat, expressing his belief that what the boys would have to say about Christianity in Europe on their return to Japan would carry much weight and give 'very great authority to our affairs' because they were themselves Japanese and persons of quality. See *Cartas*, II, f. 232v; *Documenta Indica*, XIV, pp. 654, 669–70. From Goa too, Mancio wrote to Sixtus V informing him of their safe

Mancio: Among the worthy literary exercises we can include the one which our Martin undertook. He gave a graceful and elegant oration, a polished composition in the Latin tongue, before the Father Visitor and others at the Goa college, on the subject of our voyage and its fruits.

Martin: My dear Mancio, I suspect you are trying to add savour to this lengthy colloquium with the salt of these witticisms, and to make fun of the insipidity of my discourse.

Julian: Mancio would never do any such thing; for your oration, Martin, gave such satisfaction that it was immediately printed, and it is manifest testimony to your accomplishment as a speaker.[1]

Michael: Indeed. But let us bring this long colloquium to an end. At the end of our time in Goa we were very glad to receive letters sent from here the previous year to the Father Visitor in India, letters which reported to the Father how many and how great were the victories which Quambaquundono had won over his enemies, and how rapidly and successfully he had unified the kingdom of Japan under his jurisdiction and had assumed the pre-eminent position. They reported, besides, the favour with which he always treated the fathers and all the Christians, ceding nothing to Nobunaga in this regard, and therefore urged the Father Visitor not only always to be mindful of these benefits, but also to ask the viceroy to send a legation and some form of remuneration, so as in some way to bring back an expression of our gratitude. The Father agreed with this recommendation, and the viceroy, with the benevolence which he always showed towards the Society, gave him all he asked for. From the viceroy he received those extremely valuable gifts together with a letter to present to Quambaquundono and the commission entrusted to us.[2] When all these arrangements had been made we left the port of Goa on

---

arrival and thanking him for his many kindnesses (ARSI, Jap.Sin 33, ff. 46–7). The letter is in Mesquita's hand but with Mancio's autograph and a note in his hand '*Desculatur humiliter vestra sanctitatis Pedes*'.

[1] The oration was made on 4 June and was published the following year as *Oratio habita a Fara D. Martino Iaponio*, Goa, 1588. It is considered to be the first book printed on the press brought from Europe for use in Japan. During the envoys' sojourn in Europe, Jorge Loyola and Constantino Dourado had studied matrices and printing, skills which they later put to good use (Laures, *Kirishitan Bunko*, pp. 21, 29–30). The oration is printed in Schurhammer, 'Uma obra raríssima impressa em Goa no ano 1588: A "Oratio habita a Fara D. Martino"', *Orientalia*, pp. 743–53, esp. pp. 749–53.

[2] In February 1587 Hideyoshi had succeeded in pacifying Kyushu and was very much the master of Japan. Until then the Jesuits had enjoyed what seemed to be good relations with him. The mission in Japan appeared to be flourishing. Reports indicated 15,000 baptisms in Bungo alone between 1585 and 1586. See *Cartas*, II, f. 233v; *Documenta Indica*, XIV, p. 669; Kleiser, 'P. Alexander Valignanis Gesandtschaftsreise nach Japan', p. 78. However, this rosy scenario was about to change. The idea of sending an emissary from the viceroy to Hideyoshi had been mooted previously by Gaspar Coelho. De Meneses supported the idea and an impressive letter addressed to the *kampaku* (preserved in Myoho-in Temple in Kyoto) was drawn up and dated April 1587, although this was subsequently altered to 1588, thanking him for allowing the Jesuits to preach and teach the law for the saving of men's souls. As a token of thanks the viceroy sent as presents: two broadswords, two suits of armour, two stallions with trappings (as mentioned above, one died before reaching Japan), a machete, two pairs of gilded tapestries and a field tent. The presents finally given differed slightly and included some of the items given to the boys in Europe. See ARSI, Jap.Sin 11: Ia, f. 46; Fróis, *História de Japam*, V, p. 299; Cooper, *Rodrigues the Interpreter*, pp. 75, 77–8 and plate 4 for a photographic reproduction of de Meneses's letter.

22 April 1588, in a very well-equipped ship, in which a nobleman named Aires Gonçalves de Miranda[1] arranged excellent quarters for all of us, and he gave the ship into our hands and put it at our disposal. Together with us and the Father Visitor seventeen other fathers and brothers boarded the ship, all heading for Japan and filled with zeal.

Mancio: You could add, Michael, that those who stayed behind were equally eager to come, and were convinced that those who did come with us had been blessed with all the good fortune they could wish for.

Martin: One of the many things which surprised me in the course of our voyage was certainly that zeal which was manifest in all the European fathers. As Michael has already said on another occasion, although they have available every kind of convenience, their ardour to convert all peoples to the Christian religion is such that they are astonishingly eager to leave their own country and hasten here to us.

Leo: After we accepted the Christian religion we were indeed much struck by the love the fathers showed to us, but as yet we had no deep understanding of their things; now, however, as a result of your colloquia and the many things you have spoken of, we have been able to see into them and consider them much more thoroughly, and I have come to hope that even the pagans themselves may escape from the darkness of their false superstitions and acknowledge the light of the truth.

Lino: It will be so, without doubt; for the truth, which until now has been unknown and suppressed, is beginning to emerge, and to be set out openly before the eyes of all.

Miguel: I hope that will happen more and more as time goes on; but now let us bring this colloquium to its close. After we left the port of Goa we took seventy days on the journey to Malacca, even though it often takes no more than thirty days. We spent twelve days there in the college of the Society, experiencing great kindness from all the fathers, and then boarded the same ship again, and in twenty-nine days reached the port of Macao in the kingdom of China.[2] On that journey we were in very considerable danger, for we ran in among the rocks and shallows of an island which the Malays call Pulo Sisio,[3] but eventually, through the goodness of God, we managed to get out. Now it remains for us to treat of the kingdom of China, and we shall deal with that subject in another colloquium.

---

[1] A fidalgo who had been in Asia since the 1550s. He made two voyages, as captain-major, from Macao to Nagasaki in 1583 and 1584. He had married and lived in Thane, now part of Mumbai and was a great friend and supporter of the Jesuits. He was still alive in 1620. See *Documenta Indica*, XIV, p. 699; Boxer, *Great Ship*, pp. 45–6.

[2] The chronology is confused here. The journey from Goa to Malacca took no more than 60 days. See *Documenta Indica*, XIV, p. 899, letter of Oliverio Toscanello (who sailed with Valignano from Goa) to Aquaviva, Malacca 22 June 1588. Valignano and his party reached Macao on 28 July 1588 (Schütte, *Valignano's Mission Principles*, I: 1, p. xviii).

[3] Pulo Cecir, off the coast of southern Vietnam. John Saris mentions the island on his return voyage to Bantam from Japan (Satow, *Voyage of Captain John Saris*, p. 188) and it is included in Linschoten's map of the eastern seas (ibid., facing p. 192).

COLLOQUIUM XXXIII

The kingdom of China, its customs and administration[1]

Lino: We have heard and do hear daily so many things about the kingdom of China that what we want you to tell us, Michael, is the truth about these things, rather than a great number of them. And if you know anything other than what reaches us in the form of persistent rumours we shall be only too pleased to hear about that as well.

Michael: Because the fame of this most celebrated country is spread so wide among us, I shall keep to the truth received from the fathers of the Society who are in China, and bring some order to the multiplicity and variety of the reports about it. In the first place, then, it is known that the kingdom of China is the furthest inclined to the east of all the parts of the main continent, although if you include islands then Japan and Manila are further to the east. We can regard an island commonly known as Hainan as the first boundary of China to the west, and it is sited at a point from which the North Star appears at nineteen degrees above the horizon.[2] The mainland adjoining this island juts out to the east, especially at the promontory of the city called Nimpo,[3] but then soon bends north and stretches out over an immense distance, to a point from which the inhabitants view the North Star at an elevation of fifty degrees and perhaps more; and from this it is easy to appreciate how very extensive is the latitude (to use the language of the astronomers) of this kingdom, for it runs directly north for about five hundred and forty

---

[1] A loose translation of this colloquium was published by Hakluyt under the title 'An excellent treatise of the kingdome of China, and of the estate and government thereof: Printed in Latine at Macao a citie of the Portugals in China, An. Dom. 1590. and written Dialogue-wise. The speakers are Linius, Leo, and Michael' (Hakluyt, *Principal Navigations*, VI, pp. 348–77). For a modern edition of Hakluyt's version, with Portuguese translation, see Loureiro, *Um tratado*. Valignano had become interested in China after first arriving in India. He had read Gaspar de la Cruz's *Tractado* and wrote about the celestial empire in the *Sumario de la India* (1580), in which he said that entering China appeared to be like entering 'a new world' but one which resembled Europe, and, at greater length, in the *Historia*. See *Documenta Indica*, XIII, pp. 195–201 esp. pp. 196–7; Valignano, *Historia*, pp. 214–70; *Sumario*, pp. 34*, 41*. De la Cruz's *Tractado* is printed in Boxer, *South China*, pp. 45–239. After returning to Macao in August 1588, Valignano's opinion of Japan soured while, obversely, his assessment of China, and its missionary potential, rose. In a letter to Aquaviva of 10 November 1588, he compared Japan highly unfavourably with China. He praised China's governance, institutions and cultural attributes and denigrated those of Japan. See ARSI, Jap.Sin 11: I, f. 7v, printed in Álvarez-Taladriz, 'El proyecto de embajada', p. 92. The causes of this revision of his previous high regard for Japan were, primarily, the news from Japan of Hideyoshi's order (issued the previous year) expelling the missionaries and, more immediately, what appeared to be the promising beginnings of the Jesuit mission to China. Valignano's new-found enthusiasm for the celestial empire and his anxiety about the future of the mission in Japan explain the apparent extraneity of this colloquium to *De Missione*.

[2] The latitude of Hainan is 18°–20°N.

[3] Ningbo (Wade-Giles, Ningpo, also previously known as Liampo), Zhejiang province.

leagues.¹ With regard to its length measured from east to west, that has not yet been sufficiently investigated for it to be possible to give it in degrees of longitude. It is certain, however, that on the chart which the Chinese use to illustrate the shape of their kingdom the latitude is somewhat greater than the longitude.

This kingdom, therefore, is, beyond any argument, the largest in the whole world. Many other kings, indeed, have extended their jurisdiction far further and more widely, and possess many kingdoms in places far apart from each other, but there is none in possession of one single kingdom so large, so vast, as that enjoyed by the most puissant king of China. But when we come to income and taxes, it is certain that the same king has these in the greatest and most opulent abundance, because of the great fertility of the land, the immense reach of his jurisdiction, and the extraordinary severity with which these taxes are exacted; for a royal tax is imposed on these people not only on fields, houses, and the transportation of merchandise, but on every single family. Furthermore, there is hardly any ruler with the right to levy his own taxes within his own jurisdiction, for everything belongs to the king. In Europe, however, exactly the opposite is very often the case, as we have said many times already.²

This vast region contains fifteen provinces, each of which could stand as a kingdom of no small size. Six of these are maritime provinces, namely (and I use the actual Chinese names) Guangdong, Fujian, Zhejiang, Nanjing, Shandong, Beijing; the others are inland, and are Jiangxi, Huguang,³ Henan, Shanxi, Shaanxi, Sichuan, Guizhou, Yunnan, Guangxi. Two out of all of these provinces are called royal courts, namely Beijing, i.e. northern court, and Nanjing, i.e. southern court.⁴ Formerly the kings normally resided in the southern court, but later, because of the frequent bellicose insurrections raised by the Tartars they were obliged to fix their seat in the other most northerly province.⁵ As a result it is those borders of the kingdom which boast by far the greater number of defences, instruments of war, and military garrison posts.

---

¹ Cf. Valignano's previous conjectures (*Historia*, pp. 215–16) which are revised here in the light of Ricci's more recent observations. Ricci, using an astrolabe during his travels and Chinese lunar records, was more confident about determining latitude, less so about longitude which was, of course, finally calculated accurately only in the 18th century. Rodrigues's later, and better-informed, estimate of the size of China is more accurate. The northern border of the Ming empire was at 42ºN. See Ricci, *China in the Sixteenth Century*, p. 8; Cooper, *João Rodrigues's Account*, p. 27.

² In fact the tax burden fell mainly on the poor as the gentry tried to avoid paying taxes. During the 1580s the Ming ran budget deficits. Bankruptcy was avoided because the Ming emperors were able to tap their private silver reserves. Tottering on the verge of bankruptcy, the Chinese state was not at all blessed with 'opulent abundance'. See Miller, *State Versus Gentry*, pp. 37–9, 44–6, 66–7; *Cambridge History of China Volume 8*, ch. 2, *passim*.

³ Partitioned under the Qing dynasty into Hubei and Hunan provinces.

⁴ There were in fact 13 provinces or *sheng*. The areas around Beijing and Nanjing were the Northern Metropolitan region and the Southern Metropolitan Region, the latter used in deference to the memory of the first Ming emperor, Hongwu, who established his capital there. See Hucker, 'Governmental Organization', pp. 5–8; *Cambridge History of China Volume 8*, pp. 10–13.

⁵ Nanjing became the capital for the first time in 229 CE and at various times thereafter. Under the Mongol Yuan dynasty (1271–1368), the capital was located in present-day Beijing, and called Dadu in Chinese and Khān Bāliq or Cambaluc by the Mongols, the name by which it was known to Marco Polo and Ibn Baṭṭūṭa. See *Travels of Marco Polo*, I, pp. 374–8; Gibb and Beckingham, *Travels of Ibn Baṭṭūṭa*, IV, pp. 906–7. In 1356, before the official establishment of the Ming dynasty, Hongwu made Nanjing the capital but in 1420 the imperial court moved to Beijing and from 1421 imperial documents give Beijing as the official capital of the empire (*Cambridge History of China Volume 7*, p. 241).

Leo: I have heard that those military defences include an astonishing wall with which the Chinese hold back and repel the Tartars who would invade their borders.

Michael: This wall of which you have heard fully deserves to be wondered at, for it runs the full length of the three northern provinces, Shaanxi, Shanxi, and Beijing, and is said to stretch for almost three hundred leagues, and nevertheless is so constructed that there is no obstruction to the courses of the rivers, the channels of which are defended with massive bridges and fortifications.[1] It seems probable, however, that it is so constructed that only the lower parts and possible routes through are obstructed by it, and in the spaces in between the mountains themselves with their natural defences block off all access to the enemy.

Lino: Tell us, Michael, is the kingdom very densely populated with Chinese, as we have often heard?

Michael: Yes, Lino, it is, very densely indeed, as we learned from the fathers of the Society; for though they have seen many European provinces known for the great numbers of their inhabitants, they are more than a little impressed by how populous the kingdom of China is. And these multitudes are not spread just anywhere, casually, in the countryside, but excellently distributed in their towns and famous cities, and among the Chinese these centres of population are of several different kinds. Some which are the principal cities are known as *fu*.[2] Other lesser ones are called *cheu*.[3] Those of a third kind are *hien*,[4] which are walled towns, but whose populations are not accorded the distinction of being cities. Besides these three there are two more types of minor town, which are villages and military garrisons. An example of the first kind is that most celebrated city, near the port of Macao, which is called Coancheufu by the Chinese,[5] and by the Portuguese is commonly known as Canton, which really is the word for the province rather than the city. To the third kind belongs a town even closer to the port of Macao, which the Portuguese call Ansàm and the Chinese Hiansanhien.[6] So all the provinces have major cities named *fu* and lesser cities called *cheu*, and the other towns are subject to both of these.

There is besides in each province a principal city, usually known as the metropolis, in which the chief magistrates are placed, one of these cities being the one I just mentioned, which is the head of the whole province called Guangdong. The number of major cities in the whole country is more than a hundred and fifty, and of minor cities about the same

---

[1] This is an early reference to the Great Wall of China. The wall (in fact a series of walls) is largely a Ming creation built to stem Mongol attacks on the north of the empire. Construction, using brick and stone rather than earth and mud, reached its peak under the Ming in the second half of the 16th century and the beginning of the 17th. For another reference to the wall, see Waldron, *Great Wall of China*, pp. 24–6, 140–69; Valignano, *Historia*, p. 216.

[2] Prefecture (Cooper, *João Rodrigues's Account*, pp. 31–2; *Cambridge History of China Volume 8*, pp. 15, 89). The term was also used in Japan. Rodrigues equated it with the *kuni* which made up the 66 'kingdoms' of Japan (*Arte da lingoa de Iapam*, f. 210).

[3] *Chou*, sub-prefecture.

[4] *Hsien*, county.

[5] Canton or Guangzhou (Cantonese: Gwong zau). The Portuguese also called it Cantão and Cantam.

[6] Hsiang-shan Hsien meaning Hsiang-shan, now Zhongshan.

or perhaps larger. Walled towns which are not yet ranked as cities number more than eleven hundred and twenty, and the number of villages and military garrisons is almost beyond reckoning.[1] Apart from these centres of population it would be almost impossible to say how many are the houses or villas in the countryside, for in this kingdom there are hardly any deserted or uninhabited places to be found.

And the number of people, and of whole families, living on the sea, on the rivers, and in boats, is so great that the Europeans themselves are astonished, and there are even a considerable number who have persuaded themselves (although this is going too far) that the water is no less inhabited by them than the land.[2] Nor was it entirely without visible evidence that they were brought to this opinion, for the entire Chinese kingdom is irrigated by rivers in every part, and a good part of it is occupied by the waters, and there are very large numbers of boats everywhere, so much so that it was not difficult to believe that the number of those inhabiting the land was equalled by the number living in boats. Nevertheless, this does not make sense without some degree of exaggeration, given that the cities are stuffed full of citizens and the fields teeming with peasants.[3]

Leo: This abundance of people of which you speak is truly extraordinary, and leads me to suppose that the land must be fertile, the climate wholesome, and the whole kingdom tranquil.

Michael: You do well, indeed, Leo, to bring up those three points, the fertility of the land, the wholesomeness of the climate, and the tranquillity of the whole kingdom, for they are so well matched that it is difficult to judge which of the three takes precedence in that kingdom. This is why it has been a widespread and popular opinion among the Portuguese that the Chinese kingdom has never been afflicted with the three most dreaded scourges of mankind, namely war, famine, and pestilence.[4] But this is a popular rather than a true opinion, for there have been very great civil wars among them, and this is recorded in many reliable historical accounts, and even in our own times people in this province or that have been afflicted with pestilence, or a contagious illness, and have suffered from famine. Nevertheless there is no doubt that the kingdom of China is indeed particularly notable for those three points.

---

[1] According to official records, under the Ming there were 159 prefectures, 240 sub-prefectures and 1,144 counties. See Hucker, 'Governmental Organization of the Ming Dynasty', p. 7; *Cambridge History of China Volume 8*, pp. 14–15.

[2] As is the case with Europe, population figures are unreliable. The Ming carried out official censuses but by the 16th century these were unreliable. Estimates for the population c. 1600 vary from 150–289 million people, See *Cambridge History of China Volume 8*, pp. 14, 436–9; Brook, *Confusions of Pleasure*, pp. 27–8, 95, 162. See also Valignano, *Historia*, p. 220, for Valignano's figure of 70,250,000. The best estimate for the population of Japan c. 1600 is 10 million, plus or minus 2 million. See Hayami and Kitō, 'Demography and Living Standards', pp. 217–18.

[3] Cf. Valignano, *Historia*, pp. 217–18.

[4] Natural disasters, causing famine and disease and other problems, were common occurrences under rulers who claimed to enjoy the mandate of heaven. A series of devastating famines and disease spread across central and southern China over the decade 1538–48 (Brook, *Confusions of Pleasure*, pp. 18–19, 103–7, 190–92). China's civil wars are associated with dynastic change. There had, of course, been foreign invasions before and conflict with the Jurchens in the north, already underway, would lead to the eventual overthrow of the Ming dynasty in 1644.

To take first the wholesomeness of the climate, the fathers of the Society themselves testify that so great is the number of the aged and those advanced in years that there is hardly any other country where more people can be found living to an infirm old age. And yet they do not use as many drugs and medicaments, nor the multiplicity of different ways of curing the body which we saw used in Europe. Among them there is no bleeding; all their curing is done with fasting, infusions of herbs, and mild potions, as here in Japan.[1] But in this, each region to its own custom. The fertility of the land is very great indeed, and is without doubt the greatest among all the countries of the Orient, but it does not compare with the abundance of Europe, of which I have already spoken copiously and at length.[2] It is very famous, however, because there is no other region in the Orient which has so many kinds of merchandise and from which so many things for sale are exported. Since this country is extremely large, and all of it is accessible on navigable rivers, so that things can easily be transported from one province to another, the Portuguese find so much merchandise in such variety and abundance in one and the same city,[3] which is perhaps the greatest emporium of the kingdom of China, that they easily persuade themselves that that one region is the most productive of merchandise. This, however, is to be understood only of the regions of the Orient, although there are certain items of merchandise in which the land of China is more abundant than all other countries.

This region, then, produces in the first place many metals, first among these in excellence and in abundance being gold, and there are so many gold bars transported from the kingdom of China to India and here to Japan that I have heard that in this present year two thousand of what the Portuguese commonly call loaves of gold,[4] made from solid gold, have been brought here to trade with, and one gold loaf is worth about a hundred ducats. Accordingly there are very many things beautifully embellished with gold in the kingdom of China, such as beds, tables, pictures, images, and the litters which the more elegant ladies use. And it is not only these loaves of gold that the Portuguese buy, but also a great quantity of gold thread and gold leaf, for the Chinese know how to draw out the gold into thread and film. There is also great store of silver, and clear proof of this, to say nothing of other evidence for it, is the fact that every year, with just the purchases made by the Portuguese merchants, forty million sesterces[5] are brought into the city of Canton (to use the name by which it is commonly known), and hardly anything is taken out from the kingdom of China, for it is certain that the Chinese people, having in abundance almost all the things that they need, are neither inquisitive about nor desirous of

---

[1] The same point was made by Mesquita in an unpublished account of Japan prepared while he was in Rome (ARSI, Jap.Sin 22, f. 96v).

[2] Cf. Valignano, *Historia*, p. 220, where the Visitor describes China as 'the most fertile and supplied kingdom of all in the world'.

[3] Canton or Cantam as it is called in the original edition.

[4] Gold and silver ingots were called *pães* or loaves in Macao. They were not uniform but had different values ranging from one to twenty cruzados. The Portuguese differentiated between 'common gold' and 'fine gold', the latter commanding a higher price in Japan (Boxer, *Great Ship*, pp. 179, 338–9).

[5] I.e.1 million ducats. The English merchant Ralph Fitch, who travelled overland to Goa in the 1580s, estimated that the Portuguese exported 600,000 cruzados worth of silver from Japan and 200,000 cruzados from India to China to finance their China trade (Hakluyt, *Principal Navigations*, V, p. 498). In 1585, Fróis estimated Portuguese exports of silver from Japan to be worth 500,000 cruzados (*Cartas*, II, f. 129). For a modern estimate, see von Glahn, *Fountain of Fortune*, pp. 129–41.

merchandise from any other country. I say nothing of the veins of silver, which are to be found in great numbers, though they are very cautious about digging the silver out from them, for the king fears that it could be an occasion for many to be tempted to cupidity and thieving. And indeed the silver which is in use is for the most part very pure, purged of all dross, and therefore they are very diligent in coining it.[1] What should I say of their iron, copper, lead, tin, and other metals, as well as quicksilver? There is a great supply of all of these in the kingdom of China, and they are exported from it to various other countries. Add to these the wondrous multitude of pearls extracted from oysters cleverly caught by fishermen at the island of Hainan, which make a considerable contribution to the royal revenues.

But let us come now to the silk or bombycine fleece, of which there is a very great abundance in the kingdom of China, so that even as the farmers busy themselves ploughing the land and sowing the rice, so also the women employ a good part of their time cultivating the silkworms and carding and weaving the silk.[2] Hence every year the king and queen make a public appearance, and in a solemn rite the one touches a plough and the other a mulberry tree, on the leaves of which the silkworms feed, and with this sign they urge men and women to their set task and labour; and apart from this no one other than the principal magistrates can have sight of the king for the whole of the rest of the year.[3] The abundance of this silken fleece is so great that the three ships normally sailing from India to the port of Macao, with at least one coming to us here every year, are laden mostly with a cargo of silk, and it is not only used in India but also exported all the way to Portugal. And it is not only the silk itself that is brought from China, but also many different kinds of things made of silk, for the art of weaving flourishes greatly among the Chinese, and their weavers are very similar to the weavers of Europe.[4]

---

[1] This is a curious and misleading reading of the economic relationship between China and the outside world. At this time China was the largest importer of silver in the world and a major exporter of gold. Most of the silver came from Japan mainly in exchange for Chinese silk. This exchange was the *raison d'être* of Portugal's Macao–Nagasaki trade. The Portuguese were the beneficiaries because China had broken official relations with Japan after 1557 and the Ming authorities banned Chinese voyages to Japan and Japanese ones to China. Silver also entered China from the New World via Manila, seized by the Spanish in 1571, and from Europe and India by sea and overland. China's own silver mines were near exhaustion and, thanks to the Single Whip reforms, taxes had to be paid in silver, thus increasing demand for the precious metal. The volume of this demand and the ability of non-Chinese producers and suppliers to satisfy it expanded intercontinental trade and, as the first stage of globalization, marks the beginning of the modern world economy. The literature on this subject is extensive. For an overview, see Findlay and Rourke, *Power and Plenty*, pp. 212–26.

[2] A 1543 gazetteer from Fujian noted this gender-based division of labour (*Cambridge History of China Volume 8*, p. 688).

[3] Traditionally, the emperor had ploughed a furrow of soil to honour the spirit of agriculture while the empress had, at a different altar, performed a sacrifice to honour the spirit of sericulture. See *Cambridge History of China Volume 7*, p. 116; *Cambridge History of China Volume 8*, p. 859.

[4] While Japan had had a domestic silk-producing industry since the 15th century, located in the Nishijin district of Kyoto, domestic output could not satisfy demand especially from the second half of the 16th century. The Portuguese profited handsomely from this situation by carrying Chinese silk to Japan until the early 17th century when they faced competition (Souza, *Survival of Empire*, pp. 46–7, 52–3). Chinese silk was exported to Portugal but the quantity was far less than that available from Persia and India (Boyajian, *Portuguese Trade in Asia*, p. 47). It should be emphasized that cotton was far more important to the Ming economy than silk (*Cambridge History of China Volume 8*, p. 502).

The region of China also produces in great abundance costly perfumes, especially cinnamon (although it does not compare with the cinnamon of Ceylon)[1] and musk, and their musk is excellent. The name comes from the animal designated by the same name, an animal similar to a beaver or *fiber ponticus*. When parts of this animal are crushed and putrefy they give off a most sweet odour, highly esteemed by the Portuguese, who commonly refer to those pieces as *papos*, because they are believed to be the gullets of fowls. Great quantities of these are transported to India and to us.[2] There is besides an almost incredible amount of cotton, from which is made a great variety of clothing very similar to linen, which we ourselves very frequently use, and which is distributed to various regions in many ships.

And now let us speak of that pliable clay material, which is white and must be judged the best in all the world, from which all kinds of vessels are beautifully fashioned. I say it is the best in the world for three reasons, its cleanness, its beauty, and its strength. Other matter can be found, indeed, more splendid and more costly, but none so free of impurities and so durable. I mention this because glass is indeed clean, but it is easily smashed and broken. This kind of material is not produced all over China but just in one of the fifteen provinces, namely Jiangxi, where a great number of artificers are continuously employed in that work; and they make not only smaller vessels such as plates, saucers, salt-cellars, jugs, and other similar things, but also certain huge jars, very finely wrought. These, however, because it is difficult to transport them, are not normally taken out of the country, but are in use only within it, and especially at the royal court. The variety of the painting which is laid on the material, with a certain colour, while it is still fresh, greatly contributes to its beauty, and gold is also added, so that these vessels are beautifully decorated. These vessels are wonderfully prized by the Portuguese, for they transport them, with considerable difficulty, not only here to us and to India, but also to various provinces of Europe.[3]

To the merchandise mentioned so far may be added many and various plants the roots of which are salutary for the body and suitable for making into medicines, and these are carried to our Japanese islands and to many other islands. Included among these is that wood known (by synecdoche) as Chinese wood, and it is excellent for expelling from the body those humours from which contagious sicknesses are wont to arise.[4] Also to be

---

[1] Original edition (p. 384) gives '*cinnamoni*'. This is confusing. The wood of the camphor tree or *Cinnamomum camphora*, native to, amongst other places, south-east China, is meant. The spice cinnamon is native to Ceylon not China. Cf. Hakluyt's translation which says that 'China aboundeth with most costlie spices & odours, and especially with cynamom (albeit not comparable to the cynamom of Zeilan) with camphire also & muske' (*Principal Navigations*, VI, p. 355). There is no mention of spices in the original.

[2] The same inaccurate information on the provenance of musk is contained in Gaspar da Cruz's account of China (Boxer, *South China*, pp. 76–7).

[3] By this time Jingdezhen in Jiangxi province was the main centre of production of porcelain especially for export. Chinese porcelain had been prized in Europe since the latter part of the 15th century; some 40,000–60,000 pieces arrived in Lisbon annually from the 1530s. Several unsuccessful attempts were made to manufacture it in Europe before the famous breakthrough at Meissen in 1708. See *Cambridge History of China Volume 8*, pp. 380, 393–4, 677.

[4] *Radix Chinae*, the tuber of various species of *smilax*. In China and Japan it was used as a treatment for syphilis and in Europe for more general medicinal purposes. The Portuguese carried it to Japan where it sold at double its cost. See *Hobson-Jobson*, p. 199; Boxer, *Great Ship*, p. 180.

mentioned are the canes from which sugar is made, for there is plenty of very good sugar in China, and great quantities of it are brought here and taken to India by the Portuguese.[1]

What I have been saying so far refers only to merchandise, in which this kingdom is most beneficial not only to itself but also to many others. As for those products which pertain to common food and sustenance throughout the year, they are almost too many to count, although in three which are held in high regard in Europe, namely those from which corn, wine, and oil are made, China is not very fruitful; indeed the Chinese do not even know the name of the olive tree, from the fruit of which oil is made, and the same can be said of the vine. The province of Beijing is not entirely devoid of wine, although I do not know whether it is made there or brought in from somewhere else, and there is an abundance of many other quite agreeable liquors which take the place of proper wine. With regard to corn, wheat does grow in all the provinces, but is not used as much as rice. Thus in these two necessities of life, corn and wine, China is comparable to Japan.

Leo: You have been speaking of the fertility of the kingdom of China, Michael, and I have often heard that it is also very agreeable, and in particular have had the same impression from maps drawn by the Chinese themselves.

Michael: For the most part the reality does match the picture. Those who have seen the inner parts of China report that it is a most pleasant country,[2] with plenty of trees, an abundance of different crops, and finally a wonderful variety of rivers, by which China is irrigated like a garden, some of these rivers flowing naturally, while others are directed to various places by art and industry. I shall treat now of the tranquillity of China, but only after saying something about the customs of the Chinese. They are a people of excellent ability in all the arts, holding very tenaciously to their own ways, and with little interest in the ways of others. They all use the same kind of clothes, but with some difference between the clothing of the magistrates and of the people. They all take care to grow the hair on their heads and, like women, comb it diligently right down to the ground. They then tie it up and cover it with a net, and on top of that wear various caps in accordance with their age and condition. The language of all the provinces seems formerly to have been the same, but because of the various ways of pronouncing it great changes took place and it divided into many different languages in the many provinces. Among the magistrates, however, and in their judgements, one and the same language is still used throughout the whole kingdom, and, as I said, the speech of each province differs greatly from this language. The people are very obedient to the king and to the magistrates, and this is the principal base on which is founded the tranquillity of China. The supreme magistrates give total obedience to the will of the king, the lower magistrates to the will of the higher, the people to the will of the lower magistrates, and each of them accommodates himself and his way of life accordingly, and it is wonderful to see how equably all of them live, and how well the laws which are promulgated are observed. This will be explained more at length later on, when we deal with government.

---

[1] Sugar was still a luxury commodity in Japan at this time and, although sugar cane had been introduced, there was as yet no indigenous sugar production (Mazumadar, *Sugar and Society*, p. 80). On increased sugar consumption in China at this time, see ibid., pp. 38–43.

[2] Europeans had seen only a very small part of China, mainly the south-east, at this time.

Lino: Now, Michael, tell us about the industriousness of the people there, for we have always been told that they are very hardworking.

Michael: Their industry can be seen especially in those arts which are performed with the hands, and in these the Chinese surpass most of the nations of the Orient. There is such a large number of artificers working ingeniously in gold, silver, and all sorts of other metal materials, likewise in stone, wood, and the other materials useful to man, that the city streets, full of their shops and their workmanship, are a wonderful sight to see. There are besides many artists using either the brush or the needle (the latter are sometimes called embroiderers), and others again who skilfully weave gold thread into linen or cotton cloth. The Portuguese are diligent in transporting various works of all these artists to India. They also display their industry in the making of cannon and gunpowder, with which they make many ingenious fireworks. They have in addition the art of printing, even though their letters are almost infinite in number and extremely difficult, and they cut the types for this in wood or in bronze, and with remarkable facility they daily produce a multitude of books.[1] To these less noble arts may be added two more, namely the nautical and the military, both of which were formerly practised most diligently by the Chinese, for, as we already said in the third colloquium, the Chinese reached as far as India with their ships, and conquered part of it, but later there was a change of policy and a decision was taken to stay within their own boundaries, to avoid having the power of the kingdom dispersed over too many places and thus spread too thinly.[2]

But even within their own borders, as I said, there was at one time a great conflagration of war, war among the Chinese themselves, and also against the Tartar king, who invaded their kingdom and held sway over it for a long time, both himself and those who came after him. When the Tartar kings were driven out, however, and their family completely destroyed, Chinese power once again seemed to lift its head and stand tall, and for two hundred years now it has enjoyed complete peace, and right up to the present the posterity of the king who expelled the Tartars hold the position of king and merit the utmost praise.[3] And although the Chinese, especially those living to the south of the province of Beijing, have been considerably softened by a life of ease and tranquillity, they would still prove themselves able soldiers if to their natural talent they but added practice and exercise. And this can be seen in those who are continually at war with the ferocious Tartar peoples.[4] But anyway the concern for military discipline in the whole of China is such that there is not a city or town without its garrison of soldiers, with commandants and

---

[1] In Macao, Valignano experimented with Chinese wood-block printing with a view to using it in Japan but found it unsatisfactory. See Laures, *Kirishitan Bunko*, p. 26; Moran, *Japanese and the Jesuits*, p. 155. The production of printed books in Japan was greatly influenced by Korean metallic movable type, especially following Hideyoshi's invasion and occupation of Korea, during which type from the Korean Printing House was taken back to Japan. The influence of the Jesuit printing press in Japan was minimal. See Kornicki, *Book in Japan*, pp. 125–35.

[2] The early Ming overseas voyages ceased after 1433.

[3] The Mongols were finally driven from Beijing in 1368 by Zhu Yuanzhang, who became the first Ming emperor, Hongwu.

[4] During the Ming dynasty the Mongol threat subsided. By the 1580s a new threat appeared from the Jurchen people of north-eastern China who would eventually unite with non-Jurchen people and transform themselves into the Manchu who swept away the Ming in 1644. The Manchu established the final Chinese imperial dynasty, the Qing, which survived until 1911. See *Cambridge History of China Volume 8*, pp. 224–41, 258–71.

captains all in order, all of whom in all the provinces are subject to the supreme commander of the army. He is called the *chumpin*,[1] but he is himself subject to the *tutan*, or viceroy.[2]

We come now to the art which the Chinese profess above all others, and which can justly be called 'letters'. Although it is widely held that many of the noble arts are cultivated by the Chinese, especially both branches of philosophy, treating respectively of the things of nature and of morals, and that they have universities where these arts are taught, this opinion should be considered to be widespread rather than true.[3] I shall explain, however, what it is that has given rise to this idea. In the first place, then, the Chinese do profess the art of letters, they study it with great diligence, and spend a very long time on it, indeed almost their entire lives. In every city and town, therefore, and even in small villages, there are teachers paid to instruct children in letters; and since the number of characters is infinite, as indeed is the case with us too in our more usual style of writing, from their infancy and tender years[4] children have books put in their hands. Those, however, who are judged to have little talent for the task have the books taken away again, and apply themselves to trade or to the manual arts, but the others devote themselves to letters so earnestly that they are wonderfully well-versed in their principal books, and can readily tell you how many characters there are on any page, and where this or that character is to be found on that page.

For greater progress in these letters, three degrees are usually assigned in the principal disciplines, as indeed they are for men in Europe, namely low, medium, and high. Graduates of the first degree are known as *siusai*,[5] of the second *quiugin*,[6] and of the third *chinzu*.[7] Now in each city or walled town there is a public building called the school, and all those from any private college or school who wish to obtain the first degree assemble there. They have to amplify a proposition put to them by a magistrate, and in each city the first degree is awarded to those who discourse more elegantly and more correctly. Those who aspire to the second degree are tested only in the metropolis or principal city of the province, where those who have the first degree gather every third year, and there, in one and the same building they make a speech dealing with another more difficult proposition, and undergo a more difficult examination. The press of men is usually very great, so much so that we have been very reliably informed that last year, in

---

[1] *Tsung-ping* or *tsung-ping kuan*, 'regional commander' (Hucker, *Dictionary*, p. 533; *Cambridge History of China Volume 8*, p. 102).

[2] *Tu-t'ang*, 'executive censors', a collective name for executive officials of the Censorate as well as Grand Coordinators and supreme commanders or viceroys (*tsung-tu*) who were dispatched from Beijing on an ad hoc basis to the provinces with extensive powers (Hucker, *Dictionary*, pp. 534, 543; *Cambridge History of China Volume 8*, pp. 79–81, 87, 186). See also Boxer, *South China*, pp. 6, 153–4; Cooper, *João Rodrigues's Account*, p. 37.

[3] In his *Historia* (p. 239), Valignano commented that Chinese knowledge ('*sciencias*') was imperfect in relation to ours ('*las nuestras*') and appeared to be at the level the Ancients had attained before Aristotle and before they were illuminated with the light of Christian doctrine.

[4] Original edition (p. 387) '*tenerisque unguiculis*', used by Cicero in *Ad familiares*, I: 6: '*a teneris, ut Graeci dicunt, unguiculis*'. The usage is proverbial. See Burnett, 'Humanism and the Jesuit Mission', p. 469 n. 86.

[5] *Hsiu-ts'ai*, 'cultivated' or 'budding talents', those deemed academically qualified to proceed to the provincial examinations in the series of examinations for appointment in the civil service (*Cambridge History of China Volume 8*, p. 36).

[6] *Chü-jen*, 'elevated' or 'recommended man', a provincial graduate (ibid., p. 37).

[7] *Chin-shih* 'presented scholar', a metropolitan graduate (ibid., p. 38).

the principal city commonly known as Canton, many of the huge multitude that converged for those public ceremonies were trampled underfoot and crushed to death at the outer entrance. Afterwards those that strive for the highest degree undergo an extremely demanding examination which is held only at the royal court. This too takes place every third year and, as you might expect, in the year following that in which the successful candidates for the second degree in each province have been announced. A predetermined number from each province is exalted to that supreme status, which is held in such honour by the king that the three, who emerge highest of all, drink from a cup proffered *honoris causa* by the king's own hand, and are graced with other distinctions. From this order (of candidates attaining to the third degree) come the principal magistrates. After a short period of training in the laws of the kingdom and the norms of urbanity they take up their various offices.[1]

This does not mean, however, that the Chinese totally lack other arts. With regard to the philosophy which treats of conduct, the books which they always have in their hands in order to study letters are full of precepts about this, pronouncements so grave and so subtle that for men lacking the light of faith they leave nothing to be desired. There are also books treating of the nature of things, but in this matter it must be supposed that their books are just as full of errors as ours are. Others can also be found dealing with herbs and medicaments, and others again with military matters. Neither can I here omit to mention that some Chinese (though few and far between) have a great knowledge of astronomy, allowing them to commit to writing and publish, correctly and properly set out, the day in every month when the new moon is to appear. Eclipses of the sun and moon are also precisely predicted, and whatever knowledge we have about those things is borrowed from them.[2]

Leo: That we freely admit, Michael, for our books dealing with that art are written mostly in Chinese characters. But now tell us about their manner of government, an art in which the Chinese are said to excel.

Michael: That is indeed their principal art, and all their exercises and erudition in letters are directed towards it. Given that the one king has dominion over so many provinces, it is remarkable how all affairs are administered by so many magistrates created by him. Leaving aside those who have jurisdiction in each town and city over the townsmen and citizens, there are three principal magistrates in each province. The first is the one who deals with criminal cases, and he is called *ganchasu*;[3] the second looks after

---

[1] With the exception of the drink proffered 'by the king's own hand', this is an accurate description of the examination system. Whether or not there was such an incident in Canton is unknown, but metropolitan graduates who had successfully passed the *tien-shih* or palace examination, held in the presence of the emperor or a specially appointed substitute, were celebrated and held in the highest esteem (ibid., pp. 37–8). For a full discussion of the examination system and the conditions of service, see ibid., pp. 30–54. For a European eyewitness description of the examination in Chaozhoufu in western Guangdong in 1625, see Girard, *Le Voyage en Chine*, pp. 196–8. See also Ricci's account of the examination system (Ricci, *Fonti Ricciane*, I, pp. 44–50; idem, *China in the Sixteenth Century*, pp. 34–41).

[2] On calendars and eclipses, see Cooper, *João Rodrigues's Account*, pp. 372–4, 397–8.

[3] *An-ch'a shih*, 'surveillance commissioner' (Hucker, *Dictionary*, p. 103; *Cambridge History of China Volume 8*, pp. 96–8).

the royal treasury and is known as *puchinsu*;[1] the third directs military matters, and has the name of *chumpin*, as I said earlier. These three have their seat in the principal city, and the first two of them also have associates of their own order, but inferior in rank, appointed to many cities and towns, and an appeal may be made to them by the governors of towns and mayors of cities, in some of the many different kinds of cases. Nevertheless those three principal magistrates are completely subject to the *tutan* or viceroy that there is in each province. And all these magistrates hold their office for three years, but in such a way that those who are appointed to the governing of each province are not themselves natives of that province but externs, men from another province. This means that the magistrates will be much more unprejudiced and incorrupt in giving their judgements than they would be if they were among their relatives and kinsfolk.

Besides all these people there is an annual magistrate, called *chaien*,[2] whose role it is to inquire into all crimes, but especially the crimes of magistrates, and to punish common crimes; but of the errors of the great magistrates he must advise the king himself. One of this order is sent out from the king's court every year to each province, and he journeys through all the cities and towns there, diligently investigating all crimes, and they inflict the due punishments on those thrown into prison, or, if their guilt is not proved, they release them without punishment. All the magistrates, accordingly, fear investigation by the *chaien*, and are careful to stay within the bounds of their duties.

In addition to all these magistrates there is in both courts, the southern and the northern, a senatorial assembly, to which are referred affairs of greater weight and moment from all provinces, taking into account the nearness or distance of the place in question, and for which various magistracies are created. The arranging and despatching of the most important affairs, however, belongs to the senate of Beijing.[3] Moreover some magistrates are normally appointed each year from each of the provinces to go to the king, and every third year all the governors of all the cities and towns visit him at the same time, and that is when the examination is held for those aspiring to the third degree, with the result that there is at that time an incredible throng of people at the royal court. With this admirable hierarchy of magistrates, subject one to another, the peace which prevails throughout the whole kingdom is such as to be very hard to describe, especially as criminals are punished with flogging after only a brief inquiry, without any long-drawn-out action or litigation.

Nor must we omit to mention that the competition for the various magistracies is open to all, with no account taken of birth, if they are learned in letters and especially if they attain to the third degree as just described. And the obedience of the common people to

---

[1] *Pu-cheng ssu*, 'provincial administration commissioner' (Hucker, *Dictionary*, p. 391; *Cambridge History of China Volume 8*, pp. 87, 185).

[2] *Tu ch'a-yüan*, 'chief investigation (or surveillance) bureau', also known as the Censorate. Early European writers on China transliterated the name of the subsection of this bureau, the Investigation Bureau or *ch'-üan*. to *chaien*, *chāe* or *chaem* and applied it to the officers (Boxer, *South China*, pp. 6, 156).

[3] This account of the imperial government is confusing. Early descriptions of Chinese government picked up the importance of metropolitan–provincial relations and the division of institutions between central and provincial administration. There was, of course, no such thing as a senate. What is meant here is the *nei-ko* or 'grand secretariat', a body of individuals whose functions included the delicate task of mediating between the emperor and the civil service (Hucker, *Dictionary*, pp. 346–7; *Cambridge History of China Volume 8*, pp. 76–9, 82). As mentioned above, the central government offices ascribed to Nanjing were symbolic. For full descriptions of the Ming government and judiciary, see ibid., chs 1 and 3 *passim*.

the magistrates is beyond description, as is the pomp and splendour with which the magistrates appear in public. For most of them have fifty or sixty guards attending upon them, going ahead of them two by two, some of them bearing halberds, maces, and battle axes, others pulling iron chains, a number of them holding long and very thick rods made from a type of cane, with which criminals are beaten; and there are two who carry a case containing the royal seal proper to each office. There are many others, finally, who have various insignia to display to the people, and in addition they shout from time to time in a terrifying manner so as to strike fear into all the people. Finally come the magistrates, borne on a chair carried by four, six, or eight men, according to their various offices.[1]

Their residences are magnificent, built at the king's expense and adorned with all the furnishings necessary for the performance of their duties, and there they live in elegance and splendour as long as they hold their office. These residences do not have storeys built high one on top of another, for in China as here in Japan such buildings are not for normal habitation, but are built as watchtowers or for relaxation, and for this they are built very high, with eight or nine storeys, or finally as fortifications for the cities. In other respects, however, these residences are very imposing, for they have very pleasant courtyards with an orderly arrangement of trees, and places designated for the administering of justice, and many rooms for their wives and families. And within the doors of these residences there are always a certain number of guards and attendants, who have small lodgings assigned to them on either side, and whenever there are cases being judged they are always at hand ready at the command of the magistrates to beat the prisoners or to extract confession of the truth by torture.[2] These magistrates also have their own special boats for travelling by water. In height and length they are like European galleys, but far inferior to them in speed and in the number of their oarsmen. The oarsmen are positioned outside the doors of these boats which they propel with their oars, and thus the central part of the boats affords ample space for the magistrates to take up their residence, with rooms almost as commodious as in their official residences, together with pantries and kitchens where food is prepared as required.[3]

Leo: All this accords with the reports we have always received about how things are in the kingdom of China. But I would like to know something about how things are arranged with regard to the obtaining of magistracies.

Michael: Your question concerns something which I omitted to mention but which is indeed well worth knowing about. The Chinese have a kind of priority list for promoting men to various magistracies, and for the most part this is arranged by the senate in Beijing. First they are made town judges, then city judges; after that they are chosen to belong either to the order which determines, without appeal, the punishment for crimes, or to the order which concerns itself with the king's treasury. Both of these orders are very honourable, but within both there are many different positions, so they rise from lower

---

[1] For a description and illustration of a mandarin's procession, see Adriano de las Cortes's account in Girard, *Voyage en Chine*, pp. 93–5, 428–9.

[2] For descriptions and illustrations of a mandarin's residence, a tribunal and the judicial punishments they could impose, see ibid., pp. 91–7, 444–57.

[3] De las Cortes gives a more detailed description of the mandarin's boats which he describes as like 'a beautiful floating house' (ibid., pp. 325–7, esp. p. 327).

to higher positions, until they reach the highest, and it is normally from there that an appointment to the post of viceroy is made. But this is not always made in the same province; when they take up their posts the places and provinces are changed. Beyond the office of viceroy they can rise to the senate of Nanjing, and from there to the senate of Beijing. This order of progress in obtaining these magistracies is so carefully observed so that everyone can understand who is a candidate for which office. And when some are to replace others it is done with such diligence that messengers from the royal court are despatched overland, changing horses as required, to reach various provinces almost twenty days distant. And finally, such is the severity in demoting those who do not give a good account of themselves from an honourable post to an inferior one, or even in depriving them altogether of any royal magistracy, that there is nothing that anyone who has been appointed to any office fears more.

More or less the same rules apply to the colonels and commandants of the army, with this one exception, that in this case birth and family do count;[1] for there are many, born of men who in the past have distinguished themselves in war, who are made centurions, tribunes, and colonels as soon as they reached the required age, and later become generals and protectors of whole provinces, but nevertheless they remain, as I said before, subject in all things to the viceroy. All these magistrates, both those who make war arrangements and those who administer justice, have a certain number of attendants assigned to them, who are paid a fixed wage and wear certain badges of their office; and in addition to the ordinary watches, which the soldiers assigned to it keep throughout the night in the citadel after they have closed the gates of the city, wherever there is a magistrate, at home, or in his boat, attendants take good care of him, never relaxing their vigil, and from time to time striking a brass cymbal.[2]

Lino: You have spoken about the magistrates, Michael. Tell us now about the king himself, whose name is so greatly celebrated.

Michael: I can say only what I have learned from certain rumours. We have no eyewitnesses of things pertaining to the royal court, for the fathers of the Society have not yet reached Beijing.[3] After they arrive there, God leading them, many things will become known to us through their letters. The king of China, then, is revered throughout his realm with a wonderful veneration, and whenever one of the supreme magistrates speaks to him he addresses him as *van sui*,[4] a name signifying that he wishes him ten thousand years of life. The succession of the kings depends on the royal family, for on the death of his father the kingdom passes to the eldest son born of the king's first and lawful wife. Nor do they abdicate their kingly office as long as they live, as is done here in Japan, but follow the same custom as in Europe. For the greater security of the health and life of the king his younger brothers and others born of concubines do not normally live at the

---

[1] 'Inherited offices' were called *shih-kuan*, 'circulating' ones *liu-kuan* (Hucker, *Dictionary*, pp. 426, 318). On the structure of the officer corps, see *Cambridge History of China Volume 8*, pp. 55–62.

[2] On the Ming military apparatus, see ibid., pp. 54–72.

[3] Ricci finally reached Beijing in 1598.

[4] *Wan-sui-yeh*, 'Lord of Ten Thousand' or 'Myriad years', one of many addresses for the emperor, used on the first day of the Chinese New Year and on the emperor's birthday. See Ricci, *Fonti Ricciane*, I, p. 80; *idem*, *China in the Sixteenth Century*, p. 68; Hucker, *Dictionary*, p 562.

royal court. The king assigns them places of habitation in various provinces, and they are distant provinces, and there they live in all comfort, hardly differing from kings in their accommodation and their income. They have no authority over the people, however, all the administration of the cities in which they live being in the hands of the magistrates. But the magistrates treat the princes with all honour, visiting them twice a month, and greeting them on their knees and with their heads bowed to the ground, but communicating to them nothing about the governing of the people. These are they who can properly be called the nobility and princes of China, for their estates and income are passed on to their posterity, and thus these royal families are continued.[1]

But to return to the king himself, he is extremely observant of the laws and customs of China, is diligent in studying letters in so far as his state requires it, makes himself available daily to the supreme magistrates, and deals with matters concerning the common good of the whole kingdom.[2] He has a palace of wondrous size, which he leaves only very rarely, and whenever he does so twelve carriages appear, all of them almost identical in workmanship and in value, so that it is impossible to know which of them carries the king. With regard to religion for the most part he follows the opinion of the magistrates, attributing supreme power to heaven and earth as parents of all, and offering sacrifice to them with most solemn rites. He has many most sumptuous temples to his ancestors, and offers divine honour to them, but this does not mean that he fails to favour the priests of other sects; on the contrary, he builds temples to their patrons, and assigns most ample revenues to them; and whenever any urgent necessity requires it he enjoins on them fasting and continual prayers. Thus he provides a degree of protection to all the sects of his kingdom, indicates that he wishes to respect all the false religions, and lives with many different kinds of superstition.[3]

Now from all these things that I have said you can readily appreciate that in large part the administration of the kingdom of China accords with the instinct of nature, since those set in positions of authority are not rude and ignorant persons but persons versed in the use and exercise of letters, and in promotion to these magistracies their greatest concern is with prudence, justice, and the other virtues which the Chinese cultivate. And because the way is open for all, without any prejudice, to aspire to these offices, this immense kingdom is preserved in complete peace and tranquillity.

Leo: At this point, Michael, I should like to know something about the kind of good manners which both the ordinary people and the magistrates use towards one another, for

---

[1] On the extended imperial clan, the generous payments it received from the state, the consequent burden on the state coffers and its dispersal away from the imperial capital to forestall intrigue, see Hucker, 'Governmental Organization', pp. 8–10; *Cambridge History of China Volume 8*, pp. 24–8. Under the Ming, non-imperial noble titles were awarded almost exclusively for military service, and were mainly non-inheritable (ibid., pp. 28–9).

[2] The imperial institution was the apex of the power structure under the Ming. It conferred legitimacy and performed essential state rituals, not unlike the imperial institution in Japan. During the formative years of the Jesuit mission, Wanli was the emperor (r. 1573–1620). Previously characterized as indolent, his reputation has been favourably revised in recent years, especially concerning his response to Hideyoshi's invasion of Korea. See Huang, *1587, a Year of no Significance*, esp. pp. 46–7, 95, 100, 110; *Cambridge History of China Volume 8*, pp. 72, 163; Miller, *State versus Gentry*, pp. 78–9; Swope, *Dragon's Head*, *passim*.

[3] On Chinese official religion under the Ming, see *Cambridge History of China Volume 8*, ch. 13 *passim*. After 1540, the emperors did not preside in person over the great sacrifices, including the sacrifice to Heaven, but delegated this responsibility (ibid., pp. 842, 860–61).

one cannot believe that, in a society where there is such concern for the administration of justice, courtesy, that so seemly human attribute, will be wanting.

Michael: That is correct, Leo, for of the five virtues which the Chinese hold in the highest regard courtesy is one, and the others are piety, remembering with gratitude benefits received, honesty in making business arrangements, and prudence in carrying them out.[1] And the Chinese books are full of praise for these virtues. With regard to their courtesy, then, it is very different from ours, but their norms of courtesy can be considered under two main headings, courtesy among equals and among unequals. If the men who meet are of equal rank they stand, bend their backs, and bow their heads towards the ground, and they do this once, twice, or three times. If the meeting is between a superior and an inferior, the one who holds the lower place generally kneels and bows his head right down to the ground. There are remarkably precise rules and prescriptions laying down just how often and when this is to be done, but it would be tedious to list them.

I'll also say something about their piety, especially towards their parents, which is so great that sons dress in sombre mourning and mourn their parents for three whole years, and this custom is punctiliously observed not only by the people but also by all the magistrates. And in order that all may devote themselves wholly to this business the Chinese, in accordance with a most strict law, insist that should their parents die magistrates must immediately resign from their official posts and live privately for a full three years for the due performance of the exequies for their parents, and this requirement is most diligently fulfilled by all, even by the senators of the supreme and royal senate. For even someone especially favoured of the king, someone with particularly important responsibilities in the administration of the kingdom, if he receives news of the death of his parents, of his father or his mother, he immediately returns to his home to perform the proper exequies; and even if the king were to insist on keeping him at his post the king himself would be considered by the people as a violator of the laws and customs of China; and it is recorded that this did once actually happen. There was a king who had a very close relationship with a certain senator and made use of him in his dealings. He was well aware of how much he needed this man, and he wanted to keep him at his post even after the death of his father. But there was another man, well versed in the laws of China, who refused to accept this and rebuked the king severely, accusing him of violation of the laws. The king was enraged, and threatened him with instant death, but when he, not a whit intimidated, persisted in speaking out, the king altered his determination, sent the senator off to mourn for his father, and elevated his admonitor to a higher rank.[2]

Lino: Michael, I appreciate that you are aiming to be brief, now that you are close to finishing these colloquia and weary from the long race you have run, but I would ask you

---

[1] The five virtues appear in Confucius's *Analects* (XVII: 6): courtesy, tolerance, trustworthiness, diligence and kindness.

[2] On Chinese funeral rites, see Ricci, *Fonti Ricciane*, I, pp. 83–5; idem, *China in the Sixteenth Century*, pp. 73–5. Later, the Rites Controversy revolved around the issue of honouring the ancestors. On Jesuit accommodation to Chinese funeral practice, see Brockey, *Journey to the East*, pp. 344–6; Standaert, *Interweaving of Ritual*, passim.

not to neglect to say something about the religion of the Chinese, the one thing which seems to be missing from this colloquium.

Michael: I confess, indeed, that I am aiming at brevity, not so much because I am tired as because I am afraid you may be finding it tedious, but I shall not shirk from completing my task, and shall do as you request and add something more about religion. Since true religion has been lacking until now in the kingdom of China, and even now is only just making a start and that within very narrow limits, this nation, which in other respects is very ingenious, has always lived in total error and in ignorance of the truth, has been misled into sundry opinions, and has followed a multiplicity of sects. Among these, however, there are three which are famous. First of these is the religion of those who profess the teaching of Confucius,[1] an outstanding philosopher. This man (as is reported in the account of his life) was extremely correct in his conduct, and he wrote discriminatingly and at length about this, and it is his writings, more than all others, which are read and studied.[2] All the magistrates follow this teaching, as do all others who devote themselves to the study of letters, and it is said that Confucius himself devised many of their letters; and their reverence for him is so great that on the days of the new and the full moon all these followers of his assemble at the common school which I mentioned earlier, and they kneel three times and press their heads to the ground before his image, which is venerated with burning of incense and lighted candles. And it is not only the ordinary scholars who do this, but also the highest magistrates. This teaching is, in sum, to take the light of nature as guide and zealously to cultivate the virtues I mentioned before, and to strive for the right ordering of family and kingdom. All of these are praiseworthy precepts, or would be if only Confucius had made some mention of God, the best and the greatest, and of the future life, and had not ascribed so much to the heavens and to fate and necessity, and if he had not treated in such detail of the veneration to be offered to the images of their forefathers. In this regard he can barely be acquitted, or cannot be acquitted at all, of the crime of idolatry. It has to be conceded, however, that there is no other teaching among the Chinese which approaches so close to the truth.[3]

---

[1] Original edition (p. 395) '*Confucii*' and then '*Confucius*'. Kongzi or Kong Fuzi (Wade-Giles, K'ung Fu-tzu), Master Kong (551–479 BCE). The Jesuits invented Confucius. Kong Fuzi was not in common usage in 16th-century China (or before), although Kongzi was. For a discussion of how the Jesuits created Kong Fuzi/Confucius, see Jensen, *Manufacturing Confucianism*, pp. 79–92. Jensen's suggestion (ibid., pp. 86–91) that the Latin name 'Confucius' was not used until 1689 is contradicted by its usage in *De Missione*.

[2] The *Sishu* or Four Books, which Ricci claimed Confucius had compiled, and the *Wujing* or Five Classics, which Ricci believed Confucius himself had written. These texts, widely read, studied and subjected to exegesis, were the foundation of intellectual debate in China and required texts for learning. Both Michele Ruggieri and Ricci worked on translations of the Four Books shortly after arriving in China. The Four Books became the focus of the Jesuits' study of the Chinese classics and the platform on which they attempted to construct their accommodation. See Ricci, *Fonti Ricciane*, I, pp. 42–4; Mungello, *Curious Land*, pp. 58–9; Jensen, *Manufacturing Confucianism*, p. 59; *Cambridge History of China Volume 8*, ch. 11 passim.

[3] Had the Jesuits adopted the harsher rather than the more liberal reading of this judgement of ancestor worship, the issue at the heart of the Rites Controversy, there would have been no controversy. The Jesuits (and a number of Jesuits disapproved of Ricci's policy) and the mendicants would have concurred in condemning ancestral rites as idolatry. As a result, the China mission would have followed quite a different course. Initially, Ricci forbade Chinese Christians from performing the rites but reversed this policy. In his *De Christiana expeditione apvd Sinas svscepta ab Societate Jesu ex P. Matthæi Ricij eiusdem Societatis com[m]entarijs*

The second sect is that of those who follow Xaca, or Xequia as the Chinese call him,[1] whose teachings there is no need for me to list, as they are sufficiently familiar to us, especially as they are admirably refuted in the catechism composed by the Father Visitor. All of those known in China as *cen*,[2] and among us as *bonzes*, follow this doctrine. Let me say briefly, by the way, that there is no word in Chinese which is not a monosyllable, and if there is any which sounds as if it has more than one syllable it should be taken to be a compound of more than one word. These *cen*, then, or *ceni* (to use the Latin form) shave their beards and heads, and generally they live with a number of associates in temples of Xaca and others of the same sect whom they number among the saints, and they offer prayers in their fashion, using books or beads, and perform other rites in the same manner as our *bonzes*. There is some mention among them of the future life, and of rewards for the good and punishment for the wicked, but everything they say is replete with errors.

The third of their sects is those known as *tauzu*, and they imitate another man who was outstanding for his sanctity,[3] or so they believe. Now because the sect of Confucius is the most celebrated of all, and the *ceni* and the *tauzuii* have little commitment to learning, and their religion flourishes only among the common people, the priests of both of these sects live most abjectly among the Chinese, so much so that they bend the knee before the magistrates, and cannot sit with them, and sometimes, if it please the magistrates, they are subjected to the punishment of beating; quite unlike here in Japan, where priests even of false religion are held in such honour.

Leo: I have heard, Michael, that the superstition of the Saracens is also to be found in China, and I would be glad if you could tell us whether or not that is true.

Michael: That superstition is foreign to the Chinese, and was introduced among them at the time when the Asiatic Sarmatians or Tartars invaded the kingdom of China and took power there. In so far, therefore, as there are Saracens among the Chinese, they have their origin in the Sarmatian people. They were very numerous and thus could not be expelled entirely from the kingdom of China, but though they stayed there it was their race and not their religion that they propagated. For the most part they are soldiers, and sometimes they attain to a military magistracy, but except for a few ceremonies their superstition is now obsolete and almost extinct, and they live entirely in the Chinese

---

(Augsburg, 1615), Ricci, as edited by Nicolá Trigault, went out of his way to assert the secular nature of such rites, in particular the ceremonies to venerate Confucius's memory. See Sebes, 'Precursors of Ricci', pp. 45–8; Ricci, *China in the Sixteenth Century*, pp. 96–7; Mungello, *Curious Land*, pp. 46–9, 57, 64; Jensen, *Manufacturing Confucianism*, pp. 63–70.

[1] Shaka or Sakyamuni, the historical Buddha.

[2] *Chan* (Chinese) *zen* (Japanese), one of the schools of Mahāyāna Buddhism, first introduced to Japan in the 7th century but did not emerge as a major Japanese tradition until the 12th century.

[3] Laozi (Wade-Giles, Lao Tzu) the putative author of the *Daodejing* (Wade-Giles, *Tao Te Ching*), said to have been written in the 6th century BCE, and a central text in the Daoist canon. See Boxer, *South China*, pp. 102–4; Mungello, *Curious Land*, pp. 70–72. Daoism was not just a religion of the common people; it had a rich philosophy and was highly influential in the Ming polity (*Cambridge History of China Volume 8*, ch. 15).

way, since it is now five hundred years since their ancestors came into the Chinese kingdom.¹

Lino: Now Michael, say something of the true religion of Christ. We know it has now made its first move into that vast country and we hope the auspices are favourable.

Michael: I could say a great deal about those most welcome beginnings, were it not that it is already well known in Japan because of the letters of the Fathers, but nevertheless I shall give a summary account of all of it, lest I should appear to be evading the task. You know that from the time when the fathers of the Society, zealous for the increase of the Christian religion, first came to these our islands, they were also eager to penetrate into the interior of the Chinese kingdom. It was while eagerly straining to do this that the holy Father Francis Xavier of the same Society departed this life on the island of Sancian, which some call Sangian,² handing on the torch to other Fathers so that they would apply themselves with like zeal to instructing that people in the Christian religion. Others followed him, making praiseworthy use of every possible means or instrument to bring what had been begun to a successful outcome. They were always hindered, however, by the ancient custom of China, according to which they allow foreigners access to their country only with the utmost difficulty. They make an exception for those who have been there since ancient times in the role of ambassadors, and who attend on the king every third year, but even in admitting them they take great care not to allow them to gather intelligence about what is happening in the kingdom.³ Another consideration is the attitude of the Chinese nation, which is contemptuous of other peoples and very strongly attached to their own customs and laws. What with all this it took more than thirty years of hard work just to gain entrance, before two fathers of the same Society, both of them with a degree of learning in Chinese letters and language (humanly speaking they had lost all hope, but they were relying on divine help), managed in the year 1583 to obtain permission of the *tutan* or viceroy to set up a house and church in the city of Xauquin, which, because it is so convenient, is the seat of the viceroy himself.⁴

---

¹ The Mongol rulers of China during the Yuan dynasty were not Muslims although they did employ Muslims in various capacities. Gaspar de la Cruz identifies the Tartars, i.e. Mongols, with the Scythians, a people of Iranian origin like the Sarmatians. See Boxer, *South China*, pp. 66–70, also Cooper, *João Rodrigues's Account*, pp. 21–4. Among Europeans at this time, knowledge of China's western borders and central Asia was largely conjectural, based on the writings of the Ancients, although de la Cruz was aware of the Uighars (Boxer, *South China*, p. 219). On Islamic communities in China, which had a long history (in 1608 Ricci estimated their number at more than a million, far exceeding the number of Christians, estimated at around 2,500 in 1610), and Galeote Pereira's description of the Muslims he encountered in Fujian at the beginning of the 1550s, see ibid, pp. 36–9; Ricci, *Fonti Ricciane*, I, pp 110–11, and, II, p. 483, n. 9.

² Shangchuan, where Xavier died in 1552, and where Chinese merchants came to trade with the Portuguese. At the time of his death, Xavier was awaiting the arrival of a Chinese merchant, resident in Canton, who was prepared to take him to the city for 200 cruzados. For Xavier's letters from Shangchuan, see Xavier, *Letters and Instructions of Francis Xavier*, pp. 438–55.

³ For introductions to the philosophy behind and conduct of China's foreign relations, see Fairbank, *Chinese World Order*, passim; *Cambridge History of China Volume 8*, chs 4–8.

⁴ Zhaoqing. Various attempts were made by Jesuits, and mendicants, to enter China in the years following Xavier's death. In 1580 Ruggieri, who had arrived in Macao the previous year and applied himself to the study of Chinese, visited Canton in the company of Portuguese merchants. Two years later, he was given permission to reside in Zhaoqing, 80 km to the west. In 1583 he was joined by Matteo Ricci and later by António Almeida

In the first years after their work there had started, and because of the novelty of it, those two fathers were well treated by the magistrates, so much so that two others sent from India easily gained access, and then two of them stayed in the house in Xauquin and two went for the first time into the interior provinces, intending to set up a new residence. Later on, however, other magistrates did not approve of this, and they were forced to withdraw. Now in all the time when the Fathers were living in Xauquin (which was more than five years) some of the common people were brought from false superstition to the Christian religion, and seventy persons were baptized. But since the enemy of the human race, in order to impede the progress of Christianity, leaves no stone unturned, he prompted the Chinese (who, as I said, are much inclined by nature to reject intercourse with other peoples and to be darkly suspicious of foreigners) to present the *chaien* and the *tutan*, their chief magistrates, with petitions asking for the expulsion of the fathers from Xauquin. And these magistrates came to the house and church of the fathers and deliberated about whether they should be expelled from Xauquin. They used great moderation in this matter and did not offend the fathers with any kind of acerbity, indicating that they were concerned only with what would benefit their country. The *tutan* summoned the Fathers (I omit other things that happened), spoke with them courteously, and gave many reasons to show that it was not appropriate for them to live in the city of Xauquin, especially as there were so many magistrates coming and meeting in the city, and they would not be tolerant of the presence there of foreigners. He therefore told them that part of the money spent on building the house would be restored to them, and that they were to return either to their own country or to the port of Macao. But the fathers' appeal was so effective and so deserving of sympathy that the *tutan* decided on a new residence for the fathers in the part furthest inland of the province of Guangdong, in a city called Xaucheo,[1] and he commended them to a magistrate who had come from there to greet him. The fathers therefore made their way there, not without sadness and many tears on the part of the Christians, and, as we know from recent letters, they have laid the foundations of their first house there, and they write that they are going to be able to live there much more peacefully and with a much better prospect of spreading Christianity. These are the first beginnings for the Chinese harvest, and there is no doubt that, as in other parts of Christendom, the seeds are to be sown with great labour and tears so that the hoped for fruit may be gathered in gladness and joy.[2]

---

and Duarte de Sande, who became the mission superior. Initially the Jesuits adopted Buddhist attire, later discarded in favour of Confucian clothing. On Valignano's orders, Ruggieri left China for Rome in 1588 in the expectation that he would be appointed papal ambassador to the Chinese emperor. He never returned and no such ambassador was appointed. In 1589 Ricci moved the Jesuit residence to Shaoguan, in the north of Guangdong province. He reached Nanjing in 1595 and Beijing in 1598. On the early history of the Jesuit mission to China, see Dunne, *Generation of Giants*, pp. 15–37; Sebes, 'The Precursors of Ricci', pp. 19–61; Jensen, *Manufacturing Confucianism*, pp. 35–48; *Cambridge History of China Volume 8*, pp. 793–8; Brockley, *Journey to the East*, pp. 29–41.

[1] Shaoguan, whither Ricci and Almeida moved in 1589, while de Sande returned to Macao to become rector of the Jesuit college and to work on *De Missione*.

[2] Hakluyt's translation breaks off here (*Principal Navigations*, VI, p. 377), although he adds a final comment, a note of thanks from Leo, quite different from Leo's interjection in *De Missione*. Valignano's awareness of the formidable challenge facing the China mission, especially in dealing with the mandarins, and his policy recommendations are set out in his letter of 10 November 1588 to Aquaviva (ARSI, Jap.Sin 11: I, ff. 1–8v *passim*, printed in Álvarez-Taladriz, 'El proyecto de embajada').

Leo: Oh that those beginnings may have the hoped for increase, and that everywhere on earth the name of Christ, hitherto unknown to many, may be worshipped by all peoples. One thing remains, however, about which you should speak, a matter of the most burning concern to us, namely whether you judge that China or Europe should be awarded the prize, given that you have been fulsome in praise of both.

Michael: I have been careful to avoid this kind of comparison up till now, but I am in duty bound to provide a proper answer to your honest and sincere question. Although the kingdom of China is the most celebrated in all the Orient, there is no doubt that it is much inferior to Europe, the most illustrious place in the whole world. I am going to speak about this in the next colloquium, but here I'll make a brief comparison of China with Europe. In the first place then, Europe is much larger, for it stretches from thirty-eight degrees to about ninety degrees north, and some books tell us that there are peoples in Europe who see the North directly above their heads.[1] And if you consider the multitude of cities and towns, and the abundance of population, it is clear that those of Europe are much more numerous, larger, and more populous, given that in Italy alone, and it is just one of the provinces of Europe, cities number more than four hundred and towns more than two thousand, and this does not include minor camps and villages, of which there is an almost infinite number. From that you can readily appreciate just how large the number of cities and the population is in the whole of Europe. And these European cities must be considered much nobler and much more elegant if you think of their magnificence and nobility, since in Europe the structure of the houses and other buildings is so sumptuous, with so much fine workmanship, and the cities themselves can boast such numbers of aristocracy, of nobles, and of men of wealth, whereas the cities of China are content with humbler buildings and less splendour.

With regard to fertility, we have to say that the land of Europe offers more things really useful for human life, and with these the Europeans, as I said earlier, live with much more luxury and style than the Chinese, who are accustomed to a general way of life common to all, and do not have the same degree of costly ornamentation in their dress, nor the same retinues of servants, nor do they have the use of similar magnificent items of gold, silver, and so on. In addition to this if all other things are considered, military science, the exercise of the arts humble and noble, and finally good government, all of these things flourish far better and more excellently in Europe. For proof of this I refer you to the past colloquia, to avoid being drawn into repeating the same thing too often. As well as all this there is the European nobility, distributed in its various grades and orders, the multitude of the illustrious aristocracy held in respect in each of the different countries, and the wide-ranging practice of so many disciplines.

To all of this add the Christian religion, which, as I have mentioned from time to time, totally perfects and adorns nature. Fifteen hundred years ago it was gradually spread throughout Europe, and in a wonderful way it ennobled the character and the customs of the Europeans. So all that you have been hearing about the kingdom of China is to be understood in such a way as not to detract in the least from the worth and fame of Europe,

---

[1] The Ming empire was much smaller than the present-day People's Republic whose borders are very much a result of China's westward expansion under the Qing dynasty (Purdue, *China Marches West, passim*). Today, China and Europe are roughly the same size.

which I have endeavoured to bring home to you in so many colloquia. I could also put Japan ahead of China for the order of its nobility and its military discipline, but that I might appear to be pleading our own cause; but the facts are so well known that the claim could be made without there being any suspicion of bias in our own favour. Where other things are concerned, however, with regard to knowledge of letters and of nature, and also of other things useful for our lives which derive from the merchandise brought to us, there is no denying that we owe a great deal to the kingdom of China.

Leo: Indeed, Michael, it is so, and there is no denying that we are also much in your debt for the pleasure your talk has given us.

COLLOQUIUM XXXIV

A summary description of the whole world, and a statement as to which is its principal and noblest part

Leo: Up till now, Michael, you have told us, in the colloquia so far, about the different parts of the world. Today, however, we have come together no less eagerly to hear you speak about the world as a whole, but first I would like to know why it is that although you set out from Goa in the year eighty-eight, you spent two years on the voyage and staying in Macao, and only came to us here in the year ninety.[1]

Michael: First of all, as you know, it is quite normal for the voyage from India to here to take a year, for it takes three months from India to the port of Macao, and when the ship arrives there the opportune time is already past and it is necessary to wait at least ten months for the time in the following year when the south wind blows. The cause of our staying there a further year, however, is that there was no voyage in the year eighty-nine, for a number of reasons. The first was that the ship which had sailed to us the previous year reached the port of Macao late, so that there was too little time to prepare and buy the merchandise. The second point was that the Portuguese had not made the profit they hoped for from the sale of the previous year's merchandise, and preferred to have no voyage for one year rather than to make the voyage with only limited prospects of advantage. As a result they were slow to head for Canton to buy and assemble the merchandise, and what with them waiting for the Chinese merchants, and the Chinese for them, time passed, and with it the opportunity for the voyage. There was also the political disturbance in Japan, with the fathers sent into exile, and this was very upsetting for the Portuguese. For all these reasons the annual voyage was cancelled, and for us this meant a delay of a year and no little trouble.[2]

---

[1] Valignano and the boys, by now young men, left Macao on 23 June 1590 and reached Nagasaki sometime between 18 and 22 July, to much joy and relief. They had 'grown up and changed' since they left Japan and were not recognizable to their families. See Fróis, *História de Japam*, V, pp. 186–8, esp. p. 188; *Documenta Indica*, XV, p. 518; Boxer, *Great Ship*, p. 54.

[2] Another reason was the death of the captain-major of the planned voyage, Jerónimo Pereira. The suggestion that disappointing profits from the 1588 voyage, also captained by Pereira, was one of the reasons is not credible. Although Hideyoshi had irritated the Portuguese in Nagasaki by stopping sales in Nagasaki until his factor had bought silk on his behalf, the Jesuits, in their annual letter, gloated that, by good fortune, Hideyoshi's factor, Joachim Konishi Ryūsa, was a Christian much in favour with Hideyoshi. Konishi conspired with the Jesuits to ensure that, despite Hideyoshi's orders, the Portuguese received a good price for their silk, a price with which they were quite satisfied. See *Documenta Indica*, XV, pp. 323–4; Fróis, *História de Japam*, II, p. 113; ibid., V, p. 493; Boxer, *Great Ship*, p.52.

Lino: The fathers and the Christians found the delay hard to bear, but there is one thing that greatly consoled us, namely that last year is known to have been plagued by many storms and tempests, so that if you had embarked on the journey your lives would have been in the greatest danger, which shows that even the fact that there was no voyage is to be ascribed to Providence.

Michael: We did indeed so ascribe it, when letters reached us, brought on Chinese ships at the end of last year, from which we understood how severe and violent were the storms all around Japan. And given that the Father Visitor had tried every possible way for us to make the journey and still the only result was that the voyage was cancelled, we realized that without any doubt we always had the help of Divine Providence, and this was why we had been so fortunate and successful in avoiding so many dangers throughout the whole course of our pilgrimage.[1]

Lino: But you must have been frustrated during those two years spent in the port of Macao, when your aspirations were directed to your native land as your aim and your end.

Michael: As long as the journey undertaken is not completed, especially if it is a question of returning home to one's country, it is only natural that the traveller should feel some frustration, but we always had various expedients for reducing or even removing

---

[1] This is an astonishing understatement. In fact, following Hideyoshi's order of 1587 that the fathers should leave Japan the mission was in crisis, even although the edict was not enforced. Uncertain of the future, and uncertain about when, or if, Valignano, should he still be alive, would return, the vice-provincial, Coelho, held a consultation at Katsusa at which it was decided to seek counsel and possible military assistance from abroad. Melchior de Mora was instructed to proceed to Macao to find out about Valignano. If, for whatever reason, the visitor was not there, de Mora was to proceed, not to Goa, the seat of Portuguese authority in the *Estado da Índia*, but to Manila, in the hope of securing a small expeditionary force to secure a fortified enclave for Christianity in Japan. From Manila he was to proceed to New Spain and Europe to speak directly with the Jesuit general and Philip II about the situation in Japan. Mora left Japan for Macao on Jerónimo Pereira's ship at the end of February 1589, reaching Macao at the beginning of April. There he found Valignano very much alive, awaiting passage to Japan. He gave the visitor a copy of the Katsusa minutes and other documents relating to his assignment. Valignano reacted with horror and outrage. In his covering note to the general, enclosing the minutes, he asserted that what the signatories were contemplating was 'so dangerous, scandalous and improper that I am astonished that they came to such conclusions'. On 12 June, in a letter to the general, he added that he was proceeding to Japan as the viceroy's ambassador (Hideyoshi had made it clear that he would receive Valignano in this capacity) and had ordered Mora to return with him. Once there, he would convene 'a legitimate congregation' to settle the details of his embassy and, if necessary, to agree to send a procurator to Rome to discuss with the general alone, and not with viceroys or the king, the state of the Japan mission and the remedies that should be undertaken in the light of recent developments. There were indeed 'severe and violent ... storms all around Japan' literally and metaphorically. On Hideyoshi's decree ordering the missionaries to leave Japan, see Boxer, *Christian Century*, pp. 145–52; Elison, *Deus Destroyed*, pp. 115–20. On the Katsusa consultation and Valignano's response, see Álvarez-Taladriz, '¿Resistencia armada a la persecución de 1587?', pp. 71–86, esp. p. 76; idem, 'El padre vice-provincial Gaspar Coelho', p. 76; Massarella, 'Exceptionalism versus Universalism', pp. 141–2. The annual letter, which puts a gloss on Mora's mission, makes it clear that the Jesuits in Japan knew of Valignano's appointment as the viceroy's legate from letters, dated 1587, brought by Pereira, and that the latter passed on this information to Hideyoshi when he met with the *kampaku* in Kyoto, together with misinformation that he knew for sure that Valignano had reached Macao. Neither Pereira nor the Jesuits in Japan could have known this because the captain-major left Macao before the visitor and the boys had arrived there. See *Cartas*, II, ff. 238v, 243v–244, 258v; Boxer, *Great Ship*, p. 51.

this dissatisfaction, however great, namely our various exercises connected with the study of the arts, together with the excellent lodgings which we had.¹

Leo: Now that with your arrival here all the labours and difficulties of your journey are at an end, it remains for you to put before our eyes the picture of the whole of the world which we were promised in the first colloquia, and to tell us about the difference between its principal parts.

Michael: That is why I had the *Theatrum Orbis* brought. You will find it a great pleasure to study the various maps in it. First of all, then, take a look at this picture, which contains a representation of the whole of the world, in which you can easily discern the five principal parts into which, as I said at the beginning, the whole globe of the world is divided, namely Europe, which was the end of our voyage, Asia, which we also reached, Africa, where we kept to one port, America, to which we have referred a number of times, and finally the unknown southern land which I said had often been seen by Portuguese sailors travelling past it.

Lino: I am delighted to see this picture of the world, but tell me, where is there a picture of Japan?

Michael: We usually include in the name 'Japan' all the islands which you see positioned beside the kingdom of China, and which, together with it, are part of Asia.

Leo: Oh! Is our Japan limited to such a small space? That really shows me just how easily outsiders will talk nonsense about things with which they are not familiar; and I feel that finding this mistake detracts considerably from the pleasure which I had been taking in viewing this picture.

Michael: Don't say that the map is wrong, Leo, but that we are. It is the Japanese who see this map for the first time who always make this mistake, for they don't understand how scientifically it has been measured; and you should know that the same thing happened with us the first time we were presented with the world set out in this way.²

---

¹ During their stay in Macao, they pursed their studies in the liberal arts and music, and gave Japanese lessons to the European Jesuits bound for Japan. Even Valignano attended these classes. Mesquita informed Aquaviva that Martin, in particular, showed great aptitude in the liberal arts and would be able to teach them in Japan and that he was also gifted in music. Michael and Mancio wrote to the Jesuit general about their journey from Goa. In reply to a letter from Aquaviva, Michael also wrote about the persecution by 'deste tyranno', this tyrant (i.e. Hideyoshi), in Japan, and his hope that the relics which the boys had brought back from Europe, and which, he claimed, had protected them from many dangers during their travels, might be used to grant indulgences in Japan (ARSI, Jap.Sin 11: I, ff. 9–11v, 46; 11: II, ff. 173–4, 192).

² These comments on Japanese cartography might not be out of place in a text for teaching the young but they do not reflect the extent of Japanese cartographical knowledge at the time. The Japanese, like the Chinese and the Koreans, had their own cartographical knowledge. The famous Kangnido map of 1402 was far superior to anything available in Europe at the time. From an early stage in their encounter, Japanese and Portuguese seafarers exchanged knowledge about their respective traditions. Japanese portolanos of this time incorporated Portuguese knowledge but, when it came to depicting Japan and neighbouring countries, they amended their representations in the light of their own more accurate knowledge. See Nakamura, 'Japanese Portolanos', pp. 24–44, esp. pp. 31, 34–5; Ledyard, 'Kangnido', pp. 329–32.

But to help you move away from that false opinion cast your eyes on those islands which are not smaller than the islands of Japan, but which here occupy only a very limited area. This is one of them, which used to be called Madagascar but now takes its name from São Lourenço.[1] It looks very small here, but in reality it is about three hundred leagues in length. Almost as large is this other called Taprobane, commonly known as Sumatra. Or take these, Britain and Ireland, which are entire kingdoms, but which appear on the map as quite small portions of land. The same can be said of Sicily, which is a noble kingdom, and even of Italy itself, such a famous province, and including many provinces within itself, and yet drawn here in such a small space. So you should understand that the map shows our Japan as large rather than small.

Lino: Those examples do indeed remove some of our doubts, but I don't think they satisfy them completely. Japan is much larger than those islands you have mentioned, for it extends over about five hundred leagues.

Michael: But our leagues, Lino, as we noted once earlier, are smaller than European leagues, so that three hundred and fifty European leagues correspond to more than five hundred of ours. To have a better grasp of this you must remember what we said in the sixth colloquium, namely that the world is divided up into degrees for purposes of measurement, and these degrees are each of seventeen and a half leagues on an exactly south to north path. Now this length of a league is absolutely certain, so whether it is a large or a small map that you draw the measurement is always the same, even though more space is assigned to each degree on the larger chart and less on the smaller, since whether the degree occupies a larger or a smaller space on the map it is always to be understood as representing seventeen and a half leagues. Thus on the next map Europe alone is depicted, and it takes up the same space as the whole world does on this one. That does not mean that a mistake has been made. It merely means that different amounts of space are allotted (on the two maps) to the degrees, though the degrees themselves are always the same, for in both cases the name or sign of a degree always signifies that same number of leagues which I have specified.

Leo: From the explanation you have given I do now understand that the accuracy of measurement is always the same, even though the space allowed for depicting it may vary, and that this means that the whole world may be shown sometimes on a large map, sometimes on a small one.

Michael: Now you've got it, Leo. You were on the wrong lines before, thinking that the mistake was in the picture rather than in yourself, for you were not familiar with these things. That is the fundamental point that you have to understand if you are to profit at all from studying this book. You will often see a large area given over to some small province, just as large as the area on which the whole world is mapped out, but this makes absolutely no difference to the measuring of the degrees. It merely shows the shape or picture as sometimes larger, sometimes smaller, without implying that there is any

---

[1] First reached by the Portuguese on St Laurence's day, 10 August, 1506. See Camões, *Os Lusíadas*, 10: 137; Boxer, *Tragic History*, p. 54 n. 4.

variation in the thing itself. Coming back to Japan, then, although it is shown here in quite a small space, when you look at the degrees it appears clearly that it runs from the thirty-first to the fortieth, going directly from south to north,[1] and that in longitude, from west to east, it takes in more than three hundred European or five hundred Japanese leagues.

Lino: Procede then, Michael, with what you intended to say, and if you have more to say about Japan let us hear it.

Michael: It occurs to me to compare our Japan and part of the kingdom of China with Europe with regard to their position when you look at the Great Bear.[2] The most elevated position at which the Great Bear can be seen from Japan and that part of China is similar to the position at which it can be seen from Italy or Spain, so it is not surprising if there are similarities between these regions in certain things.

Lino: If the wealth and the ways of behaving of Europe are so different from ours, how can you maintain that Europe, Japan, and a region of China are similar?

Michael: I did say 'similar', not 'the same'. If you consider the potential of the crops, meat, fish, etc., to nourish the body, and also the intelligence, civility, and degree of nobility of our people, our Japan is to some degree similar to Europe.

Leo: I am glad to hear you say so. But now tell us more also about the kingdom of China, which is next to Japan, if anything further suggests itself.

Michael: The kingdom of China is this one, which looks across to Japan, but is much larger than it, for it extends north from nineteen degrees to fifty degrees. Its latitude, then, is easy to learn, as I said before, and covers approximately five hundred and fifty European leagues, and from west to east it stretches for more or less the same distance.

Leo: But if you just look at the shape of it on this chart you wouldn't think it was so very large.

Michael: That's true, and for that reason the Chinese too, when they consider just the size, and not the measurement in degrees, complain to the Fathers who are with them

---

[1] This is an improvement on the *Historia* (p. 126) where Valignano gives the position of Japan as between 30° and 36° or 38°. The northern parts of Honshu and Hokkaido, or Ezo as it was called, were largely, but not entirely, unknown to the Jesuits. The first European, a Jesuit, Gerlamo de Angelis, reached Hokkaido in 1618 and made a second visit in 1621 following which he wrote a short account of Hokkaido confirming that it was an island although this was not finally established in European cartography until 1787 by La Pérouse's expedition. In the *Principio*, Valignano admitted that previous estimates of the geographical position of Japan, including this very passage in *De Missione*, were wrong and, relying on Ignacío Moreira's work, tried to come up with an accurate figure. See *Principio*, ch. 2, printed in Valignano, *Adiciones*, pp. 380–91; *Documenta Indica*, XV, p. 63. See also Cooper, *João Rodrigues's Account*, p. 43. On Hokkaido, see Schilling, 'Il contributo dei missionari cattoliche', pp. 139–214; Dunmore, *Journal*, II, pp. 323–4, 513; Cooper, *João Rodrigues's Account*, p. 29, n. 8; Walker, *Conquest of Ainu Lands*, pp. 31–5; Boscaro, *Ventura e sventura*, pp. 141–6; 222–34.

[2] Original edition (p. 403) '*Septentrione*', the seven principal stars of the Great Bear or Plough.

about the very small scale on which their country is drawn on a map like this, for they are persuaded that the country in which they live is the largest part of the earth. But if they thought about the measurement in degrees they would find that in fact more space is allowed to the region of China on this map than to the whole of Spain, France, Italy, and Germany, which is a remarkable thing, given that in those provinces so many kingdoms are contained, and so many different jurisdictions, namely those of the pope, the emperor, and the kings of Spain and of France.

Lino: From this reasoning it would seem to follow, and the same thing occurred to me during the previous colloquium, that the king of the Chinese must be the most powerful king of all.

Michael: If only the size of the kingdoms is taken into consideration it is easy to fall into error, as can readily be shown by an example. America is a vast land, and Spain can in no way compare with it in size, yet no one would say that America has the same value as Spain, and the same would apply to Africa as compared to Italy. So although we said earlier that the kingdom of China is much larger than any other one kingdom, it does not follow that it is the most powerful kingdom, both because there are others whose lands, though not in one and the same kingdom, extend much further and wider, and because the power of kings is based on the bravery of their soldiers, the sophistication of their armaments, the number of their fleets, their military planning, the defences of their cities, and other things, in which the Chinese are far inferior to the Europeans. But let us say no more on these points and move on to a description of our journey.[1]

We left the port of Nagasaki, which you see here, and entered the gulf of Macao, which you see here set in the kingdom of China, and hemmed in with many islands. We embarked at this port and sailed past the regions of Cochinchina, Cambodia, Champa, and Siam, and then went in among the islands of Malacca which you see here, went through the famous straits of Singapore here, and put in at Malacca. From there we took ship again, sailed over the open sea for a long way, reached the island of Ceylon, and then went on to round Cape Comorin in India, reaching Cochin, where we spent the winter. After the winter we reached Goa, the capital of the Portuguese jurisdiction in India. From Goa we came back to Cochin and started on the voyage to Portugal. We were carried over this immense ocean, and after crossing the equinoctial line from north to south and passing the edge of the land of Madagascar or São Lourenço, we were glad to round safely this very long promontory, called the Cape of Good Hope. Then, when we had proceeded further, we rested for some little time on this island of St Helena, which provides a most welcome refuge. From there we again crossed the equinoctial line, this time from south

---

[1] In the case of China, Ricci used his world map to impart the same geographical and didactic information. He completed his first, rough, world map in 1584, although no copy has survived. The third edition in 1602, with annotations in Chinese on different parts of the world, of which four copies are extant, is huge. The map, including counterfeit versions, circulated widely in China, and copies made their way to Japan. Ricci also made a globe which no longer survives. See Ricci, *Fonti Ricciane*, I, pp. 207–12; II, pp. 50, 169–73, 474; D'Elia, 'Recent Discoveries', pp. 114–16; Spence, *Memory Palace*, pp. 96–7, 148–9; *Cambridge History of China Volume 8*, pp. 814–15; Hostetler, *Qing Colonial Enterprise*, pp. 18–19, 52–6; Standaert, *Handbook of Christianity in China Volume One*, pp. 754–6. The 'Anon-Moreira' map, more modest in scale, was intended to serve the same purposes in Japan as Ricci's world map in China (see Fig. 1).

to north, and we saw Europe, which we had so much looked forward to seeing, and entered Lisbon, here, the celebrated port of Portugal, which is a part of Spain. From here we journeyed overland through Spain, and took ship for Rome at this port of Alicante. From Rome we came back again to Portugal and set sail from the port of Lisbon, again travelled across this immense ocean and round the Cape of Good Hope, and then sailed between the continent of Africa and the island of São Lourenço. There, as I said earlier, we were dragged towards extreme danger in the Shallows of Sofala, but afterwards made this port of Mozambique, and then reached Goa. From there we sailed first to Malacca on the same route as before, then to the kingdom of China, and from there, happily, we eventually reached this our homeland.

Leo: Dear Lord, what a long voyage, a voyage in which, with the circumnavigation that you did, you can be said to have covered the whole world.

Michael: It would have been a complete circumnavigation if we had taken this other route, and sailed back to our country via New Spain, but the circular course of our voyage was indeed very long, for on our way to Europe we passed much of Asia and Africa, and on our way there and back we crossed the equinoctial line four times. In the same way we travelled to both Tropics, namely Cancer and Capricorn. At the Equator or equinoctial line we had to contend with blazing heat, and beyond the tropics we saw the south and the north rise to more than thirty-six degrees and were afflicted by severe cold, and thus we experienced a remarkable variety and alteration of conditions.

Leo: Michael, I have been considering now for quite some time the five parts of the world which you put before us, and I see that Europe is the smallest of all of them. This suggests to me that if Europe has in abundance the resources and supplies that you have been telling us about, those other parts too may have an abundance of the same things.

Michael: It is vain and futile to try to demonstrate the fertility and opulence of a country by arguing from its size, for these two things depend on the nature of the soil and the industry of the people rather than on the area of the country.

Leo: That is so, admittedly. But you, since you have been to three of the parts of the world with your two companions, and have heard a great deal about the other two parts, can more easily judge which is the most outstanding part, and can explain your conclusion to us. If it was left to us to settle it we would certainly give the first place to Japan and to the kingdom of China, as you know, but now when I look at this representation of the world and see Africa placed between the other parts I suspect that it should be accorded the primacy, since we are accustomed to say that virtue consists in the mean.[1]

Michael: Your reasoning there too is not very well grounded, since 'mean' in that case refers not to the site or position but to what right reason judges. So although Africa occupies the central position it does not follow that it is superior to the others, and it may perhaps be the lowest of all. For since much of it falls within the circles known as the

---

[1] Aristotle, *Nicomachean Ethics*, bk II, ch. 6.

Figure 13. *Newe Zeyttung/ auß der Insel Japonien*, Augsburg, 1586.
By permission of Kyoto University Library.

Tropics it is subject to the more extreme heat of the sun, so much so that almost all of this region was judged by the Ancients to be a desert. Even if this is not so, since there is no part of the world, though it be under the equinoctial line or under the poles, which is not habitable,[1] Africa is nevertheless extremely hot, arid, with an abundance of sand and desert places, and is therefore lacking in many of the things necessary to life. Because of this its inhabitants are mostly wild and barbarous men, black in colour, and strangers to all human refinement, especially those who keep to the interior parts. To some degree those who live close to the coast which is near Europe approach the elegance of Europe, and we know that in former times Christianity flourished there and they had many illustrious men.

But you want me to give my judgement as to which part of the world is the most outstanding, and I shall do this gladly. I shall put aside my Japaneseness and pretend that I am worldly, a cosmopolitan, an inhabitant and citizen of the whole world, as the European philosopher Socrates gloried in being,[2] without special attachment to or excessive love for any particular region. Setting aside, then, a certain native affection for my country to which I am not, I know, indifferent, and with all things considered and

---

[1] The same point, refuting the Ancients, is made in Acosta's, *Natural and Moral History of the Indies* (p. 37).
[2] Cicero, *Tusculan Disputations*, V: 37.

weighed in an equal balance, I judge and frankly declare that Europe is the most excellent of all the parts of the world, the part on which God with most generous hand has conferred the most and the best good things. Accordingly it stands out among all the other regions for its climate, for the abilities, the industry, and the nobility of its nations, for its organization of life and of government, and for the multiplicity of its arts.

Various considerations can be adduced to confirm this. In the first place Europe is outside the circles called the Tropics, and is therefore not exposed to fierce or torrid heat from the sun. Moreover, the greater part of it, and perhaps all of it with the exception of the most distant islands, is outside the Arctic Circle, so neither is it subject to being frozen by the biting cold, but is always agreeably temperate, the cold and heat varying within a tolerable range, something which cannot be said of the other parts, which generally swelter in extreme heat, the exception being the unknown land to the South, which, the latitude being far south, cannot but be grievously afflicted by the cold. It also seems sufficiently established that the men of that region are in no way the equal of the Europeans who are in the North. It seems possible, indeed, that they are almost totally uncivilized, since they have never emerged from their own lands nor provided any indication of their abilities, industry, or fortitude, whereas the Europeans have done so to an admirable degree, filling the whole world with the fame of their name and with their splendid exploits.

In the second place if we compare Europe with Asia and Africa we find the inhabitants of Europe to be white in colour, fair of face, and with comely features, but the Africans mostly black, and the Asiatics at least dark, on the whole, and blackish. This means that although there are some who are endowed with a white colour and who can be said to be clever, all the others, who are almost black, are by nature crude and unrefined.

In the third place the true and Christian religion, which is so flourishing in Europe, contributes above all else to the more refined civilization of the people of Europe. For since men are distinguished from the brute animals by their reason and intelligence, and the more acute and discerning their intelligence the more civilized and refined they are, it is manifestly clear that the Christian religion, which illuminates the mind most brightly with the light of truth, promotes understanding, and imbues the mind with a knowledge of eternal things, greatly conduces to human refinement and civilization. From this fount, therefore, flow in abundance most just government of the people, observance of law and justice, the exercise of peace, of charity, and of all the other virtues, and many other good things noted by me in previous colloquia. In other parts of the world, however, where those who follow the Christian religion are few, and the great majority are steeped in false superstition, there is no doubt that all the opposite evils flourish, namely the subverting of law, the unjust occupation of kingdoms, the coveting of another man's property, hatred, malevolence, and all the other things which cast the human mind down from its proper state and make it most like to the brute animals. Thus, since idolatry and false religion is the mother of all errors and vices, those who are given over to it are inhuman, barbarous, superstitious; they are often poisoners, and are enveloped in other innumerable evils. It follows also that their princes are despots, imposing unjust laws, harassing the people, giving in to their own unbridled cupidity, and carried off with a blind impetus towards whatever strikes them as desirable.

But to what purpose am I dwelling on these reasons, when the whole progress of our colloquia has clearly shown the same thing? If you care to go over the earlier colloquia in your minds, and set once again before the eyes of your minds all that I have said about the papal and imperial rank, of the princes sacred and secular, of the way of waging war and governing the people, of the provision of servants, of the magnificence of the cities, the multitude of the arts, and the other ornaments of Europe, you will surely find that no further proof or witness of any kind is needed for what I have been telling you. You have generously given me your attention up till now, and in this and other matters you must have confidence in me. But in confirmation of it add this, that the all-provident God has set the capital of an empire formerly secular but now sacred in the city of Rome and in Italy and Europe. Whereas in times past a good part of the world was conquered from there and put under the yoke of the Romans, in our time the worldwide Christian republic recognizes the Supreme Pontiff as its supreme moderator and prince, and we should believe that the best and most suitable part of the world has been appointed to him by God, the greatest and best.

Leo: You win, Michael, and I declare myself entirely convinced by the reasons you give, for if the kingdom of China, to which we used to concede first place, yields it wholly to Europe, no further reason remains for doubt, especially when we consider the fruits which, as you have demonstrated, grow from the Christian religion.

Lino: That is also my opinion, and I would say frankly that no nation on which the light of Christian truth has not shone can flourish truly and perfectly with just administration, virtue, and other good things.

Mancio: You do well to agree with Michael, for the reasons he gives are excellent, and if you could see the thing itself with your own eyes there would be no question of your hesitating at all about something so manifestly clear.

Martin: If you need my testimony as well to the truth which Michael has put before you, I give it and proclaim it, from my heart and without any pretence.

Julian: My opinion is exactly the same. I have no wish to deviate in the slightest from what Michael has said, and I feel that no doubt should remain in your minds about this matter.

Michael: Now that the truth of this is accepted among us I want to explain the other parts of the world to you rather more briefly. Here you see America, very large, but its inhabitants are a most abject people, dark in colour, all of whom were conquered by a small number of Europeans and now live under their power, so much so that they accept them as naturally their masters. This second part here is Africa, most of the interior of which, and also this area bordering the ocean, is inhabited by negroes, barbarous men with no civilization to refine them. This third part is Asia. From the promontory of Malacca to the kingdom of Cochinchina, and also to India, it has people who are dark, low, and of little culture, but it does include noble provinces, Persia, Arabia, and others bordering on them, where the nations are white in colour, but not fully instructed in culture and liberal studies. Beyond the kingdom of Cochinchina you see the huge area of China, and our Japanese islands, of which I'll say only that the Chinese are ahead of us in the size of their country, and in peace, tranquillity, administration, wealth, and abundance of things, while we are superior to them in military science, greatness of spirit, the observance of forms of courtesy, and grades of nobility.

But let us return now to Europe, where you see many most noble provinces, namely Spain, within which is Portugal, mother of all the Portuguese who come to us, and many other kingdoms which the most powerful king Philip possesses. Also there is France, another very flourishing kingdom, Germany, in which the emperor has his seat, and Italy, where the Supreme Pontiff has his place. Round Germany are the provinces of Poland, Hungary, and the one now called Bohemia, provinces which formerly belonged to Sarmatia and Pannonia. In the ocean are the celebrated islands of Britain and Ireland, which are excellent kingdoms. Besides all these provinces you can see others towards the north, namely the Cimbrian peninsula, now known as Denmark, Gothia, Norway, and others which I omit. Now if we come down a little to the Mediterranean Sea, many other splendid provinces can been seen, namely Illyria, Dalmatia, Epirus, the Pelopponese, Attica, Macedonia, Thessaly, Aetolia, Phocis, Boeothia, Acarnania, Thrace, and other similar ones. I have said these things about Europe in general, but since I have spoken about the sea route traversed in our voyage I shall now show you, on the detailed maps of Spain and Italy, the principal cities which we visited on our overland journey.

Look now. This is Spain, which includes Portugal. Here you can see the royal city of Lisbon, from where, on our overland journey, we passed through first Évora, then Vila Viçosa and Elvas, and afterwards Badajoz, Mérida, Toledo, Madrid the seat of King Philip, Alcalá de Henares, Murcia, Orihuela, Elche, and many other towns, as we have already said, and passing through the middle of Spain, as you can see, we arrived at Alo or Alicante. I say nothing here about the other cities of this outstanding province, populous and noble though they are, so much so that formerly this one province could accommodate many powerful kings, as you can see from this map, which marks off the many different kingdoms. But, as I say, I think it is better to leave aside this and many other points, worthy of mention though they are, for my intention now is to show you the overland route which we took. At Alicante, then, we embarked on a very fine ship, crossed over the broad deeps of the Mediterranean, and reached the port of Livorno, in Italy. You can see Livorno here on this other map, which is a map of the province of Italy. From here we passed through Pisa, Florence, Siena, and the rest of Etruria, and travelling via Ancula, popularly known as Acquapendente, Viterbo, and other towns belonging to the papal jurisdiction, we came at last to Rome, seat of the Supreme Pontiff, to which we had been so looking forward.

On our way back from there we passed through the noble cities of Narni, Terni, Spoleto, Foligno, Assisi, Perugia, Camerino, Macerata, Recanati, and entered this celebrated town of the Most Blessed Virgin of Loreto. We departed from there and were taken to Ancona, Senigaglia, Fano, Pesaro, Rimini, Cesena, Forlí, Ímola, Bologna and Ferrara, these too being famous cities, and then we headed for Venice, the most famous of all of them, situated, as you can see, in the middle of the sea. When we departed from there we travelled on to Padua, Vicenza, Verona, Mantua, Cremona, Lodi, Milan, Pavia and Dertona, and then at last embarked on a galley in this most noble city of Genoa and sailed back to Spain, arriving at Barcelona. After that we saw Montserrat, Monzón, Zaragoza, Daroca, and many other Spanish towns as we made our way back to Madrid and thence to Portugal. There, in addition to the towns already mentioned, we passed through Santarém, Tomar, Coimbra, Leiria, Alcácer do Sal, Setúbal, and other places in Portugal.

From here we embarked once again on the voyage, and were happy indeed to arrive back at last, as to the longed-for embrace of a most dear mother, here in our own Japan. And as that was the end of our journey, so also it will be the end of our colloquia. It only remains for me to ask your pardon for what I have said being, on the one hand so longwinded, on the other so boring and inadequate. But you do know that my concern has been that it should be generally useful to us rather than eloquent or ornate.

Leo: I can't tell you, Michael, how indebted to you I feel for all that you have done for us, putting aside, as you did, everything else, and devoting yourself to complying with our entreaties and labouring for so many days to give us no inadequate account, as you term it, but a very full account of all the various things of Europe.

Lino: I too thank Michael from my heart, and will continue to thank him as long as I live, for I am convinced that I cannot possibly repay him. I have learned more from his talks than from the teaching of other masters, and I hope that I can now go out from here better informed and can pass on this so necessary knowledge to many others who are ignorant about Europe.

Mancio: It is right that you have both expressed the profound gratitude that you feel towards Michael for accepting your request, gladly undertaking and completing this difficult task, and treating each point in detail and with an exactitude that exceeded our hopes or expectation, for we feared that it might not be possible to explain things so various, so detailed, and so little discussed, with such perspicacity and lucidity.

Martin: I also believe that Divine Providence has been with us in this matter, and has brought us, at the end of these colloquia, so useful and so necessary for the Japanese church, to the desired conclusion.

Julian: No one can doubt it, for it was very difficult even to keep the things themselves in our memories and to record them in our journal throughout the many and various difficulties of the journey.

Leo: All that remains is to discuss with the reverend Father Visitor how these colloquia which we have held with one another are to be written out in elegant Japanese and printed.

Lino: The Father himself will make sure that is done, for he acquired a printing press from Europe for us and has brought it here.

Michael: I give unceasing thanks, in my own name and in the names of all of you, to God, the greatest and the best, who has assisted me in this work which I took upon myself not as a pointless exercise but in the hope that it would be of value to all; and I hope that not only our happy return to our own land, but also this account, frequently recalled among ourselves and remembered by many in the future, may redound to the benefit of our people and of the whole Japanese church, and bring joy to all the fathers.

THE END

BIBLIOGRAPHY

MANUSCRIPT SOURCES

Archivum Romanum Societatis Iesu (ARSI), Rome
Jap.Sin 8: I; 8: II; 9: I; 9: II; 10: II; 11: I; 11: II; 22; 23; 33; 46; 51; 186a
Ital. 159
Instit. 40
Real Academia de la Historia Madrid (RAHM)
Jesuítas 7236
MS 09-02663

PRINTED PRIMARY AND SECONDARY SOURCES

Abranches Pinto, João do Amaral and Bernard, Henri, 'Les instructions du Père Valignano pour l'ambassade japonaise en Europe', *Monumenta Nipponica*, 6: 1/2, 1943, pp. 392–403.

Acosta, José de, *De Procuranda Indorum salute*, ed. L. Pereña et al., 2 vols, Madrid, 1984.

—, *Natural and Moral History of the Indies*, ed. Jane E. Mangan, with intro. and comm. by Walter D. Mignolo, Durham NC, 2002.

Acta Consistorii Publice Exhibiti A S.D.N. Gregorio Papa XIII. Regum Iaponiorum Legatis Romae, Die XXIII Martii MDLXXXV, Rome, 1585.

Agostinho, Nicolau, *Relaçam summaria da vida do illvstrissimo, et reverendissimo Senhor Dom Theotónio de Bragáça*, Évora, 1614.

Alden, Dauril, *The Making of an Enterprise: The Society of Jesus in Portugal, Its Empire and Beyond, 1540–1750*, Stanford, 1996.

Allsen, Thomas T., *The Royal Hunt in Eurasian History*, Philadelphia, 2006.

Álvarez-Taladriz, José Luis, 'El Escorial visto por un japanes el siglo XVI', *Osaka Gaikokugo Gakuhō*, 14, 1963, pp. 12–20.

—, 'Opinión de un teólogo de la Compañía de Jesús sobre la pluralidad de ordenes religiosas en Japón (1593)', *Tenri Daigaku Gakuhō*, 17, 1971, pp. 1–19.

—, 'El padre viceprovincial Gaspar Coelho: ¿"Capitan de armas o pastor de almas"?', *Sapientia*, 6, 1972, pp. 41–79.

—, 'Relación del P. Alejandro Valignano, S.J. sobre su embajada a Hideyoshi (1591)', *Osaka Gaikokugo Gakuhō*, 28, 1972, pp. 43–60.

—, 'El proyecto de embajada del Papa a la China y el Padre Alejandro Valignano, S.J.' *Tenri Daigaku Gakuhō*, 89, 1973, pp. 60–94.

—, 'De arboricultura occidental en Japón durante el siglo XVI', *Tenri Daigaku Gakuhō*, 87, 1973, pp. 1–19.

—, 'A cada cosa su nombre y a dios el que corresponde', *Osaka Gaikokugo Gakuhō*, 32, 1974, pp. 1–20.

—, 'La persecución de 1587 y el viceprovincial Gaspar Coelho, segun el visitador Alejandro Valignano', *Sapientia*, 9, 1975, pp. 95–114.

—, 'Il relación de la embajada de Valignano a Hideyoshi (1593)', *Tenri Daigaku Gakuhō*, 110, 1977, pp. 1–21.

—, 'De la primera visita del P. Alejandro Valignano, S.J. a la Cristiandad de Japón (1579)', *Tenri Daigaku Gakuhō*, 124, 1980, pp. 80–92.
—, 'Apendice documental para el estudio del *Sumario de las cosas de Japón*', *Osaka Gaikokugo Daigaku Gakuhō*, 46, 1980, pp. 51–64.
—, 'El Padre Diogo de Mesquita, S.J.: Entre la obediencia y la conciencia (1593)', *Sapientia*, 15, 1981, pp. 97–106.
—, 'En el IV centenario de la embajada Cristiana de Japón a Europa: las "Instrucciones" del Visitador Alejandro Valignano, S.J. (1583)', *Sapientia*, 16, 1982, pp. 125–86.
—, '¿Resistencia armada a la persecución de 1587?', *Tenri Daigaku Gakuhō*, 140, 1983, pp. 71–86.
—, 'En el IV centenario del breve "Ex Pastorali Officio" (1585–1985)', *Sapientia*, 20, 1986, pp. 93–115.
—, ed., *Juan Rodríguez Tsuzu S.J.: Arte del cha*, Tokyo, 1954.
—, ed., *Documentos Franciscanos de Cristiandad de Japón (1593–1597)*, Osaka, 1973.
Arasaratnam, Sinnappah, ed., *François Valentijn's Description of Ceylon*, London, 1978.
Aristotle, *Nicomachean Ethics*.
—, *The Politics*.
Bailey, Gauvin Alexander, *Between Renaissance and Baroque: Jesuit Art in Rome, 1565–1610*, Toronto, 2003.
Barata, Antonio Francesco, *Évora antiga*, Évora, 1909.
Bartoli, Daniello, *Dell' Historia della Compagnia di Giesù, il Giappone*, Rome, 1660.
Beckingham, C. F. and Huntingford, G. W. B., eds, *The Prester John of the Indies*, Hakluyt Society, 2nd ser., 114 and 115, Cambridge, 1961.
Bedini, Silvio A., *The Pope's Elephant*, Nashville, 1998.
Berchet, Gugleilmo, 'Le antiche ambasciate giapponesi in Italia', *Archivo Veneto*, 13, 1877, pp. 245–85.
—, 'Documenti del saggio storico sulle antiche ambasciate giapponesi in Italia', *Archivo Veneto*, 14, 1877, pp. 150–203.
Bernard, Henri, 'Valignani ou Valignano, l'auteur véritable du récit de la première ambassade japonaise en Europe (1582–1590)', *Monumenta Nipponica*, 1: 2, 1938, pp. 86–93.
Bernard-Maitre, Henri, 'L'orientaliste Guillaume Postel et la découverte spirituelle du Japon en 1552', *Monumenta Nipponica*, 9, 1953, pp. 83–108.
Berry, Mary Elizabeth, *Hideyoshi*, Cambridge MA, 1982.
Bertini, Giuseppe, 'The Marriage of Alessandro Farnese and Maria of Portugal in 1565: Court Life in Lisbon and Parma', in K. J. P. Lowe, ed., *Cultural Links between Portugal and Italy*, Oxford, 2000, pp. 47–59.
Bésineau, J, ed., *Les jésuites au Japon: Relation missionaire (1583)*, Paris, 1990.
Bireley, Robert, *The Jesuits and the Thirty Years War: Kings, Courts, and Confessors*, Cambridge, 2003.
Blackburn, Robin, *The Making of New World Slavery: From the Baroque to the Modern 1492–1800*, London, 1997.
Blair, Dorothy, *A History of Glass in Japan*, New York, 1973.
Blastenbrei, Peter, 'Violence, Arms and Criminal Justice in Papal Rome, 1560–1600', *Renaissance Studies*, 20: 1, 2006, pp, 68–87.
Bodart-Bailey, Beatrice, ed., *Kaempfer's Japan: Tokugawa Culture Observed*, Honolulu, 1999.
Boncompagni-Ludovisi, Francesco, *Le prime due ambasciate dei giapponese a Roma (1585–1615)*, Rome, 1904.
Bonifacio, João, *Christiani Pveri Institvtio, Adolescentiaeqve perfugium: autore Ioanne Bonifacio Societatis Iesv*, Macao, 1588.
Borao Mateo, José Eugenio et al., eds, *Spaniards in Taiwan (Documents) Volume 1: 1582–1641*, Taipei, 2001.
Boscaro, Adriana, 'La visita a Venezia della prima ambasceria giapponese in Europa', *Giappone: Rivista trimestrale a cura del centro di studi di cultura giapponese*, V, 1965, pp. 19–32.

—, 'Manoscritto inedito nella Biblioteca Marciana di Venezia relativo all'ambasciata Giapponese del 1585', *Giappone: Rivista trimestrale a cura del centro di studi di cultura Giapponese*, 7, 1967, pp. 9–39.
—, 'The First Japanese Ambassadors to Europe: Political Background for a Religious Journey', in *Kokusai Bunka Shinkokai Bulletin*, 103, August–September 1970, pp. 1–20.
—, *Sixteenth Century European Printed Works on the First Japanese Mission to Europe: a Descriptive Bibliography*, Leiden, 1973.
—, *Ventura e sventura dei gesuiti in Giapppone (1549–1639)*, Venice, 2008.
Botsman, Daniel V., *Punishment and Power in the Making of Modern Japan*, Princeton, 2005.
Bouchon, Geneviève, 'L'évolution de la piraterie sur la côte Malabare au cours du XVIe siècle', in G. Bouchon, *L'Asie du sud à l'époque des grandes découvertes*, London, 1987, XII.
—, 'Sixteenth Century Malabar and the Indian Ocean', in Ashin Das Gupta and M. N. Pearson, eds, *India and the Indian Ocean 1500–1800*, Delhi, 1987, pp. 162–84.
Bourdon, Léon, *La Compagnie de Jésus et le Japon 1547–1570*, Paris, 1993.
Bouza, Fernando, *D. Filipe I*, Lisbon, 2008.
Bovill, E. W., 'The *Madre de Dios*', *The Mariner's Mirror*, 54: 2, 1968, pp. 129–52.
Boxer, C. R., *The Tragic History of the Sea 1589–1622*, Cambridge, 1957.
—, *The Great Ship from Amacon: Annals of Macao and the Old Japan Trade, 1555–1640*, Lisbon, 1959.
—, *Fidalgos in the Far East 1550–1770*, Hong Kong, 1968.
—, *Jan Compagnie in Japan 1600–1817*, Tokyo, 1968.
—, *The Christian Century in Japan 1549–1650*, Berkeley, 1974.
—, *The Portuguese Seaborne Empire 1415–1825*, London, 1977.
—, 'The Taking of the *Madre de Deus*, 1592', *The Mariner's Mirror*, 67: 1, 1981, pp. 82–4.
—, *From Lisbon to Goa*, London, 1984.
—, 'The *Carreira da Índia* (Ships, Men, Cargoes, Voyages)', repr. in *From Lisbon to Goa*, London, 1984, I.
—, 'The Principal Ports of call in the "Carreira da Índia" (16th–18th Centuries)', repr. in *From Lisbon to Goa*, London, 1984, II.
—, 'Moçambique Island and the "Carreira da Índia"', repr. in *From Lisbon to Goa*, London, 1984, III.
—, 'An Introduction to the *História Tragico-Marítima*' repr. in *From Lisbon to Goa*, London, 1984, V.
—, ed., *South China in the Sixteenth Century*, London, 1953.
— and Azevedo, Carlos de, *A Fortaleza de Jesus e os Portugueses em Mombaça*, Lisbon, 1960.
Boyajian, James C., *Portuguese Trade in Asia under the Habsburgs, 1580–1640*, Baltimore, 1993.
Braga, Isabel M. R. Mendes Drumond, 'Poor Relief in Counter-Reformation Portugal: The Case of the *Misericórdias*', in O. P. Grell, A. Cunningham and J. Arrizabalaga, eds, *Health Care and Poor Relief*, London, 1999, pp. 201–14.
Bramanti, Vanni, ed., *Filippo Sassetti: Lettere da vari paesi 1570–1588*, Milan, 1970.
Brandão, João, *Grandeza e abastança de Lisboa em 1552*, ed. José da Felicidade Alves, Lisbon, 1990.
Braudel, Fernand, *The Mediterranean and the Mediterranean World in the Age of Philip II*, 2 vols, London, 1976.
Braun, Georg and Hogenberg, Frans, *Civitates orbis terrarum*, 6 vols, Cologne, 1572–1617.
Brayman, Heidi and Mancall, Peter C., 'Richard Hakluyt the Younger's Notes for the East India Company in 1601: A Transcription of Huntington Library Manuscript EL 2360', *Huntington Library Quarterly*, 67: 3, 2004, pp. 423–36.
Brinton, Selwyn, *The Gonzaga Lords of Mantua*, London 1927.
Brito, Bernardo Gomes de, *História Tragico-Marítima compilado por Gomes de Brito*, ed. Damião Peres, 3 vols, Porto, 1942.
Brizzi, Gian Paolo, 'Les jésuites et l'école en Italie (XVIe–XVIIIe siècles)', in L. Giard, ed., *Les jésuites à la Renaissance*, Paris, 1995, pp. 35–53.

Brockley, Liam Matthew, *Journey to the East: The Jesuit Mission to China, 1579–1724*, Cambridge MA, 2007.
Broderick, John F., 'The Sacred College of Cardinals: Size and Geographical Composition (1099–1986)', *Archivum Historiae Pontificiae*, 25, 1987, pp. 7–71.
Brodrick, James, *The Progress of the Jesuits (1556–79)*, Chicago, 1986.
Brook, Timothy, *The Confusions of Pleasure: Commerce and Culture in Ming China*, Berkeley, 1998.
Brown, Judith C., 'Courtiers and Christians: The First Japanese Emissaries to Europe', *Renaissance Quarterly*, 47: 4, 1994, pp. 872–906.
Bruijn, J. R., Gaastra, F. S. and Schöffer, I., *Dutch-Asiatic Shipping in the 17th and 18th Centuries*, volume 1, The Hague, 1987.
— and Gaastra, F. S., eds, *Ships, Sailors and Spices: East India Companies and their Shipping in the 16th and 17th Centuries*, Amsterdam, 1993.
Brunon, Hervé, 'Pratolino: art des jardins et imaginaire de la nature dans l'Italie de la seconde moitié du XVIe siècle', doctoral thesis, Université Paris I Panthéon-Sorbonne, 2008.
Burckhardt, Jacob, *The Civilization of the Renaissance in Italy*, trans. S. G. C. Middlemore, Vienna, n.d.
Burke, Peter, 'The Renaissance Dialogue', *Renaissance Studies*, 3: 1, 1989, pp. 1–12.
—, 'Southern Italy in the 1590s: Hard Times or Crisis?' in Peter Clark, ed., *The European Crisis of the 1590s*, London, 1985, pp. 177–90.
—, *The Historical Anthropology of Early Modern Italy*, Cambridge, 1987.
Burnett, Charles, 'Humanism and the Jesuit Mission to China: The case of Duarte de Sande (1547–1599)', *Euphrosyne*, new ser., 24, 1996, pp. 425–71.
Bury, J. B., 'The Italian Contribution to Sixteenth Century Portuguese Architecture, Military and Civil', in K. J. P. Lowe, ed., *Cultural Links between Portugal and Italy*, Oxford, 2000, pp. 77–107.
Butler, Lee, *Emperor and Aristocracy in Japan, 1467–1680*, Cambridge MA, 2002.
Cambridge History of China Volume 7: The Ming Dynasty, 1368–1644, Part 1, ed. Frederick W. Mote and Denis Twitchett, Cambridge, 1998.
Cambridge History of China Volume 8: The Ming Dynasty, 1368–1644, Part 2, ed. Frederick W. Mote and Denis Twitchett, Cambridge, 1998.
Cambridge History of Japan Volume 4: Early Modern Japan, ed. John Whitney Hall, Cambridge, 1991.
Cambridge History of Medieval Political Thought c. 350–c. 1450, ed. H. Burns, Cambridge, 1988.
Cambridge History of Southeast Asia Volume 1: From Early Times to c. 1800, ed. N. Tarling, Cambridge, 1992.
Cambridge Modern History, vol. 3, ed. A. W. Ward et al., Cambridge, 1907.
Camões, Luís de, *Os Lusíadas*, ed. Arnaldo de Mariz Rozeira, Lisbon, 2001.
Carneiro, Roberto and Matos, Artur Teodoro de, eds, *O século Cristão do Japão: Actas do colóquio internacional comemorativo dos 450 anos de amizade Portugal-Japão (1543–1993)*, Lisbon, 1994.
Carroll, Stuart, *Blood and Violence in Early Modern France*, Oxford, 2006.
Cartas que os padres e irmãos da Companhia de Jesus escreverão dos reynos de Japão e China, 2 vols, Évora, 1598; facs. edn, Maia, 1997.
Carter, Charles H., 'The Ambassadors of Early Modern Europe: Patterns of Diplomatic Representation in the Early Seventeenth Century', in Charles H. Carter, ed., *From Renaissance to Counter-Reformation: Essays in Honour of Garrett Mattingly*, London, 1966, pp. 269–95.
Carvalho, José Adriano de Freitas, 'Os recebimentos de relíquias em S. Roque (Lisboa 1588) e em Santa Cruz (Coimbra 1595). Relíquias e espiritualidade. E alguma ideologia', *Via Spiritus: Revista de História de Espiritualidade e do Sentimento Religioso*, 8, 2001, pp. 95–155.
Casale, Giancarlo, 'Global Politics in the 1580s: One Canal, Twenty Thousand Cannibals, and an Ottoman Plot to Rule the World', *Journal of World History*, 18: 3, 2007, pp. 267–96.
—, *The Ottoman Age of Exploration*, New York, 2010.

Castellani, Marcello, 'A 1593 Veronese Inventory', *The Galpin Society Journal*, 26, 1973, pp. 15–24.

Certeau, Michel de, 'La réforme de l'intérieur au temps d'Aquaviva', in Michel de Certeau et al., *Les Jésuites, Spiritualité et activité; Jalons d'une histoire*, Paris, 1974, pp. 53–69.

Cervantes, Fernando, 'Cervantes in Italy: Christian Humanism and the Visual Impact of Renaissance Rome', *Journal of the History of Ideas*, 66: 3, 2005, pp. 325–50.

Cervantes Saavedra, Miguel de, *Obras completas*, ed. Ángel Valbuena Prat, 2 vols, Madrid, 1975.

Chase, Kenneth, *Firearms: A Global History to 1700*, Cambridge, 2003.

Chatellier, Louis, *The Europe of the Devout: The Catholic Reformation and the Formation of a New Society*, Cambridge, 1989.

Chaudhuri, K. N., *Trade and Civilisation in the Indian Ocean: An Economic History from the Rise of Islam to 1750*, Cambridge, 1985.

Ciappi, Marc'Antonio, *Compendio delle heroiche, et gloriose attioni, et santa vita di Papa Greg. XIII*, Rome, 1596.

Cicero, *Cato Maior de Senectute*.

—, *Topica*.

—, *Tusculan Disputations*.

Cieslik, Hubert, *Publikationen über das Christentum in Japan*, ed. M. Dietrich and A. Schwade, Frankfurt, 2004.

—, 'Laienarbeitin der alten Japanmission', repr. in *Publikationen über das Christentum in Japan*, pp. 165–89.

—, 'The Training of a Japanese Clergy in the Seventeenth Century', repr in *Publikationen über das Christentum in Japan*, pp. 303–24.

—, 'Zur Geschichte der kirchlichen Hierarchie in der alten Japanmission', repr in *Publikationen über das Christentum in Japan*, pp. 191–245.

Clark, Peter, ed., *The European Crisis of the 1590s: Essays in Comparative History*, London, 1985.

Cocks, Richard, *The Diary Kept by the Head of the English Factory in Japan*, ed. The Historiographical Institute, The University of Tokyo, 3 vols, Tokyo, 1978–80.

Collcutt, Martin, *Five Mountains: The Rinzai Zen Monastic Institution in Medieval Japan*, Cambridge MA, 1981.

Confucius, *The Analects of Confucius*, trans. Burton Watson, New York, 2007.

Cooper, Michael, 'The Mechanics of the Macao-Nagasaki Silk Trade', *Monumenta Nipponica*, 27: 4, 1972, pp. 423–33.

—, *Rodrigues the Interpreter: An Early Jesuit in Japan and China*, New York, 1974.

—, *The Japanese Mission to Europe, 1582–1590*, Folkestone, 2005.

—, ed., *They Came to Japan: An Anthology of European Reports on Japan, 1543–1640*, London, 1965.

—, ed., *João Rodrigues's Account of Sixteenth-Century Japan*, Hakluyt Society, 3rd ser., 7, London, 2001.

Correia, Pedro Lage Reis, 'Father Diogo de Mesquita (1551–1614) and the Cultivation of Western Plants in Japan', *Bulletin of Portuguese/Japanese Studies*, 7, 2003, pp. 73–91.

Cortesão, Armando, *Cartografia e cartografos Portugueses dos séculos XV e XVI*, 2 vols, Lisbon, 1935.

Coryate, Thomas, *Coryat's Crudities* (1611), repr., London, 1978.

Costa, João Paulo Oliveira e, 'The *Misericórdias* among Japanese Christian Communities in the 16th and 17th Centuries', *Bulletin of Portuguese/Japanese Studies*, 5, 2003, pp. 67–79.

—, 'Os Jesuítas no Japão (1549–1598): uma análise estatística', in *Portuguese Voyages to Asia and Japan in the Renaissance Period: Proceedings of the International Conference Sophia University, Tokyo September 24–26, 1993*, Tokyo, 1994, pp. 298–333.

Couto, Diogo do, *Da Ásia de João de Barros e de Diogo do Couto: dos feitos que os portugueses fizeram no descobrimento dos mares e terras do Oriente*, 24 vols, Lisbon, 1777–88, Decada 5, pt 1, Lisbon, 1779.

Coutre, Jacques de, *Andanzas asiáticas*, ed. E. Stols et al., Madrid, 1991.

Cox, Virginia, *The Renaissance Dialogue: Literary Dialogue in its Social and Political Contexts, Castiglione to Galileo*, Cambridge, 1992.

Crook, David, '"A Certain Indulgence": Music at the Jesuit College in Paris, 1575–1590', in J. O'Malley et al., eds, *The Jesuits: Cultures, Sciences, and the Arts*, Toronto, 2000, pp. 461–78.

Crouzet-Pavan, Elisabeth, *Venice Triumphant: The Horizons of a Myth*, Baltimore, 2002.

Cummins, J. S., 'The Dominican Mission in Japan (1602–1622) and Lope de Vega', in *idem, Jesuit and Friar in the Spanish Expansion to the East*, London, 1986, II.

Curran, Brian, et al, 'A Fifteenth Century Site Report on the Vatican Obelisk', *Journal of the Warburg and Courtauld Institutes*, 58, 1995, pp. 234–48.

Cushner, Nicholas P., *Why Have You Come Here?: The Jesuits and the First Evangelization of Native America*, New York, 2006.

Dai Nihon Shiryō, ed. The Historiographical Institute, The University of Tokyo, Tokyo, 1901– .

Dandelet, Thomas James, *Spanish Rome 1500–1700*, New Haven, 2001.

Davis, Robert C., *Christian Slaves, Muslim Masters: White Slavery in the Mediterranean, the Barbary Coast, and Italy, 1500–1800*, Basingstoke, 2003.

D'Elia, Pasquale M., 'Recent Discoveries and New Studies on the World Map in Chinese of Father Matteo Ricci, SJ', *Monumenta Serica*, 20, 1961, pp. 82–164.

—, 'I primi ambasciatori giapponese venuti a Roma (1585)', *La Civiltà Cattolica*, CIII, 1952, pp. 43–58.

Delumeau, Jean, *Vie économique et sociale de Rome dans la seconde moitié du XVIe siècle*, 2 vols, continuous pagination, Paris, 1957–9.

Demoustier, Adrien, 'La distinction des fonctions et l'exercise du pouvoir selon les règles de la Compagnie de Jésus', in L. Giard, ed., *Les jésuites à la Renaissance*, Paris, 1995, pp. 3–33.

Descrittione della Porta di San Benedetto della città di Ferrara, de' luoghi delitiosi, che erano attorno le mura di essa, e del ressiduo de giardini ducali, Padua, 1671.

DeSilva, Jennifer M., 'Senators or Courtiers: Negotiating Models for the College of Cardinals under Julius II and Leo X', *Renaissance Studies*, 22: 2, 2008, pp. 154–73.

Diccionario histórico de la Compañía de Jesús: biográfico-temático, ed. Charles, E. O'Neill, and Joaquín Dominguez, 4 vols, Madrid, 2001.

Dicionário de história dos descobrimentos Portugueses, ed. Luis de Albuquerque, 2 vols, Lisbon, 1994.

Diffie, Bailey W. and Winius, George D., *Foundations of the Portuguese Empire 1415–1580*, Minnesota, 1977.

Disney, A. R., *A History of Portugal and the Portuguese Empire From Beginnings to 1807*, 2 vols, Cambridge, 2009.

Documenta Indica, ed. Josef Wicki, and John Gomes, 18 vols, Rome, 1948–88.

Documenta Mexicana, ed. Félix Zubillaga, 8 vols, Rome, 1956–91.

Documentos para la historia de la demarcación comercial de California 1583–1632, ed. W. Michael Mathes, vol. 2, Madrid, 1965.

Doi, Tadao, 'Das Sprachstudium der Gesellschaft Jesu in Japan im 16. und 17. Jahrhundert', *Monumenta Nipponica*, 2: 2, 1939, pp. 437–65.

Duffy, James, *Shipwreck & Empire*, Cambridge MA, 1955.

Dunmore, John, ed., *The Journal of Jean-François de Galaup de La Pérouse 1785–1799*, Hakluyt Society, 2nd ser., 179 and 180, London, 1995.

Dunne, George H., *Generation of Giants: The Story of the Jesuits in China in the Last Decades of the Ming Dynasty*, Notre Dame, 1962.

Eden, Richard, *The Arte of Nauigation Translated out of Spanyshe into Englyshe*, 1561.

Elias, Norbert, *The History of Manners*, New York, 1978.

Elison, George, *Deus Destroyed: The Image of Christianity in Early Modern Japan*, Cambridge MA, 1973.

— and Smith, Bardwell L., eds, *Warlords, Artists and Commoners: Japan in the Sixteenth Century*, Honolulu, 1981.

Elisonas, J. S. A., 'An Itinerary to the Terrestrial Paradise: Early European Reports on Japan and a Contemporary Exegesis', *Itinerario*, 20: 3, 1996, pp. 25–68.
—, 'Acts, Legends, and Southern Barbarous Japanese' in Jorge M. dos Santos Alves, ed., *Portugal e a China; Conferências nos encontros de história Luso-Chinesa*, Lisbon, 2001, pp. 15–60.
—, 'Fables and Imitations: *Kirishitan* Literature in the Forest of Simple Letters', *Bulletin of Portuguese/Japanese Studies*, 4, 2002, pp. 9–36.
—, 'Journey to the West', *Japanese Journal of Religious Studies*, 34: 1, 2007, pp. 27–66.
Elliott, J. H., 'The Spanish Monarchy and the Kingdom of Portugal, 1580–1640', in Mark Greengrass, ed., *Conquest and Coalescence*, London, 1991, pp. 48–67.
—, *Empires of the Atlantic World: Britain and Spain in America 1492–1830*, New Haven, 2006.
Erasmus, Desiderius, *De civilitate morum puerilium*, Antwerp, 1530.
Fairbank, John K., ed., *The Chinese World Order: Traditional China's Foreign Relations*, Cambridge MA, 1968.
Farrell, Allan P., *The Jesuit Code of Liberal Education: Development and Scope of the* Ratio Studiorum, Milwaukee, 1938.
Farrington, Anthony, ed., *The English Factory in Japan 1613–1623*, 2 vols, London, 1991.
Farris, William W., 'Shipbuilding and Nautical Technology in Japanese Maritime History: Origins to 1600', *The Mariner's Mirror*, 95: 3, 2009, pp. 260–83.
Fasoli, Gina, 'La coscienza civica nelle "Laudes civitatum"', in *La coscienza cittadina nei comuni Italiani del duecento*, Atti dell'XI Convegno del Centro di Studi sulla Spiritualità Medievale, Todi, 1972, pp. 9–44.
Faure, Bernard, *The Red Thread: Buddhist Approaches to Sexuality*, Princeton, 1998.
Fenlon, Iain, *Music and Patronage in Sixteenth-Century Mantua*, 2 vols, Cambridge, 1980.
—, *Music and Culture in Renaissance Italy*, Oxford, 2002.
—, *The Ceremonial City: History, Memory and Myth in Renaissance Venice*, New Haven, 2007.
Fichtner, Paula S., *Emperor Maximilian II*, New Haven, 1981.
Findlay, Ronald and O'Rourke, Kevin, *Power and Plenty: Trade, War, and the World Economy in the Second Millennium*, Princeton, 2007.
Fontana, Domenico, *Della trasportatione dell'obelisco Vaticano et delle fabriche di Nostro Signore Papa Sisto V, fatte dal cavallier Domenico Fontana architetto di Sua Santita*, Rome, 1590.
Fosi, Irene, 'Justice and its Image: Political Propaganda and Judicial Reality in the Pontificate of Sixtus V', *Sixteenth Century Journal*, 24: 1, 1993, pp. 75–95.
—, 'Court and City in the Ceremony of the *possesso* in the Sixteenth Century', in G. Signorotto and M. A. Visceglia, eds, *Court and Politics in Papal Rome*, Cambridge, 2002, pp. 31–52.
Fróis, Luís, *Segunda parte da História de Japam*, ed. João do Amaral Abranches Pinto and Yoshitomo Okamoto, Tokyo, 1938.
—, *La première ambassade du Japon en Europe, 1582–1592*, ed. João do Amaral Abranches Pinto, Yoshitomo Okamoto and Henri Bernard, Tokyo, 1942.
—, *História de Japam*, ed. José Wicki, 5 vols, Lisbon, 1976–84.
—, *Europa/Japão: Um diálogo civizacional no século XVI*, ed. José Manuel Garcia, Lisbon, 1993.
Frugoni, Chiara, *A Distant City: Images of Urban Experience in the Medieval World*, Princeton, 1991.
Fujita Midori, 'Edo jidai ni okeru Nihonjin no Afurika kan', *Nihon Chūtō Gakkai Nenpō*, 2, 1987, pp. 239–90.
Gairdner, James, ed., *Letters and Papers, Foreign and Domestic, Henry VIII*, vol. 6, London, 1882.
García Cárcel, Ricardo, 'Las relaciones de la monarquía de Felipe II con la Compañía de Jesús', in E. Belenguer, ed., *Felipe II y el Mediterráneo*, vol. 2, Madrid, 1999, pp. 219–42.
García Mahíques, R., *Empresas morales de Juan de Borja. Imagen y palabra para una iconología*. Valencia, 1998.
Garnett, R., 'On the "*De Missione legatorum Japonensium*," Macao, 1590', *The Library*, new ser., 2, 1901, pp. 172–7.

Giard, Luce, ed., *Les Jésuites à la Renaissance*, Paris, 1995.
— and Vaucelles, Louis de, eds, *Les Jésuites à l'âge baroque (1540–1640)*, Grenoble, 1995.
Gibb, A. A. R. and Beckingham, C. F., eds, *The Travels of Ibn Baṭṭūṭa AD 1325–1354*, Hakluyt Society, 2nd ser., 108, London, 1994.
Gibson-Hill, C. A., 'Singapore: Notes on the History of the Old Strait, 1580–1850', *Journal of the Malayan Branch of the Royal Asiatic Society*, 27: 1, 1954, pp. 163–214.
Gillman, Ian and Klimkeit, Hans-Joachim, *Christians in Asia Before 1500*, Richmond, Surrey, 1999.
Girard, Pascale, ed. and trans., *Le voyage en Chine d'Adriano de las Cortes S.J. (1625)*, Paris, 2001.
Glahn, Richard von, *Fountain of Fortune: Money and Monetary Policy in China, 1000–1700*, Berkeley, 1996.
Godinho, Rui Landeiro, *A Carreira da Índia: Aspectos e problemas da Torna-viagem (1550–1649)*, Lisbon, 2005.
Godinho, Vitorino Magalhães, *Os descobrimentos e a economia mundial*, 4 vols, Lisbon, 1991.
—, 'The Portuguese and the "Carreira da India", 1497–1810', in J. Bruijn and F. S. Gaastra, eds, *Ships, Sailors and Spices*, pp. 1–47.
Góis, Damião de, *Urbis Olisiponis descriptio* (1554).
—, *Crónica de Dom Emanuel*, Lisbon, 1749.
—, *Lisbon in the Renaissance: A New Translation of the* Urbis Olisiponis descriptio, trans. and ed. Jeffrey S. Ruth, New York, 1996.
—, *Descrição da cidade de Lisboa*, trans. and ed. José da Felicidade Alves, Lisbon, 2001.
Goldenberg, David M., *The Curse of Ham: Race and Slavery in Early Judaism, Christianity, and Islam*, Princeton, 2005.
Gomes, Rita Costa, *The Making of a Court Society: Kings and Nobles in Late Medieval Portugal*, Cambridge, 2007.
Goy, Richard J., *Building Renaissance Venice*, New Haven, 2006.
Greengrass, Mark, ed., *Conquest and Coalescence: The Shaping of the State in Early Modern Europe*, London, 1991
Greenlee, William B., ed., *The Voyage of Pedro Álvares Cabral to Brazil and India*, London, 1938.
Gregory, Brad S., *Salvation at Stake: Christian Martyrdom in Early Modern Europe*, Cambridge MA, 2001.
Grell, O. P., Cunningham, A. and Arrizabalaga, J., eds, *Health Care and Poor Relief in Counter-Reformation Europe*, London, 1999.
Grendler, Paul F., *Schooling in Renaissance Italy: Literacy and Learning, 1300–1600*, Baltimore, 1989.
—, *The University of Mantua: The Gonzaga and the Jesuits, 1584–1630*, Baltimore, 2009.
Grove Dictionary of Art, ed. Janet Turner, 34 vols, Oxford, 2003.
Gualtieri, Guido, *Relationi Della Venvta De Gli Ambasciatori Giaponesi à Roma, sino alla partita di Lisbona*, Venice, 1586.
Guarini, Elena F., '"Rome Workshop of all the Practices of the World": From the Letters of Cardinal Ferdinando de'Medici to Cosimo I and Francesco I', in G. Signorotto and M. A. Viseglia, eds, *Court and Politics in Papal Rome*, Cambridge, 2002, pp. 53–77.
Guilmartin, John F., *Gunpowder & Galleys: Changing Technology & Mediterranean Warfare at Sea in the 16th Century*, London, 2003.
Gutierrez, B., *La prima ambascieria giapponese in Italia*, Milan, 1938.
Gutiérrez, Fernando G., 'A Survey of Nanban Art', in M. Cooper et al., eds, *The Southern Barbarians: The First Europeans in Japan*, Tokyo, 1971, pp. 147–206.
Guzman, Luis de, *Historia de las missiones qve han hecho los religiosos de la Compañia de Iesvs, para predicar el Sancto Euangelio en la India Oriental, y en los reynos de la China y de Iapon*, 2 vols, Alcalá, 1601.
Haar, James, 'Value Judgements in Music of the Renaissance', in T. Knighton and D. Fallows, eds, *Companion to Medieval and Renaissance Music*, Berkeley, 1997, pp. 15–22.

Hakluyt, Richard, *The Principal Navigations Voyages Traffiques & Discoveries of the English Nation*, 12 vols, Glasgow, 1903–5.
Hale, J. R., 'War and Public Opinion in Renaissance Italy', in E. F. Jacob, ed., *Italian Renaissance Studies*, London, 1960, pp. 94–122.
—, *The Civilization of Europe in the Renaissance*, New York, 1995.
—, *Florence and the Medici*, London, 2001.
Hall, John Whitney et al., eds, *Japan before Tokugawa: Political Consolidation and Economic Growth, 1500 to 1650*, Princeton, 1981.
Hamada Kōsaku, *Tenshō ken-Ō shisetsu ki*, Tokyo, 1931.
—, et al., eds, *Tenshō nenkan ken'Ō shisetsu kenbun taiwaroku*, Tokyo, 1942.
Hanke, Lewis, *Aristotle and the American Indians: A Study of Race Prejudice in the Modern World*, Chicago, 1959.
Hannaford, Ivan, *Race: The History of an Idea in the West*, Baltimore, 1996.
Hanshi daijiten, 8 vols, Tokyo, 1988.
Hare, Augustus J. C., *Florence*, London, 1896.
Harich-Schneider, Eta, 'Renaissance Europe through Japanese Eyes: Record of a Strange Triumphal Journey', *Early Music*, January 1973, pp. 19–26.
—, *A History of Japanese Music*, London, 1973.
Harris, Steven J., 'Mapping Jesuit Science: The Role of Travel in the Geography of Knowledge', in J. O'Malley et al., eds, *The Jesuits: Cultures, Sciences, and the Arts*, Toronto, 2000, pp. 212–40.
Hayami, Akira and Hiroshi Kitō, 'Demography and Living Standards', in A.Hayami et al., eds, *Emergence of Economic Society in Japan 1600–1859: Early Modern*, Oxford, 1999, pp. 213–46.
Hazart, Cornelius. *Kerckelycke historie van de gheheele wereldt, namelyck vande voorgaende ende teghenwoordighe eeuvwe*, vol. 1, Antwerp, 1667.
Headly, John M., 'Geography and Empire in the Late Renaissance: Boter's Assignment, Western Universalism, and the Civilizing Process', *Renaissance Quarterly*, 53, 2000, pp. 1119–55.
Hillgarth, J. N., *The Mirror of Spain, 1500–1700: The Formation of a Myth*, Ann Arbor, 2000.
Hirsch, Elizabeth Feist, *Damião de Góis: The Life and Thought of a Portuguese Humanist*, The Hague, 1967.
História dos mosteiros, conventos e casas religiosas de Lisboa, vol. I, Lisbon, 1950.
Holanda, Francisco de, *Da fábrica que falece à cidade de Lisboa*, ed. José da Felicidade Alves, Lisbon, 1984.
Höpfl, Harro, *Jesuit Political Thought: The Society of Jesus and the State, c. 1540–1630*, Cambridge, 2004.
Horace, *Epistles*.
Hostetler, Laura, *Qing Colonial Enterprise: Ethnography and Cartography in Early Modern China*, Chicago, 2001.
Huang, Ray, *1587, a Year of no Significance: The Ming Dynasty in Decline*, New Haven, 1981.
Hübner, Alexander, *Sisto Quinto dietro la scorta delle corrispondenze inedite*, vol. I, Rome, 1887.
Hucker, Charles O., 'Governmental Organization of the Ming Dynasty', *Harvard Journal of Asian Studies*, 21, 1958, pp. 1-66.
—, *A Dictionary of Official Titles in Imperial China*, Stanford, 1985.
Hufton, Olwen, 'Altruism and Reciprocity: The Early Jesuits and their Female Patrons', *Renaissance Studies*, 25: 3, 2001, pp. 328–53.
Hyde, J. K., 'Medieval Descriptions of Cities', *Bulletin of the John Rylands Library*, 47: 2, 1966, pp. 308–40.
Ippolito, Antonio Menniti, 'The Secretariat of State as the Pope's Special Ministry', in G. Signorotto and M. A. Viseglia, eds, *Court and Politics in Papal Rome*, Cambridge, 2002, pp. 132–57.
Iwao Seiichi, *Shuinsen bōeki-shi no kenkyū*, 2nd edn, Tokyo, 1985.
Izui Hisanosuke et al., eds, *De·Sande Tenshō ken-Ō shisetsu ki*, Tokyo, 1969.
Jami, Catherine, *The Emperor's New Mathematics: Western Learning and Imperial Authority during the Kangxi Reign (1662–1722)*, Oxford, 2012.

Janetta, Ann Bowman, *Epidemics and Mortality in Early Modern Japan*, Princeton, 1987.
Jeffery, Violet M, 'Shakespeare's Venice', *Modern Language Review*, 27, 1932, pp. 24–35.
Jensen, Lionel M., *Manufacturing Confucianism: Chinese Traditions and Universal Civilization*, Durham NC, 1997.
Jordan, Annemarie, 'Portuguese Royal Collecting after 1621: The Choice between Flanders and Italy', in K. J. P. Lowe, ed., *Cultural Links between Portugal and Italy*, Oxford, 2000, pp. 264–93.
Jorisssen, Engelbert, *Das Japanbild im 'Traktat' (1585) des Luís Fróis*, Münster, 1988.
Jouvency, Joseph de, *Historiae Societatis Jesu Pars Quinta, Tomus Posterior: Ab anno Christi MDXCI ad MDCXVI*, Rome, 1710.
Kaempfer, Engelbert, *The History of Japan Together with a Description of the Kingdom of Siam 1690–1692*, 3 vols, London, 1906.
Kamen, Henry, *The Spanish Inquisition: An Historical Revision*, London, 1998.
—, *Spain's Road to Empire: The Making of a World Power 1492–1763*, London, 2003.
Kantorowicz, Ernst H., *The King's Two Bodies: A Study in Medieval Political Theory*, Princeton, 1997.
Katsumata Shiuzuo and Collcutt, Martin, 'The Development of Sengoku Law', in John Whitney Hall et al., eds, *Japan before Tokugawa*, Princeton, 1981, pp. 101–24.
Kawamura Shinzo, 'Humanism, Pedagogy and Language: Alessandro Valignano and the Global Significance of Juan Bonifacio's Work Printed in Macao (1588)', online at http://www.humanismolatino.online.pt/v1/pdf/C003-001.pdf.
Keen, Maurice, *Chivalry*, New Haven, 1984.
Kennedy, T. Frank, 'Jesuits and Music: Reconsidering the Early Years', *Studia Musicali*, 17, 1988, pp. 70–95.
Kirishitan kanagaki in *Shiryō kenkyū Sessō Sōsai: Zen to kokka to Kirishitan*, ed. Ōkuwa Hitoshi, Kyoto, 1984.
Kleiser, Alfons, 'P. Alexander Valignanis Gesandtschaftsreise nach Japan zum Quambacudono Toyotomi Hideyoshi 1588–1591', *Monumenta Nipponica*, I:1, 1938, pp. 70–98.
Kohl, Benjamin G. and Witt, Ronald G., eds, *The Earthly Republic: Italian Humanists on Government and Society*, Philadelphia, 1978.
Kōjien, 5th edn, Tokyo, 1998.
Kornicki, Peter, *The Book in Japan: A Cultural History from the Beginnings to the Nineteenth Century*, Honolulu, 2001.
Kowall, David M., 'Innovation and Assimilation: The Jesuits and Architecture in Portuguese India', in J. O'Malley et al., eds, *The Jesuits: Cultures, Sciences, and the Arts*, Toronto, 2000, pp. 480–504.
Kubler, George, *Building the Escorial*, Princeton, 1982.
Lach, Donald F., *Asia in the Making of Europe*, 3 vols, Chicago, 1965–93.
LaMay, Thomasin K., ed., *Musical Voices of Early Modern Women: Many-Headed Melodies*, Aldershot, 2005.
Lamers, Jeroen, *Japonius Tyrannus: The Japanese Warlord Oda Nobunaga Reconsidered*, Leiden, 2000.
Lane, Frederic C., *Venice: A Maritime Republic*, Baltimore, 1973.
—, *Venetian Ships and Shipbuilders of the Renaissance*, Baltimore, 1992.
Laures, Johannes, ed., *Kirishitan Bunko: A Manual of Books and Documents on the Early Christian Mission in Japan*, 3rd edn, Tokyo, 1957.
Lazar, Lance Gabriel, *Working in the Vineyard of the Lord: Jesuit Confraternities in Early Modern Italy*, Toronto, 2005.
Lazure, Guy, 'Perceptions of the Temple, Projections of the Divine, Royal Patronage, Biblical Scholarship and Jesuit Imagery in Spain, 1580–1620', *Calamus Renascens: Revista de Humanismo y tradición clásica*, I, 2000, pp. 165–73.
Ledyard, Gari, 'The Kangnido: A Korean World Map, 1402', in Jay Levenson, ed., *Circa 1492: Art in the Age of Exploration*, New Haven, 1991, pp. 329–32.

Leturia, Pedro, 'Un significativo documento de 1558 sobre las misiones de infieles de la Compañia de Jesús', *Archivum Historicum Societatis Iesu*, 8, 1939, pp. 102–17.
Leupp, Gary P., *Servants, Shophands, and Laborers in the Cities of Tokugawa Japan*, Princeton, 1992.
—, 'Images of Black People in Late Medieval and Early Modern Japan, 1543–1900', *Japan Forum*, 7: 1, 1995, pp. 1–13.
Levin, Michael J., *Agents of Empire: Spanish Ambassadors in Sixteenth Century Italy*, Ithaca, 2005.
Lewis, Andrew W., 'Anticipatory Association of the Heir in Early Modern France', *American Historical Review*, 83: 4, 1978, pp. 906–27.
Lightbown, R. W., 'Oriental Art and the Orient in Late Renaissance and Baroque Italy', *Journal of the Warburg and Courtauld Institutes*, 32, 1969, pp. 228–79.
Linschoten, John Huyghen, *The Voyage of John Huyghen Linschoten to the East Indies*, ed. Arthur Coke Burnell and P. A. Tiele, 2 vols, London, 1935.
Liu, Xinru, *Ancient India and Ancient China: Trade and Religious Exchanges AD 1–600*, Delhi, 1988.
Livermore, H. V., *A New History of Portugal*, Cambridge, 1966.
Lopes, António, *Roteiro historico dos Jesuitas em Lisboa*, Braga, 1985.
López-Gay, Jesús, *El catecumenado en la mision del Japón del s. XVI*, Rome, 1966.
—, 'El código de un samurai. Traducción y comentario del "Iroha-uta" de Shimizu Tadayoshi (1545)', *Boletin de la Associación Española de Orientalistas*, 19, 1983, pp. 245–59.
—, 'Don Pedro Martins, SJ (1542–1598), el primer obispo portugués que visitó el Japón', in Roberto Carneiro and Artur Teodoro de Matos, eds, *O século Cristão do Japão*, Lisbon, 1994, pp. 79–94.
Loureiro, Rui Manuel, ed., *Um tratado sobre o reino da China: Dos padres Duarte Sande e Alessandro Valignano (Macau 1590)*, Macao, 1992.
Lowe, K. J. P., ed., *Cultural Links between Portugal and Italy in the Renaissance*, Oxford, 2000.
—, 'Understanding Cultural Exchange Between Portugal and Italy in the Renaissance', in *Cultural Links between Portugal and Italy*, Oxford, 2000, pp. 1–16.
—, 'Rainha D. Leonor: Of Portugal's Patronage in Renaissance Florence and Cultural Exchange', in *Cultural Links between Portugal and Italy*, Oxford, 2000, pp. 225–48.
—, '"Representing" Africa: Ambassadors and Princes from Christian Africa to Renaissance Italy and Portugal, 1402–1608', *Transactions of the Royal Historical Society*, 6th ser., 17, 2007, pp. 101–28.
Lucena, P. Afonso de, *Erinnerungen aus der Christenheit von Ōmura*, ed. Josef Franz Schütte, Rome, 1972.
Luk, Bernard Hung-Kay, 'A Serious Matter of Life and Death: Learned Conversations at Foochow in 1627', in Charles E. Ronan and Bonnie B. C. Oh, eds, *East Meets West*, Chicago, 1998, pp. 173–206.
Lynch, John, 'Philip II and the Papacy', *Transactions of the Royal Historical Society*, 5th ser., 11, 1961, pp. 23–42.
—, *Spain under the Habsburgs Volume One: Empire and Absolutism 1516–1598*, Oxford, 1965.
Machiavelli, Niccolò, *The Art of War*, rev. edn of Ellis Farneworth trans., with intro. by Neal Wood, Cambridge MA, 2001.
Maffei, Giovanni Pietro, *Historiarum Indicarum libri XVI*, Florence, 1588.
Magino, Leo, *Pontifica Nipponica*, 2 vols, Rome, 1947.
Magnuson, Torgil, *Studies in Roman Quattrocento Architecture*, Stockholm, 1958.
Maher, Michael W, 'Jesuits and Ritual in Early Modern Europe', in J. Rollo-Koster, ed., *Medieval and Early Modern Ritual*, Leiden, 2002, pp. 192–218.
Malekandathil, Pius, *Portuguese Cochin and the Maritime Trade of India 1500–1663*, Delhi, 2001.
Mallett, M. E. and Hale, J. R., *The Military Organization of a Renaissance State: Venice c. 1400 to 1617*, Cambridge, 1984.
Mallett, Michael, *Mercenaries and their Masters: Warfare in Renaissance Italy*, London, 1974.
Malm, William P., 'Music Cultures of Momoyama Japan', in G. Elison and B. L. Smith, eds, *Warlords, Artists and Commoners*, Honolulu, 1981, pp. 163–85.

Marcuse, Sibyl, *Musical Instruments: A Comprehensive Dictionary*, London, 1966.

Marques, Alfredo Pinheiro, 'A cartografia portuguesa e o Japão. Visão global e apresentação de uma nova carta', in Roberto Carneiro and Artur Teodoro de Matos, eds, *O século Cristão do Japão*, Lisbon, 1994, pp. 315–46.

—, *A Cartografia Portuguesa do Japão (séculos XVI–XVII): Catálogo das cartas Portuguesas*, Lisbon, 1996.

Marques, João Francisco, 'Confesseurs des princes, les jésuites à la cour de Portugal', in Luce Giard and Louis de Vaucelles, eds, *Les Jésuites à l'âge baroque*, Grenoble, 1995, pp. 213–28.

Massarella, Derek, *A World Elsewhere: Europe's Encounter with Japan in the Sixteenth and Seventeenth Centuries*, New Haven, 1990.

—, 'James I and Japan', *Monumenta Nipponica*, 38: 4, 1983, pp. 377–86.

—, '"Ticklish Points": The English East India Company and Japan, 1621', *Journal of the Royal Asiatic Society*, 3rd ser., 2: 1, 2001, pp. 43–50.

—, 'Exceptionalism versus Universalism: Jesuit and Friar Rivalry in Sixteenth-Century Japan', *Journal of the Institute of Cultural Science, Chuo University*, 51, 2004, pp. 131–60.

—, 'What was Happening in East Asia around 1600?', *The Transactions of the Asiatic Society of Japan*, 4th ser., 21, 2007, pp. 13–33.

Matos, Artur Teodoro de, 'The Financial Situation of the State of India during the Philippine Period (1581–1635)', in Teotonio R. de Souza, ed., *Indo-Portuguese History*, New Delhi, 1985, pp. 90–101.

Matos, Luís de, *L'expansion portugaise dans la littérature latine de la renaissance*, Lisbon, 1991.

Matsuda Kiichi, *Kinsei shoki Nihon kankei Nanban shiryō no kenkyū*, Tokyo, 1967.

—, *Tenshō ken-Ō shisetsu*, Tokyo, 1999.

Mattingly, Garrett, *Renaissance Diplomacy*, repr. New York, 1988.

Mazumdar, Sucheta, *Sugar and Society in China: Peasants, Technology and the World Market*, Cambridge MA, 1998.

McCall, John E., 'Early Jesuit Art in the Far East V: More Discoveries', *Artibus Asiae*, 17: 1, 1954, pp. 39–54.

McGowan, Margaret M., 'Impaired Vision: The Experience of Rome in Renaissance France', *Renaissance Studies*, 8: 3, 1994, pp. 244–55.

McKelway, Matthew Philip, *Cityscapes: Folding Screens and Political Imagination in Late Medieval Kyoto*, Honolulu, 2006.

McMullin, Neil, *Buddhism and the State in Sixteenth-Century Japan*, Princeton, 1984.

Medina, José Toribio, *Nota bibliográfica sobre un libro impreso en Macao en 1590*, Seville, 1894.

Memorias de Fray Juan de San Gerónimo, ed. Miguel Salvá and Pedro Sainz de Baranda, in *Colección de documentos inéditos para la historia de España*, vol. 7, Madrid, 1845.

Mendeiros, José Filipe, *Roteiro histórico dos Jesuítas em Évora*, Braga, 1992.

Mey, C. Viñas, 'La asistencia social a la invalidez militar en el siglo XVI', *Anuario de História Económica y Social*, 1, 1968, pp. 598–605.

Miller, Harry, *State Versus Gentry in Late Ming China, 1572–1644*, New York, 2009.

Mills, J. V. J., ed., *Ma Huan* Ying-Yai Sheng-Lan *'The Overall Survey of the Ocean's Shores' (1433)*, Cambridge, 1970.

Mish, John L., 'Creating an Image of Europe for China: Aleni's *Hsi-Fang Ta-Wen*', *Monumenta Serica*, 23, 1964, pp. 1–87.

Moffett, Samuel Hugh, *A History of Christianity in Asia Volume 1; Beginnings to 1500*, New York, 1998.

Moniz, Manuel Carvalho, *Dominicais Eboreneses*, Évora, 1999.

Montaigne, Michel de, *Essais*, ed. Maurice Rat, 3 vols, Paris, 1952.

—, *Journal de voyage*, ed. Fausta Garavini, Paris, 1983.

Montesquieu, Charles-Louis Secondat, Baron de, *The Spirit of the Laws*, ed. Anne Cohler et al., Cambridge, 1989.

Moran, J. F., *The Japanese and the Jesuits: Alessandro Valignano in Sixteenth Century Japan*, London, 1993.

—, 'The Real Author of *De Missione Legatorum Iaponensium ad Romanam Curiam. Dialogus*', *Bulletin of Portuguese/Japanese Studies*, 2, 2001, pp. 7–21.

Moura, Carlos Francisco, 'Notícias da visita feita a algumas terras do Alentejo pela premeira Embaixada Japonesa à Europa (1584–1585)', in *A cidade de Évora: Boletim da Comissão Municipal de Turismo*, 51–2, January–December 1968–9, pp. 40–42.

Muir, Edward, 'Images of Power: Art and Pageantry in Renaissance Venice', *American Historical Review*, 84: 1, 1979, pp. 16–52.

—, *Civic Ritual in Renaissance Venice*, Princeton, 1981.

—, *Ritual in Early Modern Europe*, Cambridge, 2005.

Munday, Anthony, *The English Roman Life*, ed. Philip J. Ayres, Oxford, 1980.

Mundy, Peter, *The Travels of Peter Mundy, in Europe and Asia, 1608–1667*, ed. Richard Carnac Temple, Hakluyt Society, 2nd ser., 45 and 46, London, 1919; 55, London, 1925.

Mungello, D. E., *Curious Land: Jesuit Accommodation and the Origins of Sinology*, Honolulu, 1989.

Munitiz, Joseph A., 'Francisco Suárez and the Exclusion of Men of Jewish Descent from the Society of Jesus', *Archivum Historicum Societatis Iesu*, 73, 2004, pp. 327–40.

— and Endean, Philip, eds, *Ignatius of Loyola: Personal Writings*, London, 2004.

Najemy, John M., *A History of Florence 1200–1575*, Oxford, 2006.

Nakamura, Hirosi, 'The Japanese Portolanos of Portuguese Origin of the XVIth and XVIIth Centuries', *Imago Mvndi*, 18, 1964, pp. 24–44.

Nakayama, Shigeru, *A History of Japanese Astronomy: Chinese Background and Western Impact*, Cambridge MA, 1969.

Nalle, Sara T., *God in La Mancha: Religious Reform and the People of Cuenca, 1500–1650*, Baltimore, 1992.

Navarro, Julian J. Lozano, *La Compañía de Jesus y el poder en la España de los Austrias*, Madrid, 2005.

Nebenzahl, Kenneth and Marques, Alfredo Pinheiro, 'Moreira's Manuscript: A Newly Discovered Portuguese Map of the World – Made in Japan', *Mercator's World*, 18, 1997, pp. 18–23.

Needham, Joseph, *Science and Civilisation in China*, Cambridge, 1954– .

Neill, Stephen, *A History of Christian Missions*, Harmondsworth, 1986.

Nelson, Thomas, 'Slavery in Medieval Japan', *Monumenta Nipponica*, 59: 4, 2004, pp. 463–92.

New Grove Dictionary of Music and Musicians, ed. Stanley Sadie and John Tyrrell, 29 vols, Oxford, 2003.

Newitt, M. D. D., 'The Early History of the Sultanate of Angoche', *Journal of African History*, 13: 3, 1972, pp. 397–406.

Nishida, Hiroko, 'A History of Japanese Porcelain and the Export Trade', in *The Burghley Porcelains: An Exhibition from the Burghley House Collection and Based on the 1688 Inventory and 1690 Devonshire Schedule*, New York, 1986.

Nussdorfer, Laurie, 'The Vacant See: Ritual and Protest in Early Modern Rome', *Sixteenth Century Journal*, 18: 2, 1987, pp. 173–89.

Oishi Kazuhisa, *Tenshō ken-Ō shisetsu: Chijiwa Migeru no boseki hakken*, Nagasaki, 2005.

Okamoto Yoshitomo, *Porutogaru o tazuneru*, Tokyo, 1930.

Olin, John C., ed., and O'Callaghan, Joseph, trans., *The Autobiography of St Ignatius of Loyola with Related Documents*, New York, 1992.

Oliveira, Cristóvão Rodrigues de, *Summario em que brevemente se contem algumas cousas assim Ecclesiasticas, como Seculares, que ha na Cidade de Lisboa*, Lisbon 1755.

—, *Lisboa em 1551: Sumário em que brevemente se contêm algumas coisas assim eclesiásticas como seculares que há na cidade de Lisboa, (1551)*, ed. José da Felicidade Alves, Lisbon 1987.

Oliveira, Francisco Manuel de Paula Noguiera Roque de, 'A construção de conhecimento europeu sobre a China, c. 1500–c. 1630', doctoral thesis, Universitat Autònoma de Barcelona, 2003, online at http://www.tesisenred.net/bitstream/handle/10803/4951/fmpnro1de4.pdf?sequence=1.

Oliver, Roland and Atmore, Anthony, *Medieval Africa, 1250–1800*, Cambridge, 2001.

O'Malley, John, *The First Jesuits*, Cambridge MA, 1993.

—, 'The Society of Jesus', in R. Po-Chia Hsia, ed., *A Companion to the Reformation World*, Oxford, 2004, pp. 223–36.

— et al., eds, *The Jesuits: Cultures, Sciences, and the Arts, 1540–1773*, Toronto, 2000.

Osório, Jerónimo, *De Rebus Emmanuelis regis Lusitaniae invictissimi virtuae et auspicio gestis libri duodecim*, Lisbon, 1571.

Osswald, Maria Cristina, 'The Society of Jesus and the Diffusion of the Cult and Iconography of Saint Ursula and the Eleven Thousand Virgins in the Portuguese Empire during the Second Half of the 16th Century', in *A Companhia de Jesus no Peninsula Iberica nos sécs. XVI e XVII: Espiritualidade e cultura: Actas do Colóquio Internacional, Maio 2004*, vol. II, Porto, 2004, pp. 601–10.

Ōta Gyūichi, *Nobunaga kōki*, 2 vols, Tokyo, 1991.

Outhwaite, R. B., 'Dearth, the English Crown and the "Crisis of the 1590s"', in Peter Clark, ed., *The European Crisis of the 1590s*, London, 1985, pp. 44–66.

Pacheco, Diego, 'Diogo de Mesquita, S.J. and the Jesuit Mission Press', *Monumenta Nipponica*, 26: 3–4, 1971, pp. 431–43.

—, 'Los cuatro legados japoneses de los daimyos de Kyushu despues de regresar a Japón', *Boletín de la Asociación Española de Orientalistas*, 1973, pp. 19–58.

—, *Os quatro legados dos dáimios de Quiuxu após regressarem ao Japão*, Macau, 1990.

Padberg, John W., et al., eds, *For Matters of Greater Moment: The First Thirty Jesuit General Congregations*, Saint Louis, 1994.

Pagden, Anthony, *The Fall of Natural Man: The American Indians and the Origins of Comparative Ethnology*, Cambridge, 1990.

Pagès, Léon, *Bibliographie japonaise ou catalogue des ouvrages relatifs au Japon*, Paris, 1859.

Palladio, Antonio, *Palladio's Rome: A Translation of Andrea Palladio's Two Guidebooks to Rome*, ed. and trans. Vaughn Hart and Peter Hicks, New Haven, 2006.

Palomo, Federico, 'Para el sosiego y quietud del reino. En torno a Felipe II y el poder eclesiástico en el Portugal de finales del siglo XVI', *Hispania*, 64: 1, 2004, pp. 63–94.

Parker, Geoffrey, *The Army of Flanders and the Spanish Road 1567–1659*, Cambridge, 1975.

—, *The Military Revolution: Military Innovation and the Rise of the West, 1500–1800*, Cambridge, 1988.

—, *The Grand Strategy of Philip II*, New Haven, 1998.

Partner, Peter, 'Papal Financial Policy in the Renaissance and Counter-Reformation', *Past & Present*, 88, 1980, London, 1991, pp. 17–62.

—, 'The Papal State: 1417–1600', in M. Greengrass, ed., *Conquest and Coalescence*, pp. 25–47.

Pastor, Ludwig, Freiherr von, *The History of the Popes from the Close of the Middle Ages*, vol. XIX, London, 1930; vol. XX, London, 1931; vol. XXI, London, 1932.

Pearson, M. N., *The New Cambridge History of India: The Portuguese in India*, Cambridge, 1987.

—, *Port Cities and Intruders: The Swahili Coast, India, and Portugal in the Early Modern Era*, Baltimore, 1998.

Pérez-Mallaína, Pablo E., *Spain's Men of the Sea: Daily Life on the Indies Fleets in the Sixteenth Century*, Baltimore, 1998.

Petrarch, *Epistolae Seniles*.

Phillips, Carla Rahn, *Six Galleons for the King of Spain: Imperial Defense in the Early Seventeenth Century*, Baltimore, 1986.

Pinson, Yona, 'Imperial Ideology in the Triumphal Entry into Lille of Charles V and the Crown Prince (1549)', *Assaph: Studies in Art History*, 6, 2001, pp. 205–32.

Pinto, Ana Fernandes and Remédio Pires, Silvana, 'The "Reposta que alguns padres de Japão mandaram perguntar": A Clash of Strategies?', *Bulletin of Portuguese/Japanese Studies*, 10/11, 2005, pp. 9–60.
Pliny the Elder, *Natural History*.
Polanco, Juan Alfonso de, *Vita Ignatii Loiolae et rerum Societatis Jesu historia*, 6 vols, Madrid, 1894–8.
Polo, Marco, *The Travels of Marco Polo: The Complete Yule-Cordier Edition*, 2 vols, New York, 1993.
Prakash, Om, ed., *Portuguese in India*, 2 vols, New Delhi, 2002.
Prodi, Paolo, *The Papal Prince: One Body and Two Souls*, Cambridge, 1987.
Prosperi, Adriano, 'The Missionary', in Rosario Villari, ed., *Baroque Personae*, Chicago 1995, pp. 160–95.
Pullan, Brian, *Rich and Poor in Renaissance Venice: The Social Institutions of a Catholic State, to 1620*, Oxford, 1971.
—, 'The Counter-Reformation, Medical Care and Poor Relief', in O. P. Grell, A. Cunningham, and J. Arrizabalaga, eds, *Health Care and Poor Relief*, London, 1999, pp. 18–39.
Purchas, Samuel, *Hakluytus Posthumus or Purchas his Pilgrims*, 20 vols, Glasgow, 1905–1907.
Purdue, Peter C., *China Marches West: The Qing Conquest of Central Eurasia*, Cambridge MA, 2005.
Pyrard, François, *Voyage de Pyrard de Laval aux Indes Orientales (1601–1611)*, ed. Xavier de Castro, 2 vols, Paris, 1998.
Quemado, José Manuel, *Alentejo glorioso: Évora suas ruas e seus conventos*, Évora, 1975.
Quevedo, José, *Historia del Real Monasterio de San Lorenzo: Llanado comumente del Escorial*, 2nd edn, Madrid, 1854.
Quinn, D. B., ed., *The Hakluyt Handbook*, Hakluyt Society, 2nd ser., 144 and 145, London, 1974.
Ramalho, Américo da Costa, 'Portugueses e Japoneses no *Dialogus* de Duarte de Sande (1590)', in Roberto Carneiro and Artur Teodoro de Matos, eds, *O século Cristão do Japão*, Lisbon, 1994, pp. 347–68.
—, 'Aspectos da vida escolar Ibérica, segundo o *De Missione Legatorvm Iaponensivm ad Romanam Cvriam*', *Biblos*, 70, 1994, pp. 155–69.
Ranke, Leopold von, *History of the Popes: Their Church and State*, 3 vols, repr. New York, 1966.
Ravina, Mark, *Land and Lordship in Early Modern Japan*, Stanford, 1999.
Reid, Anthony, *Southeast Asia in the Age of Commerce 1450–1680 Volume Two: Expansion and Crisis*, New Haven, 1993.
Rekers, B., *Benito Arias Montano (1527–1598)*, London and Leiden, 1972.
Resende, Garcia de, *Vida e Feitos D'El-Rey Dom João Segundo*, chs CXIV, CXVII in *Lyuro das obras de Garcia de Rese[n]de que trata da vida & grãdissimas virtudes: & bõdades magnanimo esforço: excele[n]tes costumes & manhas & muy craros feitos do christianissimo Rey dõ Ioão o segundo deste nome*, [Lisbon], 1545; 2nd edn 1554.
Rhodes, Elizabeth, 'Join the Jesuits, See the World: Early Modern Women in Spain and the Society of Jesus', in J. O'Malley et al., eds, *The Jesuits: Cultures, Sciences, and the Arts*, Toronto, 2000, pp 33–49.
Ribadeneira, Pedro de, *Bibliotheca scriptorvm Societatis Iesv*, Antwerp, 1608.
Ricci, Matteo, *Fonti Ricciane: Storia dell'introduzione del Cristianesimo in Cina*, ed. Pasquale D'Elia, 3 vols, Rome, 1942–9.
—, *China in the Sixteenth Century: The Journals of Matthew Ricci 1583–1610*, trans. Louis J. Gallagher, New York, 1953.
Ridolfi, Carlo, *The Life of Tintoretto and of His Children Domenico and Marietta*, trans. Catherine and Robert Enggass, University Park PA, 1984.
Robertson, Clare, *'Il Gran Cardinale': Alessandro Farnese, Patron of the Arts*, New Haven, 1992.
Robinson, O. F., *Ancient Rome: City Planning and Administration*, London, 1992.
Rodd, Rennell, *Rome of the Renaissance and To-day*, London, 1932.
Rodrigues, Francisco, *História da Companhia de Jesus na Assistência de Portugal*, 7 vols, Porto, 1931–50.

Rodrigues, João, *Arte da lingoa de Iapam*, Nagasaki, 1604–8.

—, *Arte breve da Lingoa Iapoa*, Macao, 1620.

Rollo-Koster, Joëlle, ed., *Medieval and Early Modern Ritual: Formalized Behavior in Europe, China and Japan*, Leiden, 2002.

Ronan, Charles E. and Oh, Bonnie B. C., eds, *East Meets West: The Jesuits in China, 1582–1773*, Chicago, 1988.

Rosa, Mario, 'The "World's Theatre": The Court of Rome and Politics in the First Half of the Seventeenth Century', in G. Signorotto, G. and M. A. Viseglia, eds, *Court and Politics in Papal Rome*, Cambridge, 2002, pp. 78–98.

Roscioni, Gian Carlo, *Il desiderio delle Indie: Storie, sogni e fugue di giovani gesuiti italiani*, Turin, 2001.

Rubiés, Joan-Pau, *Travel and Ethnography in the Renaissance: South India through European Eyes, 1250–1625*, Cambridge, 2000.

Ruggiero, Guido, *The Boundaries of Eros: Sex Crime and Sexuality in Renaissance Venice*, New York, 1985.

Ruiz-de-Medina, Juan, ed., *Documentos del Japón*, 2 vols, Rome, 1990–95.

Russell, Peter, *Prince Henry 'the Navigator': A Life*, New Haven, 2000.

Sá, Isabel dos Guimarães, 'Ecclesiastical Structures and Religious Action', in Francisco Bethencourt and Diogo Ramada Curto, eds, *Portuguese Oceanic Expansion, 1400–1800*, Cambridge, 2007, pp. 255–82.

—, 'Charity and Discrimination: The *Misericórdia* of Goa', *Itinerario*, 31: 2, 2007, pp. 51–70.

Saastamoinen, Timo, 'The Use of History in late Medieval Guidebooks to Rome', paper presented to the XIV International Economic History Congress, Session 48, 2006, online at http://www.helsinki.fi/iehc2006/papers2/saastamoinen.pdf.

Sacchini, Francesco, *Historiae Societatis Iesv Pars Qvinta*, Rome, 1661.

Sánchez, Javier Burrieza, 'La Compañía de Jesús y la defensa de la monarquia hispánica', *Hispania Sacra*, 60, 2008, pp. 181–229.

Sande, Duarte de, *Diálogo sobre a missão dos embaixadores Japoneses à Cúria Romana*, ed. Américo da Costa Ramalho, Macao, 1997.

—, *Embaixadores Japoneses à Cúria Romana*, ed. Américo da Costa Ramalho and Sebastião Tavares de Pinho, 2 vols, Coimbra, 2009.

Sanesi, Giuseppe, 'I principi Giapponesi a Siena nel 1585', *Bulletino Senese di Storia Patria*, vol. 1, 1894.

Sansovino, Francesco, *Venetia città nobilissima et singolare descritta en XIIII libri*, ed. Giustiniano Martinioni, Venice, 1663.

Satow, E. M., 'The Origin of Spanish and Portuguese Rivalry in Japan', *The Transactions of the Asiatic Society of Japan*, 1st ser., 18, 1890, pp. 133–56.

—, *The Jesuit Mission Press in Japan 1591–1610*, [Tokyo], 1888.

—, ed., *The Voyage of Captain John Saris to Japan, 1613*, Hakluyt Society, 2nd ser., 5, London, 1900.

Schalow, Paul Gordon, 'Kūkai and the Tradition of Male Love in Japanese Buddhism', in José Ignacio Cabezón, ed., *Buddhism, Sexuality, and Gender*, Albany, 1992, pp. 215–30.

Schilling, Doroteo, 'Il contributo dei missionari cattolice nei secoli XVI e XVII alla conoscenza dell'Isola di Ezo e degli Ainu', in *Le Missioni cattoliche e la cultura dell'Oriente: Conferenze 'Massimo Piccinini'*, Rome, 1943, pp. 139–214.

Schmidt, Petra, *Capital Punishment in Japan*, Leiden, 2002.

Schurhammer, Georg, *Shin-tō: The Way of the Gods in Japan*, Bonn, 1923.

—, *Das Kirchliche Sprachproblem in der Japanischen Jesuitenmission des 16. und 17. Jahrhunderts*, Tokyo, 1928.

—, *Orientalia*, Rome, 1963.

—, *Xaveriana*, Rome, 1964.

—, *Francis Xavier: His Life, His Times*, 4 vols, Rome, 1973–82.
Schütte, Josef Franz, 'Christliche Japanische Literatur, Bilder und Drückblätter in einem unbekannten Vatikanischen Codex', *Archivum Historicum Societatis Iesu*, 11, 1940, pp. 226–80.
—, *Valignanos Missionsgrundsätze für Japan*, vol. I, 2 pts, Rome, 1951, 1958.
—, 'Der Lateinische Dialog: "De Missione Legatorum Iaponensium ad Romanam Curiam" als Lehrbuch der Japanischen Seminare', *Analecta Gregoriana*, 70, 1954, pp. 247–90.
—, *Kulturgegensätze: Europa-Japan (1585)*, Tokyo, 1955.
—, ' A "História inédita dos bispos da Igreja do Japão" do P. João Rodriguez Tçuzu SJ', in *Actas de Congesso internacional de história dos Descobrimentos*, 5, Lisbon, 1961, pp. 297–327.
—, 'Ignacio Moreira of Lisbon, Cartographer in Japan 1590–1592', *Imago Mundi*, 16, 1962, pp. 116–28.
—, 'Die Wirksamkeit der Päpste für Japan im ersten Jahrhundert der Japanischen Kirchengeschichte (1549–1650)', *Archivum Historiae Pontificiae*, 5, 1967, pp. 175–261.
—, ed., *Monumenta Historica Japoniae I*, Rome, 1975.
—, ed., *Introductio ad Historiam Societatis Jesu in Japonia 1549–1650*, Rome, 1968.
—, *Valignano's Mission Principles for Japan*, volume I, 2 pts, St Louis MI, 1980, 1983.
Sebes, Joseph, 'The Precursors of Ricci', in Charles E. Ronan and Bonnie B. C. Oh, eds, *East Meets West*, Chicago, 1988, pp. 19–61.
'*Sei Yo Ki-Bun* or Annals of the Western Ocean', trans. S. R. Brown, *Journal of the North-China Branch of the Royal Asiatic Society*, new ser., 2, 1865, pp. 53–84; 3, 1866, pp. 40–62.
Selfa, José Guillén, *La primera embajada del Japón en Europa y en Murcia (1582–1590)*, Murcia, 1997.
Selwyn, Jennifer D., *A Paradise Inhabited by Devils: The Jesuits' Civilizing Mission in Early Modern Naples*, Aldershot, 2004.
Sepúlveda, P. Fr. Jerónimo de, 'Sucesos del reinado de Felipe', ed. P. J. Zarco, *La Ciudad de Dios*, 111, 1917, pp. 488–500.
Signorotto, G. and Visceglia, M. A., eds, *Court and Politics in Papal Rome, 1492–1700*, Cambridge, 2002.
Skinner, Quentin, *The Foundations of Modern Political Thought*, 2 vols, Cambridge, 1978.
Smith, Webster, 'Pratolino', *Journal of the Society of Architectural Historians*, 20: 4, 1961, pp. 155–68.
Snyder, Jon R., *Writing the Scene of Speaking: Theories of Dialogue in the Late Italian Renaissance*, Stanford, 1989.
Souza, George Bryan, *The Survival of Empire: Portuguese Trade and Society in China and the South China Sea, 1630–1754*, Cambridge, 1986.
Souza, Teotonio R. de, ed., *Indo-Portuguese History*: *Old Issues, New Questions*, New Delhi, 1985.
Spence, Jonathan, *The Memory Palace of Matteo Ricci*, London, 1984.
Standaert, Nicholas, *The Interweaving of Rituals: Funerals in the Cultural Exchange Between China and Europe*, Seattle, 2008.
—, ed., *Handbook of Christianity in China Volume One: 635–1800*, Leiden, 2001.
Stinger, Charles L., *The Renaissance in Rome*, Bloomington, 1998.
Strabo, *Geography*.
Strathern, Alan, *Kingship and Conversion in Sixteenth-Century Sri Lanka: Portuguese Imperialism in a Buddhist Land*, Cambridge, 2007.
Subrahmanyam, Sanjay, *The Portuguese Empire in Asia 1500–1700: A Political and Economic History*, London, 1993.
Swope, Kenneth M., *A Dragon's Head and a Serpent's Tail: Ming China and the First Great East Asian War, 1592–1598*, Norman, 2009.
Takase Kōichirō, 'A carta do Vice-Rei da Índia D. Duarte de Menezes a Toyotomi Fideyoxi: Perspectiva japonesa', *Ryūtsū Keizai Daigaku Ronshū*, 32: 3, 1998, pp. 47–93.
Tamburello, Adolfo et al., eds, *Alessandro Valignano S.I.: Uomo del rinascimento*, Rome 2008.

Taveira da Fonseca, Fernando, 'The Social and Cultural Roles of the University of Coimbra (1537–1820): Some Considerations', *e-Journal of Portuguese History*, 5: 1, 2007, pp. 1–21.

Teixeira, Manuel, *Macau e a sua diocese Volume II: Bispos e governnadores do bispado de Macau*, Macao, 1940.

Thompson, I. A. A., *War and Government in Habsburg Spain 1560–1620*, London, 1976.

—, 'The Impact of War', in Peter Clark, ed., *The European Crisis of the 1590s*, London, 1985, pp. 261–84.

Toby, Ronald P., *State and Diplomacy in Early Modern Japan: Asia in the Development of the Tokugawa Bakufu*, Princeton, 1984.

Tominaga, Michio, 'On the Nomenclature and Problems of Identification of Period Instruments', *Shōgakubu Ronsan (Chūō Daigaku)*, 51: 5–6, 2010, pp. 1–25.

Trexler, Richard C., *Public Life in Renaissance Florence*, Ithaca, 1991.

Triguero, Carmen Soriano, 'Fundación y dote del convento del Nuestra Señora de los Maria de los Ángeles de Madrid. Peculiaridades de un modelo diferente de patronato regio', *Cuadernos de Historia Moderna*, 11, 1991, pp. 41–56.

Tsang, Carol Richmond, *War and Faith: Ikkō Ikki in Late Muromachi Japan*, Cambridge MA, 2007.

Tuohy, Thomas, *Herculean Ferrara: Ercole d'Este, 1471–1505, and the Invention of a Ducal Capital*, Cambridge, 1996.

Turnbull, Stephen, *Samurai Armies 1550–1615*, Oxford, 1979.

Üçerler, Antoni J., 'Sacred Historiography and Its Rhetoric in Sixteenth-Century Japan: An Intertextual Study and Partial Critical Edition of *Principio y progresso de la religión christiana en Jappón* [...] (1601–1603) by Alessandro Valignano', 2 vols, unpublished DPhil thesis, University of Oxford, 1998.

Ullmann, Walter, *The Growth of Papal Government in the Middle Ages: A Study of the Ideological Relation of Clerical to Lay Power*, London, 1955.

Valignano, Alessandro, *Catechismus Christiannae Fidei*, Lisbon, 1586.

—, *Historia del principio y progresso de la Compañía de Jesús en las Indias Orientales (1542–64)*, ed. Josef Wicki, Rome 1944.

—, *Il cerimoniale per i missionari del Giappone*, ed. Giuseppe Fr. Schütte, Rome, 1946.

—, *Sumario de las cosas de Japón (1583)*, ed. José Luis Álvarez-Taladriz, Tokyo, 1954.

—, *Adiciones del Sumario de Japón (1592)*, ed. José Luis Álvarez-Taladriz, Tokyo, 1954 (printed but unpublished).

—, *Apología de la Compañia de Jesus de Japón y China*, ed. José Luis Álvarez-Taladriz, Osaka, 1998.

Valla, Lorenzo, *Discourse on the Forgery of the Alleged Donation of Constantine*, trans. Christopher B. Coleman, New Haven, 1922.

Vaporis, Constantine Nomikos, *Tour of Duty: Samurai Military Service in Edo, and the Culture of Early Modern Japan*, Honolulu, 2008.

Vassberg, David E., *The Village and the Outside World in Golden Age Castile: Mobility and Migration in Everyday Rural Life*, Cambridge, 1996.

Vega, Lope de, *Obras completas de Lope de Vega: Poesía, IV*, Madrid, 2004.

Vergil, Polydore, *On Discovery*, ed. and trans. Brian P. Copenhaver, Cambridge MA, 2002.

Verwilghen, Albert-Felix, 'Christian Music in Japan from 1549 till 1614', *KBS Bulletin on Japanese Culture*, 1969, pp. 1–13.

Virgil, *Aeneid*.

Vivero, Rodrigo de, *Du Japon et du bon gouvernement de l'Espagne et des Indes*, ed. and trans. Juliette Monberg, Paris, 1972.

Vlam, Grace A.H., 'Kings and Heroes: Western-Style Painting in Momoyama Japan', *Artibus Asiae*, 39: 3/4, 1977, pp. 220–50.

Vocabvlario da lingoa de Iapam com adeclaração em Portugues, feito por algvns padres, e irmaõs da Companhia de Iesv, Nagasaki, 1603–4.

Volcker, T., *Porcelain and the Dutch East India Company: as Recorded in the Dagh-registers of Batavia Castle, Those of Hirado and Deshima and Other Contemporary Papers, 1602–1682*, Leiden, 1954.

—, *The Japanese Porcelain Trade of the Dutch East India Company after 1683*, Leiden, 1959.

Vries, Jan de, *European Urbanization 1500–1800*, London, 1984.

Wade, Geoff, 'The Zheng He Voyages: A Reassessment', *Journal of the Malaysian Branch of the Royal Asiatic Society*, 77: 1, 2005, pp. 37–58.

Wakabayashi, Bob Tadashi, *Anti-Foreignism and Western Learning in Early-Modern Japan: The New Theses of 1825*, Cambridge MA, 1986.

Waldron, Arthur, *The Great Wall of China: From History to Myth*, Cambridge, 1990.

Waley-Cohen, Joanna, *The Sextants of Beijing: Global Currents in Chinese History*, New York, 1999.

Walker, Brett L., *The Conquest of Ainu Lands: Ecology and Culture in Japanese Expansion 1590–1800*, Berkeley, 2001.

Waterhouse, David, 'Southern Barbarian Music in Japan', in Salwa El-Shawan Castelo-Branco, ed., *Portugal e o mundo: O encontro de culturas na música*, Lisbon, 1997, pp. 351–77.

Waters, D. W., 'Science and the Techniques of Navigation in the Renaissance', in Charles S. Singleton, ed., *Art and Science in the Renaissance*, Baltimore, 1967, pp. 187–237.

—, *The Art of Navigation in England in Elizabethan and Early Stuart Times*, 2nd edn, London, 1978.

Wheatley, Paul, *The Golden Khersonese: Studies in the Historical Geography of the Malay Peninsula Before AD 1500*, Kuala Lumpur, 1961.

Wicki, Josef, 'Der einheimische Klerus in Indien (16. Jahrhundert)', in Johannes Beckmann, ed., *Der einheimische Klerus in Geschichte und Gegenwart*, Schöneck-Beckenreid, 1950, pp. 17–31.

—, *Missionskirche im Orient*, Immensee, 1976.

—, 'Die unmittelbaren Auswirkungen des Konzils von Trent auf Indien (ca. 1565–1585)', in *Missionskirche im Orient*, pp. 213–52.

—, 'Gesang, Tänze und Musik im Dienste der alten indischen Jesuitenmissionen (ca. 1542–1582)', in *Missionskirche im Orient*, pp. 138–52.

—, 'Die "Cristãos-Novos" in der Indischen Provinz der Gesellschaft Jesu von Ignatius bis Acquaviva', *Archivum Historicum Societatis Iesu*, 46, 1977, pp. 342–61.

—, 'Philip II und die Jesuiten der Indischen Provinz (einschliesslich Molukken, China und Japan) 1580–1598', *Archivum Historicum Societatis Iesu*, 50, 1981, pp. 161–211.

Wiesner-Hanks, Merry E., *Christianity and Sexuality in the Early Modern World: Regulating Desire, Reforming Practice*, London, 2000.

Williams, Glyndwr, *The Great South Sea: English Voyages and Encounters 1570–1760*, New Haven, 1997.

Wilson, Peter H., *Europe's Tragedy: A History of the Thirty Years War*, London, 2009.

Wood, Diana, *Medieval Economic Thought*, Cambridge, 2002.

Worcester, Thomas, ed., *The Cambridge Companion to the Jesuits*, Cambridge, 2008.

Wright, A. D., *The Early Modern Papacy: From the Council of Trent to the French Revolution, 1564–1789*, Harlow, 2000.

Xavier, Ângela Barreto, *A invenção de Goa: Poder imperial e conversões culturais nos séculos XVI e XVII*, Lisbon, 2008.

Xavier, Francis, *The Letters and Instructions of Francis Xavier*, trans. and ed. M. Joseph Costelloe, Anand, 1992.

Yūki, Ryōgo, 'Arima-ke no kirishitan daimyō no keizu o megutte', *Nagasaki Dansō*, 63, 1980, pp. 1–24.

—, *Roma wo mita: Tenshō shōnen shisetsu*, Nagasaki, 1982.

—, 'Atarashiku hakken shita Itō Manshio no nitsū no tegami', *Nagasaki Dansō*, 67, 1983, pp. 9–26.

—, 'Shinshiryō Tenshō shōnen shisetsu, 1590-nen–1990-nen', *Kirishitan Kenkyū*, 29, 1990.

—, *Tenshō shōnen shisetsu: Shiryō to kenkyū*, Nagasaki, 1992.
—, 'A Present of Arabian Horses', *Crossroads*, Nagasaki, II, 1994, unpaginated.
Yule, Henry and Burnell, A. C., *Hobson-Jobson: being a Glossary of Anglo-Indian colloquial Words and Phrases*, London, 1969.
— and Cordier, Henri, eds, *Cathay and the Way Thither: Being Recollections of Medieval Notices of China*, Hakluyt Society, 2nd ser., 33, 37, 38, 41, London 1913–16.

INDEX

abdication, 187, 236, 240
Acapulco, 27, 181n
Acarnania, 448
Accursius, protomartyr, 390
Acosta, José de, 23, 82n, 84n
Acquapendente, 269, 448
acrobatics, 371
Acta Consistorii, 22, 276n–7n
Adam and Eve, 82, 86
Adjutus, protomartyr, 390
Aetolia, 448
Africa, 18, 45–6, 60, 63, 65n, 71–2, 82, 123, 140–41,
    183, 201, 203, 207, 217, 234–6, 251n, 284n,
    390, 407n, 408, 410n, 413, 440, 443–7
Afonso IV, 201
Afonso V, 189–90, 201
Afonso Henriques, king, 220n, 390, 395, 398
Agamemnon, king, 191
Alaejos, Miguel de la, prior of El Escorial, 247
Albert of Austria, cardinal archduke, 78, 106, 141n,
    207n, 223, 225, 239n, 323n, 381, 385
Albuquerque, Afonso de, 75
Alcacer do Sal, 384, 448
Alcalá, 251–2, 383
    university, 251–2, 392, 448
Alcobaça, 398
Alcudia, 255
Aleni, Giulio, 25
Alentejo, 225, 227
Algarve, 396, 413
Alicante, 22, 254–5, 444, 448
Alifi, bishop, 320
Almeida, João de, 56
Almeirim, 222
alphabet, compared with Chinese and Japanese
    characters, 195–6
Álvares, Afonso, 215n
Álvares, Francisco, 2
Álvares, Manuel, 16n
Álvarez-Taladriz, José Luis, 17
America, 46, 155n, 234, 236, 440, 443, 447
Ancients, the, 84n, 87, 123, 160, 201, 265, 425n,
    434n, 445
Ancona, 313, 329, 448
Angoche, 407

Angola, 235
Anne, St, 217
'Anon–Moreira' world map, xv, 18–19, 47n, 443n;
    see also, maps
Anthony of Padua, St, 210n, 221, 362, 390
Antoninus Pius, emperor, 298
Antunes, Diogo, 21–2, 36
Apostolic Camera, 111, 319
Aquaviva, Claudio, 3, 4n, 6n, 7n, 11n, 12–15, 16n,
    17, 26, 38, 77n, 80n, 112, 193n, 237n, 250n,
    272, 293, 314n, 324n, 325n, 360n, 366n, 381n,
    409n, 410n, 411n, 415n, 416n, 435n, 440n
Aquaviva, Rodolfo, 3
Arabia, 81, 235, 447
Arabian Gulf (Persian Gulf), 63
Aragon, 115 n, 202n, 235, 290, 380–81, 394n
Arai Hakuseki, 31
Aranjuez, 245
Arctic Circle, 84, 446
Arestino, cardinal, 299
Arima domain, 43–4, 295n
Arima Harunobu, Protasio, 8–9, 13, 29, 39, 49, 77,
    79, 242, 273, 276, 322, 397
Arima Sumizane, Leo, 9, 30
Aristedes, Aelius, 25
Aristotle, 89, 107n, 425n, 444
Arzila, 235
Asia, 3, 5, 17, 20, 27, 46–7, 59–60, 62–3, 65n, 72–3,
    82, 123, 140–41, 183–4n, 234, 235, 236, 396,
    434n, 440, 446–7
Assisi, 325, 448
astrolabe, 100–101
Ataíde, Jorge de, 398
Attica, 448
Aveiro, D. Jorge de Lancastre, duke of, 242
    his widow and daughter, 242n
Ávila, Nicolão de, 21, 36
Ayala, Pedro López de, 239
Azores, 18, 401n
Azpilcueta Navarro, Martín de, 393
Azuchi, 3n, 8, 173n, 224n, 237n, 295n, 301n, 331n

Badajoz, 230, 448
Baixos da Judía, *see* Shallows of Sofala
Balearic Islands, 255, 390n

banquets, 143–4
Barcelona, 379–80, 448
Barco, 332
Bartoli, Daniello, 17
Bavaria, 375
Belém, 203–4, 214
  Jerónimos monastery, 203–4
Belmonte, 9n, 252
Benedict of Nursia, St, 204n, 210
Benedictine order, 215, 368, 380–81, 387
Bethlehem, 203, 297
Boeothia, 448
Berard, protomartyr, 390
Bevilacqua, Mario, 331, 364
Bohemia, 125, 448
Boleyn, Anne, 333n
Bologna, 2, 329–31, 364n, 448
Bolsena, 269
Boncompagni, Filippo, cardinal, 278
Boncompagni, Giacomo, duke of Sora, 278, 304
bonzes (Japanese Buddhist clergy), 85, 111, 114, 433
Borja, Francisco de, St, 5, 112, 293
Borja, Juan de, duke of Ficallo and Maylade, 215n, 245
Borja, Juan de, duke of Gandía, 112n
Bosphorus, 60
Brabant, 234
Bragança, Catarina de, 228, 384
Bragança, João de, 245, 387, 397
Bragança, Teodósio de, duke, 228–30, 384
Bragança, Teotónio de (archbishop of Évora), 7n, 223n, 225, 227, 384
Bragança family, 217
Brandenburg, 125
Brazil, 72n, 186n, 206, 211, 219, 326n, 234, 394–5, 401
Britain, 441, 448
Bruni, Leonardo, 25
Buddha, 46n, 47n, 433
Buddhism
  in China, 83n, 433
  in Japan, 5, 6, 16, 26, 30, 48n, 85, 110–11, 114–15, 184n, 208n, 433
Budé, Guillaume, xviii
Bungo, 3n, 8, 10, 12, 44, 49, 58, 242, 273–4, 276, 290n, 322, 397, 414n
Burgos, 211, 239
Burke, Peter, 14

Cabo Verde, 235
Cabral, Francisco, 26, 72–3, 184n, 399n
Cabral, Pedro Álvares, 70n, 72
Caesar, Julius, 123, 160, 298

Calicut, 65n, 70n
  zamorin of, 74–5
Cambodia, 63, 443
Camerino, 326, 448
Campion, Edmund, 292
Cananore, 74
Canary Islands, 211
Canton, 420
Cape Agulhas, 403
Cape Comorin, 65–7, 90, 443
Cape of Good Hope, 71, 85, 99, 103–4, 403, 409, 443–4
Capello, Filippo, 334
Carafa, Antonio, cardinal, 11n, 13, 322–3
Carneiro, Melchior, 5
Carreira da Índia, 55n, 93n, 99n, 104n, 204, 254n, 401n, 405n, 408n, 410
carriages, 142–3, 147–8, 205, 233, 244, 257, 288, 324, 330–31, 362, 365, 370, 376
Castel Sant'Angelo, 276, 284, 298, 313, 430
Castelo Branco, Afonso de, bishop of Coimbra, 387
Castile, 380–81, 396, 398
Catalina Micaela, daughter of Philip II, 239
Catalonia, 112, 379–80
Catherine, St, 215, 250
Catherine of Bologna, St, 331
Cecil, Sir Robert, 18
Cerqueira, Luis, 30
Cesena, 330, 448
Ceuta, 201, 235
Ceylon, 18, 62n, 64–5, 422
chaien, 427, 435
Champa, 63, 443
chanoyu, 140
Charles V, emperor, 2, 80n, 179n, 189n, 190–91, 232, 236, 249, 310, 373
Chaul, 74
cheu, 418
Chiavari, Gerolamo, 378
Chieti, 3, 322n
Chijiwa Seizaemon, Michael, 8–9, 12n, 13, 18, 24, 29–30, 39
  illness, 231, 233
  in Milan, 371
  in Rome, 274, 277, 302, 321–2
China, 47
  army, 425, 429
  Christianity, 434–5
  cities and towns, 418–19
  compared with Europe, 345, 436–7, 442
  economy, 424
  emperor, 429–30
  examinations, 425–6
  filial piety, 431

government, 426–30
Great Wall, 418
Jesuits in, 420, 434–5
language and letters, 423, 425, 430
mandarins, 427–9
medicine, 420, 422
natural resources, 419–23
population, 418–19
provinces, 417
religion, 432–3
size, 46
Chinese, appearance, 87, 423
in Japan, 56
chinzu, 425
Chioggia, 334
chopsticks, 143
Christian religion, 7, 36, 38, 56, 71–2, 75–6, 114–15, 120, 122, 124, 127–8, 168, 184, 194, 199–200, 209, 228–9, 245, 273, 287, 292, 295, 306, 354, 395, 415, 434–6, 446–7
Christian rulers, 76–7
chumpin, 425, 427
Cicero, 23, 107n, 144, 151, 302, 425, 445
Cimbrian peninsula, 448
cinnamon, 64, 74, 422, 443
cities
 Chinese, 418–19
 European, 7, 24–5, 106, 131, 136, 173–4, 191–9
 Japanese, 192, 199
Clare of Montefalco, St, 325
clavicimbalum, 270, 384
Clement VII, 2, 261, 298n
Clement VIII, 27, 116n
Clement, St, 387
climate, 47, 60, 63, 104, 203, 237, 399, 419–20, 446
clocks, 266
 Toledo, 232, 266
 Venice, 341, 343, 351
Clothes
 Chinese, 423
 European, 9, 78–9, 139, 141, 283, 324
 Japanese, 28, 78, 229, 240n, 257, 269n, 278n, 284, 333n, 360n, 369n
cloves, 74
Cochin, 3, 6n, 9n, 16n, 65, 68–9, 70n, 74, 77, 81, 89–90, 93, 443
 king of, 69, 72–3
Cochinchina, 63, 443, 447
Coelho, Gaspar, 9n, 12, 13, 119n, 186n, 187n, 302n, 414n, 439n
Coimbra, 22, 220, 385, 387–98, 448
 Jesuit college, 393–7
 university, 391–3
College of Cardinals, 108–9, 111, 307, 315, 351

Cologne, 125
Colombo, 64
Colonna, Ascanio, 383
Colonna, Marcoantonio, 183, 290
compass, 101–2, 103
Confucius, 431–3
Congo, 235
Congregation of the Annunciation, 294
Constantine, emperor, 127–8
Constantinople, 127, 346, 347n
copper, 249, 265, 268, 345–6, 421
Corsica, 377
Coryate, Thomas, 344n, 357n, 358n, 361n, 362n, 363n, 364n, 373n, 374n
cotton, 74, 421n, 422, 424
Cox, Virginia, 23–4
Cranganore, 74
Cremona, 232, 369–70, 448

dairi, 106, 129–30, 172, 199
Dalmatia, 178, 313n, 448
dance/dancing, 156–7, 257–8, 265, 371
Dangōjima, 30
Daoism, *see tauzu*
Daroca, 383, 448
David, king, 151, 246
Denmark, 448
Dertona, 448
Dinis, king, 201, 390–91
Divine Providence, 116, 235, 398, 405, 439, 449
Dominic, St, 202
Dominican order, 213, 219n, 253, 270, 284, 374, 387, 398
Dorea, Andrea, 377n, 378
Doria, Gianandrea, admiral, 377n, 378
Dourado, Constantino, 9, 53n, 230n, 414n
Douro, river, 215
Drake, Sir Francis, 401n
drama, 157, 363, 395–7
Duarte, king, 71, 201
Dum ad uberes, papal brief, 27

East China Sea, 54
Eleanor of Austria, 368
Elisonas, Jurgis, 11, 12, 14, 30
Elizabeth I, 277n
Elizabeth of Aragon, St, 390
Elvas, 230, 448
embassies, 1–2
Emilia, 330
Engracia, St, 382
Epirus, 448
Equator, the, 62, 100, 401, 444
Escorial, 192n, 204n, 246–8, 374

Este, Alfonso II d', duke of Ferrara, 331–3
Ethiopia, 2, 18, 117
　embassy from, 2
Ethiopians, 60, 82, 84–7, 143
Etna, Mount, 151
Europe, 37–8, 45–7, 141, 147, 228, 286, 320, 329, 334, 395–6, 399
　artisans, 198
　buildings, 191, 198–9
　education, 145, 196–8
　fertility, 73
　food, 143–5, 207, 218, 278
　furniture, 137, 261
　income, 133–4
　knowledge of Japan, 49
　law, 159–63
　medicine, 420
　punishment, 163–8
　sacred power, 107–8, 128–9, 231, 301
　secular power, 107–8, 122–9, 159–60, 172, 234, 417
　succession, 189–90
　superiority, 445–7
　wealth, 133–7, 399–400, 420, 444
Europeans, appearance, 60, 87
Évora, 225–8, 384, 391, 398n, 448
　Jesuit college, 226–7
Ex pastorali officio, papal brief, 27
Ezechias, king, 246

Fano, 329, 330, 448
Farnese, Alessandro, 271, 289, 311n, 314–15
Ferdinand, king of Aragon and Castile, 152, 235–6
Ferrara, 331, 333, 366, 448
Fiamma, Gabriello, 334
Figueroa, Jerónimo Manrique, bishop of Salamanca, 243
fireworks, 252, 313, 334, 367, 375, 424
Fishery Coast, 66–7, 81, 90
Flanders, 234
Florence, 25, 256, 259–61, 263, 267–8, 448
Foligno, 325, 448
forks, 143, 144
Forlì, 330, 448
France, 124, 166n, 206, 245, 291, 302, 321, 331, 349, 356, 382, 443, 448
Francis of Assisi, St, 210, 325, 390
Franciscan order, 202, 210, 213, 216, 313, 390
　rivalry with Jesuits, 27–8
Fróis, Luís, 10, 15, 29, 46n, 107n, 129n
fu, 418
Funai, 10, 35n, 295n
funerals/funeral rites, 190, 309–11, 431
Further India, 235

Gama, Vasco da, 72, 204n, 408n
Gambara, Cesare, bishop of Tortona, 375
Gambara, Gianfrancesco, cardinal, 270
ganchasu, 426
Ganges, river, 62
gardens, 205, 261, 301, 363, 423
Gavi, 377
Gazzuolo, 369
Genji, 172
Genoa, 211, 256, 323n, 355n, 369, 374, 376–9, 448
Germany, 124, 127–8, 206, 215, 291, 352, 443, 448
Gesualdo, Alfonso, cardinal, 326
Ghilandino, Melchior, 363
ginger, 74
glass, 248, 356, 359–60, 422
Goa, 1, 3, 6, 9n, 10, 20, 26, 29, 35n, 50n, 57, 69, 75, 77, 80n, 81, 90–93, 106, 225n, 366n, 394n, 398, 399n, 403n, 407n, 408–11, 413–15, 420n, 438–40n, 443–4
Góis, Damião de, 22, 201n
Golden Chersonese, 59, 61–2, 64, 75
Goliath, 151
Gómez, Pedro, 58, 63n
Gonçalves, Gaspar, pilot, 406n
Gonçalves, Gaspar, S.J., 277
Gonzaga, Aloysius, 39n, 112n
Gonzaga, Guglielmo, duke of Mantua, 365, 366n
Gonzaga, Margherita, 332
Gonzaga, Muzio, 365
Gonzaga, Scipione, 365
Gonzaga family, 14, 112, 368n, 376n
Gothia, 448
gozan (Five Mountain monasteries), 5, 111n, 114n
Granada, Luis de, 213
Granvelle, Antoine Perrenot de, 238–9, 245, 311n
Great Bear, 442
Greek, 25, 62, 294, 296, 345, 394
Greeks, 201, 292
Greenland, 18
Gregory I (Gregory the Great), 228, 277n, 296
Gregory XIII, 1, 3, 9–10, 14, 22, 27–9, 116, 119, 183n, 224n, 225, 269n, 281, 283, 287, 289–92, 295, 300–301
　death, 306–8
　funeral, 309–11
　receives the Japanese embassy, 273–8
Grimaldi, Domenico, 349
Guadalupe, Nuestra Señora de, 230
Gualtieri, Guido, 2, 22, 269n
Guangdong, 417–18, 426n, 435
Guastavillani, Filippo, cardinal, 278
Guinea, 401
gunpowder, 358, 424
Guzman, Luis de, 9n, 18, 252n

Hadrian, emperor, 298
Hainan, 416, 421
Hakluyt, Richard, 18, 401n, 416n
Hara, Martin, 9, 30, 39
   illness, 250
   in Milan, 371
   oration in Goa, 414
   in Rome, 274, 302, 321–2
heathen nations, 287
heavens, 83–4, 86, 100–101
Hebrew, 294, 296, 394
Heike, 172
Hellespont, 60
Henrique, king, 11n, 12n, 201, 219, 226–7, 236
Henry III, king of France, 245, 302, 331, 335n, 361n
Henry, Prince (Henrique), the Navigator, 71–2
Hieronymites, 203, 230, 237, 246, 382
Herod, king, 396–7
Hohenems, Mark Sittich von, 321
Holland, 234
Holy Roman emperor, 106, 113, 123–7, 129n, 234, 236, 278–9, 285, 302, 319, 356, 443, 448
horses, 127, 141, 176, 206, 213, 217, 229, 248–9, 253, 260–61, 271, 274–6, 284, 288, 319, 324, 330, 332, 339, 342, 347, 350, 360–61, 365, 371, 377, 399, 413, 429
horsemanship, 141, 145–53, 217
hotoke, 47
houses/palaces
   in China, 428
   in Europe, 106, 135–7, 153, 192–3, 203, 211, 214, 260, 288, 299, 336, 339, 373, 378, 417, 436
   in Japan, 237
Hungary, 448
hunting and fowling, 105, 149, 153–4, 207, 222, 229, 246–7, 270, 330, 332–3, 368n, 397, 413
Hyde, J. K., 24
Hyūga, 8, 12, 13

Illyria, 327, 448
India, 22, 46, 54, 57–9, 62–79, 89–93, 99, 103–4, 106, 120, 136, 144–6, 186, 203, 205–8, 217, 219, 225, 228, 244, 249–50, 253, 384, 394, 395–6, 398, 404, 409–10, 413, 420–24, 435, 438, 443, 447
   Indians, 81–2, 120, 447
   see also, Jesuits
Iphigenia, 191
Ireland, 441, 448
Irene, St, 387
Isahaya, 30, 50n, 53n
Isabella of Castile, 235
Isabella Clara Eugenia, daughter of Philip II, 329
Itō Sukemasu, Mancio, 8–13, 29–30, 39

illness, 63–4
in Milan, 371
in Rome, 274, 277, 302, 315, 321–2
skill at hunting, 368n
Itō Suketaka, 12, 13
Itō Yoshikatsu, Jerónimo, 8, 11–13
Itō Yoshisuke, 8, 12

Japan
   abortion and infanticide, 194
   bishop for, 5, 27, 30, 35n, 118, 225, 318n, 407n
   buildings, 199, 428
   Christianity, 38, 76, 128, 199, 229, 273, 292, 306, 363, 395, 415, 434
   climate, 88, 399
   compared with Europe, 45, 76, 107, 114, 133–4, 156, 164–5, 345, 442
   education, 90, 196
   food, 121, 144
   government, 130–31, 134, 163, 171, 189, 199, 429
   income, 133
   isolation of, 78, 128, 144, 273
   law, 163, 165
   medicine, 420, 422
   nobility, 129–31, 134
   papacy and, 277, 301, 307, 314, 322–3
   Portuguese in, 70, 137–8, 143–4
   punishment, 163, 165–70
   servants, 142, 169–70
   ships, 55
   size, 440–42
   see also, Jesuits; Portugal; war/warfare
Japanese, appearance, 87, 269n
Jerome, St, 174, 249, 296
   order of St Jerome, *see* Hieronymites
Jerusalem, 132, 189, 295, 396
   patriarch of, 365
Jesuits (Society of Jesus), 109–11, 117–21
   accommodation policy, 4–5, 24, 26–7, 31, 90n, 120
   in China, 434–5
   correspondence, 223–4
   India, 89–91, 120
   Institute, 3, 118, 293, 394
   irmãos, 8, 16
   Italy, 269, 330, 364, 372, 377
   Japan, 47–8, 111, 115–16, 119–21, 223–4, 292, 305, 434, 438
   Macao, 57
   Portugal, 106
   Ratio studiorum (1599), 24
   rivalry with mendicants, 27–8
   social status, 110–12

Spain, 250, 252
  writing about Japan, 7–8, 224
  see also, Coimbra; Lisbon; Philip II; Rome
Jews, 184, 366, 385
Jiménez, Francisco, cardinal and archbishop of Toledo, 251
João I, 71, 201, 213, 228
João II, 152, 201, 218
João III, 117n, 201, 203, 210, 212, 219, 226, 391n, 393n, 394
John Chrysostom, St, 296
John the Baptist, St, 344
Jordan, river, 396
Josias, king, 246
Juan, king of Castile, 398
Judea, 396
Julia, St, 210
Justus, St, 252

Kaempfer, Engelbert, 167n
Kaffirs, 82, 404, 407-8
kami, 47, 48n
kampaku, *see* Toyotomi Hideyoshi
Knights of St Stephen, 258–9
Kirishitan kanagaki, 30
koku, 133
kokugaku, 31
kubō, 106, 130–31, 172
kuge, 106, 130
kunishū, 106, 130, 134, 171
Kyoto, 8, 12, 13, 29, 43n, 86n, 121n, 131n, 137n, 141n, 154n, 155n, 172n, 199n, 248n, 301n, 399n, 421n, 439n

Lainez, Diego, 251n, 366n, 293
Lambert, St, 382
Latin, 14–17, 20–21, 37, 39, 62, 77n, 99, 149, 196n, 197, 218, 226, 269n, 294, 296, 345, 394, 414, 433
Laurence, St, 296–7
Lebna Dengel (David II), emperor, 2
Legatio Dauid Aethiopiae Regis, ad Sanctissimum D. N. Clementem Papā VII, 2
Leiria, 398n, 448
Leo, *see* Arima Sumizane
Leo X, 193n, 261, 274n, 286
León, Francisca Ponce de, 252
Lepanto, battle of, 178n, 182–3
Liguria, 377
linen, 73, 136, 212, 263, 311, 378, 422, 424
Lino, *see* Ōmura Suminobu
Lisbon, 202–21, 222, 225, 231–2, 249, 288n, 321, 362, 383, 387, 391, 398, 401, 402n, 404, 409–10, 444, 448

Jesuit colleges and houses, 14n, 215–16, 219, 224, 245, 384–5, 394
Livorno, 255–6, 448
Lizza Fusina, 361–2
Lodi, 370–71, 448
Loreto, 325, 326–7, 329
Loyola, Ignatius of, St, 4, 5, 17, 80n, 112n, 119n, 155n, 160n, 193n, 194n,195n, 233n, 251n, 289n, 294n, 335n, 366n, 388n, 394n
Loyola, Jorge, 9, 12, 17, 50, 53, 410n, 414n
Lucena, Afonso de, 13
Luzon, 18

Ma Huan, 65n
Macao, 1, 5, 6, 9, 12, 15–18, 20, 21, 28, 30, 35, 36n, 37n, 50n, 53–4, 56–8, 62–3, 80n, 141n, 155n, 208n, 233, 245, 305n, 306n, 326n, 345n, 399n, 415, 416n, 418, 420n, 421, 424n, 434n, 435, 438–9, 440n, 443
Macerata, 326, 448
Macedonia, 448
Madagascar, 441, 443
Madre de Dios, ship, 18
Madrid, 22, 225, 233, 237–46, 248–50, 253, 384, 448
Magi, adoration of the, 2, 284n, 343, 386
Mahomet (Muhammad), 183
Mahometans (Muslims), 183
Mainz, 125
Macerata, 53n, 326, 448
Malabar Coast, 69, 75n, 185n
Malacca, 53n, 59, 62–4, 75, 81, 235, 415, 443–4, 447
Malindi, 410
Mallorca, 255
Manasseh, 246
Manila, 27, 28, 306n, 416, 421n, 439n
Manomotapa, *see* Mutapa
Mantua, 14, 112n, 364–9, 448
Manuel I, 72–3, 201
maps, 103, 440–43, 448; *see also*, 'Anon–Moreira' world map
marble, 209, 227, 260–61, 268, 296, 327, 339, 342, 344–5, 347–8, 350, 364, 374, 376,
Margaret of Austria, 113
Maria of Austria, 106, 384
Mark, St, 288, 343, 346, 347n, 348
Martins, Pedro, 35n, 407
martyrs/martyrdom, 28n, 210, 216, 221, 252, 296–7, 354, 382, 390
Mascarenhas, Francisco, 77, 80–81, 384
Mascarenhas, Francisco, count of Vila da Horta, 80, 384
Mascarenhas, Leonor, 244

Mascarenhas family, 80n
Matsuda Kiichi, 11, 12
Matthew, apostle, 113
Mattingly, Garrett, 2
Maxima, St, 210
Maximilian I, 236
Maximilian II, 223, 256n
Mazagão, 235
Medici, Alessandro Ottaviano de', cardinal archbishop of Florence, 259
Medici, Bianca Capello de', 257
Medici, Chiara de', 321n
Medici, Cosimo de', 189n
Medici, Eleonara de', 361
Medici, Ferdinando de', 299
Medici, Francesco I de', duke of Tuscany, 256–7, 259
Medici, Giovanni de', 261
Medici, Isabella de', 304
Medici, Pietro de', 257
Medici family, 260n, 261, 311n
Medici-Orsino, Isabella de', 260n
Medina, 211
Mediterranean Sea, 63, 181, 188n, 235, 254–5, 336, 358n, 378, 448
Melegnano, 371
Melo, Francisco de, count of Tentúgal, 245
Mendoza, Iñigo Lopez de, third marquis of Mondéjar, 233
Mendoza, Iñigo Lopez de, son of third marquis of Mondéjar, 251
Mendoza, Juan Hurtado de, 232
Meneses, Duarte de, 411–13
Meneses, Jorge Telo de, 408
Meneses, Miguel Luís de, 411
Meneses family, 411
Mercurian, Everard, 293
Mérida, 230, 448
Mesquita, Diogo de, 3, 4, 16n, 17, 21–2, 28, 30, 50, 53, 63, 67, 93, 196n, 225, 248n, 277, 314n, 351n, 360n, 420n, 440n
Mexia, Lourenço, 21–2, 121n, 237n
Mexico, 234
Milan, 236, 360n, 369, 370–76, 448
Minho, river, 215
Mirabilia Urbis Romae, 24
miracles, 87, 221, 226, 230–31, 267, 270, 297, 327, 348, 356, 362, 368, 380, 382–3, 385–6, 390
Miranda, Aires Gonçalves de, 56n, 415
Mogadishu, 410
Molino, Constantino, 356
Moluccas, 91, 235
Mondego river, 391, 397
Mongols, 417n, 424n, 434n
Montagnola, 332–3

Montaigne, Michel de, 126n, 167n, 180n, 263n, 270n, 271n, 276n, 277n, 284n, 286n, 297n, 299n, 305n, 333n, 361n, 362
Montalto, Felice Peretti, cardinal, *see* Sixtus V
Monte, Urbano, 269n, 360n, 363n
Montefalco, 325
Montes Pietatis, 193
Montserrat, 380, 448
Monzón, 380–81, 448
Morais, Sebastião de, 35n, 93n, 118, 225, 384
Moreira, Ignacio, 18, 63n, 84n, 100n; *see also*, 'Anon–Moreira world map'
Moura, Cristóbal de, 240n
Moura, Cristóvão de, 238
Mozambique, 35n, 104, 118n, 204n, 235, 398, 404, 406–10, 411n, 413, 444
Munday, Anthony, 291n, 295n
Murano, 356, 359
Murcia, 252–3
Muscovy, 18
music/musical instruments, 14, 29, 57, 99, 149, 154–7, 197, 205, 212, 229, 238, 246–7, 252–3, 266, 270, 274, 299, 314, 329, 334, 338, 349, 363–4, 365n, 366–7, 378, 383, 387–8, 392, 440n
musk, 422
Mutapa, empire, 407n, 408

Nagasaki, 1, 3n, 7, 8, 11n, 12–13, 18n, 28n, 30, 43, 50n, 53, 63, 86n, 138n, 193n, 208n, 266n, 306n, 326n, 345n, 415n, 421n, 438n, 443
Nakaura, Julian, 8, 9, 30, 39, 271, 302
  illness, 300, 302, 379
  in Milan, 371
  in Rome, 321–2
nambanjin, 46
Nanjing, 417, 429
Naples, 3, 166n, 235, 256, 288n, 322n, 323–5, 373
Narni, 325, 448
Natal, 404
navigation, 100–104
  charts, 103
Nearer India, 62–3, 66, 69, 235
Nero, emperor, 347
New Spain, 181n, 236, 326n, 439n, 444
Nichijō Shōnin, 266n
Ningbo, 416
Noronha, Andres de, bishop of Plasencia, 243
Noronha, Nuno de, 392
Norway, 448
Nossa Senhora de Baluarte, Mozambique, 408

Oda Nobunaga, 8, 55n, 86n, 119n, 129n, 130n, 131n, 133n, 134n, 137, 140n, 161n, 163n, 174n, 224n, 237n, 266n, 301, 331n, 345n, 414

477

Olivares, Enrique de Guzmán, count of, 250–51
Ōmura Suminobu, 9, 30
Ōmura Sumitada, Bartolomeu, 8–9, 12n, 13, 28, 39, 49, 77, 242, 273–6, 306n, 322, 397
Ōmura Yoshiaki, Sancho, 9, 13, 79, 322n
Ōmura domain, 9, 13
Oran, 235
organ, 227n, 265, 270, 299
Orihuela, 253, 448
Ormuz (Hormuz), 75, 235
Oropesa, 384
Orsini, Paolo Giordano, 260
Orsini, Virginio, 260, 304, 330n
Orsini family, 135n
Ortelius, Abraham, 363
   Theatrum Orbis Terrarum, 363, 440
Otagio, 377
Otho, protomartyr, 390
Ōtomo Yoshimune, 9–10, 168n, 189n
Ōtomo Yoshishige (Sōrin), Francisco, 8–11, 13, 49, 77, 174n, 189n, 242n, 274, 290n, 322, 397
Ottoman empire, 18, 184n

Pacheco, Alfonso, 3–4
Padilla y Guevara, Sancho de, governor of the fortress of Milan, 375
padroado, 28, 35n
Padua, 221, 361–3, 448
pagans/pagan superstition, 3, 56, 115, 122–3, 184, 210, 287, 296, 298
Pagès, Léon, 20
Palatine, 125
Paleotti, Gabriele, cardinal, 330
Palladio, Andrea, 22, 288n
Pannonia, 448
papacy, 49, 108, 117, 126–9, 301, 320
Paros, 204, 261, 268, 339, 374
Pastor, St, 252
patronato, 27–8
Paul IV, 17, 322n, 366n
Paul V, 28
Paul, St, 115, 296–7, 353, 393
Pavia, 376, 448
Pedro I, 201
Pedro, duke of Coimbra, 213
Pedro, count of Urgell, 390
Pelopponese, the, 448
Peñon de Velez, 235
pepper, 74
Peralonga, 222
Perpinhão, Bernardo, 253
Perpinhão, Luís, 253
Pereira, Roque de Melo, 62
Persia, 75, 81, 235, 421n, 447
Perugia, 325–6, 448
Pesaro, 329–30, 448
Peru, 234
Peter, protomartyr, 390
Peter, St, 108, 279–80, 296–7, 353, 393
Philip II, 1, 3, 4, 8, 10n, 13–14, 17, 18n, 27, 30, 58n, 135n, 139n, 175n, 188n, 189n, 190, 201n, 207n, 220n, 234–5, 237n, 238n, 244–6, 248n, 249–50, 251n, 253–4, 272n, 304, 311n, 323–4, 367n, 368, 370n, 371, 373–4, 377n, 378, 387, 393n, 399, 413, 439n, 448
   audiences with, 240–43, 381
   and Jesuits, 8
   oaths of allegiance to Prince Philip, 237–9, 380
Philip IV, 251n, 253
Philip, prince (Philip III), 237–9, 380
Philippines, 31, 235
Phocis, 448
Piceno, 313, 329
Pilate, Pontius, 295
pirates, 46n, 68, 181, 255, 259
Pisa, 256–9, 448
Pius V, 112, 194n, 290, 313
Pizzighettone, 370
Plasencia, 243
Plato, 23
Po, river, 333
Polanco, Juan Alfonso de, 4, 290n, 294n
Poland, 277n, 448
porcelain, 422
Portugal, empire in Asia, 68–9, 71–6
   military orders, 206, 207n
   trade, 73–4
      trade with China, 56
      trade with Japan, 7, 27, 116n, 143, 185–7, 345n, 420, 421n
   see also, *Carreira da Índia*; Japan
pottery, 140–41
printing, in China, 424
printing press, 15, 424n, 449
puchinsu, 427
Pulo Cecir, 415

Quambaquundono, *see* Toyotomi Hideyoshi
Quilon, 68, 74, 90
Quiroga y Vela, Gaspar, archbishop of Toledo, 238, 384
quiugin, 425

Ramón, Pedro, 10–12
Recanati, 326, 448
Regimento que se ha de guarder nos semynarios (1580), 16

relics, 80, 204, 210, 215, 221, 228, 245–7, 249–51, 259, 267n, 269, 281, 295–7, 322, 327–9, 331, 333, 338, 348, 354n, 360n, 369–71, 376, 380–82, 440n
religious orders, 109–11, 114–15
Ribadeneira, Pedro de, 18
Ricci, Mateo, 83n, 84n, 326n, 417n, 426n, 429n, 432n, 434n, 435n, 443n
Rimini, 330, 448
Rinaldi, Gian Carlo, 343
Rodrigues, Nuno, 6, 7n, 21–2, 51n, 93, 225, 272n, 324n, 360n, 377n, 374n, 381n, 401, 405
Rodrigues, Simão, 22, 219n, 394
Rome, 1, 4, 6, 8–10, 13–16, 20–22, 27–9, 49, 92, 109, 111–12, 118, 123, 126–8, 148, 166n, 194n, 219, 225, 245, 251, 254, 256–7, 263, 271–321, 323–4, 326–7, 364, 370, 373–4, 384, 387, 393, 396, 444, 447–8
   ancient ruins, 287–8, 298
   Apostolic Palace, 279–80, 288
   Gesù, Jesuit church, 111n, 215n, 227n, 281n, 289, 293n
   Japanese entry into, 273–6
   Jesuit colleges and houses, 14n, 289–95
   senate, 304–5
   see also, Castel Sant'Angelo; Gregory XIII; St John Lateran; St Peter's basilica; Sixtus V
Roman empire, 123, 127–8, 256, 296
Rosa of Viterbo, St, 270
Rosier, Bernard du, 2
Rossi, Ippolito de, bishop of Pavia, 376
Rota, Sacra Romana, 319
Rovere, Domenico della, 290n
Rovere, Francesco Maria II della, 329
Ruggieri, Michele, 432n, 434n
Rusticucci, Girolamo, 323

Sá, Leonardo de, 35–6, 56
Sacred Scripture, 87, 115, 132, 151, 294, 348
St Helena, 99, 104–5, 443
St John Lateran, 296–7, 317
St John Lateran, church, papal procession to, 317–20
St Peter's, basilica of, 281, 288, 300, 312–15, 374
St Peter's Square, 298
Sala del Pappagallo, 314
Sala Regia, 183n, 276, 278n, 280
Salsete, 3, 413
Salviati, Antonmaria, cardinal, 330
samurai, 130
San Benedetto in Polirone, 368
San Giorgio in Alga, 334, 361
San Qurico d'Orcia, 269
Sancho I, 201, 390

Sancho II, 201
Sande, Duarte de, 14n, 15, 17, 20–22, 35–9, 366n, 389n, 435n
Sansovino, Francesco, man of letters, 22–3
Sansovino, Jacopo, sculptor and architect, 344n, 345n, 347n, 348n
Santa Casa da Misericórdia, 208
Santa Maria da Vitória na Batalha, 398
Santa Maria in Aracoeli, 321
Santa Maria sopra Minerva, 284
Santarém, 385–6, 398, 448
Santiago, ship, 93n, 105n, 404, 406, 407n, 411n
São Felipe, ship, 401
São Jorge da Mina de Ouro, 401
São Lourenço, *see* Madagascar
São Lourenço, ship, 409
São Sebastião, fort, 203,
São Sebastião (St Sebastian), 220
São Tomé, 211, 235
Saracens, 71–3, 75, 81, 182–5, 216–17, 219, 382–3, 389, 398, 411, 433
Sarmatia, 448
Saturn, 232
Saul, king, 151
Savoy, Charles Emmanuel, duke of, 139
Saxony, 125
Scheuchzer, J. G., 20
Schütte, Josef Franz, 16
Sebastião, king, 55n, 145, 181–2, 201, 220n, 226, 249, 413
secular clergy, 109, 192, 289
Segovia, 246
Senigallia, 329–30, 448
Sertorius, Quintus, 225
servants, 132, 139, 142–3, 169
Seville, 211
Sfondrati, Niccolò, 369
Sforza, Francesco, 236
Shaka, 433
Shangchuan (Sangian), 434
Shallows of Sofala (Baixos da Judía), 404, 444
Shaoguan (Xaucheo), 435
Sheba, queen of, 132
ships, 181–3
shipwreck, 55, 58–9, 104, 116n, 280, 327, 402n, 404–7
Siam, 46–7
Sicily, kingdom of, 235, 441
Sidotti, Giovanni Battista, 31
Siena, 268–9
silk, 27, 56n, 73, 116n, 136–7, 139, 141, 145, 147, 152, 199, 204, 211, 228, 238, 247, 261, 263, 283, 304, 310, 319, 324, 334, 337, 348, 353–5, 360, 372, 374, 392, 406n, 421, 438n

silver/silver decoration/silverware, 73–4, 81, 134, 136, 139, 143–4, 152, 175, 198–9, 204, 212–13, 227, 229–31, 236n, 245–9, 252, 261, 263, 268–9, 288, 299, 305, 319, 320, 322, 332, 338, 345–9, 353, 362, 369, 374, 376, 381–2, 392, 424, 436
   in China, 420–21
Singapore, Straits of, 59–60, 62, 443
Sintra, 222, 225n
siusai, 425
Sixtus V, xviii, 1, 14, 27, 109n, 116–17, 119, 194n, 233, 287n, 292, 298, 304n, 305n, 313
   audience with Japanese, 321–2
   cavalcade to St John Lateran, 317–20
   consecration, 314–16
   election, 311–13
skin colour, 60, 67, 81–7, 89, 143, 185, 445–7
slavery, 86n, 145, 167–8, 184–7
   in Japan, 184–7
Society of Mercy (*Misericórdia*), 208
Socrates, 445
Sofala, 235, 405–6
Solomon, king, 132, 246, 404n
Sophia, St, 391
soto, 24, 31
Sousa, Martim Afonso de, 217
Spain, 1, 4, 8, 27, 108n, 112, 135n, 175n, 176n, 177n, 183n, 202, 208, 223n, 228, 230, 233–5, 237, 239, 249, 251–2, 305n, 311n, 366n, 369, 374, 377n, 378–9, 381, 442–4, 448
Speciano, Cesare, bishop of Novara, 375
Spinola, Filippo, cardinal, 326
Spinola, Giannettino, 378
Spoleto, 325, 448
spoons, 143–4
Stephen, St, 209, 296, 386
sugar, 211–12
Sumatra, 62, 441
Swiss guards, 375

Tagus, river, 202–3, 208, 219, 225, 231, 385, 387, 402
Tangier, 201n, 235, 413
tapestries, 136, 147, 228, 237, 261, 263, 335, 372, 377, 384, 395, 414n
Taprobane, 62, 64, 441
Tartars, 417–18, 424, 433, 434n
tauzu, 433
tenshu, 174
temperate zone, 88, 399, 446
Tenka, 134, 159, 163n, 172
tennis, 158
Terni, 325, 448
Terra incognita (Oceania), 46–7
Theodore, St, 346

Thessaly, 448
Thomas Christians, 90
Thrace, 127, 448
Throna, Franciscina, 23
Timante, 191
Timothy, St, 296
Tintoretto, Jacopo, 183n, 353n, 360n, 361n
Toledo, 230–33, 239, 266, 343, 448
Toledo, Juan Álvarez de, count of Oropesa, 384
Tolentino, 326
Tokugawa Hidetada, 154n
Tokugawa Ieyasu, 30, 79n, 129n, 161n, 266n
Tokugawa shogunate, 28, 31, 133n, 163n, 174n, 181n, 186n, 189n, 237n, 240n, 345n
tono, 86n, 130n, 133, 172–3
Torrespinaldo, 252
torrid zone, 83–4, 86–9, 446
Toscanello, Oliverio, 53, 415n
tournaments, *see* horsemanship
Toyotomi Hideyoshi (Quambaquundono, *kampaku*), 5n, 11, 13, 17–18, 28–31, 35n, 43n, 119n, 124n, 129n, 131n, 133n, 134n, 136n, 140n, 141n, 155n, 161n, 163n, 165n, 168n, 173n, 178n, 181n, 185n, 186n, 199n, 224n, 237n, 240n, 266n, 306n, 322n, 331n, 345n, 369n, 399n, 411n, 413n, 414n, 416n, 424n, 430n, 438n, 439n, 440n
trade, Chinese, European and Japanese attitudes to, 400
Trajan, emperor, 298
Travancore, 67, 90
Trent, council of, 3, 5, 90n, 291
Trichanduri, 64
Trier, 125
Tropic of Cancer, 84, 444
Tropic of Capricorn, 84, 444
Turriano, Gianello, 232
Tuscany, 259
tutan, 425, 427, 434–5
Tutocorin, 67
Tyrrhenian Sea, 259

uchi, 24, 31
Ulysses, 201, 210
universities, 195–7, 425
   Alcalá, 251
   Coimbra, 391–3
   Évora, 226
   Lisbon, 220
   Madrid, 251–2
   Padua, 362–3

Valencia, 221, 380
Vale do Rosal, 384

Valignano, Alessandro (Father Visitor), 36–7
    Introduction, *passim*, 39, 45–6, 49–50, 53, 59, 64–6, 68, 77–8, 92–3, 137, 146, 301, 409, 411, 414–15, 433, 439, 449
Valladolid, 211
van sui, 429
velvet, 136–7, 139, 147, 152, 211, 238, 261, 263, 276, 278, 283, 300, 304, 317, 324, 334, 337, 353, 360, 365, 367, 371–2, 374, 392, 397
Vengurla Rocks, 411
Venice/Venetian Republic, 14, 22–3, 128, 175n, 177n, 182–3, 211, 238, 256, 288n, 302, 315n, 321, 329, 333–61, 363–5, 366n, 373, 375, 377–8, 448
    arsenal, 357–8
    audience with doge, 351–2
    doge's palace, 349–50
    government, 336–7
    Libreria di San Marco, 344–5
    Mint (Zecca), 345–6
    Piazza San Marco, 341–6
    Rialto, 352–3
    St Mark's basilica, 346–9
    sodalities, 354–5
Veniero, Sebastiano, 183
Vergil, Polydore, xviii
Verissimo, St, 210
Verona, 364, 448
Vicenza, 363–4, 448
    Olimpico theatre, 360n, 363
Vila Viçosa, 21n, 228–30, 384, 448
Villa Caprarola, 271
Villa d'Este, 299

Villa Giulia, 274
Villa Lante, 270
Villa Pratolino, 263–7, 270
Villa São Martinho, 397
Villafranca, 364
Villarejo, 252
Visconti, Gaspare, archbishop of Milan, 371, 374–6
Visconti, Gian Galeazzo, tomb of, 376
Viterbo, 269–71, 448
Voghera, 376

war/warfare
    in Europe, 135, 150, 170–71, 173–81, 188–9
    in Japan, 76, 130, 171–3, 175, 180, 189, 356, 399
    naval, 182–3, 187
women
    in China, 421
    in Europe, 113, 115, 139, 147, 156–7, 192, 194, 206n, 212–13, 239, 243, 257, 268n, 276, 310, 371

Xavier, St Francis, 5, 6n, 12, 31, 48n, 66n, 85n, 114n, 129n, 219, 266n, 290n, 335n, 386n, 393n, 434

yakata, 10, 11n, 106, 129, 130, 133–4, 142, 171–3
Yushima, *see* Dangōjima
Yusuf II, 390

Zaragoza, 381–2, 448
Zeeland, 234
Zhaoqing (Xauquin), 434–5
Zheng He voyages, 65, 424
Zodiac, the, 232, 343